NECESSARY BUT NOT SUFFICIENT

Necessary But Not Sufficient

THE RESPECTIVE ROLES OF SINGLE AND MULTIPLE INFLUENCES ON INDIVIDUAL DEVELOPMENT

Theodore D. Wachs

AMERICAN PSYCHOLOGICAL ASSOCIATION
WASHINGTON, DC

Published by
American Psychological Association
750 First Street, NE
Washington, DC 20002

Copies may be ordered from
APA Order Department
P.O. Box 92984
Washington, DC 20090-2984

In the U.K., Europe, Africa, and the Middle East, copies may be ordered from
American Psychological Association
3 Henrietta Street
Covent Garden, London
WC2E 8LU England

Typeset in Goudy by Monotype Composition, Baltimore, MD
Printer: Port City Press, Inc., Baltimore, MD
Jacket Designer: Berg Design, Albany, NY
Technical/Production Editor: Eleanor Inskip

Library of Congress Cataloging-in-Publication Data

Wachs, Theodore D., 1941–
   Necessary but not sufficient : the respective roles of single and
multiple influences on individual development / by Theodore D. Wachs.
     p.   cm.
   Includes bibliographical references and index.
   ISBN 1-55798-611-8 (hardcover)
   1. Developmental psychology.   I. Title.
   BF713.W33   1999
   155.2′34—dc21   99-37473
                                              CIP

British Library Cataloguing-in-Publication Data
A CIP record is available from the British Library.

Printed in the United States of America
First Edition

For Carol, who is both necessary and sufficient.

CONTENTS

Preface ix

Chapter 1. Necessary But Not Sufficient: The Problem of Variability
in Individual Outcomes 1

Chapter 2. Evolutionary and Ecological Influences 13

Chapter 3. Genetic, Neural, and Hormonal Influences 31

Chapter 4. Biomedical and Nutritional Influences 69

Chapter 5. Phenotypic Influences 97

Chapter 6. Proximal Environmental Influences 125

Chapter 7. Distal Environmental Influences 153

Chapter 8. Linkages Among Multiple Influences 183

Chapter 9. Temporal and Specificity Processes 217

Chapter 10. Integrating Multiple Influences, Midlevel Processes, and
Systems 261

Chapter 11. From Principles to Practice 317

References 335

Author Index 407

Subject Index 427

About the Author 439

PREFACE

"Truth is rarely pure and never simple."
Oscar Wilde, *The Importance of Being Earnest*

This volume may be regarded as the third in a trilogy. In 1982, I coauthored a volume (*Early Experience and Human Development*, G. Gruen, coauthor) that essentially dealt with the contributions of the environment to children's development. Ten years later, I wrote a second volume (*The Nature of Nurture*), which, although still focused on the environment, also stressed how environmental contributions to development could not be understood without reference to covariations and interactions between environmental and nonenvironmental developmental influences. In this volume, my focus is no longer on the environment per se but rather on environment as part of a system of multiple influences on individual human behavioral–developmental variability.

In spite of Oscar Wilde's warning in the previous century, and many similar warnings in the current century, all too many human developmental scientists have focused on the simple. All too often, we have tried to conceptualize individual human behavioral–developmental variability by explanations that are essentially based on the impact of a single class of influences taken in isolation. The infamous, persistent, and ultimately fruitless nature-versus-nurture controversy is perhaps the most obvious manifestation of this approach. Our deep seated tendency to look for "simple" truths is also illustrated by attempts to explain and deal with the epidemic of school shootings that occurred in 1998–1999. Common explanations included the easy availability of guns, or a lack of prayer in schools, or low parental involvement with their children, or the high levels of violence portrayed on television, movies, and the Web, or peer group influences, or mental illness. The solutions proposed to deal with the problems of school violence were equally simplistic, as seen in the fact that separate bills were introduced in Congress to reduce access to guns and to reduce exposure to media violence. Rarely was the possibility considered that the increase in school shootings was the result of a convergence among a number of the above factors, and that any solution must go beyond dealing with a single potential cause. This volume is my attempt to show how the overwhelming weight of available scientific evidence illustrates how most aspects of individual human behavioral–developmental variability can be understood only with reference to the action of linked influences from multiple domains operating over time.

Each of the various influences that affect individual human behavioral–developmental variability, *although necessary, are not sufficient* as an explanation of such variability. In and of itself, such a conclusion is not unique. What is unique in this volume is the range of influences on human development that is considered, the emphasis on underlying processes that are common to the operation of influences from multiple domains, and the use of principles derived from systems theory as a way of conceptualizing and organizing the impact of linked influences from multiple domains.

This volume may be regarded as loosely organized into five sections. Chapter 1 illustrates the range of individual human behavioral–developmental variability and how the range observed is incompatible with explanatory models based on the operation of a single isolated developmental influence. The second section, comprising chapters 2–7, focuses on the various influences on individual human behavioral–developmental variability and documents how each influence, although necessary, is not sufficient when considered in isolation. Specifically, chapter 2 deals with evolutionary influences and the role played by features of the physical ecology. Chapter 3 includes genetic, neural, and hormonal contributions, whereas chapter 4 encompasses the impact of biomedical and nutritional factors. Chapter 5 illustrates how specific individual characteristics act to influence subsequent individual development. Chapters 6 and 7 document environmental contributions, with chapter 6 focusing on the proximal environment and chapter 7 on the distal environment. The two chapters of the third section focus on what I have called *midlevel processes,* namely those underlying processes common to the operation of the various influences reviewed in chapters 2–7. Chapter 8 focuses on the various functional and structural linkages among developmental influences from various domains, whereas chapter 9 deals with the operation of these influences over time and how such influences tend to be specific rather than general in their impact. In chapter 10, I document how the operation of multiple developmental influences and midlevel processes meet the criteria for a system and how principles derived from dynamic and general systems theories form an additional level of influences on individual behavioral–developmental variability. In chapter 10, I propose that at a certain point in their development, individuals begin operating in a manner akin to a general system, and I make specific reference to general-systems principles involving centralization and self-stabilization. In addition, given the sensitivity of systems to context, I also illustrate interrelationships between the individual functioning as a system and contextual processes involving niche closures and openings. In the final section of this volume, chapter 11, I attempt to show how principles derived from the impact of multiple developmental influences and midlevel and systems processes can be applied to assessment of and intervention with children at risk for developmental problems.

Portions of this volume were researched and written while I was a Golestan Foundation Fellow at the Netherlands Institute for Advanced Study (NIAS). The Golestan fellowship gave me the gift of time with no outside responsibilities. NIAS and its staff provided the gift of a unique scholarly context that encourages going outside of one's own area of expertise and thinking about old problems in alternative ways. I wish to acknowledge the necessary role played by NIAS and the Golestan Foundation, for without their gifts this volume would not have been written.

Even when there is only a single author, a volume of this type bears the imprint of many individuals in addition to the author. In this regard I am deeply grateful to a number of colleagues who took the time and effort to read various chapters in this volume and give me the benefit of their wisdom. Where wisdom is present, I am more than happy to share collaboration; where wisdom is lacking, I accept full responsibility. Specifically, my thanks and appreciation go to the following individuals: chapter 3, Robert Meisel, Charles Nelson, and Robert Plomin; chapter 4, Betsy Lozoff, Ernesto Pollitt, and Robert Karp; chapter 5, Jack Bates; chapter 8, Michael Rutter; chapter 9, Avshalom Caspi; chapter 10, Alan Fogel; and chapter 11, Carol Czaja.

In addition, I owe a deep debt of thanks to Cris Pecknold, who patiently and efficiently typed multiple opening drafts and revised drafts, getting close to the end drafts and final drafts of each chapter. Thanks also are due to Peggy Treece for her typing of tables and to Jennifer Ferguson for her translating my scrawl into readable figures. Finally, I very much appreciate the patience of Mary Lynn Skutley and the staff at APA during what I am sure seemed an eternity before this manuscript finally appeared.

1

NECESSARY BUT NOT SUFFICIENT: THE PROBLEM OF VARIABILITY IN INDIVIDUAL OUTCOMES

As science and scientists have become more specialized, the tools, concepts, and methods used within a subdiscipline become less accessible and perhaps even less understandable to researchers working in different domains (Hinde, 1990). Although there may be overall "paradigms" that are almost universally accepted by researchers within a discipline, such paradigms only emerge over time (Kuhn, 1970). Furthermore, the rate of acceptance of these paradigms may well be inhibited by higher specialization and a lack of communication among researchers in different subdomains within a discipline. For example, the validity of a Darwinian paradigm was still a subject of intense debate among biologists even through the 1930s. Mayr (1980) documented how this debate was a function of a lack of communication among both experimentalists and naturalists, as well as among different subgroups of experimentalists (e.g., embryologists and geneticists). Lack of communication resulted in an inability to see both commonalities in the problems researchers in different domains were working on and what research findings from one domain could mean to interpretation of results in a second domain.

The fragmentation described by Mayr (1980) occurred even when there was a potential common framework—evolution—that could have linked researchers in different camps. Except for the lack of a potential underlying paradigm, the situation just described for biology in the 1930s clearly mirrors the situation faced today for those working in what might be called the *human develomental sciences*, or the study of how individual human behavior develops over time and the processes underlying this development. Certainly there is fragmentation. The majority of human developmental researchers tend to focus primarily on the identification of specific developmentally relevant influences taken in isolation (e.g., genes, age, learning, hormones, societal stresses, or culture). When more than one influence is considered, paired combinations tend to be the norm (e.g., genes vs. environment or genes interacting with environment) (Wachs, 1993a), with little concern for how these combinations fit into a larger systems framework encompassing multiple processes acting together (Magnusson, 1988).

Developmental scientists working with isolated specific elements or with isolated specific subprocesses sometimes justify this approach by noting the success of the physical sciences, which often focus on small specific elements or processes taken in isolation. Alternatively, the "holy grail" of parsimony is dragged out, using the argument that simultaneously focusing on multiple elements or processes results in models that are either too vague or too complex to be empirically testable (Spitz, 1996; L. Thompson, 1996). However, when examined closely, each of these justifications has major flaws.

There are a number of reasons for questioning the generalizability to the human developmental sciences of approaches used in more fundamental sciences like physics and molecular biology, which work with a relatively limited number of potential influences and explanatory processes. Both physicists (Anderson, 1972) and biologists (Oster & Alberch, 1982) have argued that explanatory principles are organized hierarchically. This hierarchy means that as we move from the physical to the biological, and from the biological to the psychosocial, new laws are necessary for adequate explanation. The requirement for new laws at each level does not compromise the relevance of more fundamental laws as part of the explanatory process. Hypotheses developed for understanding human behavior and development cannot contradict the laws of physics or of molecular biology. However, lower level physical and molecular biological laws, by themselves, are not sufficient to explain human behavior (Anderson, 1972). Rather, a satisfactory explanation of human behavior must also involve additional principles that are unique for human development. The hierarchical nature of explanatory principles means that researchers interested in human development must deal not only with more general physical and biological explanatory principles but also with explanatory principles that are unique to the study of human development.

The need for multilevel explanatory principles in studying human development becomes especially obvious when we look closely at the "successes" found when attempting to predict variability in human behavioral development on the basis of single-influence or single-process models. For example, research has shown the importance of (a) early *attachment* characteristics for a number of social–emotional outcomes, including subsequent peer relations and resilience under stress (e.g., Elicker, Englund, & Sroufe, 1992); (b) replicated *genetic influences* on a variety of developmental outcomes, including cognitive functioning, personality, and psychopathology (Plomin & McLearn, 1993); and (c) the stability and consequences associated with *individual characteristics*, such as behavioral inhibition (Kagan, 1994) or early aggressive behavior (Moffitt, 1993). However, as will be shown later, the level of prediction, although impressive across a large group of participants, becomes more attenuated when we consider the degree of intragroup variability associated with specific genetic, environmental, or individual-characteristic predictors. Single-influence or single-process models, although easily testable, are all too often not potentially productive in terms of understanding variability in individual behavior and development, or in terms of predicting specific developmental outcomes and consequences. Individual variability in developmental outcomes represents one of the major challenges for the viability of single-influence, single-process approaches to the study of human development.

In regard to the argument that complex, multiple-influence models are nonparsimonious, too vague, or too difficult to test, it is true that when treated as a "heap" of unrelated elements, complex models can be vague and problematical to test. However, it is also important to remember that parsimony does not require the simplest explanation possible but rather the simplest explanation for the phenomenon under study. Biological organisms by their very nature evolve toward greater complexity (Shatz, 1985), which requires more complex explanatory models (Gould, 1980). Although it is theoretically and empirically possible to treat processes and predictors in isolation, such an approach may not be desirable because such approaches tend to result in an overly narrow focus wherein the multiple coaction of different processes and elements will be missed when only one level or element is the focus of study (Oster & Alberch, 1982). The interrelation among multiple elements and processes may be of far greater importance for understanding human behavior and development than the influence of specific elements or processes taken in isolation. Indeed, it is a major thesis of the present volume that *individual variability is a necessary consequence of complex interactions among multiple influences that are each necessary but not sufficient contributors to behavioral development*. Such individual variability in behavior and development would be much less likely to occur if single developmental influences were both necessary and sufficient.

INDIVIDUAL VARIABILITY AND OUTCOMES ASSOCIATED
WITH PREDICTORS OR PROCESSES

I have written above about the degree of outcome variability found when we attempt to use individual elements or processes as predictors of individual development. Many lines of evidence converge to support this assertion. For example, although there is an increased probability of adult criminality in the offspring of individuals whose fathers have a serious criminal history (39% vs. only 7% of those whose fathers have no criminal record), 61% of children whose fathers had a serious criminal record themselves have no criminal history (Kandel et al., 1988). Similarly, although there is greater risk for schizophrenia in the offspring of people with schizophrenia, more than 90% of children reared by schizophrenic biological parents will not manifest schizophrenia during their life time (Masten, Best, & Garmezy, 1990). Although there is significant consistency from a history of early childhood aggressive oppositional behavior to subsequent peer rejection and then to adult antisocial behavior and adult personality disorder, the large majority of children with chronic aggressive oppositional behavior do not suffer from subsequent peer rejection (Hartup & van Lieshout, 1995), adult antisocial behavior (Magnusson, 1988), or adult personality disorder (Gottesman & Goldsmith, 1994; Rutter, 1988). A similar pattern of modest predictability also is shown when using a history of psychiatric treatment in childhood as a predictor of later psychiatric care (Magnusson, 1988), when looking at the relation between measures of difficult temperament in infancy and the preschool years and subsequent adjustment (Bates, 1989), when looking at the impact on children's mental health of continued exposure to intrafamily violence (McCloskey, Figueredo & Koss, 1995), and when looking at relations between stress and subsequent physical illness (Boyce & Jemerin, 1990). For example, following a major earthquake, 30% of kindergarten children showed an increase in respiratory illness, whereas 25% showed a decrease in the incidence of such illnesses (Boyce et al., 1991).

Notable intragroup variability also occurs when extreme groups are studied, as in the subsequent social and classroom adjustment of those children who in infancy had extremely inhibited temperaments (Gersten, 1989) or in the long-term developmental outcome of those individuals who grew up in "underclass" homes characterized by cross-generational unemployment, criminality, and substance abuse (Long & Vaillant, 1984). Variability in the subsequent growth and development of preterm infants or infants who are small for gestational age has been a continual theme in the literature for more than a quarter of a century (Falkner, Holzgreve, & Schloo, 1994; Sameroff & Chandler, 1975). For example, on the basis of the available literature, preterm infants can be characterized either as highly different or highly similar on state profiles, as more or less state mature, more or less irritable, or as showing more or less arousal than full-term infants (Thoman, 1990). Notable intragroup variability also is the norm when individual positive rather than risk characteristics are used as predictors (Freitas & Downey, 1998). For example, 36% of children who were securely attached as infants were below average on measures of social competence when tested at 11 years of age (Elicker et al., 1992; also see Sroufe & Jacobvitz, 1989, for similar findings in regard to the prediction of later ego resilience for children who were securely attached as infants).

This variability, although perhaps disquieting to researchers who use single-risk approaches, is not necessarily surprising, and perhaps could be dismissed through the usual appeals for better measurement of individual predictors. What is surprising is the degree of variability found when extremely potent biological or environmental influences are used as predictors. For example, preterm birth, perinatal asphyxia, a 15-minute Apgar score of less than 3, and neonatal seizures are all documented major risk factors for cerebral palsy. However, the majority of children with a history of these risk factors do not have cerebral palsy, and more than 75% of children with cerebral palsy do not have such a risk history in their record (Task Force on Joint Assessment, 1985). Notable variability in outcomes also has been shown for children exposed prenatally to a variety of teratogens. Thus, although the average IQ of children with fetal alcohol syndrome is 70, the reaction range for this group is IQ 20–108 (Streissguth, Sampson, & Barr, 1989). Similarly, the mean school age IQ for children exposed prenatally to heroin is 87.5; however, the IQ reaction range is from 50 to 124 (G. Wilson, 1989). A similar wide reaction range is found when looking at the long-term consequences of prenatal infections such as rubella (Rubenstein, Lotspeich, Ciaranello, 1990; Scola, 1991).

High variability also can be documented from the impact of major postnatal risk factors. For example, although there is an elevated risk rate for adult adjustment problems associated with chronic childhood illness such as diabetes, the majority of children with these types of chronic illness do not appear to show major adult adjustment problems (Cadman, Boyce, Szatmari, & Offord, 1987; Johnson, 1988). In extreme poverty conditions in third-world countries, where the overwhelming majority of children are growth retarded and have a high incidence of biomedical problems, some children somehow manage to grow and develop adequately (Zeitlin, 1991). In the nonbiomedical sphere, although institutional rearing during childhood is a strong predictor of later adult adjustment difficulties, only about one third of children who were institution-reared show significant impairment in adult adjustment (Rutter, Quinton, & Hill, 1990). Case reports of children reared in extreme-isolation situations for extended periods of time also show notable outcome variability in both social and cognitive competencies (Skuse, 1984). Even in the case of adult or child Holocaust survivors, although the overall outcome picture in regard to emotional development is grim, nonetheless, there are still subgroups of individuals who were less affected (Bar-on et al., 1998; Moskovitz, 1985). When multiple biological (Nelson & Ellenberg, 1986) or multiple psychosocial risk factors (Werner, 1990) are used, high levels of variability continue to appear. For example, of 63 children with a history of early conduct disorders plus parental criminality and high family stress, only 31 children with this profile became criminals as adults (Clarke & Clarke, 1988).

When controlled interventions or manipulations are used rather than naturally occurring conditions, there is also high evidence for significant outcome variability (Dance & Neufeld, 1988). For example, among low-income African American children, all of whom had participated in a highly successful preschool intervention program, the ultimate level of schooling ranged from 6 1/2 to 18 years of education (Luster & McAdoo, 1996). Similarly, wide outcome variability also is seen when the intervention involves tightly controlled experimental biological manipulations (Jacob, 1998).

What is perhaps most dramatic is the degree of outcome variability found among individuals with major genetic or chromosomal disorders, conditions that should result in a very narrow range of outcomes. For example, IQs for men with the single-gene disorder of fragile X syndrome range from severe to mild retardation (Israel, 1987); the IQ range for individuals with Trisomy 21 (Down's syndrome) varies from severe to low average, whereas the IQs for individuals affected with either Trisomy 8 or Trisomy 18 deletion syndromes range from severe to mild retardation (Pueschel & Thuline, 1991). Even when we are dealing with single-gene dominant disorders, a situation in which one would expect the greatest restriction of outcome variability, surprisingly high variability is seen for a number of outcomes. For example, only 40% of individuals with tuberosis sclerosis are retarded, whereas the IQ range for those with Apert's syndrome ranges from severe retardation to normal intelligence (Abuelo, 1991).

THE NATURE OF DEVELOPMENTAL OUTCOME VARIABILITY

The level of outcome variability documented here is clearly not consistent with a simple, main-effect predictor model involving either single specific predictors or combinations of isolated predictors. Why is there such outcome variability? Some developmental scientists have correctly noted that there is variability within variability; that is, some developmental outcomes may be more variable than others (Clarke & Clarke, 1988). For example, for a few genetically based disorders like Huntington's chorea, there is virtually a 100% probability of terminal neuromotor degeneration for those individuals carrying the gene for this disorder (although there is variability in the age of onset of Huntington's) (Bailey, Phillips, & Rutter,

1996). Similar limited variability is seen in the case of neuromotor degeneration associated with the single-gene disorder Tay-Sachs disease or for the behavioral consequences of the X-linked disorder of Lesch-Nyhan syndrome (Abuelo, 1991). In contrast, for schizophrenia, the individual risk occurrence may range from 0 to 55% (Gottesman & Goldsmith, 1994). Similar variability within variability also is seen in the functional consequences associated with a given disorder. In disorders such as autism or profound mental retardation, there is likely to be low variability in the degree and number of specific skills that are learned, retained, and generalized across different contexts, such that independent living is improbable (although even here, see Lovaas, 1987). In contrast, for other disorders, like Down's syndrome, greater variability in skill attainment and generalization is possible, as is some degree of independent living. What is apparent, however, is that disorders for which there is little outcome variability tend to be extremely rare (e.g., Huntington's chorea, Tay-Sachs, autism, and profound mental retardation). For the great majority of developmental disorders, variability tends to be the rule rather than the exception.

One possible exception to the rule of limited outcome variability being confined to rare developmental disorders comes from those behavioral patterns that have been labeled "universals." *Universal behaviors* are defined as those that appear for most individuals in most settings and that most individuals use in their daily activities (e.g., motor behaviors such as walking, spoken language, and the ability to accurately decode and interpret emotional cues) (Horowitz, 1992). The onset of such universal behaviors usually appears within a relatively restricted time span (often early in life), and these behaviors are thought to involve evolution-driven genetic influences. Obviously, whether we are dealing with universal or nonuniversal behaviors depends on the level we are looking at. Most people demonstrate the ability to use spoken language (a universal), but the extent of language usage and the complexity of language used can vary widely across individuals (a nonuniversal individual difference). Similarly, even for what are regarded as clearly universal aspects of development, namely early motor development, there is surprising developmental variability both in terms of age of acquisition and what is acquired at different ages (Super, 1980). In part this may reflect the operation of what some researchers have called "universal experiences" or "experience-expectant development" (Greenough & Black, 1992; Miller, 1997). By this I refer to the hypothesis that universal developmental patterns may occur because most individuals have a high probability of encountering certain critical experiences during a given developmental period. When such experiences are not encountered within a restricted time range, then we may see surprising variability in what we would normally think of as universal behavior pattern. (For further discussion of this point, see chap. 2.) I would agree with Horowitz (1992) that the acquisition of behavioral universals may be a necessary condition for the acquisition of behavioral nonuniversals. However, I also would agree with those theorists who consider universal and nonuniversal aspects of development to be quite distinct, involving different underlying process mechanisms (Hardy-Brown, 1983; McCall, 1981). The fact that there appear to be different underlying process mechanisms for universals and nonuniversals—and the inherent variability even in supposedly universal developmental patterns—means that universals cannot be considered a sufficient condition for the acquisition of nonuniversal behavior and development.

Some researchers have argued that variability may be due to imprecise measurement of specific influences. What may look like a single homogeneous predictor may in fact be quite heterogeneous, resulting in variability in developmental outcome. Certainly, this critique is applicable to what Bronfenbrenner (Bronfenbrenner & Crouter, 1983) has called "social-address predictors" or global, demographic composites under which a variety of potential predictors are nested, such as social class. An excellent example of the heterogeneity underlying social-address predictors is seen in a study by Pungello, Kupersmidt, Burchinal, and Patterson (1996) that examined developmental outcomes of children coming from poverty backgrounds. In addition to the social-address measure of poverty, these authors also obtained measures of the number of major stressful life events encountered over a 4-year period by the children in their sample (i.e., stressful life events defined along dimensions such as parental loss or major family illness). Even though all children were living in poverty, 53% of the sample had experienced no major stressful life events over the 4-year period of the study, 29% of the sample had experienced one stressful life event, and 18% had experienced two or more stressful life events. Given the variability nested under the global social address of poverty, it is not surprising that wide outcome variability is associated with predictors such as poverty. However, the same problem also holds when more precise developmental influences are studied. What look like homogeneous individual characteristics, such as a need for autonomy (Steinberg & Silverberg, 1986), or homogeneous environmental contexts, such as being reared in highly controlled state orphanages (Langmeier & Matejcek, 1975), turn out to be quite multifaceted in nature. Even research designs that appear to offer the promise of groups with distinct developmental influences, such as monozygotic twins reared apart, also turn out to be quite multifaceted in terms of variability in what is meant by being reared apart (Bronfenbrenner, 1986).

At a more fundamental level, Gottesman (1993) has shown that even with genetic-based disorders, such as phenylketonuria, there may be multiple mutant conditions that result in varying degrees of deficit in the functioning of the phenylalinine hydroxylase gene, which thus leads to variation in subsequent intellectual functioning. Indeed, one of the most dramatic examples of such biological heterogeneity within a supposedly homogeneous population comes from research showing major discordance for muscular-dystrophy in a monozygotic female twin pair (with zygosity defined by blood group analyses), who shared the same placenta and who showed no major differences in birth weight (Burn et al., 1986). One of the twins in this pair began to show neuromuscular degeneration by the second year of life; the co-twin, in contrast, showed no such degeneration in functioning, and in fact went on to become one of her country's leading gymnasts. (There was also an 18-point IQ difference between the two twins.) Molecular analysis of the chromosomal structure for these twins showed that the normal co-twin's X chromosomes contained one type of alternative gene form (allele), whereas the affected co-twin's X chromosomes contained a totally different allele. The mechanism for this remarkable difference appears to be a genetic process called "Lyonization," wherein there is inactivation of one of the X chromosomes in each female cell. Normally, such inactivation is random, such that some of the X chromosomes inactivated are paternal whereas others are maternal. However, in this particular case, all of the active X chromosomes in one twin came from the mother, whereas all of the active X chromosomes in the other twin came from the father (Burn et al., 1986). In addition to muscular dystrophy, Lyonization discordancies also have been shown for other rare X-linked genetic disorders (Israel, 1987). Similarly, cognitive variability in fragile X syndrome may be due to variability in specific biochemical processes (e.g., methylation) that influence degree of gene activity (McConkie-Rosell et al., 1993).

Undoubtedly, some of the outcome variability associated with specific developmental predictors may well be reduced as more precise measurement techniques are developed. It is unlikely, however, that more sensitive measurement techniques will account for all of the variability just described, given the range of variability demonstrated and the use of highly precise aggregated predictor combinations in some studies. Furthermore, from the perspective of dynamic-systems ("chaos") theory, in systems in which developmental patterns are a function of initial conditions, it is unlikely that we will ever know with total accuracy all relevant initial conditions (Crutchfield, Farmer, Packard, & Shaw, 1986; Nowak & Lewenstein, 1994). Within such a framework, even with the best measurement possible, variability of outcome will still be inherent over the course of development.

Furthermore, given high levels of within-species variation, it may well be that outcome variability is built into individual development as a fact of nature (Goodman, 1994). The value of such variability may be rooted in the greater adaptive value associated with allowing individuals within a species to have the capacity to follow different developmental pathways or to use different adaptive tactics to reach a specific goal, depending on current contextual conditions (Bateson, 1985; Caro & Bateson, 1986; Warner, 1980). For example, even for highly biologically programmed organisms like insects, at least three alternative tactics have been demonstrated that can lead to successful mating (Caro & Bateson, 1986). Mammals also have shown a high sensitivity to environmental conditions, as seen in evidence indicating that maternal rearing strategies appear to be based on both availability of food (Bateson, 1985) and predictability of food sources (Rosenblum, 1998). Along the same lines, biological theorists have described brain development as a process in which fundamental genetic and cellular mechanisms produce general blueprints or maps of the central nervous system, with specific adjustment to these maps (i.e., fine tuning of the central nervous system) occurring as a function of postnatal influences, including chance (Edelman, 1989; Goodman, 1991b). In a similar vein, more psychologically oriented theorists have argued that the dynamic and systemic quality of human development and the need to respond to multiple inputs naturally predisposes to variability in outcome (Gleick, 1987; Thelen & Smith, 1994). All of these different theoretical orientations converge on a similar point, namely that *variability of outcomes as a function of specific developmental influences may be inherent in the nature of the developmental process itself.* Within this framework, rather than attempting to act like physicists and look for point-to-point predictions, human developmental scientists should assume that there will be variability in individual developmental outcomes and begin to look for conceptual and methodological approaches that help us understand why such variability is occurring.

Developing such approaches is a major goal of this volume. It is my belief that we can understand variability associated with individual developmental outcomes only by systematically integrating the contributions of multiple influences from multiple domains.[1] Even with such integration, I would not expect highly precise prediction; indeed, from a dynamic-systems viewpoint, highly precise prediction may be impossible in regard to human development (Thelen & Smith, 1994). Rather, as Sroufe and Jacobvitz (1989) have suggested, we may need to be satisfied with predicting general classes of outcomes rather than specific outcomes. Ultimately, we may have to accept a certain degree of unexplained variability in developmental outcomes.

Although prediction as used in the physical sciences may be impossible, understanding why variability occurs is a viable goal. In this sense, our root metaphor may be meteorology rather than physics. This is not to say that we should not attempt to predict. However, rather than prediction being our primary goal, prediction should be used as one of the ways to test the validity of our explanatory frameworks for understanding how multiple influences converge to influence developmental variability. In using prediction in this way, it is important to keep in mind the argument made by

---

[1] It is also important to note that within a dynamic-systems framework it has been argued that one can produce complexity from relatively simple interactions among a few elements in a system (Thelen, 1989). As will be noted in chapter 10, the application of this approach to human development has been primarily descriptive and may not map well onto most elements of human behavior and development.

Dawes (1993) in regard to the asymmetrical nature of backward and forward prediction. Both for statistical and logical reasons, we are more likely to find stronger links when we start with outcome variability and try to understand the etiology of such variability than when we start with etiological antecedents and try to predict subsequent outcome variability.

In attempting to understand why developmental variability occurs, there will be three major lines of inquiry that will be taken up in this volume. The first line of inquiry will involve identifying the multiple types of influences that have been shown to be related to individual variability in human development. In contrast to other reviews, which typically focus only on one or two major classes of determinants, I will be casting a wider net, ranging from the distal to the proximal and from the biological to the cultural. As an essential part of this first line of inquiry, I will attempt to show how individual influences, although necessary, can rarely be considered sufficient explanations for variability in human behavioral development. Sufficient causes are those for which a specific outcome is the inevitable result of the operation of a particular influence acting alone (Buka & Lipsitt, 1994). Necessary causes are those for which some, but not all, outcome variability is uniquely associated with a specific influence. For necessary causes, other influences also are needed to more fully explain outcome variability. In distinguishing necessary from sufficient causes, readers should keep in mind that single sufficient causes may be caused by a group of necessary causes (Buka & Lipsitt, 1994; Scott, Shaw, & Urbano, 1994). In addition, because most behavioral aspects of human development are quantitative in nature (e.g., intelligence, personality), necessary explanations may provide a better fit to the data.

Second, I will attempt to demonstrate that the multiple determinants that I have identified function together in specific yet common ways to influence individual development. I will refer to such underlying commonalities by the term *midlevel processes*. Finally, and perhaps most speculatively, I hope to demonstrate that multiple determinants acting together form a system. This approach allows us to apply general-systems properties, both as a means of increasing understanding and as a guide to future research directions.

The first goal will be considered in the next six chapters, which identify specific determinants that have been shown to be related to developmental variability and illustrate why each of these specific determinants can be considered as necessary, but not sufficient, conditions for individual behavioral–developmental variability.

2

EVOLUTIONARY AND ECOLOGICAL INFLUENCES

Like culture, the influences discussed in this chapter are relevant primarily for group rather than individual differences. Unlike culture, the influences discussed in chapter 2 derive primarily from natural rather than constructed world characteristics. Two such influences will be considered. The first is historical: evolutionary influences on development; the second is concurrent: physical ecological features.

EVOLUTIONARY INFLUENCES

Although there are differences among the various approaches to the evolutionary interpretation of human behavior, such as sociobiology versus evolutionary psychology (Symons, 1992), common to all these approaches is a central focus on interpreting current social transactions among humans from principles derived from evolutionary theory. Some of the differences among the various evolutionary approaches to human behavior and development are of interest primarily to evolutionary theorists and have little relevance to an understanding of variability in individual human behavioral development. One example of this type of issue is whether the unit of analysis during selection should be the gene (Dawkins, 1980; Rushton, 1984) or the individual (Chisholm, 1990; Keller, 1987; Sober & Lewontin, 1982).

The origins of evolutionary approaches to the study of human behavior and development come from three distinct sources (Barlow, 1980). First, there is evolutionary genetics, the study of changes in population gene frequencies over time as a function of different genotypes being associated with differential reproductive success (fitness). Genotypes that are more fit will become more frequent over time. A second domain of influence is from ecology, with particular emphasis on ecological features that influence the growth and development of populations, such as resource availability or stability of ecological conditions. For example, if food resources were scarce and birds laid too many eggs, large numbers of their offspring would be undernourished and thereby unable to compete for what resources were available. However, if individual birds were to lay too few eggs given the available food level, the fitness of these individual birds would be less than the fitness of birds who laid a more optimal number of eggs. The final relevant discipline, ethology, emphasizes the adaptiveness of species behavioral patterns in terms of the impact of these patterns on reproductive advantage, both for the individual and for the species as a whole.

Evolutionary approaches to human behavior and development have focused primarily on understanding the nature of human social interactions in areas that are thought to be influenced by reproductive fitness strategies, such as dominance, gender differences, and social relations (Ember, 1980; MacDonald, 1996; Wilson, Near, & Miller, 1996). Attempts have been made to connect human studies with more traditional evolutionary studies using infrahuman populations by looking for common underlying processes influencing both human and infrahuman species (e.g., Chapais, 1996). However, as Caplan (1980) has pointed out, similarity of traits across species in no way proves that these traits served the same evolutionary goals in the two species. Although infrahuman data will be used for illustrative purposes, for the most part, discussion on the extent and nature of evolutionary contributions to human behavior and development will be based primarily on the human evidence.[1]

Fundamentals in Evolutionary Approaches to Human Behavioral Development

There are two fundamental points common to evolutionary explanations of human behavior and development: *selection* and *inheritance*. In regard to selection, evolutionary approaches to human behavioral development follow the Darwinian principle of differential reproduction operating within a population existing over time (Rushton, 1984). On occasion, tem-

---

[1] Readers wishing to explore potential infrahuman–human linkages within an evolutionary framework can find an excellent discussion of this topic in a volume by Hinde (1987).

poral changes in population gene frequency may reflect random conditions, with perhaps the most extreme example being the mass extinction of the dinosaurs (Raup, 1986). However, in the great majority of cases, changes in gene frequencies are not random but rather reflect the fact that some organisms have genotypes that are associated with behavioral patterns or strategies that are better able to cope with existing environmental characteristics, stresses, and supports. As a result, there will be significantly greater cross-generational reproduction or greater offspring survival for individuals with these genotypes (Buss, 1991; Dawkins, 1980). Among the behavior patterns or strategies associated with differential reproductive success are the ability to obtain a greater share of available resources, the ability to choose a mate with high reproductive potential, the ability to adapt behavioral patterns to current conditions, and the use of rearing or social interaction patterns that act to maximize survival rate of existing offspring (Archer, 1996; Crawford & Anderson, 1989; Hinde, 1987).

Selection processes also can function at the level of the group, specifically groups of biologically related individuals (kin) sharing common genes or gene combinations (Noonan, 1987; Rushton, 1984). Behavioral patterns that allow an increased chance of survival of groups of individuals who share genes in common (e.g., formation of close social alliances with kin) also can result in changes in gene frequency over time, thus providing a vehicle for the maintenance of these types of social behavioral patterns.

To the extent that different genes or gene combinations are selected for in a population, and to the extent that human behavior and development are influenced by the genetic factors that are selected for (i.e., inheritance of behavior), evolutionary influences can be maintained in a population over time (Lickliter & Berry, 1990; Lumsden, 1983). There are a number of mechanisms through which historical evolutionary influences can be translated into current behavior and development in a population. One way is when gene patterns become fixed over generations. Fixed gene patterns can act as a constraint, either through restricting the types of learning that can occur or through increasing the probability that some types of learning or some types of response patterns are more likely to occur than others (Edelman, 1989; Hinde, 1987; Smith et al., 1985). "Universal" response patterns directed by adults to young infants may be one example of this type of mechanism (Hinde, 1987). Alternatively, genes or gene combinations that have been selected may act to shape the kinds of stimulus information we can process or select to process. For example, from an evolutionary viewpoint, bonding signals, kin recognition signals, or signals that identify existing environmental resources may be of particular perceptual salience (Charlesworth, 1996; Lumsden, 1983; Tooby & Cosmides, 1992).

Because of the historical nature of evolutionary processes, experimental studies typically have been restricted to infrahuman populations. For example, differential infrahuman learning as a function of the evolutionary history of the species is a well-documented phenomenon (Edelman, 1989). Stimuli that have provided cues for danger or resources in the history of the species may be particularly salient cues in current learning situations (e.g., the predisposition of rats to avoid tainted or poisoned food) (Hinde, 1987). However, even in these studies, current experience also may be important. For example, the preference of young rats for the diet eaten by their mothers during lactation, which could have an evolutionary basis, in fact appears to be mediated by the taste of the mother's milk (Slater, 1983).

There are very few data of this sort at the human level, although results showing fear of snakes by children who have had little experience with snakes is not inconsistent with the concept of an evolutionary predisposition (Hinde, 1987). Similarly, infrahuman studies indicate that when behavioral patterns that are atypical for the species are experimentally induced (e.g., cross-species attachment), these patterns are likely to change back to species-typical behavioral patterns when external pressure is relaxed (Cairns, Gariepy, & Hood, 1990). The greater propensity of men to show aggressive behavior patterns, even in cultures that have strong social pressures against the expression of aggression (Ekblad, 1989), could be the human parallel to these infrahuman data, suggesting that potential human-evolution-based predispositions may be less easy to extinguish.

Most investigations on evolutionary influences on human behavior and development are based on "arguments from design," namely that a specific behavioral pattern must have an evolutionary adaptive function because it appears so well fitted to fulfill this function (e.g., Tooby & Cosmides, 1992). Researchers working from within an evolutionary perspective are particularly likely to emphasize that evolutionary approaches provide unique predictions that no other approach can provide (MacDonald, 1996). For example, from an evolutionary perspective, it is argued that men are more likely to show sexual jealousy than women, because in the history of our species, men could never be sure of whether their offspring were actually theirs (i.e., carried their genes); in contrast, women should be more likely to show emotional jealousy, because male flirtations could mean that resources may be diverted from their children, thus reducing their chances of survival (DeKay & Buss, 1992). The problem, of course, is that there may be multiple alternative explanations besides evolutionary adaptive value for the phenomenon under study. For example, Gould (1991) has argued that some features or traits that evolved for one function become "coopted" for an alternative function (exaptation). Alternatively, some features or traits are maintained in a population not because they once had adaptive value but rather because they were associated with features or traits that did have adaptive value (spandrels). In either case, the current usage of the feature or trait does not reflect the influence of natural selection. The fact that there may be alternative explanations in and of itself does not necessarily negate the value of an evolutionary explanation for a phenomenon.

In some cases, an evolutionary explanation provides a reasonably good fit for the data. One example of such a good fit is seen in Chagnon's (1980) detailed description of how aid in village ax fights among the Yanomamo Indians of southern Venezuela was more likely to come from those who were closely biologically related to individual fighters. (Though see Kitcher, 1985, for a somewhat less evolution-based alternative interpretation.)

Although many evolutionary theorists would accept the idea that not every current behavioral or developmental pattern has evolutionary significance, most would argue that behavior patterns that are related to increasing reproductive success and offspring survival are most likely to have evolutionary underpinnings (MacDonald, 1987). Examples of such patterns would include group living patterns, differential parental investment in children, helping biological relatives, and choosing friends on the basis of their similarity to oneself (Lickliter & Berry, 1990; MacDonald, 1996; Noonan, 1987; Symons, 1992). These patterns do not mean that individuals consciously strive to maximize their reproductive fitness. Many goals may have very proximal causes (e.g., sexual pleasure). Rather, what is meant is that some of the mechanisms underlying current behaviors are those that have evolved to maximize fitness (Smith, 1987). Within this framework, what this means is that a full understanding of current behavioral and developmental patterns requires an understanding of what has been selected for in our species (Buss, 1991; DeKay & Buss, 1992; Smith, 1987).

Evolutionary Contributions to Individual Human Behavioral Development

Conceptual Aspects

It seems clear that evolutionary principles have potential validity when applied to explain group differences or similarities. Group similarities (universals) come about when different population groups are subjected to similar selection pressures, whereas group differences emerge when different population groups are subjected to different selection pressures (Rushton, 1984; Tooby & Cosmides, 1992). Thus, the relatively late dispersion of humans from what is thought to be their point of common origin could result in a common set of selection pressures and hence behavioral universals; however, available evidence also suggests that prior to the initiation of agriculture as a way of life (12,000 or so years ago), humans lived in relatively isolated small population groups (Ulijaszek, 1994), which could have resulted in regional (group) differences in selection pressures. However, evolution-based, group-level explanations of similarities or differences do not easily fit when attempting to understand similarities or differences in individual behavior or development (Gould, 1980; MacDonald, 1987). For example, although evolutionary theory predicts that young children will be predisposed to form alliances to gain resources, evolutionary theory would find it difficult to predict who will form alliances with whom or what the specific nature of the alliances will be (Krebs, 1996). One reason why evolutionary theory has problems in dealing with individual behavior and development is that the forces that influence an individual's current behavior or development may be very different from the forces that led to the evolution of the individual's ancestors (Bateson, 1985; Hinde, 1987). Unfortunately, all too often, individual differences in domains such as social relation patterns, which require individual-level explanations, are inappropriately translated into group-level explanations (e.g., it is thought that the individual behaves socially in this way because such behaviors were adaptive for the population the individual came from during his or her evolutionary history) (Ember, 1980).

Although there are major difficulties in translating what is essentially a population level of explanation to the individual level, there are potential evolutionary mechanisms that could be applied to individual developmental differences. One such potential mechanism is frequency-dependent selection (Noonan, 1987; Partridge, 1983; Wilson, 1994). When we consider changes in gene frequency over time, the traditional emphasis is on some genes or gene combinations increasing in frequency while others decrease, to the point where some genotypes are highly characteristic of a population whereas others rarely occur in this population. In contrast, *frequency-dependent selection* refers to a situation wherein alternative genes or gene combinations can be maintained in a population across time (Partridge, 1983). Such maintenance occurs because the success of a behavior pattern associated with a particular gene or gene combination is, in part, related to the frequency of expression of other gene-related behavior patterns in the population (Noonan, 1987).

For example, if all birds in a population gather resources by fishing except for one that gathers resources by stealing from other birds, then the thief (and its descendants) will have a reproductive advantage given that there are many birds available to steal from. However, if other birds also adopt a stealing strategy and the number of thieves increases while the number of fishing birds decreases, thieves will do more and more poorly because there are fewer and fewer fishing birds to steal from. What this pattern means over time is a fluctuating balance between the number of fishing birds and thieving birds, depending on the relative frequency of each type in the population (Dawkins, 1980).

Thus, it is not the individual's behavior per se that leads to greater accumulation of resources or greater offspring survival rate but rather the individual's behavior in regard to what others in the population are doing. Once the frequency of a genotype and the behaviors associated with this genotype increase in a population past a critical point, the fitness of this genotype and its associated behaviors will begin to decline. This decline will continue until the point when expression of an alternative behavior pattern becomes so frequent that the adaptive value of the alternative behavior, in turn, is lost (Partridge, 1983).

Frequency-dependent selection may be a major force for maintaining individual genetic variability within a population, because multiple gene-influenced traits can be maintained under these conditions but no one trait can ever be eliminated (Noonan, 1987). For example, D. Wilson (1994) has developed a model illustrating how the genotypes predisposing to the emergence of *developmental specialists* (behavior very adaptive in some conditions, far less in other conditions) and *developmental generalists* (behavior moderately adaptive in all situations) can both be maintained at viable levels in a population. Selection mechanisms such as frequency-dependent selection also can be supported by cultural practices that encourage optimal rather than extreme patterns. One example is seen in the Kung San Bushman culture, in which individual attempts to accumulate high levels of resources are viewed as culturally inappropriate, leading to cultural pressure favoring those who accumulate only modest resource levels (Lumsden, 1983). Such coevolution of evolutionary and cultural influences (Lumsden, 1983) may thus act to promote behavioral and developmental heterogeneity rather than homogeneity within a population.

Besides allowing for population heterogeneity in behavioral strategies, evolutionary processes also may act to promote individual differences in the individual's ability to shift behavioral patterns to take account of changes in his or her immediate context (Chisholm, 1990; Crawford & Anderson, 1989). Such an ability to shift strategies would undoubtedly have evolutionary advantages, at least up to a point (impulsiveness as the extreme point of the ability to shift strategies would be less likely to confer such an advantage) (MacDonald, 1996). Individual differences in the ability to shift strategies may reflect inherited differences in sensitivity to frequency-dependent conditions (e.g., how many other individuals in the population are also using this strategy; Caro & Bateson, 1986). Underlying such individual differences in sensitivity may be the operation of evolved environmental tracking and monitoring mechanisms, based on the individual's perception of the impact and scope of environmental changes and the impact of one's own behavior on the environment (Chisholm, 1989). Viewed in this way, evolutionary influences may act to provide individuals with a set of potential strategies that can then be selectively applied to solve evolution-relevant problems, such as the most optimal child-rearing patterns, mate selection, or manipulation of others to gain resources (Buss, 1991; Wilson et al., 1996). For example, within many infrahuman species, physically small individuals may adopt a mating strategy different from those used by large individuals, given that individual mating tactics used by large members of the population simply do not work well for those of small stature (Dawkins, 1980). From evolutionary history, it is known that some strategies will be more likely to be in the set from which the individual chooses (Dawkins, 1980; Smith, 1987; Wilson, 1980), but underlying evolutionary mechanisms do allow for variability in the individual's ability to choose and implement appropriate strategies.

Empirical Evidence

Although conceptually logical, attempts to test evolution-based explanations can be particularly problematical when applied to the question of variability in individual behavior and development (Krebs, 1996).[2] Even in situations where evolutionary principles are consistent with outcomes, the results also often illustrate the necessity of integrating nonevolutionary influences as part of the explanatory model. One example of this situation is seen in evolutionary approaches to individual differences in parental involvement with offspring. From an evolutionary perspective, men should be more likely to forgo heavy involvement with individual offspring in favor of reproducing maximal number of offspring (an r reproductive strategy), given the uncertainty of whether the offspring are really theirs. In contrast, because women have virtual certainty that their offspring will be genetically theirs, they are more likely not only to heavily invest in these offspring but also to select a mate who has more likelihood of being heavily invested in her offspring (a k reproductive strategy) (Draper & Belsky, 1990; Noonan, 1987). However, women with a life history that predisposes them to view adult relationships as essentially transitory (e.g., father absence, family conflict during childhood) should be more likely to adopt an r strategy than women who have family experiences predisposing them to view such relationships as stable. One manifestation of a female r strategy would be early puberty, allowing for more reproductive time. This evolutionary hypothesis was tested by Moffitt, Caspi, Belsky, and Silva (1992), who related age of female pubertal onset to measures of paternal absence, family stress, and behavioral problems in childhood. Results indicated that 49% of women with fathers who were absent during their childhood had early pubertal onset, compared with father absence rates of 33% for women with on-time puberty and 24% for women with late-onset puberty. A history of family conflict during childhood also was found to be predictive of early onset of puberty. These results could be used to argue for the operation of evolution-based mechanisms on individual maturational variability.

However, there also are valid alternative explanations (Graber, Brooks-Gunn, & Warren, 1995). For example, pointing to evidence for a

---

[2] The problem of individual variability for evolutionary explanations can also be seen when the unit of analysis becomes the species. In discussing species extinction, Gould (1989) has clearly documented how evolutionary principles, although essential in explaining why species extinction occurred, were not particularly helpful in post hoc predicting from the fossil record which species should have survived and which should have become extinct.

genetic contribution to pubertal onset, plus evidence of the consequences of early marriage, Moffitt et al. (1992) proposed that early-maturing women are more likely to date, have sex, and marry earlier than late-maturing women. Because early marriage is more likely to result in divorce, father absence is a more likely consequence of having a mother who reached puberty earlier. The genetic factors that influenced the mother's early puberty will be passed along to her daughter, who as a result also will mature earlier. In this case, father absence is a consequence rather than an evolutionary sensitive signal that triggers off alternative reproductive strategies.

Similar conclusions also can be drawn from studies of parental-resource allocation. Time is a finite resource, so that time allotted to one child means less time available for other children in the family (Noonan, 1987). From an evolutionary viewpoint, particularly under low-resource conditions, parents should tailor their investment time in their children on the basis of the degree of genetic resemblance or reproductive potential they see in each child. Within this framework, children perceived as having greater genetic resemblance to the parent or more reproductive potential should receive more parental investment (Smith, 1987). The increased risk for infanticide found for adopted or stepchildren (no shared genes), infants with disabilities (low reproductive potential), and unwed mothers or families undergoing economic hardship (low resource availability) could easily fit within an evolutionary framework (Daly & Wilson, 1984). However, the influence of changes in governmental policy on rate of female infanticide in China (Potter, 1987) or culture-based preferences for male offspring in northern India, where resource availability is not a problem (Miller, 1987), suggests that nonevolutionary, cultural mechanisms also are operative here.

Along the same lines, McCloskey et al. (1995) have shown that although there was an increased risk of aggression by stepfathers toward their stepchildren in families in which the stepfather had a biological child, the effect size associated with paternal biological resemblance was relatively small as compared with more proximal nonevolutionary predictors. Similarly, Mann (1992) documented maternal behavior toward high-risk twin offspring, one of whom was sicker than the co-twin. Although mothers allotted equal basic-care time to each twin, congruent with an evolutionary prediction, mothers directed more positive reactions toward the healthier of their two twins. However, Mann's results also showed that degree of maternal involvement with the healthier twin was positively related to degree of involvement with the sicker twin. This latter result does not neatly fit into a framework emphasizing evolutionary mechanisms; rather, it implicates the importance of nonevolutionary influences, such as individual differences in maternal responsivity.

Evolutionary Approaches to Individual Behavioral Development: Necessary But Not Sufficient

I have described potential mechanisms that could explain a relation between our species' evolutionary history and current variability in behavioral development. For example, it would be difficult to question the potential relevance of evolutionary processes for the development of certain species-wide human traits, such as infant categorical perception, gender stereotyping, and some aspects of language development (Hinde, 1987). Evolutionary processes, although historical in nature, can operate in the present through their shaping of the human genotype and central nervous system. Such shaping may be manifested in developmental constraints and predispositions, making some behaviors easier or harder to acquire or extinguish. To the extent that there is genetic heterogeneity underlying these constraints and predispositions, mechanisms influenced by evolutionary history could operate at the individual as well as at the species level.

However, evidence for the simultaneous operation of alternative nonevolutionary mechanisms makes it difficult to ascribe explanatory power essentially to historical evolutionary influences. For example, the possibility that evolutionary processes predispose men to be more aggressive than women in no way negates the relevance of social learning as an important influence on male aggression (Smith, 1987). It is not surprising that many evolutionary theorists accept a necessary-but-not-sufficient role for evolutionary influences on variability in human behavioral development (e.g., Bateson, 1985; Crawford & Anderson, 1989; DeKay & Buss, 1992; Hinde, 1987; Smith, 1987). However, there are still those who stress the idea that evolutionary influences per se are sufficient.

> For human cultural forces are biological, social forces are biological, physical forces are biological, and so on . . . . Every environmentalist explanation about the influence of a given part of the environment on humans will—if it is to be considered coherent—need to be accompanied by a specific nativist hypothesis about the evolved developmental and psychological mechanisms that forge the relationship between the environmental input and the hypothesized psychological input. All environmentalist theories necessarily depend upon and invoke nativist theories. (Tooby & Cosmides, 1992, pp. 86–87)

Within such a framework, it is argued that current problem-solving strategies have evolved from adaptive solutions developed during the hunter–gatherer period of human evolutionary history and that these adaptive hunter–gatherer solutions are universal and are built into the human species. Thus, if there are differences between the nature of the current context and our historical hunter–gatherer past, we will revert to "ancestral conditions" (Tooby & Cosmides, 1992).

There are two major implications that follow from this framework. First, such a framework means that a diverse set of disparate behavioral patterns are linked together by a common underlying universal adaptive mechanism, focused on promoting reproduction and offspring survival (Warner, 1980). For example, women working outside the home, offspring spacing (Smith, 1987), extroverted behavior (Buss, 1991), and acquisition of wealth (Irons, 1980) all can be viewed as examples of the working of this universal adaptive mechanism. Second, within this framework, development is viewed primarily as due to historical information encoded in the genes, which unfold through predetermined maturational sequences (Lickliter & Berry, 1990).

There are multiple reasons to question the validity of this framework, and by implication the hypothesis that evolutionary influences are both necessary and sufficient. Obviously, there is the question of how much we really know about the adaptiveness of specific behaviors and mechanisms in our ancestral past. For example, evolutionary explanations of gender differences in intelligence may be based on incorrect assumptions about the range of female activities in ancestral hunter–gatherer societies (Halpern, 1997). Furthermore, biological changes that result from evolutionary selection pressures, such as a larger human central nervous system, may allow for a variety of new reaction patterns that have little to do with original selection conditions (Gould, 1991). One example would be the ability to effectively use a highly complex and symbolic environmental system (Gould, 1982). Similarly, the rapid pace of cultural evolution, particularly when contrasted with the relatively slow pace of genetic evolution, means that previously adaptive behaviors may no longer have adaptive value (Hinde, 1989, 1991; Symons, 1992). Along the same lines, the assumption that changes in adaptive strategies derived from our ancestral past can occur only over very long time periods also has been questioned. Specifically, D. Wilson (1994) has postulated that the speed of change in an evolution-based trait will vary as a function of the heritability of the trait, what type of trait is being considered, and the strength of current selection pressure on that trait, including cultural evolutionary pressures.

An emphasis on relatively invariant, evolution-driven, universal behavioral patterns also is particularly problematical. First, as discussed by D. Wilson (1994), universality of a trait depends in part on the level one is dealing with. Thus, even if there is a universal predisposition to aggressive behavior, as suggested by evolutionary psychologists, wide individual variability will exist in what it takes to elicit aggressive behavior from a given individual or the purposes for which a given individual displays aggression. Second, the criteria for accepting behaviors as innate and universally invariant are extremely stringent (Papousek & Papousek, 1991). Even a single discordant example is enough to lead to questions about universality, and discordant examples are relatively easy to find. For example, Tooby and

Cosmides (1992) have argued that infants the world over show essentially similar developmental processes and behavioral patterns. This sweeping conclusion is contradicted by evidence by Lewis, Ramsay, and Kawakami (1993) showing distinctly different biological–behavioral reactions to stress by Japanese and American infants, with Japanese infants being more biologically reactive but behaviorally inhibited and American infants showing the reverse pattern. The universality of patterns of early motor development can be called into question from detailed research by Super (1976) that shows how culturally based rearing differences can have a strong influence on such patterns.

Going beyond infancy, we find multiple lines of evidence contradicting the hypothesis that evolutionary explanations are sufficient. Avoidance of incestuous relations is thought to be a universal evolutionary predisposition of the human species (Lumsden, 1983). However, there are examples of human cultural groups, as in south India, that support incestuous uncle–niece marriages with little evidence of phyletic consequences such as inbreeding depression (Livingstone, 1980; Rao & Inbaraj, 1977). A central aspect of many sociobiological theories is that altruistic behavior developed because it was evolutionarily adaptive. That is, aiding those who are genetically related to oneself gives a selective advantage to those individuals sharing a common genotype, the mechanism of kin selection. However, evidence at both the infrahuman and human levels documents multiple examples of altruistic behavior among individuals who are genetically unrelated (Guisinger & Blatt, 1994). From an evolutionary viewpoint, both sibling rivalries and competition among children should be a universal predisposition, based on individuals attempting to maximize their share of critical but limited resources, such as parent investment (Charlesworth, 1996; Noonan, 1987). However, there are sufficient examples from cross-cultural research to demonstrate that if there are evolutionary predispositions for sibling rivalry and individual competition, these predispositions are easily overwhelmed by cultural pressure toward cooperation, both among unrelated children (Smith, 1996) and among siblings (Watson-Gegeo & Gegeo, 1989). Indeed, as Cole (1992) has suggested, what may be the universal predisposition among humans is a relatively broad ability to function within some type of cultural context. Other examples of inconsistent findings have been noted earlier in this chapter.

A similar point can be made in regard to discussions of direct evolutionary pressures on the development and functioning of the human central nervous system (Edelman, 1989). Although evolutionary influences may act as an influence on the evolution of the human brain, there may be indirect influences as well, based on the coevolution over time of culture and the human central nervous system (Hinde, 1987; Noonan, 1987). One function of culture is to provide cross-generational regularity of experiences for individuals within the culture (Cole, 1992). Under conditions of coevolution between culturally stable experiences and central nervous system development, the central nervous system may evolve in the direction of being predisposed to incorporate information that has a high probability of occurring at certain developmental periods (*experience-expectant development*) (Greenough, Black, Chang, & Sirevang, 1990). Within an experience-expectant framework, development is not a direct function of either evolutionary pressures on the central nervous system or of individual experiences. Rather, development results from a probabilistic covariance between a maturing central nervous system influenced by evolutionary history and the occurrence of certain critical experiences during certain developmental time periods. Evidence of what happens when such experiences do not occur when expected is seen in infrahuman studies. A number of studies have documented how so called "innate" universal behavioral patterns can be disrupted when nonobvious but pervasive environmental conditions are not allowed to occur during the time or place they normally would do so (Lickliter & Gottlieb, 1985; Miller, 1997).

The concept of experience-expectant development, incorporating both historical and current conditions, offers an alternative view to the traditional evolutionary view of universal processes of development. For the most part it has been assumed that human "universal" developmental–behavioral patterns, including early language development (Shatz, 1985), vocalization patterns of parents to infants (Jacobson, Boersma, Fields, & Olson 1983; Papousek & Papousek, 1991), and caregiver behavioral patterns to children of different ages (Edwards, 1992), result from evolution-based predispositions. However, the operation of experience-expectant development not only offers a specific mechanism whereby "universal" behavior patterns can occur, but it also allows for individual variation within these universals, which the traditional evolutionary view of invariant universal processes does not do. Experience-expectant developmental processes are based both on central nervous system maturation and the "expectation" by the central nervous system that the child will be exposed to certain stimuli, such as language, during maturational periods when central nervous system structures involved in the processing of these stimuli come on line. This co-occurrence is probabilistic, in that the appropriate stimulation has high probability of occurring but the occurrence is not guaranteed. At the human level, an excellent example of the nonoccurrence of experience-expectant development is seen in the case of the preterm infant, who is thrust out into the noisy, bright, unpredictable world of the intensive care unit well ahead of the time an infant would normlly encounter such stimulation from the evolutionary history of our species (Als, 1992). (The developmental consequences of preterm birth are discussed in chap. 4.) Similarly, focusing on the universality of behavioral patterns tends to ignore the informational content contained in such behavioral patterns. For example, in the case of the "universal" patterns of parental vocalization patterns to infants, the characteristics of such vocalizations act to make vowels more distinct to the infant, thus increasing the infant's ability to categorize and imitate adult speech patterns (Kuhl et al., 1997). Although the universality of adult speech patterns to infants may have an evolutionary basis, the functional implications of these patterns are better viewed within the framework of experience-expectant development. Even within an evolutionary framework, variations in timing or nature of critical stimulation may be reflected in differential development for individuals within a given population (Archer, 1996; Buss, Haselton, Shackelford, Bleske, & Wakefield, 1998).

Finally, even the traditional viewpoint linking genetic change to evolutionary changes has been questioned (Gottlieb, 1987, 1992). Rather than assuming that genetic change is the driving force behind evolutionary change, Gottlieb has argued that the driving force may be individual behavioral variability. Specifically, Gottlieb has hypothesized that over the evolution of our species, contextual changes due to migration or climatological changes resulted in new sources of stress and support for individuals. The resulting changes in behavioral patterns to meet these new stresses and supports led to individual biological changes. Such biological changes, although inherent in our species genotype, had not been previously elicited. (See Gottlieb 1992 for discussion of how, under the correct conditions, chickens can grow teeth.) Behavioral stability is maintained across generations by stability in the contextual conditions that produced the original behavioral changes. Although there is traditional genetic selection as a result of individual variability in adapting to changing conditions, in Gottlieb's framework the evolutionary changes have preceded the changes in gene frequency.

Even if one is not willing to accept Gottlieb's alternative view of linkages between genes, evolution, and behavior, there still remains the paradox that adaptation of a strict evolutionary genetic model (wherein selection drives variations in gene frequency and the resulting genotype drives current behavior) severely limits the potential contributions of evolutionary approaches to understanding human behavior and development. This limitation comes from the fact that under severe directional selection pressure, additive genetic contributions (the combined influences of multiple genes on a trait—why offspring resemble parents) will essentially drop to zero over multiple generations, because directional selection pressure acts to restrict genetic variability in the population (Symons, 1992). This restriction means that unless a case can be made for nondirectional selection pressure, evolutionary contributions to our understanding of human behavioral development may be limited to those human traits that show relatively low additive heritability (Crawford & Anderson, 1989). Because the vast majority of human behavioral traits show at least moderate additive genetic influence (see chap. 3), this would severely restrict the relevance of evolutionary explanations to a relatively limited number of traits. A similar point was argued by Chisholm (1990) when he noted that evolution-guided genetic processes such as canalization (self-righting tendencies) are most adaptive when there is a relatively narrow range of environments, wherein the ability to be able to respond flexibly to novel situations is unimportant.

Ultimately, I would agree with the conclusion by Smith (1987), who views evolutionary influences as laying down broad predispositions or blueprints, whereas more proximal influences act to channel and actualize these evolutionary predispositions. Viewed within this framework, evolutionary influences may be considered necessary but in no way sufficient for understanding individual variability in human behavior and development.

PHYSICAL ECOLOGICAL INFLUENCES

As noted earlier, variability in physical ecology and the individual's ability to adapt to this variability are major driving forces behind evolutionary selection. In addition, there is also the possibility that physical ecological influences can have concurrent as well as historical influences on human behavior and development. Like evolutionary influences, these effects are more useful in explaining group rather than individual differences, although tentative links to individual development will be noted as well.

Direct Consequences of Physical Ecology

High-altitude living is one physical ecological feature that has been studied as a potential biological stressor (Frisancho, 1975). Using a traditional cutoff of altitude greater than 3,000 meters, it is estimated that between 20 and 30 million individuals live at high altitudes (Pawson & Jest, 1978). Living at high altitudes involves exposure to reduced oxygen concentration and reduced barometric pressure and humidity, a lack of critical trace minerals in the soil (e.g., iodine), increased radiation, and highly variable temperatures (Saco-Pollitt, 1989). Even after controlling for potential confounds like diet, socioeconomic level, and availability of medical facilities, high-altitude living conditions are associated with a variety of physical consequences. These consequences include greater lung capacity, smaller stature, and increased risk for low birth weight and infant mortality. In addition, the greater need for blood oxygen saturation at high altitudes and the fact that the curve relating hemoglobin concentration to altitude appears to be exponential rather than linear means that for diagnosing iron-deficiency anemia, different cutoff points may be needed for individuals living at high altitudes (Berger et al., 1997). High-altitude living is also associated with variability in neonatal neuromotor behavior, including less orienting to stimuli, less responsivity, and less adequate state control (Saco-Pollitt, 1989), as well as with delays in early motor development (Pollitt & Saco-

Pollitt, 1996). However, many of the neuromotor consequences of high-altitude living appear to occur primarily during the first few days of life, and associated motor delays tend to disappear after the first year of life. These results suggest that there may be behavioral adaptation to these types of conditions. Similarly, the physical consequences of high-altitude living can be moderated to some degree by individual behavioral patterns, such as level of vigorous activity (Frisancho et al., 1995). However, as I note below, there do appear to be child-rearing consequences associated with living at high altitudes.

In general, seasonal influences have received little study in the behavioral literature. One notable exception is replicated evidence indicating a small but significant tendency for people with schizophrenia to have been born in the winter months (Crow, 1989). Although this effect may be related to an increased risk of maternal illness or increased maternal intake of medication during flu season affecting fetal central nervous system development, particularly during the second trimester (Mednick, Machon, Huttenen, & Bonett, 1988), not all of the increased seasonal risk for schizophrenia can be associated with increased flu risk per se (Sham et al., 1992). Evidence also indicates seasonal effects on a variety of biological outcome parameters. For example, there is an increased incidence of gastrointestinal illness for children living in tropical climates during the hot rainy season (Sepulveda, Willett, & Munoz, 1988). As will be seen in chapter 4, gastrointestinal illness is a risk factor for adequacy of individual growth and development.

Seasonal influences on physical growth in less developed countries also have been documented. Seasonal influences are related to maternal weight gain during pregnancy, incidence of low birth weight, and the impact of nutritional supplementation during pregnancy on infant birth weight (Prentice, Cole, Foord, Lamb, & Whitehead, 1987). However, it also appears that seasonal influences do not fit a simple cyclical model (Ferro-Luzzi, Pastore, & Sette, 1988). The complex nature of relations between seasonal influences and child growth may reflect the moderation of seasonal effects by factors such as characteristic child rearing practices, individual level of morbidity (Ferro-Luzzi et al., 1988), season-related work load (Prentice et al., 1987), and maternal nutritional status (Adair & Pollitt, 1985). Moderation of seasonal influences by individual child-rearing, morbidity, or nutritional factors illustrates how seasonal influences can be associated with variability in individual as well as population behavior. However, such moderation also illustrates why seasonal influences, although necessary, will not be sufficient.

It is also important to note that seasonal influences are not restricted to just the less developed countries of the world. In the United States, in a poverty sample of children in the first and second year of life, the risk of a child being below the fifth percentile in weight for age was significantly greater in the 3 months following the coldest months of the year than in any other time block (Frank et al., 1996). What may underlie this relation is the choice poor families may have to make between using scarce financial resources to pay for heating or food during the winter (Brown & Sherman, 1995). Parental choice in regard to resource allocation may well be another mechanism whereby group influences like seasonality translate down to the individual level.

Indirect Influence of Physical Ecology on Development

The relation of features of the physical ecology to features of the culture nested within that physical ecology is a well-researched theme (Pandey, 1990). For example, changes in physical ecology can act to change the adaptive value of specific cultural practices, as in the case of cultures that emphasize high fertility even though there are decreases in available land (LeVine & LeVine, 1988). One well-documented indirect linkage is through physical ecology (e.g., resource availability) influencing characteristic group-subsistence patterns. These patterns in turn influence cultural beliefs, which are then translated into specific child-rearing patterns. One portion of this causal chain is seen in the link from subsistence patterns to cultural beliefs. For example, hunter–gatherer cultures are typically more likely to stress independence, self-reliance, and resourcefulness as child-rearing goals, whereas agriculturally based cultures are more likely to stress cooperation, social sensitivity, and obedience (Berry, 1990; Pandey, 1990; Witkin & Berry, 1975). Although the link between culturally based belief systems and actual caregiving practices can act to promote group differences, the probabilistic nature of this linkage allows considerable room for individual variability in both rearing styles and developmental outcomes (Goodnow, 1985, 1992).

A second portion of this causal chain is seen in links between physical ecological factors and characteristic caregiver behavior patterns. Ecologically related variability in caregiving behavior patterns can act to influence offspring variability in behavior and development. For example, average temperature and temperature range have been related to differences in the amount of physical contact between adults and children, as well as the types of carrying procedures used by caregivers with children (Whiting, 1981). Thus, the characteristic practice of tightly swaddling infants in high-altitude cold climates, while acting to maintain body warmth and conserve calories, also has the effect of restricting motor activity and stimulation (Tronick, Thomas, & Daltabuit, 1994). In addition to potential consequences on cognitive performance, it has been speculated that this type of rearing situation predisposes to a more passive personality, either directly or through cultural–ecological–evolutionary covariation (i.e., those infants who can best tolerate swaddling are more likely to be favored by parents in this culture) (Greenfield & Childs, 1991).

In tropical climates, where food sources may involve increased levels of fruit and roots and lower protein availability, young children may be more dependent on nursing. This may mean a longer period until weaning, which in turn may also mean a stronger mother–child bond (Pandey, 1990). The location of food resources also may influence the degree to which young children are expected to do chores; the further away the available food resources, the fewer demands that are placed on young children for chores (Draper & Cashdan, 1988). As we shall see in chapter 7, chore activities can be a major influence on children's development, through both socialization and instructional experiences while the child is doing chores (Whiting & Edwards, 1988). Natural physical hazards also may have a direct impact on child-rearing practices and thereby on individual development, by influencing the degree to which caregivers restrict the child's attempts at locomotion and independent exploration of the environment (Kaplan & Dove, 1987; McSwain, 1981).

Physical Ecological Influences: Necessary But Not Sufficient

Although physical ecological features would seem to act primarily as an influence on group differences in caregiving practices rather than individual differences within the group, what must be emphasized is that not all parents in a given ecological setting will use techniques like swaddling, chore assignment, or restriction of exploration to the same degree. Individual child characteristics, like how well the child adapts to swaddling or to parental demands, can act as feedback mechanisms, tempering caregiver rearing patterns within a given physical ecology (Chisholm, 1983; Goodnow, 1985). Moderation of specific caregiving practices within a given physical ecology allows for both group differences as a function of physical ecological features and individual variability within the group. As noted earlier, such moderation means that physical ecological features, although a potentially necessary influence on human development, cannot be viewed as sufficient for a full understanding of the etiology of individual variability in development.

3

GENETIC, NEURAL,
AND HORMONAL INFLUENCES

Although the development and functioning of genetic, central nervous system, and hormonal influences may be triggered, channeled, or moderated by extrinsic factors, at least initially these influences fundamentally have an intra-individual origin. This origin is in contrast to biomedical and nutritional influences, which are covered in the next chapter, whose origins are more likely to come from outside the individual.

GENETIC INFLUENCES

The focus of this section will be on known and potential linkages between individual genetic variability and individual behavioral–developmental variability. Findings from molecular genetics will be discussed only briefly, primarily because much of the available research has been done using infrahuman populations (McClearn, Plomin, Gora-Maslak & Crabbe 1991). For readers wishing an introduction to potential applications of molecular genetic methods to the study of human development, an excellent source is a chapter by Plomin and Saudino (1994).

Molecular Genetic Action

The fundamentals of gene action are a well-known story (McClearn, 1993; Plomin, 1990). A few highlights of this story that are of special relevance to the present chapter will be discussed. Genes (self-duplicating neuclotide base pairs) are carried on chromosomes, of which there are normally 23 pairs in each cell of the human body. As a result of chromosomal reduction and division processes during reproduction, each individual inherits pairs of genes, one from each parent. Disruptions in chromosomal transmission processes can result in disruption of normal genetic functioning either at the chromosomal level (e.g., too much or too little genetic material) or at the gene level (Pembrey, 1991). Normally, in an ordered sequence of multiple steps, genes translate into amino acid sequences, and amino acid sequences in turn translate into specific structural proteins and enzymes. In this process, certain genes (structural genes) primarily code for amino acids. The function of other genes (regulator genes) appears to involve turning on or off, or even enhancing, the operation of the structural genes (Plomin, DeFries, McClearn, & Rutter, 1997). The operation of the structural genes appears to be insensitive to anything except the biological action of regulator genes. In contrast, the operation of regulator genes can be influenced by factors that are not intrinsic to the organism, such as nutrition or exposure to heavy metals (Plomin, 1994).

There are a number of implications of these molecular processes in regard to understanding genetic contributions to human development. First, given the number of steps, there are many places in this complex process where things can go wrong. Second, genes do not directly code for behavior. Rather, what genes code for are amino acid sequences. Thus, in talking about genetic influences on behavior and development, it must be emphasized that this is only a convenient short-hand term, meaning that genes code for amino acids that interact over time with a variety of other genetic and nongenetic influences; it is this complex interaction that ultimately influences behavioral developmental variability (Plomin, 1991). An example of this complex interaction process whereby genetic variability is ultimately translated into behavioral variability is shown in Figure 3-1. As can be seen from Figure 3-1 there is a complex, multilevel, nondirect pathway from genes to individual differences in behavioral development. Finally, although structural genes are in place at the moment of conception, this does not mean that they are all operating. Depending on the functioning of regulator genes, the influence of specific structural genes on behavior and development may be delayed to a point well past birth; similarly, structural genes that operate early in life may not be the same genes that are operating later in life (Gottesman & Goldsmith, 1994).

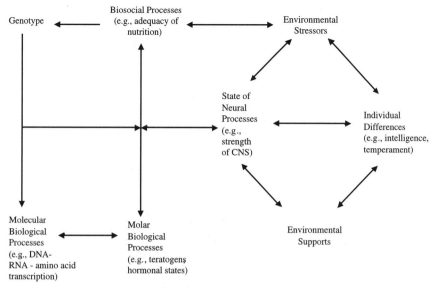

Figure 3-1. Example of a multilevel pathway from genes to behavior. CNS = central nervous system.

Chromosomal and Single-Gene Processes

Historically, the study of genetic influences on human behavior has focused primarily on the action of chromosomes or single genes. Characteristics thought to be dichotomous in nature, such as alcoholism or mental retardation, were viewed as being particularly sensitive to the action of single genes or chromosomes (McClearn, 1993). Family-pedigree studies, tracing disease characteristics within families and looking for distributions that fit Mendalian laws on inheritance, were initially used to identify single-gene influences. More recent approaches within this tradition have used linkage analysis, which allows for assessment of single-gene influences even when these influences are moderated by other genetic or nongenetic factors. This approach has been particularly productive in regard to identifying single-gene influences on a number of diseases, including cystic fibrosis, Duchenne muscular dystrophy, Huntington's chorea, and some forms of kidney disease (McClearn et al., 1991).

What have also been shown, however, are the many potential complexities involved in understanding the nature of links between single-gene action and behavioral development. On a behavioral level, the increasing use of highly complex statistical modeling procedures can mean that by making certain assumptions, highly ambiguous data can be made to fit an existing single-gene model. The pitfalls of such modeling approaches are beautifully illustrated by McGuffin and Huckle (1990) with their "discovery" that a single major recessive gene is responsible for medical school attendance. On a molecular level, infrahuman data have indicated the operation of a phenomenon called *genomic imprinting*, meaning that even with the same gene, there may be differential expression depending on whether the gene comes from the mother or the father (Solter, 1988). In recent years, a small number of rare genetic-based human disorders have been shown to be influenced by genomic imprinting (Pembrey, 1991). For example, the most severe congenital form of mytonic dystrophy is found in children who inherit the gene mutation from their mothers, whereas the rare early-onset form of Huntington's disorder is found primarily in those children who inherit the mutant gene from their father. Both Prader–Willi syndrome (mild to moderate retardation, short stature, obesity, and compulsive eating) and Angelman syndrome (severe retardation, little speech, positive disposition, and puppet-like motor behavior) involve a Chromosome 15 deletion, with the molecular areas deleted appearing to be identical. What distinguishes these two syndromes is that the Prader–Willi deletion is primarily paternal in origin, whereas the Angelman deletion appears to be maternal. More recent evidence suggests that a more common single-gene disorder, fragile X syndrome, may also be influenced by genomic imprinting (Hagerman, 1996). The implications of processes such as genomic imprinting for understanding the nature of chromosomal and single-gene contributions to development remains an open question at present.

Multiple Gene Processes

Although a number of single-gene influences on dichotomous characteristics have been identified, the vast majority of human traits are continuously distributed. For continuously distributed traits, a more likely mode of inheritance involves the operation of multiple genes, with each gene having a modest influence on the behavior in question. To assess the role of multiple genes, there are a variety of techniques that have been developed, based on looking at the degree of resemblance among individuals with varying degrees of biological relationship (McClearn et al., 1991). Standard behavioral genetic research designs are shown in Table 3-1. Variants on standard behavioral genetic designs also have been developed that allow more precise estimation of the nature of genetic influences (Cardon & Cherny, 1994). For example, analyzing for correlations between monozygotic and dizygotic twin performance on a specific outcome measure and their cotwin's performance on a different outcome measure allows us to estimate the degree to which similar genes may underlie performance on two different measures (Plomin & Rende, 1991). In recent years, approaches derived from molecular and behavioral genetics have been integrated (e.g., quantitative trait loci studies), which have enabled identification of multiple genes underlying continuously distributed traits (Plomin, DeFries et al., 1997).

TABLE 3-1

Common Designs and Potential Methodological Problems Found with Traditional Approaches to Studying Influences of Multiple Genes

Type of Study	Assumptions	Limits
Twin	MZ twins share common genes and common environment; DZ twins share half of their genes and common environment. Extent of genetic influence defined by degree to which MZ intertwin correlations exceed DZ intertwin correlations (Mzr > DZr).	MZ twins are more likely to share a more common environment than are DZ twins. Uniqueness of twin population may limit generalizability to nontwin populations.
Family	Trait resemblance among relatives differing in degree of genetic relatedness. Compare observed resemblance to what one would expect from genetic models.	Relative share both genes and environment, making it dfficult to separate out unique genetic contributions.
High-risk	Follow-up of children whose parents have a disorder believed to have a biological basis. Do children with type of risk have a higher incidence of the disorder? Can be combined with adoption studies.	Potential confounding of genetic and environmental risk. Not all children in risk population have the genetic liability for the disorder.
Adoption	Early-adopted children receive their genes from their biological parents and their environment from their adoptive parents. Greater resemblance to biological parents, greater influence of genetic factors. Can be combined with twin studies (reared-apart MZ twins).	Conclusions depend on statistics used (correlations versus mean differences between adopted child and biological and adoptive parents). Restruction of range of environments in adoptive families. Question of what does reared apart mean in terms of nature of environment (e.g., selective placement). Importance of early adoption, otherwise there can be confounding of genetic and environmental influences.
Inbreeding	Inbreeding increases probability that recessive genes will be expressed. Recessive genes are more likely to be deleterious. Greater inbreeding depression suggests a greater influence of genetic factors.	Natural confounding between inbreeding depression and parental deviance or social class in many societies.

Note. MZ = monozygotic; DZ = dizygotic.

Obviously, there are many potential methodological pitfalls that need to be considered when attempting to estimate the degree and nature of genetic influences on development. Some of the more common pitfalls are shown in Table 3-1. Other, less obvious problems are associated with specific study populations or specific methods. For example, it seems clear that estimates of genetic influence based on studies with twin populations often will be significantly higher than estimates based on family or adoptive populations (Gottesman, 1993; McCartney, Harris, & Bernieri, 1990; Plomin, 1991), perhaps reflecting the salience of a common prenatal environment for twins (Devlin, Daniels, & Roeder, 1997). Also problematic is the fact that monozygotic twins who share a common placenta will be more similar than monozygotic twins who do not, indicating a source of increased monozygotic twin resemblance that is nongenetic in nature (Rose, 1995). Selection of adoptive parents with higher educational or intellectual levels may reduce the degree of relation between adoptive parent and adopted child characteristics, because of restriction of the range of environments in adoptive families (Cavalli-Sforza & Feldman, 1981; Stoolmiller, 1999).

Finally, as a prelude to points that are raised later in this chapter, there are developmental scientists who question the traditional behavior genetic strategy of partitioning variance, with so much variance accorded to genes and so much to environment. The argument made is that development is rarely a function of such neatly partitioned categories (Oyama, 1989) and that genetic influences cannot really be understood in isolation from the role of other multiple influences on development (Bronfenbrenner & Ceci, 1994; Cairns, 1993). Although I would agree with this alternative viewpoint in regard to the processes underlying genetic influences on development, it is important to recognize that this argument is not as serious an objection when we ask a different question: Is there evidence for a genetic influence on individual behavior and development per se, regardless of how this influence occurs? Determining whether there are genetic influences is a necessary first step. If answered in the affirmative, we can then ask the more critical question: How does genetic variability translate into developmental variability? The next section will focus on the former question, Do genetic factors influence development? Discussion of potential mechanisms whereby genetic influences may occur will be found later in this chapter and in later sections of this volume.

Genetic Influences on Individual Behavior and Development

Genetics and Intelligence

It is well established that chromosomal deviations can result in mental retardation (for reviews, see Pembrey, 1991; Pueschel & Thuline, 1991). One of the most common causes of moderate mental retardation is chromosomal in nature, namely Down's syndrome (Rubenstein et al., 1990). Chromosomal deviations associated with mental retardation can involve either extra autosomes (trisomy 21, Down's syndrome), extra sex chromosomes (Kleinfelter's syndrome, XXY), autosome deletions (Chromosome 5 deletion, cri du chat syndrome), or sex chromosome deletions (Turner syndrome, XO). Although some chromosomal disorders such as Down's syndrome are associated primarily with deficits in general intellectual functioning, other chromosomal disorders are related primarily to deficits in specific cognitive functioning. For example, additional sex-chromosomal material (XXX, XXY) tends to be associated with decreased verbal abilities relative to the individual's level of spatial abilities; in contrast, missing X chromosomal material (XO) appears to be associated with relatively poorer spatial abilities (Netley & Rovet, 1988; Newcombe & Dubos, 1987). A few points are worth noting in regard to chromosomes and mental retardation. First, the overwhelming majority of chromosomal disorders are extremely rare in nature; even the most common of these disorders, such as Down's syndrome, has an incidence rate of only 1 to 2 per 1,000 live births (Rubenstein et al., 1990). Second, as discussed in chapter 1, there can be tremendous variability in the cognitive outcomes associated with some types of chromosomal abnormalities (Pueschel & Thuline, 1991).

A similar set of conclusions can be drawn in regard to the role of single-gene influences on abnormal levels of intellectual functioning. Many single-gene disorders have been associated with intellectual deficits, though, again, these disorders appear to be extremely rare (Abuelo, 1991). The single-gene mutation associated with fragile X syndrome may be the most common of these disorders (Hagerman, 1996), though even here incidence rates are no greater than 1 per 1,250 births for men, who are most likely to be affected (Plomin, DeFries et al., 1997). Probably the best-understood single-gene-based disorder leading to mental retardation is phenylketonuria. Phenylketonuria (PKU) is a relatively rare (1 in 10,000 live births) single-gene recessive disorder associated with an enzyme deficiency, leading to an inability to metabolize the amino acid phenylalanine. Resulting biochemical abnormalities act to damage the developing central nervous system (Belmont, 1994). Although strict dietary restriction of phenylalanine intake blocks the occurrence of retardation, even with this type of diet, PKU children can still average 8 to 11 IQ points below what would be expected from their family circumstances (Fuggle & Graham, 1991). This decrement reflects the fact that even with a restricted diet, there can be a residual influence of higher than normal phenylalanine levels on the development of the prefrontal cortex and on specific cognitive functions associated with the functioning of the prefrontal cortex (Diamond, Ciaramitaro, Donner, Djali, & Robinson, 1994). As a result, even for PKU children who can successfully stay on the recommended diet, there may still be deficits in those specific cognitive functions that are mediated by the prefrontal cortex, such as working memory and inhibitory control (Diamond et al., 1997).

As noted earlier, genetic contributions to intellectual variability in the normal range appear to be better explained by the action of multiple genes. Four consistent lines of evidence demonstrate the necessary role of genetic influences for general cognitive function in the normal range (Abuelo, 1991; McGue, Bouchard, Iacono, & Lykken, 1993): (a) monozygotic (identical) twins consistently show greater cognitive similarity than do dizygotic (fraternal) twins; (b) for nontwin populations, significant correlations have been found in the IQ scores of biologically related relatives who are reared apart; (c) as genetic resemblance increases, so does the IQ resemblance; and (d) as degree of parental biological resemblance increases (inbreeding), IQ score of offspring decreases. Within the past decade, reviews generally have concluded that the heritability of general intelligence is in the .5 range (Plomin & Rende, 1991; Rose, 1995).

In regard to specific abilities, there does appear to be greater genetic influence on verbal and spatial abilities than on memory (Cardon & Fulker, 1993), though these estimates may need to be qualified as a function of the age of the individual (Rose, 1995). Given linkages between school achievement and intelligence, we would expect at least some degree of genetic influence on school achievement, either as a function of commonality among measures or as a result of genetic influences common to both intelligence and achievement performance. At least for twins, the heritability of school achievement appears to fall in the .4 range (Thompson, Detterman, & Plomin, 1993). At least some of the genetic contribution to school achievement may reflect genetic contributions to general cognitive functioning (Plomin, DeFries et al., 1997). Evidence also indicates a consistent genetic influence on reading achievement (Wadsworth, 1994). This influence appears to be the result of multiple genetic mechanisms, with different types of reading disability influenced by different genetic mechanisms (DeFries & Gillis, 1993). At present, there is less agreement in regard to math achievement, with twin studies suggesting considerably stronger genetic influences than do adoption studies (Wadsworth, 1994).

Genes and Personality

Although there is ample evidence for the cognitive consequences of chromosomal or single-gene disorders on cognitive functioning, remarkably little parallel evidence exists in the area of personality. Available studies indicate a wide range of temperamental variation in Down's syndrome children, which makes it difficult to associate a unique temperament style with this syndrome (Goldberg & Marcovitch, 1989). Other evidence suggests social adjustment problems and feelings of loneliness in girls with Turner syndrome, whereas boys with Kleinfelter syndrome are rated as less assertive and less aggressive (Netley & Rovet, 1988). Poorer social skills, greater shyness, and a higher level of fear also have been reported as characteristic of girls with fragile X syndrome (Fruend, Baumgardner, Mazzocco, & Reiss, 1995), which may account for their higher social-anxiety levels (Rutter et al., 1990). However, it must be kept in mind that such conclusions are based on a very small number of studies.

In regard to multiple-gene influences, moderate heritabilities in the .2 to .4 range have been consistently demonstrated for a variety of personality and temperament traits (Loehlin, 1992; Plomin & Rende, 1991; Rose, 1995). Personality traits that appear to be most sensitive to genetic influences include extroversion, emotionality, sociability, and emotional stability (Loehlin, 1992; Plomin, 1991; Rowe, 1993). Negative affectivity and activity level appear to be the domains of infant temperament that are most sensitive to genetic influence (Goldsmith, 1989). Significant but perhaps less salient genetic influence also has been shown for a variety of other personality and temperament traits, including agreeableness, distress to limits, inhibitory control, sensation seeking, impulsivity (Gottesman & Goldsmith, 1994), and masculinity–femininity (Jacklin & Reynolds, 1993). In evaluating the role of genetic influences, it is important to note that the significance and extent of such influences on personality will vary as a function of the population studied (e.g., parent offspring or adopted sample vs. twins; Plomin, 1991; Schmitz, 1994), how personality or temperament are measured (e.g., self-report vs. other report vs. behavioral observations; Rose, 1995; Schmitz, 1994), and the age of participants studied (Viken, Rose, Kaprio, & Koshenvino, 1994).

Psychopathology

Controversy continues over the role of chromosomal damage and the influence of single major genes on the major forms of psychopathology (Plomin & Rende, 1991). For example, although fragile X syndrome has been linked to autism, less than 5% of cases of autism manifest fragile X syndrome (Rutter et. al., 1990). Some evidence does suggest that a single autosomal dominant gene may relate to the presence of obsessive–compulsive disorders, adult Tourette's syndrome, and the presence of motor tics (Rutter et al., 1990).

We appear to be on more solid ground when we look at evidence for multiple-gene contributions to psychopathology. The evidence for a genetic contribution to schizophrenia seems quite well established (Gottesman, 1993; Plomin, 1991). For example, although the lifetime risk rate for schizophrenia in the general population is about 1%, the average risk rate is just below 50% for the co-twin of a monozygotic twin with schizophrenia, about 13% for offspring of parents, with schizophrenia and approximately 9% for siblings of indviduals with schizophrenia, with decreasing resemblance thereafter as biological resemblance further declines (Gottesman, 1993).

Twin data have consistently supported the importance of genetics to the etiology of infantile autism (Rutter, Bailey, Bolton, & LeCouteur, 1993). Even given the rarity of this disorder in the population, the risk rate of siblings of autistic children may be 50 times greater than the risk rate for autism in the general population (Rutter et al., 1990). Although the exact nature of genetic contributions to autism is unclear, the excess of autistic men suggests that genetic influences on autism probably are not autosomal, whereas the high concordance rate for monozygotic twins compared with dizygotic twins and the rapid fall off of autism when going from first- to second-degree relatives suggest that more than a single gene is involved (Bailey et al., 1996).

Twin studies suggest a role for genetic influences in regard to the onset of adult bipolar and serious unipolar depression (McGuffin & Katz, 1993). In addition, some evidence also indicates a complex relation between age of onset of the disorder for parents and offspring risk for depression. Specifically, offspring appear to be at greater risk for depression if parents become depressed before age 20; however, offspring were not at greater than expected risk if parental depression occurred in childhood or after age 40 (Plomin, DeFries et al., 1997).

There is a strong consensus in the literature on the relevance of genetic influences for adult antisocial criminal behavior (Gottesman & Goldsmith, 1994; Plomin, 1991; Rutter et al., 1990). For example, criminal concordance rate increases as the degree of biological resemblance increases among adults from adoptive to half to full siblings. Similarly, the proportion of nonviolent criminal convictions for men who were adopted as children increases as the criminal recidivism rate of their biological, but not their adoptive, parents also increases (Mednick, Gabrielli, & Hutchings, 1984). In contrast, there appear to be only weak links between genetic influences and childhood antisocial–delinquent behavior (Gottesman & Goldsmith, 1994; Plomin, 1991; Rutter et al., 1990). However, the chronicity of antisocial behavior in some individuals (e.g., more than half of adult crimes are committed by 6% of adolescents with a history of six or more convictions) has led some researchers to suggest that genetic influences may be more likely to be manifest in individuals with early and chronic antisocial problem behaviors than in the child population at large (Gottesman & Goldsmith, 1994). Along the same lines, the comorbidity between childhood conduct disorder and attention deficit disorder with hyperactivity (which also has a genetic basis) appears to be related to the operation of a common set of genes in younger (8–11 years) but not in older children (12–16 years), again suggesting the need to consider age when looking at the nature of genetic contributions to antisocial behavior in childhood (Silberg et al., 1996).

The extent of genetic contributions to alcoholism appears to be strongly moderated not only by gender but also by the type of alcoholism under consideration. For alcoholism that is characterized by biological fathers but not biological mothers having a history of serious, early-appearing alcohol use and criminal behavior, there appears to be a definite genetic influence on the alcoholism of sons, though not of daughters (McGue, 1993). This could be attributed to common family-rearing influences except for the fact that the same pattern also appears in adopted children (Bohman, Cloniger, Sigvardsson, & Von-Knorring, 1987). In contrast, for late-onset alcoholism, the extent and nature of genetic influences appear to be much less salient (McGue, 1993).

Some Unanswered Questions

Given the evidence just presented, a necessary role of genetic influences on human behavior and development cannot be denied. However, a number of questions about the nature of genetic influences still remain. For example, there are studies on both sides of the issue of whether there is differential heritability for intelligence in the lower and upper IQ ranges (Thompson, Detterman, & Plomin 1993).

Results also indicate a very complex pattern of relations between genetic influences and age (Devlin et al., 1997; Fulker, Cherny, & Cardon 1993). For example, increases in the heritability of intelligence from childhood through adulthood do not reflect changes in the level of monozygotic twins' resemblance in intelligence, which essentially stays stable over time, but these increases are associated with decreasing dizygotic similarity (Brody, 1993; McCartney et al., 1990). This difference could be genetic in nature, or this pattern could be the result of more differentiated environments for older dizygotic twins (Rose, 1995). Evidence of the increasing correlation between adopted children and their biological parents on tests of general and specific cognitive abilities, as the children go from infancy to adolescence, suggests at least some level of contribution from genetic influences (Plomin, Fulker, Corley, & DeFries, 1997). Available evidence also suggests that changing patterns of genetic influence over time may be a function of the specific trait being considered. For example, dizygotic twins' resemblance on performance abilities increases over time, whereas their resemblance on verbal abilities decreases (McGue et al.,1993). In contrast to intelligence, genetic influences on personality measures tend either to remain stable (Brody, 1993; McCartney et al., 1990) or to decline across the lifespan (Plomin & Rende, 1991; Rose, 1995; Viken, Rose, Kaprio, & Koshenvino, 1994).

Only a limited amount of evidence is available in regard to the question of whether extreme scores on a trait reflect the operation of gene systems that are different from those involved in scores in the normal range (Plomin & Saudino, 1994). Evidence suggests that a multiple-gene model appears to provide a better fit than a single-gene model for understanding genetic contributions to the development of high levels of cognitive ability (Plomin & Thompson, 1993). What evidence is available on this question also suggests that for cognitive performance, similar genetic influences appear to be occurring when comparing a population at the high end of the intellectual distribution with a population having a full range of intellectual scores (Petrill et al., 1998). However, there may be differences in relevant genetic influences for those at the lower end of the intellectual continuum (Petrill et al., 1997). For neuroticism and somatic complaints (Plomin & Rende, 1991), the same genetic influences seem to be operating at both the extremes of the trait distribution and in the middle. In contrast, reading disabilities may reflect a different set of genetic influences than is found for individual variation in reading skills in the normal range (DeFries & Gillis, 1993).

Genetic Influences: Necessary But Not Sufficient

Given the evidence that has been presented, there seems little doubt that genetic factors are a necessary influence on human behavior and development. However, the available evidence also documents that genetic influences, except perhaps in the case of very rare genetic syndromes such as Huntington's chorea or Tay-Sachs, cannot be considered a sufficient influence. The high level of individual variability usually found when genetic influences are related to behavior and development is one reason why these influences may be viewed as necessary but not sufficient. (See chap. 1 for more detailed discussion of this question.) As discussed previously (see Figure 3-1), the source of such variability is likely to be found in the complex indirect molecular and molar pathways between gene action and behavioral–developmental outcomes, which allow multiple opportunities for nongenetic influences to shift developmental trajectories (Cairns, 1993). For example, the transformation of cells into structures depends partly on the genes but also on nongenetic molecular processes such as cytoplasmic influences, cell location, and interactions among neighboring cells (Partridge, 1983). At a molecular level, the expression of structural genes will depend in part on the action of regulatory genes, which are directly sensitive to a variety of nongenetic influences, such as nutritional status (Natori & Oka, 1997) or even mild sensory stimulation of the organism (Mack & Mack, 1992). It is therefore not surprising to find that the heritability of genetically linked outcomes like physical growth can be moderated by prevailing sociodemographic conditions (Harrison & Schmitt, 1989; Mueller & Malina, 1980), whereas the heritability of IQ will vary to the extent that the contributions of prenatal influences are considered (Devlin et al., 1997).

In the linkages between genes and behavioral development, what we have is a process wherein genes essentially provide predispositions toward the probability of occurrence of a specific outcome. For example, available evidence indicates that genes do not code for autism per se but rather predispose the individual to specific cognitive and social deficits that under certain conditions translate into autism (Rutter et al., 1990; 1993). The same pattern also holds in schizophrenia, wherein children of parents with schizophrenia are more likely to show a characteristic pattern of attentional and information-processing deficits (Erlenmeyer-Kimling & Cornblatt, 1987). What leads to the actualization of genetic predisposition to schizophrenia are often nongenetic factors, such as early biomedical complications (Casaer, DeVries, & Marlow, 1991), family communication patterns (Goldstein, 1988), or level of exposure to environmental stressors (Tienari, Sorri, Lahti, & Naarala, 1987).

The probabilistic nature of genetic influences is perhaps most clearly seen in studies looking at the expression of genetically influenced traits in highly restrictive environments, either at the level of the proximal environment (e.g., degree of monozygotic–dizygotic behavioral similarity in highly restrictive versus highly permissive classrooms; Fischbein, Guttman, Nathan, & Esrachi, 1990) or at the sociocultural level (e.g., variability in the heritability of aggressive behavior as a function of community differences in the level of violent behavior; Gottesman & Goldsmith, 1994). In these situations, where there is strong environmental restriction or a strong psychosocial coercion toward certain forms of behavior, the expression of genetic predispositions is found to be far less than is found in more permissive or noncoercive situations.

Situations such as those just described can be viewed as illustrating a more general process, namely moderation of genetic influences by nongenetic factors (e.g., gene–environment interaction; Wachs & Plomin, 1991). Moderation of genetic predispositions by specific nongenetic influences means that we must go beyond just genetic contributions if we are to fully understand individual behavioral–developmental variability. For example, although the intelligence level of adopted children correlates significantly with the IQ level of their biological parents, adopted children from disadvantaged backgrounds adopted into high-quality adoptive homes are found to have intellectual levels nearly one standard deviation above that of children from similar backgrounds who remain with their biological parents (Capron & Duyme, 1989).

Given evidence for the operation of moderating processes like gene–environment interaction, one critical question is how genes contribute to such processes. One potential mechanism is through genes predisposing to differences in the degree or nature of individual reactivity to specific features of the environment (Wachs, 1992). (For further discussion, also see chap. 8 of this volume.) For example, there is clearly a genetic contribution to temperament. A number of studies have consistently reported that children with difficult temperaments show significantly greater negative reactivity than do children with easy temperaments to a variety of environmental stressors, including family chaos or family stress, maternal anger, birth of a younger sibling, and stressful medical procedures (Wachs, 1992). Similarly, Bender, Linden, and Robinson (1987) have demonstrated that children with sex chromosomal abnormalities appear to be more susceptible to adverse environmental influences than are matched controls who do not have these abnormalities.

Genetically influenced differential reactivity also can operate by lessening rather than increasing reactivity to input. For example, children with noncriminal biological parents who were reared by criminal adoptive parents show a level of later criminal behavior (14.7%) that is not significantly different from children whose biological and adoptive parents were both noncriminal (13.5%). The implication is that because of their biological (genetic) background, these children were less sensitive to the adverse impact of a criminal rearing environment (Mednick et al., 1984). The operation of moderating processes such as gene–environment interaction does not lessen a necessary status for genetic influences on behavioral development. What such processes do illustrate is the probabilistic (i.e., nonsufficient) nature of gene action once we go beyond the level of amino acids to the behavioral–developmental level.

A second process illustrating the role played by genes as well as why genetic influences are necessary but not sufficient comes from a body of evidence summarized by Plomin (1994). Among the findings summarized are the following:

- Monozygotic twins' perceptions of the degree of warmth and acceptance in their family environment or ratings of their own parenting as adults are significantly closer than the ratings of dizygotic twins. This difference occurs even when the twins are living in different families.
- Biological siblings perceive significantly less differential treatment by their parents than do unrelated siblings living in the same family, particularly on measures of parental affection.
- Similar patterns are found when we look at biological and adopted sibling perceptions of nonfamily situations, including peer-group orientation, social support networks, and the number of negative life events encountered.

Plomin (1994) concluded that these data indicate that genetic and environmental influences are nonindependent from each other (i.e., there is nonrandom covariance between genetically influenced individual characteristics and characteristics of the environment). The operation of gene–environment covariance means that interpretation of genetic influences on individual developmental variability cannot be understood without reference to the operation of covarying environmental circumstances, and vice versa (Wachs, 1992). As Plomin described this process:

> The genetic contribution to measures of the environment should not be considered part of the environmental component of variance nor the genetic component of variance because it is a combination of the two. It involves a different component of variance called genotype-environment-correlation. (Plomin, 1994, p. 50)

Gene–environment correlation can be passive in nature: Parents who transmit certain genes to their offspring have an increased probability of also transmitting certain environmental characteristics as well. For example, the offspring of more competent parents are more likely to be placed in high-quality day care than the offspring of less competent parents (Clarke-Stewart, 1991). Alternatively, gene–environment covariance can be reactive in nature: differential reactivity to the child by other individuals as a function of the child's genetically influenced individual characteristics. For example, in families where parents are mentally ill, fussy irritable children are more likely to bear the brunt of parental hostility and criticism than are more calm, placid siblings (Rutter, 1988). Finally, gene–environment covariance can be active in nature: Children with specific genetically influenced characteristics may actively seek out environmental microcontexts that best match their individual characteristics. For example, Gunnar (1994) has documented how children with inhibited temperaments who are faced with new social-group situations stay on the fringes of the group, observing others interact and actively soliciting adult help, until they begin to feel more comfortable about the situation. Similarly, Werner (1990) has documented how resilient children, in part, achieve such resilience from their ability to elicit support from others in the environment. (See Plomin, 1994, for a more detailed review of gene–environment covariance.)

The operation of gene–environment covariance does not mean that genes directly "drive" environments, as some have argued (Pike, McGuire, Hetherington, Reiss, & Plomin, 1996; Rowe, 1994; Scarr, 1992). As documented earlier, genes directly drive only amino acids. Rather, the pathway between genes and the environment is indirect and probabilistic in nature (Wachs, 1996a, 1996b). What gene initiated pathways can do is increase or decrease the probability that an individual is more or less likely to encounter a specific environment. Although the genetic components of gene–environment covariance are a necessary part of a "causal chain" operating over time, they do not form the whole chain. Genetically influenced individual characteristics can act to influence the characteristics of the child's subsequent environment, but these subsequent environmental characteristics can, in turn, act to influence subsequent individual development (Wachs, 1996b). One such example of a causal chain of genetic and individual influences resulting in the emergence of antisocial behavior in childhood is seen in Figure 3-2.

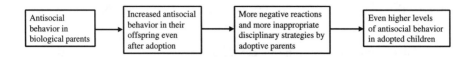

| Antisocial behavior in biological parents | → | Increased antisocial behavior in their offspring even after adoption | → | More negative reactions and more inappropriate disciplinary strategies by adoptive parents | → | Even higher levels of antisocial behavior in adopted children |

Figure 3-2. A causal chain linking genes and environment to antisocial behavior. Sequence taken from GE, Best, Conger, & Simons (1960).

Although available evidence clearly shows the necessary role genes play in individual developmental–behavioral variability, the nature of gene action and the nature of the mechanisms by which genes influence such variability (interaction and covariance) also demonstrate that genes per se are not sufficient. This viewpoint has been expressed most clearly by Richard Rose, himself a distinguished behavioral geneticist:

> With rare exceptions (e.g., Huntington's Disease) genes do not mandate life outcomes. Less than half the variance observed in typical behavioral phenotypes is attributed to heritable effects and these effects are largely indirect, from gene–environment interactions and correlations. (Rose, 1995, p. 648)

CENTRAL NERVOUS SYSTEM FUNCTIONING AND INDIVIDUAL DIFFERENCES

It seems all too obvious that human behavior is dependent on the functioning of the central nervous system (Gray, 1994). Going beyond this very general statement, neuroscience researchers have been able to implicate specific areas of the central nervous system (CNS) as mediators of specific behavior. For example, the prefrontal cortex is thought to be essential for focused attention, success in delayed-response tasks, inhibition when faced with new stimuli, and planning (Diamond, 1990b). Maturation of specific temporal cortex areas is associated with development of explicit memory (Nelson, 1995) and visual recognition memory (Bachevalier, 1990), whereas maturation of frontal lobe areas is associated with the onset of the ability to regulate emotion and voluntary control of motor behavior (Dawson, 1994). The hippocampus has been linked to development of preferences for novel stimuli (Nelson, 1995) and to new memory formation, whereas the amygdala has been associated with processing of fear stimuli and autonomic learning (Steinmetz, 1994).

Links between differentially maturing CNS structures have implications for behavioral development (Steinmetz, 1994). For example, the early maturity of the hippocampus and amygdala, which are structurally linked to the later developing prefrontal cortex, may result in the infant being able to experience and encode emotionally eliciting events but remain unable to display consistent reactions to these events as they continue to occur (Nelson, 1994).

The action of CNS-influenced neurotransmitter activities is also relevant for understanding behavior and development. Acetylcholine—found in regions of the cortex and cerebellum—is thought to mediate cognitive, sensory, and motor functions, whereas dopamine—found in the limbic system, basil ganglia, hypothalamus, and prefrontal cortex—is thought to be involved with emotions, motor behavior (Krassner, 1986), and executive-function abilities (Diamond, Prevor, Callender, & Druin, 1997). A detailed example showing how linkages between specific CNS structures and between CNS structures and neurochemical processes relate to one domain of behavior, temperament, is shown in Table 3-2.

Although a central role of the CNS for the development and expression of behavior seems all too obvious, what is less often appreciated is the role the CNS plays in individual differences in behavior and development. What I will attempt to document is how individual differences—in CNS micro- and macrostructure, in the efficiency of CNS processes, and in the complex linkages among CNS processes and structures—function as necessary influences on individual variability in behavioral development. However, what I will also argue is that the multiplicity of factors producing individual CNS

TABLE 3-2
Central Nervous System—Biochemical Links with Temperament

Temperament-dimension-trait	Relevant structures and neurochemicals
Positive negative affect, approach/ behavioral inhibition	Frontal cortex and amygdala.
Stress vulnerability	System influenced by various structures including the amygdala and its projections to the motor system, cingulate, and motor cortex and hypothalamus.
Approach/positive affect; reactions to novelty	Amygdala, temporal pole orbitoprefrontal cortex, ventral stratum, ventral pallidum, motor cortices.
Withdrawal/negative affect; reactions to novelty	Hippocampal formation and its surrounding structures, prefrontal cortex, portions of the motor system.
Arousability	Cortex, reticular formation, limbic system, autonomic nervous system, neurotransmitter, enzyme, hormones.
Impulsive unsocialized (inhibition), sensation seeking	Dopamine (approach), serotonin, norepinephrine (arousal attention focusing).

Note. Table taken from Wachs & King, 1994.

variability is a major reason why CNS variability, in and of itself, is not a sufficient explanation for understanding individual differences in behavior and development.

The Nature of CNS Variability

To understand CNS variability, it is essential to understand the developmental processes producing such variability. It is not the purpose of this chapter to give a detailed review of CNS development. (For reviews in this area, see Goodman, 1991a, 1994; Nelson & Bloom, 1997.) What will be done, however, is to highlight three aspects of CNS development that seem most relevant to the question of individual variability in behavior and development.

Sequential Order and Structure

Originally it was thought that CNS growth was based on a prespecified, hard-wired genetic program that served to guide all aspects of brain development, with such development occurring in a relatively restricted time period. More recently, a less predeterministic framework for CNS development has emerged. This new framework is based on evidence indicating that although genetic factors are necessary for the overall form of the CNS and the construction of the various CNS macrostructures, genetic influences are not a sufficient explanation either for brain development occurring later in life or for the development of the microstructure of the CNS (Killackey, 1990; Nelson & Bloom, 1997; Rakic, 1989; Rubenstein et al., 1990). Although CNS development is initially based on innate anatomical prenatal and early postnatal maturational sequences, such initial sequences are followed by a bidirectional, experience-driven organization of neural functions that ultimately stabilizes into more integrative higher order neural hierarchies (Merzenich, Allard, & Jenkins, 1991).

Complex Developmental Processes

Although the overall structure of the CNS is species-specific, there is ample room for individual CNS variability, both in regard to macro- and microstructures. Individual variability is inherent in the complex, multistep processes by which these structures are formed. As an example, we can consider the structure of the cortex, which, according to Rakic (1988), is partitioned into column-like regions with specific connections and biochemical characteristics called "cytoarchitectonic areas." Cortical structures emerge from a complex sequence of specific microprocesses, starting with the generation and replication in the ventricular zone of what will eventually become cortical neurons. Neuronal cells destined for the deepest areas of the cortex are formed first, with surface-area cortical cells formed later. After formation, neural cells initially migrate to the deepest levels of the cortex, with later migrations going to the cortical surface. The migration process is highly complex, involving the functioning of various cell units (e.g., radial glial cells) operating under relatively tight time controls (e.g., generation begins approximately 6 weeks postconception, and migration continues until 24–25 weeks of gestation). Cortical neurons appear to commit to a specific cell type sometime after generation but before they reach their final target position. Once they reach their ultimate destination, cortical neurons differentiate, enlarge, and interconnect with neurons in the same area. It is this generation–migration–commitment–enlargement–interconnection process that underlies the formation of cortical regions. (For a more detailed description of the overall process, see Caviness, Misson, & Gadisseux, 1989; Rakic, 1988.) Given the complexity of the underlying processes, it is not surprising to find that cortical column frequencies are different, both across species (Killackey, 1990) and among individuals within a species (Rakic, 1988).

Frequency of cortical columns is one reflection of individual CNS variability at the macrostructure level. At the microstructure level, individual variability is reflected in two distinct phases of neuronal growth. Starting in the first trimester, and continuing at least past infancy, there is a major overproduction of both neurons and interconnections among neurons. However, this overproduction is followed by nonrandom pruning back of both individual neurons and neuronal interconnections, with this pruning process continuing at least through adolescence (Greenough & Black, 1992; Lyon & Gadisseaux, 1991; Rakic, 1989). Although the phase of neuronal overproduction appears to be relatively autonomous (Bourgeois, Jastreboff, & Rakic, 1989), the pruning back process appears to be quite sensitive, both to a variety of individual characteristics (e.g., state of electrical activity in the CNS) and to individual interactions with the environment that act to strengthen certain synaptic connections, modify others, and eliminate still others (Greenough & Black, 1992; Rakic, 1989). For example, infrahuman studies show that increased neural branching is associated with early pain; such increased branching may be one reason why individuals encountering early pain are more sensitive to noxious stimulation later in life (Barr, Boyce, & Zeltzery, 1994). Other examples of neural plasticity at the microstructure and neurochemical levels are presented by Nelson and Bloom (1997). Given the complexity of the processes involved, it is not surprising to find significant variability in CNS microstructure, even in individuals who are genetic clones (Edelman, 1989).

CNS Development Over Time

It is well established that different areas of the CNS mature at different times (Diamond, 1990a; Goodman, 1991a; Thatcher, Walker, & Guidice, 1987). For example, the hippocampus and the amygdala are structures that mature relatively early, whereas the frontal cortex matures relatively late. A pattern of differential maturation also is seen for cortical microstructures. For example, the individual's level of neuronal and glial cells are fixed relatively early in development, whereas myelinization (i.e., synthesis of a lipid-protein substance that coats axons and increases transmission speed) occurs at a far slower rate.

Although the idea of differential rates of development of specific CNS areas is well established, what is less well appreciated is the increasing evidence for plasticity in CNS development well into maturity. Although much of the macrodevelopment of the CNS is finalized by the end of the second year of life, development of some CNS areas and interconnections among neural circuits is extended well beyond this period (Goodman, 1991a). Adult synapse levels in the frontal cortex may not be reached until late childhood or even adolescence (Diamond, 1990b; Nelson, 1994), whereas myelinization of the associative cortex may continue until middle adulthood (Casaer, 1993). One consequence of later neural development is the possibility of some degree of CNS reorganization in response to either injury or changes in sensory input in adult organisms (Nelson & Bloom, 1997).

The genesis of individual variability in CNS structure and efficiency is most likely a result of the three processes just described: complex, sequential, multidetermined steps underlying CNS development, the operation of mechanisms such as nonrandom pruning, and a prolonged period of development and plasticity for some CNS areas. Individual differences in behavioral development are one consequence of individual differences in CNS structure and mechanisms. In the following sections, I will document examples of how disruption of these complex developmental processes can lead to CNS variability.

The Etiology of Individual CNS Variability

The complex sequential steps involved in the formation of CNS structures have been described briefly. Given the number of factors that could act to adversely influence CNS structural development, such development is remarkably robust (Caviness et al., 1989). For example, even though severe malnutrition can reduce brain weight, when compared with other body organs, the CNS seems to be relatively spared under malnutrition conditions (Ballabriga, 1990). However, although well protected, CNS development is not totally protected. Deviations from normal developmental pathways can have potential consequences, both for CNS structural development and ultimately for functions that are dependent on normal CNS structural development (Casaer, 1993; Lyon & Gadisseaux, 1991). Factors that have been shown to lead to such deviation are shown in Table 3-3. (For a more detailed review of lethal and nonlethal consequences of deviations from the normal developmental pathway, see Nelson, in press.) Such structural deviations are one cause of individual variability in CNS development.

TABLE 3-3
Factors Associated with Central Nervous System (CNS) Structural Deviations and Extent of Recovery from CNS Trauma

Influence	Disruption	Reference
Deviations		
Chromosomal deletion	Disruption of normal neural migration patterns.	Rubenstein et al. (1990)
Prenatal X-ray exposure	Disruption of neuronal generation.	Caviness et al. (1989)
Prenatal alcohol exposure	Disruption of neuronal generation, migration, or differentiation.	Caviness et al. (1989)
Chronic malnutrition	Reduced myelinization and CNS DNA; changes in neurotransmitter receptors and cell type ratios.	Ballabriga (1990); Levitsky & Strupp (1995)
Traumatic head injury	Damage to CNS structures more likely to occur with injuries associated with sudden deceleration and sharp rotation.	Satz et al. (1997)

Influence	Relation	Reference
Recovery		
Age at injury	The developing CNS may have more flexibility to compensate for damage, but the mature CNS may be less sensitive to the impact of trauma.	Goodman (1991a); Lyon & Gadisseaux (1991)
Nature of injury	Functional recovery more likely to occur if CNS damage was caused by injury to existing structure than if caused by factors interfering with normally occurring CNS development.	Temple (1997)
Location of injury	Chances of recovery less if damage bilateral than if unilateral. Less recovery of speech than spatial skills with left hemisphere damage; reverse pattern with right hemisphere damage.	Goodman (1991a); Temple (1997)

Although recovery of the CNS from structural damage can be documented both at the neural (Goodman, 1989; Leiderman, 1988) and the behavioral levels (Goodman, 1994), individual differences in the rate and extent of recovery processes offer another means for promoting CNS variability. As shown in Table 3-3, variability in recovery of CNS function is related to age at injury, nature of injury, location of damage, and how recovery occurs. The recovery process is further complicated by the fact that some compensatory mechanisms may lead to inappropriate neural connections, thus inhibiting rather than facilitating subsequent development (Goodman, 1989).

Influences on individual difference in CNS fine structure go beyond just those causing insults to the system, as described in Table 3-3. A large body of infrahuman research has demonstrated how individual differences in postnatal environmental circumstances can result in individual differences in CNS microstructure and functioning (Greenough & Black, 1992; Rakic, 1989; Spear & Hyatt, 1993).[1] For example, Juraska (1990) has shown how exposure of rats to either enriched general stimulation or to specific learning experiences can result in a larger and heavier occipital cortex as well as more synapses per neuron, more dendrites, and greater CNS support structures such as capillaries, which provide greater blood flow. These effects are not restricted to stimulation early in life. Given recent evidence on the prolonged development of CNS fine structure, it is not surprising to find that such effects are shown in adult organisms as well (Juraska, 1990; Nelson, in press).[2] Differential patterns of CNS development also have been reported as a function of individual differences in prenatal (Witelson, 1991) and postnatal levels of hormone exposure (Forget & Cohen, 1994).

What this pattern suggests is that individual variability in the fine details of CNS structure can arise either through low-level insults to the system or as a function of either extrinsic psychosocial or biological influences on the organism. As Rakic has argued, "The responsiveness of the developing brain to environmental influences, including experience, may be the anatomical basis of diversity in human behavior, talent and creativity" (Rakic, 1989, p. 454).

Variability in CNS fine structure also may occur as a result of intrinsic as well as extrinsic influences. For example, nerve conduction velocity appears to be heritable (Rose, 1995). In a more speculative view, Goodman (1994) has argued that random CNS variability that cannot be attributed to known genetic, environmental, or biomedical influences may be inherent in the developmental process itself.

What have been discussed above are factors underlying individual differences in CNS structure and efficiency of function. Individual differences in either CNS structure or efficiency can relate to individual variability in critical fundamental mechanisms such as processing speed, selective attention, executive function, flexibility in changing situations, or emotional re-

---

[1] Selectionist models (e.g., Edelman, 1989) would argue that postnatal environmental influences do not create but mainly prune or select among existing structures. However, much of the evidence supporting the selectionist position is based on studies of immune system function. The generalizability of immune processes to CNS function does not appear to provide a good match for understanding environmental contributions to CNS development (Plomin, 1994).

[2] Obviously, because the overwhelming majority of research in this area involves infrahuman species, caution in generalizing to the human level is always warranted. However, our ability to generalize across species may depend on which species are involved. As Easter, Purves, Rakic, and Spitzer (1985) have indicated, a critical distinction may lie between invertebrates and vertebrates. Invertebrates appear to have more rigid and predetermined programs of CNS development, which matches their more limited ability to adapt to changing environments. Synaptic plasticity appears to be much more characteristic of vertebrates, and particularly of higher primates such as humans.

activity. Individual differences in these fundamental mechanisms can, in turn, result in variability in a wide range of developmental–behavioral outcomes (Strupp & Levitsky, 1995). Evidence documenting linkages between CNS variability and behavioral–developmental variability is considered in the following section.

The Interrelation of Neural and Behavioral Variability

Examples of behavioral patterns associated with major or subtle CNS damage are shown in Table 3-4.[3] The evidence presented in Table 3-4 is related only to indexes of CNS deficit or dysfunction. Evidence for relations between CNS variability in the normal range and population or individual behavioral–developmental variability is reviewed in the following two sections.

CNS Variability and Gender Differences

Going back to the old brain-weight studies, the idea that CNS differences may underlie at least some gender differences has a long and controversial history (Gould, 1981). Recent evidence on this question suggests that gender differences in behavior may have some basis in neuroanatomical gender differences (Kimura, 1987). Although the functional conse-

TABLE 3-4
Behavioral Patterns Associated With Markers of Damage
to the Central Nervous System (CNS)

Damage	Behavioral Pattern	Reference
Childhood CNS tumors	Increased lethargy, apathy, aggression, or irritability.	Graham (1984)
Moderate to severe childhood head injury	Increased risk for lower intelligence and psychiatric disorders; recovery rate slower for psychiatric disorders.	Rutter (1988); Rutter, Chadwick, & Schaffer (1984)
Seizure disorders	Increased risk of general cognitive deficit, poor school performance, and behavioral problems.	Steinhausen & Rauss-Mason (1991)
Excess neuronal clusters	Increased risk of dyslexia.	Lyon & Gadisseaux (1991)
"Minor neurological dysfunction"—problems in coordination of fine motor movements	Deficit in perceptual timing skills; poor school performance.	Keele & Ivry (1990); Soorani-Lunsing et al. (1993)

---

[3] CNS structural damage associated with major gene effects has been discussed earlier in this chapter. CNS structural damage associated with teratology will be considered in the next chapter.

quences of many specific gender-related anatomical differences are not yet known, the hypothalamic sexual dimorphic nucleus is larger and contains more cells in the male CNS than in the female CNS, whereas the massa intermedia, which connects the right and left halves of the thalamus, is more likely to be absent in men (Witelson, 1991). Evidence also exists indicating that men show significantly greater hemispheric asymmetries than women (Breedlove, 1994; Witelson, 1991), which may be related to sex difference in the shape and volume of the corpus callosum (Halpern, 1997). In regard to functional consequences, the percentage of CNS gray matter is related to left- versus right-handedness in men but not in women, whereas the temporal–parietal region appears to be less involved in speech functions in women than in men (Witelson, 1991). Speech skills appear to depend more on the influence of anterior than posterior cortical regions in women but not in men (Kimura, 1987). Furthermore, spatial-processing performance in gifted men is associated with a greater ability to inhibit left hemisphere functioning than is spatial processing performance in nongifted men, whereas the inhibition differences between gifted and nongifted women is nonsignificant (Benbow & Lubinski, 1993).

Gender-related differences in CNS structure and processes may underlie what some have referred to as a *paradoxical finding*, namely that although men appear to have larger brains than women, even after controlling for body size, gender differences in general intelligence are often not found, and women clearly are superior to men in certain specific skills, such as verbal abilities and perceptual speed (Rushton & Ankney, 1996). On the basis of evidence indicating that brain size predicts cognitive performance in men but not women, it has been hypothesized that other CNS indexes, such as potentially greater neuron density in women, may be more salient for explaining female cognitive performance than brain size per se (Willerman, Schultz, Rutledge, & Bigler, 1992). Recent evidence demonstrating 11% greater neural cell density in women than in men in the posterior temporal cortex supports the hypothesis that gender differences in CNS structure may underlie gender differences in information-processing skills (Witelson, Glezer, & Kigar, 1995).

Given the overlap of distributions, inconsistency of results in some areas, and small effect sizes in studies that do show significance (Breedlove, 1994; Byne & Parsons, 1994), it could easily be argued that these gender-related neural differences are really an epiphenomenon, and that gender differences essentially are social–cultural in nature. However, several lines of evidence do not support this alternative conclusion. First, gender differences in CNS structure appear early in life, which tends to minimize the potential consequences of gender-related social–cultural differences in rearing (Witelson, 1991). Second, gender differences in CNS structure appear in infrahuman populations, which again suggests that something more than just social–cultural factors are involved (Reinisch, Ziemba-Davis, & Sanders, 1991). Third, as will be discussed in the final section of this chapter, there is a potential biological mechanism that could explain gender differences in CNS structure, namely the differential effects of prenatal hormones on the development of the CNS in men and women (Breedlove, 1994).

Variability in CNS Processing and Individual Behavioral Variability

Studies using direct measures of brain electrical activity illustrate how individual variability in human CNS processing relates to variability in concurrent or subsequent cognitive task performance. In terms of quantitative differences, higher levels of intellectual performance have shown a modest but significant association with faster neural conduction velocity (speed of information processing; Reed & Jensen, 1992) and with length of cortical pathways involved in information processing (shorter pathways being viewed as a marker of more cortical efficiency; Reed & Jensen, 1993). Similar findings are shown also in regard to stimulus-onset latencies of specific brain wave patterns, which have been associated with selective attention and decision making (e.g., P 300; McGarry-Roberts, Stelmack, & Campbell, 1992).

Individual differences also can be qualitative in terms of what cortical areas are activated during information processing. For example, Benbow and Lubinsky (1993) measured the electroencephalograph (EEG) activity of gifted and nongifted individuals while they were being tested on verbal and spatial processing tasks. On verbal tasks, gifted individuals showed more frontal lobe activity, whereas nongifted individuals showed more temporal lobe activity. On spatial processing tasks, gifted men showed more ability to inhibit left-hemisphere activity, resulting in a correspondingly greater influence of the right hemisphere. Looking for qualitative changes over time, Fox and Bell (1990) used measures of both frontal cortex electrical activity and the ability to tolerate delay during memory tasks in a group of infants who were followed from 6 to 12 months of age. Results indicated that those infants who could successfully solve Piagetian A–B tasks under delay conditions were the same infants who showed EEG changes indicating increased frontal lobe activation and increased coherence of EEG activity between the frontal and occipital cortical areas. Extending the time span, Molfese and Betz (1988) have reported that neonates who were shown to have greater left-hemisphere activity when discriminating between different consonants also showed significantly better language skills at 3 years of age than did neonates who did not display this earlier differentiation. Similarly, Sigman, Cohen, Beckwith, Asarnow, and Parmelee (1992) have reported that low birth weight infants with an EGG pattern indicative of state control during quiet sleep had higher IQ scores at 8 and 12 years of age.

Although the database is not totally consistent, some studies also have reported that individual differences in CNS functioning are related to individual differences in antisocial behavior. For example, early-onset, aggressive psychopathic individuals tend to be characterized by low sympathetic nervous system activity and low activity in the hypothalamic–pituitary adrenal axis; in contrast, early-onset, nonaggressive conduct-disordered children appear to have higher sympathetic and hypothalamic–pituitary adrenal activity (Lahey, McBurnett, Loeber, & Hart, 1995). Individual differences in neurotransmitter activity also may be relevant, given evidence showing that individuals who are high in sensation seeking (which can include drug use or criminal activities) have an overactive dopamine system, whereas individuals who are low in dopamine synthesis tend to be low in sensation seeking (Zuckerman, 1994).

A number of theorists also have attempted to link individual differences in reactivity to the environment, both with individual differences in the excitability threshold of the amygdala and with linkages between the amygdala and other subcortical and cortical areas (Kagan, 1994). For example, Rothbart, Derryberry, and Posner (1994) have postulated that interconnections between the amygdala and the frontal and occipital cortical regions may underlie why anxious individuals see more threats in their world and experience more intense feelings when under stress. Other human research on individual variability in temperament has indicated that individual differences in inhibition are related to differences in activation of the right versus left frontal hemispheres, with inhibited infants showing significantly more right frontal activation and significantly less left frontal activation in novel situations, whereas uninhibited infants show significantly more left frontal activation (Calkins & Fox, 1994; Davidson, 1993; Fox & Bell, 1990). Differential frontal hemisphere activation also has been associated with individual differences in preschool children's level of social competence in play situations (Fox et al., 1995). Other studies have implicated frontal lobe activation as relevant for individual differences in distress following separation from the primary caregiver, though disagreements remain about the nature of the frontal lobe pattern associated with greater or lesser distress (Davidson, 1993; Fox, 1994).

CNS Influences on Behavior and Development: Necessary But Not Sufficient

What the evidence just documented has shown is (a) development of specific behavioral functions is linked to development of the CNS, (b) there is clear variability in individual CNS structure and processing efficiency, (c) this variability arises in part from the nature of CNS development and in part from the impact of intrinsic and extrinsic influences on CNS development and processing efficiency, and (d) variability in CNS structure and function is associated with variability in human behavior and development. It seems clear from this evidence that variability in the human CNS is a necessary condition for variability in human behavior and development. The question to be dealt with in this section is whether individual CNS variability per se is a sufficient explanation for individual behavioral developmental variability. I will argue that multiple lines of evidence converge on a conclusion of "necessary but not sufficient" in regard to CNS influences.

One of the major lines of evidence supporting the conclusion of necessary but not sufficient is that CNS structure and processing efficiency does not develop in isolation from other influences, influences that also can result in individual variability in behavior and development. As outlined earlier, these other influences can include genetics, nutrition, or rearing environment. For example, Lahey et al. (1995) have reported that conduct-disordered children show abnormal catecholamine levels. This abnormality could suggest a direct link between neurotransmitter levels and behavior, except for the fact that abnormal catecholamine levels are also associated with disturbed mother–infant relations, which could also act to influence later conduct disorder (Lahey et al., 1995). Similarly, variability in infant inhibition has been related to differential neural frontal activation patterns, but individual differences in infant inhibition also have been associated with patterns of mother–infant attachment (Calkins & Fox, 1994). Evidence also indicates that variability in infants' frontal cortical activation patterns can occur as a function of whether the infant's mother is depressed or nondepressed (Dawson, 1994). Hence, links between infant frontal activation and infant affect could be direct or could be mediated by depression-related genetic or environmental transmission factors (e.g., decreased responsiveness in depressed mothers). Even accidents, including head injuries, may not be truly accidental. As Matheny (1986) has documented, there is a higher likelihood of physical injury for highly active boys with poor attentional skills who are living in poorly organized chaotic family environments. Evidence for the role played in development by these individual and environmental characteristics will be shown in chapters 5 and 6.

A second line of evidence relates to developmental outcome variability within conditions associated with abnormal neural development. The wide range of outcomes associated with indirect measures of CNS efficiency, such as minor neurological dysfunction, has been noted previously (Barsky & Siegel, 1992). Even more dramatic are those conditions in which major neural structural malformations appear not to be associated with any type of clinical deficit (Lyon & Gaddisseaux, 1991). For example, microcephally is a structural disorder associated with both very small head size and mental retardation; the smaller the head size, the lower the IQ. Yet, there are some forms of genetically related microcephally wherein even with a head size 4 standard deviations below the population mean, normal intelligence can still occur (Rossi et al., 1987). It could be argued that such high functional variability reflects imprecise measurement of relevant CNS indicators and that with more sensitive measurement, level of functional variability would be reduced (C. Nelson, personal communication, July, 1997). Although this is a viable argument, it is of interest to note that when state-of-the-art measurement is used, results consistently show the exquisite sensitivity of CNS microstructures and processes to extrinsic influences such as repeated sensory input (Ungerleider, 1995). Thus, even if the CNS represents a final common pathway mediating individual behavioral–developmental variability, as noted in chapter 1, the nature of this final sufficient common pathway may well be the result of the prior action of multiple necessary influences. As a result, although one consequence of more precise measurement may be stronger associations between outcomes and CNS structure and function, a second consequence is likely to be increased understanding of the role of multiple influences on individual variability in CNS structure and function.

A third reason why I view CNS influences as necessary but not sufficient has to do with the translation process from CNS activity to individual behavioral variability. Potential mechanisms for such translation have been developed (e.g., Calkins, 1994), but these mechanisms typically require something in addition to neural activity per se. For example, as shown in Figure 3-3, neural regulatory functions form the first link in a longitudinal chain. In this chain, individual neural patterns influence infant characteristics, which in turn act to influence patterns of caregiver reactivity to the child, which in turn can influence subsequent child behavioral outcomes. Stable individual patterns of behavior may have their genesis in individual differences in initial neural structure and function, but the ultimate outcome pattern emerges as part of a chain of events caused by many factors, and not as a direct translation of CNS structure or activation.

Direct evidence for this hypothesized causal chain process is seen in a number of studies. For example, stronger prediction of individual differences in inhibited behavior occurs when EEG patterns are combined with individual behavioral characteristics, such as activity level or high distress, rather than when only EEG patterns are used to predict (Fox, 1994). This may partially reflect the fact that stability of ongoing neural processes, such as differential frontal activation patterns, although significant, are relatively modest (.40 over a 10-month period; Fox & Bell, 1990). Furthermore, evidence is available indicating that environmental characteristics can act to directly moderate the degree of association between indexes of neural functioning and subsequent outcomes. For example, although a relation has been reported between criminal behavior and minor physical anomalies (as an index of minor CNS dysfunction), up to one third of individuals with multiple minor physical anomalies show no evidence of criminal behavior (Kandel, Brennan, Mednick, & Michelson, 1989). Those individuals with minor physical anomalies who do not display subsequent criminal behavior are far more likely to have been raised in stable family environments, suggesting that such environments can act to break the link between minor CNS dysfunction and subsequent antisocial behavior (Mednick, Brennen, & Kandel, 1988).

Similarly, for children with neurologically mediated language impairments involving an inability to accurately discriminate rapidly presented

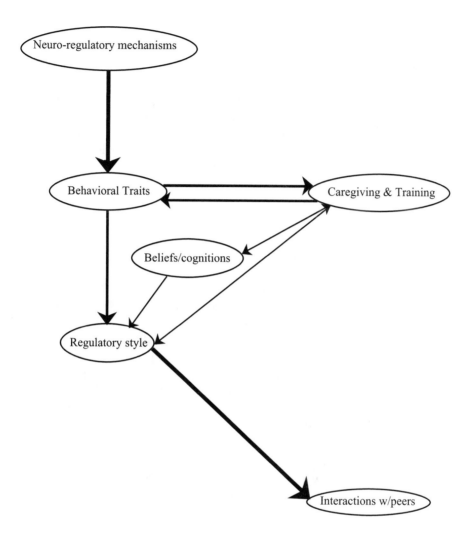

Figure 3-3. Pathway linking central nervous system processes to children's peer interactions.

speech sounds (as occurs in normal speech), significant gains in speech sound recognition occurred following 4 weeks of intensive audiovisual training (Merzenich et al., 1996). As noted earlier, low birth weight infants who do not develop EEG patterns indicative of state control during quiet sleep are more likely to show lower cognitive performance later in life. However, there is an exception to this finding. Low birth weight infants who do not develop quiet-sleep EEG state control patterns, but who are reared by responsive and sensitive caregivers, are at no greater risk for subsequent IQ deficits than low birth weight infants who do demonstrate quiet-sleep EEG state control patterns (Sigman et al., 1992).

These findings do not deny the importance of variability in CNS functioning for individual developmental–behavioral variability. Variability in CNS functioning is a crucial and necessary link in a longitudinal chain of factors that ultimately result in individual variability in developmental and behavioral outcomes. However, except in the case of extreme and pervasive damage, CNS variability, although a necessary link, in and of itself is not a sufficient link in terms of understanding variability in individual human behavior and development.

HORMONAL INFLUENCES

Hormones are biochemical substances that act to regulate physiological status and internal states. Hormone production forms part of a complex, multiple-level feedback system involving both specific areas of the CNS (e.g., the hypothalamus) and specific glands (e.g., pituitary, thyroid, adrenal, and sex glands). Within this complex system, regulation of hormone production is driven both by internal processes, such that some hormones act to regulate the production of other hormones, and by outside influences, such as stress. The very complexity of the hormonal system means that there is great potential for individual variability in hormonal levels. In addition, individual differences can exist in sensitivity to hormonal influences (Buchanan, Eccles, & Becker, 1992), perhaps as a function of individual differences in the number of specific types of hormonal receptors in the CNS (Stansbury & Gunnar, 1994). Hormonal influences on behavior and development have been viewed as acting in two ways: prenatally, through their influence on CNS organization, and postnatally, through an activation function wherein current levels of hormones act to mediate ongoing behaviors (Bancroft, 1991; Collaer & Hines, 1995). Both aspects will be considered in the following sections.

Prenatal Hormonal Influences

As noted earlier, available evidence suggests that there may be subtle gender differences in both CNS structure and function. For example, there appear to be gender differences both in hippocampal characteristics and in the responsivity of serotonin receptors in the hypothalamus (McEwen, 1989). The traditional model used to explain these differences is based on the hypothesis that male CNS structure and organization is developed during a hormonally sensitive period, as a function of prenatal exposure to threshold levels of androgen (Meyer-Bahlberg, Feldman, Cohen, & Ehrhardt, 1988). Although both boys and girls possess neural receptors that are sensitive to androgen, it has been argued that only boys are exposed to sufficient levels of androgen to produce gender-related neural changes (Breedlove, 1994). The impact of prenatal hormonal factors on gender differences in the CNS are viewed less in terms of differences in gross morphology and more in terms of the "fine tuning" of CNS structure and organization (Witelson, 1991). However, the exact mechanism whereby this fine tuning occurs is still not totally clear. Recent evidence emerging from infrahuman studies has suggested that androgen hormones such as testosterone are converted by a process called *aromatization* into estradiol, an estrogen-based hormone. It is the interaction of estradiol with estrogen receptors in the male brain that acts to masculinize the CNS; in women, specific proteins act to inhibit this process so that masculinization will not occur (Breedlove, 1994).[4]

Although the nature of the specific mechanisms underlying prenatal hormonal action at the human level is still an open question, sufficient evidence is available to document the behavioral consequences of such action. One line of human research on prenatal hormonal influences is based on studies of individuals with rare syndromes that affect level or reactivity to prenatal hormones (Reinisch et al., 1991). One example of this type of study would be research on women with congenital adrenal hyperplasia, a rare autosomal recessive disorder resulting in excessive prenatal androgen exposure for the offspring of these women. A second example would be androgen insensitivity syndrome, a gene-based disorder wherein men can produce sufficient amounts of androgens but are unable to react to the androgen they produce. A third example would be 5-alpha-reductase syndrome, which results in deficits in testosterone production. A second line of research is based on studies of hormonal treatments given to pregnant women to reduce pregnancy problems such as spontaneous abortion (Bancroft, 1991). Evidence suggests that administration of either natural or synthetic estrogen or progestin hormones during pregnancy can act to either feminize or demasculinize the fetus.

One difficulty with both of the lines of research just described is that either prenatal hormonal disorders or prenatal treatments can act to produce individuals with some physical resemblance to the other sex (e.g., genetic men with genitalia resembling that of women or genetic women with

---

[4] In understanding how prenatal hormonal process mechanisms can act to influence CNS development, one caution must be emphasized. The overwhelming majority of research in this area is based on infrahuman studies, usually using rodents rather than primates (e.g., Breedlove, 1994; Erhardt, 1985; Meyer-Bahlberg et al., 1988). However, there may be different prenatal hormonal processes in different species. For example, the estrogenic masculinization process described earlier may be less salient for primates in which direct androgen effects are more likely (Breedlove, 1994). Furthermore, there may even be limited generalization among rodents species (e.g., connectivity among hypothalamic subregions is needed for estrogen feedback mechanisms to work in rats but not in guinea pigs) (Byne & Parsons, 1993). These possible differences suggest the need for great caution when attempting to generalize conclusions across species (Meyer-Bahlberg et al., 1995).

genitalia resembling that of men, Erhardt, 1985). Under these conditions, it may be difficult to establish whether outcome differences result from differential exposure to prenatal hormones or to differential postnatal treatment resulting from differential physical characteristics (Meyer-Bahlberg et al., 1988). Examples of studies on both sides of this question will be cited below.

Cognitive Consequences of Prenatal Hormonal Exposure

Studies using lower order primates clearly document relations between prenatal hormonal influences and subsequent cognitive development. For example, the superiority of male infant rhesus monkeys on discrimination-reversal learning problems disappears when female infant monkeys are prenatally exposed to androgen (Bachevalier & Hagger, 1991). In contrast, human data on relations between exposure to prenatal sex hormones and subsequent offspring cognitive performance tend to be less consistent (Collaer & Hines, 1995). What consistency exists is found in the domain of spatial abilities, with results suggesting higher than expected levels of spatial performance in prenatally androgenized women and lower than expected levels of spatial performance for prenatally androgen-deficient men (Berenbaum & Snyder, 1995).

As will be discussed in the next chapter, prenatal deficits in synthesis of thyroid hormones can result in certain forms of mental retardation, such as cretinism (Schurch, 1995). One example would be congenital hypothyroidism, a hormonal disorder characterized by reduced levels of thyroxine and triiodothyronine. Low levels of these hormones can impair the synthesis of structural proteins essential for CNS development, resulting in cognitive and attentional deficits (Fuggle & Graham, 1991).

Social and Behavioral Consequences of Prenatal Hormonal Exposure

Interest in the influence of prenatal hormones on subsequent gender-related behaviors at the human level was stimulated by the provocative results of Imperato-McGinley, Peterson, Gautier, and Sturla, (1979), who followed up 19 genetic men who were reared as women because they had external female genitalia resulting from the prenatal hormonal disorder 5-alpha-reductase syndrome. At puberty, with the development of male secondary sexual characteristics, nearly all of these individuals changed both to a male gender identity and to adaptation of a male gender role. Imperato-McGinley et al. interpreted these findings as illustrating the dominance of hormonal influences over subsequent rearing experiences. Since the time of the original Imperato-McGinley study, there have been a number of other studies on the role played by prenatal hormones in the development of gender-related postnatal behavioral patterns. (For a detailed review, see Collaer & Hines, 1995.) Available evidence indicates increased masculinization of girls exposed to prenatal androgen, along such dimensions as higher activity levels and lower levels of nurturance (Ehrhardt, 1985), greater "tomboy" behavior, greater preference for male clothes (Bancroft, 1991), increased propensity toward aggressive behavior (Collaer & Hines, 1995), and greater preference for male toys during play (Berenbaum & Hines, 1992), though not for male playmates (Berenbaum & Snyder, 1995). Of importance is that there was no relation between toy play behavior and degree of physical masculinization in girls, which minimizes the potential role of physically based differential treatment. Berenbaum and Hines (1992) have suggested either direct effects of prenatal androgen exposure on female toy play patterns or indirect effects based on greater activity level for androgenized girls, given that male toys typically require more activity during play.

In regard to boys with congenital adrenal hyperplasia, no differences in toy play behavior have been shown (Berenbaum & Hines, 1992), though exposure of boys to excessive levels of prenatal androgen is significantly related to precocious puberty and to somewhat higher levels of aggressive behavior (Bancroft, 1991). There appear to be few significant social–behavioral differences for boys who are exposed only to low levels of prenatal androgen (Berenbaum & Snyder, 1995).[5]

Beyond childhood, significant but modest differences in gender preference are shown, with prenatally androgenized women showing same-sex attraction (Meyer-Bahlberg et al., 1995). In contrast, the consequences for men of low prenatal androgen exposure appear to be highly complex, with results varying as a function of the type of disorder and gender-related rearing patterns (Collaer & Hines, 1995).

Postnatal Hormonal Influences

Postnatally, after 5 years of age, there is increased activation of the hypothalamic–pituitary adrenal (HPA) axis, resulting in increased production of adrenal steroid hormones. Estradiol production in girls starts at about age 9 to 10 years, with increases continuing through midadolescence. Testosterone production begins to increase in boys by about age 10 and continues increasing through age 17. These hormonal changes underlie the well-known physical changes that are characteristic of adolescence: height and weight spurts, growth of pubic and facial hair, changes in body fat distribution, and stimulation of egg and sperm production (Richards, Abell, & Peterson, 1993). By promoting variability in physical growth functions like

---

[5] Significant findings in this area typically involve prenatal syndromes. Although similar patterns of results are shown for studies involving prenatal hormonal treatments, the overall majority of results found for these studies tend not to be statistically significant (Meyer-Balhberg et al., 1988; Reinisch et al., 1991). One potential explanation may be the relatively low level of hormone exposure in treatment studies as compared with levels found when medical syndromes are the source of exposure.

size or strength, hormonal influences in adolescence may have an indirect impact on subsequent behavioral variability. Evidence of such indirect influences will be summarized in chapter 5 in the section on physical maturation.

Although postnatal hormonal changes and the behavioral consequences associated with these changes are thought to be synonymous with adolescence, many relevant hormonal changes begin to occur both before and after this time period (Buchanan et al., 1992). For example, the gastrointestinal tract secretes hormones (e.g., gastrin, somatostatin) that act to influence digestive functioning. Secretion of gastric hormones can be triggered by behavioral and environmental events. Thus, when infants are physically ill, sharp increases in somatostatin occur and act to slow down digestion and subsequent physical growth (Unvas-Moberg, 1989). Also, greater hypothalamic–pituitary–adrenocortical reactivity is found to be consistently associated with greater infant distress when limits are placed on the infant's personal control (Stansbury & Gunnar, 1994).

Postnatal Hormonal Influences on Cognitive Performance

At present, there is all too little evidence of postnatal hormonal influences on cognitive performance. Infrahuman studies have shown complex patterns of relations between sex hormones, gender, and type of cognitive performance task (Bachevalier & Hagger, 1991). At the human level, boys with hormonal disorders that limit postnatal production of androgen show significantly lower spatial abilities at puberty as compared with normal boys or boys whose lower androgen production occurs only after puberty. Because these types of disorders are rarely detected until puberty, differential rearing does not seem to be a likely explanation (Breedlove, 1994). In adulthood, hormonally related menstrual cycle fluctuations have been related to changes in women's performance on dichotic listening and visual perception tasks (Forget & Cohen, 1994) as well as to variability in cognitive tasks that have been found to be gender-related, such as spatial abilities, verbal performance, and fine motor skills (Hampson, 1990; Hampson & Kimura, 1988).

Postnatal Hormonal Influences on Social and Behavioral Outcomes

It is not surprising that increments in testosterone, estrogen, and gonadotropic hormones are related to both sexual interest and sexual activity in both sexes (Bancroft, 1991; Richards et al., 1993). Higher testosterone levels also appear to be consistently associated with greater sensation seeking, higher irritability, and lower frustration tolerance in male adolescents. For male adolescents, increments in gonadotropic hormones also have been associated with greater anger and more social interaction, whereas androgen increases have been associated with acting out behavior (Richards et al., 1993). Lower estrogen and progesterone levels in girls tend to be consistently associated with more emotionality and mood swings, whereas higher estrogen levels are associated with more positive moods. In adolescent girls, increments in testosterone and estrogen also are reported to be associated with more acting out and more behavior problems, whereas higher levels of gonadotropic hormones have been linked to greater anger and depression (Richards et al., 1993). However, available evidence also suggests, particularly for girls, that behavioral changes may be more associated with changes over time in female hormonal levels rather than actual levels at a given point in time. This may be why relations between hormonal fluctuations in adolescence are associated with adolescent mood fluctuations and why in early adolescence higher estrogen levels are associated with negative rather than positive mood states for girls (Brooks-Gunn & Warren, 1989; Buchanan et al., 1992).

Hormonal Influences on Behavior and Development: Necessary But Not Sufficient

The evidence just cited documents the relevance of pre- and postnatal hormonal variability for understanding individual variability in human behavior and development. However, available evidence also leads to a conclusion that hormonal influences, although necessary, are clearly not sufficient. Support for this conclusion comes partly from the nature of hormonal influences. Hormonal changes are enmeshed in a complex system that goes beyond just hormones per se (McEwen, 1989). Taking the hypothalamic–pituitary–adrenocortical (HPA) system as an example, a primary product of this system is the hormone cortisol, which is involved in stress regulation. Although cortisol is directly produced by the adrenal glands, the production process is regulated by a complex interlinked network encompassing cortical activity, hypothalamic activity, and activity of the pituitary glands. This complex system can be set into motion through stimuli carried to the hypothalamus from the brain stem (e.g., pain) or from the cerebral cortex (e.g., threat). (For further details on the HPA system, see Stansbury & Gunnar, 1994.) Both the complexity of this system and individual variability in reactivity of this system offer ample room for the impact of nonhormonal influences.

Furthermore, a fundamental aspect of hormonal action involves its bidirectional nature. Hormones can influence behavioral variability, but behavioral variability in turn can also influence hormonal levels (Bancroft, 1991). This is clearly shown in regard to sexual behavior for a variety of infrahuman species (Meisel & Sachs, 1994). At the human level, the link between testosterone and dominance behavior is clearly bidirectional in nature. Although testosterone levels act to influence individual differences in dominance, degree of dominance in turn feeds back and influences testosterone levels (Bernhardt, 1997; Erhardt, 1985). Similarly, although hormonal activity influences stress reactivity, the individual's evaluation of the stress situation can, in turn, influence levels of hormonal activity (Stansbury

& Gunnar, 1994). The prenatal hormonal environment of the fetus also can be influenced by extrinsic stress conditions, such as loss of spouse while the mother is pregnant (Huttunen & Niskanen, 1978). This bidirectional pattern makes it difficult to assign primary causality just to hormonal influences.

In addition to bidirectional influences, the impact of hormones on individual variability in behavior and development at both the human and infrahuman levels can be moderated by a variety of nonhormonal influences, involving either individual or contextual characteristics (Collaer & Hines, 1995; Meisel & Sachs, 1994). For example, the degree of relation of hormonal activity to adolescent depression or aggression can be moderated by the adolescent's history of depression or aggression prior to puberty (Buchanan et al., 1992). The extent of HPA response to stressful situations by young organisms can be reduced significantly if there is a familiar caregiver present in the stress situation, particularly if the individual has a secure attachment with the caregiver. Similar findings also are found if there is an unfamiliar but warm and supportive caregiver present or if the individual believes that he or she has the ability to control the stressful event (Stansbury & Gunnar, 1994). Furthermore, associations between cortisol level in the first year of life and toddlers' inhibited behavior in the second year will vary as a function of the degree of parental attention to infant distress and parental limit setting occurring between the first and second years (Arcus & Gardner, 1993). Such moderation may result in modest or inconsistent findings. In the case of relations between social–emotional behavior patterns and hormonal status, individual studies show high variability of results both across and within studies (Buchanan et al., 1992). For example, Paikoff, Brooks-Gunn, and Warren (1991) have reported that although there was a linear relation between estradiol and self-report measures of depression in 10- to 14-year-old girls, the significance of this relation depended on how depression was measured; in contrast, curvilinear relations were found between estradiol, aggression, and delinquency.

Even when moderation is not occurring, available evidence also indicates that the impact of hormonal influences is typically far less than the impact of psychosocial conditions (Bancroft, 1991). For example, although 4% of unique variance in adolescent female affect is predicted by hormonal levels, depending on the type of affect studied, 2 to 4 times more unique predictive variance is associated with psychosocial factors (Brooks-Gunn & Warren, 1989).

In regard to changes in gender role and behavior for male adolescents with prenatal hormonal disorders who were previously reared as girls, conclusions seem far less definitive when more detailed investigations are conducted on the individual's rearing conditions and outcome variability (Erhardt, 1985). For example, Herdt and Davidson (1988) studied gender-role development with a population of men having the same disorder

(5-alpha-reductase syndrome) as those studied by Imperato-McGinley et al. (1979) who had grown up in a very different society. The Sambia Society of New Guinea, used by Herdt and Davidson, is strongly male dominant and gender differentiated. In terms of characteristic rearing conditions, 9 of the 14 men studied were gender typed as male hermaphodites by midwives, whose role in the Sambia culture is to assign gender at birth. The remaining 5 men were incorrectly gender typed and were reared as women. In contrast to the findings of Imperato-McGinley et al., although these 5 men did attempt to change to the male role after puberty, such changes occurred only under extreme cultural pressure, and even then their behaviors were not regarded as male by others in the society. These data, plus the results summarized in more recent reviews (e.g., Collaer & Hines, 1995), call into question the idea that prenatal hormonal activity alone is a sufficient influence on subsequent gender-role adjustment. Overall, the research reviewed in the final section of this chapter illustrates how hormonal influences, although a necessary influence on individual behavioral–developmental variability, cannot be considered a sufficient influence per se.

4

BIOMEDICAL AND NUTRITIONAL
INFLUENCES

BIOMEDICAL INFLUENCES

Pre- and Perinatal Complications

It is estimated that pre- and perinatal complications account for about
13% of all cases of severe mental retardation and about 18% of all cases of
mild mental retardation (Casaer, DeVries, & Marlow, 1991). Some of the
major pre- and perinatal complications associated with behavioral and developmental deficits like mental retardation are described next. For purposes
of the present discussion, inadequate size for gestational age will be treated
as an index of intrauterine growth retardation and discussed later in this
chapter in the section on nutritional influences.

Birth Weight

A summary of findings relating birth weight to developmental outcomes is shown in Table 4-1. Given the overlap between short gestational
age and low birth weight (LBW), children with short gestational ages show
developmental problems similar to those seen with LBW (Casaer et al.,

TABLE 4-1
Consequences of Low (LBW) and Very Low Birth Weight (VLBW)

Cognitive consequences	Educational consequences	Behavioral consquences
LBW (1501–2500 grams)[a]		
Majority of LBW normal IQ but 16% have low-average/borderline range.	20% have mild educational problems.	Increased risk of later overactivity, short attention span, and emotional immaturity
VLBW (750–1500 grams)[b]		
10–20% have below-average IQ, lower perceptual, quantitative, visual–motor, and memory problems.	34% have academic problems, increased risk for attention deficit disorder and learning disabilities.	Increases risk for impulsivity poor self-control, low ego resilience, more irritable, and less soothable.

[a] Buka, Lipsitt, & Tsuang (1992); Cohen et al., (1992); Friedman & Sigman (1992); Magyary et al., (1992); Rauh & Brennan (1992).

[b] Barsky & Siegel (1992); Carran et al. (1989); Casaer et al. (1991); Friedman & Sigman (1992); Greenberg et al. (1992); Hack et al. (1992); Hunt, Tooley, & Cooper (1992); Minde (1992); Sostek (1992); Telzrow (1991).

1991; Largo et al., 1989). Cognitive–behavioral or educational problems such as those shown in Table 4-1 are more likely to occur in LBW children with early illness or early neurological problems (Greenberg, Carmichael-Olson, & Crnic, 1992), in LBW infants growing up in less developed countries (Grantham-McGregor, Lira, Ashworth, Morris, & Assuncao, 1998), and when LBW children move into the higher grades (Carran, Scott, Shaw, & Beydouin, 1989). Although as a group LBW children are at a greater risk, the overwhelming majority of LBW children do not appear to have cognitive, behavioral, or educational problems. However, given that 6–7% of all live births have LBW in developed countries (McCormick, 1992), with rates rising as high as 30% in less developed countries (Goldberg & Prentice, 1994), in terms of absolute numbers, LBW children represent a major source of developmental problems (Carran et al., 1989; Rauh & Brennan, 1992). In addition, there is suggestive evidence that some of the cognitive consequences of LBW may continue into adulthood (Sorenson et al., 1997). Of interest is that children with higher than expected birth weight also may be at risk for biomedical problems (Kleinman, 1992) and chronic delinquency (Buka et al., 1992).

Findings for very low birth weight infants (VLBW) also are summarized in Table 4-1. It is not surprising that as birth weight declines, the risk for developmental problems increases. At particular risk for cognitive problems in infancy and at school age are those VLBW infants who show slower than expected gains in head circumference in the first year of life (Eckerman & Ohler, 1992; Hack et al., 1993). In addition to being at greater risk for developmental problems, VLBW infants are also at greater risk for a variety of postnatal biomedical complications than are infants with more adequate birth weight.

Although survival rates of extremely low birth weight infants (ELBW) of 750 grams or less have been climbing in recent years, their risk for subsequent cognitive problems (e.g., 20% are mentally retarded) has not changed appreciably (Hack, Friedman, & Fanaroff, 1996). Furthermore, even when equated for level of cognitive ability, ELBW infants are still at greater risk for deficits in academic performance than are VLBW or normal birth weight children (Taylor, Hack, Klein, & Schatschneider, 1995). However, as with LBW infants, it is important to keep in mind that a large percentage of ELBW infants show no obvious cognitive, academic, or behavioral problems as they develop.

Perinatal Complications

A number of studies have implicated perinatal complications in a variety of undesirable behavioral outcomes, including child conduct disorder (Cohen, Vele, Brook, & Smith, 1989), violent crimes in adulthood (Kandel & Mednick, 1991), and an increased risk of autism (McCurry, Silverton, & Mednick, 1991), and schizophrenia (McNeil, 1987). Common to many of these reports of perinatal problems is a loss of oxygen supply to the fetus or neonatal anoxia (Buka et al., 1992). As a group, infants with fetal anoxia are more at risk for later cognitive deficits than nonanoxic infants, but again, the great majority of children with this condition seem to show essentially normal cognitive development over time (Aylward & Pfeiffer, 1991; Menke, McClead, & Hansen, 1991). Although there may be subtle influences of early anoxia on later educational performance, these influences tend to fade over time (Telzrow, 1991). Research suggests that the presence or absence of anoxia per se may be less critical than the duration of oxygen deprivation, with a greater chance of central nervous system damage as oxygen deprivation increases (Aylward & Pfeiffer, 1991). In evaluating this pattern of findings, it is important to keep in mind the possibility that perinatal complications may be a marker for earlier prenatal problems rather than a cause for later postnatal problems (Rutter et al., 1993). For example, neonatal respiratory problems may be more likely to occur for an infant whose development already has been compromised while in utero.

It also is important to recognize that the developmental risks associated with preterm birth may be related to perinatal complications that covary with prematurity (Gross, Brooks-Gunn, & Spiker, 1992). One such complication is bronchopulmonary dysplasia (BPD). BPD is a complex disorder characterized by acute lung injury and less efficient functioning of the lungs. Biomedical consequences associated with BPD include a lack of resistance to respiratory infections, a high risk of overstressing the heart due to inadequate lung function, and an increased caloric requirement due to the increased work of breathing. Fifty percent of VLBW infants in the range of 900 to 1000 grams are at risk for BDP, and almost all infants below 900 grams will be affected (Als, 1992). Behavioral consequences associated with BDP are shown in Table 4-2.

Another major perinatal risk factor is intraventricular hemorrhage (IVH). IVH refers to ruptures of the blood vessels of the cortical germinal matrix layer. Fifty percent of infants born prior to 21 weeks gestational age develop IVH versus only 10–20% born between 32 to 36 weeks (Menke, McClead, & Hansen, 1991). The main causes of IVH in preterm infants are elevated blood pressure and an immature anatomical system (Als, 1992). Minor IVH (Grade 1) is confined to the germinal matrix area alone, whereas more severe hemorrhages (Grades 3 and 4) extend into the lateral ventricles, resulting in dilation of these ventricles. Severe IVH is far more likely to result in long-term behavioral developmental consequences than are the less severe grades (Casaer et al., 1991; Menke et al., 1991). Behavioral consequences associated with IVH also are shown in Table 4-2.

Given the multiple clinical conditions that fall under the category of perinatal problems, there are a variety of potential mechanisms linking such problems to later developmental outcomes. Although a detailed discussion of potential mechanisms is beyond the scope of the present chapter, certain mechanisms may be particularly relevant for understanding individual variability in behavior and development. One such mechanism is the extent of covariance among birth weight and other biomedical risk factors. As discussed earlier, VLBW infants who also have BDP or more serious IVH are more likely to have more adverse developmental outcomes than VLBW infants for whom there is only limited covariance with other biomedical risks. Similarly, LBW or VLBW infants with repeated hospitalizations in the first year of life or who are rehospitalized for more than 50 days are at greater risk for school-age academic problems than are preterm infants who either are not rehospitalized or are not rehospitalized for lengthy time periods (Caughy, 1996; Scott et al., 1994).

Disease

Pre- and Perinatal Infections

The pre- and perinatal infections that appear to be most salient for variability in behavioral development are the TORCH disorders: toxoplasmosis, other, rubella, cytomegalovrus, and herpes. TORCH disorders are maternal infections that affect the fetal central nervous system and, through this pathway, result in behavioral consequences such as mental retardation. The exact level of mental retardation associated with TORCH disorders is highly variable, ranging from no effect to severe and profound retardation (Scola,

TABLE 4-2
Behavioral Consequences Asociated With Various Perinatal Complications
That Covary With Low Birth Weight

Complication	Consequence	Reference
Bronchopulmonary dysplasia	Cognitive and motor delay; hypersensitivity to stimulation; greater incidence of neuropsychological problems.	Als (1992); Barsky & Siegel (1992); Singer, Yamashita, et al. (1997)
Hyaline membrane disease/respiratory distress syndrome	Childhood cognitive deficits.	Hunt et al. (1992); Rose & Feldman (1996)
Intraventricular hemorrhage	Deficits in early gross motor performance and early expressive communication related to severity of IVH; severe IVH related to later delays in cognitive performance, school readiness, motor performance, and visual recognition tasks.	Bendersky & Lewis (1994); Sostek (1992)

1991). As noted in chapter 2, evidence also indicates that the association of winter births with an increased risk for later schizophrenia may be a function of second-trimester maternal viral infection. Maternal viral infections may disrupt normal fetal neural migration processes, leading to localized migration deficits that predispose to adult schizophrenia (Goodman, 1994).

Acute Postnatal Infection

From the frequency of acute mild illness found in children living in developed countries (8–9 morbidity episodes per year in 1–3 year olds, 4–6 morbidity episodes in 4–10 year olds), Parmelee (1986) has argued that common childhood illnesses such as colds can have potentially beneficial developmental consequences. Parmelee's conclusion is based on the hypothesis that children feel a loss of personal self during illness, which is then restored when the child recovers. Parmelee also has suggested that feelings of identification with parents or siblings who also may be ill can lead to the development of a sense of empathy. Although provocative, there is little empirical evidence supporting these hypotheses. On the contrary, particularly for acute severe infections that have the potential to influence central nervous system functioning (e.g., meningitis or encephalitis), there is a significantly higher risk of mental retardation, learning disabilities, hyperactivity, and acting out behavior (Anderson et al., 1997; Graham, 1984).

Chronic Postnatal Illness

At least in Western countries, it is estimated that at least 10% of children may have chronic health impairments, including respiratory disorders, metabolic problems, seizure disorders, or cardiac problems (Shonkoff, 1994). For children in less developed countries, incidence figures appear to be even higher (Miller, Kiernan, Mathers, & Klein-Gitelamn, 1995). In addition to incidence differences, the pattern of chronic illness may differ in developed and developing countries. In developing countries, chronic illness is more often cyclical in nature, with children alternating between periods of illness and nonillness as they develop. Although disorders such as malaria and respiratory infections have been associated with growth faltering of children in less developed countries (Neumann & Harrison, 1994), perhaps the most well-documented linkage is between cyclical chronic gastrointestinal disorder and physical growth faltering (L. Allen, 1994; Golden, 1994; Keusch, 1977). This linkage is most likely due to chronic gastrointestinal illness reducing the child's ability to absorb necessary dietary nutrients (Prentice & Bates, 1994). Delayed physical growth may in turn result in differential treatment from caregivers, who treat the growth-delayed child as if he or she were younger (Pollitt, Gorman, Engle, Martorell, & Rivera, 1993). Whether as a result of biological (nutrition) or psychological (differential treatment) influences, early chronic postnatal disorders have been related to both cognitive and behavioral deficits for children living in less developed countries (L. Miller et al., 1995; Wachs et al., 1993).

In developed countries, both epidemiological surveys (Cadman et al., 1987) and meta-analyses (Lavigne, Faier, & Routman, 1992) indicate that children with chronic illness are at elevated risk for internalizing and externalizing behavior disorders. Children with chronic illness are also at greater risk for problems in school achievement (Howe, Feinstein, Reiss, Mollock, & Berger, 1993). Chronic neurological disorders, such as seizure disorders, and disorders that have an unpredictable course may be especially detrimental to children's adjustment (Howe et al., 1993; Perrin, Ayoub, & Willett, 1993). Particularly for men, chronic illness in childhood may influence level of adjustment in the adult years in a variety of areas, including increased risk for mental health problems, lower educational level, and greater likelihood of unemployment (Pless, Power, & Peckham, 1993).

Although most studies on the impact of chronic illness focus on the more severe disorders, even mild disorders can have behavioral–developmental consequences. One such disorder is chronic otitis media, an accumulation of fluid in the middle ear. Epidemiological surveys suggest that more than 30% of young children have three or more episodes of otitis media in the first several years of life (Webster, Bamford, Thyer, & Ayles, 1989). The sound distortion caused by chronic otitis media may act to cause impairments in hearing efficiency, which in turn may delay language development and associated functions in the young child (Shonkoff, 1994). It is therefore not surprising that many studies report that children with chronic otitis media have significantly lower verbal IQ, word recognition skills, and slower language development in the early school years (Webster et al.,

1989). The increased likelihood of missing school due to chronic ear infections also may be a reason why retrospective reports suggest a greater incidence of otitis media in children who have been diagnosed as learning disabled (Shonkoff, 1994). However, evidence also suggests that the impact of otitis media in the preschool years may attenuate as children move into adolescence (Roberts, Burchinal, & Clarke-Klein, 1995).

Chronic Postnatal Metabolic Disorders

In chapter 3, I discussed how hormonal or genetic disorders such as congenital hypothyroidism (CH) and phenylketonuria (PKU) can have a direct impact on central nervous system (CNS) development and thus have a long-term effect on subsequent behavior and development. Even when there are no direct effects on CNS structure, there can be behavioral consequences associated with metabolic disorders. For example, although only a minority of diabetic children have adjustment problems, there is still an elevated risk rate for adjustment problems in this population (Johnson, 1988).

In addition, some of the behavioral problems associated with metabolic disorders like diabetes and PKU may reflect the need for continual monitoring of metabolic status to avoid further physical damage. Although it was originally thought that PKU children could safely go off their restricted diet once peak CNS development had occurred, more recent evidence suggests that this may not be so (Clarke, Gates, Hogan, Barrett, & MacDonald, 1987). Even for PKU children who are treated early in life, their subsequent level of executive functioning (e.g., impulse control, sustained attention, flexibility of thought) is related to measures assessing adequacy of current dietary control, such as serum phenylalanine level (Diamond et al., 1997; Welsh, Pennington, Ozanoff, Rouse, & McCabe, 1990). In addition, there also can be devastating prenatal effects on infants born to PKU mothers who went off the restricted diet before or during pregnancy (Belmont, 1994).

Parasitic Infection

Although rarely considered a problem in developed countries, a major chronic biomedical problem in less developed countries is parasitic infection. Although exact figures are difficult to come by, it is estimated that 200 million–1.4 billion individuals may be infected, depending on the parasite (Connolly, 1998; Watkins & Pollitt, 1997). Infection by multiple parasites may be particularly common, and reinfection following treatment is often highly likely for children living in areas with high parasite levels (Watkins & Pollitt, 1996). One of the major consequences of infection by parasites such as ascaris, hookworm, or trichuris is interference with normal nutritional processes through blood loss, malabsorption, or anorexia (Connolly, 1998; Pollitt & Saco-Pollitt, 1996; Rosenberg, Solomons, & Schneider, 1977). Direct CNS damage also can occur as a result of infections from other forms of parasites, such as schistosomes (Connolly, 1998). Although humans can adapt to parasitic infections, there is often a cost to this adaptation, as seen in the higher rates of lethargy and reduced motor activity in children who are infected by parasites (Connolly & Kvalsvig, 1993). Beyond lethargy and reduced motor activity, the results from studies on the cognitive impact of parasitic infection tend to be inconsistent (Connolly, 1998; Connolly & Kvalsvig, 1993). Differences among studies may reflect differences in degree of parasitic burden. As reviewed by Watkins and Pollitt (1997), cognitive impairment is most likely to occur when there is heavy parasitic infection, but it is rarely seen when the parasite burden is light. Moderate levels of infection will influence cognitive performance only when combined with other biological risks, such as undernutrition. Inconsistencies also may reflect the fact that not all aspects of cognitive performance may be equally influenced by parasitic infection. Although memory retrieval seems particularly sensitive to parasitic infection, individual differences in reaction time or school performance appear to be far less affected (Watkins & Pollitt, 1997).

Toxic Conditions

Prenatal exposure to teratogens occurs through maternal ingestion of alcohol, drugs, chemicals, or heavy metals. Postnatal influences are most commonly associated with exposure to lead or other heavy-metal pollutants. Some of the exposure of young children to environmental pollutants may be the result of breast milk contamination if the mother has been continually exposed to certain environmental toxins (Somogyi & Beck, 1993). This may be particularly true in those less developed countries that still rely heavily on more toxic pesticides. Given that the prenatal and early postnatal period is a time of maximal CNS development, individual differences in exposure to teratogens during this time may be a potentially critical influence on individual differences in behavioral development.

Fetal Alcohol Syndrome

Recent analyses suggest that some developmental disorders that run in families may be due to familial patterns of maternal alcohol abuse rather than heredity alone (Karp, 1993). One of the major consequences of maternal alcohol use during pregnancy is fetal alcohol syndrome, which has been estimated to occur at a rate of 1–3 births per 1,000 (Vorhees & Mollnow, 1987). Developmental consequences associated with fetal alcohol syndrome are shown in Table 4-3. It has been hypothesized that the results associated with maternal drinking during pregnancy may be a function of alcohol crossing the placental barrier and interfering with fetal neural cell growth, neural migration patterns, and neurotransmitter production. In addition, prenatal alcohol exposure also may adversely affect the nutritional status of the fetus (Karp,

Qazi, Hittleman, & Chabrier, 1993). The question of how much maternal alcohol use during pregnancy is acceptable remains unanswered at present. It is worth noting, however, that children whose mothers had three or more drinks per day during pregnancy were three times more likely to have IQs below 85 than were children whose mothers had less than three drinks per day during pregnancy (Olson, Streissguth, Bookstein, Barr, & Sampson, 1994).

Exposure To Environmental Toxins

Although much of the evidence on exposure to environmental toxins such as heavy metals has focused on health-related issues, there is an increasing awareness that there may be behavioral consequences as well. Exposure to environmental lead has been of particular interest, in part because of the hypothesized vulnerability of infants and young children to lead exposure (Schroeder & Hawk, 1987). The immature organism appears to have a less effective blood–brain barrier, so lead can more easily enter the CNS. Behavioral characteristics of the young child (mouthing and playing close to the ground) are the kinds of activities that can increase exposure to ambient lead. Furthermore, the high metabolic rate associated with the fast physical growth rate of the young organism may mean that the young assimilate lead at a faster rate than do older individuals. The developmental consequences of lead exposure also are shown in Table 4-3.

In evaluating the impact of lead exposure on development, it is important to recognize that such exposure covaries with exposure to a variety of other psychosocial stressors, such as poverty, making it difficult to separate out the unique effects of lead exposure (Dietrich, Kraft, Shukla, Bornschein, & Succop, 1987). However, lead effects are found even after controlling for covarying sociodemographic risk factors (Fergusson, Fergusson, Harwood, & Kinzett, 1988; Wasserman et al., 1994). Similarly, increased exposure to lead can adversely affect the metabolism of critical nutrients like iron, calcium, and zinc, making it difficult to determine whether functional consequences are a direct result of lead exposure or are due to poor micronutrient status associated with lead exposure (Miller, Massaro, & Massaro, 1990). However, it is also important to recognize that, like other environmental toxins, the impact of lead on development will vary as a function of the neuromaturational level of the individual at the time of exposure (Shaheen, 1984).

Maternal Drug Use

When we think of the influence of maternal drugs on offspring development, illegal drugs are usually what first come to mind. Obviously, as with other toxins, it becomes difficult to separate out the effects of the drug use per se from all of the other developmental influences that may covary with illegal drug use. In addition, because substance abusers often use multiple drugs, it is often very difficult to isolate the impact of a single drug on

TABLE 4-3

Developmental Consequences Associated With Pre- or Postnatal Exposure to Toxic Substances

Substance	Consequences	References
Alcohol in utero	Microcephally, flat midface, deficits in IQ, attention, memory, academic performance.	Olson et al. (1994); Streissguth et al. (1989); Taylor (1991)
Lead	Low-level but significant negative effects on cognitive performance, attention, school achievement, behavioral adjustment.	Bellinger et al. (1994); Needleman & Gatsonis (1990); Taylor, (1991).
Mercury	Increased risk of preterm birth and mental retardation.	Pearson & Dietrich (1985); Vorhees & Mollnow (1987).
PCB	Modest but significant deficits in motor maturity, visual processing speed and short term memory; abnormal reflexes in the neonatal period.	Jacobson et al. (1984, 1992).
Multiple heavy metals	Cognitive deficits.	Lewis et al. (1992).
Maternal drug use during pregnancy	Infancy: neonatal irritability and tremors, physical features resemble fetal alcohol syndrome, increased risk of mild intraventricular hemorrhage, slower habituation to repeated stimuli, hypersensitivity to stimulation, attention regulation.	Dalterio & Fried (1992); Dow-Edwards, Chasnoff, & Griffith (1992); Fried (1989); Kaplan-Sanoff & Leib (1995); Mayes et al. (1993); Pearson & Dietrich (1985); Singer et al. (1994); Vorhees & Mollnow (1987); G. Wilson (1992).
Maternal smoking during pregnancy	Oxygen reduction to the fetus, increased risk of low birth weight, small for gestational age, and postnatal respiratory disorders, early auditory impairment, modest but significant deficits in cognitive performance, school achievement, social adjustment and attention.	Abel (1980); Leftwich & Collins (1994); Martin (1992); Wachs & Weizmann (1992).
Postnatal parental smoking	Increased risk of poor achievement, behavior problems, and attention deficit disorder.	Leftwich & Collins (1994).

individual development. The impact of maternal use of illegal drugs is seen in Table 4-3. Although results presented in Table 4-3 show a number of early detrimental consequences associated with the mother's use of illegal drugs during the prenatal period, studies also show high levels of variability, with many prenatally drug-exposed infants not showing significant developmental deficits (Hawley & Disney, 1992; G. Wilson, 1989).

Less evidence is available on the long-term consequences of prenatal exposure to illegal drugs, and what evidence is available suggests major variability in the developmental outcomes of exposed children as they get older (Dalterio & Fried, 1992; Hawley & Disney, 1992; G. Wilson, 1992). Although many prenatally drug-exposed children show levels of cognitive performance that are in the normal range, developmental deficits may appear as these children become exposed to more difficult demands from their school environment or when more subtle aspects of cognitive performance are assessed (Hawley & Disney, 1992; Kaplan-Sanoff & Leib, 1995; G. Wilson, 1989).

Illegal drug use is not the only drug risk factor to which children are exposed. Legal and prescription drug use during pregnancy also can act as risk factors. The physical consequences for the fetus of maternal thalidomide use have been clearly documented (J. Wilson, 1977), as have the behavioral consequences of maternal aspirin use during pregnancy (Barr, Streissguth, Darby, & Sampson, 1990) and the use of analgesia during labor (Pearson & Dietrich, 1985). Although avoidance of drugs during pregnancy would seem an obvious solution, such a course of action is not always possible. For example, for epileptic women, taking anticonvulsive drugs during pregnancy can be a risk factor for their developing fetus, but so can maternal seizures (Vorhees & Mollnow, 1987). Under these circumstances, the question is not one of whether to take drugs but rather which drug is least likely to have behavioral consequences for the fetus.

In terms of other legal but potentially toxic substances, prenatal caffeine exposure does not appear to be a major behavioral risk (Barr & Streissguth, 1991), although an infant's consumption of coffee is related to slower physical growth and the ability to metabolize supplemental iron (Dewey et al., 1997a, 1997b). Evidence on the physical and behavioral consequences of maternal smoking during the prenatal period also are shown in Table 4-3. It is important to note that many behavioral consequences associated with maternal smoking are less obvious when socioeconomic status is statistically controlled (Martin, 1992; Pearson & Dietrich, 1985; Rush & Callahan, 1989). Furthermore, many relations hold only when the mother is a very heavy smoker (e.g., more than three packs per day during pregnancy; Barr et al., 1990) or continues smoking through pregnancy (Martin, 1992).

Biomedical Influences: Necessary But Not Sufficient

There are many biomedical conditions that have been identified in this chapter as influences on variability in behavioral development. As discussed in chapter 1, because biomedical conditions contribute to variability in human behavioral development, they can be regarded as a necessary influence on development. However, as will be shown next, with rare exceptions, biomedical influences are not sufficient in and of themselves to uniquely explain variability in individual behavioral development. A number of reasons support this conclusion.

Effect Size

One reason why biomedical influences cannot be considered sufficient is the wide variability of outcomes associated with biomedical risk factors (see chap. 1). For example, children with prenatal infections like cytomegalovirus or rubella may show outcomes ranging from asymptomatic to severe mental retardation (Rubenstein et al., 1990; Scola, 1991). Similarly, not all children whose mothers drink get fetal alcohol syndrome, and among those who do, IQ scores range from normal to severe retardation (Olson et al., 1994). Although children with very low birth weight or who are small for gestational age are clearly at risk, the majority of children with these problems do not show developmental deficits (Als, 1992), even when followed up into adulthood (Hunt et al., 1992). Wide levels of outcome variability also are associated with prenatal drug exposure (Wilson, 1992), maternal smoking (Martin, 1992), postnatal exposure to environmental toxins (Dietrich et al., 1987), and parasitic infection (Connolly & Kvalsvig, 1993). The relatively modest level of prediction associated with most biomedical risks makes it difficult to ascribe developmental variability simply to biomedical influences per se.

Covariance Among Risk Factors

Biomedical influences often covary with nonbiomedical factors that also can act to influence development. In understanding the nature of covariance among biomedical and nonbiomedical influences, what must be stressed is that we are dealing with probabilities and not certainties. Thus, although drug-addicted mothers may have an increased likelihood of being less involved or more nonresponsive to their child, not all drug-addicted mothers function in this way (Brinker, Baxter, & Butler, 1994). As shown in Table 4-4, multiple examples of biomedical covariance can be documented. As discussed in the next section of this chapter, and in chapters 5–7, the covariates described in Table 4-4 can also act to influence individual behavioral–developmental variability. For example, one study found that 80% of children exposed to heroin in the prenatal period were living with someone other than a biological parent by the time they were of preschool age, as compared with only 5% of matched controls (Wilson, 1992). Over and above the impact of prenatal drug exposure, the potential impact of such early family disruption cannot be disregarded. Similarly, the increased incidence of hospitalization associated with pre- or perinatal risk conditions or severe and chronic disease

TABLE 4-4
Covariance Among Biomedical and Nonbiomedical Risk Factors

Biomedical risk factor	Covariate	References
Lead exposure	Increased risk of child abuse; minority group and/or poverty status; lower maternal IQ; lower maternal involvement and maternal responsivity.	Bithoney, Vandeven, & Ryan (1993); Dietrich et al. (1987); Milar et al. (1980); Schroeder & Hawk (1987); Vorhees & Mollnow (1987).
Prenatal exposure to illegal drugs	Increased risk of prenatal infection and pregnancy problems; increased risk of maternal adjustment problems.	Dow-Edwards et al. (1992); Kaplan-Sanoff & Leib (1995); Singer et al. (1997).
Maternal smoking	Family socioeconomic status; increased risk of parental depression.	Leftwich & Collins (1994); Rush & Callahan (1989).
Low birth weight	Poverty background; single mother; compromised nutritional status; less adequate home environment.	Fuchs (1990); Kleinman (1992); Grantham-McGregor et al. (1998).
Parasitic infection	Residence in communities with poorer medical care and lower educational levels; rearing in less adequate home environments; increased risk of undernutrition.	L. Allen (1994); Connolly (1998); Connolly & Kvalsvig (1993); Rosenberg et al. (1977).
Chronic disease	Compromised nutritional status, increased family stress, restriction of normal childhood activities.	L. Allen (1994); Fuchs (1990); Holaday, Swan, & Turner-Henson (1997); Prentice & Bates (1994).

also can act to adversely influence the course of development (Douglas, 1975; Quinton & Rutter, 1976; Zeskind & Iacino, 1987), perhaps as a function either of understimulation (Friedman, Maarten, Streisel, & Sinnamon, 1968) or inappropriate overstimulation associated with hospital environments (Gottfried, Hodgman, & Brown, 1984). Besides the contextual covariates associated with parasitic infection in children, individual characteristics also may be important as an influence on which children in a given community are infected. For example, in a population at overall risk for parasitic infection, more sociable children were more likely to be infected than were less sociable children (Kvalsvig & Becker, 1988).

Covariance also can occur for fundamental biological processes underlying susceptibility to illness, as seen in the well-documented relation between environmental stress and alterations in immune-system functioning (Maier, Watkins, & Fleshner, 1994). High family stress can reduce the child's resistance, thus increasing the child's susceptibility to infectious agents (Barr et al., 1994; Boyce & Jemerin, 1990). For example, children living in families that had 12 or more negative life stresses over a 4-year period were found to be six times more likely to be admitted to hospitals, even after covarying out demographic factors like socioeconomic status (Beautrais, Fergusson, & Shannon, 1982).

Naturally occurring covariance among biomedical and nonbiomedical influences means that we cannot automatically assign primary causation to biomedical influences. One can, of course, attempt to statistically separate covarying biomedical and nonbiomedical influences, but such artificial separation is more likely to mask rather than reveal the nature of processes influencing developmental variability.

Moderating Conditions

Even when biomedical and nonbiomedical influences do not covary, the influence of specific biomedical factors can be moderated by a variety of other nonbiomedical factors. Such moderation can act either to attenuate or accentuate the impact of specific biomedical influences. Sameroff and Chandler (1975) were among the first to point out how the long-term detrimental impact of pre- and perinatal biological risks can be attenuated when infants are reared in more adequate psychosocial circumstances. Evidence reported since the time of the original Sameroff and Chandler review has done little to change the nature of this conclusion (Als, 1992; Casaer et al., 1991; Landry, Smith, Miller-Loncar, & Swank, 1998; C. Miller & White, 1995; Minde, 1992; Olson et al., 1994; Werner, 1994). Risk attenuation also can occur well beyond the infancy period. For example, the ability of parents to deal with the increased independence needs of adolescent children with conditions requiring strict dietary monitoring, such as PKU or diabetes, can act to influence the subsequent biological functioning and psychosocial development of these children (Shonkoff, 1994). Even if family resources are inadequate, attenuation of pre- and perinatal biomedical risk influences can occur when intervention programs are provided for biomedically vulnerable children (Telzrow, 1991). For example, preschool cognitive deficits associated with maternal use of marijuana during the prenatal period were not found for exposed Caucasian children who had attended preschool (Day et al., 1994). The fact that similar attenuation did not occur for Black children who had prenatal marijuana exposure supports a suggestion by Latham (1998) that, in very-high-risk populations, interventions may have to occur at multiple levels to have an effect. Thus, it makes little sense to treat a child's parasitic infection with the goal of improving school performance if the school the child attends is of extremely low quality.

The impact of biomedical influences also can be accentuated as well as attenuated by other influences (Cohen et al., 1989). The adverse impact of early repeated rehospitalization on certain aspects of later school performance occurs primarily for children living in less adequate home environments (Caughy, 1996). For children with gastrointestinal disorders, if starchy foods are a common feature of the child's culture, or if cultural practices dictate that starchy foods be given to children with gastrointestinal disorders, the link between morbidity and poor dietary status may be strengthened (Rosenberg et al., 1977). Similarly, although chronically ill children are nearly two times more likely to be at risk for peer isolation, anxiety, depression, or attention deficit disorder than children who are not ill. If the child has both a chronic illness and sensorimotor impairment, the risk rate for these disorders rises to nearly five times the population average (Cadman et al., 1987).

Finally, the impact of biomedical risk factors may vary as a function of individual characteristics. For example, the relation of pre- and perinatal complications or maternal winter infections to subsequent schizophrenia is more likely to occur for those who have a familial predisposition to schizophrenia (McCurry et al., 1991; McNeil, 1987; Mednick et al., 1988). Similarly, boys may be more at risk than girls for long-term negative consequences of both chronic illness in childhood (Pless, Power, & Peckham, 1993) and prenatal heroin exposure (Hans, 1995). Differential reactivity to biomedical risk may further interact with outcome domains and risk categories to produce highly complex patterns of behavioral variability (McMichael et al., 1992). For example, the moderating impact of maternal and child characteristics on adjustment of chronically ill children can vary according to the nature of the child's illness (Perrin et al., 1993).

The findings just presented illustrate high outcome variability associated with biomedical risk characteristics, covariance of biomedical and nonbiomedical conditions, and moderation of biomedical influences by nonbiomedical influences. This pattern of results does not mean that biomedical conditions are not a necessary influence on individual behavioral–developmental variability. Rather, this pattern indicates that biomedical risk factors, although necessary, are not sufficient.

NUTRITION AND DEVELOPMENT

In this section, the primary emphasis will be on the relation between nutritional deficits and behavioral development. Studies on the relation of food allergies or megavitamin supplementation to development will not be considered, primarily because of inconsistent results and continued difficulties in replicating initial findings (Kaplan, 1988; Ricciuti, 1993; Taylor, 1991; Toller, 1992). Furthermore, the number of children with documented food allergies appears to be quite small compared with the number of children suffering from either general malnutrition or from deficits in trace minerals or vitamins.

Scope of the Problem

Available evidence suggests that approximately 35% of infants and preschool children in less developed countries are showing levels of growth retardation indicative of moderate to severe deficits in protein-energy intake (Engle, Zeitlin, Medrano, & Garcia, 1996; Pollitt & Gorman, 1994), with even greater incidence rates in certain areas such as Southeast Asia (Waterlow, 1994a). Moderate to severe malnutrition may be just the "tip of the iceberg," with even higher incidence figures for individuals showing mild, subclinical malnutrition (Pollitt & Gorman, 1994). The potential incidence rates for nutritional deficits is increased even further when we also include individuals with micronutrient deficits (deficits in trace minerals and vitamins). For example, it has been estimated that more than 180 million children in less developed countries are suffering from iron deficiency anemia (Pollitt & Gorman, 1994). Although much of the available evidence comes from less developed countries, nutritional deficits are not a problem just for third-world countries. Cook and Martin (1995) have presented data suggesting that up to 1 million low-income children in the United States fall below the 70th percentile in regard to recommended energy intake. Evidence also indicates that 20–30% of U.S. infants from low-income families may have iron-deficiency anemia (Pollitt & Gorman, 1994). Given these numbers, if adequate nutrition is a necessary influence, then individual nutritional status may be one of the most prominent causes of individual differences in behavioral and developmental variability.

Why Are Nutritional Influences Likely to be Necessary?

A number of reasons explain why either protein-energy or micronutrient deficits can act to influence behavioral development. The fact that the CNS has little energy storage capacity means that efficient CNS functioning is particularly dependent on an adequate supply of nutrients (Krassner, 1986; Landsberg & Young, 1983). For example, inadequate nutritional status can adversely affect CNS efficiency through its impact on neurotransmitter metabolism, as in the case of iron-deficiency anemia adversely influencing both the synthesis and uptake of dopamine and y-amino-butyric-acid (GABA; Pollitt, 1995).

In addition, undernutrition also can influence the development of the CNS itself. As a general statement, relative to other organs of the body, the CNS appears to be relatively well protected against nutritional insult, particularly during the prenatal period (DeLong, 1993). However, this general statement needs to be qualified in some critical ways. First, the fact that the CNS may be less sensitive than other body systems to nutritional insult does not mean that it is invulnerable. Infrahuman data show that early protein-calorie malnutrition can produce permanent deficits in certain CNS structures, as seen in malnutrition-related reductions in cortical volume, dendritic spine density, cortical cell width, number of glial cells, and number of corti-cal synapses (Levitsky & Strupp, 1995). Malnutrition also can affect CNS process mechanisms, such as the degree of myelination, number of norepi-nephrine receptors, and level of neural DNA (Ballabriga, 1990; Strupp & Levitsky, 1995). Second, certain aspects of CNS development may be par-ticularly sensitive to early deficits in specific nutrients such as iron (Lozoff, 1998; Pollitt, 1995; Youdim, Ben-Shachar, & Yehuda, 1989), iodine (Schurch, 1995), and essential fatty acids (Uauy et al., 1996). Third, to some extent the degree of protection depends on the stage of development of dif-ferent neural systems relative to when malnutrition occurs (Ballabriga, 1990; Bell, Whitmore, Queen, Orband-Miller, & Slotkin, 1987). Finally, at least in the case of protein-calorie malnutrition, some CNS macro- (e.g., brain size and width) and microstructures (e.g., synapse–neuron ratio) have shown re-markable recovery after nutritional rehabilitation. One reason for such reha-bilitation may be malnutrition-induced delays in CNS maturation, which can act to increase the time period during which maximal CNS development can occur (Levitsky & Strupp, 1995). The fact that nutritional deficits can adversely affect individual CNS development and the fact that some degree of nutritional rehabilitation of the CNS is possible have clear implications for individual variability in behavior and development.

In addition to direct CNS effects, nutritional deficits also can indirectly influence behavioral development. Individual adaptation to energy imbal-ance (degree to which energy intake does not meet the organism's energy needs) is typically handled by reducing energy output. However, some aspects of energy output, such as basal metabolism, are less changeable than other as-pects, such as voluntary activity (Scrimshaw & Young, 1989). Thus, one of the potential consequences of nutritional deficits is a reduction in the child's physical activity, exploratory activities, or responsivity to the environment (i.e., functional isolation) (Pollitt et al., 1993; Riccuiti, 1993; Simeon & Grantham-McGregor, 1990). Nutritionally driven reductions in activity and exploration can act to reduce the child's interactions with the environment and the opportunities the child has to learn from the environment, further hindering development (Pollitt et al., 1993; Strupp & Levitsky, 1995). The increased levels of inhibition and fearfulness seen for anemic infants and children would be one example of such an indirect influence (Lozoff, 1998). However, changes in children's cognitive performance following nutritional supplementation have been found to be independent of changes in their ac-tivity level (Meeks-Gardner, Grantham-McGregor, Chang, Himes, & Powell, 1995). These results suggest that activity level per se may be less crit-ical in determining the consequences of functional isolation than other child characteristics, such as reduced exploration, lower reactivity, or increased levels of inhibition (Wachs, 1989). Given these potential causal links, what is the empirical evidence on the relation of nutritional deficits to behavioral development?

Moderate to Severe Malnutrition and Development

Physical Growth

Moderate to severe malnutrition in children is characterized by a variety of physical signs, such as intrauterine growth retardation (below the 10 percentile in growth for gestational age), potential growth faltering (height or weight for age 2 standard deviations or more below international growth standards), and edema (swelling associated with a buildup of bodily fluids) (Grantham-McGregor, 1995). Intrauterine growth retardation, also called "small for gestational age" (SGA), typically is defined at birth, although, ideally, repeated growth measurements are taken during pregnancy to assess growth rates. Postnatal growth faltering leading to stunting typically occurs in a restricted age range from 3 to 30 months, with the greatest degree of growth retardation occurring between 8 and 18 months (Engle, 1991; Martorell, Khan, & Schroeder, 1994). A variety of reasons explain why growth retardation appears primarily in this period: These include the very high growth velocity characteristically found in this time period, the fact that food typically given to children in this age range is often either energy poor or too bulky for adequate digestion, and the increasing susceptibility of children in this age range to gastrointestinal infections resulting in inhibited nutrient absorption (Engle, 1991; Martorell et al., 1994). Biochemical analysis also has related stunting to the nutrient quality of the mother's breast milk (Allen, 1994). Contrary to popular belief, although intrauterine-growth-retarded or stunted children can show some degree of catch-up growth, complete growth recovery is the exception rather than the rule (Golden, 1994; Martorell, Ramakrishnana, Schroeder, Melgar, & Neufeld, 1998). Furthermore, stunting tends to run in families (Waterlow, 1994a), and although supplementation of stunted mothers can result in increased size for their infants, such infants are still smaller than infants whose mothers were not stunted. These results suggest that stunting may be cross-generational and that more than one generation of adequate nutrition may be needed before stunting can be eliminated (Falkner et al., 1994).

Behavioral Consequences

The behavioral and developmental consequences associated with moderate to severe malnutrition are described in Table 4-5. In terms of prenatal malnutrition, although there are a number of increased risks associated with being born SGA, as shown in Table 4-5, the majority of SGA children do not appear to show any major long-term behavioral problems. The SGA children at greatest risk for long-term problems appear to be those at the lower extreme of the birth weight distribution who show a failure to achieve catch-up postnatal physical growth (Grantham-McGregor, 1998; Hack, 1998).

TABLE 4-5
Behavioral and Developmental Consequences Associated With Moderate
to Severe Malnutrition

Consequences	References
Prenatal malnutrition	
Cognitive and learning deficits in adolescence and adulthood	Hack (1998)
Adult schizophrenia	Susser et al. (1996)
Adult cardiovascular, lipid and insulin disorders.	Barker et al. (1993)
Acute postnatal malnutrition	
Lower activity level, limited affect, decreased attention, less exploration, lower cognitive performance, increased apathy and irritability.	Ballabriga (1990); DeLong (1993)
Long-term postnatal consequences	
Lower IQ; lower performance on tests of spatial abilities, motor performance, and intersensory integration; poor school performance; increased risk of emotional and behavioral problems, poor emotional control and lower responsivity . to the environment.	Ballabriga (1990); Grantham-McGregor (1995); Martorell et al. (1994); Simeon & Grantham-McGregor (1990)

Although a variety of behavioral signs are associated with moderate to severe acute postnatal malnutrition, with the exception of lower exploration and lower cognitive performance, many of these acute signs tend to disappear after nutritional rehabilitation (Grantham-McGregor, 1995). The transitory nature of these behavioral signs may reflect either short-term metabolic effects associated with moderate to severe protein energy malnutrition or the impact of hospitalization on young children while they are being nutritionally rehabilitated (Grantham-McGregor, 1993).

Long-term consequences of prior moderate to severe malnutrition also are shown in Table 4-5. Although some studies suggest that early growth faltering may have more severe consequences than later growth faltering (Skuse, Reilly, & Wolke, 1994), the overall pattern of research is not highly consistent on this point (Simeon & Grantham-McGregor, 1990). However, it does seem clear that the negative impact of early moderate to severe malnutrition is accentuated if the individual is nutritionally rehabilitated and then sent back to the same environment that produced the original malnutrition (Grantham-McGregor, 1995).

Micronutrient Deficits

In understanding the impact of moderate to severe malnutrition, it is important to recognize that moderate to severe deficits in protein-energy intake are often (though not always) accompanied by moderate to severe micronutrient deficits, such as an increased risk of iron-deficiency anemia.

This naturally occurring covariance has led some researchers to hypothesize that some of the developmental consequences associated with protein-energy deficits may be attributed to micronutrient deficits (Pollitt, 1995). It is clear that some micronutrient deficits are associated with biomedical problems that can affect subsequent development. For example, severe prenatal deficits in maternal intake of folate is associated with an increased risk of neural tube abnormalities in offspring (DeLong, 1993). Similarly, growth faltering can also occur as a result of severe deficiencies in zinc, iron, iodine (L. Allen, 1994), and Vitamin B_{12} (Neumann & Harrison, 1994), even when total protein-energy intake is adequate. The critical question is whether there are also behavioral consequences associated with severe micronutrient deficits.

One of the most prevalent forms of behaviorally relevant micronutrient deficits involves prenatal iodine levels (Pollitt & Saco-Pollitt, 1996). Maternal iodine deficiencies, particularly during the first and second trimesters of gestational life, can have major detrimental consequences on the developing fetal CNS (Grantham-McGregor, Fernald, & Sethuraman, 1999). Unless treated, moderate to severe prenatal iodine deficiency can result in postnatal mental retardation (Schurch, 1995; Simeon & Grantham-McGregor, 1990). Less severe prenatal iodine deficits may result in more specific postnatal cognitive deficits (Connolly & Pharoah, 1989).

Iron-deficiency anemia (IDA) refers to alterations in red blood cells and hemoglobin production, both of which are usually preceded by iron-store depletion and then by reduction in serum iron and iron-binding capacities (Pollitt & Gorman, 1994). IDA is associated with significant decrements in general cognitive performance, discrimination learning and attention (Pollitt, 1993), as well as an increased risk of mental retardation in low income families (Hurtado, Claussen, & Scott, 1999). Behaviorally, children with IDA are characterized as more fearful, more irritable, less responsive, and less active (Wachs, in press). Establishment of a causal role for IDA in developmental variability is seen in the results from intervention studies. For IDA children less than 2 years old, short-term iron-repletion treatment (for 2 weeks or less) seems to have few developmental benefits (Simeon & Grantham-McGregor, 1990), perhaps because it takes about 8 weeks of treatment to get hemoglobin levels back to normal (Pollitt, 1993). For both younger and older IDA children, long-term iron-repletion treatment is found to promote significant improvement in both general and specific cognitive abilities, affect, and behavioral inhibition (Pollitt, 1993; Simeon & Grantham-McGregor, 1990). Young children who do not fully respond to iron-repletion treatment tend to be more developmentally at risk than those that do fully respond (Lozoff, 1998). Furthermore, when compared with controls, even successfully iron-repleted children still scored lower on tests of nonverbal performance, visual motor integration, and motor coordination. These differences may reflect long-term effects of early IDA on brain myelination (Lozoff, 1998).

Although monkeys reared on a zinc-deprived diet show lower motor activity, poorer-visual attention performance, and poorer visual-discrimination learning, nutritional remediation of children with severe zinc deficiencies often produce no clear gains in cognitive performance (Golub, Keen, Gershwin, & Hendricks, 1995). Zinc deficiency and zinc supplementation have been related to alterations in motor performance and activity levels of infants and toddlers (Black, 1998). However, the fact that one of the consequences of severe zinc deficiency is anorexia makes it difficult to determine whether outcomes are unique to zinc deficiency per se or are associated with general nutritional deficits caused by the anorexia.

Mild Nutrient Deficits

General Undernutrition

Available evidence indicates modest but significant relations between direct (food intake) or indirect (anthropometric measures) markers of mild chronic postnatal undernutrition and deficits in general or specific cognitive performance, school achievement, and adaptive behavior for children living in developing countries (Simeon & Grantham-McGregor, 1990; Wachs, 1995b). Such relations hold even when statistically controlling for obvious confounders like socioeconomic status. Similarly, nutritional supplementation of infants and young children at risk for chronic undernutrition has been shown to result in small but significant gains, particularly in regard to motor performance in infancy and general cognitive performance in the preschool years (Gorman, 1995). Early supplementation of nutritionally at risk infants and preschool children also has been shown to result in small but significant long-term increments in both psychoeducational performance and information-processing task performance when assessed in late adolescence and early adulthood (Pollitt et al., 1993).

Though not all studies show significant results after controlling for the appropriate covariates, some studies do report modest but significant variance (3–7%) in subsequent cognitive performance associated with having been breastfed in infancy (Schurch, 1995; Uauy & deAndraca, 1995). In addition, drought-related temporary food shortages have been associated with lower activity level, less positive peer interaction, and more off-task classroom behavior in a population of chronically undernourished Kenyan school children (McDonald, Sigman, Espunosa, & Neumann, 1994). This latter set of results may parallel data suggesting that children with a history of chronic undernutrition may be more sensitive than adequately nourished children to temporary disruptions in food intake, such as missing breakfast (Pollitt & Mathews, 1998).

Dietary Quality

High food intake in and of itself may not guarantee adequate nutrition if the diet consists of low-quality nutrients lacking critical trace minerals or vitamins, has low bioavailability and thus is not easily digested by the individual, or contains high levels of nutrients such as phytates that can inhibit absorption of essential trace minerals such as iron (L. Allen, 1994). Foods that come from animal sources are more likely to be richer in trace minerals and vitamins and have greater micronutrient bioavailability than foods that come from plant sources. In undernourished populations, studies have identified animal-source food intake as a more salient predictor of certain aspects of behavioral development than total amount of energy intake (Wachs, 1995b). For example, neonatal habituation and orienting performance are uniquely related to maternal intake of animal-source protein and fat rather than total maternity energy intake (Kirksey et al., 1991), whereas child intake of animal protein from 18 to 30 months has been shown to be a stronger predictor of 5-year cognitive performance than total protein intake during this same period (Sigman, McDonald, Neumann, & Bwibo, 1991).

In terms of mild micronutrient deficits, reviews suggest an association between mild deficits in B vitamins and lower neonatal consolability and responsivity, lower infant vocalization and alertness, lower level of symbolic play by toddlers, and lower activity levels for school-age boys (Wachs, 1995b). In contrast, there has been little consistent evidence indicating behavioral deficits in children who are iron deficient but not IDA (Pollitt, 1993; Watkins & Pollitt, 1998).

One feature characterizing many micronutrient intervention studies or studies relating mild micronutrient deficits to variability in behavior and development is that these studies look at micronutrient deficits in isolation, rather than as part of the individual's overall nutrient intake. However, individuals typically consume diets containing multiple nutrients. As noted earlier, the bioavailability of specific micronutrients can be facilitated or compromised, depending on the presence or absence of other nutrients in the individual's diet. For example, dietary iron becomes more available to the individual when there is also an adequate intake of Vitamin C, whereas high levels of dietary phytate or tannin can act to block individual iron absorption (Hallberg, 1989; Schurch, 1995). Studies that have looked at the impact of variability in dietary quality have suggested that stronger prediction of functional outcomes may occur when we focus on the role of bioavailability-related micronutrient combinations rather than single micronutrients taken in isolation (Kirksey et al., 1995; Wachs et al., 1995). Recent experimental studies using uni- versus multinutrient supplements have shown a similar pattern of findings (Merialdi, Caulfield, Zavaleta, Figueroa, & Di Pietro, 1998).

Taken as a whole, although the influence of mild micronutrient deficits on behavioral development may be less dramatic than the impact of moderate to severe malnutrition, available evidence does document that such an influence exists. Given the far greater extent of mild nutrient deficits, it seems clear that such deficits can be a potential source of individual variability in behavioral development for large numbers of individuals within a given population.

Nutritional Influences On Development: Necessary But Not Sufficient

Data on the developmental impact of malnutrition, chronic undernutrition, and micronutrient deficits clearly point to the necessary status of these influences. However, available data also suggest that nutritional influences, although necessary, in and of themselves cannot be considered a sufficient explanation for individual behavioral–developmental variability. There are three reasons for this conclusion: (a) the etiology of nutritional deficits, (b) covariance between nutrition and other developmental influences, and (c) evidence showing stronger prediction when we integrate nutritional and nonnutritional influences on development.

Causes Of Undernutrition

Although a common assumption is that undernutrition is essentially due to population food scarcity, in reality undernutrition is often the end result of a long chain of necessary causal influences (Immink, 1988). In a given population, the risk of undernutrition can vary as a function of either extrinsic (e.g., seasonal workload) or intrinsic (e.g., growth rate) energy demands on the individual. For example, extrinsic work demands on mothers can act to reduce breastfeeding of their infants during the first 6 months of life (Perez-Escamilla et al., 1995). Even when adequate food is available, undernutrition may still occur as a function of nonnutritional influences such as feeding practices, cultural beliefs, family structure, or individual characteristics. Cultural belief systems, family structure, or individual characteristics that predispose to poor nutritional status also can act as necessary influences on individual behavioral–developmental variability (see chaps. 5–7).

Feeding practices found in different cultures, although perhaps appearing strange when viewed from outside the culture, may have a very rational basis. For example, data from New Guinea indicate that individuals with poorer nutritional status have a lower probability of contracting malaria, and when they do, the malaria is less severe. This decreased vulnerability may occur because the malaria parasite is more nutrition sensitive than its human host (Lepowsky, 1987). Hence, food taboos that result in a child being undernourished may be one way of protecting the child against malaria.

Research also has documented a variety of cultural beliefs that influence which foods and how much food is distributed to individuals. In some cultures, animal-source foods are not seen as appropriate for pregnant women, because of fear that animal characteristics inherent in these foods may be transmitted to the fetus (Cole, 1992). In other cultures, such as Nigeria, it is thought that giving food to those who do not contribute to family survival may result in these individuals being spoiled. Hence, young children may not get an appropriate share of available food in order to promote child obedience or to ensure that these children are not spoiled (Zeitlin, 1991, 1996). Even when equating for regional differences in availability of nutritional resources, greater malnutrition is found in those regions that have stronger cultural taboos against children eating animal proteins or fresh fruits and vegetables (Lepowsky, 1987).

Besides influencing the level of nutritional intake, cultural beliefs also can act to influence how children at risk for nutritional deficits are treated. Mull (1991) has reported that although 90% of Pakistani mothers were able to identify a severely nutritionally wasted child on the basis of only photographs, only 3% of these mothers saw the wasting as due to a lack of food. The overwhelming majority of mothers (70%) saw the wasting as caused either by other persons who had violated religious rituals or as a function of supernatural activities. Therefore, it is not surprising that an overwhelming majority of these mothers said that they would use religious treatment if their child had symptoms of nutritional wasting (Mull, 1991). In Nicaragua, a prevalent belief is that the young child should be able to regulate his or her own feeding; children will eat when they are hungry. In an area of Nicaragua characterized by chronic nutritional inadequacy, only 10% of mothers either demonstrated appropriate feeding techniques to their young infants or offered their young infants additional food (Engle et al., 1996). Therefore, mothers who thought that it was appropriate to help their infants eat had children with higher heights for age than did mothers who followed traditional cultural feeding practices.

Variability in allocation of food resources within a culture also can occur as a function of family structure, such as who is responsible for child care (Leslie, 1989). In less developed countries, young children left in the care of preteen siblings have a poorer nutritional status than young children cared for either by teenage siblings or by adults other than their parents. This pattern holds even after controlling for factors such as maternal educational level and child gender (Engle, 1991).

Within a given culture, individual characteristics also can act to influence whether individuals get allocated more or less equal portions of available food. During temporary food shortages, young infants may be less nutritionally deprived than older children (McDonald et al., 1994). In cultures that favor men, we find boys having greater access to available food (Zeitlin, 1996) and female infants being significantly more likely to die of nutritional deficits (Mull, 1991). Similarly, under conditions of food scarcity, in some cultures highly intense, fussy children may receive a greater share of available food then do calm, placid infants (DeVries, 1984; Scheper-Hughes, 1987a, 1987b).

Nutritional Covariance

A description provided by Grantham-McGregor (1995) illustrates how malnutrition does not operate in isolation from other biological and psychosocial risk factors.

> Malnourished children usually come from families who suffer many disadvantages. . . . These include poor physical and economic resources, such as overcrowded homes with poor sanitation and water supply, few household possessions and low income. They also tend to have unstable family units, with large numbers of closely spaced children. Parental characteristics associated with infant malnutrition include poor health and nutritional status, poor obstetric history, extreme youth or age, low intelligence and educational levels, little media contact, few social contacts, traditional life styles and low skilled occupations. The stimulation in the home is poor with few toys or books and little participation by the parents in play activities. (Grantham-McGregor, 1995, p. 2234S)

This list, although considerable, is not exhaustive. For example, malnourished mothers have a higher probability of giving birth to a low birth weight infant than do nonmalnourished mothers (Scrimshaw & Young, 1989).

A similar set of conclusions also could be drawn in regard to children with chronic mild undernutrition or children with micronutrient deficits (Pollitt, 1988; Wachs, 1995b). As has been shown earlier in this volume, and as will be shown in subsequent chapters, many of the factors that covary with malnutrition also can have a necessary influence on behavioral development. Given the linkage between malnutrition and these other risk factors, it may be more proper to speak of malnutrition and its covariates than of malnutrition in isolation.

Carried out over time, the covariance between nutrition and other risk factors may result in negative feedback loops that act to further inhibit the development of the malnourished child. At a physiological level, one classical negative feedback loop involves the linkage between malnutrition and gastrointestinal illness. As noted earlier, gastrointestinal illness not only reduces the child's appetite, it also adversely affects absorption of those nutrients the child does take in (Martorell, 1989). Children with acute diarrhea and vomiting are more likely to be given less food or given heavily starched foods that have lower dietary quality. As a result of loss of appetite, malabsorption, and foods of lower dietary quality, energy losses of up to 600 kilocalories per day may occur for the young physically ill child in less developed countries (Rosenberg et al., 1977). The result is a negative cycle of covarying malnutrition and gastrointestinal illness, resulting in a physiological state that only increases the risk of further malnutrition and greater suscep-tibility to subsequent gastrointestinal infection. Although extra energy and protein intake can help to moderate such a negative feedback cycle, such in-creased levels are less likely to be available in less developed countries (Keusch, 1990). Although less evidence is available, there also may be par-allel linkages in the behavioral domain, with undernourished parents being less able to provide appropriate child care for their offspring (Scrimshaw & Young, 1989) and undernourished children in turn less able to act in ways that elicit more appropriate caregiving behavior from their parents (Wachs et al., 1992).

Although it may be statistically possible to separate out nutritional from nonnutritional influences, such an exercise would yield only a very limited picture of the complex cycle of interrelated risk influences that are associated with malnutrition and its impact on the malnourished child. As will be noted in the next section, a more complete picture of the develop-mental consequences of malnutrition occurs when we look at malnutrition and its covariates in combination rather than in artificial isolation.

Nutrition in Isolation and in Combination

If nutritional influences were both necessary and sufficient, we would expect to see major gains associated with nutritional interventions for mal-nourished children. However, except for the case of iodine treatment (L. Allen, 1994), the overwhelming majority of studies report that the devel-opmental effects associated with nutritional supplementation are not always consistent and, although often statistically significant, are relatively modest in terms of effect size (L. Allen, 1994; Norgan, 1988; Ricciuti, 1993; Simeon & Grantham-McGregor, 1990). For example, in what is perhaps the most well-designed study on the long-term effects of early supplementation, Pollitt et al. (1993) reported that although there were significant supple-mentation effects, the amount of unique predictive variance associated with nutritional supplementation ranged between 1% and 4% for psychoeduca-tional measures and 1% and 2% for information-processing outcomes. A sim-ilar level of effect size also has been shown in studies attempting to increase children's nutritional status through simple strategies like providing extra income to families with malnourished children (Engle et al., 1996).

Similarly, if nutritional influences were both necessary and sufficient, we would expect to see a major influence of nutrition, even in conditions where nutritionally related covariates were absent. An excellent test of this hypothesis is seen in the case of children from developed countries who are malnourished due to disease conditions that result either in reduced food in-take (e.g., inflammatory bowel disease, congenital heart disease), malab-sorption (Crohn's disease), or increased energy expenditure associated with disease conditions (e.g., cystic fibrosis) (Fuchs, 1990). What the data show are remarkably few behavioral consequences for children from advantaged circumstances who are malnourished due to disease conditions, as compared with malnourished children from less developed countries who typically are living in conditions of poverty, inadequate schooling, and increased risk of morbidity (Pollitt, 1988). The relatively low effect sizes associated with purely nutritional influences on behavior and development (with the possible exception of severe prenatal iodine deficiency) clearly signal that other influences besides nutrition also are acting to influence developmental variability.

A prominent nonnutritional influence that also covaries with nutrition is the quality of the child's psychosocial rearing environment. Evidence from intervention studies consistently shows significantly stronger gains associated with the combination of nutritional supplementation and environmental stimulation than with either supplementation or stimulation taken in isolation (Pollitt, 1988; Simeon & Grantham-McGregor, 1990; Zeitlin, 1991). For example, Grantham-McGregor (1993) compared the cognitive development of severely malnourished children who received neither nutritional supplementation or psychosocial stimulation, either stimulation or supplementation, or a combination of supplementation and stimulation. Results showed that the control group declined in cognitive development across time, whereas those receiving either stimulation or supplementation stayed at about the same developmental level. Cognitive gains occurred only for those children who received both supplementation and stimulation.

Evidence further indicates that the extent of gains associated with nutritional supplementation, or relations between measures of nutritional status and development, can be moderated by a variety of nonnutritional factors including gender (Norgan, 1988), illness (Heywood, Oppenheimer, Heywood, & Jolley, 1989), family size, parental occupational level, and quality of psychosocial rearing environment (Wachs, 1995b). For example, Pollitt et al. (1993) reported that the long-term effects of nutritional supplementation of undernourished Guatemalan children were strongest for those coming from families with low socioeconomic status and for those individuals who managed to achieve higher educational levels following the supplementation.

Conclusion

As with biomedical influences, the available evidence clearly documents that nutritional influences play a necessary role in individual behavioral and developmental variability. However, the evidence also indicates that nonnutritional factors may have an important impact on the child's dietary intake, that there is covariance among nutritional and nonnutritional risk factors, that there are significantly stronger influences of nutrition plus stimulation than nutrition taken in isolation, and that nutritional influences can be moderated by a variety of nonnutritional factors. Taken in totality, this pattern of evidence clearly indicates that nutritional influences, although necessary, cannot be considered a sufficient influence on individual variability in behavior and development.

5

PHENOTYPIC INFLUENCES

The focus of this chapter is on individual characteristics as influences on behavioral development. Such a focus may be curious in a volume that treats variability in individual characteristics primarily as an outcome. Focusing on individual characteristics as an influence could be seen as either an exercise in circular thinking (e.g., tantrums mean the child is in the tantrum stage because the child is displaying tantrums) or of descriptive statistics (e.g., autocorrelation of traits across time). However, I would argue that individual characteristics can function both as outcomes and as sources of influence on subsequent development. To the extent that we can document underlying processes illustrating how individual characteristics act to influence subsequent behavior and development, we go beyond both circularity and descriptive statistics. In this chapter I will document the types of individual characteristics that can serve as influences on subsequent development, illustrate the processes whereby individual characteristics can serve this function, and demonstrate why individual characteristics constitute a necessary but not sufficient influence on subsequent behavioral development.

MATURATIONAL INFLUENCES

Maturation refers to age-related, intrinsic, intra-individual biological processes that culminate in the emergence of individual physical and behavioral characteristics. Three aspects of maturational influence will be considered: early physical maturation, functional–cognitive maturation, and puberty.

Early Physical Maturation

Early physical maturation typically is seen in the emergence of a variety of specific behavioral skills, such as the ability to grasp objects, and increasing locomotor mobility. Physical maturational influences on emerging behavioral–developmental competencies typically involve multiple systems. Thus, changes in locomotor behavior are mediated through maturational changes in a number of physical systems, including the motor, perceptual, and skeletal–muscular systems (Lockman & Thelen, 1993). Emerging physical competencies serve to expand the child's horizons and thus further facilitate development. For example, the emergence of locomotion has been associated with a variety of cognitive changes, such as better performance in spatial memory tasks (Kermoian & Campos, 1988).

Although physical maturation generally acts to facilitate behavioral development, there are instances in which early physical maturation can inhibit psychosocial development. One such example is the increased risk of higher lead exposure for young infants who display early motor maturation (Dietrich et al., 1985). Infants showing early locomotor maturation also are more likely to encounter greater parental interference with their actions and less positive affectivity from their parents than are infants with later locomotor maturation (Biringen, Emde, Campos, & Appelbaum, 1995). Infrahuman data (Turkewitz & Kenny, 1985) have suggested that delayed maturation of some central nervous system (CNS) areas acts to reduce inter-area competition for limited sensory input. Similarly, data from artificial intelligence studies (Elman, 1993) and from infrahuman and human studies on early learning and language development (Bjorklund, 1997) suggest that maturationally based limited memory capacity in young organisms can actually facilitate development. The proposed mechanism is through limited capacities that act as a filter to reduce information flow to a point that is congruent with the organism's capacities.

Functional Cognitive Maturation

Like early physical maturation, changes in individual cognitive competencies are determined by multiple causes. Such changes, in and of themselves, also can act to influence the course of the individual's subsequent behavioral development. One clear example is seen in changes in mothers' behaviors as infants show age-related changes in cognitive maturation (Kuczynski & Kochanska, 1995). For example, from detailed observational data of 9, 12 and 21 month old infants, Kindermann (1993) has shown how mothers adapt their caregiving patterns to fit the young child's emerging functional capacities. Thus, as infants show increasing competence in age-appropriate developmental tasks, mothers decrease their dependency-fostering behavior (e.g., complying with the child's requests for help) and increase their independence-fostering behaviors (e.g., refrain from helping the child as the child attempts the behavior).

Another example of the impact of functional maturation is seen in the 5 to 7 year shift. In multiple Western and non-Western cultures, parental beliefs commonly shift toward the idea that the 5–7 year old child now has developed common sense and can be taught, or that the child can be viewed as responsible and thus can be punished for transgressions (Rogoff, 1980; Whiting & Edwards, 1988). As a result, depending on the culture, 5 to 7 year olds may be given new responsibilities for animal care or for household chores. Common to both infancy and the 5 to 7 year age period is a process whereby individual cognitive maturational changes can act to trigger changed caregiver behaviors and expectancies toward their children, which in turn can act as a source of influence on behavioral developmental variability.

Puberty

Puberty is a multidimensional phenomenon involving both hormonal and physical changes (e.g., onset of menstruation, development of male secondary sexual characteristics, adolescent growth spurt). The role of hormonal changes have been discussed in chapter 3. In this chapter, I concentrate on puberty as a physical–maturational event.

An increased interest in cross-sex peer relations, changes in self-perceptions, increased aggressive behavior in boys, and an increase of depressive affect in girls are just some of the psychological changes occurring during pubertal maturation (Paikoff & Brooks-Gunn, 1991; Petersen, Sariagiani, & Kennedy, 1991). At least within Western societies, puberty is also a time when there is a decrease in the amount of time the child spends with his or her parents, a decrease in emotional closeness to the parent, and an increase in adolescent–parent conflict. For the most part, such conflicts are relatively trivial in nature (or at least they can be viewed so when looking back), with no more than 10% of adolescents showing severe family conflict patterns (Paikoff & Brooks-Gunn, 1991).

Although virtually all adolescents go through puberty, there are individual differences in pubertal maturational timing. Examples of individual differences associated with early pubertal maturation are shown in Table 5-1.

TABLE 5-1
Outcomes Associated With Early Pubertal Maturation

Outcomes	References
Small but significant elevation in general IQ Greater sense of social responsibility (non-Western societies).	Petersen (1988) Richards, Abell, & Petersen (1993)
Higher social prestige and better self-image (Western societies). Increased probability of depression and psychological distress for early-maturing girls.	Peterson (1988); Savin-Williams (1995) Ge, Conger, & Elder (1996); Petersen et al. (1991)
Increased probability of behavioral problems, norm violations, and delinquent behavior for early-maturing girls. Increased probability of higher anxiety levels.	Caspi & Moffitt (1991); Magnusson (1988); Paikoff et al., (1991) Buchanan et al. (1992)
Increased probability of having more children and dropping out of school for early-maturing girls.	Magnusson (1988)

As shown in Table 5-1, although there are certain developmental advantages associated with early pubertal maturation, these initial advantages may fade over time. One reason for such fading of effects may be that many of the pubertal changes found for adolescent boys in Western societies (e.g., increased strength), although an asset in highly prestigious high school activities like athletics, are less salient after high school (Petersen, 1988; Savin-Williams, 1995).

Negative consequences of individual differences in pubertal maturational timing also have been found. One reason for some of the negative consequences shown in Table 5-1 is that the increased weight and onset of menstruation associated with pubertal maturation may be viewed as more negative by early-maturing girls, who may be less prepared for such changes (Petersen, 1988). A second reason may be because late maturers are less likely to model delinquent peers than are early maturers. In part this may reflect the fact that the gap between maturational level and the opportunities associated with being viewed as an adult may be seen as less dramatic by later maturing adolescents. For example, although early physically maturing junior high school girls felt a greater need for input into family and classroom decision processes than later-maturing girls, greater input opportunities were not often provided to early maturers (Eccles et al., 1993). For early maturers, one way of closing such a perceived gap would be through association with delinquent peers, who may be viewed as having greater access to adult resources and privileges (Moffitt, 1993). Although some of the negative consequences associated with early pubertal maturation may be transient, not all such consequences are. For example, given the increased emphasis on postsecondary education in technological societies, early-maturing girls in such societies who do not complete their education may be at a disadvantage in their adult years.

Maturational Influences on Development: Necessary But Not Sufficient

It seems clear that maturational variability can influence behavioral development, either through changes in specific physical structures or processes underlying development, or through the psychosocial consequences associated with variability in maturational timing. On the other hand, maturational influences, although potentially necessary, cannot be regarded as sufficient in and of themselves. There are a number of reasons for this conclusion. First, other necessary developmental influences, such as genetic factors, adequacy of nutrition, family relationship patterns, and environmental stress, can also influence maturational characteristics like pubertal onset (Graber, Brooks-Gunn, & Warren, 1995; Paikoff & Brooks-Gunn, 1991) or locomotor maturation (Biringen et al., 1995). Second, even when significant, the amount of variance accounted for by functional or pubertal maturation tends to be relatively modest (Buchanan et al., 1992; Morrison, Griffith, & Alberts, 1997; Newcombe & Dubos, 1987; Paikoff & Brooks-Gunn, 1991). The relatively small amount of variance accounted for by maturational status per se clearly suggests the importance of nonmaturational influences. Third, naturally occurring covariances can act to accentuate the salience of maturational influences. For example, to minimize the likelihood of adolescent depression, evidence suggests that it is better to go through puberty after rather than before or during the change from junior to senior high school (Petersen et al., 1991). However, due to a generally earlier age of onset of pubertal maturation, particularly in Western societies, the covariance between the onset of puberty and school change is greater for girls than for boys. As a result, adolescent girls are at greater risk for depression than are same-age adolescent boys.

Fourth, even when maturational influences do occur, their impact can be moderated by a variety of nonmaturational factors. For example, the relatively restricted range at which infants reliably show avoidance of heights (between 5 and 7 months) has been attributed to maturational influences. However, the onset of fear of heights can be accelerated by giving the infant extra locomotor experience (e.g., through walkers), or it can be retarded by reducing the level of locomotor experience (e.g., as when infants are in casts) (Rutter & Rutter, 1992). In adolescence, the relation of pubertal status to family discord can be moderated by higher order cultural influences. For example, Molina and Chassin (1996) have reported that pubertal onset tends to increase parent–son tension in Anglo-American households but tends to bring greater parent–son closeness in Hispanic households. Other identified moderators of maturational influences include gender (Eaton & Richot, 1995), maternal overprotection (Skuse, 1987), whether the individual's peer group is same or mixed sex (Ge, Conger, & Elder, 1996), and whether the individual has a history of previous behavioral problems (Buchanan et al., 1992).

In some cases, both covariance and nonmaturational moderators can be seen as operating together. For example, nearly 75% of early-maturing girls have older friends and are more likely to be involved with boys, as compared with 39% of late-maturing girls (Magnusson, 1988). Early-maturing girls with older friends are significantly more likely to be norm violators than are early-maturing girls who have friends of the same age. These differences may reflect older peers' being less sensitive to norm violations than are same-age peers, older peers' being more likely to push younger peers into norm violations, or older peers' being more likely to model antisocial behaviors (Caspi & Moffitt, 1991; Caspi, Lyman, Moffitt, & Silva, 1993; Magnusson, 1988). However, the chances that an early-maturing female adolescent will get involved with delinquent peers depends not just on maturational level but also on whether the individual is attending a mixed-gender school (probability increases) or a same-gender school (probability decreases; Caspi et al., 1993). Such complex patterns involving nonmaturational influences do not mean that maturational influences are unimportant. What they do mean is that maturational influences also fall under the heading of necessary but not sufficient.

INDIVIDUAL BIOSOCIAL AND PSYCHOLOGICAL CHARACTERISTICS

Two situations clearly illustrate the importance of individual characteristics as an influence on subsequent variability in individual behavioral development. The first refers to the importance of chance, random events in the lives of individuals (Bandura, 1982). In understanding the role of chance events, what is often not considered is how individual characteristics may well be essential for determining whether chance encounters have major, minor, or no impact on subsequent development (Clausen, 1991; Magnusson, 1993). For example, when free intervention services are offered to high-risk families or to families with medically or psychologically fragile children, up to 50% of eligible families will not use such services (Affleck, Tennen, Rowe, Roscher, & Walker, 1989; Homel, Burns, & Goodnow, 1987; Osofsky, Culp, & Ware, 1988; Rauh & Brennan, 1992). These findings illustrate that not all individuals are willing or able to use resources that are made available to them. Such differential usage of resources has been described both in folk sayings ("you can lead a horse to water, but you can't make him drink") and in poetry ("Yet they, believe me, who will wait no gifts from chance, have conquered fate"; Matthew Arnold: *Resignation*).

A second situation illustrating the salience of individual characteristics occurs at times when individuals encounter transition points in their lives that involve high ambiguity, require novel responses, or demand individual reorganization for optimal functioning. Situations of this type can reflect the commonplace (entering a new school) or the extraordinary (the Nazi Holocaust). Across multiple age periods, what is consistently shown at these time points are not sudden personality changes. Rather, the modal response of individuals appears to involve behaviors that reflect preexisting, stable individual characteristics (Caspi & Bem, 1990; Caspi & Moffitt, 1991). For example, detailed observations of the behavior of children at summer camp indicated that as situational demands increased, children with a history of aggressive behavior problems became more aggressive, whereas children with a history of inhibition became more withdrawn (Wright & Mischel, 1987). Similarly, evidence indicates that increases in marital problems following economic stress occurs primarily for those families that have had a history of marital problems prior to the economic depression (Elder & Caspi, 1988).

One argument against considering individual traits as a necessary influence on subsequent development is that observed linkages may simply reflect trait continuity/stability or individual characteristics across time. Although there is long-term continuity for some individual traits, as seen in the continuity of childhood conduct disorders to adult antisocial behavior (Quinton, Rutter, & Gulliver, 1990), the hypothesis that we are dealing simply with autocorrelation of traits across time seems insufficient on both conceptual and empirical grounds (Vuchinich, Bank, & Patterson, 1992). For example, a pure autocorrelation hypothesis would be insufficient to explain why culturally desirable traits are more stable over time than are culturally undesirable traits (Asendorpf & Van Aken, 1991).

In the following section of this chapter, I will review six broad domains of individual characteristics that have been related to subsequent behavioral–developmental variability: physical characteristics, cognitive capacity, temperament and personality characteristic, self-perceptions, interpersonal styles, and multiple trait combinations. A variety of individual characteristics will be reviewed within each domain.

Individual Characteristics That Serve as Developmental Influences

Physical Characteristics

The multiple behavioral and psychological differences between the genders are shown in Table 5-2. Although there are multiple significant gender differences, such differences are small and male–female distributions are highly overlapping (Collaer & Hines, 1995). On the other hand, significant gender differences in domains such as early language development remain

TABLE 5-2
Physical Characteristics Associated With Individual Behavioral Developmental Variability

Characteristic	Outcome	Reference
Gender	Boys > girls on rough and tumble play, activity level, aggression, spatial abilities, variability in quantitative and spatial visualization abilities, externalizing reactions to stress, susceptibility to developmental disorders.	Breedlove (1994); Feingold (1992); Finkelstein, Von Eye, & Preece (1994); Gjerde, Block, & Block (1988); Maccoby (1988); Raz et al. (1995)
	Girls > boys on verbal fluency, fine motor skills, interest in social interactions, prosocial behavior, sensitivity to affective cues.	Benbow & Lubinski (1993); Radke-Yarrow (1994); Witelson, Zahn-Waxler, Richardson, Susman, & Martinez (1991)
Physical size	Increased social withdrawal for adolescents who are small for chronological age; increased stress for female adolescents whose body shape does not fit their aspirations.	Petersen (1988); Skuse (1987)
Physical attractiveness	More positive emotional interactions by mothers of more attractive newborns; unattractive children more likely to be viewed in negative terms and rejected by peers; less family support for unattractive female adolescents during times of stress.	Coie, Dodge, & Coppotelli (1982); Elder, Nguyen, & Caspi (1985); Hoffman (1991); Langlois, Ritter, Casey, & Sawin (1995); Rutter & Rutter (1992)
Physical handicaps	Lower levels of aspiration and poorer self-concept found for individuals with visible but less serious physical handicaps than for individuals with more serious but nonvisible medical conditions.	Engfer, Walper, & Rutter (1994)

even after controlling for possible confounds such as family risk, maternal interactive style, or child attachment security (Morisset, Barnard, & Booth, 1995).

From a process standpoint, what is most interesting is the possibility of differential reactivity to experience by boys and girls. Although greater male vulnerability to stressors is not shown for all outcomes (Brody et al., 1994; Cadman et al., 1987; Conger, Ge, Elder, Lorenz, & Simons, 1994; Evans, Lepore, Shejwal, & Palsane 1998), in general boys do tend to show greater reactivity to biological and psychosocial stressors than do girls, particularly in the time period prior to adolescence (Hetherington, 1989; Jacklin, 1989; Masten et al., 1990; Wachs, 1992). For example, when looking at outcomes associated with neurological disorders (e.g., seizures), obstetrical complications (e.g., placenta previa), and perinatal complications (e.g., pulmonary infection), in 33 out of 34 comparisons boys were more likely to have adverse consequences than were girls (Gualtieri, 1987). At the same time, when girls did show adverse consequences following biological insult, they were more likely to have a higher probability of being more severely affected than were boys. For example, although boys were more likely to be mentally retarded than girls following biological insult, the average IQ for boys with retardation was 55 versus 41 for girls (Gualtieri, 1987).

Ethnic–racial differences clearly refer to physical characteristics (e.g., skin color, facial features). Ethnic–racial differences in a variety of outcomes like cognitive performance have been documented (Neisser et al., 1996), and they also have consequences that can affect subsequent behavioral development, such as the increased probability of school dropout among ethnic minorities (Finn, 1989). Attempts often have been made to tie ethnic–racial differences in behavior and development to biological factors (e.g., Rushton & Ankney, 1996). However, the heterogeneity among different ethnic–racial groups and the linkages of ethnic–racial physical characteristics to social stratification, prejudice, family structure, and cultural histories make such attempts exceedingly problematical (Garcia-Coll et al., 1996; Neisser et al., 1996; Slaughter-DeFoe, Nakagawa, Takanishi, & Johnson, 1990). For these reasons, I have chosen to treat ethnic–racial characteristics as an example of macrosystem influences rather than an example of the role of individual physical characteristics (see chap. 7). Other examples of individual differences associated with physical characteristics are shown in Table 5-2.

Cognitive Capacity

Available evidence suggests that individual differences in cognitive abilities can act to influence subsequent noncognitive behavioral developmental outcomes. Lower intelligence can be a risk factor, increasing the chances of an adverse outcome for the individual. For example, children with lower IQs not only are more likely to show inhibited behavior but also appear to be less able to shift toward a less inhibited behavior pattern (Asendorpf, 1994).

Perhaps the most consistent body of evidence involves the association between lower IQ and subsequent antisocial delinquent behavior (Cohen et al., 1989). On average, the IQ of delinquents is approximately $\frac{1}{2}$ standard deviation below that of nondelinquents, even after controlling for effects of socioeconomic status and race (Moffitt, 1990). Viewed in terms of a risk factor, evidence indicates that a deficit of 1 standard deviation in IQ results in nearly a threefold risk for later conduct disorders (Schonfeld, Shaffer, & O'Connor, 1988). IQ deficits are particularly noticeable for those individuals whose delinquency begins in early childhood and continues on through adolescence.

Available evidence further indicates that an increased risk for subsequent conduct disorders is not associated just with general cognitive deficits. Deficits in executive-function capacities (i.e., expressive and receptive verbal ability, memory, attention span) have been shown to be particularly salient risk markers for subsequent antisocial behavior patterns (Moffitt, 1990, 1993; Schonfeld et al., 1988). Executive-function deficits predict subsequent delinquency even after controlling for overall general IQ level (Moffitt & Henry, 1989), minority status, or level of reading achievement (Moffitt, 1990). In addition to executive-function deficits, individual differences in emotional conditionability (i.e., the individual's ability to form conditioned emotional responses reflecting an anticipatory fear of punishment) also have been identified as a specific cognitive factor relevant to the stability of conduct disorders. For adolescents with similar childhood delinquent histories, individual differences in emotional conditionability at age 15 were found to differentiate those individuals who stopped criminal activities after adolescence from those who continued their antisocial activities on into adulthood (Raine, Venables, & Williams, 1996).

Although the link between cognitive deficits and subsequent conduct disorders seems well established, the processes underlying such linkages remain a matter of speculation. General or specific cognitive deficits may decrease the chances of school success, and lack of school success in turn can create a greater likelihood of antisocial behavior (Moffitt, 1990). Having a low IQ also may mean a greater chance of being placed in classes with other low-ability children (Weinstein, 1991), who may also be delinquent. Alternatively, general or specific cognitive deficits may reflect underlying neural deficits. These deficits may result in the individual having difficulty relating his or her ongoing behavior to long-term goals (Moffitt & Henry, 1989) or in applying regulatory strategies, such as inhibition of dominant responses, to govern his or her behaviors (Calkins, 1994; C. Patterson & Newman, 1993).

High cognitive abilities also can act to protect individuals against the detrimental impact of either biological or psychosocial risk. Children with higher intelligence are more able to generate alternative strategies in social-problem situations than are children who are lower in intelligence (Asendorpf, 1994). Children with higher intellectual skills also show good school achievement regardless of the degree of life stress encountered, whereas declines in school achievement are found for lower ability children as their life stress increases (Garmezy, Masten, &Tellegen, 1984). Having a higher IQ may be particularly important for the subsequent development of children from severely disadvantaged backgrounds (Long & Vaillant, 1984; Werner & Smith, 1992) and for children whose parents are mentally ill (Masten et al., 1990) or have a history of serious criminality (Kandel et al., 1989).

Temperament and Personality Characteristics

As shown in Table 5-3, temperament and personality characteristics also can function either as a risk or a protective factor. In Western industrialized societies, children with a difficult temperament are often characterized as displaying high intense negative moods across a variety of situations (Bates, 1989). Although having a difficult temperament does not automatically mean an adverse outcome, as a group, infants and preschool children whose difficultness takes the form of negative emotionality and resistance to parental control may be at particular risk for externalizing problems at later ages (Bates, Wachs, & Emde, 1994).

In contrast to traits that are perceived as difficult in Western societies, in developing countries such as Taiwan and Brazil, difficult children are more likely to be characterized as being weak, fretful, and frequently ill (Mull, 1991). The importance of this cultural distinction is seen in the observation by DeVries (1984) that fussy irritable Masai infants from Kenya were more likely to survive under famine conditions than were calm, placid infants. This study illustrates that although there may well be cultural differences in defining which children are considered difficult, within a given culture, children who are defined as difficult are more likely to be at risk for adverse developmental outcomes than children who are not so defined.

Difficult temperament is a composite measure of several individual temperamental characteristics. Individual temperament and personality dimensions also can influence subsequent behavioral development. However, it is important to recognize that although different temperament dimensions will be discussed separately, in reality there may be biological or functional linkages between individual domains of temperament, as will be discussed later. One of the most studied individual temperament dimensions is behavioral inhibition. In infancy, *inhibition* refers to children who are characteristically quiet, shy, vigilant, and tending to avoid or act highly restrained in new situations (Kagan, 1994). The association of such behaviors with inhibited temperament becomes less clear as children get older. For some older children, shy or overanxious behavior may in fact reflect stability of inhibited temperament from infancy into childhood (Gersten, 1989; Kagan, Arcus, & Snidman, 1983). However, not all childhood shyness or overanxiety is due to inhibited temperament. Some children may show inhibited behavior around peers because they are socially rejected or ignored by their peers (Olweus, 1993). As shown in Table 5-3, risks are associated with having this type of temperament. However, even though there may be some long-term negative consequences associated with having an inhibited temperament in childhood, overall, inhibited children do have satisfactory work histories and interpersonal relations once they finally enter into these types of situations (Newman, Caspi, Silva, & Moffitt, 1997). Furthermore, early inhibition also can serve as a protective factor, as seen in evidence showing

TABLE 5-3
Developmental Consequences of Individual Differences
in Temperament and Personality

Dimension	Outcome	Reference
Difficult temperament	Increased risk of later internalizing and externalizing behavior problems; boys with difficult temperament less likely as adults to continue formal education, more likely to show downward social mobility; as adults difficult-temperament girls will have greater marital conflict.	Bates, Wachs, & Emde (1994); Caspi, Elder, & Bem (1987); Caspi, Elder, & Herbener (1990); Hartup & van Lieshout (1995)
Inhibition	Increased risk of internalizing behavior problems in childhood; less likely as adults to be assertive or to have social supports but more likely to withdraw in response to frustration and to be delayed in getting married and entering a stable job track.	Caspi et al. (1987); Caspi et al. (1990); Newman et al. (1997); Rothbart & Bates (1998)
Reactivity	Hyperreactivity associated with an increased risk of schizophrenia; hyporeactivity associated with an increased risk for antisocial behavior.	Cannon, Mednick, & Parnas (1990); Magnusson (1988)
Self-regulation	Low self-regulation related to low peer acceptance, lower prosocial behavior; higher rates of adolescent delinquency and behavior problems, poor academic achievement; less likelihood of developing an internalized conscience.	Brody & Flor (1997); Eisenberg & Fabes (1992); Feldman & Weinberger (1994); Kochanska, Murray, & Coy (1997)
Ego control and ego resilience	Ego-resilient children rated as more empathetic, more prosocial, more academically and socially competent, more able to break away from substance abuse; low ego-control children more at risk for drug and alcohol abuse; adolescents who are high in ego control and ego resilience are more intelligent, more able to delay gratification, and less likely to have behavior problems or be delinquent.	Block, Block, & Keyes (1988); Funder & Block (1989); van Aken (1995)

that inhibited children are at lower risk for delinquency in adolescence than are less inhibited peers, perhaps because more inhibited children are less likely to be accepted socially by delinquent peers (Moffitt, 1993).

Another temperament trait with the potential to influence subsequent behavioral developmental variability is individual differences in the degree of reactivity and sensitivity to stimulation (Strelau, 1994). Conceptually, Strelau (1994) has linked high reactivity to inhibited behavior, as in the situation when moderate levels of stimulus input are overwhelming to a highly reactive individual, who then withdraws from the situation. As shown in Table 5-3, evidence suggests that either extreme high reactivity or extreme low reactivity may be equally problematical for subsequent development. However, whether an individual is classified as hyperreactive or underreactive may depend on the stimuli or outcome measures that are being assessed (Asendorpf, 1994). For example, Caucasian infants appear to be more behaviorally responsive and less physiologically responsive to physical stress, whereas the reverse pattern is shown for Japanese infants (Lewis et al., 1993). Similarly, preterm or Down's syndrome infants appear to be oversensitive to highly intense stimulation while simultaneously being underresponsive to parental soothing (Field, 1987). This complex pattern makes such infants very difficult to parent, because it is relatively easy to elicit highly negative emotions from these infants when they are stressed but far more difficult to soothe them once they are aroused.

The relevance to developmental variability of individual differences in reactivity may be further moderated by individual differences in self-regulation abilities (Rothbart, 1989). Although behaviors reflecting self-regulation and inhibition may seem similar, they are quite distinct in terms of both neural underpinnings and psychological structure. As discussed by Rothbart et al. (1994), inhibition involves differences in emotional reactivity, whereas self-regulation refers to how individuals deal with their emotional reactivity. A number of studies have looked at interactions between reactivity and self-regulation. For example, individual differences in negative reactivity become more predictive of adjustment problems as the individual's level of self-regulation declines (Eisenberg et al., 1996). Similarly, boys who are low in emotional reactivity and high in self-regulation show better classroom behavior and have fewer behavioral problems than boys with the reverse pattern of high reactivity and low self-regulation (Eisenberg et al., 1995). Over and above potential interactions with reactivity, individual differences in self-regulation also can directly influence subsequent behavioral–developmental variability, as shown in Table 5-3.

Individual differences in regulation capacities may go beyond temperament to also involve personality dimensions such as ego control and ego resilience (Rothbart & Bates, 1998). Ego control reflects variability in the individual's ability to contain and control feelings, impulses, and desires (e.g., delay of gratification), whereas ego resilience reflects variability in the individual's ability to respond flexibly to changing situations (e.g., degree of stereotyped responses to new situations; Block & Block, 1980). Individuals with a greater capacity for controlling their own impulses, or with a greater capacity to adapt their control strategies to meet current conditions, would be expected to have better developmental outcomes and be more able to make use of environmental opportunities than individuals who are less able to control impulses or to develop flexible coping strategies. Support for this prediction comes from a variety of sources, as also shown in Table 5-3. Use of flexible coping strategies such as ego resilience also has been one of the characteristics that distinguishes children who can make maximal use of resources to better adapt to highly disadvantaged biological and psychosocial backgrounds (Werner, 1990). The influence of low flexibility is seen in children from highly disorganized families who were unable to make use of remedial intervention opportunities and persisted in the same nonadaptive routines despite several years of nursery school enrichment (Pavenstedt, 1967).

Self-perceptions

Individual differences exist in the degree to which persons think they can influence their environment and how competent they think they are likely to be when attempting to do so. This type of self-perception is characterized by a number of terms, including *internal locus of control, perceived controllability, mastery motivation, learned helplessness,* and *sense of self-efficacy.* Having a sense of perceived control over the environment has been shown to have both physiological and behavioral consequences. Persons who believe they have potential control over their environment are found to be less physiologically reactive when exposed to stressors than are individuals who are exposed to similar stressors but do not have a sense of perceived control (Stansbury & Gunnar, 1994). Behaviorally, having a sense of perceived control has been associated with the use of more active coping strategies during times of stress (Compas, 1987; Masten et al., 1990), higher levels of academic achievement (Bandura, Barbaranelli, Capara, & Pastorelli, 1996), better coping when living with a mentally ill parent (Masten et al., 1990), greater persistence following rejection, greater motivation to take on an unfamiliar task, and a higher level of ability to tailor one's behavior to situational differences (LaFromboise, Coleman, & Gerton, 1993). In contrast, children who have a sense of learned helplessness (i.e., who believe their actions will have little effect on outcomes) show less effort in problem solving activities and lower levels of problem solving competency, particularly during stress episodes or following failure experiences (Compas, 1987; Finchim & Cain, 1986).

It also is important to note that there may be situations in which a strong belief in perceived self-efficacy (i.e., internal control) is not necessarily desirable in terms of developmental outcomes. For individuals with a high sense of perceived control who must deal with stress situations that are beyond individual control, attempts at control may only increase the individual's level of stress and thereby increase individual vulnerability (Masten et al., 1990). Similarly, in cultures where a passive coping style is the cultural norm, an individual with a belief in active control may show greater than expected achievement, but there may well be a cost in terms of subsequent adjustment problems (Diaz-Guerrero, 1977).

One individual trait associated with a sense of self-efficacy, or perceived controlability, is *planfullness*. Individuals who believe they can control their own destiny are more likely to set up realistic goals and consider the types of action that will allow them to have a realistic chance of achieving these goals (Clausen, 1991). Longitudinal data indicate that the level of planfullness shown by male adolescents was a better predictor of subsequent educational and occupational levels than either family socioeconomic status or individual IQ. For female adolescents, planfullness was a strong predictor of not only higher education levels but also a greater likelihood of stable marriages and more marital satisfaction (Clausen, 1991). Similarly, for girls who were reared in disorganized homes and then in institutions, one of the major factors associated with better adult adjustment was quality of marital relationship, which was predicted by the level of planfullness shown prior to marriage (Rutter et al., 1990).

Another individual personality pattern that may be linked to the combination of perceived controllability and planfullness is a higher positive self-concept. A positive individual self-concept may serve to enhance subsequent behavioral development, whereas a negative self-concept may leave the individual less able to cope with subsequent negative events (Rutter & Rutter, 1992). Available evidence indicates that children with a more positive self-concept are more able to cope with either acute (Compas, 1987) or chronic family stresses (Radke-Yarrow & Sherman, 1990).

Interpersonal Style

One interpersonal relationship pattern that has clear long-term consequences is aggressive behavior. There appears to be a relatively strong linkage between early persistent aggressive behavior in childhood and adult criminality or antisocial behavior (Parker & Asher, 1987; Quinton et al., 1990). For example, in a sample of 85 men who at age 13 were rated as persistently and highly aggressive, nearly half were found to have adult criminal records, compared with only 14% of nonaggressive matched controls (Magnusson, 1988). The continuity of aggressive behavior appears especially strong when it covaries with high motor activity (Magnusson, 1988) or when it occurs both in preadolescence and adolescence, as opposed to just in adolescence (Moffitt, 1993). Early aggressive behavior also predisposes to both peer rejection (Olweus, 1993), an increased probability of dropping out of school (Cairns, Cairns, Neckerman, Gest, & Gariepy, 1988), and adult problem behaviors such as alcoholism (McGue, 1993) and poor work performance (Newman et al., 1997).

Although there appear to be fewer developmental consequences resulting from peer rejection that is not aggression based (Cillessen, van Ijzendoorn, Van Lieshout, El Hartup, 1992), there are still unique consequences associated with such rejection. Children who are actively rejected (e.g., bullied by peers) are more likely to become withdrawn and develop a poorer self-image (Olweus, 1993). Nonaggressive peer rejected children also are more likely to view social interactions as not being influenced by their own actions, to perceive the world as a hostile place (Dodge & Feldman, 1990), and to be less able to generate alternative social-problem-solving strategies (Richard & Dodge, 1982).

The developmental consequences of developing a secure versus insecure attachment in infancy have been discussed extensively in a variety of publications, with differences in attachment history predisposing to a variety of differences in developmental outcomes. Examples of some of the outcomes associated with differences in early attachment status are summarized in Table 5-4.

One reason for observed relations between attachment differences and individual developmental variability may be differential treatment of children with different attachment patterns. For example, without any knowledge of the child's attachment history, preschool teachers are more likely to react to children with a history of secure attachment with age-appropriate demands, high expectations, and positive affect. In contrast, children with a history of anxious–avoidant attachment are more likely to elicit anger and low warmth from their preschool teachers, whereas those with a history of anxious–resistant attachment are more likely to elicit both high warmth and controlling–infantalizing behaviors (Sroufe & Egeland, 1991). Alternatively, securely attached children living in high-risk environments may be more responsive to supportive aspects of the environment and thus more resilient under stress than are insecurely attached children living in such environments (Greenberg, Spelt, & DeKlyen, 1993). Low resilience may be particularly characteristic for children with a disorganized attach-

TABLE 5-4
Developmental Consequences of Early Attachment Differences

Age Period	Consequences
Infancy	Compared with insecurely attached infants, securely attached infants are more sociable and show more appropriate social responses, greater empathy in peer interactions, higher levels of exploration, and higher levels of play competence.
Preschoolers	Compared with preschoolers with a history of secure attachment, preschoolers with a history of insecure attachment are lower in impulse control, more likely to be aggressors, more likely to be the target of peer aggression.
Preadolescents	Compared with preadolescents with a history of insecure attachment, preadolescents with a history of secure attachment are higher in social competence, self-esteem, self-confidence, interpersonal skills, sensitivity, and independence.

Note. Consequences have been summarized from Belsky & Cassidy (1994); Belsky & Nezworski, 1988; Cassidy & Berlin (1994); Elicker et al. (1992); Rutter & Rutter (1992); Sroufe, Egeland, & Kreutzer (1990); and Sroufe & Jacobvitz (1989).

ment pattern, who may not have an organized set of attachment coping responses and thus may be particularly vulnerable to the effects of stress (Hertgaard, Gunnar, Erickson, & Nachmias, 1995).

Multiple Trait Characteristics

The role of individual characteristics in influencing subsequent individual developmental variability, although well documented, may nonetheless be of less salience than combinations of individual traits (Eisenberg & Fabes, 1992). One example of the simultaneous operation of multiple traits would be individual resilience. Resilient individuals are those who appear to show adequate development in the face of multiple biological and environmental risk factors. Characteristics associated with resiliency at different ages are shown in Table 5-5. As shown in Table 5-5, although the specific traits associated with resilience change over the age span, a number of common dimensions keep appearing. Resilient children appear to be more intelligent and have a greater sense of self-concept and self-efficacy and greater flexibility than nonresilient children. In addition, resilient children have interpersonal characteristics that draw others to them: "Resilient children seem to be especially adept at actively recruiting surrogate parents, even if they are not kin" (Werner, 1990, p. 107). Thus, even in the most disadvantaged or disorganized families, resilient children are more likely to receive whatever warmth or support is available in these situations (Radke-Yarrow & Sherman, 1990). The combination of traits that produce resilience means that children with these multiple traits will have different developmental pathways than children without these traits, even when facing similar sets of risk conditions.

The mirror image to resilience may well be a combination of traits that result in increased vulnerability to risk or stress. For example, the combination of aggressive behavior, high motor activity, low school performance, low motivation for school work, and negative ratings by peers at age 13 proves to be a much more potent predictor of adult alcoholism, criminality, and mental illness than are single characteristics like peer relations or low school achievement per se (Magnusson, 1988). Similarly, compared with adolescents who reduced their alcohol intake, adolescents who continued drinking as they moved into adulthood were more likely to be male, to be less concerned with future plans, to have a lower sense of self-efficacy and internal control, and to have a lower need for social conformity (Schulenberg, Wadsworth, O'Malley, Bachman, & Johnston, 1996).

Combinations of vulnerability characteristics also predispose to lifestyle changes, which in turn may be associated with subsequent problem behaviors. For example, individuals who are more likely to be enticed into cults share a common set of characteristics, including a feeling of aloneness, depression, a sense that life has little meaning, and a lack of career skills (Bandura, 1982).

TABLE 5-5
Individual Traits Associated With Resilience at Different Ages

Age Period	Traits
Infancy	High activity level Alertness Affectionate disposition Responsiveness to people Responsiveness to objects
Early childhood	Sociability Sense of autonomy Sense of self-reliance Independence Good communication skills Good self-help skills Ability to use adults as resources
Middle childhood	Sense of competence Sense of self-efficacy Sense of self-control Sociability Flexible coping strategies
Adolescence	Internal locus of control Positive self-concept High achievement orientation Sense of responsibility Interpersonal sensitivity

Note. List taken from Werner (1990).

How Individual Characteristics Act as a Developmental Influence

What has been shown up to now is that a variety of individual characteristics have the potential to influence subsequent individual developmental variability. Some mechanisms by which these individual characteristics can act as influences have been briefly noted. In this section, I will discuss potential and existing mechanisms in greater detail. Examples of such mechanisms are shown in Table 5-6. One such mechanism involves direct biological consequences associated with physical characteristics such as gender. The greater susceptibility of men to X chromosome-linked disorders would be one such example.

As also shown in Table 5-6, individual characteristics also can act to moderate individual reactivity to current situations. One such example noted earlier involves the higher levels of adaptive responding to later environmental challenges shown by securely attached as compared with insecurely attached infants.

One hypothesized process whereby individual characteristics can act as moderators occurs when such characteristics function as an internal working model. The concept of an *internal working model* refers to integrated sets

TABLE 5-6

Potential Processes Whereby Individual Characteristics Translate Into
Individual Developmental Variability

Process	Examples	References
Direct consequences	Maternal immune system more likely to react against male than female fetus, resulting in greater incidence of pregnancy complications and higher risk of developmental disorders for boys.	Gualtieri (1987)
Moderation of reactivity	Difficult-temperament children show greater reactivity than less difficult children when faced with stress.	Wachs (1992)
	Girls with a history of pre-adolescent behavior problems have more adjustment problems at puberty than girls without such a history.	Caspi & Moffitt (1991); Caspi et al. (1993)
	Linkage of adolescent stress to depression is stronger for girls than boys, even when equated for level of stress. Easier emotional conditionability reduces the probability of continued criminality in adolescents at risk for criminal behavior.	Ge, Lorenz, Conger, Elder, & Simons (1994) Raine et al. (1996)
Event chains/ cumulative spirals	Difficult or oppositional children more likely to elicit negative reactions from caregivers, which only increases the child's oppositional behavior.	Ge, Conger, & Elder (1996); Vuchinich et al. (1992)
	Mothers who perceive themselves as low in child-rearing capability are more likely to withdraw from their difficult infant, who becomes more difficult, which further compromises the mother's sense of efficacy.	Rauh & Brennan (1992)
	Inhibited children are less likely to enter novel peer play situations and thus less likely to learn appropriate social behaviors toward peers, who are more likely to react negatively, further increasing the child's inhibition.	Caspi et al. (1988)
Individual niches	Stable aggressive behavior patterns tend to restrict children to peer niches composed primarily of other aggressive children.	Cairns et al. (1988)
	Individuals who are low in self-regulation and high in impulsivity are less likely to find stable interpersonal or occupational niches.	Moffitt (1993)
	Inhibited individuals are more reluctant to enter into new niches or niches that contain unfamiliar people.	Caspi (1998)
	Dependent individuals are more likely to restrict niches only to those that provide them with approval and aid.	Caspi et al. (1990)

of memories, expectancies, and associations between stimuli and affectual responses. Current experiences are filtered through such an integrative structure and interpreted on the basis of what is stored in the internal working model (Calkins, 1994; Hofer, 1994). These interpretations lead the child to selectively attend to certain stimuli and be more likely to react to experiences in a specific way. Thus, relationship experiences with primary caregivers result in the child's developing expectancies about how the interpersonal world functions. If his internal working model predisposes the child to assume a supportive environment, the child will attend and react to the environment in ways that increase the probability of future support. On the other hand, children who have been rejected by their primary caregivers will assume that adults are rejecting, and they will be more likely to attend to adult cues that could signal rejection (Belsky & Cassidy, 1994). The differential occurrence of future support or rejection for children in these two groups feeds back and confirms the original internal working model. Similarly, children whose behavior patterns lead to a consistent history of peer rejection may come to expect rejection by peers, thus reducing their motivation to change their behavior in ways that could increase peer acceptance (Coie, 1990). Along the same lines, children with aggressive characteristics are more likely to perceive aggression from other people in ambiguous situations and act aggressively on the basis of these perceptions (Dodge & Feldman, 1990). Although there is no direct evidence for the operation of internal working models, the construct does provide a useful organizing device for understanding how variability in individual characteristics can translate into variability in behavioral development.

Another way in which individual characteristics can act to influence subsequent behavioral development is through initiating *event chains*, which are spirals of continuing consequences that can cumulate across time (Caspi et al., 1990; Moffitt, 1993). One such example, shown by Sameroff and Chandler's (1975) transactional model, occurs when a child's individual characteristics influence parental reactions, which in turn act to further influence child characteristics. Such event chains can spiral outward, as in the case of negative parent–child spirals that begin in the home, generalize to the child's relation with peers, and then affect the child's performance in school (Henry, Caspi, Moffitt, & Silva, 1996).

With the proper longitudinal design, such cumulative spirals can be traced from early childhood to adulthood. For example, women with early adverse rearing experiences (e.g., family disruption, institutional rearing) are less likely to show planful behavior. Less planful behavior is more likely to result in hasty marriages, which in turn increase the chances of adult behavior problems for these women (Rutter et al., 1990). Thus, even when there is no direct link between individual characteristics and subsequent developmental outcomes, we still can trace the causal chains whereby individual characteristics increase the probability of specific behavioral outcomes.

Another way in which individual characteristics can act to influence behavioral–developmental variability involves the availability of appropriate niches in the environment for individuals with specific characteristics. The niche concept is based on the hypothesis that individuals self-select into certain groups or contexts that match their own individual characteristics. In traditional approaches to the niche concept, it is assumed that multiple niches are easily available and that it is simply a matter of the individual's selecting the particular niche that is best for him or her (Scarr & McCartney, 1983). However, an alternative possibility exists, namely that individual characteristics can act either to close off or increase available niches for the individual, thus reducing or augmenting an individual's ability to self-select appropriate niches for themselves (Wachs, 1996b). Within this alternative approach it is assumed that the fewer niches available to the individual the more he or she will be locked into a restricted set of behavioral characteristics that will be maintained across time by restricted opportunities. For example, given that the more desirable adult niches (jobs) require specific training or educational credentials (Clausen, 1991), behaviors that increase the likelihood of an individual's dropping out of school, such as high aggression, automatically close off many future occupational niches (Caspi et al., 1987). Such niche closing limits aggressive individuals to the types of low-status jobs that are often most problematical for individuals with impulsive, overreactive characteristics who have difficulty handling frustration (Caspi et al., 1990). Other examples of niche restriction are shown in Table 5-6. In reviewing these data, it is important to keep in mind that positive characteristics such as planning or a secure attachment history may act to open up rather than close potential niches for the individual (Wachs, 1996b).

Individual Characteristics and Development: Necessary But Not Sufficient

The relevance of individual characteristics as a source of influence on subsequent individual developmental variability seems well established. Particularly when we integrate initial individual characteristics and the event chain processes that these individual characteristics help set into motion, it would seem that we have very powerful explanatory mechanisms, which may well be both necessary and sufficient. For example, individuals with difficult temperaments or individuals who are highly aggressive, have a low sense of self-efficacy, or are not ego resilient may find themselves locked into rigid behavioral cycles that are very difficult to break, even when new, potentially facilitative opportunities emerge. In contrast, individuals who are securely attached, ego resilient, or more intelligent may be more able to make adaptive use of new situations and opportunities. However, there is also evidence indicating that individual characteristics, even when operating over time, may well be necessary but not sufficient. Five lines of evidence supporting this conclusion will be discussed.

Effect Sizes and Individual Heterogeneity

Relations between initial variability in individual characteristics and subsequent variability in individual behavioral development, although significant, tend to be relatively modest in size. For example, although early chronic aggression has clear linkages to later antisocial behavior, approximately 50% of children with chronic early aggression have no criminal record as adults (Magnusson, 1988). Results showing significant but relatively modest effects also can be documented for the impact of child intellectual capacities (Moffitt, 1990), maturationally related educational readiness (Morrison et al., 1997), and difficult temperament (Bates, 1989).

One reason for these modest effect sizes may be because, all too often, predictive relations are driven by a small group of individuals within a larger sample, rather than by the whole sample per se (Magnusson, 1988). A second reason may be because relations are moderated by gender, as in the case of continuity between intelligence and adult personality occurring for men but not for women (Caspi et al., 1987), or relations between age of pubertal onset and adjustment problems occurring primarily for women (Ge, Conger, & Elder, 1996), or adolescent differences in planfullness being more predictive of subsequent educational or occupational level for men than for women (Clausen, 1991).

A third reason may involve the complex nature of individual characteristics. Such complexity is seen in the question of whether children labeled as resilient are equally resilient in all areas of functioning. To answer this question, Luthar et al. (1993) identified 25 resilient children based on their level of functioning in one of three outcome domains during high-stress periods. Of the 25 children who showed the highest level of functioning in one domain, 15 showed lower levels of functioning in the remaining two domains. Overall, only approximately 15% of this sample showed superior performance in one domain and no problems in other domains. Similar conclusions can be drawn from evidence showing a lack of behavioral consistency by the same children when assessed in different contexts, such as home and school (Hinde, 1990). The modest levels of variance accounted for by individual characteristics and the variability in intraindividual outcomes associated with individual characteristics are difficult to reconcile with a conclusion that molar individual characteristics are both necessary and sufficient.

Covariance Across Influences

From what has been discussed in previous chapters, it is not surprising to find that there are covariances between individual characteristics and other influences on individual behavioral developmental variability. A variety of such covariances involving individual characteristics also have been documented in this chapter. For example, differential educational opportunities also have been associated with individual differences in cognition level and aggression. In terms of temperament, children who are inhibited or highly reactive are likely to have different patterns of peer-group relationships than children who are less inhibited or less reactive. Perhaps one of the most well-documented examples of covariance involves differential experience associated with being male or female. In terms of differential experience, at least in Western developed countries, it remains an open question as to whether there is a systematic difference in the treatment of boys and girls by their parents (Hoffman, 1991; Jacklin & Reynolds, 1993). However, particularly in non-Western countries, from early childhood on there appear to be clear-cut differences in the types of contextual settings in which boys and girls find themselves (Whiting & Edwards, 1988). In both Western and non-Western countries, one clear setting difference is gender composition of the peer group, with same-sex peer groups being the norm even in Western societies (Edwards, 1992; Maccoby, 1988). As will be shown in chapter 7, such setting characteristics can be a major influence on variability in behavioral development.

Evidence also suggests gender-related differences in life stress, with greater stress encountered by boys in the preteen years and girls in the adolescent period (Masten et al., 1990). Gender-related differential experience also may occur through differential reactivity by caregivers to gender-characteristic behavioral patterns, as in the case of greater male oppositional behavior being more likely to elicit negative reactions from others (Rutter, Quinton, & Hill, 1990).

Particularly in non-Western societies, differential resources may be allocated to boys and girls. One example is seen in the relation between gender and educational opportunities. In a detailed review of this subject, Stromquist (1989) has reported that in 66 out of 108 less developed countries, women's educational level was at least 10% below that of men. In these countries, when boys failed in schools, the typical response was for them to repeat the grade, whereas for girls it was to remove them from school. Given the potential importance of education as a major influence on developmental variability (see chap. 7), gender-related differences in education level can be seen as a crucial mechanism through which a physical individual characteristic translates into subsequent behavioral differences. Preferential resource allocation favoring boys also has been documented in regard to feeding patterns (Engle et al., 1996; Miller, 1987) and access to medical care (Miller, 1987). (Though see Cronk, 1993, for a description of a society where women receive preferential allocation.) Given the relevance of both nutritional and biomedical status to behavioral variability (see chap. 4), such preferential allocation also may be a means whereby gender can translate into variability in behavioral development.

Such naturally existing covariances do not negate the importance of individual characteristics as an influence on behavioral–developmental variability. Rather, what such naturally occurring covariances emphasize is the importance of not artificially isolating the impact of individual characteristics from the impact of other developmentally relevant covarying, influences such as context.

Proximal Contextual Moderators

It also seems clear that aspects of the proximal context, like caregiver behavior, can act to modulate and influence the nature and consequences of even strongly biologically based individual characteristics, like temperament (Rothbart & Bates, 1998; Wachs & King, 1994). For example, outcomes associated with infant difficultness (Engfer, 1986), inhibition (Kagan et al., 1993), state regularity (Horowitz, 1992), and reactivity (Fox, 1989; Gunnar, 1994) can be moderated by variability in caregiver sensitiveness, limit setting, and responsivity, as well as by overall level of environmental stress. It is not surprising that variability in individual traits like attachment, which are less strongly biologically based, also can be traced to proximal environmental characteristics (Teti, Gelfand, Messinger, & Isabella, 1995). For example, the level of relation between early attachment status and later behavioral problems will vary as a function of the nature of intervening parent and teacher behaviors toward the child (e.g., support, encouragement, limit setting) (Greenberg et al., 1993). Similarly, links between adolescent planfullness and later educational achievement can be moderated by the degree of parental support for the child's activities (Clausen, 1991).

Moderation of the impact of individual characteristics also can occur as a result of the influence of contextual characteristics other than caregiver behavior patterns. For example, the relation between gender and educational level in less developed countries may partly depend on contextual characteristics, such as the amount of chores girls are expected to do (Stromquist, 1989). For children who are socially unpopular with their peers, changing schools may be one way to block the negative consequences associated with interpersonal problems (Engfer, Walper, & Rutter, 1994). The relation to development of individual characteristics like physical attractiveness or cognitive skills may, to some extent, vary as a function of the characteristics of the individual's reference group. Thus, if a majority of the individual's reference group is physically attractive, the contribution of the individual's own physical attractiveness to their individual development may be different than in situations where only a minority of those in the individual's reference group are perceived as physically attractive (Engfer et al., 1994).

Temporal and Cultural Moderators

Relations between individual characteristics and individual developmental variability also can be moderated by historical factors, such as the time period in which the individual grows up (Kerr, 1996). For example, evidence showing that childhood inhibition is related to later age of marriage for men but not for women may reflect the fact that the data were collected at a time when men but not women were supposed to be active in courtship (Caspi et al., 1988).

Relations between individual characteristics and individual developmental variability also can be moderated by the nature of the culture within which the individual grows up, with different outcomes being associated with the same individual characteristic in different cultures. For example, gender-related differences in specific intellectual abilities or gender-related differences in variability of intellectual performance found in Western cultures are not always found in non-Western cultures (Feingold, 1992) or even in minority groups in Western cultures (Born, Bleichrodt, & van der Flier, 1987). Similarly, gender-related differences in aggressive behavior can disappear when boys and girls are exposed to high levels of ongoing societal violence (Day & Ghandour, 1984; Farver & Frosch, 1996). The most dramatic evidence supporting the importance of cultural moderation is the lower survival rate in certain third-world countries for infants with characteristics that would be considered highly desirable in developed Western countries (e.g., calm, placid, temperamentally easy infants; DeVries, 1984; Scheper-Hughes, 1987a, 1987b). One reason may be that in less developed countries with high infant mortality rates, fussy, intense infants are more valued than calm, placid infants because mothers see the former group of infants as having a stronger will to live.

Less dramatic but equally important for the necessary-and-sufficient question are studies on potential cultural moderation of individual differences in attachment characteristics. In Western countries, secure attachment to a primary caregiver has been shown to be an individual characteristic that has a variety of positive developmental consequences. However, there are other cultures wherein other forms of attachment may provide a more desirable social prototype (Belsky & Cassidy, 1994; Mizuta, Zahn-Waxler, Cole, & Hiruma, 1996). For example, primary attachment to a single caregiver may be less adaptive in cultures like the Efe, where simultaneous infant attachments to multiple primary caregivers can promote both physical survival and culturally desirable traits like sociability and sensitivity to interpersonal relations (Tronick, Morelli, & Winn, 1987). Similarly, weak maternal attachment to infants may be appropriate in less-developed countries where there is a high infant mortality rate (DeVries, 1984). Furthermore, cultural moderation need not be restricted only to less developed countries. As noted earlier, in the United States men who were shy and inhibited as children were found to have a delayed entrance into stable occupational roles. One explanation for this finding is that inhibition is not a valued trait for men in the United States, so inhibited men are at a disadvantage when competing for job openings. No such relation between childhood inhibition and adult occupational entry is seen for Swedish men, in part because inhibition is viewed as a culturally appropriate male trait in Sweden (Kerr, 1996).

Event Chains: Probabilistic, not Deterministic

In a framework within which individual characteristics like temperament or intelligence are viewed as setting off an unalterable chain of events, the influence of such characteristics can be sufficient (Scarr, 1992). Such a deterministic framework does not fit the nature of the processes underlying human development as we know them (Wachs, 1995a). In part this is because ascribing sufficient causality to individual characteristics ignores the fact that individual differences in characteristics such as self-efficacy beliefs or self-regulatory capacity may themselves be the result of extrinsic influences like family routines or family values (Bandura, Barbaranelli, Capara, & Pastorelli, 1996; Brody & Flor, 1997). Even more critical is the fact that there are multiple points along an event chain wherein other developmental influences can act to change the initial course of development. A hypothetical example (but based on actual data on each point of the chain) is shown in Table 5-7. As can be seen from this table, two children may start out equally inhibited but end up at very different points because of intervening events. Though simplified, this diagram does represent the probabilistic nature of event chains. Individual characteristics can increase the probability of a specific event occurring further along the chain, but individual characteristics cannot guarantee which subsequent events will actually occur for an individual.

As discussed in chapter 1, although it is relatively easy to generate correct explanatory scenarios when we start with the outcome and work our way backward along a causal chain, it is far more difficult to predict both causal chain links and outcomes when we are at the starting point of such an event chain (Dawes, 1993). There are all too many situations in which outcomes predicted from the starting point of an event chain are not what we would expect. For example, it would be relatively easy to hypothesize a causal chain wherein childhood dependency was associated with a variety of negative adult outcomes. In fact, adults who were highly dependent children are more likely to be rated as calm, empathic, at ease in new situations, poised, and nurturing, and to have very stable marriages (Caspi et al., 1990). What transforms dependent children into mature, nurturant adults is unclear, but the nature of the transformation is not one that could be easily predicted from any existing event-chain model.

Influences that lead to probabilistic links between earlier and later events in causal chains have been demonstrated. For example, although difficult infant temperament should act to increase the likelihood of negative transactions between parent and infant, at least within the first year of life,

TABLE 5-7
Proposed Transition Paths Between Early Temperament and
Later Personality

| Intervening Context | Initial Temperament Trait: Inhibition | |
	Child A	Child B
	Intervening events	
Social microenvironment	Caregivers (parents) who are sensitive, accepting, and let child set his or her own pace.	Caregivers who use inappropriate "low level control" and attempt to force the child into new situations.
Physical microenvironment	Presence of "stimulus shelters" or "defensible spaces," that the children can retreat to when there is too much stimulation.	The child continually encounters noisy, chaotic environments that allow no escape from stimulation.
Nonfamily: Peer groups	Peer groups have other inhibited children with common interests, so the child feels accepted.	Peer groups consist of athletic extraverts, so the child feels rejected.
Mesosystem: School environment	School is "undermanned" so inhibited children are more likely to be tolerated and feel they can make a contribution.	School is "overmanned" so inhibited children are less likely to be tolerated and more likely to feel undervalued.
	Personality outcomes	
	As an adult, individual is closer to extraversion and has high emotional stability.	As an adult, individual is closer to introversion and has a higher level of neuroticism.

Note. Table taken from Wachs (1994).

studies show low and inconsistent relations between infant temperament and caregiver behavior patterns (Slabach, Morrow, & Wachs, 1991). In part this is because nontemperamental factors, like the parent's experience with infants and parental preferences for certain types of infant behavior, can also influence how the parent reacts to an infant with a difficult temperament (Slabach et al., 1991). Going beyond infancy, girls who are reared in highly disorganized family environments or in institutions tend to lack planfullness, which in turn can adversely influence their subsequent adult development. However, if a girl from this type of background happens to attend a school that provides her with support and success in her social and educational activities, then the link between early disruption and later impulsivity is strongly reduced, resulting in a very different set of adult outcomes (Rutter et al., 1990). Although causal-event chains may be a powerful explanatory model to help us understand why variability in individual characteristics translates into later developmental variability, the probabilistic nature of the connections between links in causal chains means that individual characteristics are, in reality, only one necessary link.

CONCLUSIONS

In this chapter, I have identified many (but not all) of the individual characteristics that have been documented as being related to subsequent individual developmental variability. I also have shown some of the mechanisms that are important in the translation of individual characteristics into subsequent individual behavioral variability. Finally, I have shown that developmental outcome variability cannot be understood just by the actions of individual characteristics per se. Across time, multiple factors both covary with and act to moderate the impact of individual characteristics on individual behavioral development. Taken as a totality, the evidence presented in this chapter makes it clear that individual characteristics, although a necessary influence for individual behavioral developmental variability, are not necessarily sufficient.

6

PROXIMAL ENVIRONMENTAL INFLUENCES

Proximal environmental influences are specific social, physical, or symbolic contextual characteristics that directly impinge on the child (Bronfenbrenner & Ceci, 1994). Although studies of proximal environmental influences most often have emphasized specific behavioral transactions between a child and his or her parents, proximal influences are not limited just to parent–child relationships. Transactions between the child and other children, transactions with nonparental adults such as teachers, and the child's relationship with physical characteristics of the immediate environment, such as object availability, object variety, and noise level, also qualify as proximal influences (Wachs, 1992). Cumulative caregiver characteristics such as commitment to a relationship or openness to other persons (Hinde, 1989), a cumulative parental rearing style such as authoritative versus authoritarian rearing (Darling & Steinberg, 1993), and specific parental beliefs, values, and goals, although not necessarily directly observable, nonetheless directly affect the child. As such, these influences also will be considered as part of the child's proximal environment.

Proximal environmental characteristics can be contrasted with descriptive "social address" terms. Social address terms may include proximal characteristics, but they do not reveal the nature of the specific proximal processes encountered by the child. One such social address would be birth order, which has been directly or indirectly associated with a variety of outcome differences (Eaton, Chipperfield, & Singbeil, 1989; McHale, Crouter, McGuire, & Updegraff, 1995; Pine, 1995; Zajonc & Mullally, 1997). For example, Tarullo, DeMulder, Ronsaville, Brown, Radke-Yarrow, (1995) reported that the relative contributions of maternal psychopathology and family environment to children's adjustment varies as a function of the child's birth order. However, the descriptive term *birth order,* in and of itself, tells us little about what specific proximal processes are operating to influence development. Understanding the role played by social address characteristics will require specification of the specific proximal processes associated with these characteristics, such as differential treatment of first versus later born children. Rather than focusing on broad descriptors, this chapter will discuss specific proximal processes. Other examples of environmental social addresses include cultural or social institutions such as schools or social class, which describe broad-based events or settings but do not detail the social, physical, or symbolic characteristics of these settings. Such cultural or social institutions will be considered as distal rather than proximal environmental influences. Thus, specific school characteristics that act to influence a child's academic achievement would constitute an example of a proximal process, whereas the impact of attending or not attending schools would be considered a distal influence. Discussion of the role of distal environmental influences will be deferred until the following chapter.

Given several detailed volumes on the characteristics and nature of environmental influences (Detterman, 1996; Wachs, 1992), the focus of this chapter will be less on listing those specific proximal characteristics that are relevant to variability in individual development (though there will be some of this) and more on how proximal processes operate to influence development.

CAREGIVER BELIEF SYSTEMS

Relevant Caregiver Belief Systems

Parental belief systems can include parent values—the goals that parents see as desirable for their children to achieve—as well as parent beliefs and ideas about how their children can achieve these goals (Luster, Rhodes, & Haas, 1989). Although a complete survey of the multiple dimensions encompassing belief and value systems is well beyond the scope of this chapter (see Miller, 1995, or Sigel, 1985, 1992, for more detailed reviews), I will present a few of the parent belief dimensions that have been considered as being especially relevant to individual variability in children's behavioral development.

One major dimension involves the values that parents think are important for their children to acquire. For example, a traditional distinction is between cultures that value the importance of communality (i.e., the individual's needs should be subordinated to the needs of the family and society) and cultures that value individuality (i.e., the individual's needs and uniqueness should be primary; Kagitcibasi & Berry, 1989). Within cultures there also can be individual differences among parents in regard to the degree to which they emphasize their children's developing a sense of conformity versus a sense of individualism and self-direction (Schooler, 1984). For example, Japanese mothers value the early appearance of children's emotional control, politeness, and obedience, whereas Australian and North American mothers value the early appearance of verbal and social assertiveness in their children (Goodnow, 1985).

Parents also have beliefs about the causes and characteristics of children's development. Thus, parents can differ on whether they see children's development as being due to intrinsic factors, such as genes, personality, or biological maturation, or as being due to extrinsic factors, such as peer pressure or direct instruction from adults (Miller, 1995).

Finally, it is also important to recognize that parent beliefs can operate as an interrelated system. This fact has led to attempts to categorize parental belief and value systems in complex multidimensional clusters. One example would be the distinction between modern and traditional parental belief systems (Palacios, Gonzalez, & Moreno, 1992; Schaefer & Edgerton, 1985). The modernity cluster would consist of parents who deemphasize conformity and gender stereotyping as appropriate rearing goals, see development as determined by multiple causes, believe in a flexible approach to child rearing, and believe that they can influence their child's development. Parents falling into the traditional cluster would be those who assume innate influences on development, emphasize conformity and traditional gender roles as appropriate values for children to develop, and have lower expectations about their ability to influence their child's development (Sigel, 1992). It is important to recognize that such distinctions are not absolute. For example, parents who believe in extrinsic influences can differ in the degree to which they think they can influence their child's development (Miller, 1995). Furthermore, parental beliefs may vary depending on the developmental domain with which they are dealing (Miller, 1995). For example, Tanzanian mothers tend to believe that children develop motor skills as a result of direct instruction from parents. However, these same mothers also believe that children develop language skills not from direct instruction but rather from being in the presence of older siblings (McGillicuddy-DeLisi & Subramanian, 1996).

Parental Beliefs and Parent Behaviors

Underlying much of the research on parental belief systems is the assumption that parental beliefs, values, and child-rearing goals should directly influence specific parental child-rearing practices, which in turn should influence child outcomes (Darling & Steinberg, 1993). Within this framework, parental behaviors are seen as the outward manifestation of latent parental belief systems. For example, in some societies young infants are awakened when guests arrive and the activities of older children are regulated so that they fit in with family meal times. Underlying these practices is the belief that the needs of the family are more important than the needs of the individual members of the family (Goodnow, 1992).

In reality, however, the correspondence between parental beliefs and parental actions is not always significant and, when significant, the level of association is relatively modest (Kohn, 1983; S. Miller, 1988, 1995). Although individual studies exist that show a clear relation between parental beliefs and parental action (e.g., Bugental, Blue, & Cruz-sosa, 1989; LeVine, Miller, Richman, & LeVine, 1996; Luster et al., 1989), there are all too many other studies that show little relation between beliefs and actions, (e.g., Belsky, Crnic, & Gable, 1995; Engle et al., 1996; Mize, Pettit, & Brown, 1995). Furthermore, when linkages between parent beliefs and parent behaviors are observed, too often these linkages do not lend themselves to easy interpretation (Kochanska, 1990). As a result, even in anthropology traditional assumptions about strong linkages between parental beliefs and parents' behavior are being reexamined (Harkness & Super, 1992).

Several reasons explain the modest level and inconsistent nature of relations found between parental beliefs and parental behaviors. First, parents may have difficulty in clearly describing the nature of their belief systems (New & Richman, 1996), particularly when parental belief systems are deeply embedded in the culture (D'Andrade, 1987). In this case, asking parents to describe deeply embedded belief systems may be the equivalent of asking a fish to describe water. Second, we are likely to find stronger or more consistent relations between parental beliefs and parental actions when there is a close fit between the content of the belief and the content of the action (Goodnow, 1988b; Kochanska, 1990; Sigel, 1985). For example, we would expect a closer fit between parental beliefs about the relative effectiveness of positive versus negative reinforcement as a disciplinary tool and parental reinforcement patterns than between parental beliefs about general parenting goals and the parent's reinforcement patterns. Third, parental beliefs may change over time (e.g., the well-known observation that parents believe in the importance of environment with their first child but become nativists after their second child is born).

Parental Beliefs and Individual Developmental Variability

Although strong relations between parental beliefs and individual variability in children's behavioral development have not always been demonstrated, a number of individual behavioral outcomes have been shown to be sensitive to the influence of caregiver belief systems (Miller, 1995). For example, individual variability in physical growth patterns has been related to maternal beliefs about appropriate child-feeding strategies (Engle et al., 1996), whereas the religious beliefs of rural African American parents have been shown to be related to fewer behavioral problems in off-spring (Brody, Stoneman, & Flor, 1996). Rather than reviewing all examples of how variability in belief systems can relate to individual behavioral developmental variability, I have chosen one developmental outcome as an example, namely variability in children's cognitive and academic achievement. Examples of studies showing an association between individual variability in children's cognitive and academic achievement and variability in parental, teacher, and community belief systems are shown in Table 6-1. As can be seen from Table 6-1, parent beliefs about the desirability of educational achievement and teacher beliefs about the ability of specific children to succeed academically each contribute to variability in children's academic achievement. In addition, both parent and teacher beliefs about the importance of active parent and child effort act to facilitate both cognitive performance and academic achievement.

Caregiver Beliefs: Necessary But Not Sufficient

Although the relevance of caregiver beliefs and values for variability in children's development has been just documented, what also can be documented is the fact that belief systems, in and of themselves, are insufficient as a primary explanation for variability in development. In part, this conclusion is based on the fact that caregiver belief systems are nested within larger systems and processes that also can act to influence variability in behavioral development. Such nesting is most clearly documented in the linkage between parental belief systems and family demographic or cultural characteristics (Goodnow, 1988b; Luster et al., 1989; also see chap. 7).

More critically, the relation of caregiver belief systems to children's behavioral development may be bidirectional in nature. That is, caregiver beliefs and values may act to influence specific child characteristics, but child characteristics in turn can act to influence caregiver belief systems. For example, mothers tend to attribute their sons' success in mathematics to ability rather than effort, whereas their daughters' success in mathematics tends to be attributed to effort rather than ability (Miller, 1995). Although parents may hold certain educational goals for their children, feedback from the school about the child's competencies and capacities may act to raise or lower parental educational expectations (Seginer, 1983). A similar process also is seen in regard to child competencies and teacher expectations about the child (Brophy, 1983).

TABLE 6-1
Relation of Parental Beliefs to Children's Cognitive
and Academic Performance

Outcomes	Beliefs	Direction of Relationship	Study
Cognitive performance	That children's development is determined by multiple causes and that parents can influence their child's development		Benasich & Brooks-Gunn (1996); Palacios et al. (1992)
	That early appearance of verbal assertiveness and school-related skills is important	+	Hess, Kashiwaga, Azuma, Price, & Dickson (1980)
Teacher ratings of child's intelligence and creativity	That child learns from observation and experimentation	+	McGillicuddy-DeLisi & Subramanian (1996)
	That children acquire knowledge through biological maturation	−	McGillicuddy-DeLisi & Subramanian (1996)
Child school performance	That child's conforming to external standards and respect for authority are important	−	Brody & Stoneman (1992); Okagaki & Sternberg (1993)
	That education and child's academic success associated with degree of child's effort are important	+	Kim & Chun (1994); Chen & Stevenson, (1995)
	That education is important for children	+	Fuligni (1997); Luster & McAdoo (1996)

The relation between parental belief systems and variability in children's behavioral development is further weakened by the nature of parental belief systems. As noted earlier, parental beliefs typically are not monolithic in nature. Parents and even cultures typically offer children a range of values and goals, some of which are preferred, some of which are tolerated, and some of which are rejected (Goodnow, 1992; Lightfoot & Valsiner, 1992). To the extent that children are allowed to choose among competing belief systems, there may well be divergencies between the beliefs that parents cherish most and the values and goals that are adopted by their children. One such example is seen in the case of conflicts between immigrant parents and their children, where there is a clear contrast between the nature of parental belief systems and the belief systems held by the larger culture or by the peer group (Goodnow, 1992).

TABLE 6-1 (*continued*)

Outcomes	Beliefs	Direction of Rela-tionship	Study
Child school performance	That child's succeeding academically is important	+	Brody & Stoneman (1992); Seginer (1983)
	That women are capable of succeeding educationally and that education for women is desirable	+	Gustafson (1994); Holloway (1986)
	That development of a sense of self-respect in the child is an important child rearing goal	+	Brody & Stoneman (1992)
	That poorly functioning minority children do not have the capacity to succeed in school (Teacher expectation)	–	Alexander & Entwisle (1988); Brophy (1983)
	That school inhibits a woman's ability to function as wife and mother in traditional society (Cultural belief)	–	Stromquist (1989)
Child expectations of academic success	That teachers can teach adolescents technical subject matter (Teacher expectation)	+	Eccles et al. (1993)

Finally, the necessary but not sufficient nature of belief systems also is inherent in the tenuous linkage between parental beliefs and parental behaviors, as noted earlier. One reason for this tenuous linkage is the existence of many potential moderators that can operate to attenuate or accentuate the linkage between parent beliefs, parent behaviors, and child outcomes. For example, there is an attenuation of the influence of parental belief systems on parental behaviors when parents are depressed (Kochanska, 1990) and a strengthening of such links when there is a combination of specific parent beliefs (e.g., low perceived control) and specific child characteristics (e.g., difficult temperament; Miller, 1995).

Moderation of the impact of parental belief systems also can result from the influence of higher order contextual factors. For example, relations between maternal beliefs about what can influence children's development and their children's actual cognitive performance can vary systematically as a function of ethnic group membership (Benasich & Brooks-Gunn, 1996).

Higher order moderators also can operate within ethnic groups. Thus, the positive relation between offspring school achievement and the attitudes of Asian American parents on the importance of education may be attenuated when nonattitudinal conditions come into play, such as whether the adolescent is working or dating (Chen & Stevenson, 1995). Taken together, all of the factors just listed document that caregiver belief systems, although necessary, in and of themselves cannot be considered a sufficient explanation for individual behavioral–developmental variability.

PROXIMAL ENVIRONMENTAL INFLUENCES

As noted earlier, proximal environmental influences include not only parental beliefs but also parental rearing styles, the child's social interactions with other children and nonparental adults, and physical environmental characteristics that directly impinge on the developing child. These diverse proximal influences, although conceptually distinct, often interact in complex ways. For example, parental rearing styles can act as moderators, predisposing the child to be more or less receptive to specific parental rearing techniques (Darling & Steinberg, 1993). Similarly, linkages between parental rejection and children's peer relations may be mediated through relationship patterns among siblings (MacKinnon-Lewis, Starnes, Volling, & Johnson, 1997), whereas schools characterized as authoritative and structured in nature can serve to attenuate the negative developmental consequences associated with parental divorce (Hetherington, 1989).

The Necessary Nature of Proximal Environmental Influences

Although proximal environmental influences would seem to be obvious and necessary contributors to variability in children's behavioral development, such necessity is not universally accepted. A small number of developmental researchers either deny the relevance of the family environment for individual developmental variability (Lytton & Romney, 1991; Harris, 1995) or argue that proximal environmental influences are relevant for individual variability only under conditions of extreme environmental deprivation or enrichment (Rowe, 1994; Scarr, 1992). The multiple fallacies in these lines of argument have been extensively pointed out in previous publications (e.g., Hoffman, 1991; Wachs, 1995a). A brief review of some of these fallacies is discussed next, if only to help readers avoid the incorrect conclusion that nonextreme proximal environmental influences are not a necessary condition for variability in individual behavioral development.

There are four lines of converging evidence that clearly illustrate why such a position is fallacious. First, all too often researchers who deny the salience of nonextreme environmental influences do so on the basis of very selective reviews of the evidence. For example, Harris (1995) has denied the role of family environment for variability in personality development but is willing to accept a role for peer-group influences. What Harris does not consider is evidence showing how parents can act to influence peer-group acceptance and peer-group choices of their children (Brown, Mounts, Lanborn, & Steinberg, 1993; MacKinnon-Lewis et al., 1997). In addition, these researchers often tend to ignore the wealth of data found in infrahuman studies indicating significant effects of nonextreme environmental conditions on behavior, development, and central nervous system (CNS) growth and function (e.g., Bateson, 1983; Rubenstein et al., 1990; also see chap. 3).

Second, conclusions denying the role of nonextreme influences too often are based on methodologically flawed studies, such as studies on family environmental influences that never directly measure the family environment (Rowe, 1994). Even in the same study with the same population, significant environmental influences that are found when environmental influences are directly measured vanish when environmental influences are only indirectly inferred (Kendler, Neale, Kessler, Heath, & Eaves, 1992).

A third line of evidence consists of studies of psychosocial interventions with risk populations. What must be emphasized is that successful interventions do not require extreme changes in the environment. Rather, many successful psychosocial interventions do nothing more than provide good rearing conditions to children at biological or psychosocial risk who previously have not been exposed to such conditions (Grantham-McGregor, 1995; Gross et al., 1992; G. Patterson & Bank, 1989; Ramey & Ramey, 1998; Rauh & Brennan, 1992).

Finally, a consistent body of evidence documents the importance of variability in naturally occurring but not extreme proximal conditions for children who are at developmental risk due to biomedical or psychosocial risk conditions. Such children often show better than expected development as a function of naturally occurring nonextreme protective factors, such as responsive parents, the presence of stimulus objects in the home, or having a warm and supportive relationship with another adult, such as a grandparent, neighbor, or teacher (Bradley et al., 1994; Farber & Egeland, 1987; Masten et al., 1990; Werner, 1990). Similarly, children in good-quality, center-based day care or good-quality schools show more adequate social and cognitive development than do children attending lower quality home-based day care or poor-quality schools (Caughy, DiPietro, & Strobino, 1994; Ceci, 1991; Clarke-Stewart, 1991). Behavioral variability also has been associated with nonextreme physical environmental characteristics, such as community television access (Signorelli, 1990), and with more indirect environmental changes, such as the hiring of new principals for schools with a history of generally low academic achievement (Rutter, 1988). Even such a fundamental biomedical outcome as longevity has been found to be related to whether an individual's parents were divorced during his or her childhood (Friedman et al., 1995).

All of this evidence clearly documents how nonextreme proximal environmental influences, both within and outside of the family, can act to influence individual developmental behavioral variability. Given that variability in proximal environmental influences has been shown to be a necessary influence on variability in behavioral development, a critical question to be considered in the next section is that of which specific proximal factors operate in this way.

Specific Proximal Contributions to Individual Variability

A survey of the available literature indicates that too little is known about specific proximal environmental contributions to a number of outcome domains such as temperament, mastery motivation, and human CNS development. However, there are a number of other behavioral–developmental domains where the evidence is sufficiently consistent to allow conclusions to be drawn about the role of specific proximal influences. A summary of evidence relating proximal environmental contributions to individual variability in children's cognitive and academic competence, social behavior, personality, and resilience is shown in Table 6-2. It is important to

TABLE 6-2
Proximal Environmental Characteristics Contributing to Individual
Developmental Variability in Different Domains

Proximal Characteristics	Directionality
Cognitive and academic competence	
Family environment[a]	
Tactual kinesthetic stimulation	+
Caregiver responsivity	+
Verbal stimulation	+
Restriction of exploration	−
Variety of age appropriate age stimulation	+
Adult scaffolding	+
Parental support for children's achievement (e.g., monitoring, involvement)	+
Opportunities for concentrated practice on a given skill	+
Parental rearing styles	
Authoritative	+
Authoritarian	−
Permissive	−
Peer, class, and school characteristics[b]	
Peer support for academic achievement	+
Teacher's structuring of material	+
Time spent on academic activities	+
Appropriate teacher's expectations for students' achievement	+
Frequent evaluation of student progress	+
Teacher's support of students	+
Teacher's commitment to education	+
Strong educationally oriented administrative school leadership	+
Emphasis on basic skills	+

TABLE 6-2 (*continued*)

Proximal Characteristics	Directionality
Cognitive and academic competence	
Collegiality and a sense of shared learning among teachers	+
Providing a safe and organized environment	+
Allowing older students to have responsibilities for school functioning	+
Fewer students than positions available for students ("undermanned setting")	+
Higher proportion of low-ability students	−
Prosocial behavior[c]	
Use of authoritative rearing strategies	+
Use of reasoning and joint negotiation as a way of dealing with family problems	+
High levels of parent activity in arranging and monitoring young children's peer contact	+
Antisocial behavior[d]	
Marital and family conflict	+
Parental rejection of the child	+
Parental monitoring of the child's activities	−
Parental use of coercive, inconsistent, or ineffective disciplining strategies	+
Personality	
Secure attachment[e]	
Responsive parenting	+
Sensitive parenting	+
Parental rejection	−
Self-regulation, internal conscience[f]	
Sensitive parenting	+
Parental support	+
Reciprocal discipline strategies (reasoning, responsive to child)	+
Power-assertive discipline strategy (physical punishment)	−
Resilience[g]	
Presence of warm, responsive, accepting caregivers	+
Rules and structure in the child's household	+
Social network of supportive nonfamily members available to the child	+
Presence of same-gender role models	+
Opportunity to demonstrate competence in nonfamily situations	+
Caregiver responsivity to child	+
Child attendance at school that sets high but appropriate standards, offers feedback, and allows students positions of trust and responsibility	+
Having teachers available to serve as role models	+

[a] Dornbush, Ritter, Leiderman, Roberts, & Fraleigh (1987), Ericsson & Charness (1994), Rogoff (1990), Wachs (1992)

[b] Coie (1990), Eccles et al. (1993), Kindermann (1993a), Maughn (1994), Schoggen (1991), Talbert & McLaughlin (1999)

[c] Cooper & Cooper (1992), Hartup & van Lieshout (1995), Parke & Bhavnagri (1989), Putallaz & Heflin (1990)

[d] Bryant & DeMorris (1992), Cooper & Cooper (1992), Hartup & van Lieshout (1995), Putallaz & Heflin (1990), Sampson & Laub (1994)

[e] Isabella (1993), Pedersen & Moran (1995)

[f] Calkins (1994), Crockenberg & Litman (1990), Holden & West (1990)

[g] Werner (1990)

note that most of the conclusions about classroom or school influences shown in Table 6-2 are based on studies in Western developed countries. What evidence is available from non-Western or less developed countries suggests that other school characteristics also may be critical, including when teachers actually arrive for class, availability of school uniforms, or basic learning materials, such as pencils and paper and whether textbooks are free (Gorman & Pollitt, 1992; Grantham-McGregor & Walker, 1998).

As shown in Table 6-2, many of the contributions to children's antisocial behavior involve the contribution of parental and family characteristics, such as an increased probability of modeling inappropriate parental behavior patterns. Antisocial behavior patterns in children also can be promoted by nonfamily factors, such as exposure to television violence (Quinton, 1994) and high levels of interaction with delinquent peers (Moffitt, 1993), or can be reduced by attending schools with a strong academic focus (Maughn, 1994). Furthermore, the contribution of family factors may be only the first step in a long event chain. Thus, children's anger with coercive, inconsistent, and rejecting parents may spill over into their relations with peers (Rubin, LeMare, & Lollis, 1990). Subsequent negative reactions by peers can serve to maintain the child's antisocial behavioral patterns across time (Coie, 1990).

Some Emerging Environmental Domains

What have been documented in Table 6-2 are conclusions about the role of well-established proximal environmental influences. However, such established findings do not represent all of our knowledge about proximal environmental contributions to individual variability in children's behavior and development. Research also has begun to identify potential new domains of proximal environmental influences that ultimately may prove to be equally salient. Examples of some of these "emerging domains" are noted next.

Prenatal Stimulation

For the most part, when we think of proximal environmental stimulation, we think primarily about stimulation occurring after birth. Although postnatal stimulation may be of greater salience, infrahuman studies show that there is no a priori reason to restrict the role of environmental influences to just the postnatal period. For example, in infrahuman species, even strongly biologically programmed behavioral characteristics can be reduced or even eliminated when normally occurring prenatal auditory stimulation is eliminated (Miller, 1997). Although little evidence is available at the human level, there are some tantalizing hints that suggest the potential salience of stimulation occurring prior to birth. For example, neonatal language preference and language discrimination have been shown to be related to the characteristics of the language to which the fetus was exposed while in utero (DeCasper & Spence, 1986; Mehle et al., 1988). Offspring of mothers who were highly stressed during the prenatal period have been shown to have a higher incidence of adult adjustment problems than offspring of mothers who were stressed in the early postnatal period, even after controlling for potential biomedical influences like birth complications (Huttunen & Niskanen, 1978).

Environmental Chaos

There is growing interest in the impact of a cluster of environmental characteristics that includes high noise levels, high-density living conditions, high home-traffic patterns (i.e., many people coming and going in the home), a lack of temporal and physical structuring in the home (e.g., little is scheduled, nothing has its place), and unpredictable and repeated changes in the child's environment (e.g., high number of family moves). Taken together, these dimensions define what can be called *environmental chaos* (Wachs, 1989; Wohlwill & Heft, 1987). Environmental chaos also can occur in nonfamily settings, as in the case of high stimulus levels in neonatal intensive care units (Als, 1992). A summary of relations between indexes of environmental chaos and individual behavioral–developmental variability is shown in Table 6-3.

A number of mechanisms exist through which environmental chaos can act to adversely influence developmental variability. Children may adjust to chaos by filtering out unwanted stimulation, a process that unfortunately can also result in children's filtering out more desirable stimulation, such as language (Evans, Kliewer, & Martin, 1990). Alternatively, high levels of environmental chaos have been repeatedly associated with decrements in the quality of caregiver behaviors toward the child (Matheny, Wachs, Ludwig, & Phillips, 1995; Wachs, 1993b). For example, Evans, et

TABLE 6-3
Relations Between Environmental Chaos and Individual
Behavioral–Developmental Variability

Association with Environmental Chaos	Reference:
Lower cognitive, academic, and linguistic competence	Wachs (1992), Wohlwill & Heft (1987)
Neonates' difficulty in maintaining state control	Als (1992)
Difficult temperament	Matheny, Wilson, & Thoben, (1987), Wachs (1988)
Reduced mastery motivation	Wachs (1987)
Increased risk of childhood injuries	Matheny (1986)
Increased risk of elevated blood pressure and learned helplessness in childhood	Evans, Hygge, & Bullinger (1995)

al., (1990) have shown how high-density living conditions result in an increase in family conflict, which in turn adversely influences children's adjustment at school.

Shared and Nonshared Environmental Processes

From evidence indicating that siblings may have different developmental outcomes, behavioral genetic researchers have postulated a distinction between *shared environmental influences* (those aspects of the environment that act to make siblings similar) and *nonshared environmental influences* (those aspects of the environment that act to make siblings different) (Plomin & Daniels, 1987). Behavioral–genetic researchers further argue that nonshared environmental influences represent a unique, previously unknown environmental dimension (Plomin & Daniels, 1987) and that nonshared environmental influences are the major means through which the environment operates to influence development (Rowe, 1994).

Although outcome differences among siblings appear to be a well-established fact, such differences do not occur for all aspects of development. Across a number of outcome domains, such as antisocial behavior (Goodman, 1991b; Pike et al., 1996), development of attitudes (Hoffman, 1991), and reading achievement (Thompson, 1996), significant sibling similarity is shown, suggesting the operation of shared environmental influences. Furthermore, the operation of shared and nonshared environmental influences appears to be partially age dependent, with nonshared influences more likely to be found in older populations, even at the adult level (Gatz, Pedersen, Plomin, Nesselroade, & McClearn, 1992).

Even when sibling differences are found, attributing such differences to the operation of nonshared environmental processes remains an open question. Dividing the environment into shared and nonshared components implies that these are distinctly different aspects of the environment. Such a distinction may be misleading given that the same environmental dimensions can be either shared or nonshared, depending on whether the dimension is common to one or all of the siblings in the family (Goodman, 1991b; Wachs, 1995a). An excellent example illustrating this point is seen in studies of risk versus protective environmental factors. Although the risk-protective dichotomy suggests there are two distinct environmental domains involved, Stouthamer-Loeber et al. (1993) have documented how the same environmental variable can act either as a risk or as a protective factor. For example, the absence of adequate parental supervision may constitute a risk factor, whereas its presence can act as a protective factor. Researchers espousing the importance of nonshared environmental influences often ignore the potential overlap of shared and nonshared components by making the assumption that siblings living under the same roof must, of necessity, be sharing the same environment. The validity of such an assumption is problematical, given evidence that a variety of individual characteristics such as comparative age of siblings, sibling gender, and sibling temperament can act to ensure that siblings are encountering nonsimilar environments (Dunn, 1991; Hoffman, 1991; Rose, 1995; Wachs, 1995a). For example, if mothers are "seductive" toward their sons, they are much more likely to show diametrically opposed behavioral patterns toward their daughters, even when both sons and daughters are living under the same roof (Sroufe, Jacobvitz, Mangelsdorf, De Angelo, & Ward, 1985).

The conceptual problem of overlap of dichotomous categories is further compounded by a second conceptual problem, namely failure to distinguish between the weak and strong forms of the shared–nonshared hypothesis (Wachs, 1996b). The strong form of this hypothesis (Harris, 1995; Rowe, 1994) is based on the assumption that even if siblings are encountering similar environments, such environmental similarity will be irrelevant for variability in behavioral development. Little if any evidence is available to support the strong form of this hypothesis. The weak form of the shared–nonshared hypothesis asserts that sibling outcome differences are a function of siblings encountering differential treatment. What evidence is available favors the weak form of the hypothesis (Wachs, 1996b). If the weak form of nonshared environmental influences is correct, what such influences may reflect is not the operation of a new dimension of the proximal environment but rather one manifestation of a known environmental action process, namely environmental specificity (discussed later).

Processes of Proximal Environmental Action

Research on proximal environmental influences has allowed us not only to define which aspects of the environment are relevant or potentially relevant for subsequent individual developmental behavioral variability, but also to illustrate the mechanisms through which the proximal environment acts as an influence. Previous discussion of proximal environmental action processes have focused primarily on relations between the individual and his or her immediate microcontext. For example, the environment has been viewed either as a setting within which the child learns appropriate social relationship patterns, as a source of stimulation for the individual, or as a context that provides the child with opportunities to practice specific skills (Horowitz, 1987; Wohlwill, 1973). In the following sections, I emphasize a broader approach to defining the processes through which proximal environmental factors act to influence individual behavioral developmental variability.

The Proximal Environment Has A Defined Structure

From the pioneering work of Bronfenbrenner (1989, 1993), it is clear that the environment is organized into a multilevel higher order structure,

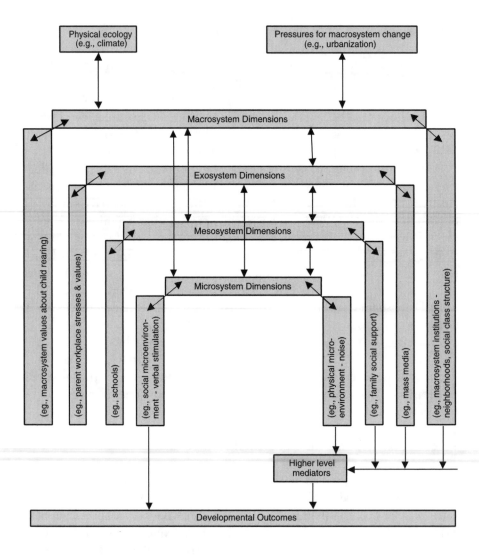

Figure 6-1. The structure of the environment. Double headed arrows refer to bidirectional levels of influence across the environment. Single headed arrows refer to direct or mediating influences of the environment on development.

with bidirectional patterns of influence both across and within levels. As shown in Figure 6-1, the environment is hierarchically organized into five levels: (a) *physical ecology*, (b) the *macrosystem* (culture, subcultures, societal institutions), (c) the *exosystem* (aspects of the environment that affect the child's development but that the child does not directly encounter), (d) the *mesosystem* (links between proximal settings that are directly encountered by the child), and (e) the *microsystem* (proximal settings that contribute to individual variability in children's development).

Within this framework, proximal environmental influences cannot be understood simply as a function of the isolated operation of microsystem processes. Rather, proximal environmental processes function as part of a coordinated system, involving reciprocal influences both among and within the various levels illustrated in Figure 6-1. There are two ways in which the multilevel nature of the environmental structure can influence the operation of proximal environmental processes (Wachs, 1992). First, higher level contextual characteristics can act to influence the nature of the proximal environment encountered by the individual. For example, a number of studies have shown how macro- and exosystem economic and social stressors can influence parental characteristics (e.g., irritability, marital relations). Parental characteristics in turn influence proximal parent–child relations, which ultimately influence variability in children's behavioral development (Brody et al., 1996; Conger, Patterson, & Ge, 1995; Elder & Caspi, 1988; Patterson, Griesler, Vaden, & Kupersmidt, 1992). Other evidence documents linkages between the extent of the parent's social network, the number of adults to whom the child is exposed, and the child's language development (Salzinger, 1990).

Second, the hierarchical structure of the environment also allows for the operation of moderation processes, wherein the impact of proximal microsystem influences is accentuated or attenuated as a function of proximal influences from other levels of the environment (Wachs, 1992). For example, the beneficial influences of parental authoritativeness are accentuated when the parents of children's peers also are authoritative in their rearing style (Fletcher, Darhny, Dornbush, & Steinberg, 1995). Similarly, specific neighborhood characteristics can act either to attenuate or to accentuate the impact of positive parental practices like parent involvement and parental monitoring on children's development (Cauffman & Steinberg, 1995). At an even higher level of the environmental structure, we see that the impact of father absence during an individual's childhood will vary, depending on the overall extent of father absence as a function of factors like compulsory military service during wartime (Grundman, 1996).

One potential mechanism underlying moderation occurs when value systems change the meaning of proximal environmental variables. For example, American adolescents perceive high parental control in a negative fashion, whereas Chinese adolescents view the same level of control as an appropriate means for parents to promote traditional cultural goals like family organization and cohesion (Lau & Cheung, 1987). The degree of incongruity between what schools demand of the child and the behavioral patterns taught in the child's home is another mechanism by which higher order moderation of proximal processes can occur. For example, a typical North American classroom based on teacher control of participation, low levels of peer interaction, and a requirement of individual verbal presentations will be particularly problematical for children coming from Native

American or Hawaiian homes, where peer interactions are an important means of learning and young children are given the opportunity to participate or not as they wish (Weinstein, 1991).

What must also be emphasized, given the nature of the environmental system illustrated in Figure 6-1, is that environmental moderation is bidirectional in nature, going up as well as down the hierarchy (Wachs, 1992). Although evidence is limited, some studies do show how higher order environmental influences can be moderated by microsystem characteristics. For example, the detrimental impact of macrosystem stressors like sectarian conflict, poverty, or societal violence can be attenuated when the child's proximal family environment is supportive and when sensitive, responsive caregiving practices are used (Bradley et al., 1994; Dawes, 1990; Masten et al., 1990). Similarly, although high social support has been shown to attenuate the detrimental impact of crowding on individual psychological distress, high-density living in turn erodes the individual's level of social support (Evans, Palsane, Lepore, & Martin, 1989; Lepore, Evans, & Schneider, 1991).

Specificity Of Environmental Action

Earlier in this chapter, I noted the possibility that what have been called nonshared environmental influences may simply reflect the operation of a broader process of environmental action, namely environmental specificity (Wachs, 1992). As originally conceived, environmental specificity assumes that environmental influences are relatively specific in nature, such that different aspects of development are influenced by different aspects of the environment (Wachs & Gruen, 1982). An illustration of the weak and strong forms of environmental specificity are shown in Figure 6-2. Examples of environmental specificity are shown in Table 6-4. (For a more detailed review of environmental specificity, see Wachs, 1992.) More recently, the concept of specificity has been extended to the process level, on the basis of the hypothesis that different proximal environmental processes may underlie development in different domains or different contexts (Wachs, 1996b). Examples of process specificity also are shown in Table 6-4.

Both environmental and process specificity may underlie proximal environmental contributions to variability in individual behavior and development. Given that the environment appears to function in a relatively specific fashion, unique individual developmental patterns can occur as a function of the unique environmental characteristics encountered by individuals.

Critical Proximal Processes Covary

If proximal processes are the "engines" that drive development (Bronfenbrenner & Ceci, 1994), one major reason why is because critical proximal processes tend to covary. Such covariance means that the impact of a specific proximal influence will be strengthened by the cumulative im-

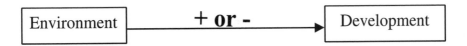

Conditional Specificity

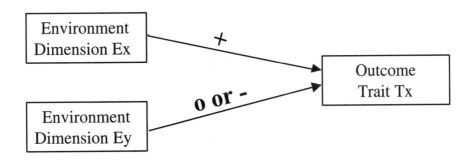

Strong Specificity

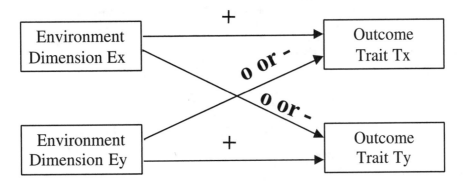

+ = positive influence
- = negative influence
0 = no influence

Figure 6-2. Illustration of weak and strong forms of environmental specificity. Ex and Ey refer to two different environmental dimensions. Tx and Ty refer to two different outcome dimensions.

TABLE 6-4
Examples of Environmental and Process Specificity

Domain	Findings	Reference
Family environment	Variability in maternal language related to level of toddler language but not to toddler play; variability in maternal play behavior related to variability in toddler play level but not to toddler language.	Tamis-LeMonda & Bornstein (1994)
	Caregiver verbal behavior related to variability in toddler language but not to amount of toddler distress; caregiver responsivity to distress related to level of toddler distress but not to toddler language.	Wachs et al. (1993)
Nonfamily environment	Number of adults in child social network related to complexity of child's speech, whereas number of peers in network related to amount of child's social use of speech.	Salzinger (1990)
	Relative salience of neighborhood characteristics versus kin network varies, depending on whether outcome involves antisocial behavior or academic competence.	Cochran & Bo (1989)
	Schools that facilitate academic achievement are not necessarily those that facilitate behavioral or emotional adjustment.	Maughn (1994)
	For children in high-risk families, residence in a good neighborhood decreases the likelihood of aggressive behavior and increases the likelihood of peer rejection.	Kupersmidt, Griesler, DeRosier, Patterson, & Davis (1995)
Process specificity	Whether later developmental outcomes are a function of early, later, or cumulative experiences depends on the outcome dimension.	Bradley, Caldwell, & Rock (1988)
	Depending on the outcome dimension, behavioral variability related to single main effect, two-variable additive coaction, or nonlinear interactions.	Bendersky & Lewis (1994)
	Level of associations between child adjustment and child characteristics, family characteristics, or transactional processes depends on the nature of family orientation.	Mink & Nihara (1986)

pact of similar covarying proximal influences. The covarying nature of proximal processes is most clearly seen in evidence indicating that environmental risk and protective factors rarely occur in isolation. Rather, exposure to a specific risk or protective factor often means a higher probability of exposure to other proximal risk or protective factors as well (Wachs, 1992). For example, children experiencing one negative family life event over the previous 12 months (e.g., parental divorce) were two times more likely to experience peer rejection than children not exposed to such family risk factors; children encountering two negative family life stressors in this time period were three times more likely to experience peer rejection (Patterson et al., 1992). Similarly, children whose parents use negative disciplinary styles, such as poor monitoring and coercive discipline, have a greater likelihood of being in peer groups that are primarily antisocial in nature (Cooper & Cooper, 1992; Dishion, Patterson, Stoobmiller, & Skinner, 1991; Hartup & van Lieshout, 1995). Linkages between environmental chaos and poor-quality caregiver–child relationship patterns have been described earlier.

On the protective side, adolescents whose parents use authoritative rearing styles are more likely to have friends whose parents also use authoritative rearing styles (Fletcher et al., 1995). To the extent that peer-group characteristics mirror the nature of parent–child relations (Brown et al., 1993), children will be getting similar types of messages on appropriate values, goals, and behaviors from both parents and peers.

The cumulative impact of covarying proximal environmental sources is shown in studies documenting how poorer developmental outcomes are more likely to occur as increasing numbers of risk factors impinge on the individual (Magyary et al., 1992; Sameroff, 1994; Sameroff, Seifer, Barocas, Zax, & Greenspan, 1987; Sameroff, Seifer, Baldwin, & Baldwin, 1993). In addition, stabilization of proximal environmental influences can occur when covariance between different proximal dimensions means that information a child has received from one source will be reinforced by similar types of information from other sources (Super & Harkness, 1986b).

Proximal Environmental Factors Also Operate Across Time

Under some conditions, early proximal experiences can have long-term consequences, even after controlling for the impact of subsequent proximal processes. For example, early parental disruption (marital separation, family discord) in the first 2 years of life can be directly linked to later problems in adult adjustment, over and above the impact of later experiences (Rutter et al., 1990). Similarly, conditions associated with differences in early attachment status have been found to be associated with differences in social competence and peer relationships well past the infancy period (Sroufe & Egeland, 1991). In other situations, long-term consequences occur as a function of proximal experiences cumulating over time (Rutter & Rutter, 1992). For example, evidence on the differential impact of chronic versus acute environmental stressors on children's behavior problems (Bolger, Patterson, Thompson, & Kupersmidt, 1995) or on the impact of regular cyclical periods of disruption in maternal behavior (e.g., maternal depression) on subsequent offspring adjustment (Radke-Yarrow et al., 1994) illustrate the consequences that occur as proximal processes cumulate over time.

There are a variety of mechanisms underlying the action of proximal environmental influences operating over time. One such mechanism is *anticipatory socialization* (Corsaro & Rizzo, 1988). This mechanism refers to situations where children acquire values and behavioral patterns that mirror the values and behavioral patterns of the adult world they will enter into later in life. The source of such anticipatory socialization is usually the child's play patterns in their peer group, which often are characterized by activities and interactions commonly seen among adults in the child's culture. By allowing the child to practice and ultimately to make sense of adult routines, the peer group serves as the child's bridge to the adult world.

Another potential mechanism is *temporal moderation*, such that the impact of later proximal experiences may depend on the nature of prior proximal experiences. For example, the same level of concurrent stress may be associated with positive outcomes in individuals with a positive developmental history and negative outcomes in individuals with a troubled developmental history (Gore & Eckenrode, 1994).

A third potential mechanism consists of *spiraling processes* that escalate positively or negatively over time. Both negative and positive spiraling can be seen as examples of "causal chain" models (Rutter & Rutter, 1992). In causal chain models, the impact of early proximal experiences can be accentuated or attenuated, depending on what happens to the individual across the life course. However, the nature of prior experiences increases the probability that the individual will encounter certain types of later experiences. One classic example of negative spiraling is seen in situations where angry, coercive, inconsistent parental discipline patterns lead to mutually coercive spirals of negative parent–child interactions. Such negative interactions can not only escalate over time in intensity and frequency, but they also can spill out to adversely affect the nature of the child's relations with peers, leading to an increased probability of long-term antisocial behavior patterns (G. Patterson & Bank, 1989; Rubin et al., 1990).

In contrast, positive spiraling can occur when early environmental interventions act to promote the child's initial school success. One consequence of initial school success is teachers' having higher expectations of the child's scholastic ability, which in turn can act to increase the probability of later academic success (Maughn, 1994). A particularly striking demonstration of the potential power of positive educational spiraling processes can be seen in a long-term follow-up study of 60 children attending an urban school of very low quality, who were randomly assigned to one of three first-grade teachers (Pedersen, Faucher, & Eaton, 1978). Nearly 60% of first graders initially assigned to one specific teacher subsequently completed more than 10 years of education, compared with just over 40% of pupils assigned to the other two teachers. More than two-thirds of the children who happened to be assigned to the facilitative first-grade teacher had high levels of occupational success, compared with less than 40% of the children who had been assigned to the other two teachers. The potential operation of positive spiraling is supported by teacher records in later school years, where children coming from the facilitative first-grade class were consistently rated as higher in effort than were children coming from the other two classes. Of interest is that although most of the children in the sample who were assigned to the other first-grade teachers remembered little about these teachers, every one of the children assigned to the facilitative teacher had strong and positive memories about this teacher 25 years later.

Proximal Environmental Influences Are Probabilistic In Nature

Although many of the mechanisms just described can act to strengthen and stabilize the impact of proximal processes, ultimately the impact of proximal processes is probabilistic in nature. For example, the long-term impact of early psychosocial adversity on female adult adjustment will vary as a function of the characteristics of subsequent influences, including whether childhood school experiences were positive or negative in nature and the quality of the individual's marital relationship after school (Rutter, 1988). Similarly, Engfer et al. (1994) have documented how potential linkages between peer rejection and subsequent problematical outcomes can be broken by naturally occurring ecological shifts, such as the child's transferring to a new school where his or her previous peer history is unknown. Even in extreme cases involving severe proximal trauma, the probabilistic nature of proximal influences holds out the hope that such trauma can be partially offset by later positive experiences. In one of the most dramatic examples of this process, Kinzie, Sack, Angell, Manson, & Rath, (1986) assessed the adjustment level of Cambodian adolescents who had spent 4 years of their childhood in concentration camps during the Pol Pot era. The impact of this incredibly stressful childhood experience on subsequent adjustment depended partly on the child's later family placement. Specifically, for those children who subsequently moved to the United States and were reunited with their biological families, only 46% were considered to have behavioral difficulties, as compared with 90% who lived either with foster families or on their own after migration to the United States.

At this point, readers may have detected a curious phenomenon, namely that certain early proximal processes appear to have long-term consequences over and above the impact of subsequent proximal experiences, whereas other early proximal processes function as part of a causal chain, with their influence depending on the nature of subsequent proximal experiences. This distinction leads to the question, What conditions lead to some early proximal experiences being uniquely associated with long-term effects? Common to many explanations is the idea that some proximal early experiences contain self-stabilizing components that act to maintain their impact over time. For example, Hinde (1989) has argued that the impact of early proximal experiences are more likely to be maintained if they provide individuals with information about what they can expect from the environment later in life. Through encountering such information, individuals may develop in ways that anticipate their encountering certain types of environments later in life. (Also see discussion in chap. 5 on internal working models.) Evidence of the potential long-term impact of experiences producing secure attachments may be one example of how these types of self-maintaining expectancies may operate over time (Sroufe & Egeland, 1991). Similarly, being a victim of school bullies in the middle grades may act to promote a negative view of the world and a lower sense of self-esteem. Such self-maintaining worldviews may carry the negative impact of early victimization into the adult years, even when the individual is no longer being victimized (Olweus, 1993). Exposure to moderate levels of early stress that the child can successfully handle may act to make children more stress resistant (Rutter & Pickles, 1991), perhaps as a function of such children becoming more sensitized to or more active in searching out positive or supportive aspects of their environment (Sroufe et al., 1990). Although these types of self-stabilizing mechanisms are cumulative in nature, the source of the cumulation is the individual's acting on or interpreting his or her early proximal environment.

Proximal Environmental Influences: Necessary But Not Sufficient

Up to this point, I have shown that proximal environmental influences can act to influence variability in individual behavioral development, which specific proximal influences promote individual variability, and the processes underlying the contributions of proximal environmental variables to individual behavioral–developmental variability. The evidence cited illustrates why proximal environmental factors are a necessary influence. However, available evidence also illustrates why proximal environmental influences, in and of themselves, cannot be considered sufficient. Part of the reason for this conclusion is based on the probabilistic nature of proximal environmental influences, as discussed earlier. In addition, four additional points are critical for understanding why I view proximal environmental influences as necessary but not sufficient: (a) The impact of proximal environmental influences can be moderated by higher order contextual factors, (b) proximal environmental influences covary with a variety of nonenvironmental influences that also can act to influence behavioral developmental variability, (c) proximal environmental processes are transactional, and (d) proximal environmental influences can interact with a variety of nonenvironmental influences, such that similar proximal environmental influences may produce different outcomes for different individuals with different characteristics.

Higher Order Moderators

As noted earlier in this chapter, proximal environmental processes are nested within a hierarchical environmental system encompassing higher order cultural, demographic, and contextual characteristics (see Figure 6-1). By being part of such a network, the impact of proximal environmental factors on individual developmental variability can be moderated by the action of higher order nonproximal contextual influences, such as cultural, ethnic, or social-class membership. For example, the positive benefits of authoritative parenting on children's academic achievement can vary as a function of ethnic group membership, with different patterns found for Caucasian Americans, African Americans, and Asian Americans (Steinberg, Dornbusch, & Brown, 1992). Ethnic group membership also can act to moderate linkages between parental disciplinary strategies and children's acting out behavior (Deater-Deckerd, Dodge, Bates, & Pettit, 1996). Similarly, although parent–child interaction patterns act as the link between maternal depression and children's externalizing disorders in Caucasian American families, a parallel linkage is not seen in African American families (Harnish, Dodge, & Valente, 1995). Social-class differences also can function as moderators, as seen in evidence indicating a greater facilitative effect of attending a developmentally oriented day care center for children from groups of lower rather than higher socioeconomic status groups (Caughy et al., 1994). Alternatively, different cultures may offer alternative pathways to a specific developmental outcome. For example, although adult scaffolding has been seen as an essential proximal process in terms of children's learning object and verbal skills, there are some cultures (e.g., Kung San) in which parental scaffolding is not evident and yet children develop appropriate object and verbal skills (Bakeman, Adamson, Konner, & Barr, 1990). All of the evidence just presented is illustrative of how the impact of proximal environmental factors on individual developmental variability depends, in part, on the nature and operation of higher order contextual characteristics.

Covariance

As discussed in previous chapters, one of the major reasons why nutritional or biomedical factors, genetic background, or individual characteristics are viewed as necessary but not sufficient is because these individual influences covary with other influences that also can affect individual behavioral–developmental variability. The same probabilistic covariance also holds in regard to proximal environmental influences (Wachs, 1992). For example, given that children receive both genes and environments from their parents, there is a built-in covariance between genetic and environmental influences (Braungart, Fulker, & Plomin, 1992; Plomin, 1994). Thus, children whose parents suffer from major psychological disturbances like schizophrenia are more likely to receive both "risk" genes for schizophrenia and inadequate or inappropriate treatment from their mentally ill parents (Walker, Downey, & Bergman, 1989). Covariances between inadequate proximal environments and nutritional deficiencies (Pollitt, 1988; Powell & Grantham-McGregor, 1985), an increased risk of childhood morbidity (Joffe, 1982), and greater exposure to environmental toxins (Schroeder & Hawk, 1987) also have been documented. In addition, proximal environmental factors can covary with a variety of individual characteristics that also can influence subsequent individual developmental–behavioral variability. For example, in chapter 5 I reviewed evidence indicating the importance of early-appearing antisocial behavior patterns for later developmental outcomes. Children with antisocial behavioral patterns are far more likely to receive harsh discipline (Elder & Caspi, 1988) and lower levels of support from their families (Stice & Barrera, 1995), and they also are more likely to be in peer groups characterized by a high proportion of other children with antisocial characteristics (Caspi et al., 1993).

The covariance between proximal environmental and nonenvironmental characteristics means that relations between environmental influences and subsequent individual behavioral–developmental variability must be interpreted within a framework of environmental covariance rather than main-effect environmental influences. An environmental covariance framework means that any discussion of environmental influences on behavioral developmental variability will be incomplete without simultaneous consideration of the actions of covarying nonenvironmental factors. Within such a framework, developmental variability is best viewed as a function of the covariance among multiple developmental elements, rather than as being due to the actions of just one of these elements (Wachs, 1996c). It is in this sense that covariance means that environmental influences, although necessary, are not sufficient.

Transactional Processes

Organism–environment covariances operating over time become bidirectional transactional processes. When transactional processes are operating, the proximal environment influences the course of individual developmental and behavioral variability, but changes in individual behavioral development in turn influence subsequent variability in the proximal environment (Sameroff & Fiese, 1990). Individual characteristics that have been shown to influence variability in proximal environmental characteristics include difficult temperament (Maccoby, Snow, & Jacklin, 1984), aggressive behavior (Moffitt, 1993), gender and physical appearance (Hoffman, 1991), inhibited behavioral patterns (R. Bell & Chapman, 1986; Gersten,

1989), sociability (Pianta, Sroufe, & Egeland, 1989), attachment status (Elicker et al., 1992), and social competence (Kuczynski & Kochanska, 1995; Mink & Nihara, 1986). Transactional linkages from child characteristics to the environment may be particularly critical for so called "resilient" children, who are reared under extremely disadvantaged circumstances and yet display adequate or more than adequate developmental outcomes. Resilient children typically are found to have a specific set of individual characteristics, including high social skills, cognitive competence, and a strong sense of self-esteem (Wachs, 1992). Children with these characteristics not only are less likely to be the target of parental anger or abuse (Hetherington, 1989) but are also more able to elicit whatever psychological resources are available in their extremely dysfunctional families, even when availability of these resources is minimal (Radke-Yarrow & Sherman, 1990).

In understanding the nature of transactional processes, it is essential to avoid the fallacy that because children's individual characteristics can influence their subsequent environment, all environmental influences really are due to variability in individual characteristics (Scarr, 1992). In part this viewpoint is fallacious because the influence of individual characteristics on the individual's subsequent proximal environment is truly probabilistic in nature. For example, although children with a difficult temperament have a higher probability of eliciting negative reactions from their parents, other influences, such as parental anxiety level, child rearing experience, and preference for individual child characteristics, can serve to accentuate or attenuate linkages between a difficult temperament and the environment (Slabach et al., 1991). Even more critically, although individual characteristics can serve to influence the nature of the individual's subsequent environment, environmental changes in turn can act to influence the subsequent development of individual characteristics (Wachs, 1996b). For example, although a high level of individual academic self-esteem can foster school achievement, academic achievement in turn can foster greater academic self-esteem (Maughn, 1994). For many developmental outcomes, a mutual influences model, encompassing both child and environmental characteristics, provides a far more powerful explanation of developmental variability than do models based just on child or environmental effects per se (Ge, Conger et al., 1996; Stice & Barrera, 1995).

Organism–Environment Interaction

Proximal environmental and individual characteristics also can interact so that the same proximal environmental influence may have radically different effects, depending on the characteristics of the individual. Although the study of interactions between organism and environment is both conceptually and methodologically complex, certain consistencies do appear (Wachs & Plomin, 1991). Individual characteristics that have been

TABLE 6-5
Examples of Specific Organism–Environment Interaction

Individual Characteristic	Interaction Pattern	Reference
Family biosocial-risk history	Children of schizophrenic parents more adversely affected by maltreatment or deviant family communication than children of non-schizophrenic parents.	Goldstein (1988), Walker et al. (1989)
Gender	Schools or family environments that are well structured are more protective for boys than for girls who are at developmental risk.	Brody & Flor (1997), Werner (1990)
	Boys more reactive than girls to parental loss and to aggressive cues.	Levy-Shiff (1982), Quinton (1994)
Temperament	Difficult-temperament children show more negative reactivity under stress than easy children.	Hetherington (1989)
	Different discipline styles needed for inhibited and uninhibited children.	Kochanska (1993)

shown to interact with the proximal environment include biosocial risk history, gender, and temperament (Wachs, 1992). Examples of these types of organism–environment interaction are shown in Table 6-5.

Interactions between organism and environment mean that although both organism and environmental characteristics are necessary, neither can be viewed as sufficient. Like organism–environment covariance, higher order contextual influences, and transactional processes, organism–environment interactions serve both to promote individual behavioral variability and to limit the role of environment to a necessary but not sufficient influence.

CONCLUSIONS

The fact that proximal environmental influences are necessary but not sufficient is a major reason why some children living in violent proximal environments turn out to be nonviolent and some children living in warm, supportive environments turn out to have highly violent antisocial personalities (Hartup & van Lieshout, 1995), or why the same level of stress is developmentally facilitative for some children but has major negative developmental consequences for other children (Aldwin & Stokols, 1988). As with all other influences discussed in this volume, a satisfactory explanation of complex developmental outcomes occurs only when we view individual influences, such as proximal environmental processes, as part of a complex, multilevel system wherein all of the elements of this system are necessary but none is sufficient.

7

DISTAL ENVIRONMENTAL
INFLUENCES

Under the heading of distal environmental influences are included cultural and subcultural characteristics, societal institutions, societal disruptions, place of residence, social class, and parental work situation or social support networks. These characteristics fit within Bronfenbrenner's structural model (see Figure 6-1) under the headings of exosystem and macrosystem influences. Although each of these domains will be reviewed individually, it is important to remember that some social scientists question the legitimacy of "unpackaging" higher order dimensions such as culture into individual elements, arguing that distal environmental influences are best viewed as a prevasive "medium" within which the individual functions (Cole, 1992; Super & Harkness, 1999). Although this chapter will not attempt to settle this longstanding debate, two aspects of the operation of higher order distal environmental influences need to be stressed at the outset.

First, there are clearly social–cultural group differences in values, goals, beliefs, and actions (Odum, 1983; Super & Harkness, 1999; Weisner, Matheson, & Bernheimer, 1996; Whiting, 1980). However, even within a given social cultural group, we typically find moderate to high levels of intragroup variability in values, goals, beliefs, and actions (Fogel, 1993;

Quinton, 1994; Slaughter-DeFoe et al., 1990). Variability within higher order distal environmental contexts may be one reason why we find high levels of intraindividual variability coexisting with significant intercultural differences in outcomes like infant attachment (van Ijzendoorn & Kronenberge, 1988).

Second, implicit in many definitions of higher order distal environmental influences is the idea that these influences will remain stable across generations (Bronfenbrenner, 1989; Cole, 1992; Roopnarine et al., 1992). In some cases, once viable traditional cultural practices like polygamy and high population growth continue to be maintained, even in the face of changing ecological conditions that result in these practices being associated with highly detrimental outcomes like overcrowding, child malnutrition, and increased poverty (LeVine & LeVine, 1988). However, generational shifts in a variety of cultural practices and values also have been documented. Such shifts encompass changes concerning respect and obedience to elders (Edwards, 1992; Liddell, Kvalsvig, Shabalala, & Masilela, 1991), belief in the appropriateness of education for women (Stromquist, 1989), feeding practices (Howrigan, 1988), parents' values and goals for their children (Lee & Zhan, 1991), and degree of tolerance for individual autonomy (Kagitcibasi, 1989). Conditions that result in generational shifts in the nature of higher order distal environmental characteristics include changing economic conditions (Roopnarine et al., 1992; Stromquist, 1989), political changes such as the Chinese cultural revolution (Lee & Zahn, 1991), changes in climatological conditions (LeVine, 1988), and migration of people or ideas into a different culture (Cavalli-Svorza & Feldman, 1981).

One potential consequence of cross-generational shifts in higher order distal environmental characteristics is embodied in the conclusion that cultural evolution may be more important for current changes in the human species than is traditional Darwinian evolution. This conclusion is based on the assumption that modifications of complex population traits are spread faster under conditions of cultural evolution than under conditions governing traditional Darwinian evolution (Gould, 1980). It is surprising that some of the strongest evidence for this line of reasoning comes from studies on the operation of "cultural transmission" processes in infrahuman populations, documenting how a new discovery by one member of a species can spread throughout the population at a rate that far exceeds what can be explained by natural selection. Examples include population-scale changes in bird behavior following the discovery by individual birds of how to open milk bottles with their beaks, or changes in the behavior of primate groups following discovery by an individual animal of how to wash sweet potatoes (Slater, 1983). Implications of intragroup variability, cultural stability, and generational shifts will be considered later in this chapter.

In the following section of this chapter, I will discuss the types of distal environmental characteristics that have the potential to influence population and individual developmental variability. This section will be followed by a discussion of mechanisms underlying the translation of variability in higher order distal environmental characteristics to behavioral and developmental variability, at both the group and individual levels.

DIMENSIONS OF THE DISTAL ENVIRONMENT

Culture

Like intelligence and temperament, culture is one of those domains that, although widely emphasized, seems to resist precise definition (Super & Harkness, 1999). Rather than going into the intricacies of definition, I will use a working definition of culture, as suggested by Quinton (1994, p. 159): ". . . beliefs, conventions or approved behaviors and symbolic representations that are shared by a group of people, have some persistence over time and are transmitted to new members of a society or institution." In addition to aspects of culture encompassed by this definition, I also include acculturation processes involving contact between different cultures, which result in population and individual changes in culturally driven values, beliefs, and behaviors in one or both cultures (Berry, 1990).

A discussion of all the differences in specific behavioral developmental outcomes associated with variability in cultural characteristics could well fill this volume and several others as well. Examples of outcome differences related to cultural differences are seen in Table 7-1. As a specific example of cultural influences, let us consider cross-cultural differences in self-concept and values. A major distinction in this area is between cultures that focus on collectivistic values versus cultures that are individualistic in orientation (Tietjen, 1989; Triandis, 1990). Collectivistic cultures emphasize that the needs of the family or kin group take precedence over the needs of the individual, stress close physical and psychological proximity to others in the family or kin group, and define an individual's worth as a function of his or her social role. Thus, when individuals in collectivistic cultures are asked to define who they are, their answers often are tied into family or kin terms (e.g., "I am the child of X"). In contrast, in individualistic cultures, the interests of the individual are thought to transcend those of the family or kin group. In these cultures physical and psychological distance from others is encouraged, and a person's worth is seen as a function of his or her individual characteristics. When asked the same question, a person from this type of culture is more likely to reply using individual attributes (e.g., "I am a highly motivated person").

TABLE 7-1
Examples of Outcome Variability Associated With Distal Environmental Dimensions

Distal dimension	Outcome	References
Culture	Value preferences	Bonta (1997); Chen et al. (1998); Feldman et al. (1991)
	Specific intellectual skills or cognitive style	Dasen, (1984); Witkin & Berry (1975)
	Level of academic achievement	Chen & Stevenson (1995)
	Infant and child play behavior patterns	Gaskin (1996); Sutton-Smith & Roberts (1980)
	Child rearing patterns	Bonta (1997); Hewlett et al. (1998)
	Occupational patterns	Weisner & Wilson-Mitchell (1990)
	Long-term consequences of individual differences in temperament	Kerr, Lambert, & Bem (1996)
	Changes in weaving patterns, female education level and level of child neglect associated with acculturation	Bevers (1986); Greenfield & Childs (1991)
Minority status	Biomedical problems	Kleinman (1992)
	Level of educational achievement	Alexander & Entwisle (1994)
	Risk of illegal drug abuse	Nettles & Pleck (1994)
	Exposure to discrimination and residential segregation	Garcia-Coll et al. (1996)
Urban–rural residence	Cognitive processing strategies	Sinha (1988); Wagner (1978)
	Academic achievement	Falbo & Poston (1993); Stromquist (1989)
	Gender differentiation	Best & Williams (1993)
	Physical growth	Falbo & Poston (1993)
	Behavior problem incidence	Liddell et al. (1994); Rutter et al. (1974)
	Parent teaching strategies	Levy (1996)
Socioeconomic status	Academic achievement and school dropout rates	Roth (1995); White (1982)
	Parental expectations and values	Hess et al. (1980); Schooler (1999)
	Parental disciplinary strategies	Mills & Rubin (1993)
	Family relationship patterns	Brody, Stoneman, & Flor (1996)

TABLE 7-1 (*continued*)

Distal dimension	Outcome	References
Societal disruption	Risk of behavioral, adjustment, mental health, or learning problems	Kostelny & Garbarino (1994); Liddell et al. (1994); Punamaki, Qouta, & Sarraj (1997); Sack, Clarke, & Seeley (1996)
	Disruption in family function	Nicassio (1985); Williams & Berry (1991)
Parental work characteristics	Child characteristics valued by parents	Crouter & McHale (1993)
	Time parents can spend with their children	Crouter & McHale (1993); Liddell et al. (1991)
	Parental disciplinary strategies	Crockenberg & Litman (1991)
	Family social network characteristics	Cotterell (1986); Tietjen (1989)
School attendance	Individual cognitive performance levels	Ceci (1991); Dasen (1984); Morrison, Smith, & Dow-Ehrensberger (1995); Maughn (1994); G. Sinha (1988); Stevenson et al. (1978); Wachs et al. (1996)
	Gains in cognitive performance following nutritional supplementation	Pollitt et al. (1993)
Social support networks	Parental physical and mental health	Boyce & Jemerin (1990); Dubois et al. (1994); Homel, Burns, & Goodnow (1987); Simons et al. (1993)
	Parental child rearing strategies	Cotterell (1986); Mills & Rubin (1993)
	Risk of child abuse	Bevers (1986); Garbarino & Sherman (1980)
	Sense of control over life events	Sandler et al. (1989)

Minority Status

One aspect of the heterogeneous nature of culture is whether an individual is part of a cultural majority or of a minority or subcultural group within a given culture. In developed countries, being a member of certain minority groups is associated with higher biological and psychosocial risk, as shown in Table 7-1. However, subcultural disadvantage is not a problem that is unique to developed countries. For example, in some third-world countries, low religious caste status confers some of the same disadvantages as does being Black in the United States (Ogbu, 1983). Nor is minority status per se necessarily associated with a greater risk of disadvantage. In spite of similar levels of poverty and low education, Hispanic American and Native American infants have birth weights that are comparable to those of the majority White population (Kleinman, 1992), whereas Hispanic American adolescents are found to have greater levels of parental support and lower levels of parental conflict during puberty than are Anglo American adolescents (Molina & Chassin, 1996). One critical factor moderating the impact of minority status is the different types of adaptive behavior strategies used by children in different minority groups as a way of dealing with the majority culture (Garcia-Coll et al., 1996; Harrison et al., 1990). These issues will be explored later in this chapter.

Place of Residence

Although traditional cultural values are more likely to be found in rural than in urban populations (Rosenthal et al., 1989), urbanization may be a particularly salient acculturation force, particularly given the accelerating pace of population shift from rural to urban areas (e.g., in the 19th century less than 3% of the world's population lived in urban areas, as compared with current levels of more than 43% of the world's population; Quinton, 1994). Developmental–behavioral differences as a function of urban versus rural residence have been found in a variety of domains as shown in Table 7-1.

Although there is ample evidence for the influence of urban versus rural residency on a variety of behavioral developmental outcomes, what also is becoming increasingly apparent is that such global dichotomies may be less useful than more specific residential distinctions (Liddell et al., 1994). For example, Black South African children reared in their rural native homeland were found to be higher in physical stature, vocabulary, mathematical skills, and self-concept than were Black South African children living on rural farms owned by Whites (Goduka, Poole, & Aotaki-Phenice, 1992). Similarly, differences in children's aggressive behavior were found to be associated with variability in the level of ambient violence in the different rural villages in which these children resided (Fry, 1988). Such critical distinctions would be lost if only global urban–rural distinctions were used as the prime means of classifying residence.

Another more precise approach to residential classification is at the level of the neighborhood. Even when children are matched for overall socioeconomic level, it has been found that living in lower quality or more dangerous neighborhoods can adversely affect the extent of their social networks and can accentuate the negative impact of existing family problems (Garbarino & Sherman, 1980; Tietjen, 1989). Even living in a more adequate neighborhood that is in close proximity to a poor-quality neighborhood can have detrimental consequences, as shown in higher levels of child abuse and neglect in areas near poor-quality neighborhoods (Coulton, Korbin, Su, & Chow, 1995).

Socioeconomic Status

Socioeconomic status (SES) traditionally is defined by a complex grouping of family income, occupational, and educational characteristics. Variability in SES has been related to a variety of developmental outcomes, as also seen in Table 7-1. The relation of social class to developmental behavioral variability is not limited just to individuals living in developed Western countries, as seen in evidence relating family income level to the extent of schooling for women in less developed countries (Stromquist, 1989) and evidence relating low family SES to greater exposure to war trauma and a greater risk of war-related injuries in Lebanon (Aber, 1994).

Particularly for children living under poverty conditions, there is decreased access to educational, social, and health care resources, coupled with an increased risk of problematical family relationship patterns (Garbarino, 1990; Karp, 1993; Sampson & Laub, 1984). It is not surprising that children living in poverty are at increased risk for a variety of negative developmental outcomes (Aber, 1994), particularly if the poverty conditions are chronic (McLeod & Shanahan, 1993). On the other hand, it is important to note that outcomes associated with living in poverty are not invariably negative. For example, at least for some individuals, growing up under conditions of widespread economic disruption (e.g., the Great Depression of the 1930s) resulted in the development of an increased sense of responsibility and industry (Elder, 1974).

Societal Disruption

Large numbers of the world's population may be at risk due to major societal disruption associated with warfare, political violence, or enforced-migration. It has been estimated that within the past decade more than 5.5 million children have been killed or physically injured by armed conflict and more than 15 million children below the age of 15 have been forced to migrate (Ladd & Cairns, 1996). Both families and children who are faced with involuntary migration and consequent residence in refugee camps as a result of massive societal disruptions like warfare or political–religious violence are at significantly greater risk for a variety of negative developmental outcomes, as shown in Table 7-1. In considering the impact of social disruption, two points need to be kept in mind. First, some researchers argue that although there may be short-term adjustment problems, over time children and their families can adapt and adjust to chronic political or sectarian violence (Cairns & Dawes, 1996; Cairns & Wilson, 1989; McWhirter & Trew, 1982). Whether there are long-term developmental consequences of societal disruption may depend on the level of chronicity or severity of violence to which children are exposed (Dawes, 1990) as well as on the degree to which there are indirect consequences of community violence, such as closing of schools (Liddell, Kemp, & Moema, 1993) or an erosion of parent–child relations (Punamaki et al., 1997). Second, in some non-Western cultures where women traditionally have fewer opportunities, violent societal disruptions may lead to greater opportunities for female independence, which in turn may result in greater female resilience in these types of situations (Garbarino & Kostelny, 1996).

Economic and Work Characteristics

Economic conditions and parental work characteristics are one example of an *exosystem* dimension in Bronfenbrenner's structural model, an aspect of the environment that can affect a child's development but one in which he or she is not directly involved. Parental unemployment has been repeatedly shown to act as a major family stressor, resulting in a variety of potentially detrimental outcomes both at the family and the individual levels (Garbarino, 1990). For example, economic stress caused by unemployment or underemployment of family members can result in greater family disorganization and a greater likelihood of detrimental child rearing strategies (Brody et al., 1994, 1996; Bryant & DeMorris, 1992; Conger et al., 1992, 1994; Elder et al., 1985; McLeod & Shanahan, 1993; Simons et al., 1993).

Parental work characteristics also can affect parental beliefs and values, which in turn can translate into variability in children's behavioral development (see chap. 6). In less developed countries, population groups involved in hunter–gatherer activities are more likely to stress independence and self-reliance and agrarian groups are more likely to stress social conformity and responsibility (Witkin & Berry, 1975). In developed countries, a variety of outcomes are associated with variability in parental work characteristics, as shown in Table 7-1.

Multilevel linkages between different levels of the distal environment also can be documented. For example, the impact of employment conditions can be moderated by a variety of culturally driven practices such as the time normally spent by fathers with their children and the activities fathers typically use when interacting with their children in a given culture (Liddell et al., 1991; Roopnarine et al., 1992).

Schooling

In chapter 6 I discussed the impact of specific school characteristics as influences on individual behavioral–developmental variability. In this chapter, schools are viewed at a more distal level, namely the impact of schooling per se, over and above specific characteristics of the school itself. Evidence cited in Table 7-1 indicates that, both in developed and less developed countries, the more education attained, the higher the individual's level of cognitive performance. Results also indicate that the impact of school attendance on cognitive performance tends to be task specific, with school-attendance influences being more likely to be shown on more abstract cognitive skills (such as understanding of classification principles) or for more school-related skills like arithmetic (Sharp, Cole, & Lave, 1979; Wagner, 1978).

Maternal education may be of particular importance for offspring survival and development in less developed countries. In these countries, level of maternal education is negatively related to family birth rates (Werner, 1988) and positively related to a mother's use of medical care during pregnancy, aspirations for her children, and responsivity to her children's behavior (LeVine et al., 1996). Higher levels of maternal education also are positively related to children's level of early language development (LeVine et al., 1996), physical growth (Aboud & Alemu, 1995; Engle et al., 1996), children's survival rates (Bicego & Boerma, 1993; Sandiford, Cassel, Sanchez, & Coldham, 1997), and the quality of children's diets (Wachs, McCabe, Moussa, & Yunis, 1999). The influence of maternal schooling in less developed countries is particularly remarkable, given evidence showing how schools in many of these countries are characterized by overcrowded classrooms, few teaching materials available, poorly trained teachers, and high dropout rates (Gorman & Pollitt, 1992; Sharma, 1996).

Social Support Networks

Social support networks can function as a proximal environmental factor directly affecting a child, as in the case of community child care networks (Liddell et al., 1991) or the presence of a nonfamily adult who has a positive relation with a child who is at risk (Werner & Smith, 1992). Social support networks also can function as an exosystem factor, as in the case of social support for parents under stress. In this latter situation, the child may not directly experience the social support, but such support can positively affect either caregiver–child relationship patterns or caregiver characteristics that in turn influence caregiver–child relationship patterns. Consequences associated with availability of social support to parents are shown in Table 7-1. For the most part, having a social support network has beneficial consequences, as shown in the relation of higher levels of social support for mothers who are under stress and school adjustment for their children (Manetti & Schneider, 1996). However, research also suggests that the beneficial effects of social support for parents does not occur under all situations. Social support to parents may have little effect when there are few stressors on parents or when there are multiple covarying stressors that either overwhelm the buffering impact of social support or severely limit the parents' ability to make use of such support (Hetherington, 1989).

OUTCOMES ASSOCIATED WITH DISTAL ENVIRONMENTS: INFLUENCE OR COVARIATE?

The listing of potential distal environmental influences on behavioral–developmental variability does not directly address the issue of whether distal environmental influences are a necessary agent for promoting such variability. Population or subpopulation groups can differ not only in terms of cultural characteristics but also in terms of differences in the frequency of specific genes (Williams, 1980; Wolff, 1977), nutritional status, and nature and extent of disease incidence (LeVine, 1989). Behavioral–developmental differences associated with residential area may be a function of area environmental characteristics, or they may be related to area differences in nutritional status (Beaton, 1989; Falbo & Poston, 1993; Goduka et al., 1992). The impact of societal disruption may be due to the disorganization that invariably follows communal or secretarian violence, or it may be related to the higher incidence rates of disease and malnutrition associated with societal violence (Liddell et al., 1993). Changes in diet or disease patterns also could underlie what look like behavioral changes associated with societal shifts due to changes in economic support systems (Ackerman, 1971; Howrigan, 1988). Even distal influences like social support to parents may be understood more as a reflection of individual difference characteristics, such as the parent's ability to develop and maintain support networks (Belsky, 1990; Diener et al., 1995).

Given evidence on covariation between higher order distal environmental characteristics and nondistal influences, can we continue to maintain the argument that distal environmental influences are necessary for understanding developmental behavioral variability? On the basis of five different lines of evidence considered below, I will argue that higher order distal environmental characteristics are indeed necessary.

Unique Variance Associated With Distal Environmental Influences

Even when we statistically partial out the influence of proximal environmental factors, individual characteristics, and markers of risk status, there still remains a consistent body of evidence showing that unique predictive variance is associated with distal environmental predictors, including culture (Bornstein, Tal, & Tamis-LeMonda, 1991; Chen & Stevenson, 1995; Feldman & Rosenthal, 1991; Feldman, Rosenthal, et al., 1991; Pomerleau, Malcuit, & Sabatier, 1991); region of residence (Godkua et al., 1992; Roth, 1995), level of societal violence (Liddell et al., 1994); schooling (Ceci & Williams, 1997); and poverty (McLeod & Shanahan, 1993).

Unfortunately, too little evidence is available on the critical question of whether unique variance associated with distal environmental group membership remains after statistically controlling for the impact of biological influences. What little evidence is available on this question suggests that cultural (Liddell, 1988), schooling (Wachs et al., 1996), and regional (Liddell, 1994) differences do remain, even when population groups are equated on dietary base or access to food resources.

Distal Environmental Influences as a Moderator

Available evidence also indicates that distal environmental characteristics can act to moderate the extent and nature of relations between development and either biological influences or individual characteristics. One such line of evidence involves cultural influences moderating the functional consequences of individual differences in nutritional status (Beaton, 1989; Scrimshaw & Young, 1989). For example, the impact of nutritional intake on children's school behavior (Wachs et al., 1995) or on children's level of aggressive or prosocial behavior (Barrett, Radke-Yarrow, & Klein, 1982) will vary as a function of culturally based values related to appropriateness of specific child behavior patterns.

Higher order distal environmental factors also can act to moderate the influence of biologically based individual characteristics, including temperament (Chen et al., 1998; Super & Harkness, 1999); puberty (Molina & Chassin, 1996); parental genetic contributions to children's physical growth (Pollitt, 1995); developmental delay (Weisner et al., 1996); gender-based differential predisposition to aggression (Day & Ghandour, 1984; Farver & Frosch, 1996); and maternal depression (Harnish et al., 1995). In one of the most dramatic demonstrations of such higher order moderation, DeVries (1984) has shown how infant survival under drought conditions is related to prevailing cultural values about what is considered to be a desirable temperament for an infant. The fact that there can be higher order moderation by distal environmental influences does not negate the covariance between such influences and biological influences or individual characteristics. However, the fact that higher order distal environmental moderation can occur does emphasize the necessary role of distal environmental influences, even when these influences covary with individual or biological factors.

Parallels Between Distal Environmental Changes and Individual Change

A third line of evidence supporting the necessary nature of distal environmental influences comes from situations where changes in individual behavioral or developmental trajectories occur following changes in higher order distal environmental context. Individual changes associated with changes in culture, region of residence, or economic conditions occur too rapidly to be easily explained by population-level influences such as genetic evolution. Examples of such changes are shown in Table 7-2. As shown in Table 7-2, one such example is acculturation, when one culture changes as a function of contact with a different culture (Werner, 1979). Results similar to those seen in acculturation situations also can occur when intrasocietal circumstances force a change in normal cultural practices. For example, in some traditional African societies, boys are rarely given caregiver responsibility for young siblings. However, when female siblings were unavailable, boys in some tribal groups were pressed into service as child caretakers. One individual consequence was a higher level of subsequent nurturance by boys who were given child care responsibilities as compared with boys from other tribal groups who did not have responsibility for younger siblings (Whiting, 1980). An unusual but related line of evidence is seen in studies of deliberate infrahuman acculturation, as when lower order primates are reared in human cultural environments (e.g., primates being reared by human parents in the same way that such parents would raise their own children). One consequence of such cross-species acculturation is a level of cognitive performance that is well above what primates display when they are reared in their own primate culture, such that there is virtually no performance overlap between acculturated and traditionally reared primates (Tomasello, Savage-Rumbaugh, & Kruger, 1993).

As shown in Table 7-2, individual change patterns also can be seen when comparing individuals from the same population group, some of whom migrate to a different culture or to a different region in the same country. Such individual-level changes could be viewed as an example of variability associated with individual characteristics (e.g., selective migration), but evidence from two sources would suggest that cultural factors may be more critical. One line of evidence involves individuals from radically different cultural groups who migrate to the same common setting, as in the case of Yemeni and Kurdish Jews migrating to Israel. In such cases individuals from radically different cultures of origin show changes in beliefs, attitudes, and family practices that reflect the nature of their common host culture (Frankel & Roer-Bronstein, 1982). Also supporting a necessary role for distal environmental influences is evidence showing positive correlations between time spent in the new culture and shifts by migrant parents toward use of parental rearing practices typically found in the new culture (Kobayashi-Winata & Power, 1989).

TABLE 7-2
Individual Changes Associated With Changes in the
Distal Environmental Context

Cause of contextual change	Individual change	References
Accculturation	Incidence of child antisocial behavior	Ackerman (1971); Yamazaki et al. (1987)
	Maternal feeding practices	Howrigan (1988)
	Level of education of women	Greenfield & Childs (1991)
	Ability to differentiate figure from ground	G. Sinha (1988)
	Typical patterns used by weavers	Greenfield & Childs (1991)
Migration	Level of cognitive competence	Kaniel & Fisherman (1991); Lieblich et al. (1972)
	Parenting practices	Chiu et al. (1992)
Changes in family economic status or work characteristics	Levels of child abuse	Garbarino (1990)
	Parenting practices	Draper & Cashdan (1988)
Intracountry change in area of residence	Figure ground discrimination	G. Sinha (1988)
	Child behavior problems	Rutter & Rutter (1992)

Stability of Cultural Patterns in the Face of Change

In the preceding section, I described changes in behavior and development associated with migration to a new culture. However, what also can be documented is that some traditional cultural values and practices are maintained among children and even among grandchildren of immigrants to a new culture (Chiu, Feldman, & Rosenthal, 1992; Feldman & Rosenthal, 1990). For example, group differences among Israeli-born Kurdish and Yemeni Jews whose grandparents migrated to Israel have been shown in regard to different beliefs about child rearing and pregnancy practices, what traits are valued in children, and in some aspects of rearing stimulation provided to young children (Frankel & Roer-Bronstein, 1982).

Cultural factors also can act to limit the degree of individual change in response to economic changes in a culture (LeVine & LeVine, 1988; Roopnarine et al., 1992).

Cultural background may act to constrain the degree of individual change in a new context by channeling such changes along pathways that are characteristic of the original culture. For example, in collectivist cultures undergoing industrialization, the collective value system may be shifted from the family to the company (Kagitcibasi, 1990), or the practice of shared rearing of children may remain even when older children are no longer available to act as caregivers (McGillicuddy-DeLisi & Subramanian, 1996).

The extent to which cultures function to limit individual change in reaction to context is not random. Rather, the extent of cultural constraint on change depends, in part, on the nature of the culture (LaFromboise et al., 1993). Individuals from cultures where traditional practices involve adaptation to a restricted number of settings are more likely to show slower and more problematic adaptation when encountering new contextual situations (Whiting, 1980). Individuals who are more able to adapt to new cultural contexts also are more likely to come from cultures characterized by multiple layers of society, where people must learn complex abstract rules of social relations to determine where they fit in the hierarchy (Levy, 1996). The extent to which cultures function to limit individual change also depends on the area of change. In general, material characteristics or parental behaviors appear to be more sensitive to contextual changes, whereas emotional values and parental ideas about what behaviors are socially inappropriate are more likely to resist contextual change (Feldman & Rosenthal, 1990; Kagitcibasi, 1990). Such differential sensitivity may reflect the fact that cultures have both core and noncore values. Core values are those that are deeply embedded in the framework of the culture and are therefore less amenable to change in new contexts (D'Andrade, 1987).

Even with these added complexities, the fact that cultural characteristics can act to limit or vary individual reactivity to changing conditions is further evidence for the necessary status of distal conditions.

Fit Between the Individual and the Culture

A final line of evidence supporting the necessary nature of distal environmental influences is seen in studies looking at differential outcomes of individuals who display behavior patterns that are concordant or discordant with traditional cultural values and beliefs. Individuals whose characteristics fit well within a given cultural context will tend to show better adaptation to this context than individuals with characteristics that run counter to the demands of their culture (Chen et al., 1998; Greenfield & Childs, 1991;

Kerr, Lambert, & Bem, 1996). A similar phenomenon can be seen in regard to changes in the incidence rates of developmental disorders in children residing in traditional cultures that are becoming urbanized or Westernized. Less cognitively able children or highly active children, who previously would have been able to adapt and assimilate into traditional cultural settings, are now more likely to be diagnosed as having cognitive problems or attention deficit disorder as a result of increased pressure for education of children (Hasan, 1977; Rahim & Cederblad, 1984). The importance of fit between individual and culture is also seen in studies documenting how personality traits that are viewed as desirable within a given cultural context show significantly more stability over time then do personality traits that are viewed as less desirable in that context (Asendorpf & Van Aken, 1991; Caspi & Bem, 1990; Kerr et al., 1996).

Taken together, these five lines of evidence document why distal environmental characteristics can be viewed as a necessary influence on behavioral–developmental variability. In the next section, I turn to the question of processes underlying how distal environmental influences translate into behavioral–developmental variability at both the group and the individual levels.

DISTAL ENVIRONMENTAL PROCESSES UNDERLYING BEHAVIORAL–DEVELOPMENTAL VARIABILITY

At a Population Level

At a population level, distal environmental influences are viewed as channeling "universal" behavioral patterns like language, regulation of bodily needs, and the development of interpersonal skills into specific pathways that enable individuals to function adequately within a given cultural context (Altman, 1977; Bonta, 1997; Cole, 1992; Goodnow, 1996; LeVine, 1989; Rogoff, 1991; Whiting & Edwards, 1988). Thus, in cultures that have a strong emphasis on the importance of interpersonal relationships, infants are more likely to be held facing away from their caregivers so that language to and from the child is directed toward others (Cole, 1992), or mothers may use objects primarily to emphasize social rituals and social exchange rather than to demonstrate object characteristics (Fernald & Morikawa, 1993). In time-driven cultures such as the United States and the Netherlands, there is an emphasis on getting the child into a regular sleep pattern, so that the child will be able to fit into the parents' work and leisure schedule (Cole, 1992; Super et al., 1996). Such a rearing pattern is less likely to be seen in a culture such as India, where time scheduling is viewed as less central (Malhotra, 1989). The results produced by such cultural channeling can be quite subtle at times. For example, in cultures characterized by multikin families, such as the Mayan Indians, children acquire the capacity to simultaneously monitor both their own actions as well as those of adults and siblings who are engaged in other activities (Rogoff, Mistry, Goncu, & Mosier, 1991).

A listing of potential distal environmental mechanisms that act to channel behavioral–developmental variability at the population level is shown in Table 7-3. One mechanism is through cultures, subcultures, or social groups influencing parental values, beliefs, and attributions about what causes child behavior and what child behaviors are desirable, which in turn influence how parents rear their children (Table 7-3, Item 1). As discussed previously, caregivers in individualistic cultures are more likely to emphasize independence, separation, individual development, and the idea that a person's worth is a function of his or her own attributes and skill. In contrast, caregivers in collectivistic cultures emphasize the importance of relatedness, cross-generational interdependence (young children depend on their parents for survival, whereas elderly parents depend on their children for survival), and the idea that a person's worth is a function of his or her social role (Chinese Cultural Connection, 1987). Thus, in collectivistic cultures, when a person transgresses, both the individual and his or her family will be held responsible for the transgression (Ma, 1988). Similarly, in hierarchical cultures that stress the need for children to be helpful or obedient, the level of children's intelligence is often defined with reference to the level of the child's responsibility (Harkness & Super, 1992). Going beyond the home, cultural characteristics also can influence socialization strategies used in preschools (Kim, 1990), the nature of the child's social network (Tietjen, 1989), patterns of peer and sibling relationships (Edwards, 1992; Whiting & Edwards, 1988), and the degree and nature of chores required of young children (Zeitlin, 1996).

Higher order distal environmental characteristics such as culture or minority group status also can influence family structure, which can either directly (Table 7-3, Item 2a) or indirectly (Item 2b) influence developmental behavioral outcomes (Garcia-Coll et al., 1996; Muret-Wagstaff & Moore, 1989). One example of an indirect influence is seen in "rational choice" theory, which proposes that there will be an optimal strategy for child rearing in a given society, which will maximize benefits and reduce risks to the family (LeVine, 1988). In agrarian societies, children are relatively low cost because the family grows its own food, shares living space, and can use young children to help with chores. In addition, in these societies typically there also is a higher risk for infant mortality. Thus an optimal rearing strategy in an agrarian society would be to produce many children; have adults focus their caregiving efforts on the early years of childhood, when mortality risks are highest; and use older siblings to care for younger children. In contrast, in urban industrialized societies, where child survival rates are higher and children cannot contribute economically to the

TABLE 7-3
Summary of Distal Environmental Processes Acting to Promote Group Differences in Behavioral–Developmental Variability

Process	References
1. Cultural, subcultural, or social class characteristics influence parental beliefs, values, goals, and behavioral norms, which in turn result in culturally characteristic child rearing practices.	Draper & Cashdan (1988); Gaskin (1996); Goodnow (1988a); Greenberger & Chen (1996); Greenfield & Childs (1991); Hoffman (1988); LeVine et al. (1996); Luster et al. (1989); McLeod & Shanahan (1993); Pomerleau et al. (1991); Richmond et al. (1988,1992); Sampson & Laub (1994)
2a. Culture influences family structure, which in turn influences child outcome.	Draper & Belsky (1990); LeVine (1988); Sutton-Smith (1986); Sutton-Smith & Roberts (1980)
2b. Culture influences family structure, which influences caregiver behaviors, which in turn influence child outcomes.	Morelli & Tronick (1991); Tronick, Morelli, & Winn (1987); Whiting & Edwards (1988)
3. Culture influences how the child perceives parents' behaviors.	Kagitcibasi (1990); Kobayashi-Winata & Power (1989); Weisner (1989)
4. Children acquire culturally appropriate behaviors and values by being placed in settings where the child can observe specific groups of people engaging in specific tasks and social relationship patterns.	Chisholm (1990); Edwards (1992); Jacklin & Reynolds (1993); Whiting (1980); Whiting & Edwards (1988)
5. Cultural and subcultural beliefs and values or social class or minority group status lead to different groups of individuals having differential accessibility to resources.	Bronfenbrenner (1989); Bryant & DeMorris (1992); Garbarino (1990); Garcia-Coll et al. (1996); Hoffman (1988); LeVine et al. (1996); Parke & Bhavnagri (1989); Zeitlin (1996)
6. Cultural values and beliefs can support the individual's ability to function in a new cultural context (e.g., cultural emphasis on education or on cross-generational family support).	Alva (1993); Ogbu (1983); Quinton (1994); Steinhausen et al. (1990)
7. The greater the discrepancy (lack of fit) between the individual's native culture and the demands of a new culture, the greater the likelihood of developmental problems.	Greenberger & Chen (1996); Kim (1990); Quinton (1994); Vogt et al. (1987); Weinstein (1991)

family until they have acquired complex skills, a more optimal strategy would be to have fewer children and invest more adult resources in them over longer periods of time (LeVine, 1989).

As also seen in Table 7-3 moderation of proximal environmental influences by distal environmental influences can occur through specific parental behaviors having different meanings in different cultures (Item 3). For example, Chao (1994) has noted that the term *guan* in Chinese refers both to firm control and to a sense of loving and caring. Thus, for Chinese adolescents, parental demands for obedience are not viewed as an attempt by the parents to dominate but rather as a means of maintaining family harmony. Chao further argued that differences in the meaning of parental control may be one reason why, unlike Western children, Asian children from authoritarian families do well in school. Again, this type of process is not restricted just to the level of culture. Using peer relations as an example, in low-crime neighborhoods, high levels of peer contact by children are viewed in positive terms, with older children being seen as a resource. In contrast, in high-crime neighborhoods, high levels of peer contact are more likely to be viewed negatively by parents, with older children being seen as potential initiators of younger children into violence or drug use (Cochran & DaVila, 1992).

The term *setting* typically is used to refer to the normal day-to-day activities of individuals in a given physically defined space (Whiting, 1980). As also shown in Table 7-3, Item 4, macrosystem influences also can operate by increasing the likelihood that developing children will repeatedly encounter specific settings. For example, culturally based differences in patterns of appropriate gender-related behaviors may be developed as the child observes how men and women relate to each other across a variety of settings, the degree of overlap of male and female tasks in specific settings, and who is absent from specific settings. Membership in a low-SES or ethnic minority group may restrict the extent of parental social support networks (Garbarino & Sherman, 1980; Sampson & Groves, 1989; Tietjen, 1989), which in turn can act to restrict the degree to which children are exposed to more varied settings (Homel et al., 1987; Parke & Bhavnagri, 1989). It is also important to keep in mind that repeated exposure to familiar settings can influence how the individual reacts to such new settings. For example, the very close proximity of Japanese mothers to their infants early in life may mean that separation from the mother is a very traumatic event for the Japanese infant (Cole, 1992).

As shown in Table 7-3, Item 5, macrosystems also can enhance the operation of proximal family processes by providing resources to the family so it can carry out its goals. Alternatively, by systematically denying availability to resources, macrosystems can act to inhibit the behavior and development of children in certain groups. In some cases, group differences may be based on differential access to physical resources like food. For example, in some Asian societies a cultural tradition of private land ownership and inheritance going through the male line favors preferential feeding of male rather female children. In contrast, in the Yoruba tribe in Nigeria, where maternal income is a major family resource and land ownership is communal (the more children there are in the family, the more land for which the family is eligible), preferential feeding may be directed more to the mother than toward the children (Zeitlin, 1996).

Differential access to resources also encompasses nonphysical resources like information or education (Goodnow, 1988a). In gender-segregated societies, significantly less secondary and higher education for women is often the norm. For example, even though Nigerian Muslim women come from more educated and affluent families than women from Nigerian Christian families, the university education rate of Muslim women in Nigeria is less than half that of women from Christian families (Stromquist, 1989). Similarly, in countries where the bride's family has to pay a dowry price to the groom to marry their daughter, it is not desirable to have a highly educated daughter because more educated daughters are more likely to marry an educated man, and an educated man would demand a high dowry (Stromquist, 1989).

Biases against minority groups also can act to influence the availability and quality of educational resources for children in these groups. Biases can act either directly, as in the case of differential government spending for education based on race (Liddell et al., 1991), or indirectly, as in the case of lower teacher expectations about the ability level of Black children in the United States (Alexander & Entwisle, 1988) or lower caste children in India (Sinha, 1990). When bias is operating at a societal level, individuals in a minority group may react to bias in ways that even further deny them access to resources. One prime example of this would be children from involuntary migrant groups (groups taken into a majority culture through conquest or slavery). These children's experiences with discrimination may lead them to turn away from education, because education is not perceived as being linked to success but rather as a representative institution of the majority culture that has rejected them (Ogbu, 1983). Alternatively, minority groups can act in ways that increase resource accessibility, as in the case of developing extended family networks that maximize the family's ability to obtain and use scarce economic resources (Harrison et al., 1990). However, one consequence of living in minority group neighborhoods characterized by high levels of poverty or neighborhood disorganization is a reduced ability of families to group together to engage in mutually supportive actions, such as supervising teenager activities, promoting crime fighting initiatives, or engaging in reciprocal child care (Garbarino & Sherman, 1980; Sampson & Groves, 1989).

Finally, characteristics of the individual's original culture can act to facilitate or inhibit adjustment to a new culture (Table 7-3, Items 6–7). In some cases, there can be temporal shifts such that the same cultural characteristics that had originally facilitated adaptation to a new culture now begin to act in an inhibitory fashion. For example, although high family cohesion in certain migrant groups may initially facilitate adjustment, over time high cohesion may result in higher levels of family conflict when adolescents begin to adopt the cultural values of their peers as opposed to those of their families (Feldman & Rosenthal, 1990).

Many of the multiple mechanisms shown in Table 7-3 through which cultural influences produce population behavioral–developmental differences are nicely integrated in the *developmental niche model* of Super and Harkness (1986b). The developmental niche consists of three elements: (a) the physical and social setting within which the child functions; (b) culturally driven customs of child care; and (c) the psychology of the caregiver (e.g., parental beliefs and goals). All three aspects of the niche are interrelated and function together, such that the developing individual in a given culture gets redundant and concordant messages from all components of the niche (Super & Harkness, 1999). For example, the development of an external locus of control orientation in rural Mexican children has been attributed to parallels between the way in which the child is rewarded by its parents, the way in which the parents are rewarded by society, and cultural beliefs about the adaptive value of an external orientation (Kagan & Ender, 1975). In China, children's political and social attitudes are shaped by similar messages from the family, school, mass media, and youth organizations (Lee & Zhan, 1991). Redundancy also can occur when schools act as a mirror of the larger society, as seen in parallel treatment of minority children in schools and in society in the United States, or in parallels between children's relations with their families and their relations and obligations toward their teachers in subsaharan Africa (Whiting & Edwards, 1988).

Although the developmental niche model is explicitly cultural in nature, examples of redundant and cumulative distal influences also can be seen operating below the level of culture. Redundant sources of input can be seen in the multiple stressors (poverty, community and family violence, minority status) that typically are encountered by children who are at risk for developing antisocial behavior patterns (Hartup & Van Lieshout, 1995). The cumulative nature of such influences can be seen in the spiraling bidirectional pattern between child and community violence, with communities characterized as violent predisposing the children in them to become more violent, and violent children in turn raising the level of community violence (Liddell et al., 1994). Although evidence is relatively sparse, one implication of the operation of cumulative influences at the exosystem level is the possibility of nonlinear relations between distal environmental characteristics and developmental outcomes. For example, in regard to distal characteristics like neighborhood violence or deterioration of neighborhood quality, there may be little impact of these characteristics on the behavior and development of groups living in violent or deteriorating neighborhoods until such influences accumulate past a critical threshold point. Once the cumulative threshold is passed, one consequence is a sharp upsurge in maladaptive behaviors in such neighborhoods (Crane, 1991; Quinton, 1994).

Going From the Population to the Individual Level

As shown in Table 7-1, there are multiple distal environmental mechanisms that promote population differences in behavior and development. A critical question is whether and how such mechanisms can operate to produce individual behavioral–developmental variability. In the present section, I will explore two characteristics of distal environments that can result in individual behavioral developmental variability, even within a given population group.

The Heterogeneous Nature of Distal Environmental Influences

As noted at the outset of this chapter, it is traditional to think that distal environmental contexts such as culture form a homogeneous monolithic structure. However, such an image is not correct. Theoretically, substantial variability is inherent in the very nature of large-scale complex systems such as culture (Fogel, 1993). Empirically, evidence shows that there can be tremendous variability in the nature of experiences encountered by individuals within a given cultural context (Maccoby, 1988; Weisner, 1989; Weisner & Wilson-Mitchel, 1990; Whiting & Whiting, 1975). For example, nearly 25% of Japanese mothers show a rearing strategy that is more characteristic of mothers in the United States (Power et al., 1992). Significant intragroup variability is seen even for strongly culturally driven practices. For example, among one small tribal group of Efe hunter–gatherers, observations made when infants were 18 weeks of age revealed that the range of multiple caregiving experiences for individual infants varied from 20% to 90% of the infant's day (Tronick et al., 1987). Differential rearing experiences within a common culture also can occur, depending on whether a family is living in an extended or a nuclear family (Chisholm, 1989) or when children's parents and day care providers have different child rearing values, goals, and strategies (Edwards, Gandini, & Giovaninni, 1996; Holloway & Gorman, 1988).

Although intracultural variability may be stronger for caregiver behavior patterns than for caregiver belief systems (Quinton, 1994), there can be significant intracultural variability when the origins of beliefs are contemporary in nature rather than historically rooted (Lee & Zhan, 1991). Furthermore, even when individuals within a given culture share a common set of beliefs, they may weight various elements of these beliefs differently, depending on the situation in which they find themselves (Wainryb, 1995). Even when functioning within a culturally driven developmental niche, children may encounter different rearing situations as caregivers adjust their rearing strategies, beliefs, and goals to correspond to the unique characteristics of their offspring (Super & Harkness, 1999). For example, among the Efe hunter–gatherers, Efe infants who initially appear to be more viable (e.g., higher birth weight, less fussy) are more likely to be cared for by caregivers other than their mothers than are Efe infants who do not have these viability signs (Tronick et al., 1987). The fact that cultures are not homogeneous in nature is one reason why we can find individual variability coexisting with intracultural similarity.

Intradistal environmental variability is not restricted just to the level of culture. Variability in individual experiences also can be seen in distal contexts like migration (Williams & Berry, 1991), *minority group status* (Gutierrez & Sameroff, 1990), depressed economic conditions (Elder & Caspi, 1988), *schools* (Maughn, 1994), social support networks (Tietjen, 1989), and living in rural versus urban communities (Fry, 1988; Liddell, Strydom, Qotyana, & Shabalala, 1993). For example, variability in an individual's experiences in institutions like schools may result partly from the complex nature of the school structure (Talbert & McLaughlin, 1999) and partly from differential attendance patterns of different children (Whiting & Edwards, 1988). Particularly in less developed countries, whether or not a woman attends school and how far she can go in school is found to be a function of a highly complex set of factors, including cultural characteristics, family education, economic status, and religious beliefs (Stromquist, 1989).

The critical point of documenting such variability in distal environmental characteristics is to show that even within a given distal environment, individuals may encounter a very wide range of experiences. It is highly unlikely that such intradistal variability would lead to homogeneous outcomes across a population (Quinton, 1994). High levels of variability both within and across given distal environmental contexts are a major mechanism through which distal environmental influences, while promoting differences among population groups, can still leave room for intraindividual outcome variability.

Linkages Among Distal Environmental Influences

Another potential source of individual variability in behavior and development within a given distal environmental context comes from the complex pattern of linkages among different dimensions of the macrosystem. Using the concept of the cultural niche as an example, the three components of the niche, although interconnected with each other, are not completely interconnected. Changes in degree of linkage among the components of the niche can occur, either as a function of intrinsic or extrinsic cultural changes or as a function of chance events (Super & Harkness, 1999). Individual variability can result when different components of the niche become more or less linked for different individuals at a given point in time.

Even without the concept of the cultural niche, it seems clear that multiple distal environmental influences are simultaneously impinging on individuals in complex ways, such that individual variability can arise from the nature and extent of linkages between different levels of the distal environment. As shown in Table 7-4, even within a given cultural group the impact of culturally driven beliefs, styles, and values on individual behavioral development will vary as a function of the operation of other distal environmental characteristics. Similar moderation also occurs for other distal environmental influences like migration, exposure to societal violence, social class membership, and neighborhood characteristics, as also shown in Table 7-4. The schematic diagram shown in Figure 7-1 illustrates how complex linkages among cultural, societal, and institutional characteristics (Items 1–5) affect child and family characteristics and child competencies in minority populations (Items 6–8).

TABLE 7-4
Distal Moderators of the Impact of Specific Aspects
of the Distal Environment

Distal influence	Moderated by	Reference
Culture	Family social class	Bronstein (1994); Ma & Leung (1990); Triandis (1990)
	Parental educational level	Bronstein (1994); LeVine et al. (1996); Ma & Leung (1990)
	Parental work characteristics	Hoffman (1988); LeVine (1988)
	Region of residence	LeVine et al. (1996)
	Parental religion	Weisner et al. (1996)
	Parental biculturalism	Gutierrez & Sameroff (1990)
Migration	Residential area	Eliram & Schwarzwald (1987)
	Adult SES level in original culture	Williams & Berry (1991)
	Parent educational level	Chiu et al. (1992)
	Tolerance and support in new culture for migrants	Williams & Berry (1991)
Societal disruption	Cultural traditions and beliefs	Dawes (1990)
	Ethnic group membership	Farver & Frosch (1996)
Social class/income	Ethnic group membership	Nettles & Pleck (1994)
	School income level	C. Patterson et al. (1992)
Neighborhood	Region of residence and ethnic group membership	Chase-Lansdale & Gordon (1996)

Note. SES = socioeconomic status.

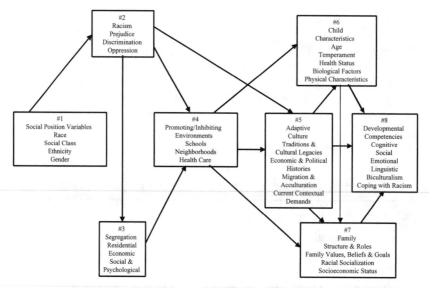

Figure 7-1. Linkages among multiple domains of distal environment influences and family and child characteristics in minority groups (figure taken from Garcia-Coll et al., 1996).

The complex linkages and moderating influences shown in Table 7-4 and Figure 7-1 allow ample room for individual variability in reaction to specific distal influences such as culture, social class, and family employment characteristics. Complex reciprocal moderating linkages between different dimensions of the distal environment provide a second mechanism through which individual behavioral–developmental variability can emerge for individuals being reared in a given macrosystem.

DISTAL ENVIRONMENTAL INFLUENCES:
NECESSARY BUT NOT SUFFICIENT

Ample evidence exists to document the necessary influence of distal environmental influences on behavior and development, at both the population and the individual levels. However, available evidence also illustrates how these influences, in and of themselves, are not sufficient to explain such variability. In the following section, I discuss three reasons for this conclusion.

Individual Reactivity to Common Distal Environmental Influences

Even if distal environmental influences had the potential to function as a "cookie cutter," differential reactivity by different individuals to similar distal environmental pressures would mean that not all cookies were identical (Valsiner & Litvinovic, 1996). The importance of differential reactivity is seen most dramatically in the extreme case of individuals exposed to massive psychosocial trauma, such as Jewish children imprisoned in Nazi concentration camps (Moskovitz, 1985) and Cambodian children imprisoned in concentration camps during the Pol Pot era (Kinzie et al., 1986). Even in the face of such overwhelming trauma, individual differences in reactivity have been documented. Differential individual reactivity also has been documented in reaction to a variety of less extreme distal environmental pressures, including culture (McGillicuddy-DeLisi & Subramanian, 1996; Whiting, 1980), acculturation pressure (Williams & Berry, 1991), ethnic group membership (Alva, 1993), schooling (Stevenson et al., 1978), family financial stress (Brody & Flor, 1997), and exposure to political violence (Cairns & Dawes, 1996; Cairns & Wilson, 1989; Liddell et al., 1993; Punamaki, 1988).

Individual characteristics that have been identified as moderators of distal environmental influences at the macro- and exosystem levels include age of the individual at the time of exposure (Cairns & Wilson, 1989; Crouter & McHale, 1993; Elder, 1986; Elder & Caspi, 1988), gender (Chen & Stevenson, 1995; Elder, Nguyen, & Caspi, 1985), individual cognitive abilities (Elder, 1974), and individual expectations (Garbarino, 1990). For example, a consistent body of evidence exists documenting a greater impact of neighborhood characteristics on male than female behavioral development (Ensminger, Lamkin, & Jacobson, 1996). Moderation of distal environmental influences also can occur as a function of interaction among multiple individual characteristics, including age-by-gender interactions in reaction to societal violence (Dawes, 1990; Liddell, Kemp, & Moema, 1993).

An excellent example of how individual characteristics act to moderate the impact of higher order distal environmental influences is seen in regard to individual variability in adjusting to two cultures. Faced with acculturation pressure or migration, some individuals attempt to become totally assimilated by rejecting the values of their own culture. In contrast, other individuals either cling to the values and traditions of their original culture or attempt to alternate between two cultures, tailoring their behavior to fit the cultural context they are in and maintaining a relation with both cultures without choosing between them (LaFromboise et al., 1993). Multiple individual characteristics act to influence how and how well individuals can adapt to two cultures. Individuals possessing a strong sense of their own individuality, a sensitivity to social nuances, and a sense of cognitive control (feeling able to develop strategies to cope with change) are better able to function in bicultural settings (LaFromboise et al., 1993) and better able to adjust to acculturation pressures (Williams & Berry, 1991). In contrast, individuals with a problematic premigration developmental history are more likely to react poorly to migration pressures than are individuals with a nonproblematic history (Aronowitz, 1984). Obviously, such individual characteristics do not arise in a contextual vacuum, as seen in the case of Navajo children who are sent to non-Navajo boarding schools. Children who have those personal characteristics that allow them to adapt to boarding school are more likely to come from families where there is a greater degree of congruence between family and Navajo community values (Boyce & Boyce, 1988).

Regardless of their origin, individual differences in reactivity are one reason why distal environmental influences, although necessary, are not sufficient. However, other reasons for this conclusion have been found.

Distal Environmental Influences Are Not Always There

If distal environmental influences are both necessary and sufficient, two sets of findings should emerge. First, variability in behavior and development associated with differences in distal environmental influences should be consistently found. In regard to this first prediction, too many studies show similarities in behavior and development for individuals living in different cultural contexts. For example, cross-cultural studies on gender find surprising similarity across different cultures in gender-related play patterns (Maccoby, 1988), processes underlying children's understanding of gender differences and similarities (Munroe, Skimmer, Pitzer, 1984), and gender-related socialization pressures (Best & Williams, 1993). Evidence linking cultural differences either to children's personality development (Hinde, 1987) or to the factor structure of parental descriptions of their children's personality (Kohnstamm, Halverson, Havill, & Mervielde, 1996) also is not consistent. Inconsistencies also are shown in regard to other distal influences below the level of culture. For example, not all ethnic minority groups in the United States show the same degree of bicultural identification (LaFromboise et al., 1993), whereas differences in parental feeding beliefs are not always associated with differences in level of maternal schooling (Engle et al., 1996).

From the viewpoint of both contextual theory (e.g., Rosnow & Georgoudi, 1986) and human ecological theory (e.g., Bronfenbrenner, 1989), a second prediction is that patterns of proximal environment–development relations should invariably and systematically vary as changes occur in the distal context in which proximal influences are embedded. Certainly there is much evidence available showing how patterns of relations between similar proximal environmental characteristics and individual developmental variability differ across different macrosystem contexts (Wachs, 1996a). However, many studies do not report such higher order moderation. Parallel patterns of relations between parental rearing practices and variability in children's behavioral development are found across widely differing cultures (Bornstein et al., 1991; Chen, Dong, & Zhou, 1997; Chiu et al., 1992;

Feldman & Rosenthal, 1991; Hart et al., 1998; Hess et al., 1980; Jose et al., 1998; Kobayshi-Winata & Power, 1989; Ninio, 1990; Wachs et al., 1993; Witkin & Berry, 1975). Similarly, parallel patterns also are found below the level of culture (Harnish et al., 1995; Pomerleau et al., 1991). Furthermore, in many studies where distal environmental moderation is found, the effect sizes associated with such moderation tend to be rather small (Feldman et al., 1991; Sampson & Groves, 1989). These findings, although not contradicting a necessary role for distal environmental influences, are difficult to reconcile with a conclusion of necessary and sufficient.

There appear to be two potential reasons why direct macrosystem influences or macrosystem moderation is not always found. The first reason involves what I will call macrosystem specificity; the second involves proximal environmental influences acting to mediate distal environmental influences.

Macrosystem Specificity

Available evidence suggests that macrosystem influences may be stronger for some behavioral or developmental outcomes than for others (Masten et al., 1990). For example, few group differences are seen between Israeli and Druse children when they have to choose between values involving justice versus authority or justice versus group orientation; group differences do appear when these children need to choose between personal and group values or personal values and obedience to authority (Wainryb, 1995). Similarly, older Native American children have been shown to prefer traditional values on community and social relations while preferring majority cultural values on school achievement (LaFromboise et al., 1993).

A variety of other studies have shown how the impact of acculturation pressures (Kagitcibasi, 1990), migration to a new culture (Aronowitz, 1984; Feldman & Rosenthal, 1990; Rosenthal, 1989), poverty (McLeod & Shanahan, 1993), neighborhood quality (Crane, 1991), and schooling (Bisanz, Morrison, & Dunn, 1995; Felner et al., 1995; Sharp, Cole, & Lave, 1979) varies as a function of the outcome variables under consideration. Indeed, under some conditions the same distal environmental influence can produce either a positive or a negative outcome. For example, children from high-risk family situations living in good neighborhoods show significantly less aggressive behavior than children from such families living in poorer quality neighborhoods; on the other hand, children from high-risk family backgrounds living in good-quality neighborhoods are more likely to be rejected by their peers than are similar risk children living in poorer quality neighborhoods (Kupersmidt et al., 1995). The operation of specificity at the macrosystem level may be one reason why the nature and extent of these influences vary across studies, with variability occurring as a function of different outcome measures being used in different studies.

Proximal Environmental Moderation

A second reason why distal environmental influences do not always behave as predicted has to do with evidence suggesting that the impact of distal environmental influence on behavior and development can drop substantially when the impact of proximal environmental influences are statistically or experimentally controlled. Distal environmental influences that appear sensitive to moderation from the proximal environment include socioeconomic status (Aber, 1994; Brody et al., 1994; Conger et al., 1992; Harnish et al., 1995; McCloskey, Figueredo, & Koss, 1995; C. Patterson et al., 1992), migration (Quinton, 1994), refugee status (Harding & Looney, 1977), cultural differences (Chen & Stevenson, 1991; Feldman et al., 1991), economic depression (Elder, 1974), social support networks (Taylor & Roberts, 1995), exposure to political sectarian violence (Kinzie et al., 1986; Liddell et al., 1994), and parent work schedules (Bryant & DeMorris, 1992). The operation of proximal environmental moderation of distal environmental influences also can account for inconsistent findings for distal influences, depending on the extent of proximal moderation that is occurring.

Covariance Between Distal and Nondistal Influences

A final reason why distal environmental influences can be considered necessary but not sufficient relates to existing covariance between distal influences and necessary nondistal influences. As discussed earlier, cultural practices covary with specific proximal environmental characteristics, which also can influence behavioral developmental variability (Chisholm, 1989; LeVine, 1989). However, such covariance is not restricted just to the level of culture. Exosystem characteristics like parent social support networks have been shown to covary with the level of sensitive caregiving of the child (Pianta et al., 1989). As noted earlier, there is ample evidence for covariance between family economic circumstances or sociopolitical violence and proximal environmental characteristics encountered by the child. In some cases, there may be transactional cycles, as seen in the situation where exposure to chronic societal violence acts to erode parent–child relationships, and low-quality parent–child relationships in turn make the child more sensitive to the detrimental impact of chronic societal violence (Punamaki et al., 1997).

Nondistal influences that covary with distal environmental characteristics are not restricted just to the proximal environment. Culturally driven rearing practices may evolve over generations on the basis of parents' experience with the reactions of individual children to such practices (Best & Williams, 1993; Lester & Brazelton, 1982). The end point of such evolutionary covariance would be a child whose individual characteristics should mesh with the predominant rearing characteristics of his or her culture (coevolution). For example, the predisposition to low motor activity of Latin American infants born in high altitude regions is elaborated on and reinforced by survival-related cultural practices such as swaddling the infant and maternal nursing when the child gets restless, as well as by long-term exposure to adults who typically display highly restricted motor movements (Greenfield & Childs, 1991). To the extent that coevolution is occurring, it becomes difficult to ascribe behavioral–developmental variability solely to culture without simultaneously considering the covarying individual characteristics of individuals functioning within that culture.

Another potential covariance is between culture and nutritional risk. Available evidence indicates a clear linkage between children's nutritional intake and culturally driven factors like age of weaning (Neumann & Harrison, 1994) and parental beliefs about the relation of certain foods to child illness (Launer & Habicht, 1989). Furthermore, in Western developed countries, approximately one-third of low birth weight children are small for generational age compared with three-quarters of low birth weight infants in less developed countries. These differences may well reflect the greater likelihood of prenatal malnutrition and infection in less developed countries (Falkner et al., 1994). The relation to subsequent behavior and development of either poor nutritional status or being small for gestational age (see chap. 4) makes it difficult to argue that differences between children from developed and less developed countries are purely cultural in nature.

CONCLUSION

In this chapter I documented processes whereby distal environmental characteristics translate into behavioral and developmental variability, at both the population and individual levels. Both empirical evidence and the nature of underlying process mechanisms illustrate why an understanding of distal environmental characteristics is necessary for a complete understanding of behavioral and developmental variability. However, what I also showed in this chapter is that there are individual differences in reaction to the distal environment, that not all developmental and behavioral outcomes are equally affected by distal environmental influences, and that distal environmental characteristics covary with, or can be moderated by, more proximal biological and environmental influences. All of this evidence taken together allows generalization to this chapter of the conclusion I drew in previous chapters; namely, in terms of understanding individual behavioral developmental variability, distal environmental influences, although necessary, are not sufficient in and of themselves.

8

LINKAGES AMONG MULTIPLE INFLUENCES

In the first section of this book, I have documented how specific influences from different domains are necessary but not sufficient conditions for individual behavioral–developmental variability. Up to the present, my focus has been on specific influences functioning in isolation from each other. In the next two chapters, I will discuss underlying processes that are common to the various specific behavioral–developmental influences discussed earlier. The importance of identifying underlying processes that are common to different disciplines has been emphasized by E. O. Wilson (1998), with specific reference to the term *consilience*. However, the biological-reductionist flavor associated with Wilson's use of consilience does not fit well with the overall "necessary but not sufficient" conclusion of this volume. To avoid misinterpretation I will use the more neutral term, *midlevel processes*, to refer to what will be discussed in these next two chapters. Midlevel processes refer to mechanisms that are common to specific developmental influences from different domains. Midlevel processes function at a level that is intermediate between that of domain specific influences discussed in chapters 2–7 and general systems principles, which will be discussed in chapter 10.

In this chapter, I present evidence showing how an explanatory framework based on individual influences functioning in isolation (a main effect framework) is not the best one for understanding individual behavioral–developmental variability. Rather, what the evidence leads to is a conclusion supporting an explanatory framework based on common midlevel processes involving either functional or structural linkages among separate influences from multiple domains. *Functional linkages* refer to situations wherein maximal prediction or explanatory power comes either from combinations of unrelated specific influences or when the contributions of one influence depend on the nature of contributions from other unrelated influences. *Structural linkages* refer to situations where separate influences from different domains tend to co-occur at a level greater than chance.

In this chapter, I first briefly review examples of those situations where an individual influence operating as an isolated main effect can provide a satisfactory explanation for individual developmental variability. I then present evidence on functional and structural linkages among individual developmental influences. The chapter concludes with a section on implications of functional and structural linkages for understanding behavioral–developmental variability, with particular emphasis on issues involving research design.

ISOLATED SINGLE INFLUENCES

In chapters 2–7, I documented that in most cases specific developmental influences taken in isolation must be considered necessary but not sufficient to adequately explain individual behavioral–developmental variability. The fact that single influences taken in isolation are rarely sufficient does not mean that single influences are never sufficient. Single isolated influences are more likely to be sufficient either when we are dealing with extremely rare outcomes that are qualitatively different from the normal range of developmental outcomes (Clarke & Clarke, 1988; Rutter et al., 1990) or when the operation of a single influence results in massive, irreversible damage to the individual (Horowitz, 1992).[1] Perhaps the best illustration of the sufficiency of a single isolated influence occurs when variability in multiple outcomes can be traced to the action of a single influence. One such example is seen in the operation of what geneticists have called *pleiotropy*, wherein a single gene can be shown to have multiple consequences (Rutter, 1993). For example, the single gene associated with neurofibromatosis can result in both seizures and skin problems; the single gene associated with Lesch-Nyhan syndrome can result in both mental retardation and self-mutilation, and the gene coding for mytonic dystrophy

---

[1] When discussing how single influences can be sufficient, I am not referring to situations in which multiple influences are aggregated under a single label that is then used to predict or explain outcomes (e.g., community disorganization; Coulton et al., 1995). In this case prediction is not due to the label but rather to the multiple predictors that are nested under the specific label.

can affect neuromuscular abilities, the cardiac system, and endocrine functioning (Abuelo, 1991).

The fact that single influences can have sufficient multiple consequences does not, in and of itself, mean that a single-influence framework offers the best explanation for understanding individual behavioral–developmental variability. As was repeatedly documented in chapters 2–7, and as will be discussed later, the great majority of behavioral–developmental outcomes appear to be influenced by multiple rather than single influences (Caplan, 1980; Horowitz, 1992; Sameroff & Fiese, 1990). For example, outcomes uniquely associated with single-gene influences appear to be restricted primarily to relatively rare disorders (Plomin, 1990). Even on a molecular level, what appears to be a single influence having multiple consequences may reflect coaction between this specific influence and multiple other influences. That is, rather than a single molecular influence operating in isolation, it may well be the potential combinations resulting from complex multiple molecular coactions among hormonal and nutritional receptors that lead to multiple outcomes being associated with a single influence (Chambon, 1996).

Furthermore, even when a single influence is sufficient to produce a specific outcome, this does not rule out the possibility of alternative routes to the same outcome. One such example is seen for *phenocopies,* specific outcomes associated with genetic mutations that can be duplicated by nongenetic influences like chemical exposure (Goodwin, 1985). Similarly, at the level of the central nervous system (CNS), we find the concept of "degenerate" neuronal groupings involving different but redundant neural cell groups, so that a specific function can be carried out by any number of different CNS micro-units (Edelman, 1989). The fact that single influences operating in isolation provide a satisfactory explanatory mechanism for only a very limited set of behavioral–developmental outcomes, that generalized effects of single influences may involve the operation of other influences, and the possibility of alternative routes necessitates our going beyond a main-effect, single-influence explanatory framework.

FUNCTIONAL LINKAGES AMONG MULTIPLE INFLUENCES

Although there are a number of examples of how a single influence can have multiple consequences, far more common is a pattern whereby multiple influences converge on a single outcome. One such pattern involves functional linkages among multiple influences, wherein unrelated influences combine to influence developmental variability. For example, whether a child is resilient under stress varies as a function of child temperament, level of cognitive skills, level of home crowding, degree of separation from caregivers in the first year of life, level of attention from adults after infancy, stability of caregiving, and having areas of competence that are valued by society (Masten, et al., 1990; Werner, 1994). Other examples of outcomes associated with multiple causation are shown in Table 8-1. What is critical to note in regard to Table 8-1 is that functional linkages among multiple influences can influence both abnormal developmental outcomes and outcome variability within the normal range.

Do we gain in understanding or prediction of developmental–behavioral variability by using midlevel processes involving the simultaneous impact of functionally linked multiple developmental influences? The answer to this question appears to be yes. Available evidence shows that both significantly better prediction of outcomes and better understanding of how developmental influences operate occurs when individual predictors are combined rather than treated in isolation (Berry, 1990; Bradley et al., 1994; Coulton et al., 1995; Dodge & Feldman, 1990; Garbarino & Kostelny, 1996; Gore & Eckenrode, 1994; Magyary et al., 1992; Nelson & Ellenberg, 1986; C. Patterson et al., 1992; Pungello et al., 1996; Sameroff et al., 1993; Wachs, 1995b). Given evidence showing better prediction or understanding occurring when individual developmental influences are combined, a second question emerges, What are the forms in which functional linkages among multiple influences occur?

Additive Coaction

One possible form of linkage is a simple additive summation of sets of independent influences. This form has been labeled *additive coaction* (Rutter, 1983). Additive coaction is essentially a linear series of multiple main effects, wherein the whole equals the sum of the parts and multiple parts are involved. Additive coaction processes may well represent one of the most common forms of functionally linked multiple influences (Rothbart & Bates, 1998). For example, the outcome domains shown in Table 8-1 are all influenced by additive coaction processes.

Although additive coaction may be a common form of functional linkage, among independent multiple influences it is not the only form. Coaction processes can be subtractive as well as additive. This is particularly so when there are competing forces operating simultaneously. One such situation occurs when the impact of developmental forces such as canalization, which acts to restrict variability in developmental outcomes or to keep development on existing tracks, is opposed by other developmental forces such as plasticity, which act to promote a range of developmental outcomes or act to shift ongoing developmental tracks to alternative pathways (Bateson, 1985; Gruber, 1985). When opposing forces are operating, the nature of individual developmental trajectories at either the biological (Edelman, 1989; Waddington, 1966) or the behavioral level (Goodman, 1991b; Werner, 1990) depends on the degree of relative balance or strength between multiple

TABLE 8-1
Examples of Outcomes Associated With Functional
Linkages Among Multiple Influences

Outcome Domain	Reference
Fitness of individual genotype	Keller (1987)
Intrauterine growth retardation	Menke et al. (1991)
Physical growth faltering	Karlberg et al. (1994), Martorell et al. (1994), Waterlow (1994b), Zeitlin (1991)
Etiology of cerebral palsy	Nelson & Ellenberg (1986)
Long-term consequences of low birth weight	Hack et al. (1995)
Psychiatric disorder	Rutter (1993)
Persistent antisocial behavior	Moffitt (1993)
Family breakdown	J. Patterson & McCubbin (1983)
Adolescent substance abuse	Schulenberg et al. (1996)
Special education placement	Holloman et al. (in press)
Intelligence	Capron & Duyme (1996)
	Hunt et al. (1992), Sigman et al. (1991), Simeon & Grantham-McGregor (1990)
Psychoeducational performance and school achievement	Gorman & Pollitt (1996)
	Grantham-McGregor & Walker (1998), Luster & McAdoo (1996)
Inhibited temperament	Kagan (1994)
Parent belief systems	Sigel (1985)
Parenting behavior	Belsky (1984), Bornstein (1991), G. Patterson & Bank (1989)
Social competence	Greenberg et al. (1992), Stormshak et al. (1996)
Patterns of peer relationships	Dishion et al. (1991), Olweus (1993), C. Patterson et al. (1992)

opposing forces. For example, the balance between the extent of right versus left hemispheric activation is a CNS process that has been suggested as underlying individual differences in approach versus inhibited-behavior patterns (Calkins & Fox, 1994).

Interaction

Multiple influences on development can interact as well as coact. Statistically, interaction refers to predictive variance remaining after main effects, including multiple main effects, are removed (Cronbach, 1991). Interaction differs from additive coaction in that interaction refers to a nonlinear process involving multiple predictors, wherein the whole does not equal the sum of the parts. Thus, with additive coaction processes, when two predictors are combined, we might expect a twofold change in the outcome variable, whereas for interactive processes, the resulting change might be fourfold. Conceptually, interaction refers to differential reactivity to similar influences by individuals with different histories or characteristics. Relevant individual characteristics may be categorical (e.g., evidence in chap. 5 showing that children with difficult temperaments are more reactive to stress than children with easy temperaments) or continuous (e.g., a given developmental influence may be salient only for individuals falling within a given range in a trait distribution; Caro & Bateson, 1986; Cronbach, 1991).

Evidence on the operation of interaction processes is repeatedly found in infrahuman studies and in biomedical research (Rutter & Pickles, 1991). However, interactions have proven to be far more difficult to capture or to replicate in human behavioral studies (Cronbach & Snow, 1977; Rothbart & Bates, 1998; Wachs & Plomin, 1991). Difficulties in detecting interactions at the human behavioral level appear to be primarily due to methodological and statistical factors, including the following:

- The insensitivity of traditional statistical procedures for detecting interactions (Wahlsten, 1990). (A major reason for insensitivity is the increased statistical power needed to detect interactions [Cronbach, 1991], particularly when multiple predictors are involved [L. Steinberg et al., 1991].)
- The fact that interactions are more likely to appear in extreme groups, which often are not adequately sampled in nonexperimental human research studies (McClelland & Judd, 1993).
- The use of inappropriate or imprecise measurement procedures (Wachs & Plomin, 1991).
- Lower order interactions may be masked by the operation of higher order interactions (Cronbach, 1991; Sackett, 1991) or by organism–environment covariance processes (McCall, 1991).
- The relatively small chances of an individual encountering the relevant variables at the same time point if outcomes are due to the interaction of two or more variables at a given point in time and the relevant variables are independent of each other (Pickles, 1993).

To illustrate the problems involved in detecting interaction processes, let us consider gender. Given the same level of biological insult, boys are significantly more likely to be adversely affected than girls by multigene inherited disorders (Pueschel & Goldstein, 1991), prenatal conditions (Largo et al., 1989), central nervous system disorders (Goodman, 1991a), and childhood illness (Greenberg et al., 1992; also see chap. 5). However, the overall pattern of results does not support a simple conclusion of greater male vulnerability (Doherty & Needle, 1991). For many psychosocial stressors, there is a consistent finding of greater male stress reactivity prior to adolescence, with a reverse pattern occurring during the adolescent period (Davies & Windle, 1997; Dawes, Tredoux, & Feinstein, 1989; Elder & Caspi, 1988; Wachs, 1992; Werner, 1990). Alternatively, boys and girls may be equally vulnerable but may use different coping strategies to deal with stress (Bancroft, 1991; Petersen et al., 1991). For some risk conditions, there appear to be either no gender differences in susceptibility (e.g., prenatal alcohol exposure, Abel, 1979; exposure to societal violence, Farver & Frosch, 1996; Punamaki et al., 1997) or girls rather than boys may be more susceptible (e.g., sensitivity to genetic influences underlying antisocial behavior; Rutter et al., 1990).

Part of the reason for such inconsistency may be the possibility that boys, although more vulnerable to risk conditions, may also be more sensitive to protective factors like nutritional supplementation (Adair & Pollitt, 1985; Weinberg, Zimmerberg, & Sonderegger, 1992). As in the case of exposure to lead, greater sensitivity of boys to both risk and protective factors can lead to what appear to be hopelessly inconsistent patterns of gender-by-risk interactions (McMichael et al., 1992). Inconsistencies also can reflect the masking effect of organism–environment covariance, as in the likelihood of greater cumulative stress for adolescent girls (Petersen, 1988). Also relevant may be the operation of higher order interactions. For example, gender differences in reaction to parental divorce may be further moderated by the age of the child and the nature of the family structure following divorce (Hetherington, 1989). Higher order interactions also can involve distal contextual factors, as in the case when culturally driven preferences for certain gender-related behavioral patterns result in higher order interactions between gender, nutritional status, and developmental outcomes (Wachs et al., 1995). These multiple lines of evidence illustrate the complexities inherent in detecting interactions, especially for broad-based categorical dimensions such as gender. However, these complexities are not unique to gender differences. Similar complexities also are found when investigating interactions in a variety of human behavioral domains encompassing both normal and abnormal development (Wachs & Plomin, 1991).

Even with all of these methodological and statistical problems, interactions have been documented in a variety of outcome domains at the human behavioral level. Evidence showing differential sensitivity to stress by individuals with certain types of genetic predispositions and the accentuation or attenuation of CNS insult by environmental characteristics have been documented in chapter 3. Differential individual reactivity to or environmental moderation of biomedical or nutritional risk conditions like anoxia or prenatal exposure to illegal drugs was illustrated in chapter 4. Differential consequences as a function of interactions between context and individual characteristics like pubertal status, gender, temperament, and attachment status were shown in chapter 5. Evidence illustrating moderation of the impact of proximal environmental influences by individual characteristics or by higher order contextual factors was documented in chapter 6. Finally, in chapter 7 we saw how the impact of higher order distal environmental influences could be moderated by individual behavioral styles or proximal environmental characteristics.

TABLE 8-2
Examples of Different Types of Interaction

Type	Examples
Categorical: Differential reactivity as a function of categorical group membership	Differential level of reactivity to environmental input shown for children with and without sex-chromosome abnormalities (Bender et al., 1987), for children with easy versus difficult temperaments (Wachs, 1992), for aggressive versus nonaggressive children (Dodge, 1986), and for LBW versus appropriate birth weight children (Grantham-McGregor, Chang, & Walker, 1998); differential reactivity to biomedical interventions as a function of ethnic group (Hamvas et al., 1996); different types of environmental input needed to produce behavioral competence in full-term versus preterm infants (Eckerman & Oehler, 1992) and in inhibited versus uninhibited infants (Bates et al., 1997; Kochanska, 1995).
Continuous: A specific influence is salient primarily for individuals falling within a given range on a trait distribution	Intervention effects on IQ stronger for heavier than for lighter LBW infants (Infant Health and Development Program, 1990); relation between earthquake exposure and subsequent illness strongest for those with higher immune reactivity (Barr et al., 1994); relation between adult adjustment and childhood family risk stronger for those who were adopted later in life (Cadoret et al., 1990); relation between parental emotionality and later temperament stronger for infants who are higher in negativity (Park et al., 1997).
Synergistic: Impact of one influence acts to increase the impact of a second influence	Contribution of stress and/or family disorganization to subsequent adjustment or psychopathology accentuated for individuals with neuropsychological deficits (Moffitt, 1993), for individuals with a family history of psychopathology (Goldstein, 1988; Kendler et al., 1995; Cannon et al., 1990), and for individuals with a history of early oppositional behavior (Henry et al., 1993); reactivity to massive social change varies as a function of individual differences in problem solving skills (Elder & Caspi, 1988); relation between malnutrition and infant development accentuated with increasing levels of tillness (Pollitt, 1983).

Evidence exists showing not only the operation of interactive processes, as documented in earlier chapters, but also the fact that interactions can come in a variety of forms (Rutter, 1983). Examples of the different forms of interaction are shown in Table 8-2. Although some forms of interaction, such as buffering, would seem to reflect coaction rather than interactive processes, the fact that buffering influences tend to have an impact only during times of stress or only for individuals with a history of risk suggests that buffering functions as something more than just a coactive facilitator of development. In addition, as shown in Table 8-2, the various forms of interaction are common to developmental influences across a wide variety of domains.

TABLE 8-2 (*continued*)

Type	Examples
Buffering: Protective influences attenuate the impact of exposure to developmental risk factors	Negative impact of institutional rearing on later development attenuated as a function of positive school experiences (Quinton & Rutter, 1988); negative impact of exposure to multiple biological and social risks reduced as a function of school experience (Gorman & Pollitt, 1996); exposure to high quality daycare reduces the developmental risks associated with having an emotionally unavailable mother (Field, 1994), or of chronic otitis media (Vernon-Feagans, Emmanuel, & Blood, 1997); developmental risks associated with a history of family schizophrenia reduced if individual adopted into a nondisturbed family (Tienari et al.,1987).
Intradomain: Interaction among influences within a given domain rather then across domains	Absorption of ingested lead will increase for children who have diets that are either calcium or iron deficient (Huber, 1991); epistasis interaction among genes from different loci (Plomin, DeFries et al., 1997).
Higher order: Interactions among more than two influences	Language decrement in infants a function of interaction between gender x family risk x attachment security (Morisset et al., 1995); delinquency rates a function of interaction among family stress level x ethnic group x neighborhood characteristics (Matsueda & Heimer, 1987).
Outcome driven: Nature and extent of interactions vary as a function of outcome	Interactive relation of family characteristics and larger environmental context to development will vary depending on whether outcome involves developmental competence or developmental dysfunction (Bronfenbrenner & Ceci, 1994); effects of maternal cocaine use in pregnancy on preterm and full-term infants varies depending on whether outcomes involve birth weight or neonatal irritability (J. Brown et al., 1998).

Note. LBW = low birth weight.

STRUCTURAL LINKAGES

In contrast to functional linkages, which involve unrelated developmental influences acting in concert, structural linkages refer to situations where two or more developmental influences co-occur at a greater-than-chance probability. Although functional linkages mean that individual developmental influences do not act in isolation, structural linkages mean that individual developmental influences neither act nor occur in isolation. In most cases, the reasons why structural linkages among different developmental influences co-occur is not known. It is possible that one influence causes the appearance of a second influence, but too often there is not sufficient theoretical or empirical justification to warrant a conclusion of a causal linkage.

Structural linkages, where there is an observed co-occurrence between two or more developmental influences but the co-occurrence is probabilistic in nature, will be referred to as *covariance* linkages. Structural linkages that are based on known mechanisms wherein the operation of one developmental influence is a necessary (but not sufficient) cause for the occurrence of a second developmental influence will be referred to as *causal linkages*.

The likelihood that we are dealing with covariance rather than causal linkages among two or more developmental influences is greater under two conditions (Salthe, 1985). The first condition is when developmental influences are relatively noncontiguous, with multiple intervening steps between them. For example, the linkage between biomedical risk factors and CNS functioning is relatively contiguous as compared with the linkage between social class status and biomedical influences. The greater the number of intervening steps, the greater the likelihood that there are other potential variables that can reduce the ability of one developmental influence to actually cause the occurrence of a second developmental influence. The criterion of contiguity is a major reason why I view the connection between genes and environments as an example of probabilistic covariance instead of causal linkage. As discussed in chapter 3, genes directly influence amino acids, with multiple intervening steps between genes and the environment.

A second condition is when there is temporal discontinuity between two different developmental influences. *Temporal discontinuity* refers to differences in the speed at which these influences function (Salthe, 1985). For example, the speed at which hormonal processes occur is far faster than the speed at which cultural processes occur. High levels of temporal discontinuity mean that a slower process is more likely to function as background for a faster process, rather than directly influencing the faster process. For example, a faster process may undergo multiple changes by the time it receives a different message from the slower process. Alternatively, different multiple messages from a faster process may reach the slower process before the slower process begins to show any change. In most cases, high levels of temporal discontinuity mean that we are dealing with covariance rather than causal linkages. The only possible exception to this rule is when temporally slower processes operate over very extended time spans, as in the case of evolutionary influences on genetic and CNS characteristics, or when there is high redundancy among messages from faster processes. When there is a question of whether we are dealing with covarying or causal linkages among developmental influences, my decision rule for choice will be based on the dual criteria of the degree of contiguity and temporal discontinuity.

Covariance Among Multiple Influences

In understanding the relation of covariance processes to individual behavioral–developmental variability, it is essential to stress the probabilistic nature of such processes. Covariance among developmental influences means a higher-than-chance probability of individuals encountering specific combinations of developmental influences, but covariance processes in no way guarantee that such linked encounters will actually occur. Thus, not all individuals from a given socioeconomic status (SES) group have an equal chance of encountering those developmental influences that covary with SES. A major reason why covariance linkages are probabilistic is illustrated in the pattern of inconsistent findings relating infant temperament to parent behavior during the first 2 years of life (Crockenberg, 1986; Plomin, 1994; Slabach et al., 1991). Available evidence indicates that the degree to which early child temperament is linked to subsequent parent caregiving practices is a function not only of individual variability in temperament but also of child characteristics such as age, gender, and risk status, as well as of individual parental characteristics, such as anxiety level, previous experience with infants, and individual parental preferences for different types of infant behavior patterns (Slabach et al., 1991). It is the operation of moderating variables that influences the degree of covariance encountered by individuals. Thus, failure to find expected covariance linkages for specific individuals may not reflect the lack of operation of covariance processes as much as the probabilistic nature of such processes.

Many examples of covariance linkages have been noted in the first half of this volume. In chapter 2, covariances between evolutionary influences and cultural characteristics were described (coevolution), as were covariances between physical ecology and nutrition, susceptibility to illness, and child rearing practices. In chapter 3, evidence was presented on the extent and nature of covariance between genetic risk factors and characteristics of the proximal environment. Chapter 4 described covariance linkages between specific biomedical and nutritional influences, between biomedical risk factors, and proximal and distal environmental risks, between inadequate nutrition and psychosocial environmental risks and between environmental stress and immune system functioning. In chapter 5, evidence was presented illustrating covariance linkages between specific individual characteristics and malnutrition, biomedical influences, and specific aspects of the proximal and distal environment. Reiterating what was noted in previous chapters, in chapter 6 evidence was presented on covariance linkages between proximal environmental characteristics and genetic, nutritional, and biomedical influences, and in chapter 7 covariance linkages were documented between distal and proximal environmental influences and between distal environmental characteristics and biomedical and nutritional factors. To refresh the reader's memory, specific examples of various types of covariance linkages are presented in Table 8-3.

Similar to the point raised earlier in regard to higher order interactions, higher order covariances also can exist. Examples of higher order

TABLE 8-3
Examples of Probabilistic Covariance Among Different
Developmental Influences

Covarying influences	Covariance pattern
Evolutionary and cultural influences	Adult caregivers are predisposed to respond to infant signals with culturally appropriate nurturing responses (Whiting & Edwards, 1988).
Physical ecology and nutritional status	Linkage of seasonality and food availability (Immink, 1988).
Genetic and proximal environmental influences	Parents with genetically influenced mental disorders less likely to provide adequate caregiving to their offspring (Goldstein, 1988; Masten et al., 1990).
Biomedical and nutritional influences	Increased risk of feeding problems for VLBW infants (Casaer et al., 1991). Micronutrient deficits and increased lead exposure in inner cities (Huber, 1991).
Biomedical and proximal environmental influences	Increased risk of child lead exposure associated with lower parental involvement and responsivity (Dietrich et al., 1985; Fuggle & Graham, 1991; Milar et al., 1980). Greater family disturbance and disruption for offspring of substance abusing mothers (Singer et al., 1994; Singer, Arendt, et al., 1997). Increased risk of family problems when child has chronic medical problems (Johnson, 1988; Shonkoff, 1994). Preterm infants at greater risk for having disturbed relationships with their parents (Beckwith & Rodning, 1992; Eckerman & Oehler, 1992).
Biomedical and distal environmental influences	Disorders like otitis media or parasitic infection more likely to occur in groups or communities characterized by low SES or low educational level (Connolly, 1998; Webster et al., 1989). Level of medical attention for male versus female children related to type and extent of gender preference in culture (Whiting & Edwards, 1988).
Nutritional status and proximal environmental characteristics	Malnourished children or children with micronutrient deficits more likely to be living in homes with low stimulation value and low parental responsivity (deAndraca et al., 1991; Lozoff, 1998).
Individual characteristics and biomedical influences	Greater risk of physical injury for individuals high in impulsivity, sensation seeking, or difficult temperament (Matheny 1986; Rutter et al., 1984).

TABLE 8-3 (*continued*)

Covarying influences	Covariance pattern
Individual characteristics and nutritional status	Higher level of weight gain in difficult temperament children (Carey, 1985).
Individual characteristics and proximal environmental influences	Anxious or depressed children more likely to encounter high levels of daily family hassles and lower levels of family support (DuBois et al., 1994). Low-achieving pupils get fewer teacher demands for achievement than do high-achieving pupils (Weinstein, 1991). Unresponsive LBW child more likely to elicit higher levels of caregiver stimulation (Field, 1987). Longer sibling spacing when older sibling has an inhibited temperament (Arcus & McCartney, 1989).
Distal environment and nutritional status	Increased risk of malnutrition in communities characterized by illiteracy or low levels of parent education (Ricciuti, 1993).
Distal environment and individual characteristics	Greater stability of individual characteristics that fit cultural values than characteristics that do not fit (Kerr, 1996).
Distal and proximal environmental influences	In lower SES find greater likelihood of parent use of punitive disciplines, lower parental responsivity and higher family stress (Hartup & van Lieshout, 1995; McLeod & Shanahan, 1993; Sampson & Laub, 1994).

covariances encompassing structural linkages among multiple influences are shown in Table 8-4. As can be seen from Table 8-4, multiple covariate linkage combinations can include biological, proximal, and distal environmental characteristics. Linked causal chains of covarying multiple influences also can occur. For example, changes in distal environmental characteristics associated with acculturation can increase the chances of changes in feeding practices, which in turn can increase children's risk of gastrointestinal illness (Howrigan, 1988). Similarly, there is a greater likelihood of better nutrition being provided to those individuals with specific characteristics that are viewed as most important for family survival in a given culture (Zeitlin, 1996).

Covariance linkages may be passive in nature, wherein children are more likely to receive specific combinations of developmental influences from their parents (e.g., "smarter" genes and a better environment). Alternatively, covariance linkages may result from others reacting in certain

TABLE 8-4
Examples of Covariation Among Multiple
Developmental Influences

Covariates	Reference
Exposure to community violence covaries with poverty and neighborhood crowding	Garberino & Kostelny (1996)
Covariance between increased lead exposure, higher rate of parental smoking, and poor-quality parental rearing patterns	McMichael et al. (1992)
Covariance between family history of biological risk, small for gestational age at birth, higher rate of maternal smoking	Klebanoff et al. (1989)
Covariance between low birth weight and increased family stress, higher work demands, lower quality parent–child relations	McCormick (1992)
Covariance between difficult temperament, parental mental illness, higher family discord, increased exposure to parental hostility	Rutter (1988)
Covariance between early appearing antisocial behavior, insecure attachment, less adequate parenting behaviors	Sampson & Laub (1994)
Covariance between child oppositional behavior at school, greater peer rejection, less on-task classroom behavior, and poorer learning	Dishion et al. (1991)
Covariance between child neuropsychological deficits and increased likelihood of aggressive behavior, difficult temperament, impulsivity, a proximal environment that accentuates these conditions, parents who are more likely to be aggressive or impulsive, and being more likely to live in poor quality neighborhood	Moffitt (1993)
Covariance between poor school attendance, and early dropout of school, being less qualified for skilled jobs, and being more vulnerable to economic downturns	Rutter (1993)

ways to individuals with specific traits (*reactive covariance*) or from individuals with certain traits seeking out certain types of contexts (*active covariance*; Plomin, DeFries, & Loehlin, 1977). In some situations, it is possible to distinguish between the passive, active, and reactive forms of covariance. Covariance linkages between child biomedical risk and poor family functioning can be viewed as an example of passive biomedical–proximal environment covariance, whereas relationship disturbances between parents and their preterm infants are better understood as an example of reactive biomedical–proximal environment covariance, particularly if the preterm infant also has other chronic medical complications (Minde, 1992). The covariance between child nutritional status and parental rearing patterns appears to reflect reactive covariance (Wachs et al., 1992), as do the consequences of differential treatment of individuals with hormonal disorders (Herdt & Davidson, 1988). However, the higher rate of parasitic interaction of more sociable children appears to be best understood as an example of active covariance (Kvalsvig & Becker, 1988).

Linking together the different forms of covariance, I would predict that we may be less likely to find active or reactive covariance for individual developmental influences that are passively linked to a variety of other developmental influences. My rationale is that multiple passive covariance links act to increase the probability of moderating factors that can weaken the consistency of reactions the individual gets from others (less reactive covariance) or can inhibit the individual's ability to freely self-select into a context of his or her choosing (less active covariance).

Initiating a theme to be elaborated on in chapter 9, covariance processes also can operate over a background of time. For example, as in the case of assortative mating, interdomain covariance between genotype and individual characteristics can have cross-generational consequences (Buss, 1985). Similarly, children of battered women are more likely to be sexually abused than children of nonbattered women (McCloskey et al., 1995). By operating across time, the strength of covarying linkages can be increased. One example is seen in a preference among adults who are more intellectually flexible for more complex work situations, which in turn enhance their level of intellectual flexibility (Kohn & Schooler, 1983). Another example is seen in the linkage of noncompliant difficult temperament toddlers with parents who respond to oppositional behavior with inconsistent harsh discipline. In this situation, each negative interchange reinforces both parental and toddler styles, thus increasing the probability of future negative interchanges (G. Patterson & Bank, 1989).

Also of interest is the nature of relations between covariance and interaction processes. As noted previously, interaction is traditionally defined as differential reactivity by individuals with different characteristics to similar developmental influences. However, to the extent that either reactive or active covariance processes are operating, children with different characteristics may be less likely to encounter similar developmental influences (Sroufe & Egeland, 1991). This negative linkage between reactive–active covariance and interaction led McCall (1991) to argue that nature may "conspire" against finding interactions, given that interaction processes may be masked by the operation of active or reactive covariance. However, this does not preclude the possibility that in some cases there can be additive coaction among passive covariance and interaction processes. Conceptually,

Kendler and Eaves (1986) postulated that genes may influence both individual sensitivity to protective and risk features of the environment (*interaction*) while also relating to the degree of exposure the individual has to environmental protective and risk factors (*covariance*). Empirically, Rahmanifar et al. (1993) showed how the level of infant alertness is influenced both by a synergistic interaction between maternal intake of animal source calories and level of crowding in the home, as well as by passive covariance between maternal animal source caloric intake and level of maternal vocalization to the infant. Other evidence indicates that although the impact on children of exposure to chronic political violence can be moderated by warm, affectionate parenting (interaction), the greater the exposure of children to such violence, the more likely they are to perceive their parents as punitive and rejecting (covariance; Punamaki et al., 1997).

There is also the possibility that interaction may be an initial and necessary condition for promoting reactive covariance. This is particularly so in terms of gender development, where it has been hypothesized that initial differences in reactivity of male and female infants to similar parental caregiving patterns (interaction) may ultimately lead to differential parental treatment of boys and girls (reactive covariance; Reinisch et al., 1991; Rutter & Pickles, 1991). A similar argument also could be made in regard to other individual characteristics. Early infant variability in biomedical status or in individual characteristics like responsivity, level of inhibitory control, distress proneness, impulsivity, or reactivity to parental control may result in differential responsivity to specific parental rearing strategies. Over time this differential responsivity may lead parents to channel their choice of disciplinary or stimulation strategies to fit their infant's characteristics (Kochanska, 1993; Minde, 1992; Rothbart et al., 1994). The possibility that interactions may be a necessary condition for the development of reactive covariance is not restricted just to the infancy period. Dodge and Feldman (1990) showed how the greater likelihood of aggressive children perceiving aggressive interactions from peers in neutral situations (interaction) is likely to lead to behavioral reactions by aggressive children, which increase the likelihood of peer rejection (reactive covariance). Within a framework of interaction → reactive covariance, a particularly critical and as yet unanswered question is how this linkage would be manifested in different cultures that vary on level of gender stereotyping or on the value placed on different types of child characteristics.

Causal Linkages

Criteria for assuming causal linkages between two or more developmental influences can be empirical (variability in one influence consistently leads to structured change in a second influence) or it can be inferred by the action of a known mechanism promoting causality. Multiple examples of known causal linkages between two or more different developmental influences have been previously noted in this volume. As one example, nutritional influences have been shown to directly influence central nervous system development and function (Georgieff, 1994; Landsberg & Young, 1983). One known mechanism associated with protein energy malnutrition is irreversible changes in the development of certain central nervous system structures like the cerebellum and hippocampus, as well as critical central nervous system processes like myelination (Levitsky & Strupp, 1995). Adequate iodine status has been shown to be a necessary condition for the development of central nervous system microstructures like the number of neurons (DeLong, 1993), whereas essential fatty acids appear to play a necessary role in the development of the visual system (Uauy & deAndraca, 1995). The efficiency of neural transmission mechanisms also has been shown to be directly influenced by deficits in both iron (Lozoff, 1998; Pollitt, 1993) and Vitamin B_6 (Guilarte, 1993).

Causal links between nutritional influences and gene action also have been documented (Groff, Gropper, & Hunt, 1995; Whitefield et al., 1995). For example, it appears as if the role of antioxidants in disease prevention may involve their altering the ability of oxidants to regulate gene expression (Palmer & Paulson, 1997). Alternatively, genetic mutations that cause deficits in the ability of the individual to metabolize specific nutrients like the vitamins, folate and B_{12} (Rosenblatt & Whitehead, 1999) also have been identified.

These linkages refer to unidirectional causally linked developmental influences (e.g., A → B). Causal linkages between different developmental influences can be bidirectional in nature, with each influence being necessary for the occurrence or nature of the other (e.g., A ↔ B). Prenatal development has been attributed to a "dialogue" between cells and the genome (Oster & Alberch, 1982; Waddington, 1966), whereas linked reversible causal cycles are a major feature of metabolic activity (Groff et al., 1995). As seen in chapter 3, other examples of bidirectional causal linkages go between the CNS and hormonal influences (e.g., CNS processes regulate hormonal secretions but hormonal action can influence synaptic production), between genetic and hormonal influences (e.g., genes turn on hormonal systems in puberty while hormonal levels influence regulator gene action), and between hormones and individual characteristics (e.g., hormones influence gender-related behavior, whereas individual behavioral differences, such as level of dominance, influences testosterone level).

A classic example of bidirectional linkage is seen in the pattern of reciprocal relations between nutritional status and gastrointestinal illness. Gastrointestinal illness influences nutritional status, both by increasing the risk of malabsorption of nutrients, as well as by increasing the individual's basal metabolism rate and thus their need for more caloric intake (Keusch, 1977; Rosenberg et al., 1977). Some studies suggest that up to 20% of energy loss can be associated with illness (Martorell, Yarbrough, & Klein, 1980). On the other hand, malnutrition can directly act to influence the individual's risk of illness through decreasing immune system efficiency, thus making the individual more vulnerable to illness (Martorell, 1989). Other examples of nutritionally related bidirectional causal linkages also have been documented. Adequate levels of anabolic hormones, which are involved in growth regulation and cell maintenance, can help buffer individuals against the negative consequence of protein-energy malnutrition through influencing the degree of breakdown of fatty tissue; however, severe protein-energy malnutrition in turn can affect secretion of anabolic hormones (Soliman et al., 1986).

Causal and Covarying Structural Linkages

Earlier in this chapter, I noted that there were instances where we could observe either the simultaneous or temporally linked operation of both covariance and interactive processes on a specific behavioral–developmental outcome. The same situation also holds in regard to causal and covarying structural linkages, which, up to the present, have been treated in isolation. At a biological level, morbidity and malnutrition linkages can involve both causal processes (e.g., malnutrition resulting in reduced immune system functioning) and covariance (e.g., fever covaries with loss of appetite). This dual process linkage has cumulative nutritional and biomedical consequences, as seen in the accelerated breakdown rate of body protein to restore energy balance for the malnourished individual, coupled with an increased need for protein synthesis to restore immune system functioning (Keusch, 1990). In infrahuman primates, higher levels of dominance behavior are causally linked to hormonal changes, which in turn covary with an increased probability of more dominance behavior (Cairns, 1993). In human populations, CNS dysfunction covaries with an increased probability of delinquent behavior patterns, including substance abuse, and substance abuse is causally linked to further CNS dysfunction (Moffitt, 1990).

FUNCTIONAL AND STRUCTURAL LINKAGES AMONG
MULTIPLE DEVELOPMENTAL INFLUENCES:
CONSEQUENCES AND IMPLICATIONS

Although there are examples of individual developmental influences functioning in isolation, it seems clear that most developmental–behavioral outcomes are a function of the operation of functionally or structurally linked multiple influences. The concept of a linked system of developmental influences occurs repeatedly across multiple domains.

Conceptualizations of the role of the CNS emphasize linked organized structures both at the cellular level (Edelman, 1989) and at the level of organized CNSs (Nelson, 1994). It has been argued that organized structures allow for coordinated action patterns when the CNS receives multiple signals from different sources (Edelman, 1989). In chapter 3, I described how links involving cortical activity, hypothalamic and glandular activity, and extrinsic stimulation allow hormonal and CNS activities to function as a complex organized structure (e.g., hypothalamic–pituitary–adrenal system). Concepts such as structural and regulator genes also suggest the operation of some type of linked system underlying patterns of gene action (Plomin et al., 1997). Within an ethological perspective, social interactions take place within an organized structural network (Hinde, 1989). Anthropological researchers focus on cultures being structurally organized to provide socialization agents who act to promote the child's acquisition of culturally appropriate action patterns (Zukow, 1989).

One of the best-known examples of a linked multiple-influence structure at the behavioral level is Bronfenbrenner's (1989) formulation of the structure of the environment (see Figure 6-1 in chap. 6). According to Bronfenbrenner, the environment is organized in a hierarchical linked fashion, ranging from macrosystem down to microsystem processes. The hierarchical framework of Bronfenbrenner's overall structure is mirrored in the organization of environmental characteristics at each level of the hierarchy. For example, families have their own structures, encompassing both hierarchical linkages (e.g., parent–child alliances) and parallel linkages (e.g., sibling or marital relations; Cooper & Cooper, 1992; Goodnow, 1988a). Similarly, societal institutions like schools also have a complex structure involving both hierarchical linkages (e.g., administration, teachers, students) and parallel linkages (e.g., peer-group cliques; Talbert & McLaughlin, 1999).

Conceptual Implications

One major implication of developmental influences functioning in an organized linked fashion is the importance of considering not only the direct impact of individual influences but also the potential indirect impact that can result from the organizational structure of multiple developmental influences. The importance of structural influences having an indirect impact is well known in the field of ecology, wherein attempts to understand the role played by an individual species in a complex ecosystem are based on knowledge of the organized relationship among the various species existing in the ecosystem (Patten, 1982). A second major implication of the fact that we are dealing with linked influences is that we are able to meet one of the fundamental criteria defining the operation of a system (Fogel, 1993). As will be discussed in chapter 10, applying systems principles is one means of bringing order to and understanding the operation of multiple linked influences (von Bertalanffy, 1968). However, prior to considering systems principles, it is essential to deal with the most often raised reactions to the assertion that developmental variability is the result of complex linkages among multiple influences. I refer specifically to the often expressed concerns that an explanatory framework based on linked multiple influences tells us that "life is complicated" but not much else (Bateson, 1985), or that such a complex framework leads to basically uninterpretable or untestable models (Thompson, 1996).

In responding to such concerns, we could of course pretend that the world is much simpler than it is and focus primarily on single influences taken in isolation. Although this is a parsimonious strategy, it is legitimate to ask whether denying the documented existence of complex linkages among multiple developmental influences is a strategy that will result in higher levels of either prediction or understanding of individual behavioral developmental variability. I would argue that we are likely to get both better prediction and better understanding when our explanatory frameworks encompass rather than ignore existing linkages among multiple developmental influences. Thus, in terms of promoting understanding, there is an increasing focus on the role of correlated or linked influences as one mechanism for explaining comorbidity of different biochemical or behavioral disorders (Pickles, 1993; Rutter, 1997). At a more applied level, let us consider children with chromosome 5 deletion ("Cri du Chat") syndrome. Such children were originally thought to have a very limited and dismal prognosis, including no language, severe retardation, and early death. However, this restricted and dismal prognosis was developed at a time when most children with this syndrome were institutionalized. A much more hopeful and varied prognosis for children with Cri du Chat syndrome occurs when they are home reared and enrolled in early stimulation programs (Carlin, 1990). This more promising outcome would not have occurred if we had focused solely on the genetics of Cri du Chat and had not considered the possibility of functional linkages between genetic and contextual influences.

At this point readers may feel a sense of being trapped between the Scylla of unrealistic parsimony and the Charybdis of unanalyzable complexity. Is there the possibility of a middle way between these extremes? I would argue that there is such a middle way. Table 8-5 shows the nature and inferred strength of structural linkages among the various development influences discussed in this volume. The nature of linkages is drawn from material reviewed earlier in this chapter. The inferred strength of linkages is drawn from the material reviewed in chapters 2–7. As can be seen from Table 8-5, not all developmental influences are linked to each other, not all developmental influences are linked in the same way, and when linked, the strength of different linkages is not the same for different influences. For example, although some developmental influences have relatively complex interconnections (e.g., genetic influences, proximal environmental influences), others have relatively sparse interconnections (e.g., evolutionary influences, physical ecology). Similarly, we see in Table 8-5 that there is a bidirectional covariance relation between the proximal environment and genetic and nutritional influences. In contrast, although evidence indicates that proximal environmental stimulation influences CNS variability, there does not appear to be a linkage path from the CNS to the objective environment. Rather, what evidence indicates is that CNS characteristics can influence the individual's perception or representation of his or her objective environment, along dimensions such as individual differences in affectual characteristics or perceptions of threat (Merzenich et al., 1991; Rothbart et al., 1994). As a result, there is a undirectional linkage from the CNS to individual characteristics. Although I have not presented similar information for functional linkages, for at least some sets of functionally linked developmental influences (e.g., Organism × Proximal Environment), we have a sufficient database to tell us what interactive combinations are most likely to occur (Wachs, 1992).

One implication of these different linkage patterns is that the interconnection density of a given developmental influence is likely to relate to the importance of that influence. Influences with denser covarying or causal structural linkages are more likely to be important in explaining individual behavioral-developmental variability than are influences with sparser linkage patterns.

Implications for Research Design

A second set of implications is seen in Figure 8-1, which is a flow chart illustrating the steps needed to generate realistic research strategies for different types of midlevel linkage processes. As seen in Figure 8-1, the first step involves a decision as to how many developmental influences to include in a research design. If we are dealing with outcomes having restricted variability, which are associated with rarely occurring specific influences, it may be valid to assume the operation of a main effect process based on a single influence operating in isolation. However, in all other cases there is a high probability that we are dealing with outcomes driven by multiple influences that are linked either functionally or structurally. If we are dealing with multiple-influence driven outcomes, then choosing to focus on a single influence puts the researcher in a situation of unrealistic parsimony. To avoid the alternative problem of unanalyzable complexity, as shown in Step 2 of Figure 8-1, it is necessary to focus primarily on those influences that are the most important sources of individual variability in a given outcome. Ideally, the choice of which developmental influences from which domains are to be included would be based on theoretical grounds For example, using

TABLE 8-5
Nature of Structural Linkages Among Multiple
Developmental Influences

Influence	Covariance linkage to	Causal linkage to	Causal linkage from	Bidirectional causal linkage
Evolution	Culture	Genetics, CNS, Individual characteristics		
Physical ecology	Biomedical factors, **Nutrition,** Proximal environment, Distal environment			
Genetics[a]	**Proximal environment**	**CNS,** Individual characteristics	Evolution, Proximal environment	Nutrition, Biomedical factors, Hormones
CNS		**Individual characteristics**	Evolution, **Genetics,** Biomedical factors, **Nutrition,** Proximal environment	**Hormones**
Hormones			Proximal environment, Biomedical factors	Genetics, CNS, Nutrition, **Individual characteristics**
Biomedical factors[a]	**Nutrition,** Individual characteristics, Proximal environment, **Distal environment**	CNS, Hormones	Physical ecology	Genetics, **Nutrition**

the developmental niche theory of Super and Harkness (1986b) as a guide for research would require taking measures of culturally driven child rearing customs, parent values and goals, and individual child characteristics that could moderate parental behavior in a given culture. Using theories derived from the field of developmental psychopathology as a guide for research would require taking measures of family genetic risk for the disorder under

TABLE 8-5 (*continued*)

Influence	Covariance linkage to	Causal linkage to	Causal linkage from	Bidirectional causal linkage
Nutrition[a]	Physical ecology, CNS, **Biomedical factors,** Individual characteristics, **Proximal environment,** Distal environment			Genetics, Hormones, **Biomedical factors**
Individual characteristics	Biomedical factors, Nutrition, Distal environment		Evolution, **Genetics, CNS**	**Hormones,** Proximal environment
Proximal environment	**Genes, Biomedical factors Nutrition, Distal environment**	CNS, Hormones		Individual characteristics
Distal environment	Evolution, **Physical ecology, Biomedical factors,** Nutrition, Individual characteristics, **Proximal environment**			

Note. CNS = central nervous system. Boldface type indicates a stronger level of linkage.
[a]Indicates both covariance and structural linkages involving the same influences.

consideration, individual stress exposure, individual attentional and reactivity characteristics, and the stress-producing characteristics of the broader context within which individuals reside (Rutter et al., 1997).

In the absence of an appropriate guiding theory, the material reviewed in chapters 2–7 can serve as a guide to which developmental influences from which domains are most likely to influence individual variability in a given outcome. Following the specificity principle discussed in chapter 6 (also see chap. 9), it is important to avoid the assumption that the same set of developmental influences will be equally salient for all outcomes. Following an inductive strategy and focusing primarily on those developmental influences that have been shown to be most strongly associated with variability in a given developmental–behavioral outcome is an alternative way to reduce the number of influences investigated

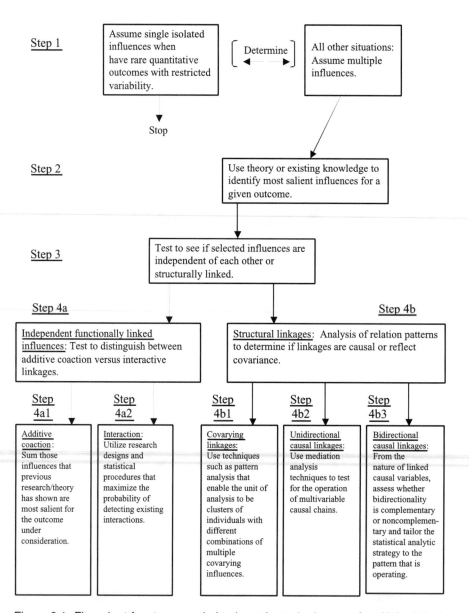

Step 1 | Assume single isolated influences when have rare quantitative outcomes with restricted variability.

[Determine ◄——►]

All other situations: Assume multiple influences.

▼

Stop

Step 2 | Use theory or existing knowledge to identify most salient influences for a given outcome.

Step 3 | Test to see if selected influences are independent of each other or structurally linked.

Step 4a

Independent functionally linked influences: Test to distinguish between additive coaction versus interactive linkages.

Step 4b

Structural linkages: Analysis of relation patterns to determine if linkages are causal or reflect covariance.

Step 4a1 | Step 4a2 | Step 4b1 | Step 4b2 | Step 4b3

Additive coaction: Sum those influences that previous research/theory has shown are most salient for the outcome under consideration.

Interaction: Utilize research designs and statistical procedures that maximize the probability of detecting existing interactions.

Covarying linkages: Use techniques such as pattern analysis that enable the unit of analysis to be clusters of individuals with different combinations of multiple covarying influences.

Unidirectional causal linkages: Use mediation analysis techniques to test for the operation of multivariable causal chains.

Bidirectional causal linkages: From the nature of linked causal variables, assess whether bidirectionality is complementary or noncomplementary and tailor the statistical analytic strategy to the pattern that is operating.

Figure 8-1. Flow chart for steps needed to investigate the impact of multiple, linked developmental influences.

to a manageable number. However, choosing a limited set of predictor variables is just the first step. The next step (3) would be to test whether we are dealing with independent or structurally linked influences. If our chosen influences covary, then we are in a situation involving some type of structural linkage. As shown in Figure 8-1, different strategies are called for, depending on whether we are dealing with functionally or structurally linked influences.

Strategies for Functional Linkages

Additive Coaction

If our Step 3 analysis indicates that we are dealing with uncorrelated independent influences, the next step is to determine whether we are dealing with additive coaction or interaction processes (Step 4a). In distinguishing between additive coaction and interaction processes, a traditional statistical test is to determine whether an interaction model provides a better fit to the data than does an additive coaction model. Additive coaction explanations are traditionally preferred if our analysis demonstrates no additional predictive variance found for the interaction term, over and above variance associated with additive coaction. This traditional approach may be problematic, given that standard statistical tests often underestimate the contribution of interactive processes (Rodgers, 1990). Even when standard statistical tests for interaction do not reach the commonly accepted $p < .05$ level of statistical significance, this does not necessarily mean that underlying functional linkages among multiple influences involve only additive coaction (Cronbach, 1987). Given this situation, a number of authors have suggested supplementing traditional statistical procedures with the use of confidence intervals to determine whether the range of values is consistent with models based on interactive processes (Cronbach, 1991; Rutter & Pickles, 1991). If confidence intervals are consistent with the possibility that interactive processes may be operating, I would argue that appropriate tests for interactions (as discussed later) should be implemented before assuming that only additive coaction processes are operating.

If our tests rule out the possibility of interactive processes operating, then the strategy for assessing the nature and impact of additive coaction processes is fairly straightforward (Step 4a1, Figure 8-1). Basically we need to determine whether better prediction of outcomes occurs from our combining theoretically or empirically derived developmental influences than from analyzing the impact of each influence in isolation. If results demonstrate better prediction from a combination of influences, then it is appropriate to deal with questions such as whether there is an *additive* effect (combining risk predictors), a *subtractive* effect (risk factors minus protective factors), or a *threshold effect* (a certain number of risk or predictive factors need to be operating to shift the pattern of development).

Interaction

If we are unable to rule out the operation of interaction processes, then it becomes necessary to test for the extent and nature of potential interactions. The possibility that interactive processes are operating becomes particularly important when predicted relations between outcome measures and specific developmental influences are found to be either nonsignificant

TABLE 8-6
Examples of Studies Reporting Dilution or Cancellation of Significant Subgroup Findings

Type	Finding	Reference
Dilution	Interventions used with preterm infants of differing birth weight and gestational age.	Infant Health and Development Program (1990)
	Relations between environmental noise and mastery motivation found for boys but not for girls.	Wachs (1987b)
	Relations between physiological reactivity and stress moderated by individual restlessness and concentration or by individual immune system reactivity.	Magnusson (1988); Barr et al. (1994)
	Genetic influences on affective disorders occurring only for individuals with a specific risk history.	Cadoret et al. (1990)
	Link between childhood institutionalization and adult schizophrenia occurring only for those with a family history of schizophrenia.	Cannon et al. (1990)
Cancellation	Level of stimulation that acts to organize state control of full-term infants acts to disorganize state control of preterms.	Eckerman & Oehler (1992)
	Daycare facilitates later adjustment of insecurely attached infants and inhibits attachment of securely attached infants.	Egeland & Hiester (1995)
	Higher levels of caregiver attention focusing behavior facilitates exploratory competence of low active infants and inhibits exploratory competence of high active infants.	Gandour (1989)

or extremely weak. Nonsignificant or low-level relations between specific predictors and outcomes may reflect a lack of influence of these predictors, or they may reflect the fact that the developmental predictors under consideration operate only for certain subgroups within a larger population (Baron & Kenny, 1986). In this situation, the impact of a specific influence on a smaller subgroup of individuals is diluted when the results for this subgroup are combined with the nonsignificant results found for the majority of individuals who are not in this subgroup (McCall & Applebaum, 1991). Nonsignificant or low-level relations also may reflect a situation where specific developmental influences significantly influence outcomes for different subgroups but in different ways. In this situation, combining the outcome scores for both groups cancels out the significant effect for each group. Examples of both of these types of situations are shown in Table 8-6.

When either theoretical or empirical guidelines alert the researcher to the possibility that interactive processes may be occurring, the situation becomes somewhat more complex than in the case of additive coaction. Earlier in this chapter, I reviewed the multiple methodological and statistical procedures that can inhibit our ability to detect interactions. A number of these potential problems can be minimized if appropriate design features are put into the research design before beginning the study (Step 4a2, Figure 8-1). Two important design features to incorporate would include the following: (a) oversampling of groups or individuals that are at the extreme end or ends of the distribution of the trait or situation that should be acting as a moderator (McClelland & Judd, 1993) and (b) use of aggregated measures of both developmental predictors and moderating variables as a means of maximizing statistical power (Wachs & Plomin, 1991).

The above discussion assumes that available theory or an empirical literature has sensitized the researcher toward specific interactions that should be tested. Unfortunately, too often it is the appearance of nonsignificant results or low effect size in an already designed study that suggest to the researcher that interactions may be a reason for disappointing main effect results. To be able to test for potentially existing interactions, even on a post hoc basis, I would argue for systematic collection of what Cronbach (1991) called "side information" in all studies in which there is the possibility of functionally linked multiple influences on a given outcome. *Side information* refers to the routine collection of relatively low-cost information that would allow for meaningful tests of the operation of unpredicted interactions. From previous research and theory on this question, I would argue that three sources of side information are particularly critical to collect as a routine part of human behavioral–developmental research (Wachs, 1991).

- Information that could be useful in terms of grouping individuals on the basis of *differential vulnerability to stressors* (e.g., gender; biological risk history, such as malnutrition or family genotype; difficult temperament).
- Information that could help classify individuals on the basis of differential ability to *make use of existing environmental supports* (e.g., activity level, intelligence, attachment).
- Information that could be useful in classifying individuals on the basis of *differential reaction patterns* (e.g., gender, history of antisocial behavior).

Strategies for Structural Linkages

When dealing with multiple structural linkages, the traditional response has been either to ignore linkages or to use statistical partialing as a way of isolating the "unique" contributions of a specific predictor (Gore & Eckenrode, 1994). The fact that statistical control can be easily done does not necessarily mean that such control is desirable, particularly when we are attempting to understand outcomes that are based on the operation of multiple structurally linked developmental influences.

As discussed previously, differentiating between covarying and causal structural linkages can be made on the basis of a number of criteria (Figure 8-1, Step 4b). One such criterion is the physical or temporal contiguity between different influences, with a greater degree of contiguity increasing the likelihood that we are dealing with causal linkages. The absence of known causal mechanisms linking together two influences or the absence of replicated patterns showing that change in a second variable consistently follows change in a preceding variable suggests that we are dealing with covarying rather than causal linkages.

Covariance

In a situation in which we have structural covarying linkages among multiple influences, one implication is that our unit of analysis should not be the individual influence taken in isolation. As shown in Figure 8-2, Step 4b1, a more appropriate unit of analysis would be the pattern of linkages among multiple influences (Rogoff, 1991; Wachs, 1996b). One such approach is through a technique called *pattern analysis*, wherein individuals with different biological, individual, and psychosocial characteristics are grouped into different clusters. Cluster membership is designed to maximize intragroup similarity while minimizing intergroup resemblance on specific biological, environmental, and individual characteristics (Magnusson, 1988; Magnusson & Bergman, 1990). Rather than an individual isolated predictor, the unit of analysis used for predicting outcomes in pattern analysis is membership in a given cluster. The advantage of such a procedure is twofold. First, it allows us to determine which clusters of covarying characteristics are most predictive of specific developmental outcomes. Second, if cluster membership significantly predicts outcome variability, by looking at cluster characteristics we can specify which linked combinations of influences are most relevant for different developmental outcomes. In this sense, pattern analysis offers a more direct way to map onto an existing reality consisting of covarying multiple influences on individual development.

Such an approach may seem dramatically antithetical to our traditional research strategy of attempting to isolate the critical influence on individual behavioral–developmental variability. However, if we are dealing with multiple linked covarying influences, then our traditional strategy may not be a good fit to the nature of the phenomenon we are attempting to understand. It would be relatively easy to test the validity of this nontraditional approach. In situations in which existing reality involves multiple linked influences, we should get stronger prediction by using pattern analysis techniques than by using statistical techniques that are based on an assumption of individual predictors acting in isolation from each other (e.g., simultaneous regression, which gives us the summed unique contribution of the predictors treated in isolation from each other). The degree of predictive gain associated with pattern analysis would be a measure of the degree of multiple linked influences, over and above the contribution of isolated multiple predictors. Although there is little direct evidence on this validation question, evidence from a few studies indirectly supports the foregoing hypothesis. For example, although both age of onset of puberty and changing schools can be risk factors for depression in adolescent girls, depression is more likely to occur when pubertal onset covaries with school change (Petersen et al., 1991). Similarly, the impact of a single protective factor may depend on the degree with which it covaries with other protective factors encountered by the individual (Bradley et al., 1994; Gore & Eckenrode, 1994).

Causal Linkages

An alternative analytic strategy is indicated when the underlying structure suggests that we are dealing with causal linkages among multiple influences. As illustrated in Table 8-2, Step 4b2, in the case of unidirectional causal linkages between two or more developmental influences, one analytic strategy involves testing for "mediation" (Baron & Kenny, 1986). Mediational analysis can be used to test whether a given developmental influence predicts outcome variability ($a \rightarrow x$) primarily through its impact on a second developmental influence ($a \rightarrow b \rightarrow x$). For example, evidence suggests that distal environmental characteristics such as economic stress do not directly influence adolescent adjustment; rather, economic pressures influence parental characteristics such as mood. Parental mood in turn influences family processes such as parental conflict and rearing strategies, which then directly influence adolescent adjustment (Conger et al., 1992, 1993). The mediated chain would thus be as follows:

Economic stress $\rightarrow$ parental mood $\rightarrow$ family processes $\rightarrow$ adolescent adjustment

When analyzing mediated causal chains, one critical error that must be avoided is interpreting results as if outcome variability were solely a function of the last link in the predictor chain (Gore & Eckenrode, 1994). Using the example just given as an illustration, this error would occur if we concluded that the only influence on variability in adolescent adjustment were family proximal processes. Such an interpretation, although perhaps parsimonious, is also misleading, because we ignore the impact of distal conditions such as economic stress and individual characteristics such as parental mood on the characteristics of the adolescent's family environment.[2] Avoiding such an

---

[2] The same error also occurs with covarying linkages when the researcher focuses on just one of the covariates as the prime cause, ignoring any contributions made by the remainder of the covariates (e.g., Dawkins, 1980; Scarr, 1992).

error is particularly critical in the most common mediating pattern encountered in human behavioral–developmental research, partial mediation, when the last link in the chain explains some but not all of the outcome variability (Evans & Lepore, 1997).

Bidirectional causal linkages among multiple developmental influences are among the most challenging processes to deal with, either analytically or conceptually.[3] Use of appropriate statistical procedures such as time series sequential analysis can be costly, requiring not just longitudinal data but also the use of multiple data points (Evans & Lepore, 1997). Furthermore, the choice of which statistical approach to use is difficult. As with interactions, we are more likely to be able to understand the nature of bidirectional causal linkages if our statistics are tailored to the nature of the linkage process. In some cases, bidirectional linkages may act in a homeostatic fashion, keeping outcome levels within a given range (Hofer, 1994). Multiple examples of homeostatic biodirectional feedback are seen in regard to biological regulatory processes, as in the case of regulation of body calcium levels under conditions of low calcium intake (Groff et al., 1995). However, bidirectional causal linkages also can act to accentuate the impact of linked influences over time, as seen in the bidirectional escalation between malnutrition and illness (Keusch, 1990). Unfortunately, too often we do not know the nature of the relationship among bidirectional, causally linked multiple influences.

In terms of tailoring analyses to underlying processes, it would be extremely useful if we had some guidelines that would allow us to decide whether we are more likely to be dealing with homeostatic or accentuation bidirectional causal linkages (Step 4b3). Borrowing liberally from a number of sources (Cairns, 1993; Lloyd-Morgan, 1902; Moffitt, 1993; Reinisch et al., 1991; Waddington, 1966), I would argue for the following speculative guidelines:

- When bidirectional, causally linked influences are operating and these influences appear to support each other (i.e., pushing the individual toward the same developmental track), then we can expect an accentuation pattern to occur.
- When bidirectional, causally linked influences are operating and these influences appear to be in opposition to each other (i.e., pushing the individual toward different developmental tracks), then we can expect a homeostatic pattern to occur.

Although this discussion is focused on causal bidirectional linkages, a similar set of predictions could be made for covarying linkages. For example, accentuation is more likely to occur when there is positive covariance

---

[3] The situation becomes even more complex, both analytically and conceptually, when there are reciprocal linkages between outcomes and predictors. Possible approaches to dealing with reciprocal linkages are found in Evans and Lepore (1997).

among developmental influences (e.g., a child's difficult temperament and the parent's coercive discipline), whereas homeostasis is more likely to occur when there is negative covariance (e.g., between risk and protective factors).

MULTIPLE INFLUENCES ON DEVELOPMENT: CONCLUSIONS

In this chapter I have documented not only that multiple influences converge on individual behavioral–developmental variability but also that these multiple influences are linked. Linkages can be functional, as in the case when the impact of one developmental influence depends on the contributions of a second influence. Alternatively, there are structural linkages, in which existing multiple developmental influences are not independent of each other. As will be discussed in chapter 10, structural linkages allow us to apply systems principles as tools for organizing and understanding how multiple developmental influences contribute to individual behavioral–developmental variability.

What must be stressed is that a research framework based on a linked system of multiple developmental influences did not arise as a plot by a small cabal of scientists who hoped to make the study of development unduly complicated. Echoing a theme raised by both Anderson (1972) and Salthe (1985), in multilevel systems each level is influenced not only by its own unique set of laws but also by laws operating at lower levels of the system. Thus, to understand human behavioral development, we must take into account the action of influences operating both at molar levels (e.g., the proximal and distal environment) as well as the action of influences operating at molecular levels (e.g., genetics and biochemistry). Although postulating the operation of linked multiple influences may seem to violate the concept of parsimony, we must remember that parsimony does not refer to the simplest explanation possible. Rather, parsimony refers to the simplest explanation that fits the phenomenon under study. Human behavioral development by its very nature is very complex. To understand such complexities, we need to understand both the extent and the nature of contributions of linked multiple influences from various domains, all of which are necessary but not sufficient.

Although most individual behavioral–developmental variability results from the operation of linked multiple influences, this fact does not rule out studies designed to test how a specific influence from a single domain is relevant to such variability. Single-influence studies are necessary, if only because it is important to document whether a specific influence is relevant for a given aspect of individual behavioral development (e.g., studies designed to test whether iron supplementation influences anemic children's level of attention; studies relating early attachment differences to later social interaction patterns). However, single-influence studies are not sufficient in and of themselves because outcomes like attention or social interaction also can be affected by other influences that covary or interact with iron status or early attachment. Studies of single specific influences taken in isolation and studies of multiple influences considered simultaneously are not antagonistic but rather complementary to each other, in the sense of asking different but nonetheless necessary questions. However, for a greater depth of understanding, we need to go beyond single-influence studies to studies of multiple linked influences.

Besides showing the operation of linked multiple influences, what I also have attempted to do in the present chapter is to lay to rest two despairing cries. The first cry is that if everything is linked to everything else, there is no way to study such complexity. What I showed in this chapter is that not all developmental influences are linked to each other. Linkages vary in their degree of strength, and different developmental influences are linked in different ways (Table 8-5). Furthermore, the nature of linkages has definite implications for how we study the role of multiple developmental influences on individual behavioral–developmental variability (Figure 8-1). The complexities defined in this chapter may be difficult to intuitively comprehend, and they do require the use of alternative research designs and statistical analyses that are different from what would be used if we were studying the impact of a single isolated influence. However, the complexities described in this chapter are nonetheless open to rigorous empirical testing. Although the exact methodologies used will vary, depending on what specific questions are being asked, the fact that similar linkage patterns occur across influences from multiple domains means that the research and analytic strategies described in this chapter may be generalizable to integrative, multidomain research.

The fact that the complexities inherent in a linked multi-influence framework are open to empirical testing of specific hypotheses does not necessarily mean that such testing is actually feasible. This concern is reflected in a second despairing cry: If we need to study linked multiple influences, then the cost of doing such research becomes prohibitive in terms of time, effort, and sample size. If one attempts to study all possible linkages, this cry is correct. However, as suggested earlier, for any given outcome we should not be attempting to test the role of all possible linked influences. Rather, for any given outcome, our focus should be on those specific influences that are most salient and most closely linked together. Identification of salience for a given outcome can be based on the information contained in chapters 2–7 in this volume. Linkage patterns among the different developmental influences are illustrated in Table 8-5. By integrating existing knowledge of salience and linkage patterns, it is possible to study combinations of linked multiple influences in ways that are feasible in terms of both cost and statistical power. For example, applying the dual criteria of salience and linkage strength to studies of developmental psychopathology would mean a focus on influences taken from the domain of genetics, individual characteristics, and the proximal environment. Studies on gender development would encompass evolutionary, genetic, hormonal, proximal environmental, and cultural characteristics. In contrast, in terms of studying variability in intellectual development, we would want to focus on genetic, biomedical, CNS, nutritional, and proximal environmental influences within a given culture.

Even with a restricted set of influence domains, given cost and sample size considerations, is it really practical to integrate measures from more than two domains? I previously have suggested how studies of proximal environmental influences can be expanded at relatively low cost to include measures of at least two subgroups of individuals, as well as one potential nonenvironmental covariate and one alternative higher order distal context (Wachs, 1992). Expanding this example across multiple domains is clearly possible. Measures of individual characteristics could include gender or easily obtained assessments of intellectual ability (IQ screening test) or temperamental difficultness (parent report). Measures of height could be used as a low-cost proxy for nutritional history in disadvantaged populations, whereas reporting of medical history by parents could be used as a low-cost covariate proxy for biomedical status in more advantaged populations. Low-cost context proxies could include parent educational level or social class, school size, and number of hours spent by the child in day care or nursery schools, or short, validated measures of caregiver perceptions of their context. By using low-cost measures, it is feasible to use larger samples, which can increase statistical power. Statistical power also can be increased by use of converging measurements that can be aggregated across measures or situations as a means of reducing errors of measurement (e.g., parent and teacher reports of child temperament; measures of objective stress and the individual's subjective perceptions of his or her ongoing stress; cumulative medical records and self-report of the cumulative number of biological and psychosocial stressors encountered by the individual). One of the benefits of such aggregation is reduced error of measurement, which can increase available statistical power.

Lest it be assumed that this is all pure speculation, I refer the reader to a living example. Talbert and McLaughlin (1999) showed how studies on school influences can include, at relatively low cost and sufficient power, measures of school characteristics, measures of pupil and teacher characteristics, and measures of higher order school-related contextual influences. There appears to be no reason why the same research framework could not be applied to other domains of developmental influence as well.

What has been shown in this chapter is that it is essential to look not just at multiple influences per se but also at how multiple influences are linked to each other and how the nature of such linkages increases our ability to understand individual behavioral–developmental variability. Can we stop here? I would argue not. Midlevel processes involving linkages among multiple influences, although necessary, are not sufficient for a complete understanding of the etiology and nature of individual behavioral–developmental variability. Three lines of evidence emphasize the need to go beyond linked multiple influences per se:

- the appearance of "turning points" in the developmental course when the individual encounters major intrinsic or extrinsic changes that act to open up new developmental niches, close down access to existing developmental niches, or alter the individual's sense of control over his or her life (Rutter, 1993; also see chap. 9).
- evidence indicating that different combinations of developmental influences may be related to individual variability for different types of outcomes (Wachs, 1992; also see chap. 9).
- evidence showing how existing developmental pathways may shift in unpredictable directions that cannot be easily explained by the nature of the various developmental influences impinging on the individual (Gottman, 1991; also see chap. 10).

9

TEMPORAL AND SPECIFICITY PROCESSES

At the close of chapter 8, I concluded that midlevel processes involving linked multiple influences, although necessary, were not sufficient for understanding individual behavioral–developmental variability. In the present chapter, I go beyond multiple influences to describe two additional midlevel processes that are also necessary for understanding the etiology and course of individual behavioral–developmental variability. Both *temporal* and *specificity* midlevel processes are common to multiple influences from different domains.

TEMPORAL PROCESSES

Evidence on the relevance of age-related maturational influences for development was discussed in chapter 5. Besides maturation, we also know that certain behavioral characteristics have been associated with a particular age period, such as an increased level of adolescent antisocial behavior and behavioral patterns that disrupt family functioning (Moffitt, 1990; Petersen, 1988). More recently, developmental theorists have focused on changes in life course trajectories as a function of changes such as school transitions or military service encountered by individuals during a given age

217

period (Ceci, 1993; Elder & Caspi, 1988; Maughn, 1994; Rutter, 1996). Concepts such as critical or sensitive periods, when the organism is particularly sensitive to the impact of extrinsic influences, have been used in a number of disciplines, including ethology, embryology, genetics, neuroscience, and developmental linguistics (Bornstein, 1989a; Cairns, 1993; Edelman, 1989; Newport, 1990).

This emphasis on age-related processes is particularly interesting, given that age itself is traditionally viewed as a proxy for more fundamental biological and experiential mechanisms (Rutter, 1988; Wohlwill, 1973). For example, as seen in chapter 4, the association of the 3–30 month age period with maximal risk for physical growth faltering in less developed countries is the result of a set of multiple conditions, including high individual growth velocity during this time, quality of food available to infants, and an increased susceptibility to gastrointestinal infections during the first 30 months of life. Similarly, the timing of individual age differences in pubertal maturation is mediated by underlying differences in nutritional status, health, genetics, ethnicity, and stress level (Paikoff & Brooks-Gunn, 1991). Age-related differences also have been related to level of demands made on the individual (Caspi & Bem, 1990), differences in the ability to attend to task-relevant information (Spear & Hyatt, 1993), differences in challenges or expectancies that need to be met by children (Erikson, 1963), availability and nature of coping strategies used by the individual (Asendorpf, 1994; Punamaki, 1988), and options that are available to the individual at different age periods (Gore & Eckenrode, 1994).

Even though many age-related differences can be reduced to differences in specific biological or psychosocial mechanisms, temporal processes per se also can uniquely act to influence individual behavioral–developmental variability. One way is through temporal influences acting at the level of the group, as in the case of cohort influences based on living during a particular historical time period (Caspi, 1998). For example, the impact of father absence on children's long-term development has been found to vary depending on whether children were in time cohorts when father absence was common (e.g., wartime) or uncommon (Grundman, 1996). In this chapter, I will focus on six midlevel temporal processes that can serve as additional sources of influence on individual behavioral–developmental variability: (a) the impact of deviations from time-locked temporal sequences, (b) age specificity, (c) temporal moderation, (d) temporal persistence, (e) cumulative influences, and (f) causal chains.

Impact of Deviations From Time-Locked Developmental Sequences

In chapter 2 the concept of experience-expectant development was presented, along with evidence illustrating the consequences when information normally available to an organism during a given developmental period is made unavailable. In chapter 3 I documented how central nervous system (CNS) development occurs in a regular temporal sequence, both at the microstructure (e.g., neural migration patterns) and the macrostructure levels (e.g., order of development of different brain regions). What was also documented in chapter 3 is how deviations from normal CNS developmental sequences can result in a variety of negative consequences. For example, Turkewitz and Kenny (1985) have hypothesized that maturationally based sensory restrictions early in life may be necessary to prevent competition for information among different sensory systems. Within this framework, premature exposure to sensory information that would normally be processed later in development can act to inhibit rather than facilitate subsequent development. Empirical validation for this hypothesis has been provided by Spear and Hyatt (1993), who show that providing young rats with a range of stimulation wider than they would normally encounter early in life results in a diminished ability to distinguish task-relevant from task-irrelevant information later in life. At a behavioral level, Gore and Eckenrode (1994) also have hypothesized that compromising the ability of the individual to fulfill developmental tasks central to a given age can have long-term negative consequences. Empirical validation for this hypothesis is seen in studies showing the consequences associated with disruption of the infant's ability to develop self-regulation and secure attachment (Elicker, Englund, & Sroufe, 1992).

These findings would seem to suggest an underlying principle, namely that temporal deviations from normally occurring biological or psychological developmental sequences, or deviations in exposure to stimulation that would normally be processed at a given age period, can constitute a developmental risk. However, the generalizability of such a principle is not well supported. As shown in chapter 4, evidence indicates that malnutrition can slow the rate of CNS development. One consequence of such slowing is an extension of the time period during which nutritional rehabilitation can occur. In this case, temporal deviation has a potential positive impact on individual development. Furthermore, the impact of temporal deviations can be moderated by individual characteristics. One such example involves individuals deviating in physical maturation rate as compared with other individuals in their age cohort (e.g., early puberty). As shown in chapter 5, the developmental consequences of boys being maturationally out of step with their peer group initially tend to be positive (e.g., higher social prestige, more likely to be a leader), whereas for girls the consequences tend to be negative (increased risk of depression, behavior problems, or lower educational level).

Overall it seems clear that there are developmental consequences at both the physical and psychological levels as a result of deviation from normal time-locked sequences. However, it also seems clear that the nature of such consequences are not necessarily obvious. One reason why involves the multiplicity of biological and experiential variables that are nested under the concept of age (Rutter, 1996). Thus, simply referring to temporal deviations is highly ambiguous unless we are able to specify what the deviation is in reference to. As Caspi has noted (A. Caspi, personal communication, February 1998), from a biological viewpoint, teen pregnancy does not necessarily represent a temporal deviation. However, from a social–cultural perspective, in Western developed societies teen pregnancy may indeed be a temporal deviation. Unless we are able to refer to what processes underlie temporal deviations, there will continue to be ambiguity in terms of what types of consequences can be expected.

Can we go beyond just age deviations from time-related developmental sequences or events to come to more specific process-based conclusions about the nature of consequences associated with temporal deviation? From what little evidence is available on this question, I offer the following tentative inductive hypotheses:

1. When temporal sequence deviations only occur for subelements of a larger biological system, then developmental consequences are more likely to be negative. This conclusion is congruent with the evidence cited earlier in regard to temporal deviations associated with specific CNS micro- and macrostructures or with premature exposure to stimulation in one modality.

2. To the extent that temporal deviations from age-linked behavioral sequences fit what is viewed as a positive consequence by the individual's macrocontext, the result is more likely to be a positive developmental outcome. When temporal deviations are viewed by the macrocontext in a negative light, detrimental developmental outcomes are more likely to result. Thus, for boys, pubertal changes such as increased strength would fit what is viewed as a desirable asset in high school, namely greater potential for athletic ability. For girls, less desirable changes such as the increased weight associated with early puberty would be more likely to produce the negative developmental outcomes reported. Similarly, in cultures where pubertal maturation means that the individual is viewed as being ready to assume adult responsibility, it is not surprising to find that early maturing adolescents are more likely to have a stronger sense of social responsibility than are later maturing adolescents (Richards et al., 1993).

3. Whether the developmental consequences of temporal sequence deviations are positive or negative will depend on the nature of subsequent structurally linked developmental influences encountered by the individual. Thus, where generalized

slowing of CNS development is followed by positive developmental influences, such as nutritional rehabilitation, positive outcomes are more likely to occur. Negative developmental outcomes are more likely to occur when temporal deviations covary with developmental risk factors (e.g., early motor maturation in an environment high in flaking lead-based paint; preterm birth into a high-stress, low socioeconomic status [SES] family).

The foregoing hypotheses, although clearly speculative, illustrate how deviations from normal temporal developmental sequences can affect subsequent behavioral–developmental variability. Although speculative, these hypotheses are empirically testable.

Age Specificity

The term *age specificity* is used in preference to terms such as *critical period* or *sensitive period* (Bornstein, 1989a), in large part because the term age specificity is less encumbered by theoretical assumptions. Age specificity is defined as follows: The impact of specific developmental influences will vary as a function of age of the individual, such that different developmental influences will be differentially salient at different ages (Wachs & Gruen, 1982).

Evidence showing how the impact of specific developmental influences may be moderated by the age of the individual is clearly seen in regard to the CNS (see chaps. 3 and 4). Evidence summarized in these chapters shows how the CNS is less sensitive to the impact of injury or environmental toxins later in life than it is earlier in life, when CNS structures are still maturing; at the same time, the more mature CNS is less able to compensate after exposure to injury or environmental toxins. Other examples of age specificity are shown in Table 9-1.

Although there is ample evidence for the operation of age specificity, what are less clear are the mechanisms underlying this temporal process. As already emphasized, age itself is a form of social address, and it is thus more useful as a descriptor than an explanation (Wohlwill, 1973). Going beyond description, in some cases we can logically assume that evolutionary mechanisms may underlie age specificity (Horowitz, 1992). For example, infant survival is more likely to occur if universal aspects of early development (walking, communication) are relatively well buffered against early social risks. In some cases, structural considerations are important, as exemplified by the concept that specific CNS areas are most sensitive to developmental influences during their period of maximal structural growth (Georgieff, 1994). Conversely, the slowing of physical growth rate over time means that the further the child is behind in physical growth, the longer the child will

Table 9-1
Examples of Age Specificity

Domain	Pattern of findings	Reference
Evolutionary influences	Experience-expectant development processes are age dependent; more likely to occur in infancy and toddler period.	Greenough et al. (1990)
Physical ecology	Ability to acclimate to high-altitude living conditions easier for those exposed in childhood than for those who must acclimate as adults.	Frisancho (1975)
Genetic influences	Extent of genetic influences on antisocial behavior varies from adolescence to adulthood.	DiLalla &Gottesman (1989)
	Same set of genes related to ADHD and conduct disorder of 8–11 year old children; different sets of genes related to each disorder after 12 years of age.	Silberg et al. (1996)
CNS	Sensitive period for development of human visual and auditory perceptual systems.	Goodman (1994)
Biomedical influences	Serum bilirubin levels that are safe for older infants are more likely to be toxic for preterms.	Menke et al. (1991)
	Young children are more sensitive to lead-exposure effects than are older children.	Schroeder & Hawk (1987)
	Exposure of pregnant women to mercury results in localized CNS damage for the mother but diffuse fetal CNS damage.	Vorhees & Mollnow (1987)
	Relation of prenatal malnutrition to adult schizophrenia seen only when malnutrition occurred in the first trimester of pregnancy.	Susser et al. (1996)

Table 9-1 *(continued)*

Domain	Pattern of findings	Reference
Nutrition	Supplementing growth-retarded infants has strongest influence in first year of life, with declining effects thereafter.	Martorell et al. (1994)
Individual characteristics	Antisocial behavior has more consistent and strongest impact when onset is early in childhood rather than in adolescence.	Clarke & Clarke (1988)
Proximal environment	Hospital admissions during age 1–4 years are a greater stressor on children than earlier or later admissions.	Rutter (1988)
	Children with XXY disorder are less influenced by parenting practices prior to puberty than during and after puberty.	Netley & Rovet (1988)
	The earlier the exposure to a second language prior to puberty, the better the level of acquisition; no such relation after puberty.	Newport (1990)
	Marriage in the teen years acts as a risk factor while marriage in the adult years acts as a protective factor.	Rutter (1996)
	In regard to cognitive development, tactual stimulation most salient over first 6 months.	Wachs (1922)
	Caregiver verbal stimulation and verbal responsivity become increasingly salient after 12 months; caregiver emotional reactivity becomes less salient after Year 4, whereas aversive instructional techniques become increasingly important.	

(continued)

Table 9-1 (continued)

Domain	Pattern of findings	Reference
Distal environment	In cultures where rearing is done primarily by peers or siblings, older children may be more influenced by rearing conditions than are younger children.	Rogoff (1990)
Multidomain influences	Maternal depression is the primary predictor of adjustment for older children; maternal depression and parental rearing patterns are both predictors of adjustment of younger children.	Tarullo et al. (1995)
	Physical growth in the first 6 months of life sensitive to level of nutritional intake; later physical growth associated with level of growth hormones and sex steroid production.	Karlberg et al. (1994); Schurch (1995)

Note. CNS = central nervous system; ADHD = attention-deficit/hyperactivity disorder.

have to show an accelerated growth rate in order to catch up. This means that even when adequate nutrition is provided, slowly growing older children may never catch up (Golden, 1994).

Age specificity also may reflect differences in the level of functional capacities. The cognitive capacities of the young child, although sufficiently developed to allow the child to retain an image of the parent, may not be sufficiently developed to allow the child to use memory processes to bridge separations from the parent. As a result, young children may be particularly sensitive to separation experiences (Rutter, 1993). Biologically, the fact that TORCH infections (toxoplasmosis, other, rubella, cytomegalovirus, and herpes) primarily affect the fetus rather than mother can be seen as due to the fetus's poorly functioning immune system (Menke et al., 1991). The greater metabolic rate seen in young organisms means that they are more likely to absorb and retain a greater percentage of lead than adult organisms (Dietrich et al., 1985). At the other end of the life span, less functional physiological support systems that influence blood-carrying capacity may limit the plasticity of the CNS to respond to experience-dependent influences (Greenough et al., 1990).

The question of the mechanisms underlying age specificity is an essential one if we are to predict which ages will interact with specific developmental influences. A number of examples in the literature show how more precise predictions can be made when we focus on potential mechanisms underlying age specificity. For example, from what is known about CNS development, Shaheen (1984) was able to make relatively precise predictions about which cognitive functions would be most influenced when children of different ages were exposed to lead. From evidence on the development of functional capacities, Wasserman (1984) has shown how different types of cognitive–behavioral therapy are differentially suited to children at different ages. From knowledge of the development of CNS areas related to temperament, it also may be possible to predict when individual differences in infant temperament should influence caregiver behavioral patterns (Wachs & King, 1994). Mechanism-based studies are critical if future research on age specificity is to go beyond just a descriptive level.

Temporal Moderation

There has been a long running debate in developmental psychology in regard to the role of early versus later experience. Some theorists emphasize the unique salience of early experience (Wachs & Gruen, 1982), whereas other theorists have concluded that early experience is just one link in a causal chain, being neither more nor less important than later experience (Clarke & Clarke, 1979, 1989).

There is certainly ample evidence documenting how developmental trajectories set in motion by early influences can be redirected as later influences come into play (see chaps. 4 and 5). For example, more adequate food intake and better environmental stimulation later in life can at least partially compensate for the effects of early childhood malnutrition (Colombo, de la Parra, & Lopez, 1992; Winick, Meyer, & Harris, 1975). The fact that many individuals who display behavior problems early in life show little trace of these problems later in life suggests that the impact of early-appearing behavioral problems can be attenuated by later influences (Rutter, 1993; Steinhausen & Rauss-Mason, 1991). Adult experiences such as divorce or becoming a parent can act as "turning points," redirecting a previously stabilized developmental life course in new directions (Caspi, 1998; Clausen, 1995). Moderation of prior environmental influences by later environmental characteristics can occur either at the microsystem level (Bradley et al., 1988) or as a function of societal changes (Elder, 1995). Regardless of the source, redirection of previously stabilized developmental trajectories is most likely to occur when later influences are of sufficient magnitude or duration, run counter to previous life trajectory, involve some type of environmental or organismic discontinuity, and carry the potential for persistence over time (Rutter, 1996).

Besides attenuation, later developmental influences also can act to accentuate the salience of prior influences. One classic example is seen in the case of children originally from dysfunctional families who are institutionally reared and then returned to their dysfunctional family of origin. Such children show a higher incidence rate of societal, school, and family problems than institution-reared children who later were reared in functional foster families (Hodges & Tizard, 1989a, 1989b). Similarly, later stress experiences may act to accentuate the salience of already existing individual characteristics, thus stabilizing an existing developmental trajectory (Rutter, 1996).

The fact that later developmental influences can act to moderate the impact of prior developmental influences is not a surprising finding, nor should it be. Both biologically and psychologically (Lerner, 1984), mammalian species such as humans possess the gift of plasticity (i.e., openness to developmental influences throughout the lifespan). Although the extent of plasticity may decline over the lifespan, both infrahuman (Juraska, 1990) and human evidence (Lawton, 1999) shows plasticity even in older aging individuals. Such plasticity underlies the ability of later developmental influences to moderate the impact of earlier influences.

Although later developmental influences can act to moderate the impact of prior influences, evidence also suggests that temporal moderation is bidirectional in nature, such that *the impact of later developmental influences can be moderated by developmental influences occurring earlier in the lifespan.* For example, as shown in chapter 7, characteristics of an individual's original culture may act to channel his or her reactivity when faced with new cultural contexts later in life.

For the most part, discussion on the moderating impact of prior developmental influences has focused on the distinction between *buffering, sensitization,* and *steeling. Buffering* refers to prior influences protecting the individual against later stress. For example, evidence from the attachment literature shows that children with a secure attachment are more likely to show competent responding when faced with later environmental challenges than are children who are insecurely attached (Sroufe & Egeland, 1991). A number of examples of the operation of buffering processes are seen in chapters 6 and 7. *Sensitization* refers to prior negative developmental influences acting to make the individual more sensitive to later stresses. *Steeling* refers to exposure to prior negative developmental influences acting to protect the individual against the detrimental impact of later stresses (Rutter, 1993). Although evidence is available showing how early exposure to stress can have later beneficial consequences in areas like physical growth and intelligence (Aldwin & Stokols, 1988), far less evidence is available on the operation of steeling than on sensitization processes. Finally, there also is evidence for a fourth process: *blunting,* wherein prior exposure to risk influences makes the individual less able to benefit from subsequent positive developmental influences. Examples of sensitization, steeling, and blunting are shown in Table 9-2.

TABLE 9-2
Examples of Studies Showing the Operation of Sensitizing,
Steeling, and Blunting Processes

Process	Example	Reference
Sensitizing	Previously malnourished children more sensitive to later short-term nutritional deprivation than non-malnourished children.	Grantham-McGregor, Chang, & Walker (1998); Jacoby, Cueto, & Pollitt (1996)
	Children with a history of developmental problems at greater long-term risk when faced with later stress than children without this history.	Chase-Lansdale et al. (1995)
	Children with greater exposure to early stress have more conduct problems when exposed to later stress than children with less early stress.	Werner & Smith (1982)
Steeling	Multiple infrahuman studies show how preweaning exposure to mild environmental stress promotes stress resistance in adulthood.	Thompson & Grusec (1970)
	Individuals who have encountered prior economic stress better able to deal with new challenges later in life than individuals who have not encountered such stress	Bronfenbrenner (1993)
Blunting	Children with poor early nutritional status less able to benefit from being reared in advantaged circumstances than children with better early nutritional status.	Morrison et al. (1995); My-Lien, Meyer, & Winick (1997); Winick et al. (1975)
	Children exposed to early institutional rearing less able to benefit from later rearing in advantaged circumstances than children not reared in institutions.	Hodges & Tizard (1989a, 1989b)
	Inability to benefit from later developmental intervention by children reared in highly disorganized family environments.	Pavenstedt (1967)

Although sufficient evidence is available to indicate that early developmental influences can act to moderate the impact of later developmental influences, what are not yet clear are the mechanisms that lead to buffering, sensitization, steeling, or blunting. Some potentially testable mechanisms have been suggested. In chapter 6, I noted evidence suggesting that children with positive developmental histories were more likely to react positively to later stress (buffering), whereas children with negative developmental histories were more likely to react negatively (sensitization). This difference may be due to the greater likelihood of children with positive developmental histories to develop positive "internalized models," whereas children experiencing negative developmental histories are more likely to develop negative internal models. Internal models may function both to filter incoming information encountered later in life by the individual, as well as to influence biological subsystems that influence individual affective reactivity and motivation (Hofer, 1994; Sroufe, 1983). For example, experimental infrahuman data indicate that long-term sensitization may be due to relatively permanent changes in neurochemical activity associated with exposure to early developmental risks (Levitsky & Strupp, 1995). The nature of the individual's internal models may influence both whether the child perceives his or her later environment as positive or negative and the degree of reactivity the child has in response to later stress and support.

Rutter (1993) has argued that a critical determinant of whether prior influences act to sensitize or steel children is based on whether the child can successfully deal with early stressors. Within this framework, successfully dealing with early stressors gives the child coping strategies that he or she can use to be able to successfully cope with later stressors (steeling); children who could not cope effectively with early stressors are less equipped to be able to cope effectively with later stressors (sensitized).

Alternatively, it may be that the question of whether individuals are sensitized, steeled, buffered, or blunted is best viewed as a function of multiple influences (Wachs, 1992). Within this framework, individual reactivity would be a function not only of how well the individual copes with earlier stressors but also the intensity of earlier stressors, the nature of the child's characteristic coping style, and the applicability of the child's earlier coping styles for dealing with current stresses and supports. Early stressors that were too strong may completely overwhelm the child, leading to individual characteristics that predispose to blunting or sensitization, such as learned helplessness. Children from highly disorganized environments may adjust by adopting a highly rigid coping style that allows them to provide their own structure in the face of chaos. Such a rigid coping style, while initially effective, may prevent the child from being flexible enough to benefit later in life when he or she is placed in better quality environments (i.e., blunting) (Pavenstedt, 1967). Alternatively, there is also the possibility that too little exposure to early stressors may predispose children to a more passive coping style later in life, resulting in behavioral patterns that resemble sensitization or blunting.

Temporal Persistence

Clearly there is a bidirectional moderating relation between early and later developmental influences. However, available evidence suggests that the impact of some developmental influences persist well beyond the time period in which they initially occurred. For example, there are unique effects on adult depression and self-esteem associated with being victimized by bullies in the middle school grades (Olweus, 1993). Similarly, the later life course of individuals who encountered severe economic circumstances in childhood often is characterized by a need to regain a sense of control that was lost while growing up during the Great Depression (Elder & Caspi, 1988). My reading of the available literature also indicates that there is something unique about the role of developmental influences encountered early in life. Given the moderating role played by later influences, it is not surprising to find that the level of unique influence associated with early influences is relatively modest (Cairns, 1993). However, if we are to understand the role played by temporal processes, what is important to recognize is that unique long-term effects of early influences do occur, even over and above the contribution of later influences. Evidence shows unique long-term effects associated with prenatal hormonal influences (chap. 3), early biomedical and nutritional influences (chap. 4), individual characteristics (chap. 5), and early characteristics of the proximal environment (chap. 6). Examples of such unique long-term effects associated with early influences are shown in Table 9-3.

Four sets of mechanisms could underlie temporally distant events exerting a unique influence on later development. These mechanisms are summarized in Table 9-4. First, as shown in Table 9-4, from the perspective of nonlinear chaos theory, such unique influences may be inherent in the developmental process itself. Second, some early influences may lead to irreversible damage to CNS macro- or microstructure (Goodman, 1991a). In this type of situation, not only may there appear to be long lasting consequences of early biological insult, but there may also be "sleeper" effects (i.e., functional consequences that may not be seen until later in life). In this second case, a likely explanation is that the functions mediated by the damaged area do not come on line until later in development (e.g., prenatal damage to the motor cortex may not be manifest until the onset of voluntary movement; Lyon & Gaddisseux, 1991).

Third, organism–environment covariance processes may be a major mechanism underlying the temporal persistence of early events or traits. As a general principle, it has been hypothesized that the greater the level of interdomain covariance, the more likely we are to find stability of behaviors

TABLE 9-3

Examples of Unique Long-Term Effects Associated With Developmental
Influences Encountered in the Early Years of Life

Nature of Influence	Pattern of results	Reference
Biological	IUGR or early growth retardation associated with delayed pubertal onset and adult body size.	Martorell et al. (1994, 1998)
	Variability in adult disease rate and mortality uniquely related to variability in fetal growth rate and neonatal size.	D. Barker (1996); Goldberg & Prentice (1994)
	Impact of neonatal IVH on later cognitive performance fades and then reappears as child enters school.	Sostek (1992)
	Prenatal nutritional supplementation of mother and postnatal supplementation of child through preschool years has unique influence on later adult cognitive performance and work capacity.	Haas et al. (1996); Pollitt et al. (1993)
Psychological	Quality of child's home environment in infancy and early childhood predicts elementary school functioning even after controlling for subsequent home or school characteristics.	Bradley et al. (1988); Sroufe et al. (1990)
	Extent of young adult post-traumatic stress disorder related to extent of early stresses in preschool years and not current stresses for Cambodians who grew up in Cambodia during the Pol Pot genocide.	Sack et al. (1996)
	Even when causal-chain processes are operating, unique long-term influence of early family disruption on adult adjustment is found.	Rutter et al. (1990)

Note. IUGR = Intra-Uterine Growth Retardation; IVH = Intraventricular Hemorrhage.

that are related to these influences (Cairns, 1993). In terms of specific covariance processes, persistence of nonbiological early influences can be the result of *reactive covariance* (children influence their subsequent environment; see chap. 8). As in the case of child behavior problems that cause parental rejection, leading to stronger child behavior problems, over time negative transactional loops between parent and child can be extended to other developmental contexts like peer groups, thus further stabilizing the impact of the original rejection (Vuchinich et al., 1992). Coevolutionary influences may act in a similar way, with selection pressures for physical features leading to new cultural adaptations, which in turn strengthen the original impact of selection pressures (Cole, 1992).

Active covariance (niche selection) processes also may act to stabilize the impact of early-occurring developmental influences (see chap. 8). In understanding the role active covariance plays in stabilizing the impact of early influences, what must be emphasized is that, for any given population, there are only a finite number of niches available (Livingstone, 1980). Even more critical, not all available niches are equally open to all individuals. Niches may be closed to individuals as a function of societal constraints such as discrimination, required prerequisites such as a certain level of education or training, or individual perceptions about how much a certain setting, like the local country club, really is open to all individuals (Goodnow, 1988a; Wachs, 1996b). Thus, one consequence of a preschool child being rejected by peers is a limitation of future options, in terms of who will be willing to be the child's friend or play with the child or the types of activities that will be open to the child (G. Patterson & Bank, 1989). Similarly, societal institutions also can act to limit niche availability, as in the case where schools place poorly achieving adolescents in classrooms containing other poorly achieving adolescents (Dishion et al., 1991). What this means in practice is that early developmental influences or early individual characteristics can be stabilized over time, either as a function of the individual selecting into niches that maintain these influences or characteristics, or by closing niches that could serve to moderate the impact of early influences or characteristics on the individual (Wachs, 1996b).

Finally, as shown in Table 9-4, persistent consequences of early developmental influences or early individual characteristics may be manifest primarily when the individual is faced later in life by conditions characterized by high demand, high stress, or high ambiguity. For example, although the impact of parental divorce occurring after age 7 may not be manifest immediately, children with preexisting behavior problems may be at greater risk for adjustment problems in adulthood as later challenges reinstate earlier divorce-related vulnerabilities (Chase-Lansdale, Lindsay, Andrew, & Kiernan 1995). Viewed in terms of dynamic system theory, contextual reactivation of previously masked coping strategies or experiences may be one way for the

TABLE 9-4

Mechanisms Underlying the Long-Term Impact of Early
Developmental Influences

Mechanism	Action process	References
Nonlinear developmental processes	Small initial differences are magnified over time, leading to widely divergent developmental trajectories.	Gottman (1991); May (1976)
Damage to the developing CNS	Early macro- or micro-structural damage to the CNS can permanently impair underlying functional mechanisms that are critical for later adaptive behavior.	DeLong (1993); Levitsky & Strupp (1995); Lozoff (1998)
Reactive organism–environment covariance	Encountering certain developmental influences early in life results in an individual with characteristic behavioral patterns that are reacted to by others in ways that set up feedback loops that act to stabilize the impact of the early influences.	Field (1987); Ge, Conger, & Elder (1996); Rutter & Rutter (1992); Sampson & Laub (1994)
Active organism–environment covariance	Children with specific characteristics behavioral patterns select into environmental niches with characteristics that act to stabilize the original behavioral patterns.	Kandel (1978): Kinderman (1993); G. Patterson & Bank (1989)
Contextual reactivation	The impact of prior influences on individual characteristics may be masked by the later use of adaptive strategies that may break down under high-demand/high-stress situations. Alternatively, exposure to novel or challenging later circumstances may serve to reactivate recovery of forgotten experiences, which are then incorporated into the individual's current behavioral repertoire.	Caspi (1998)

Note. CNS = central nervous system.

individual to attempt to restore a sense of equilibrium to a highly chaotic situation (Magnusson, 1993).

Even more dramatic, in some cases a unique impact of early developmental influences can persist across generations. Certainly there is evidence for cross-generational influences occurring at a population level, as seen for both evolutionary processes (Gottlieb, 1992) and culture (Welles-Nystrom, 1996). Cross-generational influences at the population level can sometimes span multiple generations. Thus, in discussing the nature of Iranian responsivity to the Iraq–Iran war of the 1980s, V.S. Naipaul (1997) pointed to the importance for Iranians of the defeat of Persia by the Arabs in the battle of Kadisiya in 637 A.D.

Although we typically think of cross-generational influences at the individual level primarily in terms of the inheritance of specific genes, such influences are not restricted just to genetics. Individual cross-generational persistence of early biomedical influences can be seen in findings showing that women who themselves were of low birth weight or small for gestational age (SGA) are more likely to have a low birth weight, SGA, or preterm child, even after statistically controlling for potential confounds like maternal age and smoking habits (Klebanoff et al., 1989; Kleinman, 1992). Maternal nutritional history also can have cross-generational consequences in terms of offspring stunting (Susser & Stein, 1994), with some evidence suggesting that even with nutritional rehabilitation it may take as long as three generations to compensate for early maternal growth retardation (Golden, 1994). Cross-generational influences also are seen at the level of the proximal environment, with evidence indicating that level of parental involvement (Minde, 1992), mother–child attachment (Fonagy, Steele, & Steele, 1991), quality of parenting (Beckwith & Rodning, 1992), and stability of family environment (Elder & Caspi, 1988) are all influenced by the nature of the family environment experienced by the current generation of parents when they were children themselves.

Some may be tempted to dismiss evidence from human studies showing cross-generational transmission of developmental influences on the basis of such evidence being primarily correlational. However, infrahuman experimental research shows the same cross-generational patterns in regard to the impact of early malnutrition (Galler & Propert, 1981a, 1981b), early stress (Sackett, 1991), proximal environmental stimulation, such as early handling (Dennenberg & Rosenberg, 1967), and environmental enrichment (Dell & Rose, 1987).

Although the exact mechanisms are not well understood, it may nonetheless be useful to speculate a bit about why intergenerational transmission processes can occur at an individual level. In addition to classical parent–offspring genetic inheritance, a related mechanism involves the influence of parental exposure to environmental toxins, malnutrition, or stress being transmitted across generations, either through their impact on the genetic material of the exposed parent (Vorhees & Mollnow, 1987) or by influencing the uterine environment of the fetus (Barker, 1996; Sackett, 1991). At the level of the proximal environment, growing up in a disturbed family environment can influence the individual's characteristics in ways that make them less effective parents with their own children (Beckwith & Rodning, 1992). In a nondisturbed family environment, family rituals and family "stories" can serve to transmit family values over generations (Sameroff & Fiese, 1990). For example, when families migrate to a new culture, family stories about past traumatic events (Sack et al., 1996) or about life in the country of origin (Miller, 1996) may serve to give offspring a sense of what were the characteristics, beliefs, values, and stressors in the parental culture.

Cumulative Influences

Temporal processes also can be cumulative in nature, such that developmental influences cumulate over time to promote individual behavioral–developmental variability. Unlike age specificity or the temporal moderation processes described earlier, when cumulative influence processes are operating, it is the accumulation of influences over time that are most critical, rather than influences operating at a given point in time (see chaps. 6 and 7). Examples showing the impact of cumulative influences operating over time are shown in Table 9-5.

To some readers, the concept of cumulative influences may seem to contradict a temporal process described earlier, namely the persistence of early influences across time. In fact, there is no such contradiction. It is possible to have direct influences on later behavioral development coming from both a single point in time and the accumulation of influences at multiple time points (Magnusson & Bergman, 1990). When both persistent and cumulative influence processes are occurring, we can expect to find a pattern wherein there is unique prediction from early influences, but the strongest level of prediction is associated with cumulative influences operating across time (Rutter & Rutter, 1992; Vuchinich et al., 1992). For example, the direct impact of parental divorce on children's later adjustment as adults, although significant, is far less powerful than the cumulative impact of divorce-related occurrences (Chase-Lansdale et al., 1995). Similarly, although there can be a unique direct influence of early institutionalization on later adjustment, a stronger influence is associated with continued exposure to inadequate rearing environments following institutionalization (Hodges & Tizard, 1989a, 1989b).

Also important to any discussion of cumulative influences is the idea of stable influences operating over time. One such case is when initial teacher judgments about the academic competence of a young child persist as the child moves into later grades. One consequence of the persistence of

TABLE 9-5

Examples Illustrating the Impact of Cumulative Developmental
Influences Operating Over Time

Influence	Process	Reference
Nutrition	Short periods of malnutrition are far less critical for physical growth than malnutrition that continues over extended periods.	Golden (1994); Gorman (1995)
	Nutritional supplementation that continues over extended periods has a larger and more lasting impact on cognitive development than does short-term supplementation.	Pollitt (1996)
Biomedical factors	For malnourished children, the risk for continued gastrointestinal disorder increases sharply for those individuals with a history of previous bouts of gastrointestinal disorder.	Sepulveda et al. (1988)
Individual characteristics	The use of withdrawal by a child as a strategy for coping with novel contexts becomes problematical only if this behavioral pattern continues to occur over time.	Calkins (1994)
Proximal environment	Although families can cope well with stresses occurring at a given point in time, extended coping can exhaust resources leaving the family more vulnerable to later stresses.	J. Patterson & McCubbin (1983)
	Exposure to highly unstable family environments in childhood (e.g., changes in family structure, high number of family moves) is associated with increased risk of adult behavior internalizing and externalizing problems.	Pulkkinen (1982); Pulkkinen & Saastamoninen (1986)
Distal environment	Decline in the use of active coping strategies used by children exposed to societal violence is seen as the violence continues over a period of several years.	Punamaki (1988)

teacher ratings is long-term school success for children who are rated positively (Reynolds, Mavrogenes, Bezruczko, & Hagemann, 1996). Stability also can refer to the reoccurrence over time of the same type of influence. For example, stability of the proximal environment along such dimensions as environmental demands, environmental risks, parental sensitivity, and child control strategies have been reported in a number of studies (Caspi, 1998). Stability also can refer to the reoccurrence of different variations of the same type of influence (e.g., the same cultural message repeated in different formats; see chap. 7).

In terms of potential mechanisms underlying the impact of stable or cumulative developmental influences, Bronfenbrenner and Ceci (1994) postulated that proximal processes, to be effective, must occur on a regular basis over time and that unstable contexts can act to disrupt the facilitative influence of positive proximal processes. Supporting this prediction, both infrahuman (Hofer, 1994) and human data (Eckerman & Oehler, 1992) suggest that exposure to regularly patterned stimulation may be an essential component of helping individuals organize and self-regulate their behavior. A linkage of temporal instability to high levels of family stress may be another mechanism through which instability becomes a risk factor for subsequent behavior problems. Another consequence of greater levels of family instability (e.g., repeated moves) is a reduction in the child's ability to find stable, developmentally appropriate niches. However, particularly at the microsystem level, it is critical to keep in mind that a certain level of stimulus variability also is essential for development to proceed (Wachs, 1992). Unstable contexts may be disruptive to individual development, but unchanging contexts (e.g., institutional environments) also can be disruptive. Similarly, being in a stable but developmentally inhibiting home or school environment may be more problematical for individual development than changing to a different but more facilitative home or school environment (Wachs, 1999).

Causal Chains

As discussed in chapters 5 and 6, cumulative influences may be built into developmental processes. I refer specifically to the possibility that the occurrence of certain influences earlier in the life span may increase the probability of occurrence of later types of influences, which act to maintain the impact of the earlier influences. Such patterns have been described as *cumulative spirals* or *causal chains*. Within a causal-chain framework, outcomes are not a function of any one specific prior influence. Rather, outcomes are viewed as a function of probabilistic linkages between different influences over time, which act to lock the child into a narrower and narrower developmental path. Causal chains have been documented for both populations and individuals, at both the infrahuman and human levels, and

TABLE 9-6
Examples of Causal Chains Linking Together Multiple Developmental
Influences Operating Over Time

Causal chain	Reference
Level of food available to young bees influences their physical growth, which in turn acts to influence their adult mating strategies.	Caro & Bateson (1986)
Genetically based physical sex differences influence subsequent gender-appropriate classification of individuals, which in turn increases the probability of culturally based differential treatment of men and women.	Reinisch et al. (1991)
A lack of early educational support by parents with low educational expectations increases the likelihood of children starting off poorly prepared for school, which in turn increases the probability of early school failure, which in turn decreases the child's involvement with school, which in turn increases the likelihood of school dropout.	Finn (1989)
Participation in educational preschool programs increases both parental school involvement and child school readiness. Parental school involvement directly increases the likelihood of later school success, whereas early school readiness increases the likelihood of more positive teacher ratings of the child in the early grades, which in turn increases the likelihood of later school success.	Reynolds et al. (1996)
Sexual abuse in early childhood increases the likelihood of earlier and riskier adolescent sexual behavior, which in turn increases the likelihood of adult physical and psychological sexual problems.	Browning & Laumann (1997)

for either biological or psychosocial processes (see chaps. 2, 4, & 6). Examples of documented causal chains are shown in Table 9-6.

In understanding the operation of causal chains, as shown in Table 9-6 and earlier in this volume, what is important to emphasize is how causal-chain processes are probabilistic in nature. An individual with a particular set of characteristics or an individual who encounters certain types of early developmental influences may be more likely to encounter certain types of specific developmental influences later in life. However, this does not mean that there is an ironclad law that guarantees that such later encounters actually will occur. As previously discussed in regard to reactive covariance, the complex, multidimensional nature of developmental influences means that individuals may encounter alternative sets of influences that can act to disrupt existing or potential causal chains (see chap. 8). For example, the potential causal chains associated with a lack of educational support at home in the preschool years need not occur if a child coming from such a home happens to be assigned to a first grade teacher who can compensate for the child's lack of preparation. In this situation, a completely different developmental trajectory can occur (Pedersen et al., 1978). The probabilistic nature of causal chains also is seen in the stage-risk formulation developed by Pickles (1993). In this framework, an initial necessary risk factor leads to an intermediate stage of physical or psychological vulnerability. Negative outcomes occur when an individual in such a stage of vulnerability subsequently encounters a second necessary risk factor. In such a time-linked scenario, the second risk factor will have negative consequences only when it affects an individual who is already vulnerable. However, not all individuals in the vulnerable stage will encounter the second risk factor.

As with cumulative influences, the operation of causal-chain processes in no way precludes the simultaneous operation of noncumulative, persistent long-term influences. As described by Rutter et al. (1990), follow-up of men who were institution-reared early in life reveals both long-term effects of early disruptive parenting (direct influence of early environment) as well as a higher probability of continuity of negative experiences after institutionalization (causal-chain process). As with cumulative influences, when both causal-chain and persistent influences are occurring, I would expect the strongest effects to be associated with causal-chain processes.

Although the operation of causal-chain processes seems well established, at present there is remarkably little theory or evidence on the question of the conditions under which causal-chain processes are likely to form and be maintained. Do all developmental influences have an equal likelihood of entering into causal-chain processes, or are causal chains likely to form only under certain conditions? Drawing on what little evidence and theorizing is available, as presented in previous chapters, I would hypothesize that there are five conditions favorable for initiating and maintaining causal-chain processes over time.

1. Causal chains are more likely to occur when one influence has a direct impact on or reinforces the actions of a second influence, as in the case of gastrointestinal illness and malnutrition or hormonal changes and shifts in parent–child relationships in adolescence (Pickles, 1993). However, I would go beyond this obvious conclusion to predict that the greater the extent of covariance among multiple developmental influences at a given point in time, the more likely we are to find causal-

chain processes operating. Just in terms of sheer numbers, multiple influences that covary at a given point in time have a greater likelihood of being involved in causal chains than do single developmental influences operating in isolation, even if this single influence is a relatively powerful one.

2. Biological or psychosocial developmental influences that affect the individual's processing of or reactivity to subsequent information or stimulation are also more likely to enter into causal-chain processes. Relevant biological influences could include genotype or CNS processes associated with increased arousability or higher reactivity to ambient stimulation. Potential psychosocial influences could include factors related to the nature of internal working models (e.g., attachment) or stresses like chronic abuse, which can inhibit the development of a positive self-concept, promote negative expectations of others, or inhibit self-regulation (Masten et al., 1990; Rutter, 1996). Individuals who process information or react to stimulation in certain ways are more likely to select into certain contexts or be responded to by others in ways that are related to their unique processing or reactivity style (active or reactive covariance; see chap. 8). The contexts one selects into and the nature of feedback one gets from others become subsequent links in causal-chain processes operating over time. For example, children with a sense of secure attachment to their caregivers are more likely to have positive social expectations and a more positive self-image, and are thus more likely to get positive reactions from their peers, than are individuals who have internal working models characterized by negative social expectations and have a low sense of self-worth (Elicker et al., 1992). Similarly, parents of children with chronic illness who view their children as "vulnerable" may behave in ways that, over time, result in their children also viewing themselves as vulnerable (Boyce & Jemerin, 1990).

3. Integrating conditions 1 and 2, I would further propose that causal-chain processes are even more likely to be operating if there is both covariance among different developmental influences and the occurrence of differential reactivity or processing. The consequences of protein-calorie malnutrition could easily fit this prediction, with poor nutritional status being associated with lower CNS integrity, less adequate rearing environments, and slower rates of physical growth. The covariance of low-quality rearing environments with malnutrition serves to further adversely affect CNS integrity (see chap. 3); the covariance of malnutrition with slow physical growth results in

functional isolation leading to a pattern of passive learning and relating to the environment (see chap. 4). Both impaired CNS integrity and a passive learning style predispose to a variety of subsequent links in a causal chain, such as poor school performance.

4. Negative causal chains are more likely to be maintained when developmental influences promote individual characteristics that act to restrict the availability of niches that the individual can enter. When alternative niches are restricted the characteristics of niches that are available are likely to be those that keep the person locked into self-defeating behavioral styles similar to those that functioned initially to close off niches. Furthermore, restriction of the individual's choice of niches means a reduction in the chances for the individual to encounter new and positive developmental influences that are sufficiently discordant to change his or her developmental trajectory (Wachs, 1996b).

5. The situation is somewhat more complicated in the case of positive causal chains. Although negative causal-chain niches are more likely to be forced on the individual rather than selected into, the reverse situation would hold in regard to positive causal-chain niches. The developmental influences that put the individual in a positive causal chain also are likely to promote individual characteristics that increase the probability of exposure to new developmental niches. As a general rule, exposure to a variety of developmental niches maximizes the probability of the person's encountering trajectory-altering developmental influences (Werner, 1994). This should result in a lessened likelihood of maintaining an existing causal chain. However, in this situation the individual may choose those niches that continue to reward what is positive about the person, thus maintaining the positive causal chain. As a result, we are more likely to see greater individual variability in causal-chain stability in the case of positive causal chains.

SPECIFICITY OF DEVELOPMENTAL INFLUENCES

Although we cannot fully understand the contribution of multiple developmental influences without also considering the role played by temporal processes, available evidence also indicates that we cannot understand the impact of temporal processes without also keeping in mind what developmental outcomes we are looking at and what developmental influences are operating. For example, the degree to which environmental influences persist over time will vary as a function of the outcomes under study (Bradley et al., 1988; Pungello et al., 1996; Rutter & Rutter, 1992; Sack et al., 1996). Thus, exposure to current rather than persistent poverty is a stronger predictor of children's externalizing problems, whereas the reverse pattern holds in regard to children's internalizing problems (McLeod & Shanahan, 1993). Similarly, the recovery curve associated with head injury indicates a narrower recovery window for outcomes involving psychiatric problems than for outcomes involving cognitive functioning (Rutter et al., 1984). Developmental variability is strongly associated with perinatal biomedical risks during the first year of life, with a declining salience of such risks thereafter; in contrast, a reverse pattern is shown for psychosocial contextual risk conditions such as low socioeconomic status (Molfese, Holcomb, & Helwig, 1994).

All of these diverse findings converge on a common principle, namely that we cannot assume that specific temporal influences or processes operate in the same way for all developmental outcomes. This pattern can be viewed as part of a broader principle of specificity, which is the focus of the final section of this chapter. The term *specificity* has been used in a variety of ways. For example, psychopathology researchers use this term in reference to whether individuals with a given disorder show a generalized deficit that is common to other types of disorders or a specific deficit that is unique to their specific disorder (Sher & Trull, 1996). I use the term in a specific way: to refer to the fact that different developmental influence patterns and processes are related to different developmental outcomes.

As just defined, the concept of specificity was extensively discussed in chapter 6 with regard to *environmental specificity*: different aspects of development being influenced by different aspects of the proximal environment. However, the concept that the impact of developmental influences is specific rather than general in nature is seen in theories deriving from a number of different domains in addition to the proximal environment. Evolution researchers have hypothesized that multiple adaptive mechanisms are found within a given species and that evolution-based mechanisms useful for solving problems in one domain may have only limited carryover to different domains (Buss, 1991). A number of theories describing the nature of CNS function and development are based on evidence (a) that the cortex has different functions located in different representational areas (Sur, Pallas, & Roe, 1990; Ungerleider, 1995); (b) that even within a given cortical area, individual neurons appear to be sensitive to input only from specific modalities (Rakic, 1988); and (c) that influences involved in the overall shape of neural microstructure are different from those involved in the extent of branching of the different structures (Edelman, 1989). A recurrent feature of embryological theories is the idea that forces that determine the appearance of one part of the body are different from forces influencing the development and appearance of other morphological features (Waddington,

1972). Behavioral–genetic researchers have hypothesized that there may be different genetic processes underlying severe versus mild disorders (Plomin, 1991). A similar theoretical position has been taken by researchers interested in the etiology and nature of individual differences such as mental retardation (Zigler, 1967).

The concept of specificity also appears in more general, nondomain theories. For example, Goodwin (1985) has argued that factors associated with developmental perturbations tend to destabilize only a limited set of outcomes, regardless of domain. Dynamic-systems theorists have hypothesized that the nature of the task faced by the individual can act to influence whether systems change to stable or to unstable patterns (Thelen, 1989) and that early in life many stable attractors are context specific (Thelen & Smith, 1994).

It also is important to note that some researchers have argued that specificity is an artifact, capitalizing on random variation (Belsky, 1990). It is true that when looking at the results of a single isolated study it can become very difficult to differentiate genuine specificity from random, nonreplicable variability. However, the intra- and intercultural replication of findings on the operation of specificity processes lends support to the argument that specificity reflects something more than just random variability (Wachs, 1992, 1996a).

Two major types of specificity have been hypothesized as occurring. *Developmental specificity* refers to differential salience of different developmental influences for different types of outcomes within a given domain. As will be discussed next, there are two types of developmental specificity: *conditional* and *strong*. *Process specificity* refers to different underlying processes being associated with different developmental outcomes. There appear to be three types of process specificity: *interdomain*, *initiation–maintenance*, and *range*. Each of these types is illustrated in Figure 9-1. In addition, as will be discussed next, there are two situations in which there can be *coexistence* of both generalizable and specific influence processes (also illustrated in Figure 9-1).

Developmental Specificity

As shown in Figure 9-1, the operation of developmental specificity can be seen as occurring in one of two forms. The conditional form of specificity can be inferred when a developmental influence is salient for some outcomes but not for others. The strong form requires at least two influences and two outcomes. In this situation, specificity is seen as occurring when developmental outcome Tx is predicted by developmental influence Ix, but not by developmental influence Iy, whereas the reverse pattern occurs for developmental outcome Ty. For example, epidemiological evidence indicates that an increased risk of adult death from stroke is associated with prenatal influences, an in-

I. Developmental Specificity

Conditional Specificity *

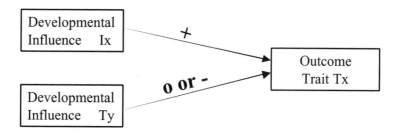

Strong Specificity *

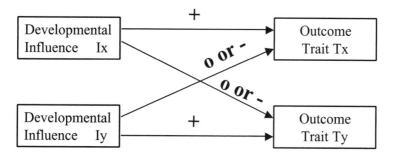

+ = positive influence
- = negative influence
0 = no influence
***** The reverse pattern would hold when
    Ix ⟶ Tx was in the negative direction
    Iy ⟶ Ty was in the negative direction

Figure 9-1. I. Forms of specificity.

creased risk of adult death from respiratory disorders is associated with postnatal influences, and an increased risk of death from heart disease is associated
with both pre- and postnatal influences (Barker, Osmond, & Law, 1989).

A number of examples of developmental specificity have been described in chapters 3, 4, 6, and 7 in this volume. Examples of the operation
of developmental specificity processes occurring across multiple domains is
seen in Table 9-7.

II. Process Specificity

Interdomain Specificity *

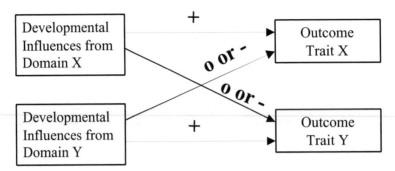

Initiation-maintenance Specificity

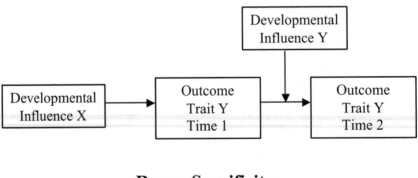

Range Specificity

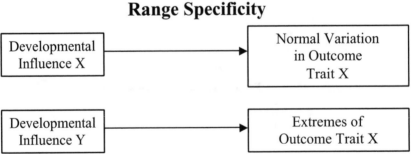

Figure 9-1. II. Forms of specificity.

Also worth noting is that developmental specificity has been shown in experimental studies with infrahuman populations. For example, studies of honey bees indicate that alleles that influence one aspect of nest-cleaning behavior are different from alleles that influence other aspects of bee be-

III. Generalizability—Specificity

Co-existence

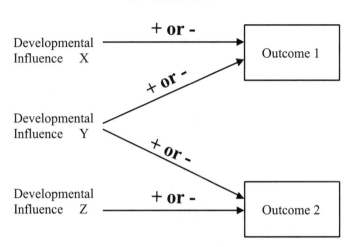

Final Common Pathway

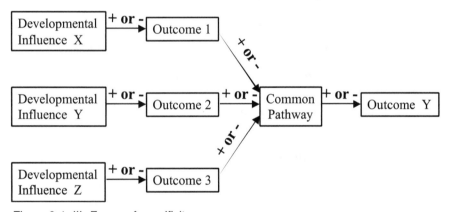

Figure 9-1. III. Forms of specificity.

havior (Bateson, 1983). Early handling or isolation of rat pups, although influencing age of initiation of exploratory behavior, does not influence the
pattern of exploration (Nadel, Wilson, & Kurz, 1993). Early exposure to
variable stimuli, although impeding acquisition performance by adult rats,
also can act to enhance adult retention of what has been acquired (Spear &
Hyatt, 1993).

The fact that developmental specificity operates across different domains, across cultures, and across species emphasizes both the generalizabil-

TABLE 9-7
Examples of Developmental Specificity

Domain	Findings	Reference
	Conditional specificity	
Evolution	Evolutionary influences appear to be more salient for specific abilities than for general learning capacity.	Roper (1983)
CNS	Early CNS damage more likely to influence general level of functioning and specific skills.	Goodman (1991a)
	Impact of head injury on cognitive performance primarily seen for timed spatial motor tasks; whereas impact on psychiatric symptomatology primarily involves lack of social inhibition.	Rutter et al. (1984)
	Relation of brain ventricle size to schizophrenia varies as a function of type of schizophrenia.	Cannon et al. (1990)
	Limbic system damage results in memory deficits but not in skill acquisition deficits.	Strupp & Levitsky (1995)
	Unique sensitivity of prefrontal cortex to phenylalanine/tyrosine ratio, resulting in unique sensitivity of cognitive function mediated by prefrontal cortex-to-ratio imbalances.	Diamond et al. (1997)
Hormonal influences	High levels of the stress-regulating hormone prolactin related to infants' affect during cognitive testing but not related to the level of task orientation during testing.	Lozoff et al. (1995)
Biomedical influences	Neurobehavioral consequences of fetal alcohol exposure greater than physical growth consequences.	Streissguth et al. (1989)

TABLE 9-7 *(continued)*

Domain	Findings	Reference
	Shape of curves relating extent of response to dose of teratogen exposure varies with outcome measured.	Vorhees & Mollnow (1987)
	Number of minor physical anomalies have a stronger impact on neurological functioning than on language or cognitive functioning.	Largo et al. (1989)
	For developmentally disabled children, behavioral impact of chronic illness most often seen for anxiety, depression, and ADHD.	Cadman et al. (1987)
	Newborn CNS more susceptible to herpes symplex infection than to anoxia.	Goodman (1991a)
Nutrition	Under conditions of inadequate dietary intake, adaptation occurs by loss of function being restricted only to certain body systems.	Scrimshaw & Young (1989)
	Development of frontal lobe structure and function particularly sensitive to nutritional deprivation.	Strupp & Levisky (1995)
Individual characteristics	Differences in maturational timing salient primarily for componental spatial tasks.	Newcombe & Dubos (1987)
Proximal environment	What teaching strategies parents believe facilitate one aspect of the child's skill performance may not be seen as useful for different aspects of skill performance.	Sigel (1992)
	Early death of parent increases risk of later panic disorder but not risk of later depression.	Kendler et al. (1992)

(continued)

TABLE 9-7 *(continued)*

Domain	Findings	Reference
Proximal environment[1]	Impact of differences in family structure varies as a function of type of offspring adjustment being considered.	Jacobvitz & Bush (1996)
	Maternal warmth buffers against adolescent depression but not adolescent conduct problems, and differentiates adolescents with comorbid adjustment problems from those with single problems.	Ge, Best, et al. (1996)
	Superiority of children's skills in a specific area was related to the degree to which their day care program stressed these and not other skills.	Clarke-Stewart (1991)
Distal environment	Schools that are most effective in facilitating academic competence are not necessarily equally effective in facilitating behavioral adjustment of emotional maturity.	
	Family emotional support more critical for physiological functioning than informational support; cardiovascular reactivity more sensitive to social support than other measures of physiological reactivity.	Uchino, Cacioppo, & Kiecolt-Glaser (1996)

	Strong specificity	
CNS	Type of infant performance deficit varies as a function of what area of CNS is damaged (e.g., hippocampal damage affects memory but not emotionality; reverse pattern for damage to the amygdala).	Diamond (1990a); Squire & Zola-Morgan (1991)
	Different neural response patterns found for animals trained on different types of tasks.	Merzenich et al. (1991)

TABLE 9-7 *(continued)*

Domain	Findings	Reference
Hormonal influences	Validity of models of influence of different gonodal hormones on human sex differences will vary, depending on what aspects of sex differences are being considered.	Collaer & Hines (1995)
	Impact of prenatal hormonal influences on CNS structure, function, and maturation depends on CNS area under consideration.	Bachevalier & Hagger (1991)
Biomedical factors	Different types of stressors affect different aspects of autonomic activation and hormonal release systems.	Boyce & Jemerin (1990); Paikoff et al. (1991)
	Differential affect on physical versus behavioral development depends on which type of teratogen the individual is exposed to.	Vorhees & Mollnow (1987)
	Different types of cerebral palsy predicted by different types of perinatal insults.	Casaer et al. (1991)
Parent beliefs	Child reading performance is associated with parents' expectancies about reading but not with expectancies about math; reverse pattern for child math performance.	Alexander & Entwisle (1988)
Proximal environment	Infant attachment relates to later social interaction with peers but not to aggressive behavior patterns; reverse pattern shown for material use of directive rearing strategies.	Rose-Krasnor et al. (1996)
	Maternal referential language use predicts subsequent toddler receptive and expressive language but not toddler symbolic play; level of maternal play interaction	Tamis-LeMonda & Bornstein (1994)

(continued)

TABLE 9-7 *(continued)*

Domain	Findings	Reference
	predicts subsequent toddler symbolic play but not toddler language.	
	Maternal verbal stimulation primarily predicts toddler language use but not toddler negative emotionality; maternal response to distress primarily predicts toddler negative emotionality but not language use.	Wachs et al. (1993)
	Infant distress associated more with maternal withdrawal than with intrusive maternal rearing; intrusive maternal rearing is primarily associated with infant avoidance.	Field (1994)
	Adult contact shapes how toddlers use language, whereas peer contact influences toddlers' motivation to use language to communicate socially.	Salzinger (1990)
	Training infants to walk on a treadmill accelerates use of alternating steps, whereas placing infants on a non-moving treadmill enhances use of parallel stepping.	Thelen & Smith (1994)
	Level of family support and stress uniquely predict child internalizing and externalizing problems but not child's school grades or school absences; school grades and absences are uniquely predicted by SES.	DuBois et al. (1994)
	Influence of parental rearing style on change in adolescent competence over a 4-year period varies as a function of what cognitive areas are assessed as well as the characteristic type of rearing style used by parents.	Steinberg et al. (1994)

TABLE 9-7 *(continued)*

Domain	Findings	Reference
	Angry and insecurely attached infants more likely to have highly interfering mothers, whereas passive and insecurely attached infants more likely to have mothers who ignore them.	Cassidy & Berlin (1994)
Distal environment	Strong family religious beliefs inhibit adolescent externalizing and internalizing problems but do not influence adolescent academic competence; academic competence is predicted by family income.	Brody et al. (1996)
	Strongest prediction of child's school achievement is number of poor, minority, female-headed households in the neighborhood; strongest prediction of child's antisocial behavior is the degree of concentration of crowded households in the neighborhood.	Aber (1994)

Note. CNS = central nervous system; ADHD = attention deficit/hyperactivity disorder.

[1] For the proximal environment, a detailed view of environmental specificity can be found in Wachs (1992). Examples shown in Table 9-7 are those that have not been covered in this earlier review.

ity of this process as well as its potential importance for understanding the nature of human behavioral–developmental variability. One implication of developmental specificity is that in evaluating contributions of a specific developmental influence, it is essential to ask, What behavioral developmental outcome are we talking about? A specific developmental influence that has a facilitative impact on behavior or development in one outcome domain may be irrelevant to outcomes in a second domain and may, under some circumstances, hinder development in a third domain. For example, depending on the outcome, the same influence can act as either a risk factor or a protective factor, as in the case of sickle cell trait being a risk factor for anemia and a protective factor for malaria, or high physiological reactivity predisposing to emotional disorders but buffering against conduct disorders (Rutter, 1996).

Process Specificity

Process specificity refers to a situation wherein different behavioral–developmental outcomes are influenced not only by different developmental influences but also by different underlying process mechanisms. Both infrahuman (Sackett, 1991) and human data (Dance & Neufeld, 1988) indicate that whether developmental influence processes involve main effects, additive coaction, or interaction varies as a function of the characteristics of the outcome variable. As shown in chapter 3, process specificity may be operating in regard to genetic influences, with genetic influences increasing with age for verbal IQ, decreasing with age for nonverbal intelligence, and either staying the same or decreasing for personality. In chapter 4, results indicated that patterns of hormonal action depend not only on the hormone under consideration but also on the outcome; for example, for female adolescents, linear relations are seen between estradiol and depression, whereas a curvilinear relation is seen between estradiol and delinquency. Evidence illustrating the operation of process specificity at the level of the proximal environment was reviewed in chapter 6. For example, in a population of children with sex chromosome anomalies, there was a nonlinear ordinal interaction between measures of family dysfunction and outcomes involving motor performance, school adaptation, and overall adjustment; in contrast, linear additive coaction patterns were found when measures of family dysfunction were related to measures of language development.

The most common type of process specificity is seen when variability in different developmental outcomes occurs as a function of the differential salience of developmental influences from different domains. This form of interdomain specificity is illustrated in Section II of Figure 9-1. Multiple examples of this type of process specificity are shown in Table 9-8.

A second type of process specificity common to a number of domains refers to different processes being associated with initiation versus maintenance of existing outcomes (see Figure 9-1). Examples include (a) different processes being involved in the evolution of specific morphological features versus the spread of morphological features within a species (Gould, 1982); (b) the development of new neural structures versus the elimination of existing neural structures (Edelman, 1989); (c) establishment of initial ranges of developmental outcomes versus influencing variability within a given outcome range (Gruber, 1985); and (d) the initiation of behavioral problems or psychiatric disorders versus the maintenance of existing behavior problems (G. Patterson & Bank, 1989) or psychiatric disorders (Goldstein, 1988).

A third type of process specificity, for which little evidence is available at present, is based on the idea that different processes may be operating in regard to outcomes at the extreme ends of the distribution of a trait versus outcomes in the middle range of the distribution (i.e., range specificity;

TABLE 9-8
Examples of Process Specificity

Type	Pattern	Reference
Biological vs. psychosocial	Different forms of alcoholism are differentially influenced by genetic or sociodemographic factors.	Plomin (1991)
	Toddler mental development equally well predicted by biomedical and environmental risks; motor development best predicted by biomedical risks; receptive communication most strongly predicted by environmental risks; expressive communication predicted by the interaction of biomedical and environmental risks.	Bendersky & Lewis (1994)
	Biological or genetic influences are more salient than proximal or distal environmental influences in the prediction of neurological status, motor performance, and somatic complaints; the reverse pattern occurs when outcomes involve cognitive, social–emotional, or affective disorders.	Gatz et al. (1992); Largo et al. (1990); Magyary et al. (1992)
Different proximal processes	Adolescent offspring of authoritative parents are more likely to be influenced by high-achieving peers in regard to achievement goals but less likely to be influenced by drug-using peers in regard to substance abuse.	Mounts & Steinberg (1995)
Proximal vs. distal environment	In disadvantaged contexts, positive proximal processes reduce maladjustment, whereas in advantaged contexts, positive proximal processes promote competence.	Bronfenbrenner & Ceci (1994)

(continued)

TABLE 9-8 *(continued)*

Type	Pattern	Reference
Proximal vs. distal environment	Distal influences highly salient for substance abuse, whereas there is greater salience of proximal influences for internalizing problems.	P. Cohen et al. (1990)
	For aggressive behavior, living in a low-risk neighborhood can be a protective factor for adolescents from high-risk families; for peer social relations, the degree of fit between family and neighborhood characteristics underlies the degree of peer rejection.	Kupersmidt et al. (1995)
Proximal vs. individual characteristics	Time-limited drinking by adolescents associated primarily with situational factors, whereas chronic alcoholism is more influenced by individual characteristics.	Schulenberg et al. (1996)
Different sets of multiple influences	Persistent antisocial behavior related to neuropsychological risk, school failure, and family environment, whereas adolescent limited antisocial behavior related to early pubertal maturation and deviant peer models.	Moffitt (1993)

see Figure 9-1). Thus, stronger genetic influences have been suggested as operating at the extremes, whereas variability in the middle may be more likely to reflect lower genetic influences and a greater influence of nongenetic factors (Plomin, 1991; Rutter et al., 1990). A similar differentiation between extreme and nonextreme processes also is seen in regard to individual characteristics, given the hypothesis that children with extreme behavioral characteristics such as difficult temperament are more likely to have an influence on their environment, whereas less extreme children are more likely both to influence and to be influenced by their environment (Clarke & Clarke, 1988).

Coexistence of Generalizable and Specific Processes

Although the operation of specificity would seem to preclude a generalizable impact of various developmental influences, such a conclusion would be an oversimplification. There is clear evidence for generalizable effects of a single developmental influence, as in the case of pleiotropy (see chap. 8), or when common influences affect a variety of different psychological disorders (Sher & Trull, 1996). Whether we find specificity or generalizability influence processes operating will partly depend on methodological considerations. Obviously, the more individual predictors or outcome domains are intercorrelated, the less likely we are to find specificity, because specificity assumes distinctly different predictors and outcomes. We also must be cautious of claims for predominance of generalizable influences when multiple predictors from different domains are combined into a single risk score, given that use of summed total risk scores are likely to dilute the predictive value of specific developmental influences (McCall & Appelbaum, 1991; Molfese, DiLalla, & Lovelace, 1996).

Evidence also suggests that, under some conditions, both specificity and generalizable process mechanisms can coexist. Coexistence of generalizable and specificity processes has been shown at the behavioral level (Nadel et al., 1993; Wachs, 1979), for the CNS (Sur et al., 1990), at the metabolic level (Palmer & Paulson, 1997), and for evolution-based adaptive mechanisms (Buss, 1991). For example, adoption study data indicate that some domains of cognitive function are primarily influenced by characteristics associated with the child's biological family, other domains are primarily influenced by characteristics of the child's postnatal adoptive family, and a third set of cognitive domains are influenced by both biological and adoptive family characteristics (Capron & Duyme, 1996).

There are two situations where genuine coexistence of both specificity and generalizable processes can be seen. As shown in Section III of Figure 9-1, the first situation is when there is a common global predictor for two or more outcomes, but the occurrence of a specific outcome depends on the operation of other specific predictors unique to that outcome (Cohen et al., 1990; Ge, Best, et al., 1996; Ge, Conger, et al., 1996; Schwartz, Dodge, Pettit, & Bates, 1997; Tarullo et al., 1995). For example, there may be a common genetic predisposition to schizophrenia, but the form of schizophrenia the individual manifests may depend on the operation of nongenetic influences, such as ventricular size, number of perinatal complications, or whether or not the individual was institutionally reared early in life (Cannon et al., 1990). Similarly, being reared in an unstable family environment or by a single parent is common to individuals with adult convictions for either violent or nonviolent criminality; what distinguishes those individuals with violent criminal convictions is also having a difficult-to-control temperament in childhood (Henry et al., 1996).

As also shown in Figure 9-1, the second type of situation where there can be a coexistence of generalizable and specific process mechanisms occurs when different specific patterns of influence ultimately converge on a final common pathway (Gore & Eckenrode, 1994). There may be multiple ways by which the individual can reach the final common pathway (specificity), but once this pathway is reached, the nature of the common pathway becomes the primary developmental influence (generalizable process). For example, there may be a variety of specific processes through which an individual develops chronic antisocial behavior, but once this individual characteristic is achieved, it becomes the primary predictor of a variety of negative adult consequences.

The Etiology of Specificity

What are the mechanisms that produce specificity? The operation of specificity may be inherent in the fact that both developmental influences and development are multidimensional in nature. When multidimensional predictor and outcome variables are involved, specificity is the logical outcome of a variety of biological and psychosocial influences acting on different outcome dimensions (Collaer & Hines, 1995; Wachs, 1992). Specificity would be less likely to occur if either predictors or outcome variables were unidimensional in nature.

Besides being inherent in the structure of developmental influences and outcomes, specificity also may be the result of our species' evolutionary history and the organization of our CNS. Levins (1973) has developed a mathematical model based on the idea that what is subject to selection pressure is not individual traits but rather individual traits clustered into related sets, with different levels and types of selection pressure being shown for different sets. The variety of different survival-related problems encountered by our evolutionary ancestors may have led to the evolution of multiple sets of adaptive mechanisms that are differentially salient for different types of adaptation problems (Buss, 1991). These different sets of adaptive solutions may have become integrated into the structure of our CNS. We know, for example, that the cortex is organized into linked but modality-specific areas, wherein specific regions act to process information from different domains (Greenough, Black, & Wallace, 1987; Rakic, 1988). Specificity also may arise from the nature of development of the CNS. Although axons have potential multiple targets, selective elimination of connections to targets through experience-dependent input may result in relatively specific patterns of neural connections (Goodman, 1994). The end result of these processes is an individual with a CNS that is primed to encode or react to specific forms of stimulation in relatively specific ways, both behaviorally and biologically.

Implications of the Operation of Specificity Processes

A major implication of the operation of specificity is that we must be very cautious in developing theories of developmental influences that are based on a specific influence affecting all aspects of development in the same way. Such theories, although parsimonious, would likely result in over-generalization of findings, even in the case where global and specific processes were cooccurring. For example, Bornstein (1989b) has hypothesized that parental responsivity to the child is likely to affect most aspects of development in a positive way. However, this global hypothesis is contradicted by available evidence indicating that one aspect of parental responsivity (caregivers responding nonverbally to children's vocalizations) acts to inhibit rather than to facilitate development (Wachs et al., 1993). The operation of specificity, either at the variable or process level, does not necessarily mean that we need a separate theory for each aspect of development. However, we must be open to the possibility that our theories about the nature and impact of developmental influences may have limited range and may be relevant only for certain classes of developmental outcomes.

A second implication deriving from the operation of specificity processes involves the often-repeated concern that explanatory frameworks based on multiple influences are too complex and too hard to conceptualize (see chap. 8). The potential complexities involved in multiple-influence frameworks are indeed daunting if everything is related to everything else. One major implication of specificity is that everything is not related to everything else. Rather, only certain classes of developmental influences are related to a given outcome. By limiting the types of linkages that specific influences are likely to enter into, specificity processes could well function as an organizational tool, helping us to organize our understanding of complex linkages between multiple influences and multiple outcomes.

The organizational function of specificity may be particularly powerful if the specificity processes illustrated in Figure 9-1 are combined with other midlevel processes described in this and the preceding chapter. In terms of understanding the impact of a given set of developmental influences, it seems clear that the nature and degree of impact will vary as a function of the nature of the time period within which the influences occur, the characteristics of the individual on whom the influences impinge, and the developmental outcome under consideration (Horowitz, 1992; Rutter, 1996). The combined operation of the various midlevel processes discussed in chapters 8 and 9 can potentially illustrate why maximal differentiation of children with antisocial behavioral problems from children with other types of behavioral problems occurs when a combination of nine specific predictors are used (Henry et al., 1993). The operation of these midlevel processes also can potentially illustrate why different combinations of predictors are necessary to distinguish children with antisocial behavior patterns limited to adolescence from individuals with long-term antisocial behavioral problems (Moffitt, 1993), or why relations between different child rearing styles and child characteristics vary as a function of differing family characteristics (Mink & Nihara, 1986).

The use of specificity processes in theory construction and as an organizational framework has potential in terms of increasing our ability to conceptualize the impact of multiple linked developmental influences. However, our ability to use specificity in this way is currently limited by the absence of a theoretical framework that would allow us to predict, in advance, the specific types of outcomes that would most likely be associated with specific types or classes of developmental influences (Nadel et al., 1993). At present, our ability to apply specificity processes is purely inductive, based essentially on replications of specific influence–outcome relation patterns. Even given replicated patterns, this situation is likely to remain until we begin to understand the mechanisms underlying specificity. One of the few examples we have in regard to understanding the mechanisms underlying specificity is seen in the work of Diamond et al. (1997) on the neural processes underlying relations between the biomedical disorder phenylketonuria and specific types of cognitive deficits. Understanding the fundamental mechanisms underlying specificity will enable us to develop theoretical frameworks linking specific influence processes to specific types of behavioral–developmental outcomes. Until such frameworks are developed, inductive use of specificity would seem to be our best approach, looking for commonalities among replicated influence–outcome relations and processes.

CONCLUSIONS

In this chapter I showed how the impact of multiple developmental influences can be moderated by temporal factors such as the age of the individual or how long a particular influence has affected the individual. I also illustrated how there is specificity for both developmental influences and the processes by which such influences affect development, with the impact of both influence and process varying as a function of the outcome dimension being considered. It also was noted that these midlevel processes do not operate in isolation from each other. Taken together, the concepts described in chapters 8 and 9 suggest a highly complex pattern of developmental influences. The implication from these chapters is that in order to adequately understand individual developmental behavioral variability, we need to take into account the impact of structurally organized, linked multiple influences from various domains, which combine in a variety of ways that result in either additive or nonlinear patterns of influence, and whose effects may vary as a function of both time and the outcome variable under consideration.

Under these complex conditions, it is not surprising when many researchers and theorists quickly retreat and refocus their efforts primarily on the role of specific individual influences considered in isolation. "Better to have over-simplification than such complexity" would seem to be a major theme for much developmental research and theory. What I hope to do in the next chapter in this volume is to suggest organizing principles that could conceptually simplify the complexities just described without losing the necessary complex nature of individual behavioral–developmental variability.

10

INTEGRATING MULTIPLE INFLUENCES, MIDLEVEL PROCESSES, AND SYSTEMS

The concept of a system as a unit of analysis arose from dissatisfaction with the classic explanatory "paradigms" of the 18th and 19th centuries, which assumed that complex phenomena were reducible to their basic elements, and that once we understood the basic elements, we could understand everything else (Fogel, 1993). When applied to individual human behavior and development a reductionist explanatory paradigm such as this has not proven to be particularly useful (Hinde, 1990). Early in this century Alfred North Whitehead (1925) suggested an alternative paradigm, the concept of a system of influences. Theoretically, the concept of *system* refers to a "complex of interacting elements" (von Bertalanffy, 1968, p. 55) or a "group of parts that are interacting according to some kind of process" (Odum, 1983, p. 4). What is common to the various definitions of a system is not the characteristics of the individual units or parts but rather the extent and nature of linkages or interrelationships among the various units. A set of unrelated individual elements, no matter how numerous, does not constitute a system; on the other hand, a set of elements that are so tightly linked to each other that the sum of the parts is equal to the functioning of the whole also would not constitute a system (Weiss, 1971).

One consequence of the operation of a system is that the variability associated with the system as a whole would be less than the variability found if the component parts of the system were studied in isolation. In part this is because variability associated with a specific element may be counterbalanced by the operation of other elements within the system (Weiss, 1971). For example, the potential variability inherent in individuals will be constrained when an individual is part of a cultural system, which tends to limit response patterns to those that are deemed to be culturally appropriate (Fogel, 1993). The fundamental characteristics of a system, as defined in previous writings, and as used in the present chapter, are seen in Table 10-1.

Do multiple developmental influences form a system? Comparing what has been presented in previous chapters on the operation of multiple developmental influences with the system criteria defined in Table 10-1 suggests a reasonable degree of fit. In chapters 2–7, I have shown how heterogeneous multiple influences impact individual behavioral development, and as shown in chapters 8–9, midlevel processes are common to a variety of different domains (criterion 1). As demonstrated in chapter 8, multiple developmental influences are either structurally or functionally linked with each other (criterion 2). Particularly in the case of functional linkages, the impact of a given influence will depend on the nature of other developmental influences (criterion 3), leading to either linear (additive coaction) or nonlinear relation patterns (criterion 3b). Further, as shown in chapter 9, individual influences operate across a background of time (criterion 4).

If multiple developmental influences are organized into a system, it becomes important to take into account system level processes when attempting to understand individual behavioral–developmental variability. This does not mean that we can ignore the impact of individual influences or mid-

TABLE 10-1
Criteria That Define a System

---

1. Elements within a system are heterogeneous in nature: coming from different classes and with different functions. However, the essential properties of a system hold regardless of the domains from which its elements come.
2. The linked elements composing a system form a structure. The nature of the structure is based on ongoing feedback and interaction among linked elements of the system.
   a. Systems tend to retain their existing organizational structure, even when there is variability in system elements or perturbations to the system. However, under certain conditions the structure of a system can change.
3. The operation of any one element in a system depends on the existence and operation of other elements in the system. Thus, the impact of a system is more than just the sum of its individual parts.
   a. There is coordination among elements of a system (and among subelements of a subsystem within the larger system) to meet functional goals.
   b. Relations between elements of a system or between the system and outcomes can be either linear or nonlinear in nature.
4. Systems operate across a background of time; therefore, the history of a system can influence ongoing system structure and function.

Note. Defining characteristics were taken from Fogel (1993), Magnusson (1993), Simon (1973), Thoman (1990), von Bertalanffy (1968), and Weiss (1971).

level developmental processes. In understanding the role of multiple developmental influences on individual behavioral–developmental variability we are operating simultaneously at a 3-level framework. Within this framework individual behavioral–developmental variability is a function of the joint contribution of level I systemwide processes (e.g., the present chapter), of midlevel (level II) processes that cut across elements of a system but do not operate at a systemwide level (e.g., chapters 8 and 9), and of domain specific developmental influences (level III, chapters 2–7). This 3-level framework is illustrated in Figure 10-1. For the most part studies of the etiology of individual behavioral–developmental variability have emphasized the contribution of influences found at level III (unfortunately all too often focusing only on a restricted subset of level III influences). Far less attention has been given to the impact of level II processes, and level I processes have been treated in a

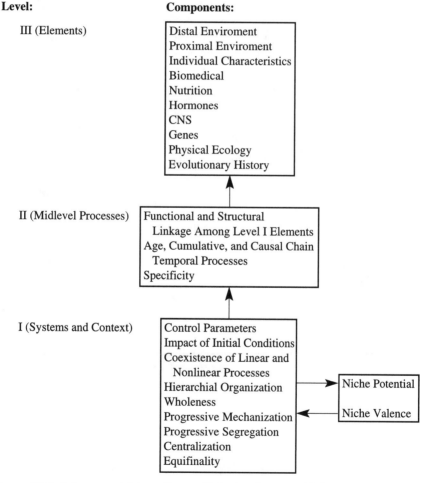

Figure 10-1. A framework integrating multiple developmental influences, midlevel processes, and system-level processes.

post hoc descriptive fashion. The fact that we are dealing with a system means that the impact of individual influences and midlevel developmental processes will be further moderated by the operation of system level processes, which impact all the elements functioning within an overall system. Identification of level I systemwide processes is a major goal of this chapter.

Before embarking on a search for system principles that are particularly relevant to understanding individual behavioral–developmental variability, a cautionary note: Although we can find a number of examples in the human developmental sciences where the concept of systems has been evoked (e.g., Als, 1992; Marvin & Stewart, 1990; van Geert, 1991), all too often the concept of system is evoked post hoc when highly complex results emerge, rather than being used to link specific principles derived from system models to the design of studies or to the types of predictions that are made (Thelen, 1989). To avoid this problem I will start with principles derived from the operation of complex systems and illustrate how such principles can be used as an organizing tool in the study of individual behavioral–developmental variability. My focus will be on the two systems approaches that have been most often discussed in regard to individual human behavioral–developmental variability; namely, *dynamic systems theory* and *general systems theory*. Dynamic and general systems theories share common assumptions. Both theories postulate that the impact of each element of a system depends in good part on the role played by other elements in the system—the whole is more than the sum of its parts (Gleick, 1987; Sameroff, 1989). Both theories also find common ground postulating that order arises from interaction among components of the system—the more elements involved in a system the more stable the system is likely to be—and the idea that systems can act either to promote developmental change or to constrain the degree and nature of change (Crutchfield et al., 1986; Fogel, 1993; Thelen, 1989).

In this chapter I first describe the characteristics of dynamic and general systems theories. These characteristics will be used as a means of deriving system level general principles that can be used as integration points for further understanding the role of multiple developmental influences and midlevel developmental processes on individual behavioral–developmental variability. Ultimately I focus on two integration points: (a) The individual as system, with particular reference to the role of stabilized central attractors (SCA) and to individual differences in self-stabilization mechanisms, and (b) the role of context, with specific reference to availability of niches for the individual.

SYSTEMS PRINCIPLES

The major principles of dynamic and general systems theories that are most relevant to human development are shown in Table 10-2. A more detailed review of dynamic systems theory and its relation to behavioral development can be found in a number of sources (Barton, 1994; Fogel, 1993; Gleick, 1987; Thelen, 1989; Thelen & Smith, 1994). Detailed reviews of general systems theory and principles from this theory that are most relevant to behavioral development are also available (J. Miller, 1978; Pattee, 1973a, 1973b; Salthe, 1985; Sameroff, 1989, 1995; von Bertalanffy, 1968). The principles shown in Table 10-2 are derived from these two sets of sources.

Dynamic systems theory (also called chaos or catastrophe theory) has most often been applied to situations where there are highly unpredictable nonlinear outcomes (e.g., outcomes that cannot be predicted by the additive sum of the various elements involved). Such outcomes, although appearing random, are nonetheless determined and may be maintained across time (Gleick, 1987; May & Oster, 1976; Skarda & Freeman, 1987). Concepts from dynamic systems or chaos theory are particularly useful in situations where the direction of system change can be modeled only by way of non-linear solutions, wherein initial outcomes feed back into the prediction equation resulting in a range of potential outcomes (Barton, 1994). One such situation occurs in attempts to model cross-generational population frequency changes in seasonally breeding species (May, 1976). Dynamic systems theory approaches also can be useful in attempting to understand the sudden transition of a system from point "a" to point "b," when transition processes or transition points are not easily predicted from the individual elements of the system or from linear combinations of such elements (Crutchfield et al., 1986; Thelen & Smith, 1994).

At the human behavioral level dynamic-systems approaches have been most often used to explain the emergence of "universal" behavioral patterns such as the onset of walking or of social smiling (Lewis, 1995). Dynamic systems theory also has been used as a model for mapping variability and change in a variety of biological and psychological phenomena including functioning of the cardiac system; cognitive growth; the role of caregiver sensitivity in the development of attachment, memory formation, family dynamics, and marital therapy; and the development of multiple personality disorders (Barton, 1994; Gleick, 1987; van Geert, 1991). What is unique about dynamic-systems explanations is the underlying assumption that system transitions are not governed either by intrinsic central blueprints (e.g., genes), or by extrinsic facilitators and controls (e.g., culture), but rather are inherent in the interplay among the elements of the system itself (Thelen, 1989; Thelen & Smith, 1994). One consequence of such interplay is that simple elements can give rise to highly complex behaviors and highly unpredictable nonlinear transitions (Gleick, 1987).

General systems theory is defined as the "formulation and derivation of those principles which are valid for systems in general" (von Bertalanffy, 1968, p. 32). Specifically, general systems theory refers to a body of specific principles that illustrate how individual elements are interconnected, how patterns of element interconnections change over time, and the implica-

TABLE 10-2
Principles of Dynamic Systems Theory (DST) and General Systems Theory (GST)

DST	GST
I. Elements (what the system comprises)	
In DST there is a deemphasis on characteristics of elements that compose the system. With one possible exception, no element in a dynamic system is favored over other elements. The one possible exception involves *rate-limiting components*, which refer to the slowest developing component in a system of components, all of which are necessary for a given behavior to occur. Because the rate-limiting component must come on line for a behavior to appear or change, the rate-limiting component acts to govern the state of the system. System elements are viewed as activity patterns and not discrete entities. For example, memory is not viewed as being due to the categorical storage of discrete units of information but rather as spatial patterns of CNS electrical activity that can be destabilized or restabilized as new information is encountered.	Individual elements of the system serve to differentiate between different levels of the system (see II. Organization). A given system level is composed of elements that are either in close physical proximity to each other, are of a similar size, or are composed of similar materials. Elements also serve specific functions that act to maintain the integrity of the system (e.g., decoder elements act to transform input to a form that is usable by all system elements). Some elements within a system may have greater salience than other elements in regard to the overall functioning of the system (see III. *Centralization.*)
II. Organization (how the system is organized)	
In DST there are a variety of ways in which a system can be organized. The organizational form of a system is described in terms of attractors. *Attractors* refer to points where system trajectories converge. Attractors are not entities but rather refer to either a mathematical description of where trajectories converge or a description of the pattern into which a system has settled. Thus, attractors may describe a system converging on a single point or organized into a closed loop cycle, multiple loop cycles, or a "chaotic" pattern. Dynamic systems have the potential to suddenly shift from one type of organization to another.	GST postulates a structure that can be defined in terms of a hierachy of linked system elements. A hierarchical structure occurs when one element is nested within another element differing in either temporal or physical scale (see chap. 6, Figure 6-1). Applied to the human level, molecular (biological) influences would be at the bottom of the hierarchy, whereas more molar influences (social–cultural) would be at the top. Within a hierarchical structure, elements are not independent of each other but neither do elements at one level totally control the actions of elements at other levels. Furthermore, there is variability in the degree of linkage among elements and between levels, with some elements or levels being tightly linked while other elements or levels are loosely linked.

TABLE 10-2 (*continued*)

DST	GST

III. Processes (how systems operate)

DST	GST
In DST fundamental processes include the following: 1. High sensitivity to the influence of initial starting conditions. 2. Self-organizational processes that result from interactions among multiple system elements. 3. System change is viewed as a function of the current state of the system (e.g., attractors, rate-limiting components) and extrinsic factors such as new information, task demands, or challenges.	Eight fundamental processes are viewed as essential in GST: 1. Centralization: In a system of multiple elements, one or more elements becomes critical for the functioning of the overall system. 2. Competition: Outcome of the action of any one system element depends on the action of other system elements. 3. Equifinality: A variety of different initial conditions can result in a similar outcome—a final common pathway. 4. Progressive mechanization: Specific elements of a system act to constrain the action of other elements of the system, thus reducing the level of free interchange among system elements. 5. Progressive segregation: Elements of a system become more specialized and begin to function independently of each other. 6. Self-reorganization: Systems encounter perturbations that cannot be compensated for by self-stabilization, resulting in system structural reorganization. 7. Self-stabilization: The system can retain its organizational structure in the face of perturbations. 8. Wholeness: The outcome of the operation of a system is more than the sum of its parts. These processes interact with each other in complex ways. For example, competition among system elements leads to wholeness, whereas one consequence of self-stabilization is equifinality. Which processes are most critical for a given system at a given time reflects both the evolution and nature of the system. Thus, self-reorganization is more likely to occur when a system has evolved to a point of progressive segregation of elements.

(continued)

TABLE 10-2 (*continued*)

DST	GST
IV. Change and stability (how systems change and when they stabilize)	
Within DST, system change is based on the stabilization or destabilization of attractor states over time. Dynamic systems with deep, strong attractors are more likely to be stable. Destabilization can occur when new attractor states emerge or when single attractor states split into multiple attractor states. Within DST, change and stability are two sides of the same dynamic processes, involving the nature of ongoing attractor processes.	Over time, general systems naturally evolve toward greater complexity. General systems also can change as a way of adapting to internal or external perturbations to the system. However, general systems also have a range of stability within which the system can correct for perturbations and thus return to its current organizational structure. The self-stabilization capacity of a general system is a function of two factors. First, the hierarchical organization of the system predisposes toward redundant pathways. Second, in evolving toward greater complexity, general systems incorporate more elements and more linkages among elements. Having more linked elements increases the probability of the system having more adaptive mechanisms available to deal with perturbations. However, the fact that general systems tend toward stability does not mean that the structure of a general system is fixed. As the number and strength of perturbations increases, the system may have to reorganize to deal with these perturbations. One way to reorganize is to alter the nature of linkages among system elements. There may be a cost if the reorganization results in a less efficient system. Under extreme conditions, parts or all of the system may break down and lose all semblance of organization.

tions of such interconnections (Sameroff, 1989). As shown in Table 10-2 the operating principles that form the basis of general systems theory include wholeness, progressive mechanization, competition, centralization, hierarchical order, and equifinality. Additional principles such as goal-directed purposeful behavior, and outputs that are more complex than inputs may be needed when describing the action of living systems (J. Miller, 1978). Concepts derived from general systems theory have been particularly attractive to researchers working in the areas of high-risk conditions and developmental psychopathology (Greenberg et al., 1992; Sameroff, 1995; Werner, 1994); the role of the family in the development of attachment (Marvin & Stewart, 1990); and the nature of mother–infant interaction (Thoman, Acebo, & Becker, 1983).

Dynamic Systems Theory (DST)

A number of points derived from dynamic- and general-systems principles are essential when attempting to understand systems contributions to individual behavioral–developmental variability. As shown in Table 10-2 the organization of a dynamic system is viewed as imposed by the nature of the system itself, rather than from some outside organizing force. The organizational form of a dynamic system is typically described in terms of attractors (Barton, 1994; see also Table 10-2). Although dynamic systems can be stable and may even "prefer" a particular type of organization, within a dynamic-systems framework the potential for sudden sharp system reorganization always exists. One example of such a sudden sharp reorganization is when a system shifts into a "chaotic" state that is intermediate between an organized pattern and pure randomness. Although there is organization underlying a chaotic state, the nature of the organizing pattern is difficult to detect (Barton, 1994).

The potential for sudden dramatic changes is inherent in dynamic systems, but this does not mean that such systems are in a constant state of flux. Although even relatively small changes in elements of a dynamic system can lead to a major system reorganization, it is also true that within a given context dynamic systems can be relatively stable (Thelen, 1989). Although system patterns may appear chaotic, this does not mean any possible pattern can emerge from a given system. Self-organizational processes can act to restrict potential system configurations. One process that serves to limit potential system configurations may involve the increasing likelihood of powerful linkages among what have been called *strong deep attractors* (Thelen & Smith, 1994). Dynamic systems initially start with broad, shallow attractors that over time may become deeper and narrower (as in the case of specialized knowledge) or deeper and broader (as in the case of well-generalized knowledge states which result in the close proximity of multiple attractors). For example, neural patterns that are repeated over time, or repeated exposure to specific experiences, can result in the formation of deep and stable attractors, which appear to draw in the trajectories associated with other attractors. Similarly, early individual differences in negative emotionality and inhibition could merge with later individual differences in effortful control to function as an integrated deep, strong attractor controlled by the balance between individual reactivity and self-regulation. With increasing linkages among strong attractors, there is a greater likelihood of compensation by other attractors when perturbations occur at one attractor site. Such compensation can result in a more stable system.

Beside attractors, systems change within a dynamic-systems framework is also associated with two other factors: First, in terms of system properties, dynamic systems can be characterized on the basis of how close they are to a transition (bifurcation) point. Being close to a transition point may mean that all system components are functional except the rate-limiting component. When the rate-limiting parameter shifts, the interactions among multiple system elements changes, and the system shifts (Gleick, 1987; Thelen & Ulrich, 1991). There appears to be general agreement among dynamic systems theorists that when a system is at a point of transition (e.g., a rate-limiting component is about to shift) even minor changes to one aspect of the system or minor extrinsic challenges may be sufficient to result in major nonlinear changes to the system as a whole (Prigogine & Stengers, 1984; van Geert, 1991). In contrast, when a system is not at a transition point, major changes to system components would be needed to evoke a system-wide change.

Second, as shown in Table 10-2, trajectories of dynamic systems are highly sensitive to the influence of even small differences in initial conditions. The fact that dynamic systems are highly sensitive to initial conditions means that widely different outcomes can result from small differences in such conditions. Initial conditions can include "built in" values involving the history of the organism, either at an evolutionary or at an individual level. Evolutionary influences that have survival value in the history of the species can result in an initial bias toward certain stimulus configurations or certain response modes, such as the tendency of human neonates to orient toward human faces (see chap. 2, this volume). Built in values also may reflect the input of recurring early experiences, resulting in strong attractors associated with these experiences. Alternatively, built in values may reflect intrinsic early individual characteristics that influence the relation of the individual to their context, as in the case of central nervous system integrity at birth (see chap. 3) or temperamental inhibition (see chap. 5, this volume).

General Systems Theory (GST)

Because of their hierarchical organizational structure combined with variable linkage among system elements, general systems have a built in propensity for stability. In a hierarchical system some elements at a given level can shift and change while other levels of the system remain stable. This allows for both system flexibility and system stability (Simon, 1973). Thus, even major disorganization at one level of the system need not compromise the whole system, because the impact of such disorganization will be attenuated when the next stable level is reached (Salthe, 1985). There is also the theoretical possibility that some parts of a hierarchical system can be totally chaotic while the overall structure of the system remains stable (Pattee, 1973b).

Although general systems have a propensity for stability, this does not mean that once formed, such systems become essentially static. As seen in Table 10-2 major forces promoting change in a general system are internal or external perturbations. Internal perturbations can occur where a critical system element fails (e.g., single gene disorders that act to disrupt normal body metabolic processes; see chap. 3, this volume). External perturbation occurs when systems encounter highly intense or chronic stressors coming from outside the system (e.g., high levels of chronic societal violence; see chap. 7, this volume).

Perturbations to a general system, particularly a living system, can be viewed in terms of the discrepancy between system input and system output (von Bertalanffy, 1968). Systems are in a state of imbalance and are under strain in situations where there is a lack of input or an excessive output, resulting in insufficient resources for the system; alternatively, systems are out of balance and under stress in situations where there is excessive input or a lack of output, resulting in an overload of resources (Miller, 1978). For example, the low bioavailability of iron found in a diet high in whole grains and vegetables can result in iron deficiency (lack of input); in contrast, genetic defects in the regulation of iron absorption may result in an individual's iron status reaching toxic levels (i.e., lack of output; Yip & Dallman, 1996).

Living systems particularly have a variety of self-stabilization mechanisms available to deal with and adjust to short-term perturbations. The relatively time limited effects on children of mild head injury can be viewed as one example of a system correcting for an external perturbation (see Satz et al., 1997). When perturbations are the result of deficiencies, systems can compensate by lowering thresholds, opening up subsystem boundaries, moving closer to input sources, or opening more input channels. In the case of perturbations associated with overload, systems can compensate by moving away from input, raising thresholds, finding additional storage facilities, or breaking input down into more easily managed chunks (J. Miller, 1978). Thus, in the case of iron deficiency, the body acts to increase the absorption rate of whatever iron is available; in the case of iron toxicity, the number of body storage sites can be increased to deal with iron overload (Yip & Dallman, 1996).

However, as noted above, systems are not totally resilient. When perturbations become too chronic or too severe, systems can lose part or all of their structure. For example, under conditions of mild nutritional energy imbalance, individuals can "adapt" by reducing nonessential activities and thus lower energy demands. If energy imbalance continues over time, a greater reduction of function may be needed to maintain energy balance. At this point critical physical (growth) or behavioral (essential activity levels) functions may be lost. In the latter situation a system will remain in balance but at a major cost to the system in terms of outcomes such as increased illness or decreased work capacity (Scrimshaw & Young, 1989). When the cost of such accommodation becomes too great, or when no further compensation is possible, systems may break down entirely and lose all semblance of organization (J. Miller, 1978).

The interplay of centralization and segregation is of particular relevance for understanding both general systems processes and contributions to individual behavioral–developmental variability (see Table 10-2). Open (e.g., living) systems wherein there is continual intake and output of energy and systems that are composed of more structurally dissimilar elements are most likely to move toward progressive segregation (J. Miller, 1978). However, systems also require at least some degree of linkage or interdependence among the various elements if the overall system is to be maintained as a whole rather then splitting into separate systems. Although centralization and segregation would seem to be diametrically opposed, the joint operation of these system-level processes does not fit a simple either/or model. Particularly for living systems, a more likely scenario is one wherein subsystems become more specialized (greater segregation), but within each specialized subsystem we find one or more centralized elements around which the operation of the subsystem focuses (greater centralization). One of the benefits of having concurrent segregation–centralization processes co-occurring is that it allows for both overall systemwide operation as well as intrasystem specialization. The central nervous system may be viewed as having these dual properties, functioning both as an overall system and as a series of specific cortical areas that control critical operations for different outcomes (see chap. 3).

Systems Theories and Development

In spite of its growing application to living systems there are a number of reasons to be concerned about the degree of applicability of DST as a general framework for understanding individual behavioral–developmental variability. Although an important function of theory is to be able to accurately describe, an equally important function is to explain. Descriptions of regularity cannot be regarded as explanations (Waddington, 1972). At the level of human development, much of what is cited as evidence for the validity of dynamic systems theory are descriptions of changes. Although such descriptions tell us what is occurring, they do not illuminate the processes underlying observed pattern shifts. For example, because all we know about attractors is that system trajectories converge around these points, it is impossible to understand why such convergence is occurring. Ascribing specific qualities to attractors (e.g., attractors act as stable mediators that select, organize, and interpret information) runs the risk of redefining mathematical descriptors into things, a usage which does not fit within the framework of dynamic systems theory (Fogel, 1993). Furthermore, the use of what passes for process mechanisms in DST, as seen in concepts like system self-organization, runs the risk of circularity: Why is the system behaving in this way? Because it is self-organizing. How do we know it is self-organizing? Because it behaves in this way. The essentially descriptive nature of DST is recognized by many dynamic systems theorists who concede that this theory does not tell us how observed patterns emerge from transaction among the elements of a system, but only that such patterns do emerge (Crutchfield et al., 1986; Fogel, 1993).

Furthermore, there are a number of situations where it seems clear that the characteristics ascribed to dynamic systems do not provide a good fit to existing empirical data. One of the most critical of these discrepancies involves the DST principle that we cannot easily predict how a complex system will react to change when the system is not in equilibrium (Prigogene & Stengers, 1984; Thelen & Smith, 1994). In spite of this principle, evidence suggests that when individuals are faced with situations involving rapid change (e.g., onset of menarche), or are placed in high-demand stress situations, their behavior often becomes *more, not less predictable*. Rather than new or unexpected developmental trajectories emerging in these types of situations, the best predictor of future behavior is most likely to be previously established behavioral patterns (Caspi & Moffitt, 1991; Wright & Mischel, 1987). Along the same lines, the dynamic-systems principle of discontinuity, when systems jump from one attractor state to another (Thelen, 1989), does not provide a good fit with the multiple illustrations of causal chain processes discussed in chapter 9. Furthermore, there is the assumption that elements of a system are of far less salience for understanding developmental variability than is the relation among elements (e.g., what we inherit are not genes or environments but rather relations between genes and environment; see Fogel, 1993). This assumption does not fit well with evidence presented in chapters 5 and 8, showing how specific elements (e.g., individual characteristics) acting over time can structure the nature of subsequent transactional relations between organism and environment.

DST appears to be most useful when we are dealing with relatively simple systems that have a small number of variables that can be easily identified and whose trajectories can be easily quantified (Barton, 1994; Fogel, 1993; Gleick, 1987). These criteria may not necessarily fit with highly complex multivariable phenomena, like individual behavioral development (Magnusson, 1993). Although it may be difficult to fully adopt DST as an overall framework, some dynamic-systems concepts are important to include when attempting to develop an integrative framework for understanding system-level influences on individual behavioral-developmental variability. This is particularly true if we accept the assumption that systems in and of themselves may have unique inherent processes that act to influence outcomes, over and above the impact associated with specific elements of the system. From a dynamic-systems framework, the following concepts may be particularly important:

1. The possibility that under certain conditions change can be sudden, linear, and nonpredictable. Sudden unpredictable changes in developmental trajectories do not necessarily mean that we are dealing with pure randomness; even a highly chaotic system may ultimately be determined (Gleick, 1987).

2. The concept that systems are highly sensitive to initial conditions. Such sensitivity is one reason why it is often difficult to make precise long-term predictions. This is especially true when there is error of measurement associated with initial conditions, a situation which is very characteristic of human developmental studies (Crutchfield et al., 1986). However, within a dynamic-systems framework it may be possible to predict *ranges of outcomes*, even if sensitivity to initial conditions means we are unable to predict specific outcomes (Barton, 1994).

3. Changes in a small subset of system parameters have the potential to shift the whole system. When sudden unpredictable shifts occur, we should be looking for changes in a small number of control parameters that result in dramatic, systemwide change (Nowak, Vallacher, & Lewenstein, 1994).

4. Unpredictable nonlinear shifts associated with a small subset of control parameters are more likely to occur when a system reaches a transition point. However, as the number of elements involved in a system increase, or when a system is not at a transition point, we should not expect to see sudden systemwide changes.

As with dynamic systems theory, there are some aspects of GST that call for caution when attempting to apply this framework as the sole basis for understanding individual human variability. First, as noted by J. Miller (1978), connections among elements of a system do not necessarily translate into a functional system. Some connections may be arbitrary and may share little relation to function. For example, Gould (1991) discussed the possibility that certain physical features evolve in a species not because they have a survival function, but rather because they were associated with other physical features that did have survival value. As a theory, GST tells us little about which interconnections among elements of a system are more likely to be functional. In addition, some principles derived from GST do not necessarily fit well with available evidence. For example, Salthe (1985) argued that hierarchical structures do not allow for bidirectional influences over more than one level. As I documented repeatedly in this volume, bidirectional linkages do exist across multiple levels (see chaps. 6–8). This contradiction need not necessarily be fatal if we are willing to assume *asymmetrical relations*, such that bidirectional influences vary in strength depending on direction and the distance between levels (Salthe, 1985).

Also of concern is the way in which GST is used, particularly in the human developmental sciences. Although specific general-systems-properties can be detailed, all too often these properties are used in a post hoc descriptive fashion. Paralleling what I said in regard to DST, specific developmental patterns are often assumed to be the result of the operation of general systems principles, rather than of general systems principles being used to predict what developmental patterns may be emerging. However, as with DST, certain concepts may be drawn from general systems theory that are especially salient for understanding systems contributions to individual behavioral–developmental variability. These concepts are listed below.

1. Individual elements (or in the present case, individual developmental influences) serve specific functions, both in the development and maintenance of a system. Elements are not interchangeable. Systems elements can vary in importance in different contexts or in different time periods (J. Miller, 1978).
2. Because of linkage patterns among systems elements at different levels, general systems have built in mechanisms that can act to compensate for either internal or external perturbations to the system. However, general systems are not infinitely flexible, and even when systems adjust, this adjustment may come at a cost (J. Miller, 1978; Salthe, 1985).
3. The operation of general-systems processes involving progressive segregation and centralization allows for a variety of system patterns. Such patterns can involve high centralization of elements, high element segregation, or a structure characterized by subsystem specialization with linkage among central elements from different subsystems (von Bertalanffy, 1968).
4. In general systems there is an ongoing tension in regard to the balance between self-reorganization and self-stabilization processes, or between segregation processes that act to drive system elements apart and the simultaneous operation of centralized processes that act to focus elements around a common point (von Bertalanffy, 1968).

In addition to specific concepts derived from DST or GST, developmentally relevant concepts common to both theories are listed below:

1. From both a dynamic-systems and a general-systems perspective, a major factor influencing the stability of an existing system is the degree of linkage among system elements, with greater stability occurring in more densely linked systems (Lewis, 1995; Sameroff, 1989).

2. Both DST and GST also allow for multiple system states. Within a general-systems framework, some systems evolve toward stability with remarkably little change, other systems may never reach this point, some systems may cycle in and out of periods of stability, and system collapse allows for sudden sharp changes to system organization (von Bertalanffy, 1968). Within a dynamic-systems framework there may be times when a system can act in a very predictable manner for long periods of time, but under certain conditions the same system may become highly chaotic (Gleick, 1987). In this sense both dynamic and general systems theory would be compatible with evidence from paleobiology showing long periods of regular predictable evolutionary change within a species, followed by relatively brief periods (geologically speaking) where there are sudden unpredictable shifts where species may suddenly appear or disappear (Eldridge & Gould, 1972).
3. Both DST and GST allow for the possibility that some elements of a system may well be chaotic, unstable, and unpredictable, even while the overall system shows both stability and predictability, or that a system element can behave in a linear predictable manner even though the overall system is chaotic (Anderson, 1972; Gleick, 1987; Pattee, 1973b; Prigogene & Stengers, 1984). For example, the molecular pattern of gene action (DNA → RNA → amino acids) is highly linear and predictable, whereas relations between genes and behavior may be nonlinear and far more difficult to predict (Weiss, 1971).

INTEGRATING DYNAMIC AND GENERAL SYSTEMS PRINCIPLES IN THE STUDY OF BEHAVIORAL DEVELOPMENT

Given the similarities in system-process mechanisms noted above, can dynamic and general systems theory be applied interchangeably to the same developmental outcomes? I would argue *not*. By its nature, dynamic-systems principles such as rate-limiting components (see Table 10-2) may be more applicable to situations where outcome changes are sudden and sharp. In contrast, GST mechanisms such as progressive mechanization and self-stabilization (see Table 10-2) are more likely to be operating when outcome changes are gradual in nature. Thus, outcomes where change is more qualitative in nature may be more likely to reflect dynamic-system processes, whereas outcomes where change is quantitative in nature may be a better reflection of general-systems processes (Nowak et al., 1994). Similarly, the distinction made by life span developmentalists (Moen, Elder, & Luscher,

1995) between coexisting discontinuity (life turning points) and continuity (consistent life themes) may reflect the differential operation of dynamic-(turning points) or general-systems processes (life themes) at different points in the life span.

The operation of GST principles such as centralization, equifinality, and self-stabilization also may be particularly applicable to individuals with extreme traits (e.g., highly aggressive children; see chap. 5, this volume), who continue to show similar behavioral patterns across time and across varying contexts. GST principles such as centralization or progressive mechanization may also be particularly relevant when individuals are living in highly stable cultural contexts, where there is strong macrosystem pressure for certain behavioral patterns (see chap. 7, this volume). On the other hand, when we have aspects of development where a particular element acts as a rate-limiting control parameter (change cannot occur until this element reaches a certain level of functioning), dynamic-systems principles may be more likely to apply (Barton, 1994). Examples of this latter case would include tasks such as discrimination or oddity learning, where a principle must be learned to solve a particular type of problem. This suggests the possibility that more molecular aspects of behavior, such as specific problem solving, may be more sensitive to the operation of dynamic-systems forces, whereas more molar aspects of behavior comprising multiple elements (e.g., intelligence) would be more sensitive to processes derived from the operation of general-systems principles. The critical point is that the operation of dynamic-systems or general-systems theory processes is not an absolute. Which framework is more salient may well depend on what level, what outcome, or what developmental influences are being looked at (Barton, 1994; Fogel, 1993). In this case the operation of systems processes may be compatible with the operation of midlevel process specificity (see chap. 9, this volume).

To illustrate the application of systems-level process mechanisms to individual behavioral–developmental variability, three mechanisms will be considered, one deriving primarily from DST (bifurcation), one primarily from GST (balance), and one from both theories (centralization).

Bifurcation Points

An important feature of dynamic systems theory is the idea that development proceeds as the organism encounters a series of bifurcation points where individual development can go in one of several specific directions (Oster & Alberch, 1982; Smith et al., 1985; Thelen, 1989). It is important to recognize that bifurcation points do not necessarily lead to sudden sharp changes in developmental trajectories. Systems at a bifurcation point also may become fixed in a highly stable pattern (Prigogene & Stengers, 1984). As Lewis (1995) has pointed out, when a system goes through a bifurcation point, some potential pathways are lost as the system branches in a certain direction. By reducing degrees of freedom of the system to develop in certain directions, some potential developmental pathways may become lost to the individual. Alternatively, because bifurcation points represent both the end of one stage and the start of a new one, and because initial stage conditions can bias the direction of change, at such points systems can also shift to a modified restructuring that encompasses many of the features of the system's prior organizational structure (Oster & Alberch, 1982). What is critical to recognize about bifurcation points is that, at such a point, small changes in a relatively restricted set of developmental influences can have a major nonlinear impact on the development or integrity of a system; in contrast, at nonbifurcation points, relatively major changes in a variety of influences are needed to have the same degree of impact (Oster & Alberch, 1982; Prigogene & Stengers, 1984). In understanding the role played by bifurcation points in individual behavioral–developmental variability answers to three questions are essential: What produces bifurcation points? How can we identify such points? And what changes are likely to result when an individual reaches such a point?

What Conditions Lead to a Bifurcation Point in Development?

Integrating the general-systems principles of self-stabilization and self-reorganization into the operation of bifurcation, I would argue that only when systems encounter perturbations that cannot be compensated for by existing stabilization mechanisms is the system likely to be approaching a bifurcation point. Perturbations that cannot be compensated for may involve high levels of stress to the individual, or they may involve major contextual changes such as a sudden monetary windfall or new information that requires the individual to change existing plans or goals (Lewis, 1995). Consistent with the necessary but not sufficient theme of this volume, I would also argue that bifurcation points can be the result of the cumulative impact of convergent multiple developmental influences. Rather then a specific extreme condition at a single point in time (e.g., sudden major central nervous system injury; forced migration), it may be that combinations of predisposing conditions occurring concurrently, or an accumulation of conditions over time can act to move an individual to a bifurcation point. This is particularly true when perturbations build on themselves and are amplified by positive feedback loop mechanisms, resulting in nonlinear amplifications of the original set of influences (Lewis, 1995). One example of combined perturbations that could result in an individual reaching a bifurcation point would be genetically influenced pubertal changes occurring at the same time as distal contextual shifts, such as a shift from primary to secondary school, or the onset of initiation rites. Another example would be changes in both diet and pattern of caregiver–child relations associated with weaning. A third example could involve new sources of repeated feedback about one's abilities or personality that are discrepant from what individuals have always believed about themselves, as may occur when an individual moves from secondary school to college. Cumulative risk factors which could have the same result are seen when a child reaches a bifurcation point as a function of long-term parental marital problems culminating in divorce and the characteristic contextual changes that are associated with divorce.

How Do We Know When a Bifurcation Point in Development Has Been Reached?

Obviously one potential group includes individuals who are undergoing major life changes as a function of biological (e.g., major illness), psychosocial (e.g., parental divorce), or macrosystem influences (e.g., migration to a different culture). Alternatively, individuals are also likely to be approaching a bifurcation point when they are exposed to cumulative multidomain perturbations that are distinctly different from what the individual has previously experienced, and that act to change the individual's self-perceptions, internal working models, or worldviews. However, as discussed in chapter 1, not all individuals react in the same way to these types of major or cumulative perturbations, so focusing just on perturbations may be a rather crude screen.

Although we have relatively few good empirical or theoretically based markers that would allow us to detect when a given individual is approaching a bifurcation point, one way is to look at variability among elements of the system. Theoretically, increases in element variability over time reflect a system that is rapidly approaching a transition point, and thus will be extremely sensitive to outside influences or changes in individual system components (Nowak & Lewenstein, 1994; Thelen & Smith, 1994). Analogously, increases in intra-individual behavioral variability may reflect individuals who are approaching bifurcation points in their development.

When a System Has Reached a Bifurcation Point in Development, Is the Response Likely to be Major Change, Graduated Change, or Little Change in Development?

Given the focus of this chapter, I frame this question in terms of individual development and ask, When an individual has reached a bifurcation point in their development, can we reliably predict the extent and nature of change at this point? As noted earlier, reaching a bifurcation point does not necessarily mean major changes in system trajectories. Although an answer to this question is not readily apparent from either dynamic or general systems theory, at an inductive level it is possible to take the evidence presented in chapters 2–7 of this volume and develop a set of hypotheses about which individuals at a potential bifurcation point are more likely to demonstrate rigid, flexible, or chaotic behavioral patterns. Such a set of hypotheses is seen in Table 10-3. Using individual characteristics as one example, individuals whose behavior is consistently characterized by traits involving a low level of reactivity or a high level of self-regulation (e.g., highly inhibited individuals), individuals who have a background predisposing to blunting (see chap. 9), individuals whose behavioral characteristics are highly valued by their culture (see chap. 7, this volume), and individuals who have a lessened ability to make use of new opportunities (e.g., low IQ) would be those who would most likely show continued stability in their developmental trajectories when encountering a bifurcation point.

In contrast, individuals whose behaviors are characterized by high reactivity or poor self-regulation skills (e.g., impulsive), individuals who do not have a sense of control over their world (e.g., learned helplessness), or individuals who do not have backgrounds that predispose to a strong internal working model or who are unable to learn from previous experience would be those whose developmental trajectories are more likely to show sharp changes on encountering a bifurcation point. As we move away from the extremes we are more likely to see individuals whose developmental trajectories are a function of the balance between competing tendencies such as reactivity and self-regulation, and who would react in a more graduated way to perturbations at bifurcation points.

Balance as a Metaphor

At the level of individual influences there are multiple references to the level of balance between competing tendencies. The role of the central nervous system in development has been conceptualized as the tension between those central nervous subsystems that promote activation versus those subsystems that promote inhibition (Calkins & Fox, 1994; Nelson, 1994). The operation of homeostatic balance control models are also seen in regard to nutritional influences, as in the case when physiological mechanisms act to compensate for dietary deficits in micronutrient intake (e.g., zinc metabolism; Cousins, 1996). Individual behavioral variability has consistently been viewed in terms of the relative balance between risk and protective biological and psychological factors encountered by the individual (Bradley et al., 1994; Bronfenbrenner & Ceci, 1994; DuBois et al., 1994; Garbarino, 1990; Kendler & Eaves, 1986; Rutter & Rutter, 1992). The quality of spousal relations is often viewed not as a function of the number of negative versus the number of positive interactions per se, but rather as the balance between negative and positive interactions (Sameroff, 1995). Alternatively, developmental variability also has been viewed as a consequence of the degree of balance between an individual's available resources and his or her level of contextual demands (R. Barker, 1968; Scrimshaw & Young, 1989). As noted earlier, in the organization and growth of general

TABLE 10-3
Conditions That Predispose to Continuity or
Discontinuity of Individual Patterns

Moderators			
Biological	Individual	Psychological	Cultural

Persons showing little change in response to perturbations			
Biologically compromised (e.g., mal-nutrition, morbidity, major CNS injury).	Extreme traits (e.g., inhibition, early appearing antisocial behavior, insecure attachment, low IQ, low stimulus reactivity).	Prior exposure to stress individual cannot deal with. Few niches available, rearing in highly chaotic environment, few social supports, background predisposes to blunting.	Culturally based passive coping style. Limited no. of culturally based options. Has character-istics that are highly valued by culture.

Persons showing gradual change in response to perturbations			
Not biologically comprised.	Self-regulation, ego control, ability to delay gratification, sense of self-efficacy, secure attachment, above average IQ, planning skills, social skills.	Adequate number of desirable niches available, prior exposure to moderate stress that could be coped with, background predisposes to buffering or steeling.	Culturally based active coping style, cultural tolerance for diversity.

Persons showing extreme change in response to perturbations			
CNS injury, rapidly fluctuating hormonal changes.	High impulsivity, poor self-regulation, inability to learn from previous experience, external locus of control, learned helplessness, limited internal working models of how to relate to the world, difficult temperament.	Niches available but dissatisfied with existing niches, low prior exposure to stress (i.e., overprotected), background predisposes to sensitization.	Change in cultural context such that old rules no longer apply, mixed mes-sages from friends and family.

Note. CNS = central nervous system. *Examples of perturbations:* biological shifts—changes in ongoing gene systems, major illness or accident, puberty; psychological shifts—family disruption, school changes; macrosystem shifts—acculturation, economic changes, migration, war.

systems, balance is a critical process, as seen in the relative strength of self-reorganization and self-stabilization processes, or in the degree of balance between progressive segregation and centralization.

In understanding the impact of balance–imbalance at either the sys-tem or individual level, it is important to recognize that outcomes are not a function just of the *difference* between reorganization and stabilization mechanisms or of protective minus risk factors. Nonlinear relations between risk and protective influences may be equally critical (Garmezy et al., 1984; Werner, 1990), as seen in evidence for the operation of organism–environment interactions (see chap. 8, this volume). Nonlinear relations are also a characteristic feature when feedback mechanisms are operating (Lewis, 1995). However, a linear conceptualization of balance may be useful when the goal is to predict potential outcome ranges rather than specific outcomes. For example, for outcomes such as personality, intelligence, and behavioral adjustment, we may not be able to predict exact levels over the course of time. However, for many outcomes we can predict reasonably well the range within which an individual will fall (Costa & McCrae, 1994; Neisser et al., 1996; see also chap. 5, this volume). If we are attempting to predict ranges rather than specific outcomes, looking at the degree of balance between competing tendencies may be a useful way of predicting the potential degree and nature of change. For example, an individual who tends toward self-stabilization is more likely to show a well-canalized developmental trajectory and a narrower range of reaction then an individual who tends more toward self-reorganization.

Centralization

The idea that system trajectories can be focused around a specific element in the system is seen both in dynamic systems theory (deep and stable attractors; Thelen & Smith, 1994) and in general systems theory (centralization; von Bertalanffy, 1968). Although deep and stable attractors are defined primarily in terms of system trajectories, in GST, central elements of a system are defined as those that are most closely linked with other elements in the system (J. Miller, 1978). Furthermore, both general systems (von Bertalanffy, 1968) and dynamic systems theory (Thelen & Smith, 1994) allow for the possibility of multiple central elements or multiple deep and stable attractors. There is also general agreement that in a noncentralized system or in a system lacking deep and stable attractors there is a greater likelihood of system breakdown or a radical change in system trajectory when perturbations are encountered (Thelen & Smith, 1994; von Bertalanffy, 1968). In contrast, a more centralized system is less likely to break down or have its trajectory radically altered, unless perturbations directly affect the central element. In this case change may be sudden and systemwide (K. Lewin, 1952; von Bertalanffy, 1968).

What are the implications of centralization principles for understanding individual behavioral–developmental variability? Anticipating a conclusion that I will elaborate on in the next sections I argue that not only system's but also individual's developmental trajectories can be characterized on the basis of degree of centralization. At an individual level high centralization refers to a single developmental influence dominating the course of the individual's life trajectory. Such an influence may be *biological* (e.g., the malnutrition morbidity cycle, major gene defect); *individual* (e.g., high level of talent in a given domain, disorganized attachment, early antisocial behavior, high level of mastery motivation); *environmental* (e.g., a history of poverty or abuse, exposure to a highly supportive teacher in the early grades); or *macrosystem–cultural* (e.g., racism, strongly held culturally supported religious beliefs, assigned cultural role). Individuals whose development is moderately centralized would be those for whom there are a limited number of developmental influences dominating the course of their life trajectory. In contrast, an individual whose development is noncentralized would be affected by many developmental influences with no single or small group of influences being especially salient. Using individual characteristics as an outcome, a hypothetical example of each type of pattern is shown in Figure 10-2-A on page 284.

INTEGRATING MULTIPLE INFLUENCES, MIDLEVEL, AND SYSTEMS-LEVEL PROCESSES

Both dynamic systems and general systems theories are based on two fundamental assumptions. First, that systems, in and of themselves, produce processes that influence growth and development. Second, that such systemwide processes cannot be understood without looking at the operation of the system as a whole. However, like all other levels of influence presented in this volume, I view the contribution of system-level processes as necessary but not sufficient. Within a necessary but not sufficient framework, a central problem in understanding the etiology of individual differences in behavioral–developmental variability is how to integrate the role of multiple influences (as discussed in chaps. 2–7), with the impact of both midlevel (as discussed in chaps. 8 and 9) and system-level processes (current chapter). To anticipate what is discussed at greater length on this issue, I start with my overall conclusions:

First, structurally and functionally linked multiple influences operating over time and impacting on specific developmental domains have two consequences:

1. The functioning of multiple developmental influences and midlevel processes leads to the development of an individual who begins to operate according to system-level principles. That is, underlying processes that characterize the functioning of general and dynamic systems also began to characterize the functioning of individuals. I will refer to this process as the *individual as system*.

2. Multiple influences and midlevel processes functioning as described above also lead to the development of an individual who has a range of contextual niches with varying characteristics open to them. I will refer to this process as *individual niche potential*.

Second, following the development of the individual as system and the stabilization of individual niche potential, the subsequent impact of multiple developmental influences and midlevel processes are moderated by individual system and niche characteristics.

System characteristics of the individual and individual niche potential, in combination with later occurring contextual and biological perturbations and supports, act to stabilize, destabilize, or redirect individual developmental trajectories that were initially set by multiple influences and midlevel processes. These conclusions are summarized in Figure 10-3.

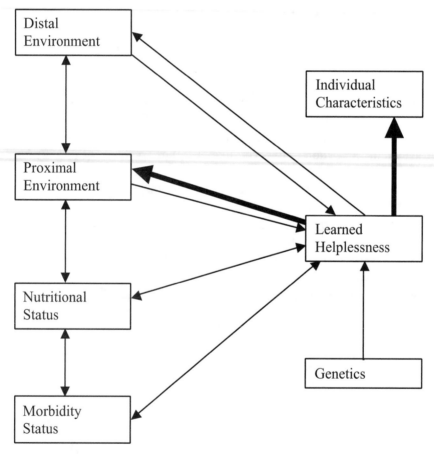

Figure 10-2-A. Example of individuals whose developmental trajectories are strongly centralized.

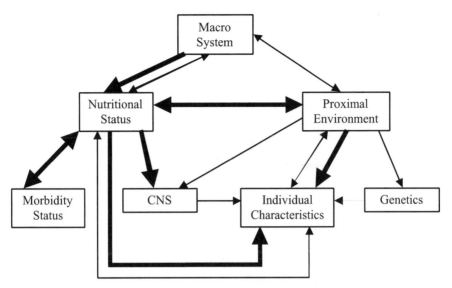

Figure 10-2-B. Example of individuals whose developmental trajectories are moderately centralized.

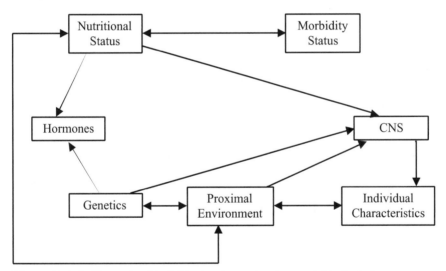

Figure 10-2-C. Example of individuals whose developmental trajectories are non-centralized.

What is essential to understand about the framework presented in Figure 10-3 is the temporal nature of this process. Initially, multiple influences and midlevel processes influence individual behavioral–developmental variability (path a). However, over time multiple influences and midlevel processes also contribute to the development of the individual functioning as a system as well as to individual niche potential (paths b & c). As a result there is a systematic shift in what drives developmental trajectories, from multiple influences and midlevel processes to the person as

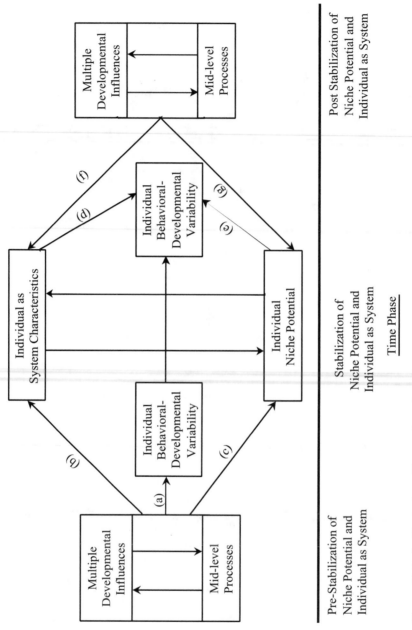

Figure 10-3. An illustration of how a three-level framework is related to individual behavioral–developmental variability.

system and the extent and nature of contextual niches available to the individual (paths d & e). Ultimately, it is the integration between these four sets of influences that acts on developmental trajectories (paths d, e, f, g). For example, as discussed in chapter 5, a variety of specific biological and psychosocial characteristics lead some children to develop early appearing antisocial behavior patterns. However, over time the very fact of a child being chronically antisocial means that the child begins to process input from the environment in very specific ways that may depend less on the nature of the input and more upon the child's organized internal working model of both himself or herself and the nature of others (e.g., expectation of rejection and hostility from others). Biological, psychosocial, and midlevel processes initially act to produce a child who is chronically antisocial. However, once this child enters into an antisocial developmental trajectory it is the organized pattern of child characteristics and the limited number of niches that are available to such a child (e.g., loss of opportunities to interact with prosocial peers, loss of educational opportunities) which become the major impetus for the subsequent developmental path these children travel.

This does not mean that multiple influences and midlevel processes function as the developmental equivalent of deism, acting to set up the individual as system and individual niche potential and then ceasing to function as an influence on development. As noted in Figure 10-3 multiple influences and midlevel processes continue to operate over the life span, but, unlike their initial impact, their subsequent impact is moderated through the characteristics of the individual as system and the niches that are available to the individual.

What is described above and shown in Figure 10-3 may induce an uncomfortable feeling of *deja vu* in many readers. Is what is described above nothing more than the all too common and all too vague statement that development is a joint function of the individual and his or her context, which tells us all too little about specific individual and contextual characteristics and how they interrelate (K. Lewin, 1952; Oyama, 1989)? What I hope to document below is how concepts derived from the above framework can be detailed in terms of their specific characteristics and can be described in ways that lead to testable predictions about the nature of the processes underlying individual behavioral–developmental variability.

The Individual As System

Particularly when related to his or her biological or cultural context the individual is regarded primarily as a cog or element in a larger system (Coleman, 1971). For example, in sociobiology the individual is regarded primarily as the carrier of genes in a larger evolutionary framework

(Dawkins, 1980; Rushton, 1984). In contrast to this view of the individual as a cog is an alternative viewpoint based initially on the writings of Alfred North Whitehead (1925) and later elaborated on by von Bertalanffy (1968) and J. Miller (1978). These authors argue that *the individual organism itself may be viewed as a living system.* That is, individuals show many of the same properties exhibited by complex general systems. These properties include the following:

1. Like systems, individuals show growth and differentiation, becoming more complex over time.
2. Like systems, individuals function as a whole rather then as a collection of separate parts (Goodwin, 1987).
3. Like systems, individuals function in an organized manner partly as a result of outside events, but partially also as a result of self-organization processes (Barton, 1994; Goodwin, 1987). This means that individuals can be characterized on the basis of coherent clusters of behavior that vary in a reliable way across different contexts (Freitas & Downey, 1998).
4. Like systems, individuals show a capacity for self-regulation, maintaining individual integrity in the face of biological and environmental shifts. Indeed, one of the critical developmental tasks for young organisms is to be able to regulate their own internal systems (Sameroff, 1995). Failure of such regulation can lead to disruption of individual (system) functions and, as in the case of mental illness, destabilization of previously stable developmental trajectories (Als, 1992; von Bertalanffy, 1968).
5. Like systems, the various unique characteristics that make up an individual interact in a variety of ways (von Bertalanffy, 1968).
6. Like general systems, individuals can also show progressive segregation, as seen in processes like automatization of some developmental functions so they are no longer under conscious control (Bargh, 1992). Individuals can also show system processes such as centralization (specific aspects of personality or behavior become a dominant feature of the individual; see chap. 5) and sensitivity to early initial conditions (see chap. 6, this volume).

How do individuals come to function in a way similar to the way a system functions? As shown in Figure 10-3, although the exact mechanisms are as yet unknown, what is proposed is the following sequence: (a) Over time, contributions of multiple developmental influences (chaps. 2–7) and the midlevel processes underlying such influences (chaps. 8–9) act to produce an individual with systemlike properties; (b) as systems-level processes begin to stabilize for an individual, the contribution of system processes become as important, if not more important, than the impact of multiple influences for subsequent individual variability.

It is at this point that our fundamental unit of analysis must shift from the contributions of specific developmental influences to the characteristics of the individual functioning as a whole (Goodwin, 1987). For example, children whose characteristics of temperament do not fit their proximal and distal contexts are more likely to have repeated rejection experiences. Such experiences cumulate over time and result in an individual who is rejection sensitive (individual begins to function as a coherent system). This internalized rejection sensitivity acts to influence how the individual processes information and reacts in situations where rejection is a possible issue (system processes begin to impact on subsequent individual behavioral–developmental variability).

How do we know when we have reached a point where individual system-level processes become important in stabilizing and influencing the course of subsequent individual development? Given that a fundamental property of a developed system is its ability to reduce the impact of perturbations to the system, I propose that we have reached such a point when the following occur:

1. In the face of changing biological (e.g., illness) and psychosocial perturbations (e.g., family disruption) individual characteristics remain either relatively stable or return to prior levels after the perturbation has passed.
2. It takes increasingly intensive multiple perturbations to deflect the individual's developmental trajectory.
3. The impact of multiple intensive perturbations is seen primarily in changes in isolated aspects of individual functioning.
4. The contributions of perturbations to individual development cannot be predicted or understood without knowledge of the system characteristics of the individual.

The criteria described above for defining when the individual begins to function in a way similar to that of a stable general system are similar to criteria used in connectionist models of development, wherein weights given to certain units increase over time so that more heavily weighted units become less sensitive to small differences in informational input (Elman, 1993). The time at which individuals begin to function according to a system's principles will vary across individuals and can be viewed as a major source of differences among individuals.

If one of the major consequences of developmental influences acting over time is to produce an individual who functions in a way that is analogous to the functioning of a complex general system, a critical question is which system properties and processes are most influential in understanding the contributions of the individual as system to their own subsequent development (Sameroff, 1995)? I propose that two complex system properties are especially salient. The first is structural; namely, what I call *stabilized central attractors*. The second process involves the operation of *self-stabilization mechanisms*.

Stabilized Central Attractors (SCA)

Stabilized central attractors (SCA) integrate the concept of centralization from GST with the concept of deep and stable attractors from DST. Although SCA may function in the same way as attractors, as a focal point for developmental trajectories, unlike attractors, SCA have specific definable properties and function as a result of their linkage to multiple other developmental influences and individual characteristics. *Stabilized central attractors* are defined as developmental influences or individual characteristics around which individuals organize their perceptions of their world and their relationship to their world. Structurally SCA refer to strongly weighted individual characteristics and developmental influences, which are densely linked to other multiple elements or influences characterizing an individual and toward which the individual's developmental trajectory converges. As discussed previously, individuals may be defined with reference to their pattern of SCA as highly centralized, moderately centralized, or noncentralized.

As shown in Figure 10-2-A (page 284) a *strongly centralized* individual is one whose characteristics and ongoing development can be essentially described on the basis of a single dominant SCA. Although the dominant SCA may have developed as the result of multiple developmental influences, over time the impact of these other influences is subsumed by the operation of the dominant SCA. The dominant SCA shown in this figure is an individual characteristic (learned helplessness), but any other biological (e.g., major illness or gene disorder), individual (e.g., early appearing antisocial behavior pattern, religious beliefs), or environmental characteristic could act as the dominant SCA (e.g., family abuse, kin group in a collectivist society, societal discrimination).

A *moderately centralized* individual is one whose developmental trajectories are influenced by the action of a set of dominant SCA (see Figure 10-2-B, page 285). As also seen in this figure, the dominant SCA (malnutrition and proximal environmental risks) are characterized in terms of both the number and the strength of linkages they have with other developmental influences. Developmental variability is seen as the combined weighted impact of both dominant and nondominant linked SCA. In contrast, for a noncentralized individual there are no dominant SCA. For such an individual any number of developmental influences can have an equal influence on behavioral–developmental variability, especially given the weak linkages among the various developmental influences (Figure 10-2-C, page 285).

Although it is possible to abstractly conceptualize individual differences in SCA patterns, can individuals actually be classified in this way? One approach would be through the use of *P*-technique factor analysis. *P*-technique factor analysis is based on the repeated measurement of different variables, such as different developmental influences. By using *P* technique, we can analyze the structure of individual change patterns across multiple variables and assess which variables covary across time as well as the nature of the covariance pattern for a given individual (Hooker, 1991; Jones & Nesselroade, 1990; Jones, Nesselroade, & Birkel, 1991; Luborsky, 1995). For individuals who are highly centralized, we would expect to find a single factor structure with one element dominating the loading pattern when applying the *P* technique. If more then one factor were identified, we would expect to find the other factors strongly correlated with the first factor and weakly correlated with themselves. For a moderately centralized individual, we would expect to find two or three factors, with each factor being dominated by a different element, and only modest correlations among the different factors. For a noncentralized individual, we would expect a highly differentiated factor pattern, with modest correlation among factors and factor loadings not being dominated by particular elements.

Alternatively, we could use a more qualitative approach such as the repertory grid technique developed from George Kelly's Personal Construct Theory (Kelly, 1955) to assess individuals' perceptions of the nature and type of elements they feel are central to them (e.g., Bower & Tylee, 1997; Sewell et al., 1992; Winter, 1993). Highly centralized individuals would define themselves by a single personal construct, whereas the construct grid of moderately centralized individuals would be defined by two or three critical constructs. In contrast, for noncentralized individuals, we would find a much more differentiated repertory grid pattern, with no single element dominating (Epting et al., 1992). Going from the individual to the group level it may also be possible to use cluster analysis techniques, as described earlier in this volume (e.g., Magnusson & Bergman, 1990), to group together individuals with similar SCA patterns.

The Nature of SCA

From a measurement standpoint SCA seem to be most easily defined by individual characteristics. However, individual characteristics are not the only form in which SCA can exist. Examples of developmental influences or individual characteristics that can act as SCA are shown in Table 10-4. It could be argued that almost any individual characteristic or developmental influence can act as an SCA. However, in defining what is an SCA, it is essential to keep in mind that the nature of individual characteristics or de-

TABLE 10-4
Examples of Individual Characteristics and Developmental Influences That Can Act as Stabilized Attractors

I. Biological influences
   A. Chronic physical illness requiring a specialized diet or restructuring of lifestyle
   B. Major central nervous system damage that either cannot be compensated for or for which compensation leads to less than optimal central nervous reorganization
   C. Major genetic anomalies resulting in inborn metabolic errors
   D. Chronic malnutrition

II. Proximal and distal psychosocial influences
   A. Nature of early attachment
   B. Cultural belief about the appropriateness of certain activities for individuals with certain characteristics (e.g., schooling for girls)
   C. Posttraumatic stress disorder following major psychosocial trauma
   D. History of school success
   E. Continued exposure to physical punishment during childhood or level of cultural support for violence as a solution to life problems
   F. Deep-seated, culturally (evolutionary) based values (e.g., incest taboo)
   G. History of rejection by caregivers or peers
   H. History of sensitive, responsive authoritative rearing

III. Individual characteristics
   A. Individual goals and values
      1. Belief in effort as important
      2. Belief in social mobility
      3. Belief about type of role that is appropriate for oneself
   B. Competence beliefs (belief in ability to influence events in one's context)
   C. Individual and situational competencies
      1. Problem-solving skills that allow the individual the flexibility to shift solutions to meet changing problems posed by the environment
      2. Sense of family cohesion (a fixed point that serves to modulate and regulate family conflict)
   D. Internal working models (How the individual evaluates his or her world)

Note. Supportive evidence for these characteristics and influences reviewed in previous chapters in this volume.

velopmental influences are not what define stable central attractors. Rather, as discussed above, what is essential as a definitional criterion is the *nature and extent of linkages* among specific individual characteristics or developmental influences. An individual characteristic or developmental influence that is not linked to multiple other individual characteristics or influences is not an SCA for a given individual. The same individual characteristics or developmental influences, if strongly linked to multiple other system elements, will function as an SCA for a different individual. The influences and individual characteristics shown in Table 10-4 are those which previous research has shown are likely to be linked with other developmental influences or individual characteristics, and thus have the capacity to function as SCA. For example, early central nervous system injury can function as an SCA to the extent that such injury results in hypersensitivity to the environment, so that the individual prefers situations with reduced stimulation and such that there is a severe reduction in emotional responsivity of the individual. Similarly, chronic illnesses that result in an individual's dependency on drugs, greater disturbances in parent–child relations, and lower school attendance are more likely to function as an SCA for a given individual than chronic illness that does not result in these types of life course changes.

Also recognize that some individual characteristics or developmental influences such as evolutionary predispositions can function as an SCA only under conditions of low resource availability. Similarly, the degree to which individual energy requirements function as an SCA may well depend on the degree of energy needs demanded by the individual's context. Furthermore, although this discussion focuses on SCA in relation to individuals, in some collectivistic cultures such as Japan, group norms or group characteristics may function as an SCA, and serve as a focal point around which the individual defines him- or herself (C. Edwards, 1992; Triandis, 1989). In this event exclusion from the group is a major perturbation for the individual (Coleman, 1971).

How Stable Central Attractors Develop

Theoretically, SCA can evolve both as a function of extrinsic multiple developmental influences as well as from the impact of intrinsic midlevel processes. In terms of the role of multiple developmental influences, we start with an individual with certain predispositions (genetic or evolutionary based tendencies, temperament, prenatal influences). Major stressors early in life such as early abuse, severe malnutrition, or major perinatal insult can also act as predispositions. How do such predispositions become SCA? Fundamentally, SCA form from the action of midlevel processes involving structural linkages among multiple developmental influences (see chap. 8, this volume) operating either cumulatively or through the mechanism of probabilistic causal chains (see chap. 9, this volume). Over time as midlevel processes combine with multiple biological, psychosocial, and cultural influences some initial predispositions or influences become stabilized, carry increasingly greater weight, and become more densely linked to an individual's other biological and psychological characteristics. Ultimately such strongly weighted and densely linked elements come to function as SCA. Underlying the increased weighting of central elements may be certain critical intrinsic processes such as categorization. As described by von Bertalanffy (1968), categorization is a process determined by multiple factors influenced by individual biology (e.g., sensory capacities), individual experience (e.g., learning what and how to categorize), and culture (e.g., what categories are emphasized in a given culture). Categorization enables individuals to organize their perceptions and thus to bring order to their experiences. The organizing and ordering functions of emergent SCAs can be strengthened as an individual's categorization skills develop over time.

As described, the development of SCA may seem to be a purely linear process, whereby the cumulative interplay of multiple developmental influences and midlevel processes builds on existing predispositions to the point where these predispositions come to function as SCA. However, this linear process is not the only means through which SCA can develop. Building on existing predispositions in a linear fashion may be an easier way to form SCA, but it is not the only way.

As for alternative pathways to SCA, I would disagree with the evolutionary model proposed by Edelman (1989), who argues that all system elements are in place initially, but some are selected against and thus disappear. In the framework presented here, based on the extrinsic input of multiple developmental influences, new SCA have the potential to appear. For example, regardless of predispositions, the opportunity for formal education can serve to open up the individual to new coping mechanisms such as abstract problem-solving abilities that have the potential to develop into new SCA (see chap. 7, this volume). Similarly, in the absence of existing predispositions sudden major illness (chap. 4) or exposure to major societal changes such as enforced migration (see chap. 7, this volume) can also act to shift developmental trajectories toward new SCA. The development of structural linkages among existing SCA also can act to produce new SCA. For example, Case and Okamoto (1996) describe an SCA-like cognitive process they call *central conceptual structure*. Central conceptual structures are networks of meanings and relations that apply to children's ability to perform cognitively in certain domains but not in others. Such structures can represent cognitive knowledge or can help to organize the individual's internal states in terms of understanding desires, beliefs, and feelings. As children develop the elements comprising central conceptual structures can broaden, deepen, and merge to form more elaborate structures, such that new central conceptual structures (SCA) can emerge.

Furthermore, even when the process of forming new SCA involves building on existing predispositions, such a building process need not necessarily be linear in nature. Intrinsic midlevel processes can act in nonlinear fashion to produce new SCA. Functional linkages among multiple developmental influences is one such intrinsic process (see chap. 7, this volume). When multiple developmental influences involved in SCA formation interact in ways that *amplify* their impact (e.g., positive feedback loops), SCA may form in a nonlinear rather than linear fashion. For example, Lewis (1995) has described how positive feedback linkages between cognition and emotion act in a nonlinear fashion to promote the development of an integrated cognitive–emotional structure. The linked structural organization of such a "cognitive affective personality system" acts as an SCA, influencing how individuals appraise their world (Freitas & Downey, 1998). In contrast, nonlinear processes involving negative feedback between cognition and emotion can result in the sudden loss of an existing SCA.

Although the initial formation and differentiation of SCAs can be driven by multiple developmental influences and midlevel processes, once SCA begin to form, their subsequent development and stabilization also will be a function of intrinsic organizational processes inherent in the working of complex systems. As described by J. Miller (1978), over time, systems evolve toward greater complexity. Furthermore, as described earlier, system evolution involves the tension between *progressive segregation*—system elements functioning with increasing independence—and *centralization*—development of centralized system elements followed by increasing linkage among centralized elements of a segregating system (von Bertalanffy, 1968). Part of the intrinsic evolution of SCA may involve their becoming deeper (stronger) and more strongly weighted over time, as a function of increasing independence (segregation). In turn, more strongly weighted SCA can attract more system elements toward themselves (increased centralization).

SCA and Individual Differences

At a systems level, one major factor that differentiates individuals is the characteristics of their SCA. Critical SCA characteristics that differentiate individuals include how centralized the individual is and what elements the individual SCA are linked to. As discussed earlier, individual differences in the characteristics, extent, and linkage of SCAs, although complex, are nonetheless measurable. Individual differences in SCA emerge as a result of the interplay of multiple developmental influences and midlevel processes, particularly specificity (see chap. 9, this volume). Within a specificity framework, differential exposure of individuals to the various multiple developmental influences described in chapters 2–7 will inevitably lead to variability in the extent and characteristics of individual SCA patterns. Interindividual variability in SCA characteristics would be expected to occur as a function of the fit between individual characteristics and cultural preferences; as a function of the nature of the proximal and biological experiences that help form an individual's internal working model (e.g., securely attached, vulnerable); and as a function of variability in the genetically and hormonally based individual predispositions from which SCA are formed. Similarly, given that coactivation of SCA by different contextual circumstances represents a primary pathway through which SCA become stronger and more densely linked (Lewis, 1995), the extent of probabilistic covariance among multiple developmental influences can be a major force in promoting individual differences in SCA and SCA patterns. For example, individuals locked into tight causal chains or transactional pathways involving multiple developmental influences are far more likely to be highly centralized than individuals for whom events are encountered in a more random fashion.

Individual differences in centralization, SCA characteristics, and SCA linkage patterns offer an alternative way of looking at individual differences in a more integrated fashion than is normally seen if we look only at individual differences in specific traits. However, the relevance of individual SCA patterns goes beyond just description. In terms of dynamics, the transaction between individual SCA patterns and the individual's biological and psychosocial context is a major influence on subsequent individual developmental trajectories. As noted earlier individual differences in SCA-based internal working models can act to influence individual differences in reactivity to contextual input. For example, individual self-perceptions such as attachment or self-efficacy beliefs, or individual behavioral styles such as persistent antisocial behavior patterns, can act as internal working models. Such models act to selectively filter the cues in the environment the individual attends to, and act to filter how the individual is likely to react to these cues (Belsky & Cassidy, 1994; Caspi & Bem, 1990).

More broadly, individual differences in the level of centralization can lead to variability in individual developmental trajectories. Individuals who are highly centralized are more likely to view the world in a relatively rigid fashion and have only a limited number of reaction patterns available to them (Gleick, 1987). Such individuals may be able to function adequately as long as their interpretation and reaction patterns are congruent with their context. If the context changes, highly centralized individuals may have a far more difficult adaptation than moderately centralized individuals with multiple SCA, who have a variety of alternative interpretations and reaction patterns available to deal with changing contexts. Furthermore, although individuals who are highly centralized may be less vulnerable to influence by perturbations, they are far more vulnerable to perturbations that directly impinge on their central SCA. If such a perturbation cannot be compensated for, we would expect to see major, perhaps chaotic, individual change, because the system integrity of a highly centralized individual is dependent on only a limited number of central elements. In addition, such individuals may be less able to use environmental supports (positive perturbations), unless the nature of the support system matches their existing SCA. For such individuals, blunting may be one consequence.

Alternatively, persons who are moderately centralized and have multiple linked SCAs are more likely to be flexible in their interpretation of life events and have a greater variety of coping strategies. Furthermore, based on general-systems organizational principles (see Table 10-2), such individuals are also more likely to have their coping strategies arranged hierarchically, so that if one coping strategy fails, they can quickly shift to the next. Such individuals also are more able to compensate for psychosocial or biological perturbations, given that the greater number of linkages across greater numbers of SCA means that more alternative pathways are available.

Not surprisingly, individuals who are noncentralized are more likely to demonstrate unstable developmental trajectories when faced with even relatively minor perturbations, because they have few fixed points that could help stabilize their ongoing developmental trajectories. Furthermore, such individuals may be open to multiple interpretations of a given event and may have greater difficult deciding among the available interpretations, perhaps because their interpretations are less likely to be organized into a hierarchical structure. Even if they are able to decide among interpretations, the choice of appropriate coping strategies for such individuals will be difficult, given that no set of strategies (SCA) are predominant.

Self-Stabilization Processes

Individual differences in self-stabilization mechanisms are a second aspect characterizing the individual as system. Self-stabilization mechanisms reflect the system's ability to respond to internal or external perturbations by altering internal relations among its components so that the overall organization and structure of the system is maintained (Sameroff, 1989). The operation of systemwide self-stabilization mechanisms at the individual level can be seen in reduced individual variability across multiple domains in reaction to biological and psychosocial perturbations encountered by the developing individual. The fact that systems have self-stabilization mechanisms that allow them to adjust to perturbations does not mean that systems are infinitely flexible. Particularly when perturbations are amplified by positive feedback loops, or when perturbations impact on central elements of a system, a system's integrity can be threatened (Lewis, 1995; J. Miller, 1978). To the extent that perturbations compromise the overall integrity of a system, there will be long-term negative consequences, either for a general system or for the individual functioning as a general system.

The Development of Self-Stabilization Mechanisms

As shown in Figure 10-3 individual differences in self-stabilization mechanisms are produced by multiple developmental influences and midlevel processes. The foundation for systemwide self-stabilization mechanisms at the individual level may well lie in initial individual differences in the neonate's ability to display and to develop state control capacities (Sameroff, 1995). Such differences are the precursors for the development of self-regulation skills in initially isolated functional domains, such as voluntary attentional focusing and voluntary inhibition of action (Ahadi & Rothbart, 1994). Subsequent variability in such self-regulation skills arises from the joint contributions and interplay of central nervous system structures; individual genetic, neurotransmitter, and temperament characteristics; and specific environmental contexts encountered by the developing child (Als, 1992; Kendler & Eaves, 1986; Rothbart, Derryberry, & Posner, 1994). For example, the development of an internalized conscience has been found to be the result of specific interactions between child temperament and parental disciplinary style (Rothbart & Bates, 1998). As with SCA, individual self-stabilization processes become generalized through coactivation, resulting in increasing linkages among system elements involved in self-stabilization. Individual characteristics such as ego control or executive function are often used to describe an individual who is functioning as a self-stabilizing system (see chap. 5, this volume).

Individual differences occur both in the type and number of self-stabilization mechanisms available to the individual. Biological influences such as frequent illness or malnutrition, individual characteristics such as insecure attachment or inhibited temperament, proximal environmental characteristics such as restrictive parental rearing, and cultural characteristics such as a highly rigid societal structure may reduce the chances for individuals to have to deal with a variety of different contexts and challenges. A reduction in the variety of contexts and challenges available to the individual can result in a reduction in the variety of self-stabilization mechanisms that the individual builds up for dealing with different contexts and challenges. Alternatively, biological, individual, proximal, or distal environmental characteristics that increase the likelihood that the individual will have to cope with a variety of different contextual challenges act to increase the likelihood of the individual's developing a wider variety of self-stabilization mechanisms.

Consequences of Individual Differences in Self-Stabilization

At an individual level, high behavioral variability may be viewed as reflecting an individual functioning in the same way as a system with poorly developed self-stabilization mechanisms; alternatively, individuals demonstrating low behavioral variability may be viewed as the individual analogue to a rigidly and overly stabilized general system (Gottman, 1991; Thoman, 1990). Individual differences in self-stabilization mechanisms may have a variety of implications for later development, particularly when the individual or system is at a transition point (Bateson, 1985). At one extreme, would be highly stabilized individuals whose development fits what some biologically oriented theorists have characterized as highly canalized developmental trajectories (Waddington, 1966). Such individuals should be relatively unreactive to external perturbations, so that once such individuals enter a particular developmental pathway, it becomes increasingly difficult for them to diverge from it. What this means is that although individuals who function as a highly stabilized system should be relatively insensitive to potential risk factors, such individuals also may be less sensitive to potential protective factors (i.e., blunted; see chap. 9, this volume). For example, an older individual's ability to profit from experience may be compromised by physiological influences such as lower vascular blood carrying capacity that inhibits central nervous system flexibility (Greenough et al., 1990). Possessing very strong self-stabilization mechanisms is thus not necessarily positive, given that the adjustments made by systems to perturbations are one way through which systems evolve.

In contrast, other individuals may have poorly functioning self-stabilization mechanisms and should be highly reactive to even minor perturbations. Children who are described as "sensitized" (see chap. 9) would fit this description. Although more sensitive to potential risk factors, individuals who function as poorly stabilized systems, also may be more sensitive to potential protective factors (Gottman, 1991; Kendler & Eaves, 1986; see also chap. 8 on interactions between gender and risk and protective factors). What this means is that functioning as a poorly self-stabilizing system is not necessarily totally negative. For example, the increased behavioral variability associated with individuals who function like a poorly stabilized system may increase the probability that such individuals will show novel forms of behavior, which may be adaptive under some circumstances (Gottman, 1991).

Is there a way of defining an optimal level of individual self-stabilization without resorting to contrast between the extremes? Expanding on concepts developed by Bronfenbrenner (1989) and Eisenberg and Fabes (1992), I will hypothesize that the critical marker for an optimally stabilized system is not level of variability per se, but rather the degree to which the system can adjust relations among its components to adapt to a variety of internal and external perturbations while keeping its overall organizational structure stable. The problems inherent in a strict variability criterion are most dramatically illustrated in the case of autistic children who can display coexisting patterns of both low behavioral variability (e.g., highly stereotyped and ritualized behavior patterns that are very resistant to change) and high behavioral variability (e.g., sudden sharp changes in behavior when the child encounters novel situations). Rather than variability per se, following the ego resilience model of Block et al. (1988), I argue that optimal self-stabilization is reflected by the degree to which individuals can adjust their behavior or coping strategies to deal effectively with a variety of internal and external perturbations, while keeping their overall SCA pattern intact. Within this framework, optimally self-stabilized individuals do not slip into chaotic patterns in the face of perturbation, nor do they show the same patterns of behavior repeatedly regardless of the nature of the perturbation. Rather, such individuals are able to use their self-stabilizing mechanisms to adjust their level of behavioral variability to match the level of contextual perturbations encountered. For example, under stress optimally self-stabilizing individuals may initially show patterns of behavior that have been adaptive in past situations (restricted variability). If such patterns are inappropriate in their current context, these individuals will have available a variety of alternative self-stabilization mechanisms. Having alternative self-stabilization mechanisms available allows such individuals to shift patterns of behavior and try alternative strategies to deal with contextual stressors (increased variability). Thus, although behavioral consistency helps define the degree of self-stabilization of the individual, for optimally stabilized individuals consistency refers not to specific behaviors but rather to the individual's ability to consistently adapt his or her behaviors and coping strategies to deal with new contextual perturbations. This definition of optimal stabilization allows me to argue that highly stabilized individuals who show low behavioral variability (blunted) and poorly stabilized individuals who show very high behavioral variability (sensitized) are both at greater risk for long-term maladaptive behavior patterns.

Integrating SCA and Self-Stabilization

So far I have treated SCA and self-stabilization system-level processes in isolation. Within a systems framework such isolation is not likely to exist. Much more likely is a bidirectional feedback loop between system-level SCA and self-stabilization processes. Specifically optimal self-stabilization, as defined by the ability of the individual to vary adaptive strategies to meet changing contextual demands, is more likely to occur for those individuals with a semicentralized system structure characterized by multiple linked SCA. An individual with multiple linked SCA has more informational resources and more potential combinations of resources to draw on when traditionally adaptive strategies do not fit current contextual demands than does an individual characterized by fewer SCA or one with more sparsely linked SCA. Conversely, the feedback gained by individuals when they effectively use self-stabilization mechanisms may act to create new SCA, deepen existing SCA, or create additional linkages among SCA. Illustrating this point evidence shows that the ability of the young school-age child to inhibit aggressive inappropriate behavior will influence what can be viewed as developing SCA; namely, their sense of self and their view of school (Alexander & Entwisle, 1988). Similarly, children who are able to adjust their problem-solving strategies to meet changing conditions are more likely to show stable personality patterns over time (SCA) than are children with less optimal self-stabilization patterns (Asendorpf & Van Aken, 1991). These types of results indicate the importance for individual behavioral–developmental variability of linkages, not only among multiple developmental influences, but also among system-level processes as well.

Contextual Niches

Common to attempts to apply DST or GST to issues involving behavioral development is the assumption that the operation of systems is linked to the context within which the system is functioning (J. Miller, 1978; Nowak & Lewenstein, 1994; Sameroff, 1989; van Geert, 1991). As discussed earlier, contextual variability is one of the conditions necessary for variability in the development of system-level processes at the individual level. In integrating context with the individual operating as a system, I propose that in addition to SCA and self-stabilization, we must also take account of the contextual niches within which the individual operates. In concert with individual differences in system processes the extent and characteristics of contextual niches that are open to a given individual (niche potential) can act to stabilize, destabilize, or redirect ongoing individual developmental trajectories.

The Nature of Niches

The concept *niche*, as derived from ecology, refers to a bounded range in a larger environment within which an individual functions (Odum, 1983). Psychologically, niches are often defined in terms of concepts such as behavior settings (Barker, 1968), or social networks (Tietjen, 1989). I use a definition of niche that expands on Bronfenbrenner's (1989, p. 277) description of the microsystem, namely, a stable "pattern of activity roles and interpersonal relations . . . in a given face to face setting with particular physical and material features, and containing other persons with distinctive characteristics", involving cognitive abilities and skills, interpersonal characteristics and attitudes, that are potentially available to a given individual. In this sense, niches encompass both physical settings and the individual and interpersonal characteristics of individuals traditionally found in such settings. Although my focus will be on the proximal characteristics of individual niches, remember that individual niches are nested in a larger social–cultural context which can act to moderate the impact of individual niches (Pianta & O'Connor, 1996; see also chap. 7).

Niches and Individual Development

As defined above, niches can vary along a variety of dimensions such as size, diversity, level of feedback, and level of interconnectedness (Salzinger, 1990; Tietjen, 1989). However, in understanding the role niches play in regard to individual behavioral development, it is necessary to go beyond these characteristics and bring in two additional criteria. First, niches are not necessarily neutral. Depending on the social and cultural context, a given niche may be regarded as having a positive, negative, or neutral valence. The valence given to a specific niche typically reflects what is valued within the society in which the niche is located. *Positive valence niches* have characteristics and contain individuals with characteristics that are valued by a given society; the reverse holds for *negative valence niches*. Exposure to negative valence niches can act to inhibit individual behavioral development, as seen in the negative consequences that occur when schools place low-achieving adolescents in the same classroom (Dishion et al., 1991), or when antisocial children select into peer groups containing other antisocial children (Cairns et al., 1988). Conversely, within a given cultural context, exposure of individuals to positive valence niches such as peer groups oriented to achievement can serve to facilitate developmental competence (G. Steinberg et al., 1992). In understanding the role played by niche valence it is important to weigh positive and negative niches in terms of developmental salience. For example, having a positive family niche may be more important for individual development than finding a niche on the high school basketball team. Furthermore, such weightings obviously will vary as a function of the age of the individual, with family niche valence being more critical for young children and peer niche valence increasing in salience as the individual moves into adolescence.

Second, to understand the role played by niches in individual behavioral development, it is necessary to go beyond the view, espoused by Barker (1968) and Scarr and McCartney (1983), that individuals are basically free to select their own niches based on their interests, talents, and preferences. From an ecological perspective, only a limited number of niches are available to a given population (Livingstone, 1980; Odum, 1983). At an individual level, the same consideration also holds. Not all available niches are equally open to all individuals in a given population (Wachs, 1996b). Those niches that are open to a given individual (niche potential) are partly a result of the number and types of niches available in a given society, but are also a function of the unique contributions of multiple developmental influences and midlevel processes operating across time for the individual. Examples of influences that can act to open up or close available niches for a given individual are summarized in Table 10-5.

Some influences such as major cultural shifts can function either to open or to close niches for individuals. Thus, war may open niches for some individuals, either directly through military service or indirectly from the subsequent benefits of military service such as an increased chance of education for veterans. Alternatively, for other individuals such shifts may act to sharply reduce niches, as when war-related migration disrupts traditional extended family rearing patterns. In addition, it is important to emphasize that although single influences are shown in Table 10-5, it is usually the combination of multiple influences acting across time that are most important in influencing the niche potential of a given individual. For example, it is the combination of inconsistent punitive parent discipline and a child with poor self-regulation capacities, leading to an escalating cycle of behavioral problems, peer rejection, school failure, and chronic antisocial behavior patterns, that ultimately act to close off a variety of potential adult niches for the individual (Wachs, 1996b). Similarly, although extreme be-

TABLE 10-5
Factors That Influence Niche Availability for a Given Individual

	Factors Process	Outcome
	Individual Characteristics	
Age	Increasing child mobility and range of experiences allowed	Opens niches
Societally nonapproved behaviors	Teen pregnancy, school dropout, and aggressive behavior all act to close down windows of opportunity	Closes niches
Cognitive deficits	Low IQ or learning disability adversely affects school competence, which in turn reduces adult economic opportunities	Closes niches
Dependency	Dependent individual can have higher social sensitivity, which can increase his or her ability to recruit help from others	Opens niches
Learned helplessness	Individual gives up trying	Closes niches
	Biological factors	
Malnutrition or chronic illness	Reduced activity; functional isolation	Closes niches
	Proximal environment	
Contextual instability	When there are a large number of family moves, a child may not be in a situation long enough to identify appropriate niches	Closes niches
Large parental social network	Increases size of child's peer network	Opens niches
	Macroenvironment	
Low parental socioeconomic status, low education level, or family poverty	Child's access to societal resources reduced as family social class, education, or economic status decreases	Closes niches
Discrimination	Limits ability of talented individuals to make full use of their talents	Closes niches

Note. Supportive evidence reviewed in previous chapters in this volume.

haviors often act to reduce individual niche potential, in contexts where more niches are available, the same behavior patterns may be viewed as less extreme and may thus have less of an impact on niche availability (Clarke & Clarke, 1988).

One question that may have occurred to readers is whether relations between niches and individuals are unidirectional or bidirectional; niches influence individuals but do individuals influence niches? As discussed in chapter 5, there is always the possibility of individuals influencing niches, particularly for individuals with extreme traits. Furthermore if there is a fit between person and niche they will reinforce each other, thus stabilizing both person and niche characteristics. However, I focus less on bidirectional relations because I view niches in system terms, which means that niches have self-stabilizing mechanisms which make them able to correct for perturbations introduced by individuals within the niche. Furthermore, if there is a poor fit between an individual and a given niche, the individual who has a choice will move out of the niche, thus reducing perturbations. Niches are likely to change as a result of individual actions only when there are large numbers of individuals who do not have a good fit and do not have the option to move out of the niche. As seen in the case of popular revolutions, under these circumstances self-stabilizing mechanisms can break down, and niches can change. However, given the operation of self-stabilizing mechanisms, niche change usually will be slow and often insensitive to the impact of a given individual. Rather, given that individual proximal microsystem niches are embedded in a larger social cultural context (Super & Harkness, 1986; see also chap. 6), niche change is more likely to be a result of higher order distal rather then individual influences.

How Niches Operate

Niches can act to either stabilize or destabilize individual behavioral–developmental patterns over time (Wachs, 1996b). In the case of individuals who can self-select into a variety of niches, it is logical to assume that such individuals will select niches for themselves that are congruent with their talents, goals, and expectations—niches that provide a good fit. In this situation some individuals may select into relatively homogeneous niches, where the individual receives the same basic message from a variety of niches. Homogeneous niches will act to reinforce and maintain individual self-expectations and goals, and thus stabilize individual developmental trajectories over time. Alternatively, based on individual characteristics such as sensation-seeking or approach tendencies (Strelau, 1994), other individuals may select into more heterogeneous niches, which means having to adapt and adjust one's behavior to a variety of circumstances. Encountering more heterogeneous niches also allows individuals to observe a wider variation in the behavioral patterns of others, thus increasing the variety of different behavioral strategies that are available to the individual. Thus, self-selection into heterogeneous niches is more likely to produce an individual who is more flexible and to support the behavioral patterns of more flexible individuals. Individuals who are more flexible and have a wider variety of behavioral strategies also have a greater potential to adaptively change the course of their developmental trajectories over time. Put in systems terms, such individuals are more likely to be semicentralized with multiple SCA available.

However, as noted above, not all individuals have the freedom to select into niches that they find congenial. Particularly for individuals with behavioral patterns or characteristics that are not valued by their society, there are likely to be contextual channeling processes that restrict the number of niches available. For example, one consequence of maladjusted behavior may be that an individual is locked into niches that serve to maintain maladjustment (Elder & Caspi, 1988). Examples of such channeling, as shown in Table 10-5, include racial bias or individual characteristics such as cognitive deficit or antisocial behavior.

What are the consequences of niche restriction for individual behavioral development? The restricted number of niches available reduces the chance of a good level of person–niche fit, which can be a source of stress. Furthermore, exposure to a limited set of niches is likely to restrict the individual's ability to change even when change is possible, if only because such individuals have less exposure to alternative ways of behavior and thinking. Even for individuals who can initially change their behavior patterns, this change needs to be supported by the opening of new and appropriate niches or the end result may be a heightened sense of frustration and learned helplessness, particularly if individual behavioral change brings no change in contextual circumstances.

However, the relevance of niches for individual behavioral–developmental variability goes beyond just availability per se. As noted above niches can have positive or negative valence. One consequence of exposure to niches with a specific type of valence is to increase the probability of the individual's accessing other similar valence niches. Looked at within a causal-chain framework, repeated exposure to positive valence niches at a given point in time increases the likelihood of availability of other positive valence niches later in time. The linkage of access to positive valence niches can serve to both initiate and facilitate positive developmental trajectories. For example, individuals who go to excellent secondary schools are more likely to get into excellent universities, which in turn increases their chances of finding more valued occupational niches. In the case of causal-chain linked negative valence niches, a mirror image process occurs, particularly when repeated exposure to linked negative valence niches also serves to restrict the availability of positive valence niches to the individual.

The Interrelation of Individual as System and Niches

The final common pathway of both multiple developmental influences and midlevel processes is the individual operating under the influence of system-level and individual niche potential processes. However, like multiple developmental influences, system processes and niche potential do not operate independently of each other. In part this is because the same unique influences that produce an individual with specific system characteristics also produce an individual with a specific level of niche potential. In addition there also can be direct overlap between individual-as-system characteristics and the individual's preferred niches. One such example is the case of an individual with strong religious values (SCA), for whom a place of worship serves as a major niche in his or her life space (Brody et al., 1996). However, the linkage between individual system characteristics and niche potential goes beyond just a common etiology or actual overlap. Niche characteristics can influence the extent and nature of individual SCA. One such example is seen in regard to peer support (niche), which can act to increase or decrease individual educational expectations and goals (SCA). In addition, as discussed earlier, evidence suggests that experience with a variety of different niches can influence the variety of individual self-stabilization mechanisms available to the individual. Furthermore, the availability and characteristics of an individual's social support network (niches) can also influence the efficiency of individual self-stabilization, through reducing or increasing the perturbations that impinge on the individual (see chap. 7).

The reverse can also hold; individual differences in SCA patterns and self-stabilization mechanisms can act to directly influence the availability of given niches for a specific individual. This statement does not contradict the argument above in regard to the greater likelihood of niches influencing persons than persons influencing niches. Although persons have a limited capacity to influence niches, individual-as-system characteristics in the form of SCA patterns and self-stabilization mechanisms can influence how many and what types of niches are available to the individual. This can occur either by individual SCA or self-stabilization characteristics influencing an individual's ability to recruit and maintain environmental support from others (interpersonal niches), or by such characteristics acting as filters and predisposing the individual toward contexts containing other individuals with similar values and beliefs. For example, individuals with a biobehavioral-based SCA centered on high inhibition to novelty will be less likely to seek out new alternative niches (Caspi et al., 1988; Gunnar, 1994). Individuals with a prior history of adequate self-regulation or more efficient self-stabilization mechanisms, as seen in higher levels of planfulness or ego resilience, may be more adaptable to finding niches (Asendorpf & Van Aken, 1991) and may be better able to break free of negative valence niches than are overly regulated or understabilized individuals (Block et al., 1988; Moffitt, 1993).

The linkage between individual-as-system and individual niche potential has a number of implications in regard to understanding individual

TABLE 10-6
Individual Change Potential

System and niche characteristics	Very high	Moderately high	Moderately low	Very low
SCA Pattern	Decentralized	Moderately centralized	Moderately centralized	Strongly centralized
Self-stabilizing capacities	Low	Moderately low	Moderately high	High
Niche availability	High	Moderate	Moderate	Low
Available niche characteristics	Heterogeneous	More heterogeneous than homogeneous	More homogeneous than heterogeneous	Homogeneous

Note. SCA = stabilized central attractors

behavioral–developmental variability. Two specific implications are discussed below.

Potential for Change

As documented previously in this volume, given the probabilistic nature of individual behavioral–developmental variability, it becomes increasingly difficult to assume that we have the ability to make precise "point to point" predictions on the course of an individual's development (Anderson, 1972; Hinde, 1989; Nowak & Lewenstein, 1994). However, as shown in Table 10-6, it may be possible to predict which individuals are more likely to change over time and the range of changes that are most likely to occur for a given individual (Clarke & Clarke, 1988; Gruber, 1985; Magnusson, 1988). Integrating what has been discussed previously, Table 10-6 illustrates how the likelihood of an individual being able to change their developmental trajectories is a joint function of self-stabilization capacities, SCA characteristics, and niche availability and characteristics. For example, Rutter and Rutter (1992) propose that current contextual circumstances that are markedly different from an individual's previous context are more likely to predispose individuals to a "turning point" in their life trajectory. However, I propose that whether the individual actually makes use of changing circumstances will be a joint function of individual self-stabilization, how strongly centralized the individual actually is, and individual niche potential. Individuals with the strongest potential for change (including chaotic changes) would be those who have few self-stabilization mechanisms, decentralized SCA patterns, and a large number of widely varying niches available to them. Individuals with the lowest potential for change would be those with highly regulated self-stabilization mechanisms, strongly centralized SCA patterns, and only a small number of functionally equivalent niches available to them. Critical differences between the two middle columns of Table 10-6 involve the role of self-stabilization capacities and niche characteristics. Semi-centralized individuals with more heterogeneous niches available to them who have lower self-stabilization capacities are more likely to have greater change potential than are semi-centralized individuals with equal niche availability who have greater self-stabilization capacity and whose available niches are more homogeneous.

Conceptually I further argue that congruent linkages between niche potential and system-level processes can be viewed as an example of a positive feedback loop. Such linkages act to amplify the combined contributions of both niche potential and system processes to maintain individual developmental trajectories over and above what would be predicted from the summed contributions of each taken in isolation.

How the Individual Reacts to Perturbations

The same system-level and niche factors discussed above in regard to potential for long-term developmental change also hold in regard to how well the individual deals with ongoing biological or psychosocial stressors, that is, perturbations to the individual as system. One form of perturbation becoming more prominent, particularly in third-world countries, involves increasing urbanization, industrialization, and acculturation pressures. Under these pressures an increasingly large number of individuals are leaving familiar contexts and moving into radically different contexts that call for different forms of adaptation (Nsamenang, 1992). When there is a lack of fit between an individual's SCA patterns and new culturally rooted criteria that define the niches available to him or her, there is likely to be an increase in perturbations to systemwide processes at the individual level. For example, evidence indicates that a major source of family conflict occurs as a result of the lack of fit between Asian American adolescents' need for autonomy (an SCA pattern) and what their parents view as appropriate forms of adolescent behavior within the family (niche), namely respect and obedience (Greenberger & Chen, 1996). When individual SCA patterns are sufficiently different from culturally defined positive valence niches there will be increasing pressure on the individual to change his or her behavior in ways that provide a better fit to culturally based positive valence niches (Caspi & Bem, 1990).

Under these conditions some individuals adapt well to such radical changes, whereas others adapt poorly. Obviously how the individual deals with perturbations will in part be a function of the nature of the perturbations, with a greater impact on the person being more likely to occur with cumulative or stronger perturbations. For example, a young child is more likely to react strongly if perturbations impact on both the child and his or her family than if the perturbations impact just on the child (Marvin & Stewart, 1990). However, for any given level of perturbation, both individual-as-system and niche characteristics also can influence the extent and nature of reactivity.

Based on what has been discussed above I hypothesize that highly self-stabilizing individuals who are characterized as having a strongly centered SCA pattern and as having few available niches will be more likely to show rigid behavioral patterns in the face of perturbations. For example, when facing acculturation pressures, such individuals would be far more likely to cling to the ways of their original culture even in the face of rapid cultural change. However, although such individuals may appear to be behaviorally unreactive even when stressors appear overwhelming, they may also be highly brittle. That is, individuals with the pattern described above may be far more likely to show sudden sharp chaotic changes in their behavior if perturbations impact on one of their limited number of SCA or existing niches. This is particularly true when niche characteristics and SCA characteristics are linked to each other.

In contrast, individuals who are moderately centralized, have more optimal self-stabilization mechanisms as defined above, and who have a variety of different niches available to them are more likely to be characterized as resilient in the face of perturbations. Such individuals can easily handle small perturbations and have the capacity to respond in flexible and adaptive ways to large perturbations. These are individuals who will bend but not break, in part because they have the ability to use their linked SCA to anticipate problems and to vary their behavior to match and deal with perturbations, even before perturbations occur (Clausen, 1991; Salthe, 1985). Although the developmental trajectories of such individuals may be temporarily deflected in the case of large perturbations, these are individuals who also have the greatest potential of returning to their previous developmental trajectories once perturbations have ceased. Such individuals can change, but for them change is more likely to be gradual in nature. Such individuals when faced with major perturbations involving acculturation would be more likely to be able to successfully adapt to different cultural contexts, tailoring their behavioral patterns to the characteristics of the specific context they are currently functioning in without losing sight of themselves as individuals from a different cultural background.

Finally, individuals who have low self-stabilization capacities, who are noncentralized, and who have few niches available to them can be characterized as vulnerable. Such individuals are much more likely to become badly disorganized even when faced with relatively minor perturbations. When faced with acculturation pressures, such individuals are more likely to drift between their original culture and the new culture without ever being able to commit to either context or to develop strategies that would allow them to function successfully in both contexts.

The Ongoing Role of Multiple Developmental Influences

I have postulated a developmental framework wherein multiple developmental influences and midlevel processes produce an individual who begins to function in a way similar to that of a general system and who has a greater or lesser potential to enter available cultural–contextual niches. The operation of system-level processes at the individual level and the availability to the individual of cultural contextual niches ultimately become unique influences on subsequent individual behavioral–developmental variability. A remaining question involves the role of multiple developmental influences on subsequent developmental trajectories, once the individual has reached a point where system and niche influences are operative. Having set system and niche processes in motion, do multiple developmental influences continue to shape individual developmental trajectories, over and above the contribution of system and niche processes?

Keep in mind evidence indicating that the developmental influences salient in initiating a behavioral trajectory may not necessarily be the ones that are salient for maintaining such a trajectory (Goldstein, 1988; Rutter & Pickles, 1991). For example, although initiation into a criminal lifestyle may be primarily a function of social factors, maintenance of criminal behavior also involves a strong biological component (Raine et al., 1996). Similarly, although child–parent problems act to initiate children's behavioral disorders, child–peer problems often serve to maintain these disorders (G. Patterson & Bank, 1989). It is also important to keep in mind that the impact of multiple developmental influences may be moderated by the action of the very processes these influences were instrumental in forming, that is, stabilized central attractors, self-stabilization capacities, and niche potential. Although multiple developmental influences may not have the same level or type of impact on individual developmental trajectories once individual-as-system and niche characteristics come into play, I argue that they nonetheless continue to be important in influencing such trajectories. Discussion of the role played by multiple developmental influences is presented below.

Perturbations and Supports

Under perturbation conditions systems may be forced to temporarily or even permanently reorganize. The degree and extent of reorganization needed will be a function of which aspects of the system perturbations act on (SCA versus non-SCA), the adequacy of system self-stabilizing mechanisms, how close the system is to a transition point, the degree to which available niches support the current organization of the system, and the strength and duration of the perturbations themselves.

Ongoing developmental influences can act either to perturb or to support the integrity of the individual functioning as a system. Perturbations to the individual as system can occur when new demands or challenges are placed on the individual. This is particularly true when previously functional self-stabilization processes are no longer valid, as in situations where highly novel contextual demands are placed on the individual (Chess & Thomas, 1990). Alternatively, ongoing biological and psychosocial demands can perturb the integrity of the individual as system by reactivating previous individual vulnerabilities or, in system terms, reenergizing dormant SCA. Although not typically thought of in general system terms, there are multiple empirical examples where such reactivation may be occurring. Examples include the sudden increase in predictive power associated with previous biomedical status when children with a history of intraventricular hemorrhage in infancy enter into kindergarten (Sostek, 1992), the increasing decrement in performance when previously malnourished children are exposed to short-term nutritional deprivation later in life (Grantham-McGregor, Chang, & Walker, 1998; Pollitt, Cueto, & Jacoby, 1998), and the maintenance into adulthood of social problems for siblings of autistic children as a function of increasing social demands (Rutter et al., 1993).

Besides being a source of perturbation, later occurring multiple developmental influences can also provide buffers or supports that act to open up previously closed niches for the individual, strengthen an individual's self-stabilization capacities, stabilize existing SCAs or promote the development of new SCAs that increase the individual's ability to successfully cope with perturbations. For example, ongoing external demands that allow the individual to develop a sense of self-efficacy (SCA) also may increase self-stabilization capacities, thus increasing the individual's ability to cope with subsequent stressors (Rutter & Rutter, 1992). Alternatively, for a child with a history of social and academic problems, a family move to a new location may expose the child to a different set of peers and teachers. When feedback from peers and teachers in this new context is different from previous feedback, this can serve to reopen closed niches and to promote a different world-view by the individual (new SCA).

Transition Points

Later occurring developmental influences can also play a role by moving the individual as system closer to a developmental bifurcation point, and thus increase individual sensitivity to internal or external perturbations. One way in which later multiple influences could move the individual as system to a bifurcation point is through closing off previously well-established niches. Established niches may be closed to the individual as a function of changing biomedical conditions (e.g., major illness or incapacity), changing proximal environmental influences (e.g., divorce or family disruption), or changes in distal environmental influences (e.g., economic downturn, forced migration).

Closing off previously well-established niches can force the individual to a turning point, because, with the closing of niches, well-established behavioral patterns or values may no longer be viable. As discussed earlier, having a restricted number of niches in and of itself is a stress on the individual as system. Further, given the previously discussed linkage between niches and SCA, closing of previously established niches may also negatively influence the integrity of what were once well-established stabilized central attractors. For example involuntary closing of niches for an individual can result in a weakening or loss of SCA based on an individual's sense of self-efficacy and belief of having control over his or her life course (Rutter, 1993). In this situation one consequence could be a shift toward an overcentralized individual, whose remaining SCA are essentially focused on a need to regain a lost sense of control. Alternatively, consistently receiving new positive feedback that is discordant with previous feedback may move the individual to a transition point that leads to a more differentiated SCA pattern and greater niche potential.

Intrarange Variability

Niche availability, centralization, and self-stabilization processes can act to define the *behavioral range* within which an individual functions, for example, adaptive or maladaptive, above average or below average, inhibited or uninhibited. When system processes or niche potential shift radically we would expect a corresponding shift in the individual's behavioral range as well. When system and niche processes are stable, we would expect individuals to remain within a given behavioral range of reaction. However, even within a stable behavioral range there is intraindividual behavioral variability across time (see chap. 1, this volume). What causes such variability? Expanding on a suggestion by Sroufe and Jacobvitz (1989), I propose that an additional role for later occurring multiple developmental influences and midlevel processes is that of influencing the degree of behavioral variability shown by individuals within a given range. Thus, whether an individual's behavior is adaptive or maladaptive in a given context is ultimately a function of ongoing system and niche processes. However, the degree of adaptive or maladaptive function the individual has, or the degree of intraindividual changes in the level of maladaptive or adaptive behavior within a given range, can be viewed as a function of the continued impact of multiple developmental influences and midlevel processes. By allowing range to be set by the operation of self-stabilizing system mechanisms, SCA and available niches, we can account for the moderate stability of individual behavioral development over time, as seen in such diverse domains as *intelligence* (Neisser et al., 1996), *personality* (Caspi, 1998), *temperament* (Rothbart & Bates, 1998), and patterns of *interpersonal relations* (Hartup & van Lieshout, 1995). By allowing for the continued impact of multiple developmental influences and midlevel processes we can also account for individual developmental variability within a given behavioral range.

CONCLUSIONS

I have presented a framework of how various levels of influence combine to impact on individual behavioral–developmental variability. Within this framework there are four major elements organized on three levels: multiple developmental influences, midlevel processes, system-level processes, and niches. This framework has been summarized structurally in Figure 10-1 and dynamically in Figure 10-3. Congruent with a major theme of this volume, each of these elements is *necessary but not sufficient* for understanding both the range and course of individual behavioral–developmental variability. As shown in Figure 10-3, multiple developmental influences moderated by midlevel processes influence initial patterns of individual behavioral–developmental variability, the characteristics of individual system-level processes, and individual niche potential. Once functional, system-level processes (SCA and self-stabilization mechanisms) and individual niche potential act to control the level of stability of individual developmental trajectories. Both system-level processes and contextual niches can change as a function of the continued operation of multiple developmental influences. Major changes in either system-level processes or availability of niches to the individual can cause major changes in an individual's developmental trajectory. Without such changes individuals will remain in a more or less stable developmental trajectory. However, individual variability within a given trajectory range will be a function of the continued operation of multiple developmental influences and midlevel processes operating over time.

The descriptive framework I am proposing integrates what is known about the role of multiple developmental influences and midlevel processes on individual behavioral development with what is understood about the processes governing the functioning of complex systems such as the individual. As discussed previously, the various elements in this framework are measurable to a greater or lesser degree. Although the operation of certain developmental influences such as evolutionary history can be only indirectly estimated through ongoing behavioral patterns, there are more direct measures for other influences found in the biological (e.g., biomedical, nutritional influences); individual (e.g., temperament); and proximal and distal environmental domains. Particularly for the domains of genetics and the central nervous system, current technology promises highly sophisticated measures of the operation of these influences. When analyzed using procedures described in chapters 8 and 9, measures of developmental influence also reveal the operation of midlevel processes such as covariance, interaction, temporal moderation, and specificity. Although we are less clear about how to measure system-level and niche processes operating at the individual level, there are a variety of potential approaches that show promise. Such approaches include *P*-technique factor analysis or repertory grid techniques for assessing SCA, changes in individual behavioral variability over time, or individual differences in ego resilience to assess the strength of an individual's self-stabilization capacities, and techniques borrowed from human ecology to assess an individual's available niches.

Our ability to understand the nature and etiology of individual behavioral–developmental variability will depend on how well we are able to integrate the necessary contributions of multiple developmental influences, midlevel and system-level processes, and individual niche potential. The framework presented in Figure 10-3 offers one approach to such integration. However, further progress in integrating the contributions to individual behavioral–developmental variability of multiple developmental influences, midlevel processes, and systemwide processes and niches will depend not only on having a more precise conceptual framework and better measurement of the operation of systemwide processes, but also on our ability to answer certain critical questions listed below.

1. For a given individual can we define a time frame when system-level processes and a stabilized set of niches become operative and begin acting as an influence on individual behavioral–developmental variability?
2. What are the signs that allow us to determine if individuals are approaching a bifurcation point in their development, where they will be particularly sensitive to the impact of multiple developmental influences?
3. What combinations of contextual perturbations and level of an individual's self-stabilization capacities place the individual as system at a point where major system reorganization must take place?
4. For the most part niches have been defined in terms of observable aspects of the individual's context. SCA are most easily defined in terms of individual characteristics. Can we develop better alternative assessments of niches or SCA that encompass individual biological parameters, such as nutritional or biomedical status?
5. We have an increasing understanding of how specific developmental influences relate to individual variability in a given domain, but much more needs to be known about the combined operation of multiple developmental influences, both on initial levels of individual behavioral variability and on the organization of system-level processes and individual niche potential.

In spite of the many questions that need to be answered, this overall framework, even in its relatively primitive state, appears to be applicable to fundamental scientific questions about understanding individual behavioral–developmental variability. The proposed framework also allows us to conceptualize the contributions of multiple linked developmental influences for individual behavioral–developmental variability in a way that takes account of existing complexities, through the contributions of multiple developmental influences and midlevel processes to system processes and niche potential. Furthermore, although complex, the present framework does not lose us in a conceptual morass where everything is related to everything else. Rather, after a certain point in development our focus becomes narrowed to the contributions of system characteristics and niche potential to ongoing individual behavioral–developmental variability. Although operating at a different level, system processes and niche potential do not necessarily add additional complexity to what has already been discussed. Rather, by focusing on the three end products of the impact of multiple developmental influences and midlevel processes (SCA, self-stabilization, and niche potential) we are able to integrate these multiple contributions under a single conceptual framework, and thus encompass complex processes within a manageable number of variables. To illustrate how the framework presented here allows us to encompass rather then lose ourselves in complexity, the final chapter of this volume is devoted to the question of whether principles derived from the framework presented here have potential applications to issues involving deviations from "normal" individual behavioral development.

11

FROM PRINCIPLES TO PRACTICE

To those working directly with children at potential or actual risk for developmental problems, concepts such as temporal moderation, specificity, or centralized attractors may seem to have little direct relevance to real-world problems such as childhood developmental delay, delinquency, dysfunctional families, and posttraumatic stress disorder. What I hope to show in this final chapter are the potential applications found when individual developmental variability is viewed as a joint function of the operation of multiple developmental influences, midlevel processes, and system-level principles. Ideally, to show real-world application, I would integrate and synthesize what is known about multiple developmental influences and midlevel and system-principles into a set of coherent and programmatic packages for assessment and intervention. Intervention specialists could then take such "prescription" packages and use them to intervene to facilitate optimal development for children with developmental problems. Unfortunately, I am not sure that such a "tour de force" is either possible or appropriate. Within a general or dynamic systems framework, prediction and control must be viewed in a probabilistic manner (see chap. 10). Similarly, the operation of midlevel processes such as causal chains and specificity means that multiple developmental influences also operate in a probabilistic and domain-specific manner.

The probabilistic nature of influences on developmental trajectories means that it will be exceedingly difficult to integrate multiple developmental influences and midlevel and systems processes into a coherent "prescriptive" package. Nor is it likely that a single intervention will work equally well for all children or even for all children with a given developmental disorder. Rather, the application to development of multiple developmental influences and midlevel and system processes may be best understood with reference to Anderson's (1972) definition of legitimate reductionism. As defined by Anderson, *legitimate reductionism* means that the unique explanatory laws found at more molar influence levels cannot violate the explanatory laws found at more molecular levels. In practice terms, this means that effective assessment and intervention programs must, of necessity, be consistent with what we know about the role of multiple developmental influences and midlevel and systems processes. Intervention and assessment programs that are consistent with what is known about the impact of multiple influences and midlevel and system processes are far more likely to be highly effective and more generalizable than programs that are not consistent with what is known.

For example, all through this volume I have presented evidence showing how, except for certain rare disorders, most developmental influences are necessary but not sufficient. Although there are successful interventions for biomedical problems that are caused by a single influence taken in isolation (e.g., prenatal administration of folate to reduce the incidence of neural tube deficits), such examples are the rare exception particularly for behavioral development. Even when dealing with single-influence biomedical problems, we can see the operation of complex multiple influences. Thus, although we can prevent certain diseases by administration of vaccines, whether or not a child is allowed to be vaccinated will depend on a variety of social and cultural factors. Even when the operation of a single developmental influence taken in isolation results in what looks like a successful behavioral intervention, in too many cases what we find is that we achieve only partial success. For example, the use of Ritalin as a treatment for children with attention deficit/hyperactivity disorder (ADHD) can increase attention, but ultimately the school success of the individual child will also be a function of the quality of the teaching environment and parental and peer support for educational achievement.

Given the complexity and the probabilistic nature of individual behavioral development, can we derive principles from the operation of multiple influences and midlevel and system processes that can be applied to the design of assessment and intervention strategies? Such principles may be viewed as the scientific foundation of empirically derived assessment and intervention strategies. Translation of such principles into specific assessment or intervention strategies, tailored for a given child in a given context for a given outcome, must ultimately be the responsibility of those who will be working directly with specific children. However, those doing the translation must be careful to ensure that there is congruence between these principles and the design of assessment or intervention strategies. Again I would stress that assessment or intervention strategies based on these principles will have a far greater likelihood of success than strategies that do not derive from what is known about multiple midlevel and system influences on individual behavioral–developmental variability. Specific principles are presented in the following section.

PRINCIPLES

Principle 1. The Focus of Assessments and Interventions Should Be Multi- and not Unidimensional

A major goal of assessment is to determine whom to target for intervention. Given that development is multidetermined, the assessment of multiple risk and protective factors as a routine part of an assessment strategy would seem to be an all too obvious recommendation. As has been repeatedly noted in this volume, better prediction occurs when multiple developmental risk factors and multiple protective factors are considered in combination rather than in isolation (e.g., Moffitt, 1993; Werner, 1994).

The fact that individual behavioral–development variability has multiple causes also leads directly to the principle that the more a given domain of development is multidetermined, the less likely we are to find maximal gains associated with a unidimensional intervention (Wachs & McCabe, 1998). Evidence of potentially greater benefits associated with multidimensional rather than unidimensional interventions has been noted throughout this volume, as in the cases of malnourished children (e.g., Brown & Sherman, 1995; Grantham-McGregor et al., 1994; Myers, 1992; Pollitt, 1998), preterm infants (e.g., Beckwith & Rodning, 1992), children with cerebral palsy (e.g., Nelson & Ellenberg, 1986), children with severe rare genetic syndromes, and children at genetic risk for psychopathology (e.g., Goldstein, 1988). For example, for preterm infants the most optimal intervention strategy would combine appropriate medical interventions; the training of parents in appropriate feeding skills, care, and expectations; the reduction of extraneous noise in the neonatal intensive care unit; and the development of the preterm infant's self-regulatory skills (Als, 1992).

Principle 2: Take Account of Structural Linkages in the Assessment Process

A traditional assessment strategy for early identification of children who are likely to show later inappropriate or inadequate levels of development is to document that a child has been exposed to a known developmental risk factor. However, as documented in previous chapters, children exposed to a single risk factor are more likely to be simultaneously exposed to multiple covarying developmental risk factors. If we accept the not-unlikely assumption that a child exposed to one developmental risk factor is also likely to have been exposed to other developmental risk factors, one critical implication is the need to assess the pattern of covarying risk factors for a given child before providing intervention.

Principles 1 and 2 suggest an answer to an important real-world problem: whether assessment efforts should be targeted toward identifying populations who are particularly vulnerable because of exposure to multiple developmental risks or toward identifying individuals within a given population. On the one hand, targeting assessment toward identification of high-risk populations has the advantage of economy of scale. Because our focus is at the population level, more easily obtained, broadly based sociodemographic assessments can be used (e.g., percentage of population showing stunting in the first 2 years of life, percentage of population exposed to parasites in childhood, and average years of education). However, as repeatedly documented in this volume, even within a given set of population risk conditions, not all individuals are at equal developmental risk (e.g., Boyce & Jemerin, 1990; Werner, 1990). For example, the idea of a specific dose–response relation between level of exposure to an environmental toxin and level of subsequent impairment is being replaced by the idea of a family of dose–response relations, with differing dose–response curves representing the impact of multiple individual moderators (genetics, nutritional status) on individual reactivity to environmental pollutants (Bellinger, 1995; Pearson & Dietrich, 1985). By focusing our assessment efforts primarily on identifying high-risk populations, we also may miss identifying individuals from outside these populations who are also at high risk, either because they are exposed to similar risks or because they are particularly sensitive to even low levels of risk exposure (Boyce & Jemerin, 1990; Brown & Sherman, 1995). However, if our focus is on identifying individuals within a population who are at particular risk for development deficits, then we are often dealing with a high-cost assessment. There are single, simple, sensitive tests that can be used to identify individuals within a given population who are at particular risk (e.g., the heel-prick test for neonatal PKU). Unfortunately, such tests are the exception and are primarily confined to identification of rare biomedical disorders. Particularly for behavioral outcomes, accurate identification of individuals usually requires the use of multiple assessments given over time, which is a high-cost strategy.

Integrating Principles 1 and 2 suggests using a dual-level assessment strategy.[1] First, we should attempt to identify populations where, for the ma-

---

[1.] I am indebted to Sally McGregor and Ernesto Pollitt for clarifying my thinking on the question of criteria defining when one should intervene at a population level versus an individual level.

jority of individuals, there is a high incidence of covarying multiple developmental risks (e.g., covariance between malnutrition, morbidity, inadequate psychosocial rearing, and poor schooling) as well as a low incidence of protective factors (e.g., no stable social network of kin who can help in child rearing if parents are unavailable). For such populations, it is a safe assumption that the majority of individuals are at some degree of developmental risk. Once identified, intervention would be at the population level and not the individual level. Even if there are individuals within these populations with greater levels of resilience, the resilience of these individuals is likely to be relatively limited given that individual resilience is, in part, a function of the previous operation of linked multiple biosocial risk and protective factors. Attempting to identify resilient individuals in populations of this type would draw away scarce personnel and financial resources that could be better used for large-scale interventions. Furthermore, even resilient individuals in a high-risk population are likely to benefit from interventions that are provided to the population as a whole.

For populations in which initial assessment shows a better balance of risk and protective factors, or in which there are high levels of some developmental risk factors but not of others (low risk covariance), a second level of assessment is needed. In these populations, our focus should be on identifying individuals who are at actual or potential risk. *Actual risk* children are those with rare, highly debilitating disorders (e.g., autism) or with serious biomedical (e.g., very low birth weight and BPD) or psychological disorders (e.g., mental retardation). *Potential risk* children fall into two groups. First, there are children who are at the high end of the distribution in terms of the combined number of encountered biological (e.g., morbidity), psychosocial (e.g., harsh rejecting parenting), and cultural risk factors (e.g., minority status) while also being at the low end of the distribution in regard to exposure to combined biological (e.g., adequate early nutritional status), psychosocial (e.g., family support networks), and cultural protective factors (e.g., having traits that are favored by the individual's culture). Second, there are children who are not at the extreme ends of the risk and protective scales but may be vulnerable to relatively low-level stressors, either as a function of biological parameters (e.g., genetic risk), individual characteristics (e.g., difficult temperament), or rearing history (e.g., poorly attached). At an individual level, our goal would be to identify those children with a major imbalance in the ratio of risk to protective factors, as well as those children who may be particularly vulnerable to even relatively low-level risk factors.

Principle 3: The Need to Bring Context Into Assessment and Intervention Strategies

In previous chapters (6, 7, 10), I have documented the importance for development of the overall context within which the individual functions.

Particularly in terms of assessment, it may be important to look at children's functioning across a variety of microcontextual situations to identify the available niches for a child with given characteristics. Identification of a child's available niches would allow us to ask the question of whether such niches are likely to facilitate or hinder the child's subsequent development. In a case where the child's available niches are likely to hinder growth, it is then important to assess what characteristics of the child should be shifted to maximize the chances that the child will be able to enter more culturally appropriate, positive valence niches.

We typically think of contextual influences on intervention primarily in terms of the differential success of psychoeducational programs (Frankel & Roer-Bronstein, 1982; Kagitcibasi, 1990). For example, low parental educational level or low family social support networks can adversely influence the degree to which mothers and fathers of preschool age developmentally disabled children actively participate in the intervention programs of their children (Gavida-Payne & Stoneman, 1997). However, the literature also contains examples of how contextual factors also play a role in interventions directed at biomedical problems. Social–cultural contextual factors can influence the degree to which parents make use of genetic screening information (Solan, 1991), the level of benefit to be gained from oral rehydration therapy for gastrointestinal illness (Scheper-Hughes, 1991), and the impact of nutritional interventions (Launer & Habicht, 1989). For example, the benefits of providing nutritional supplements to families can be attenuated in cultures where parents believe that severe child malnutrition is a result of supernatural actions (Mull, 1991) or that undernourished infants do not require any special help other than making food available (Engle et al., 1996).

The combination of contextual influences and specificity should also lead intervention specialists to question the assumption that interventions that work well in one context will generalize equally well to other contexts. We know that the level of developmental gain associated with participation in intervention can be influenced by a variety of contextually related factors, such as degree of segregation in childhood (Vogt et al., 1987), preferred mode for teaching young children (Liddell & McConville, 1994), and family demographics such as socioeconomic status, and whether a culture is family or child centered (Gorman & Pollitt, 1997). Similarly, highly chaotic microenvironments can compromise the effectiveness of successful nutritional (Grantham-McGregor, Chang, & Walker, 1998) and early educational interventions (Bronfenbrenner, 1974). Context also can reflect biological as well as social and cultural background. Thus, in populations at risk for anemia where there is a high intake of whole grain products and tea, there may be limitations on the degree of functional benefits to be found for interventions that provide only iron supplementation (Yip & Dallman, 1996). The complex impact of multiple biological and psychosocial contextual influences leads to what I regard as a fundamental and yet too overlooked principle in regard to intervention: *Never design interventions without first asking what existing conditions can interfere with the potential gains individuals can realize from proposed interventions.* Before trying a given intervention in a new context, it is essential to first look for existing conditions that could act to limit generalizability and then modify the interventions on the basis of these conditions.

Principle 4. Build on Specificity When Designing Interventions

Given the complexities inherent in human behavioral development, designing intervention programs on the basis of a false assumption that human development is both simple and easily changed is a strategy that, although economical in the short run, is less likely to be effective in regard to either long-term effectiveness or the generalization of initial gains (Myers, 1992). Given the need for multidimensional interventions to match the multilevel etiology of developmental problems, we ask. What elements from what domains should enter into our intervention efforts, because we cannot realistically intervene across all potentially relevant domains?

Obviously, there are some domains that are either not susceptible to existing interventions (e.g., evolutionary influences) or are relevant primarily at the level of primary prevention (e.g., genetic influences, congenital biomedical anomalies). Other influences, although important, are extremely resistant to change (e.g., culture, physical ecology). For these influences, the most we can do is determine the degree to which the presence of evolutionary, genetic, congenital, or cultural factors can act to compromise the impact of the interventions we do choose. Furthermore, from a general-systems perspective on intervention, not all system levels may need to enter into intervention strategies (Sameroff, 1995). For example, in dealing with the malnutrition–morbidity cycle, satisfactory intervention can occur if we focus on better sanitation and nutrition, even if we ignore molecular changes in the body that act to produce illness (see later discussion of these points).

Besides eliminating some domains, how can we make use of specificity when designing interventions? The operation of specificity processes emphasizes the need to avoid the assumption that a specific intervention, taken in isolation, will apply equally well to all outcomes. For example, school curricula that foster academic achievement may do little to foster either behavioral adjustment or emotional maturity (Maughn, 1994). As discussed in chapter 9, at present there is little in the way of available theory that we can use to determine which developmental influences will be most salient for variability in a given outcome or outcome domain. However, it is possible to use existing empirical literature on the role of multiple influences as a guide to which influence domains should be included in an intervention program designed to affect a specific aspect of development. To use specificity in this way, we need to integrate both incidence figures (reflecting to what extent this influence is occurring either at the individual or the population level), as well as existing evidence about the role played by this specific developmental influence for a given outcome. The most likely candidates around which we would design our intervention program are those that occur either at a high rate (risk) or low rate (buffer) for a given population or for a given individual and that bear a strong demonstrated relation, either as a risk factor or a protective factor, to the type of outcome we are looking to change. Developmental risks that occur at a high rate and developmental buffers that occur at a low rate, either at a population or individual level, and that have been documented as being strongly related to a specific developmental outcome would be our primary target variables for intervention.

Another implication of the operation of midlevel specificity processes is the need to detail, prior to intervention, the goals of intervention and to use those specific interventions that are most salient for a given goal. For example, Sameroff (1995) has described the distinction between psychosocial interventions that are focused on remediation, redefinition, and reeducation. The goal of *remediation* is to intervene to change the child to the point where the child can make more efficient use of what the context provides (e.g., provide Ritalin to a child with ADHD). *Redefinition* refers to interventions designed to change the parents' perceptions about the nature of their child's behavior and in so doing change the nature of the child's family context in a more positive direction (e.g., helping parents to understand that their child's oppositional behavior is not willful but instead represents the behavioral manifestation of a biologically based difficult temperament; Bates, Wachs, & Van den Bos, 1995). *Reeducation* has the goal of intervening to give parents specific skills that enable them to deal more effectively with their child (e.g., providing parents of low-birth-weight preterms with the most appropriate strategies for feeding and physically caring for their infant; Minde et al., 1980). Within a specificity framework, the same set of strategies that promote reeducation will not be the same ones that promote remediation or redefinition. Choice of strategy must follow from the specific goals of the intervention process rather than from assuming that the same strategy will work equally well for all goals (Sameroff, 1995).

A final implication derived from the operation of specificity processes is the importance of evaluating more than a single targeted intervention outcome when assessing the success of our interventions. Given the operation of specificity, the possibility always exists that gains in a specific domain associated with a specific intervention may be offset by losses in a different domain. For example, providing additional play objects to Black South African preschool children, while increasing their cognitive competence and their appropriate use of objects, also was found to decrease their use of language and increase their level of solitary as opposed to social play (Liddell, Rapodile, & Masilela, 1991).

Principle 5: Build on System and Niche Characteristics When Designing Interventions

In regard to system principles, I would argue for the importance of identifying *the characteristics of individual SCA patterns, niche potential, and self-stabilization mechanisms as a guide as to where to intervene.* As discussed in chapter 10, individuals with strongly centralized or decentralized SCA, individuals having very weak or very strong self-stabilization mechanisms, and individuals with few available positive valence niches may be those who are at particular risk, either for the occurrence of developmental deviations or for the maintenance of existing developmental problems. Individuals with decentralized SCA, weak self-stabilization mechanisms, or having few available positive valence niches will have few fixed points to help stabilize themselves under stressful or conflictual conditions. Such highly variable individuals are at risk for going off in unpredictable, chaotic directions under stress or conflict (Gottman, 1991). Highly variable individuals also may have a lessened ability to use the environment as a source of information, because they may be less able to detect contingencies between their specific behaviors and specific outcomes given the wide variability of behavior they display. In contrast, individuals with high centralized SCA, very strong levels of self-stabilization mechanisms, or only homogeneous niches available may be locked into a rigid life cycle. Such individuals may be described as blunted, in the sense of being less able to make use of developmental opportunities when they emerge (Moffitt, 1993). In addition, if perturbations impinge on their centralized SCA, such individuals also may be at risk for highly chaotic behavioral change.

For individuals who are highly decentralized, have weak self-stabilization mechanisms, and have few positive valence niches available, the goal of intervention would be to increase the number of SCA and the linkages among SCA, strengthen self-stabilization mechanisms, and increase the availability of positive valence niches. For individuals who are highly centralized, have very strong self-stabilization mechanisms, and function primarily in highly homogeneous niches, general intervention goals would be to break the individual's rigid set and expose him or her to alternative niches and behavioral patterns.

Although there is little empirical evidence or even theory on how such changes may be made at the level of the individual, certain intervention possibilities do exist. For individuals who are decentralized, understabilized, and with few available niches, one appropriate intervention strategy may be to intervene through developing external fixed points for such individuals. Following Vygotsky's developmental principles, the goal would be for the individual to use such external fixed points to develop his or her own internal stabilizing structure. Thus for individuals living in a highly chaotic family situation, family therapy designed to stabilize the family and provide a fixed family pattern could be one form of external stabilization (Gottman, 1991). Alternatively, providing social support networks could not only act as an external scaffold but could also offer alternative niches that would allow the individual to broaden his or her existing SCA through exposure to other individuals with alternative behavior patterns. Obviously, one risk of providing external support is fostering a sense of learned helplessness or dependency in which the individuals begins to believe (SCA) that their own efforts play little part in their development.

For individuals who are fixed or rigid, one radical way of inducing change is to identify the individual's central SCA and manipulate the context in ways that perturb the SCA. For example, a chronically physically ill child whose parents stress the child's vulnerability, over time, the child may begin to develop a belief in his or her own vulnerability (SCA). Training parents to treat their child as if he or she were not vulnerable could act to shake up a child's belief system and thus bring the child to a bifurcation point where developmental change is more likely. In generalizing from studies of cross-cultural adaptation (LaFromboise et al., 1993), it appears that providing overly rigid individuals with both an alternative set of skills and exposure to alternative contextual niches may not only increase their opportunities but also may give such individuals the means to behave in ways that allow them to make optimal use of new alternative niches. Perturbing overly centralized individuals in this way does, of course, increase the risk of the individual developing chaotic behavioral patterns.

Common to both midlevel processes of active covariance-transaction (see chap. 8) and to the operation of the individual functioning as a system is the concept of the role of the child as a force in his or her own development. Particularly for children with identified developmental deficits, I would argue that we need to focus our intervention efforts not just on the deficits per se but also on those characteristics that can maximize the child's ability to place him- or herself in appropriate positive valence niches that will serve to maintain developmental gains that result from our interventions. Of particular relevance would be interventions designed to facilitate less easily measured but highly important individual characteristics such as a capacity for self-regulation, the development of secure attachments, and the ability to seek out appropriate environmental supports. Although at present we have no known standard intervention strategies to promote development of these traits, working to develop such strategies will be a necessary goal if we hope to develop individual self-stabilization mechanisms that children can build on to promote their own subsequent development.

Principle 6: Build Intervention Strategies on Existing Structural Linkages Among Multiple Developmental Influences (Covariance)

Principle 2 focused on the implications of structural linkages for assessment strategies. Assessing patterns of covarying risk factors also has implications for intervention. As discussed in previous chapters, we are much more likely to maximize our chances of long-term and generalizable positive outcomes when interventions are tailored to a covarying cluster of risk factors rather than to a single risk factor taken in isolation. For example, in less developed countries, zinc deficiency is frequent (Prasad, 1996) and is linked to poor health status (Hambidge, 1997). Poor health status in turn covaries with poor school attendance and poor attention or involvement (Shonkoff, 1994). An intervention strategy building on zinc as a primary target variable with health and school involvement as covariates is illustrated in Figure 11-1.

As shown in Figure 11-1, our initial interventions would be targeted to reduce zinc deficiency. One likely consequence is better health status, which in turn increases the likelihood of greater attention and involvement with the environment. When health monitoring revealed lower morbidity, we would then expand on our unidimensional nutritional intervention (zinc) and bring in a concentrated program of psychoeducational stimulation to maximize the potential gains associated with children being more attentive, alert, and involved in their environment. Stopping just at the level of the nutritional intervention would limit potential gains, because zinc-remediated children would have fewer learning opportunities without the provision of additional psychosocial stimulation. Alternatively, just providing psychoeducational stimulation without the nutritional intervention would limit gains associated with such stimulation, because less healthy children would be less able to process, and thereby benefit from, increased stimulation. Combining both nutritional and psychoeducational interventions, as shown in Figure 11-1, maximizes our chance of promoting significant, long-term, and generalizable gains, either at a population or at an individual level.

It could be argued that when risk factors covary (e.g., child nutrition, child morbidity, adequacy of rearing conditions), improving the child's sta-

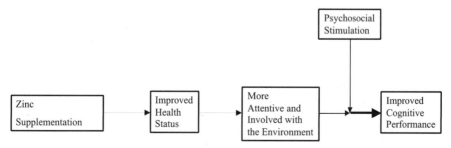

Figure 11-1. An intervention strategy integrating nutrition, health, and psycho-educational stimulation.

tus on one risk factor is likely to improve the child's status on covarying risk factors. However, as noted in chapter 8, it is essential to stress the probabilistic nature of covarying linkages. Assuming that changing one influence will lead to changes in other influences is a viable assumption only when linkages between two or more influences are "causal" in nature (see chap. 8) so that changing one influence leads to changes in the underlying mechanisms that act to change a second influence. However, too often linkages among multiple influences are truly probabilistic, as in the linkage between adequacy of child nutritional status and adequacy of caregiver–child relationship patterns, so that changing one influence may have little impact on the status of the covarying influence. Unless we have strong evidence for causal structural linkages, we cannot assume that a specific intervention targeted to a specific risk or protective factor will generalize to other risk or protective factors. A more appropriate strategy is to assume only covariance among risk and protective influences and to focus on providing multidimensional interventions targeted at the covarying risk and protective factors found in a given population or for a given child. Again, for those critics who would argue that such multidimensional interventions are too costly, I would argue that unidimensional interventions that do not generalize well or that wash out over time are even less cost-effective.

Principle 7: Build on Individual Differences in Reactivity (Organism–Environment Interaction)

When considering either assessment or intervention, there are several obvious implications that come from the operation of processes underlying individual differences in reactivity. In terms of assessment, it seems clear that some individuals will show remarkably little functional impairment even in the face of major recurrent stressors, whereas other individuals will show major impairments even when faced with relatively minor life stresses (Boyce & Jemerin, 1990; Werner & Smith, 1992). As noted earlier in this chapter, identifying children as "at risk" just on the basis of exposure to life stress factors is a strategy that is likely to result in unsatisfactory high levels of both false positives and false negatives. As described in previous chapters (5, 8), there are specific individual characteristics that increase the chances of a person showing developmental impairments even in the face of relatively low stress levels. Among those who are more likely to be overreactive to minor life stresses are children with family histories of mental or physical illness, a history of severe malnutrition, difficult temperament, insecure attachments, high reactivity and low self-regulation, and children living in contexts with few support systems or with characteristics not valued by their specific culture. In contrast, children with an adequate nutritional history early in life or who are securely attached, have adults who are available to them in times of stress, grow up in smaller families with longer birth spacing, or are more intelligent, more sociable, and able to develop flexible response patterns in response to stress are more likely to be resistant to even relatively high levels of biological or psychosocial stressors. From this pattern we can derive several implications in regard to the role of interaction processes in both assessment and intervention.

First, it seems essential that our assessments involve not only the child's level of developmental competence and the degree of exposure to biological and psychosocial risk factors but also a systematic evaluation of whether a given child has individual characteristics or exposure to contexts that would promote either individual vulnerability (e.g., sensitizing, blunting) or resilience (e.g., steeling, buffering). Second, there is the question of how we use such information. As discussed earlier, for a population of children who are exposed to cumulative and multiple risks, it is probably most economical to consider all such children as candidates for intervention, unless a given child in this population has a history of successful coping or possesses multiple protective factors of the type just described. In contrast, if a child possesses more than one of the vulnerability-promoting characteristics just described, such a child should be considered a prime candidate for intervention efforts even if he or she is exposed to only low levels of risk.

In terms of intervention principles, the most desirable strategy would be to tailor interventions to an individual child's particular characteristics rather than assuming that one form of intervention will be equally valid for all children. For example, Als (1992) found that within a population of high-risk premature infants, those who received interventions tailored to the child's initial reaction to intensive care procedures had significantly fewer days on a respirator, more rapid weight gain, earlier ability to bottle- or breastfeed, and better cognitive performance through the first 3 years of life than a sample of matched high-risk infants who all received standard biomedical intervention packages. However, the problem of providing empirically based individual intervention packages to a population of children is a daunting prospect given the number of potential individual characteristics that could act to moderate our intervention efforts. The problem is made slightly easier by what little knowledge is available on matching an intervention to a child. For example, providing increased sensory stimulation may be inappropriate for preterms who do not have the sensory or cognitive capacity to process such stimulation (Field, 1987). Similarly, fearful children appear to respond better to gentle, nonpower-based disciplinary strategies than to harsher, power-focused discipline (Kochanska, 1995). For other examples see Rothbart and Bates (1998). From a systems perspective, as discussed earlier in this chapter, different intervention strategies may be called for based on the nature of the individual's SCA patterns and self-stabilization mechanisms. Overall, however, our knowledge base on tailoring a treatment to an individual is still relatively limited.

While waiting for the appropriate knowledge to emerge, I would argue that our efforts should be focused on training intervention specialists who are sensitive to individual-difference characteristics and who can make maximal use of existing knowledge of individual-difference characteristics as they apply to the design of individually tailored intervention strategies. An essential aspect of such training would be the selection of individuals who display sensitivity to children's individual characteristics. Going beyond selection, training of these individuals would include not only exposure to standard intervention strategies but also to assessment of those individual child characteristics that the empirical literature indicates are most likely to affect the child's reactivity to standard intervention packages.

Implications of the operation of organism–environment interaction go beyond simple assessment and intervention, to also encompass evaluation of the impact of our interventions. The traditional strategy used when evaluating intervention programs is to compare the gains made by those in an intervention program with those made by a control group of individuals who did not receive the intervention. When interaction processes are operating, an additional evaluation step is called for that goes beyond focusing on just main-effect group differences. Specifically, even when there are significant group differences between individuals receiving interventions and controls who did not, it is equally critical to pay attention to the level of *intragroup variability* within the intervention group. In too many cases we see results indicating that a few children in an intervention group show major gains, the majority of children show very modest changes, and some children in the intervention group show either no change or even a regression over time (Ramey & Ramey, 1998; T. Williams, 1977). With this type of pattern, can we really say that we have carried out a successful intervention? I would argue that successful interventions are those that not only maximize differentiation between intervention and nonintervention groups but also minimize intragroup variability within the intervention group. One critical implication of Principle 7 is that identification of the level of intragroup variability should be as important a focus as assessing between-group differences when attempting to determine the success of a given intervention.

Principle 8. Intervention Efforts Operate Over a Background of Time

The operation of cumulative influences and causal-chain processes (chap. 9) suggests that one principle of intervention should be to break the operation of negative causal chains early in a sequence. If negative causal chains can be broken, then exposure to one developmental risk factor should not increase the probability of later exposure to other risk factors, thus reducing cumulative vulnerability. For example, as noted in chapter 4, inadequate caregiving patterns can increase the risk of an infant's ingestion of lead, which in turn can increase the likelihood of developmental deficits, which in turn can increase the chances of further inadequate caregiving due to parental rejection of a delayed child. By identifying those children who are encountering early inadequate caregiving in a population at risk for elevated lead exposure, and by intervening to teach more optimal caregiving patterns in these families, we may be able to minimize the cumulative negative impact of early inadequate caregiving in this population. An important benefit of interventions designed to break negative causal chains early in their sequence is relative ease of intervention. For example, as in the case of antisocial children, it is far easier to deal with an initial link in this chain (inadequate parental disciplinary strategies with a temperamentally difficult child) than to have to deal later in life with multiple cumulated links, such as mutual parent–child hostility, peer rejection, and school failure (G. Patterson & Bank, 1989), or with the need to unlearn long-term cumulative behavior patterns that may compromise ongoing intervention efforts (e.g., stealing from the person who has given the individual a job; Moffitt, 1993).

Using interventions designed to break negative causal chains before such chains have had a chance to cumulate also illustrates the importance of designing interventions that occur during periods of rapid developmental change. For example, the slowing of physical growth makes it increasingly difficult for a child to recover from early malnutrition-induced stunting, because less and less growth potential is available to the child over time (Golden, 1994). Systems principles such as increased sensitivity to extrinsic influences when the organism is at a bifurcation point also emphasize the importance of identifying contextual or individual characteristics that can serve as markers for when an individual is approaching such a point (see chap. 10). For example, Sameroff (1995) has hypothesized that the transition to school may be a period when young children who are at developmental risk may be particularly sensitive to intervention efforts.

The combination of linked multiple influences and the cumulative nature of such influences also has major implications for intervention. In populations where children are exposed to linked multiple risks, even targeting interventions early in life or at bifurcation points may be ineffectual if the interventions are either of short duration (Powell & Grantham-McGregor, 1989) or limited in scope (Hauser-Cram et al., 1991). Particularly for children who are encountering linked multiple biological and psychosocial risks, there appears to be a convergence of results indicating that a 3-year intervention period may be necessary if we wish to see long-term intervention effects (Grantham McGregor et al., 1994; Super, Herrera, & Mora, 1990).

Furthermore, even if significant gains occur following early intervention in these populations, this does not rule out the likelihood that even greater gains can occur if the interventions are continued over a longer time period. For example, research with at-risk inner-city minority children showed higher long-term academic achievement occurring when interventions occurred during both preschool and the early primary school grades rather than being restricted to just the preschool years (Reynolds, 1994;

Reynolds & Temple, 1998). In addition, as discussed in chapter 3, there is increasing evidence that the central nervous system may be relatively plastic even in late adulthood. This suggests the possibility that later occurring interventions may have both behavioral and biological effects. The bottom line appears to be intervening early and strongly during periods of rapid developmental change, with provision for later intervention to stabilize and build on existing gains. Successful cumulative interventions can involve relatively low-cost procedures, such as extra funding to provide teacher's aides or needed classroom materials (Reynolds & Temple, 1998). It is again important to stress that less costly early interventions that vanish over time may be less cost-effective than more costly cumulative interventions that do not wash out over time.

Summary

Ultimately, many of the principles just discussed can be summarized by the simple acronym IT–AT. *IT–AT* stands for *integrate, target, across time* (Wachs & McCabe, 1998). *Integrate* refers to the need to use intervention strategies based on the contributions of multiple developmental influences rather than monofocal interventions. *Target* refers to the need to tailor assessment and intervention strategies for different cultures, different risk conditions, different outcomes, and different individuals with different individual system characteristics. *Across time* refers to the need for both assessment and intervention strategies not only to consider the developmental course of the individual as a guide to how the individual will react to intervention but also to the need for early interventions that will continue over time in order to maximize the chances of long-term gains.

BRIDGING THE GAP BETWEEN PUBLIC POLICY AND RESEARCH

Too often, transactions between developmental scientists and specialists in public policy result in a mutual sense of frustration. Developmental scientists complain that public policy specialists wish to draw overly simplistic conclusions that misrepresent both the nature and meaning of their research. Public policy specialists complain that researchers wish to unduly complicate matters by endless caveats and that they fail to understand that complex solutions are not easily transcribed into large-scale assessment and intervention programs, particularly when cost is an issue. My reaction, based on both personal experience and the evidence documented in this volume, is that to some extent both sides are correct. The complex pattern of factors influencing individual behavioral–developmental variability is not an artifact. Basing policy decisions about intervention strategies on a restricted subset of potentially relevant influences and processes is most likely to produce weak effects that do not generalize and are not maintained over time. On the other hand, developmental scientists have been too slow in going beyond their own narrow disciplines to collaborate in the generation of multidimensional intervention strategies that both reflect the complexities of development and are relatively cost-effective. For example, we have wasted far more time on sterile questions like nature versus nurture (or, using more modern terminology, "my variance is greater than your variance") than on attempting to integrate and apply common genetic and environmental principles such as covariance and interaction to real-world problems like mental illness or retardation.

I would argue that several steps are essential if we are to progress in the translation of research findings involving multiple influences and midlevel and systems-level processes into accurate and effective public policy decisions about human development. First, it is essential for researchers in human development to repeat and repeat the message to public policy specialists that human behavioral development is a complex phenomenon, and that simple solutions rarely are best for such complex phenomena. One way of emphasizing this point would be to use economic concepts like *human capital* (i.e., how a healthy, well-nourished, well-educated population can contribute to a country's ability to develop economically). I believe the evidence is sufficient to make a reasonable argument that we can expect greater gains in adult productivity if multidimensional rather than unidimensional intervention strategies are used in infancy and childhood to improve cognitive, psychosocial, and motivational levels within a given population (Immink, 1988; Young, 1998). I believe this argument can be made because the evidence cited earlier indicates that multidimensional interventions are more likely to have stronger effects, be more generalizable, and have a greater likelihood of being maintained over the long term.

Second, it is equally essential for developmental scientists to find ways to translate their findings into assessment and intervention strategies that reflect existing complexities yet are relatively cost-effective. There are various ways in which this might be done. One approach would be to make better use of existing data on the extent and nature of developmental risk factors and protective factors within a given population. Combining existing data with knowledge on the role played by different developmental influences will enable us to more efficiently target the extent and nature of our intervention efforts to the extent and nature of the types of developmentally salient problems that are documented in a given population (Latham, 1998). Particularly in populations in which linked multiple developmental risk factors are operating, integrating service delivery to simultaneously target multiple risk factors would provide a natural framework for multidimensional intervention efforts. For example, in a population in which there are relatively high levels of undernutrition, morbidity, and school dropout, integrating the site and delivery of nutritional supplementation, medical intervention, and psychosocial educational programs in the preschool years would be a strategy that would not only benefit children's health and nutritional status but would also increase the likelihood that children would stay in school for longer periods and be more effective learners in their school environment.

FINAL CONCLUSION

For too long we have looked for parsimonious explanations for variability in human behavioral development, under the assumption that the simpler the explanation the better. This is a misunderstanding of the concept of parsimony. *Parsimony* does not refer to the simplest explanation possible but rather to the simplest explanation that best fits the phenomenon under study. As documented in this volume, human development and the multiple influences and midlevel and systems-level processes that underlie individual developmental variability are very complex phenomena. To deal effectively with complexity, we need to understand the nature of such complexity. Whether one is involved in research, intervention, or public policy, we need models and intervention strategies that honor existing complexities that underlie individual human behavioral developmental variability. Through understanding of these complexities, we will be better able to promote both competence and resilience for a greater number of individuals. Building on rather than denying existing complexities is a strategy that is long overdue, in terms of both research and practical application of research to solving real-world problems.

REFERENCES

Abel, E. (1979). Sex ratio in fetal alcohol syndrome. *Lancet, 2*, 105.

Abel, E. (1980). Smoking during pregnancy: A review on growth and development of offspring. *Human Biology, 52*, 593–625.

Aber, L. (1994). Poverty, violence and child development. In C. Nelson (Ed.), *Threats to optimal development* (pp. 229–272). Hillsdale, NJ: Erlbaum.

Aboud, F., & Alemu, T. (1995). Nutrition, maternal responsiveness and mental development of Ethiopian children. *Social Science and Medicine, 41*, 725–732.

Abuelo, D. (1991). Genetic disorders. In J. Matson & J. Mulick (Eds.), *Handbook of mental retardation* (2nd ed., pp. 97–114). New York: Pergamon Press.

Ackerman, L. (1971). Marital instability and juvenile delinquency among the Nez Pierce. *American Anthropologist, 73*, 595–603.

Adair, L., & Pollitt, E. (1985). Outcome of maternal nutritional supplementation. *American Journal of Clinical Nutrition, 41*, 948–978.

Affleck, G., Tennen, H., Rowe, J., Roscher, B., & Walker, L. (1989). Effect of formal support on mothers' adaptation to the hospital to home transition of high risk infants. *Child Development, 60*, 488–501.

Ahadi, S., & Rothbart, M. (1994). Temperament, development and the big 5. In C. Halverson, G. Kohnstamm, & R. Martin (Eds.), *The developing structure of temperament and personality from infancy to adulthood* (pp. 189–208). Hillsdale, NJ: Erlbaum.

Aldwin, C., & Stokols, D. (1988). The effects of environmental change on individuals and groups. *Journal of Environmental Psychology, 8*, 57–75.

Alexander, K., & Entwisle, D. (1988). Achievement in the first two years of school. *Monographs of the Society for Research in Child Development, 218*, 53.

Allen, L. (1994). Nutritional influences on linear growth. *European Journal of Clinical Nutrition, 48*, (Suppl.), S75–S89.

Als, H. (1992). Individualized family focused developmental care for the very low birthweight preterm infant in the NICU. In S. Friedman & M. Sigman (Eds.), *The psychological development of low birthweight children* (pp. 341–388). Norwood, NJ: Ablex.

Altman, I. (1977). Privacy regulation: Culturally universal or culturally specific? *Journal of Social Issues, 33*, 66–84.

Alva, S. (1993). Differential patterns of achievement among Asian-American adolescents. *Journal of Youth and Adolescence, 22*, 407–423.

Anderson, P. (1972). More is different. *Science, 177*, 393–396.

Anderson, V., Bond, L., Catroppa, C., Grimwood, K., Keir, E., & Nolan, T. (1997). Child bacterial meningitis. *Journal of the International Neuropsychological Society, 3*, 147–158.

Archer, J. (1996). Sex differences in social behavior. *American Psychologist, 51,* 909–917.

Arcus, D., & Gardner, S. (1993, March). *When biology is not destiny.* Paper presented at the annual meeting of the Society for Research in Child Development. New Orleans, LA.

Arcus, D., & McCartney, K. (1989). When baby makes four: Family influences on the stability of behavioral inhibition. In S. Resnick (Ed.), *Perspectives on behavioral inhibition* (pp. 197–228). Chicago: University of Chicago Press.

Aronowitz, M. (1984). The social and emotional adjustment of immigrant children. *International Migration Review, 18,* 237–257.

Asendorpf, J. (1994). The malleability of behavior inhibition. *Developmental Psychology, 30,* 912–919.

Asendorpf, J., & Van Aken, M. (1991). Correlates of the temporal consistency of personality patterns in childhood. *Journal of Personality, 59,* 689–703.

Aylward, G., & Pfeiffer, S. (1991). Perinatal complications and cognitive/neuropsychological outcomes. In J. Gray & R. Dean (Eds.), *Neuropsychology of perinatal complications* (pp. 128–160). New York: Springer.

Bachevalier, J. (1990). Ontogenetic development of habit and memory formation in primates. In A. Diamond (Ed.), *The development and neural bases of higher cognitive functions* (Annuals of the New York Academy of Sciences, Vol. 608, pp. 451–477). New York: New York Academy of Sciences.

Bachevalier, J., & Hagger, C. (1991). Sex differences in the development of learning abilities in primates. *Psychoneuroendrocinology, 16,* 177–188.

Bailey, A., Phillips, W., & Rutter, M. (1996). Autism. *Journal of Child Psychology and Psychiatry, 37,* 89–126.

Bakeman, R., Adamson, L., Konner, M., & Barr, R. (1990). Kung infancy. *Child Development, 61,* 794–809.

Ballabriga, A. (1990). Malnutrition and the central nervous system. In R. Suskind & L. Lewinter-Suskind (Eds.), *The malnourished child* (pp. 177–192). New York: Raven Press.

Bancroft, J. (1991). Reproductive hormones. In M. Rutter & P. Casaer (Eds.), *Biological risk factors for psychosocial disorders* (pp. 260–310). Cambridge, England: Cambridge University Press.

Bandura, A. (1982). The psychology of chance encounters and life paths. *American Psychologist, 37,* 747–755.

Bandura, A., Barbaranelli, C., Capara, G., & Pastorelli, C. (1996). Multifaceted impact of self-efficacy beliefs on academic functioning. *Child Development, 67,* 1206–1222.

Bargh, J. (1992). The ecology of automaticity. *American Journal of Psychology, 105,* 181–199.

Barker, D. (1996). Growth in utero and coronary heart disease. *Nutrition Reviews, 54,* 51–57.

Barker, D., Gluckman, P., Godfrey, K., Harding, J., Owens, J., & Robinson, J. (1993). Fetal nutrition and cardiovascular disease in adult life. *Lancet, 341,* 938–941.

Barker, D., Osmond, C., & Law, C. (1989). The intrauterine and early postnatal origins of cardiovascular disease and chronic bronchitis. *Journal of Epidemiology and Community Health, 43*, 237–240.

Barker, R. (1968). *Ecological psychology*. Stanford, CA: Stanford University Press.

Barlow, G. (1980). The development of sociobiology: A biologist's perspective. In G. Barlow & J. Silverberg (Eds.), *Beyond nature/nurture* (pp. 3–24). Boulder, CO: Westview Press.

Bar-On, D., Eland, J., Kleber, R., Krell, R., Moore, A., Sagi, A., Soriano, E., Suedfeld, P., Van der Velden, P., & Van Ijzendoorn, M. (1998). Multigenerational perspectives on coping with the Holocaust experience. *International Journal of Behavioral Development, 22*, 315–338.

Baron, R., & Kenny, D. (1986). The moderator–mediator variable distinction in social psychological research. *Journal of Personality and Social Psychology, 51*, 1173–1182.

Barr, H., & Streissguth, A. (1991). Caffeine use during pregnancy and child outcome. *Neurotoxicology and Teratology, 13*, 441–448.

Barr, H., Streissguth, A., Darby, B., & Sampson, P. (1990). Prenatal exposure to alchohol, caffeine, tobacco, and aspirin. *Developmental Psychology 26*, 339–348.

Barr, R., Boyce, W., & Zeltzer, L. (1994). The stress–illness association in children. In R. Haggerty, L. Sherrod, N. Garmezy, & M. Rutter (Eds.), *Stress, risk and resilience in children and adolescents* (pp. 182–224). Cambridge, England: Cambridge University Press.

Barrett, D., Radke-Yarrow, M., & Klein, R. (1982). Chronic malnutrition and child behavior. *Developmental Psychology, 18*, 541–556.

Barsky, V., & Siegel, L. (1992). Predicting future cognitive, academic and behavioral outcomes for very low birthweight infants. In S. Friedman & M. Sigman (Eds.), *The psychological development of low birthweight children* (pp. 275–298). Norwood, NJ: Ablex.

Barton, S. (1994). Chaos, self-organization, and psychology. *American Psychologist, 49*, 5–14.

Bates, J. (1989). Concepts and measures of temperament. In G. Kohnstamm, J. Bates, & M. Rothbart (Eds.), *Temperament in childhood* (pp. 3–27). New York: Wiley.

Bates, J., Pettit, G., Dodge, K., & Ridge, B. (1997, April). *The interaction of temperamental resistance to control and restrictive parenting in the development of externalizing behavior.* Presented at a symposium of the Society for Research in Child Development, Washington, DC.

Bates, J., Wachs, T. D., & Emde, R. (1994). Toward practical uses for biological concepts of temperament. In J. Bates & T. D. Wachs (Eds.), *Temperament: Individual differences at the interface of biology and behavior* (pp. 275–306). Washington, DC: American Psychological Association.

Bates, J., Wachs, T. D., & VandenBos, G. (1995). Trends in research in temperament. *Psychiatric Services, 46*, 661–663.

Bateson, P. (1983). Genes, environment and the development of behavior. In T. Halliday & P. Slater (Eds.), *Genes, development and learning* (pp. 52–81). Oxford, England: Basil Blackwell.

Bateson, P. (1985). Problems and possibilities of fusing developmental and evolutionary thought. In G. Butterworth, J. Rutkowska, & M. Scaife (Eds.), *Evolution and developmental psychology* (pp. 3–21). Sussex, England: Harvester.

Beaton, G. (1989). Small but healthy? Are we asking the right question? *Human Organization, 48,* 30–38.

Beautrais, A., Fergusson, D., & Shannon, F. (1982). Life events and childhood morbidity: A prospective study. *Pediatrics, 70,* 935–940.

Beckwith, L., & Rodning, C. (1992). Evaluating effects of intervention with parents of preterm infants. In S. Friedman & M. Sigman (Eds.), *The psychological development of low birthweight children* (pp. 389–410). Norwood, NJ: Ablex.

Bell, J., Whitmore, W., Queen, K., Orband-Miller, L., & Slotkin, T. (1987). Biochemical determinants of growth sparing during neonatal nutritional deprivation or enhancement. *Pediatric Research, 22,* 599–604.

Bell, R., & Chapman, M. (1986). Child effects and studies using experimental or brief longitudinal approaches to socialization. *Developmental Psychology, 22,* 595–603.

Bellinger, D. (1995). Interpreting the literature on lead and child development. *Neurotoxicology and Teratology, 17,* 201–212.

Bellinger, D., Titlebaum, L., Hu, H., & Needleman, H. (1994). Attentional correlates of dentin and bone lead levels in adolescents. *Archives of Environmental Health, 49,* 98–105.

Belmont, J. (1994). Organic mental retardation. In R. Sternberg (Ed.), *Encyclopedia of human intelligence* (Vol. 2, pp. 717–724). New York: Macmillan.

Belsky, J. (1984). The determinants of parenting: A process model. *Child Development, 55,* 83–96.

Belsky, J. (1990). Parental and nonparental child care and children's socioemotional development. *Journal of Marriage and the Family, 52,* 885–903.

Belsky, J., & Cassidy, J. (1994). Attachment: Theory and evidence. In M. Rutter & D. Hay (Eds.), *Development through life* (pp. 373–402). Oxford, England: Basil Blackwell.

Belsky, J., Crnic, K., & Gable, S. (1995). The determinants of co-parenting in families with toddler boys. *Child Development, 66,* 629–642.

Belsky, J., & Nezworski, T. (1988). *Clinical implications of attachment.* Hillsdale, NJ: Erlbaum Press.

Benasich, A., & Brooks-Gunn, J. (1996). Maternal attitudes and knowledge of child rearing. *Child Development, 67,* 1186–1205.

Benbow, C., & Lubinski, D. (1993). Psychological profiles of the mathematically talented. In G. Brock & K. Ackrill (Eds.), *CIBA Foundation Symposium 178: The origins and development of high ability* (pp. 44–59). New York: Wiley.

Bender, B., Linden, M., & Robinson, A. (1987). Environmental and developmental risk in children with sex chromosome abnormalities. *Journal of the American Academy of Child and Adolescent Psychiatry, 26,* 499–503.

Bendersky, M., & Lewis, M. (1994). Environmental risk, biological risk, and developmental outcome. *Developmental Psychology, 30,* 484–494.

Berenbaum, S., & Hines, M. (1992). Early androgens are related to childhood sex-typed toy preferences. *Psychological Sciences, 3,* 203–206.

Berenbaum, S., & Snyder, E. (1995). Early hormonal influences on childhood sex-typed activity and playmate preferences. *Developmental Psychology, 31,* 31–42.

Berger, J., Aguayo, V., Miguel, J., Lujan, C., Tellez, W., & Traissac, P. (1997). Definition and prevalence of anemia in Bolivian women of childbearing age living at high altitudes. *Nutrition Reviews, 55,* 247–256.

Bernhardt, P. (1997). Influences of serotonin and testosterone in aggression and dominance. *Current Directions in Psychological Science, 6,* 44–48.

Berry, J. (1990). Psychology of acculturation. In R. Brislin (Ed.), *Applied cross-cultural psychology* (pp. 323–353). Newbury Park, CA: Sage.

Best, D., & Williams, J. (1993). A cross-cultural viewpoint. In A. Beall & R. Sternberg (Eds.), *The psychology of gender* (pp. 215–248). New York: Guilford Press.

Bevers, C. (1986). A cross-cultural look at child abuse. *Public Welfare, 44,* 18–22.

Bicego, G., & Boerma, J. (1993). Maternal education and child survival. *Social Science and Medicine, 36,* 1207–1227.

Biringen, Z., Emde, R., Campos, J., & Appelbaum, M. (1995). Affective reorganization in the infant, the mother and the dyad. *Child Development, 66,* 499–514.

Bisanz, J., Morrison, F., & Dunn, M. (1995). Effects of age and schooling on the acquisition of elementary quantitative skills. *Developmental Psychology, 31,* 221–236.

Bithoney, W., Vandeven, A., & Ryan, A. (1993). Elevated lead levels in reportedly abused children. *Journal of Pediatrics, 122,* 719–720.

Bjorklund, D. (1997). The role of immaturity in human development. *Psychological Bulletin, 122,* 153–169.

Black, M. (1998). Zinc deficiency and child development. *American Journal of Clinical Nutrition, 68,* 464S-469S.

Block, J., & Block, J. (1980). The role of ego-control and ego-resiliency in the organization of behavior. In W. Collins (Ed.), *Minnesota Symposia on Child Psychology* (Vol. 13, pp. 39–101). Hillsdale, NJ: Erlbaum.

Block, J., Block, J., & Keyes, S. (1988). Longitudinally foretelling drug use in adolescence. *Child Development, 59,* 336–355.

Bohman, M., Cloniger, R., Sigvardsson, S., & Von-Knorring, A. (1987). The genetics of alcoholism and related disorders. *Journal of Psychiatric Research, 21,* 447–452.

Bolger, K., Patterson, C., Thompson, W., & Kupersmidt, J. (1995). Psychosocial adjustment among children experiencing persistent and intermittent family economic hardship. *Child Development, 66,* 1107–1129.

Bonta, B. (1997). Cooperation and competition in peaceful societies. *Psychological Bulletin, 121,* 299–320.

Born, M., Bleichrodt, N., & van der Flier, H. (1987). Cross-cultural comparison of sex related differences on intelligence tests. *Journal of Cross-Cultural Psychology, 18,* 283–314.

Bornstein, M. (1989a). Sensitive periods in development. *Psychological Bulletin, 105,* 179–197.

Bornstein, M. (1989b). *Maternal responsiveness: Characteristics and consequences.* San Francisco: Jossey-Bass.

Bornstein, M. (1991). *Cultural approaches to parenting.* Hillsdale, NJ: Erlbaum.

Bornstein, M., Tal, J., & Tamis-LeMonda, C. (1991). Parenting in cross-cultural perspective. In M. Bornstein (Ed.), *Cultural approaches to parenting* (pp. 69–90). Hillsdale, NJ: Erlbaum.

Bourgeois J., Jastreboff, P., & Rakic, P. (1989). Synaptogenesis in visual cortex of normal and preterm monkeys. *Proceedings of the National Academy of Sciences: USA, 86,* 4297–4301.

Bower, P., & Tylee, A. (1997). Measuring general practitioner psychology. *Family Practice, 14,* 142–147.

Boyce, W., & Boyce, J. (1988). Acculturation and changes in health among Navajo boarding school students. *Social Science and Medicine, 17,* 219–226.

Boyce, W., Chesterman, E., Wara, D., Cohen, F., Folkman, S., & Martin, N. (1991). Immunologic changes occurring at kindergarten entry predict respiratory illness following the Loma Prieta earthquake. *Pediatric Research, 29,* 8a.

Boyce, W., & Jemerin, J. (1990). Psychobiological differences in childhood stress response. *Developmental and Behavioral Pediatrics, 11,* 86–94.

Bradley, R., Caldwell, B., & Rock, S. (1988). Home environment and school performance. *Child Development, 55,* 803–809.

Bradley, R., Whiteside, L., Mundfrom, D., Casey, P., Kelleher, K., & Pope, S. (1994). Early indications of resilience and their relation to experiences in the home environments of low birthweight, premature children living in poverty. *Child Development, 65,* 346–360.

Braungart, J., Fulker, D., & Plomin, R. (1992). Genetic mediation of the home environment during infancy. *Developmental Psychology, 28,* 1048–1055.

Breedlove, M. (1994). Sexual differentiation of the human nervous system. *Annual Review of Psychology, 45,* 389–418.

Brinker, R., Baxter, A., & Butler, L. (1994). An ordinal pattern analysis of four hypotheses describing the interactions between drug-addicted, chronically disadvantaged and middle-class mother–infant dyads. *Child Development, 65,* 361–372.

Brody, N. (1993). Intelligence and the behavioral genetics of personality. In R. Plomin & G. McClearn (Eds.), *Nature, nurture, and psychology* (pp. 161–178). Washington, DC: American Psychological Association.

Brody, G., & Flor, D. (1997). Maternal psychological functioning, family processes, and child adjustment in rural, single-parent African American families. *Developmental Psychology, 33*, 1000–1111.

Brody, G., & Stoneman, Z. (1992). Child competence and developmental goals among rural Black families. In I. Sigel, A. DeLisi, & J. Goodnow (Eds.), *Parental belief systems* (pp. 415–431). Hillsdale, NJ: Erlbaum.

Brody, G., Stoneman, Z., & Flor, D. (1996). Parental religiosity, family processes, and youth competence in rural two-parent African American families. *Developmental Psychology, 32*, 696–706.

Brody, G., Stoneman, Z., Flor, D., McCrary, C., Hastings, L., & Conyers, O. (1994). Financial resources, parent psychological functioning, parent co-caregiving and early adolescent competence in rural two-parent African-American families. *Child Development, 65*, 590–605.

Bronfenbrenner, U. (1974). *Is early education effective?* (Pub. No. OHD76-30025). Washington, DC: Department of Health, Education, and Welfare.

Bronfenbrenner, U. (1986). Ecology of the family as a context for human development. *Developmental Psychology, 22*, 723–742.

Bronfenbrenner, U. (1989). Ecological systems theory. *Annals of Child Development, 6*, 187–249.

Bronfenbrenner, U. (1993). The ecology of cognitive development. In R. Wozniak & K. Fisher (Eds.), *Specific environments: Thinking in context* (pp. 3–44). Hillsdale, NJ: Erlbaum.

Bronfenbrenner, U., & Ceci, S. (1994). Nature–nurture reconceptualized in developmental perspective: A biological model. *Psychological Review, 101*, 568–586.

Bronfenbrenner, U., & Crouter, A. (1983). The evolution of environmental models in developmental research. In P. Mussen (Ed.), *Handbook of child psychology, Vol. 1: History, theory and methods* (4th ed., pp. 357–414), New York: Wiley.

Bronstein, P. (1994). Patterns of parent–child interaction in Mexican families. *International Journal of Behavioral Development, 17*, 423–446.

Brooks-Gunn, J., & Warren, M. (1989). Biological and social contributions to negative affect in young adolescent girls. *Child Development, 60*, 40–55.

Brophy, J. (1983). Research on the self-fulfilling prophecy and teacher expectations. *Journal of Educational Psychology, 75*, 631–661.

Brown, B., Mounts, N., Lanborn, S., & Steinberg, L. (1993). Parenting practices and peer groups affiliation in adolescence. *Child Development, 64*, 467–482.

Brown, J., & Sherman, L. (1995). Policy implications of new scientific knowledge. *Journal of Nutrition-Supplement, 125*, 2281S–2284S.

Browning, C., & Laumann, E. (1997). Sexual contact between children and adults: A life course perspective. *American Sociological Review, 62*, 540–560.

Bryant, B., & DeMorris, K. (1992). Beyond parent–child relationships. In R. Parke & G. Ladd (Eds.), *Family–peer relationships* (pp. 159–189). Hillsdale, NJ: Erlbaum.

Buchanan, C., Eccles, J., & Becker, J. (1992). Are adolescents the victims of raging hormones? *Psychological Bulletin, 111*, 62–107.

Bugental, D., Blue, J., & Cruz-Sosa, M. (1989). Perceived control over caregiving outcomes. *Developmental Psychology, 25*, 532–539.

Buka, S., & Lipsitt, L. (1994). Toward a developmental epidemiology. In S. Friedman & H. C. Haywood (Eds.), *Developmental follow-up* (pp. 331–350). San Diego: Academic Press.

Buka, S., Lipsitt, L., & Tsuang, M. (1992). Emotional and behavioral development of low birthweight infants. In S. Friedman & M. Sigman (Eds.), *The psychological development of low birthweight infants* (pp. 187–214). Norwood, NJ: Ablex.

Burn, J., Povey, S., Bird, Y., Munro, E., West, L., Harper, K., & Thomas, D. (1986). Duchenne muscular dystrophy in one of monozygotic twin girls. *Journal of Medical Genetics, 23*, 494–500.

Buss, D. (1985). Human mate selection. *American Scientist, 73*, 47–51.

Buss, D. (1991). Evolutionary personality psychology. *Annual Review of Psychology, 42*, 459–491.

Buss, D., Haselton, M., Shackelford, T., Bleske, A., & Wakefield, J. (1998). Adaptation, exaptations, and spandrels. *American Psychologist, 53*, 533–548.

Byne, W., & Parsons, B. (1993). Human sexual orientation. *Archives of General Psychiatry, 50*, 228–239.

Cadman, D., Boyce, M., Szatmari, P., & Offord, D. (1987). Chronic illness, disability and mental social well-being. *Pediatrics, 79*, 805–813.

Cadoret, R., Troughton, E., Mecchant, L., & Whitters, A. (1990). Early life psychosocial events and adult affective symptoms. In L. Robins & M. Rutter (Eds.), *Straight and devious pathways from childhood to adulthood* (pp. 300–313). Cambridge, England: Cambridge University Press.

Cairns, E., & Dawes, A. (1996). Children: Ethnic and political violence: A commentary. *Child Development, 67*, 129–139.

Cairns, E., & Wilson, R. (1989). Mental health aspects of political violence in Northern Ireland. *International Journal of Mental Health, 18*, 38–56.

Cairns, R. (1993). Belated but bedazzling: Timing and genetic influences on social development. In G. Turkewitz & D. Devenny (Eds.), *Developmental time and timing* (pp. 61–84). Hillsdale, NJ: Erlbaum.

Cairns, R., Cairns, B., Neckerman, H., Gest, S., & Gariepy, J. (1988). Social networks and aggressive behavior. *Developmental Psychology, 24*, 815–823.

Cairns, R., Gariepy, J., & Hood, K. (1990). Development, microevolution, and social behavior. *Psychological Review, 97*, 49–65.

Calkins, S. (1994). Origins and outcomes of individual differences in emotion regulation. *Monographs of the Society for Research in Child Development, 59*, 53–72.

Calkins, S., & Fox, N. (1994). Individual differences in the biological aspects of temperament. In J. Bates & T. D. Wachs (Eds.), *Temperament: Individual differences at the interface of biology and behavior* (pp. 199–217). Washington, DC: American Psychological Association.

Cannon, T., Mednick, S., & Parnas, J. (1990). Two pathways to schizophrenia in children at risk. In L. Robins & M. Ruttter (Eds.), *Straight and devious pathways from childhood to adulthood* (pp. 328–350). Cambridge, England: Cambridge University Press.

Caplan, A. (1980). A critical examination of current sociobiological theory. In G. Barlow & J. Silverberg (Eds.), *Sociobiology: Beyond nature/nurture* (pp. 97–121). Boulder, CO: Westview Press.

Capron, C., & Duyme, M. (1989). Assessment of effects of socio-economic status on IQ in a full cross-fostering study. *Nature, 340,* 552–554.

Capron, C., & Duyme, M. (1996). Effect of socioeconomic status of biological and adoptive parents on WISC-R subtest scores of their French adopted children. *Intelligence, 22,* 259–276.

Cardon, L., & Cherny, S. (1994). Adoption design methodology. In J. DeFries, R. Plomin, & D. Fulker (Eds.), *Nature and nurture during middle childhood* (pp. 26–45). Oxford, England: Blackwell Scientific.

Cardon, L., & Fulker, D. (1993). Genetics of specific cognitive abilities. In R. Plomin & G. McClearn (Eds.), *Nature, nurture, and psychology* (pp. 99–120). Washington, DC: American Psychological Association.

Carlin, M. (1990). The improved prognosis in cri-du-chat (5pk0) syndrome. In W. Fraser (Ed.), *Key issues in mental retardation research* (pp. 64–73). London: Routledge & Kegan Paul.

Caro, T., & Bateson, P. (1986). Organization and ontogeny of alternative tactics. *Animal Behavior, 34,* 1483–1499.

Carran, D., Scott, K., Shaw, K., & Beydouin, S. (1989). The relative risk of educational handicaps in two birth cohorts of normal and low birthweight disadvantaged children. *Topics in Early Childhood Special Education, 9,* 14–31.

Casaer, P. (1993). The human brain and longitudinal research in human development. In D. Magnusson & P. Casaer (Eds.), *Longitudinal research on human development* (pp. 51–59). Cambridge, England: Cambridge University Press.

Casaer, P., DeVries, L., & Marlow, N. (1991). Prenatal and perinatal risk factors for psychosocial development. In M. Rutter & P. Casaer (Eds.), *Biological risk factors for psychosocial disorders* (pp. 139–174). Cambridge, England: Cambridge University Press.

Case, R., & Okamoto, Y. (1996). The role of central conceptual structures in the development of children's thought. *Monographs of the Society for Research in Child Development, 61*(1–2, Serial No. 246).

Caspi, A. (1998). Personality development across the life course. In N. Eisenberg (Ed.), *Handbook of child psychology: Social, emotional and personality development* (Vol. 3, pp. 317–388). New York: Wiley.

Caspi, A., & Bem, D. (1990). Personal continuity and change across the life course. In L. Pevin (Ed.), *Handbook of personality theory and research* (pp. 549–575). New York: Guilford Press.

Caspi, A., Elder, G., & Bem, D. (1987). Moving against the world: Life course patterns of explosive children. *Developmental Psychology, 23,* 308–313.

Caspi, A., Elder, G., & Bem, D. (1988). Moving away from the world: Life course patterns of shy children. *Developmental Psychology, 24,* 824–831.

Caspi, A., Elder, G., & Herbener, E. (1990). Childhood personality and the prediction of life course patterns. In L. Robbins & M. Rutter (Eds.), *Straight and devious pathways from childhood to adulthood* (pp. 13–35). Cambridge, England: Cambridge University Press.

Caspi, A., Lyman, D., Moffitt, T., & Silva, P. (1993). Unraveling girls' delinquency. *Developmental Psychology, 29,* 19–30.

Caspi, A., & Moffitt, T. (1991). Individual differences are accentuated during periods of social change. *Journal of Personality and Social Psychology, 61,* 157–168.

Cassidy, J., & Berlin, L. (1994). The insecure/ambivalent pattern of attachment. *Child Development, 65,* 971–991.

Cauffman, E., & Steinberg, L. (1995, March). *Moderating effects of neighborhood parenting on family socialization processes.* Presented at a symposium of the Society for Research in Child Development, Indianapolis, IN.

Caughy, M. (1996). Health and environmental effects on the academic readiness of school-age children. *Developmental Psychology, 32,* 515–522.

Caughy, M., DiPietro, J., & Strobino, D. (1994). Day-care participation as a protective factor in the cognitive development of low-income children. *Child Development, 65,* 457–471.

Cavalli-Sforza, L., & Feldman, M. (1981). *Cultural transmission and evolution.* Princeton, NJ: Princeton University Press.

Caviness, V., Misson, J., & Gadisseux, J. (1989). Abnormal neuronal patterns and disorders of neocortical development. In A. Galaburda (Ed.), *From reading to neurons* (pp. 405–439). Cambridge, MA: MIT Press.

Ceci, S. (1991). How much does schooling influence general intelligence and its cognitive components? *Developmental Psychology, 27,* 703–722.

Ceci, S. (1993). Contextual trends in intellectual development. *Developmental Review, 13,* 403–435.

Ceci, S., & Williams, W. (1997). Schooling, intelligence, and income. *American Psychologist, 52,* 1051–1059.

Chagnon, N. (1980). Kin selection theory, kinship, marriage and fitness among the Yanomamo Indians. In G. Barlow & J. Silverberg (Eds.), *Sociobiology: Beyond nature/nurture* (pp. 545–571). Boulder, CO: Westview Press.

Chambon, P. (1996). A decade of molecular biology of retinoic acid receptors. *Federation of American Societies for Experimental Biology Journal, 10,* 940–954.

Chao, R. (1994). Beyond parental control and authoritarian parenting style. *Child Development, 65,* 1111–1119.

Chapais, B. (1996). Competing through co-operation in nonhuman primates. *International Journal of Behavioral Development, 19,* 7–24.

Charlesworth, W. (1996). Co-operation and competition: Contributions to an evolutionary and developmental model. *International Journal of Behavioral Development, 19,* 25–38.

Chase-Lansdale, P., & Gordon, R. (1996). Economic hardship and the development of five and six year olds. *Child Development, 67,* 3338–3367.

Chase-Lansdale, P., Lindsay, C., Andrew, J., & Kiernan, K. (1995). The long term effects of parental divorce on the mental health of young adults. *Child Development, 66,* 1614–1634.

Chen, C., & Stevenson, H. (1995). Motivation and mathematics achievement. *Child Development, 66,* 1215–1234.

Chen, X., Dong, Q., & Zhou, H. (1997). Authoritative and authoritarian parenting practices and social and school performance in Chinese children. *International Journal of Behavioral Development, 21,* 855–873.

Chen, X., Hastings, P., Rubin, K., Chen, H., Cen, G., & Stewart, S. (1998). Child rearing attitudes and behavioral inhibition in Chinese and Canadian toddlers. *Developmental Psychology, 34,* 677–686.

Chess, S., & Thomas, A. (1990). Continuity and discontinuity in temperament. In L. Robins & M. Rutter (Eds.), *Straight and devious pathways from childhood to adulthood* (pp. 205–220). Cambridge, England: Cambridge University Press.

Chinese Cultural Connection. (1987). Chinese values and the search for culture-free dimensions of culture. *Journal of Cross-Cultural Psychology, 18,* 143–164.

Chisholm, J. (1983). *Navajo infancy.* Chicago: Aldine.

Chisholm, J. (1989). Biology, culture and the development of temperament. In J. Nugent, B. Lester, & T. Brazelton (Eds.), *The cultural context of infancy* (Vol. 1, pp. 341–364). Norwood, NJ: Ablex.

Chisholm, J. (1990). Life history perspectives on human development. In G. Butterworth & P. Bryant (Eds.), *Causes of development* (pp. 238–262). New York: Harvester-Wheat Sheaf.

Chiu, M., Feldman, S., & Rosenthal, D. (1992). The influence of immigration on parental behavior and adolescent distress in Chinese families residing in two Western nations. *Journal of Research on Adolescence, 2,* 205–239.

Cillessen, A., van Ijzendoorn, M., van Lieshout, C., & Hartup, W. (1992). Heterogeneity among peer rejected boys. *Child Development, 63,* 893–905.

Clarke, A., & Clarke, A. (1979). Early experience: Its limited effect upon late development. In D. Shaffer & J. Dunn (Eds.), *The first year of life.* New York: Wiley.

Clarke, A., & Clarke, A. (1988). The adult outcome of early behavioral abnormalities. *International Journal of Behavioral Development, 11,* 3–19.

Clarke, A., & Clarke, A. (1989). The later cognitive effects of early intervention. *Intelligence, 13,* 289–297.

Clarke, J., Gates, R., Hogan, S., Barrett, M., & MacDonald, G. (1987). Neuropsychological studies on adolescents with phenylketonuria returned to phenlalanine restricted diets. *American Journal of Mental Retardation, 92,* 252–262.

Clarke-Stewart, K. (1991). A home is not a school. In M. Lewis & S. Feinman (Eds.), *Social influences and socialization in infancy* (pp. 41–62). New York: Plenum Press.

Clausen, J. (1991). Adolescent competence and the shaping of the life course. *American Journal of Sociology, 96,* 805–842.

Clausen, J. (1995). Gender, contexts, and turning points in adult's lives. In P. Moen, G. Elder, & K. Luscher (Eds.), *Examining lives in context* (pp. 365–392). Washington, DC: American Psychological Association.

Cochran, M., & Bo, I. (1989). The social network, family involvement and pro- and antisocial behavior of adolescent males in Norway. *Journal of Youth and Adolescence, 18,* 377–398.

Cochran, M., & DaVila, V. (1992). Societal influences on children's peer relation-ships. In R. Parke & G. Ladd (Eds.), *Family–peer relationships* (pp. 191–212). Hillsdale, NJ: Erlbaum.

Cohen, P., Brook, J., Cohen, J., Valez, N., & Garcia, M. (1990). Common and un-common pathways to adolescent psychopathology and problem behavior. In L. Robins & M. Rutter (Eds.), *Straight and devious pathways from childhood to adult-hood* (pp. 242–258). Cambridge, England: Cambridge University Press.

Cohen, P., Vele, C., Brook, J., & Smith, J. (1989). Mechanisms of the relation be-tween perinatal problems, early childhood illness and psychopathology in late childhood and adolescence. *Child Development, 60,* 701–709.

Cohen, S., Parmelee, A., Beckwith, L., & Sigman, M. (1992). Behavior problems and social competence during early adolescence in children born preterm. In S. Friedman & M. Sigman (Eds.), *The psychological development of low birth-weight infants* (pp. 239–258). Norwood, NJ: Ablex.

Coie, J. (1990). Toward a theory of peer rejection. In S. Asher & J. Coie (Eds.), *Peer rejection in childhood* (pp. 365–401). Cambridge, England: Cambridge University Press.

Coie, J., Dodge, K., & Coppotelli, H. (1982). Dimensions and types of social status. *Developmental Psychology, 18,* 557–570.

Cole, M. (1992). Culture in development. In M. Bornstein & M. Lamb (Eds.), *Developmental psychology* (pp. 731–789). Hillsdale, NJ: Erlbaum Press.

Coleman, J. (1971). Social systems. In P. Weiss (Ed.), *Hierarchically organized systems in theory and practice* (pp. 69–80). New York: Hafner Press.

Collaer, M., & Hines, M. (1995). Human behavioral sex differences: A role for go-nadal hormones during early development. *Psychological Bulletin, 118,* 55–107.

Colombo, M., de la Parra, A., & Lopez, I. (1992). Intellectual and physical outcome of children undernourished in early life is influenced by later environmental conditions. *Developmental Medicine and Child Neurology, 34,* 611–622.

Compas, B. (1987). Coping with stress during childhood and adolescence. *Psychological Bulletin, 101,* 393–403.

Conger, R., Conger, K., Elder, G., Lorenz, F., Simons, R., & Whitbeck, L. (1992). A family process model of economic hardship and adjustment of early adoles-cent boys. *Child Development, 63,* 526–541.

Conger, R., Conger, K., Elder, G., Lorenz, F., Simons, R., & Whitbeck, L. (1993). Family economic stress and adjustment of early adolescent girls. *Developmental Psychology, 29,* 206–219.

Conger, R., Ge, X., Elder, G., Lorenz, F., & Simons, R. (1994). Economic stress, coercive family processes and developmental problems of adolescence. *Child Development, 65,* 541–561.

Conger, R., Patterson, G., & Ge, X. (1995). It takes two to replicate: A mediational model for the impact of parent's stress on adolescent adjustment. *Child Development, 66,* 80–97.

Connolly, K. (1998). Mental and behavioral effects of parasitic infection. In *Nutrition, health and child development* (Pan-American Health Organization Scientific Monograph No. 566). Washington, DC: Pan-American Health Organization.

Connolly, K., & Kvalsvig, J. (1993). Infection, nutrition and cognitive performance in children. *Parasitology, 107,* S187–S200.

Connolly, K., & Pharoah, P. (1989). Iodine deficiency, maternal thyroxine levels and developmental disorders in children. In F. DeLong, J. Robbins, & P. Condlitte (Eds.), *Iodine and the brain* (pp. 317–331). New York: Plenum Press.

Cook, J., & Martin, K. (1995). Differences in nutrient adequacy among poor and nonpoor children. *Center on Hunger, Poverty and Nutrition Policy Monograph.* Medford, MA: Tufts University School of Nutrition.

Cooper, C., & Cooper, R. (1992). Links between adolescent's relationship with their parents and peers. In R. Parke & G. Ladd (Eds.), *Family–peer relationships* (pp. 135–158). Hillsdale, NJ: Erlbaum.

Corsaro, W., & Rizzo, T. (1988). Discussion and friendship. *American Sociological Review, 53,* 879–894.

Costa, P., & McCrae, R. (1994). Stability and change in personality from adolescence through adulthood. In C. Halverson, G. Kohnstamm, & R. Martin (Eds.), *The developing structure of temperament and personality from infancy to adulthood* (pp. 139–150). Hillsdale, NJ: Erlbaum.

Cotterell, J. (1986). Work and community influences and the quality of child rearing. *Child Development, 57,* 362–374.

Coulton, C., Korbin, J., Su, M., & Chow, J. (1995). Community level factors and child maltreatment rates. *Child Development, 66,* 1262–1276.

Cousins, R. (1996). Zinc. In E. Ziegler & L. Filer (Eds.), *Present knowledge in nutrition* (7th ed., pp. 293–306). Washington, DC: International Life Sciences Institute Press.

Crane, J. (1991). The epidemic theory of ghettos and neighborhood effects on dropping out and teenage childbearing. *American Journal of Sociology, 96,* 1226–1259.

Crawford, C., & Anderson, J. (1989). Sociobiology: An environmentalist discipline. *American Psychologist, 44,* 1449–1459.

Crockenberg, S. (1986). Are temperamental differences in babies associated with predictable differences in caregiving? In J. Lerner & R. Lerner (Eds.), *Temperament and psychosocial interaction in children* (pp. 53–72). San Francisco: Jossey-Bass.

Crockenberg, S., & Litman, C. (1990). Autonomy and competence in 2 year olds. *Developmental Psychology, 26,* 961–971.

Crockenberg, S., & Litman, C. (1991). Effects of maternal employment on maternal and two-year-old child behavior. *Child Development, 62,* 930–953.

Cronbach, L. (1987). Statistical tests for moderator variables. *Psychological Bulletin, 102,* 414–417.

Cronbach, L. (1991). Emerging views on methodology. In T. D. Wachs & R. Plomin (Eds.), *Conceptualization and measurement of organism–environment interaction* (pp. 87–104). Washington, DC: American Psychological Association.

Cronbach, L., & Snow, R. (1977). *Aptitudes and instructional methods.* New York: Halstead Press.

Cronk, L. (1993). Parental favoritism toward daughters. *American Scientist, 81,* 272–279.

Crouter, A., & McHale, S. (1993). The long arm of the job. In T. Luster & L. Okagaki (Eds.), *Parenting: An ecological perspective* (pp. 179–202). Hillsdale, NJ: Erlbaum.

Crow, T. (1989). Viruses and schizophrenia: The virogene hypothesis. *Biologist, 36,* 10–14.

Crutchfield, J., Farmer, J., Packard, N., & Shaw, R. (1986). Chaos. *Scientific American, 225,* 38–49.

D'Andrade, R. (1987). A folk model of the mind. In D. Holland & R. Quinn (Eds.), *Cultural models in language and thought* (pp. 112–148). New York: Cambridge University Press.

Dalterio, S., & Fried, P. (1992). The effects of marijuana use on offspring. In T. Sonderegger (Ed.), *Perinatal substance abuse* (pp. 161–183). Baltimore: Johns Hopkins University Press.

Daly, M., & Wilson, M. (1984). A sociobiological analysis of human infanticide. In G. Haustater & S. Hardy (Eds.), *Infanticide: Comparative and evolutionary perspectives,* pp. 487–502. New York: Aldine de Gruyter.

Dance, K., & Neufeld, R. (1988). Aptitude treatment interaction in the clinical setting. *Psychological Bulletin, 104,* 192–213.

Darling, N., & Steinberg, L. (1993). Parenting style as context. *Psychological Bulletin, 113,* 487–496.

Dasen, P. (1984). The cross-cultural study of intelligence. *International Journal of Psychology, 19,* 407–434.

Davidson, R. (1993). Childhood temperament and cerebral assymetry. In K. Rubin & J. Asendorpf (Eds.), *Social withdrawal, inhibition and shyness in childhood* (pp. 31–48). Hillsdale, NJ: Earlbaum.

Davies, P., & Windle, M. (1997). Gender specific pathways between maternal depressive symptoms, family discord, and adolescent adjustment. *Developmental Psychology, 33,* 657–688.

Dawes, A. (1990). The effects of political violence on children. *International Journal of Psychology, 25,* 13–31.

Dawes, A., Tredoux, C., & Feinstein, A. (1989). Political violence in South Africa. *International Journal of Mental Health, 18,* 16–43.

Dawes, R. (1993). Prediction of the future versus an understanding of the past. *American Journal of Psychology, 106,* 1–24.

Dawkins, R. (1980). Good strategies or evolutionary stable strategies? In G. Barlow & J. Silverberg (Eds.), *Sociobiology: Beyond nature/nurture* (pp. 331–367). Boulder, CO: Westview Press.

Dawson, G. (1994). Frontal electroencephalographic correlates of individual differences in emotion expression in infants. *Monographs of the Society for Research in Child Development, 59,* 135–151.

Day, N., Richardson, G., Goldschmidt, L., Robels, N., Taylor, P., Stoffer, D., Cornelius, M., & Geva, D. (1994). Effect of prenatal marijuana exposure on the cognitive development of offspring at age three. *Neurotoxicology and Teratology, 16,* 169–175.

Day, R., & Ghandour, M. (1984). The effects of television mediated aggression and real life aggression on the behavior of Lebanese children. *Journal of Experimental Child Psychology, 38,* 7–18.

Deater-Deckerd, K., Dodge, K., Bates, J., & Pettit, G. (1996). Physical discipline among African American and European American mothers. *Developmental Psychology, 32,* 1065–1072.

DeCasper, A., & Spence, M. (1986). Prenatal maternal speech influences newborns' perceptions of speech sounds. *Infant Behavior and Development, 9,* 133–150.

DeFries, J., & Gillis, J. (1993). Genetics of reading disability. In R. Plomin & G. McClearn (Eds.), *Nature, nurture, and psychology* (pp. 121–145). Washington, DC: American Psychological Association.

DeKay, W., & Buss, D. (1992). Human nature, individual differences and the importance of context. *Current Directions in Psychological Sciences, 1,* 184–189.

Dell, P., & Rose, F. (1987). Transfer of effects from environmental enriched and impoverished female rats to future offspring. *Physiology and Behavior, 39,* 187–190.

DeLong, G. (1993). Effects of nutrition on brain development in humans. *American Journal of Clinical Nutrition-Supplement, 57,* 286S–290S.

Dennenberg, V., & Rosenberg, K. (1967). Nongenetic transmission of information. *Nature, 216,* 549–550.

Detterman, D. (1996). *Current topics in human intelligence: Vol. 5. The environment.* Norwood, NJ: Ablex.

Devlin, B., Daniels, M., & Roeder, K. (1997). The heritability of IQ. *Nature, 388,* 468–471.

DeVries, M. (1984). Temperament and infant mortality among the Masai of East Africa. *American Journal of Psychiatry, 141,* 1189–1194.

Dewey, K., Romero-Abal, M., Serrano, J., Bulux, J., Peerson, J., Engle, P., & Solomons, N. (1997a). Effects of discontinuing coffee intake on iron status of iron-deficient Guatemalan toddlers. *American Journal of Clinical Nutrition, 66,* 168–176.

Dewey, K., Romero-Abal-M., Serrano, J., Bulux, J., Peerson, J., Engle, P., & Solomons, N. (1997b). A randomized intervention study of the effects of discontinuing coffee intake on growth and morbidity of iron-deficient Guatemalan toddlers. *Journal of Nutrition, 127*, 306–313.

Diamond, A. (1990a). Developmental time course in human infants and infant monkeys and the neural basis of inhibition control in teaching. *Annals of the New York Academy of Sciences, 608*, 637–669.

Diamond, A. (1990b). The development and neural bases of memory function as indexed by the AB and delayed response tasks in infant monkeys. *Annals of the New York Academy of Sciences, 608*, 267–309

Diamond, A., Ciaramitaro, V., Donner, E., Djali, S., & Robinson, M. (1994). An animal model of early-treated PKU. *Journal of Neuroscience, 14*, 3072–3082.

Diamond, A., Prevor, M., Callender, G., & Druin, D. (1997). Prefrontal cortex cognitive deficits in children treated early and continuously for PKU. *Monographs of the Society for Research in Child Development, 62*(4, Series No. 252).

Diaz-Guerrero, R. (1977). A Mexican psychology. *American Psychologist, 32*, 934–944.

Diener, M., Mangelsdorf, S., Contreras, J., Hazelwood, L., & Rhodes, J. (1995, April). *Correlates of parenting competence among Latina adolescent mothers*. Paper presented at the annual meeting of the Society for Research in Child Development, Indianapolis, IN.

Dietrich, K., Kraft, K., Pearson, D., Harris, L., Bornschein, R., Hammond, P., & Succop, P. (1985). Contribution of social and developmental factors to lead exposure during the first year of life. *Pediatrics, 75*, 1114–1119.

Dietrich, K., Kraft, K., Shukla, R., Bornschein, R., & Succop, P. (1987). The neurobehavioral effects of early lead exposure. In S. Schroeder (Ed.), *Toxic substances and mental retardation* (Monographs of the American Association on Mental Deficiency, Vol. 8, pp. 71–96). Washington, DC: American Association on Mental Deficiency.

DiLalla, L., & Gottesman, I. (1989). Heterogeneity of causes for delinquency and criminality. *Developmental and Psychopathology, 1*, 339–349.

Dishion, T., Patterson, G., Stoolmiller, M., & Skinner, M. (1991). Family, school, and behavioral antecedents to early adolescent involvement with antisocial peers. *Developmental Psychology, 27*, 172–180.

Dodge, K. (1986). Social information processing variables in the development of aggression and altruism in children. In C. Zahn-Waxler, E. Cummings, & R. Ianotti (Eds.), *Altruism and aggression* (pp. 280–302). Cambridge, England: Cambridge University Press.

Dodge, K., & Feldman, E. (1990). Issues in social cognition and sociometric status. In S. Asher & J. Coie (Eds.), *Peer rejection in childhood* (pp. 119–155). Cambridge, England: Cambridge University Press.

Doherty, W., & Needle, R. (1991). Psychological adjustment and substance use among adolescents before and after a parental divorce. *Child Development, 58*, 328-337.

Dornbush, S., Ritter, P., Leiderman, P., Roberts, D., & Fraleigh, M. (1987). The relation of parenting style to adolescent school performance. *Child Development, 58*, 1244–1257.

Douglas, J. (1975). Early hospital admissions and later disturbances of behavior and learning. *Developmental Medicine and Child Neurology, 17,* 456–480.

Dow-Edwards, D., Chasnoff, I., & Griffith, D. (1992). Cocaine use during pregnancy. In T. Sonderegger (Ed.), *Perinatal substance abuse* (pp. 184–206). Baltimore: Johns Hopkins University Press.

Draper, P., & Belsky, J. (1990). Personality development in evolutionary perspective. *Journal of Personality, 58,* 141–161.

Draper, P., & Cashdan, E. (1988). Technological change and child behavior among the Kung. *Ethnology, 27,* 339–365.

DuBois, D., Felner, R., Meares, H., & Krier, M. (1994). Prospective investigation of the effects of socioeconomic disadvantage, life stress, and social support on early adolescent adjustment. *Journal of Abnormal Psychology, 103,* 511–522.

Dunn, J. (1991). Sibling influences. In M. Lewis & S. Feinman (Eds.), *Social influences and socialization in infancy* (pp. 97–109). New York: Plenum Press.

Easter, S., Purves, D., Rakic, P., & Spitzer, N. (1985). The changing view of neural specificity. *Science, 230,* 507–511.

Eaton, W., Chipperfield, J., & Singbeil, C. (1989). Birth order and activity level. *Developmental Psychology, 25,* 668–672.

Eaton, W., & Ritchot, K. (1995). Physical maturation and information processing speed in middle childhood. *Developmental Psychology, 31,* 967–972.

Eccles, J., Midgley, C., Wigfield, A., Buchanan, C., Reuman, D., Flanagan, C., & MacIver, D. (1993). Development during adolescence. *American Psychologist, 48,* 90–101.

Eckerman, C., & Oehler, J. (1992). Very-low birthweight newborns and parents as early social partners. In S. Friedman & M. Sigman (Eds.), *The psychological development of low-birthweight children* (pp. 91–124). Norwood, NJ: Ablex.

Edelman, G. (1989). *Neural Darwinism.* Oxford, England: Oxford University Press.

Edwards, C. (1992). Cross-cultural perspectives on family–peer relations. In R. Parke & G. Ladd (Eds.), *Family–peer relationships* (pp. 285–316). Hillsdale, NJ: Erlbaum.

Edwards, C., Gandini, L., & Giovaninni, D. (1996). The contrasting developmental timetables of parents and preschool teachers in two cultural communities. In S. Harkness & C. Super (Eds.), *Parents' cultural belief systems* (pp. 270–288). New York: Guilford Press.

Egeland, B., & Hiester, M. (1995). The long-term consequences of infant day-care and mother–infant attachment. *Child Development, 66,* 474–485.

Eisenberg, N., & Fabes, R. (1992). Emotion, regulation and the development of social competence. In M. Clark (Ed.), *Emotion and social behavior* (pp. 119–150). Newbury Park, CA: Sage.

Eisenberg, N., Fabes, R., Murphy, B., Karbon, M., Smith, M., & Maszk, P. (1996). The relations of children's dispositional empathy related responding to their emotionality, regulation, and social functioning. *Developmental Psychology, 32,* 195–209.

Eisenberg, N., Fabes, R., Murphy, B., Maszk, P., Smith, M., & Karbon, M. (1995). The role of emotionality and regulation in children's social functioning. *Child Development, 66,* 1360–1384.

Ekblad, S. (1989). Stability in aggression and aggression control in a sample of primary school children in China. *Acta Psychiatrica Scandinavica, 80,* 160–164.

Elder, G. (1974). *Children of the Great Depression.* Chicago: University of Chicago Press.

Elder, G. (1986). Military times and turning points in men's lives. *Developmental Psychology, 22,* 233–245.

Elder, G. (1995). The life course paradigm: Social change and individual development. In P. Moen, G. Elder, & K. Luscher (Eds.), *Examining lives in context* (pp. 101–140). Washington DC: American Psychological Association.

Elder, G., & Caspi, A. (1988). Human development in social change. In N. Bolger, A. Caspi, G. Downey, & M. Moorehouse (Eds.), *Persons in context* (pp. 77–113). Cambridge, England: Cambridge University Press.

Elder, G., Nguyen, T., & Caspi, A. (1985). Linking family hardship to children's lives. *Child Development, 56,* 361–375.

Eldridge, N., & Gould, S. (1972). Punctuated equilibria: An alternative to phyletic gradualism. In T. Schopf (Ed.), *Models in paleobiology* (pp. 83–115). San Francisco: Freeman.

Elicker, J., Englund, M., & Sroufe, A. (1992). Predicting peer competence and peer relationships in childhood from early parent–child relationships. In R. Parke & G. Ladd (Eds.), *Family–peer relationships* (pp. 77–106). Hillsdale, NJ: Erlbaum.

Eliram, T., & Schwarzwald, J. (1987). Social orientation among Israeli youth. *Journal of Cross-Cultural Psychology, 18,* 31–44.

Elman, J. (1993). Learning and development in neural networks: The importance of starting small. *Cognition, 48,* 71–99.

Ember, S. (1980). Ecological determinism and sociobiology. In G. Barlow & J. Silverberg (Eds.), *Sociobiology: Beyond nature/nurture* (pp. 125–150). Boulder, CO: Westview Press.

Engfer, A. (1986). Antecedents of perceived behavior problems in infancy. In G. Kohnstamm (Ed.), *Temperament discussed* (pp. 165–180). Lisse, The Netherlands: Swets & Zeitlinger.

Engfer, A., Walper, S., & Rutter, M. (1994). Individual characteristics as a force in development. In M. Rutter & D. Hay (Eds.), *Development through life* (pp. 79–111). Oxford, England: Blackwell.

Engle, P. (1991). Maternal work and child care strategies in peri-urban Guatemala: Nutritional effects. *Child Development, 62,* 954–965.

Engle, P., Zeitlin, M., Medrano, Y., & Garcia, L. (1996). Growth consequences of low-income Nicaraguan mothers' theories about feeding one year olds. In S. Harkness & C. Super (Eds.), *Parents' cultural belief systems* (pp. 428–446). New York: Guilford Press.

Ensminger, M., Lamkin, R., & Jacobson, N. (1996). School leaving: A longitudinal perspective including neighborhood effects. *Child Development, 67,* 2400–2416.

Epting, F., Prichard, S., Wiggins, S., Leonard, J., & Beagle, J. (1992). Assessment of the first factor and related measures of construct differentiation. *International Journal of Personal Construct Psychology, 5,* 77–94.

Erhardt, A. (1985). The psychobiology of gender. In A. Rossi (Ed.), *Gender and the life course* (pp. 81–96). New York: Aldine.

Ericsson, K., & Charness, N. (1994). Expert performance. *American Psychologist, 49,* 725–747.

Erikson, E. (1963). *Childhood and society* (2nd ed.) New York: Norton.

Erlenmeyer-Kimling, L., & Cornblatt, B. (1987). The New York high risk project. *Schizophrenia Bulletin, 13,* 451–461.

Evans, G., Hygge, S., & Bullinger, M. (1995). Chronic noise and psychological stress. *Psychological Science, 6,* 333–338.

Evans, G., Kliewer, W., & Martin, J. (1990). The role of the physical environment in the health and well-being of children. In H. Schroeder (Ed.), *New directions in health psychology: Assessment* (pp. 127–157). New York: Hemisphere Press.

Evans, G., & Lepore, S. (1997). Moderating and mediating processes in environment-behavior research. In G. Moore & R. Marans (Eds.), *Advances in environment, behavior and design* (pp. 255–285). New York: Plenum Press.

Evans, G., Lepore, S., Shejwal, B., & Palsane, M. (1998). Chronic residential crowding and children's well being. *Child Development, 69,* 1514–1523.

Evans, G., Palsane, M., Lepore, S., & Martin, J. (1989). Residential density and psychological health. *Journal of Personality and Social Psychology, 57,* 994–999.

Falbo, T., & Poston, D. (1993). The academic, personality and physical outcomes of only children in China. *Child Development, 64,* 18–35.

Falkner, F., Holzgreve, W., & Schloo, R. (1994). Prenatal influences on postnatal growth. *European Journal of Clinical Nutrition-Supplement, 48,* S15–S24.

Farber, E., & Egeland, B. (1987). Invulnerability among abused and neglected children. In E. J. Anthony & B. Cohler (Eds.), *The invulnerable child* (pp. 253–288). New York: Guilford Press.

Farver, F., & Frosch, D. (1996). LA stories: Aggression in preschoolers' spontaneous narratives after the riots of 1992. *Child Development, 67,* 19–32.

Feingold, A. (1992). Sex differences in variability in intellectual ability. *Review of Educational Research, 67,* 61–84.

Feldman, S., & Rosenthal, D. (1990). The acculturation of autonomy expectations in Chinese high schoolers residing in two Western nations. *International Journal of Psychology, 25,* 259–281.

Feldman, S., & Rosenthal, D. (1991). Age expectations of behavioral autonomy in Hong Kong, Australian and American youth. *International Journal of Psychology, 26,* 1–23.

Feldman, S., Rosenthal, D., Mont-Reynaud, R., Leung, K., & Lau, S. (1991). Ain't misbehavin': Adolescent values and family environments as correlates of misconduct in Australia, Hong Kong and the United States. *Journal of Research on Adolescence, 1,* 109–134.

Feldman, S., & Weinberger, D. (1994). Self-restraint as a mediator of family influences on boys' delinquent behavior. *Child Development, 65,* 195–211.

Felner, R., Brand, S., DuBois, D., Adan, A., Mulhall, P., & Evans, E. (1995). Socioeconomic disadvantage, proximal environment experience and socio-emotional and academic adjustment in early adolescence. *Child Development, 66,* 774–792.

Fergusson, D., Fergusson, P., Horwood, L., & Kinzett, N. (1988). A longitudinal study of dentine lead levels, intelligence, school performance and behavior: II. Dentine lead and cognitive ability. *Journal of Child Psychology and Psychiatry, 29,* 793–809.

Fernald, A., & Morikawa, H. (1993). Common themes and cultural variations in Japanese and American mothers' speech to infants. *Child Development, 64,* 637–656.

Ferro-Luzzi, A., Pastore, G., & Sette, S. (1988). Seasonality in energy metabolism. In B. Schurch & N. Scrimshaw (Eds.), *Chronic energy deficiency* (pp. 37–58). Lausanne, Switzerland: International Dietary Energy Correlative Group.

Field, T. (1987). Affective and interactive disturbances in infants. In J. Osofsky (Ed.), *Handbook of infant development* (2nd ed., pp. 972–1005). New York: Wiley.

Field, T. (1994). The effects of mothers' physical and emotional unavailability on emotion regulation. *Monographs of the Society for Research in Child Development, 59*(2–3, Serial No. 240).

Finchim, F., & Cain, K. (1986). Learned helplessness in humans. *Developmental Review, 6,* 301–333.

Finkelstein, J., Von Eye, A., & Preece, M. (1994). The relationship between aggressive behavior and puberty in normal adolescents. *Journal of Adolescent Health, 15,* 319–326.

Finn, J. (1989). Withdrawing from school. *Review of Educational Research, 59,* 117–142.

Fischbein, S., Guttman, R., Nathan, M., & Esrachi, A. (1990). Permissiveness–restrictiveness for twins and controls in two educational settings. *Acta Geneticae Medicae et Gamellologiae, 39,* 245–257.

Fletcher, A., Darling, N., Dornbusch, S., & Steinberg, L. (1995). The company they keep. *Developmental Psychology, 31,* 300–310.

Fogel, A. (1993). *Developing through relationships.* New York: Harvester Wheatshaft.

Fonagy, T., Steele, H., & Steele, N. (1991). Maternal representations of attachment during pregnancy predict the organization of infant–mother attachment at one year of age. *Child Development, 62,* 891–905.

Forget, H., & Cohen, H. (1994). Life after birth: The influence of steroid hormones on cerebral structure and function is not fixed prenatally. *Brain and Cognition, 26,* 243–248.

Fox, N. (1989). Psychophysiological correlates of emotional reactivity during the first year of life. *Developmental Psychology, 25*, 364–372.

Fox, N. (1994). Dynamic cerebral processes underlying emotion regulation. *Monographs of the Society for Research in Child Development, 59*, 152–166.

Fox, N., & Bell, M. (1990). Electrophysiological indices of frontal lobe development. *Annals of the New York Academy of Science, 608*, 677–698.

Fox, N., Coplan, R., Rubin, K., Porges, S., Calkins, S., Long, J., Marshall, T., & Stewart, S. (1995). Frontal activation asymmetry and social competence at four years of age. *Child Development, 66*, 1770–1784.

Frank, D., Roos, N., Meyers, A., Napoleone, M., Peterson, K., Cather, A., & Cupples, L. (1996). Seasonal variation in weight-for-age in a pediatric emergency room. *Public Health Reports, 111*, 366–371.

Frankel, D., & Roer-Bronstein, D. (1982). Traditional and modern contributions to changing infant-rearing ideologies of two ethnic communities. *Monographs of the Society for Research in Child Development, 47*(4, Serial No. 196).

Freitas, A., & Downey, G. (1998). Resilience: A dynamic perspective. *International Journal of Behavioral Development, 22*, 263–285.

Freund, L., Baumgardner, T., Mazzocco, M., & Reiss, A. (1995). *The influence of X chromosome genes on neurobehavioral function in females*. Paper presented at the annual meeting of the Society for Research in Child Development, Indianapolis, IN.

Fried, P. (1989). Postnatal consequences of maternal marijuana use in humans. In D. Hutchings (Ed.), *Prenatal abuse of licit and illicit drugs* (Vol. 562. Annals of the New York Academy of Sciences, pp. 123–132). New York: New York Academy of Sciences.

Friedman, H., Tucker, J., Schwartz, J., Tomlinson-Keasey, C., Martin, L., Wingard, D., & Criqui, M. (1995). Psychosocial and behavioral predictors of longevity. *American Psychologist, 50*, 69–78.

Friedman, J., Maarten, S., Streisel, I., & Sinnamon, H. (1968). Sensory restriction and isolation experiences of children with phenylketonuria. *Journal of Abnormal Psychology, 73*, 294–303.

Friedman, S., & Sigman, M. (1992). *The psychological development of low birthweight children*. Norwood, NJ: Ablex.

Frisancho, A. (1975). Functional adaptation to high altitude hypoxia. *Science, 187*, 313–319.

Frisancho, A., Frisancho, H., Milotick, M., Brutsaert, T., Albalak, R., Spielvogel, H., Villena, M., Vargas, E., & Soria, R. (1995). Developmental, genetic and environmental components of aerobic capacity at high altitude. *American Journal of Physical Anthropology, 96*, 431–442.

Fry, D. (1988). Intercommunity differences in aggression among Zapotec children. *Child Development, 59*, 1008–1019.

Fuchs, G. (1990). Secondary malnutrition in children. In R. Suskind & L. Lewinter-Suskind (Eds.), *The malnourished child* (pp. 23–36). New York: Raven Park Press.

Fuggle, P., & Graham, P. (1991). Metabolic/endocrine disorders and psychological functioning. In M. Rutter & P. Casaer (Ed.), *Biological risk factors for psychosocial disorders* (pp. 175–198). Cambridge, England: Cambridge University Press.

Fuligni, A. (1997). The academic achievement of adolescents from immigrant families. *Child Development, 68,* 351–363.

Fulker, D., Cherney, S., & Cardon, L. (1993). Continuity and change in cognitive development. In R. Plomin & G. McClearn (Eds.), *Nature, nurture, and psychology* (pp. 77–97). Washington, DC: American Psychological Association.

Funder, D., & Block, J. (1989). The role of ego-control, ego-resiliency, and IQ in delay of gratification in adolescence. *Journal of Personality and Social Psychology, 57,* 1041–1050.

Galler, J., & Propert, K. (1981a). Maternal behavior following the rehabilitation of rats from intergenerational malnutrition 1. *Journal of Nutrition, 111,* 1130–1136.

Galler, J., & Propert, K. (1981b). Maternal behavior following the rehabilitation of rats with intergenerational malnutrition 2. *Journal of Nutrition, 111,* 1377–1342.

Garbarino, J. (1990). The human ecology of early risk. In S. Meisels & J. Shonkoff (Eds.), *Handbook of early childhood intervention* (pp. 78–96). Cambridge, England: Cambridge University Press.

Garbarino, J., & Kostelny, K. (1996). The effects of political violence on Palestinian children's behavior problems. *Child Development, 67,* 33–45.

Garbarino, J., & Sherman, D. (1980). High risk neighborhoods and high risk families. *Child Development, 51,* 188–198.

Garcia-Coll, C., Crnic, K., Lamberty, G., Wasik, B., Jenkins, R., Garcia, H., & McAdoo, H. (1996). An integrative model for the study of developmental competencies in minority children. *Child Development, 67,* 1891–1914.

Garmezy, N., Masten, A., & Tellegen, A. (1984). The study of stress and competence in children. *Child Development, 55,* 97–111.

Gaskin, S. (1996). How Mayan parental theories come into play. In S. Harkness & C. Super (Eds.), *Parents' cultural belief systems* (pp. 345–363). New York: Guilford Press.

Gatz, M., Pedersen, N., Plomin, R., Nesselroade, J., & McClearn, G. (1992). Importance of shared genes and shared environment for symptoms of depression in older adults. *Journal of Abnormal Psychology, 101,* 701–708.

Gavida-Payne, S., & Stoneman, Z. (1997). Family predictors of maternal and paternal involvement in programs for young children with disabilities. *Child Development, 68,* 701–717.

Ge, X., Best, K., Conger, R., & Simons, R. (1996). Parenting behaviors and the occurrence and co-occurrence of adolescent depressive symptoms and conduct problems. *Developmental Psychology, 32,* 717–731.

Ge, X., Conger, R., Cadoret, R., Neiderhiser, J., Yates, W., Troughton, E., &

Stewart, M. (1996). The developmental interface between nature and nurture. *Developmental Psychology, 32,* 574–589.

Ge, X., Conger, R., & Elder, G. (1996). Coming of age too early: Pubertal influences on girls vulnerable to psychological distress. *Child Development, 67,* 3386–3400.

Ge, X., Lorenz, F., Conger, R., Elder, G., & Simons, R. (1994). Trajectories of stressful life events and depressive symptoms during adolescence. *Developmental Psychology, 30,* 467–483.

Georgieff, M. (1994). Nutritional deficiencies as developmental risk factors. In C. Nelson (Ed.), *Threats to optimal development* (pp. 142–159). Hillsdale, NJ: Erlbaum.

Gersten, M. (1989). Behavioral inhibition in the classroom. In J. Reznick (Ed.), *Perspectives on behavioral inhibition* (pp. 71–92). Chicago: University of Chicago Press.

Gjerde, P., Block, J., & Block, J. (1988). Depressive symptoms and personality during late adolescence. *Journal of Abnormal Psychology, 97,* 475–486.

Gleick, J. (1987). *Chaos: Making a new science.* New York: Viking.

Goduka, I., Poole, D., & Aotaki-Phenice, L. (1992). A comparative study of Black South African children from three different contexts. *Child Development, 63,* 509–525.

Goldberg, G., & Prentice, A. (1994). Maternal and fetal determinants of adult diseases. *Nutrition Reviews, 52,* 191–200.

Goldberg, S., & Marcovitch, S. (1989). Temperament in developmentally disabled children. In G. Kohnstamm, J. Bates, & M. Rothbart (Eds.), *Temperament in childhood* (pp. 387–404). New York: Wiley.

Golden, M. (1994). Is complete catch-up possible for stunted malnourished children? *European Journal of Clinical Nutrition, 48,* S58–S71.

Goldsmith, H. (1989). Behavior genetic approaches to temperament. In G. Kohnstamm, J. Bates, & M. Rothbart (Eds.), *Temperament and childhood* (pp. 111–132). New York: Wiley.

Goldstein, M. (1988). The family and psychopathology. *Annual Review of Psychology, 39,* 283–299.

Golub, M., Keen, C., Gershwin, M., & Hendricks, A. (1995). Developmental zinc deficiency and behavior. *Journal of Nutrition-Supplement, 125,* 2263S-2271S.

Goodman, R. (1989). Neuronal misconnections and psychiatric disorder. *British Journal of Psychiatry, 154,* 292–299.

Goodman, R. (1991a). Developmental disorders and structural brain development. In M. Rutter & P. Casaer (Eds.), *Biological risk factors for psychosocial disorders* (pp. 20–49). Cambridge, England: Cambridge University Press.

Goodman, R. (1991b). Growing together and growing apart: The nongenetic forces on children in same family. In P. McGuffin & R. Murray (Eds.), *The new genetics of mental illness* (pp. 212–224). Oxford, England: Butterworth: Heinemann.

Goodman, R. (1994). Brain development. In M. Rutter & D. Hay (Eds.), *Development through life* (pp. 49–78). Oxford, England: Blackwell.

Goodnow, J. (1985). Change and variation in ideas about childhood and parenting. In I. Sigel (Ed.), *Parental belief systems* (pp. 235–270). Hillsdale, NJ: Erlbaum.

Goodnow, J. (1988a). Children, families and communities. In N. Bolger, A. Caspi, G. Downey, & M. Moorehouse (Eds.), *Persons in context* (pp. 50–76). Cambridge, England: Cambridge University Press.

Goodnow, J. (1988b). Parents' ideas, actions and feelings. *Child Development, 59,* 286–320.

Goodnow, J. (1992). Parents' ideas, children's ideas. In I. Sigel, A. DeLisi, & J. Goodnow (Eds.), *Parental belief systems* (pp. 293–318). Hillsdale, NJ: Erlbaum.

Goodnow, J. (1996). From household practices to parents' ideas about work and interpersonal relationships. In S. Harkness & C. Super (Eds.), *Parents' cultural belief systems* (pp. 313–344). New York: Guilford Press.

Goodwin, B. (1985). Constructional biology. In G. Butterworth, J. Rutkowska, & M. Scaire (Eds.), *Evolution and developmental psychology* (pp. 45–66). Sussex, England: Harvester.

Goodwin, B. (1987). Developing organisms as self-organizing fields. In F. Yates (Ed.), *Self-organizing systems* (pp. 167–180). New York: Plenum Press.

Gore, S., & Eckenrode, J. (1994). Context and process in research on risk and resilience. In R. Haggerty, L. Sherrod, N. Garmezy, & M. Rutter (Eds.), *Stress, risk, and resilience in children and adolescents* (pp. 19–63). Cambridge, England: Cambridge University Press.

Gorman, K. (1995). Malnutrition and cognitive development: Evidence from experimental/quasi-experimental studies among the mild-to-moderately malnourished. *Journal of Nutrition, 125*(Suppl. 85), 2239S–2244S.

Gorman, K., & Pollitt, E. (1992). School efficiency in rural Guatemala. *International Review of Education, 38,* 519–534.

Gorman, K., & Pollitt, E. (1996). Does schooling buffer the effects of early risk? *Child Development, 67,* 314–326.

Gorman, K., & Pollitt, E. (1997). The contributions of schooling to literacy in Guatemala. *International Review of Education, 43,* 283–298.

Gottesman, I. (1993). Origins of schizophrenia. In R. Plomin & G. McClearn (Eds.), *Nature, nurture, and psychology* (pp. 231–244). Washington, DC: American Psychological Association.

Gottesman, I., & Goldsmith, H. (1994). Developmental psychopathology of antisocial behavior. In C. Nelson (Ed.), *Threats to optimal development* (pp. 69–104). Hillsdale, NJ: Erlbaum.

Gottfried, A., Hodgman, J., & Brown, K. (1984). How intensive is newborn intensive care? *Pediatrics, 74,* 292–294.

Gottlieb, G. (1987). The developmental basis of evolutionary change. *Journal of Comparative Psychology, 101,* 262–271.

Gottlieb, G. (1992). *Individual development and evolution*. New York: Oxford University Press.

Gottman, J. (1991). Chaos and regulated change in families. In P. Cowan & M. Hetherington (Eds.), *Family transitions* (pp. 247–272). Hillsdale, NJ: Erlbaum.

Gould, S. (1980). Sociobiology and the theory of natural selection. In G. Barlow & J. Silverberg (Eds.), *Sociobiology: Beyond nature/nurture* (pp. 257–269). Boulder, CO: Westview Press.

Gould, S. (1981). *The mismeasure of man*. New York: Norton.

Gould, S. (1982). Darwinism and the expansion of evolutionary theory. *Science, 216*, 380–387.

Gould, S. (1989). *Wonderful life: The Burgess Shale and the nature of history*. New York: Norton.

Gould, S. (1991). Exaptation: A crucial tool for an evolutionary psychology. *Journal of Social Issues, 47*, 43–65.

Graber, J., Brooks-Gunn, J., & Warren, M. (1995). The antecedents of menarcheal age. *Child Development, 66*, 356–359.

Graham, P. (1984). Specific medical syndromes. In M. Rutter (Ed.), *Developmental neuropsychiatry* (pp. 68–82). Edinburgh, Scotland: Churchill-Livingstone.

Grantham-McGregor, S. (1993). Assessments of the effects of nutrition on mental development and behavior in Jamaican studies. *American Journal of Clinical Nutrition Supplement, 57*, 303S–309S.

Grantham-McGregor, S. (1995). A review of studies of the effect of severe malnutrition on mental development. *Journal of Nutrition, 125(Suppl.)*, 2233S–2238S.

Grantham-McGregor, S. (1998). Small for gestational age term babies in the first 6 years of life. *European Journal of Clinical Nutrition, 52(Suppl.)*, S59–S64.

Grantham-McGregor, S., Chang, S., & Walker, S. (1998). Evaluation of school feeding programs. *American Journal of Clinical Nutrition, 67(Suppl.)*, 785S–789S.

Grantham-McGregor, S., Fernald, L., & Sethuraman, K. (1999). Effects of health and nutrition on cognitive and behavioral development in children in the first three years of life. Part 2: Infectious and micronutrient deficiencies: Iodine, iron, and zinc. *Food and Nutrition Bulletin, 20*, 76–99.

Grantham-McGregor, S., Lira, P., Ashworth, A., Morris, S., & Assuncao, A. (1998). The development of low birthweight term infants and the effects of the environment in Northeast Brazil. *Journal of Pediatrics, 132*, 661–666.

Grantham-McGregor, S., Powell, C., Walker, S., Chang, S., & Fletcher, P. (1994). The long term follow-up of severely malnourished children who participated in an intervention program. *Child Development, 65*, 428–439.

Grantham-McGregor, S., & Walker, S. (1998). Health and nutritional determinants of school failure. In *nutrition health and child development* (Pan-American Scientific Monographs No. 566). Washington, DC: Pan-American Health Organization.

Gray, J. (1994). The neuropsychology of temperament. In J. Strelau & A. Angleitner (Eds.), *Exploration in temperament* (pp. 105–128). New York: Plenum Press.

Greenberg, M., Carmichael-Olson, H., & Crnic, K. (1992). The development and social competence of a preterm sample at age 4. In S. Friedman & M. Sigman (Eds.), *The psychological development of low birthweight children* (pp. 125–156). Norwood, NJ: Ablex.

Greenberg, M., Spelz, M., & DeKlyen, M. (1993). The role of attachment in the early development of disruptive behavior problems. *Development and Psychopathology, 5,* 191–213.

Greenberger, E., & Chen, C. (1996). Perceived family relationship and depressed mood in early and later adolescence. *Developmental Psychology, 32,* 707–716.

Greenfield, P., & Childs, C. (1991). Developmental continuity in bicultural context. In R. Cohen & A. Siegel (Eds.), *Context and development* (pp. 135–160). Hillsdale, NJ: Erlbaum.

Greenough, W., & Black, J. (1992). Induction of brain structure by experience. In M. Gunnar & C. Nelson (Eds.), *Developmental behavioral neuroscience* (pp. 155–192). Hillsdale, NJ: Erlbaum.

Greenough, W., Black, K., Chang, F., & Sirevang, A. (1990). Might different brain information storage processes at different developmental ages affect compensation for early developmental disabilities? In W. Fraser (Ed.), *Key issues in mental retardation research* (pp. 46–56). London: Routledge.

Greenough, W., Black, K., & Wallace, C. (1987). Experience and brain development. *Child Development, 58,* 539–559.

Groff, J., Gropper, S., & Hunt, S. (1995). *Advanced nutrition and human metabolism* (2nd ed.). Minneapolis, MN: West.

Gross, R., Brooks-Gunn, J., & Spiker, D. (1992). Efficacy of comprehensive early intervention for low birthweight premature infants and their families. In S. Friedman & M. Sigman (Eds.), *The psychological development of low birthweight children* (pp. 411–434). Norwood, NJ: Ablex.

Gruber, H. (1985). Divergence in evolution and individuality in development. In G. Butterworth, J. Rutkowska, & M. Scaire (Eds.), *Evolution and developmental psychology* (pp. 133–147). Sussex, England: Harvester.

Grundman, M. (1996). Historical context of father absence. *International Journal of Behavioral Development, 19,* 415–431.

Gualtieri, T. (1987). Fetal antigenicity and maternal immunoreactivity: Factors in mental retardation. In S. Schroeder (Ed.), *Toxic substances and mental retardation* (Monographs of the American Association on Mental Deficiency, Vol. 8, pp. 37–70). Washington, DC: American Association on Mental Deficiency.

Guilarte, T. (1993). Vitamin B_6 and cognitive development. *Nutritional Review, 51,* 193–198.

Guisinger, S., & Blatt, S. (1994). Individuality and relatedness. *American Psychologist, 49,* 104–111.

Gunnar, M. (1994). Psychoendocrine studies of temperament and stress in early childhood. In J. Bates & T. D. Wachs (Eds.), *Temperament: Individual differences at the interface of biology and behavior* (pp. 175–198). Washington, DC: American Psychological Association.

Gustafson, S. (1994). Female underachievement and overachievement: Parental contributions and long-term consequences. *International Journal of Behavioral Development, 17,* 469–484.

Gutierrez, J., & Sameroff, A. (1990). Determinants of complexity in Mexican-American and Anglo-American mothers' conception of child development. *Child Development, 61,* 384–394.

Haas, J., Murdoch, S., Rivera, J., & Martorell, R. (1996). Early nutrition and physical work capacity. *Nutrition Reviews, 54,* 541–548.

Hack, M. (1998). Effects of intrauterine growth retardation on mental performance and behavior outcomes during adolescence and adulthood. *European Journal of Clinical Nutrition 52(Suppl.),* S65–S70.

Hack, M., Breslau, N., Aram, D., Weissman, B., Klein, N., & Borawski-Clark, E. (1992). The effect of very low birth weight and social risk on neurocognitive abilities at school age. *Journal of Developmental and Behavioral Pediatrics, 13,* 412–420.

Hack, M., Friedman, H., & Fanaroff, A. (1996). Outcomes of extremely low birth weight infants. *Pediatrics, 98,* 931–937.

Hack, M., Klein, N., & Taylor, H. (1995). Long-term developmental outcomes of low birth weight infants. *Future of Children, 5,* 176–196.

Hack, M., Weissman, B., Breslau, N., Klein, N., Borawski-Clark, E., & Fanaroff, A. (1993). Health of very low birth weight children during their first eight years. *Journal of Pediatrics, 122,* 887–892.

Hagerman, R. (1996). Biomedical advances in developmental psychology: The case of fragile X syndrome. *Developmental Psychology, 32,* 416–424.

Hallberg, L. (1989). Search for nutritional confounding factors in the relationship between iron deficiency and brain function. *American Journal of Clinical Nutrition, 50,* 598–606.

Halpern, D. (1997). Sex differences in intelligence. *American Psychologist, 52,* 1091–1102.

Hambidge, K. (1997). Zinc deficiency in young children. *American Journal of Clinical Nutrition, 65,* 160–161.

Hampson, E. (1990). Variations in sex-related cognitive abilities across the menstrual cycle. *Brain and Cognition, 14,* 26–43.

Hampson, E., & Kimura, D. (1988). Reciprocal effect of hormonal fluctuations in human motor and perceptual–spatial skills. *Behavioral Neuroscience, 102,* 456–459.

Hamvas, A., Wise, P., Yang, R., Wampler, N., Noguchi, A., Maurer, M., Walentik, C., Schramm, W., & Cole, F. (1996). The influence of the wider use of surfactant therapy on neonatal mortality among Blacks and Whites. *New England Journal of Medicine, 334,* 1635–1640.

Hans, S. (1995, March). *Effects of prenatal drug exposure on sustained attention*. Paper presented at the annual meeting of the Society for Research in Child Development, Indianapolis, IN.

Harding, R., & Looney, J. (1977). Problems of southeast Asian children in a refugee camp. *American Journal of Psychiatry, 134*, 407–411.

Hardy-Brown, K. (1983). Universals and individual differences. *Developmental Psychology, 19*, 610–624.

Harkness, S., & Super, C. (1992). Parental ethnotheories in action. In I. Sigel, A. DeLisi, & J. Goodnow (Eds.), *Parental belief systems* (2nd ed., pp. 373–393). Hillsdale, NJ: Erlbaum.

Harnish, J., Dodge, K., & Valente, E. (1995). Mother–child interaction quality as a partial mediator of the roles of maternal depressive symptomatology and socioeconomic status in the development of child behavior problems. *Child Development, 66*, 739–753.

Harnish, J., Dodge, K., Valente, E., & Conduct Problems Prevention Research Group. (1995). Mother–child interaction quality as a potential mediator of the role of maternal depressive symptomatology and socioeconomic status in the development of child behavior problems. *Child Development, 66*, 739–753.

Harris, J. (1995). Where is the child's environment? A group socialization theory of development. *Psychological Review, 102*, 458–489.

Harrison, A., Wilson, M., Pine, C., Chan, S., & Buriel, R. (1990). Family ecologies of ethnic minority children. *Child Development, 61*, 347–362.

Harrison, G., & Schmitt, L. (1989). Variability in growth stature. *Annals of Human Biology, 16*, 45–51.

Hart, C., Nelson, D., Robinson, C., Olsen, S., & McNeilly-Chogue, M. (1998). Overt and relational aggression in Russian nursery school age children. *Developmental Psychology, 34*, 687–697.

Hartup, W., & van Lieshout, C. (1995). Personality development in social context. *Annual Review of Psychology, 46*, 655–687.

Hasan, K. (1977). Effect on child mental health of psychosocial change in developing countries. *International Journal of Mental Health, 6*, 49–57.

Hauser-Cram, P., Pierson, D., Walker, D., & Tivan, T. (1991). *Early education in the public schools*. San Francisco: Jossey-Bass.

Hayley, T., & Disney, E. (1992). Crack's children: The consequences of maternal cocaine abuse. *Society for Research in Child Development Social Policy Report, 6*(4).

Henry, B., Caspi, A., Moffitt, T., & Silva, P. (1996). Temperamental and familial predictors of violent and nonviolent criminal convictions from age 3 to age 18. *Developmental Psychology, 32*, 614–623.

Henry, B., Moffitt, T., Robins, L., Earls, F., & Silva, P. (1993). Early family predictors of child and adolescent antisocial behavior. *Criminal Behavior and Mental Health, 3*, 97–118.

Herdt, G., & Davidson, J. (1988). The Sambia "Turnim-man." Sociocultural and clinical aspects of gender-formation in male pseudohermaphrodites with

5-alpha-reductase deficiency in Papua, New Guinea. *Archives of Sexual Behavior,* *17,* 33–56.

Hertgaard, L., Gunnar, M., Erickson, M., & Nachmias, M. (1995). Adrenocortical responses to the strange situation in infants with disorganized attachment relations. *Child Development, 66,* 1100–1106

Hess, R., Kashiwagi, K., Azuma, H., Price, G., & Dickson, W. (1980). Maternal expectations for mastery of developmental tasks in Japan and the United States. *International Journal of Psychology, 15,* 259–271.

Hetherington, E. (1989). Coping with family transitions. *Child Development, 60,* 1–14.

Hewlett, B., Lamb, M., Shannon, D., Leyendecker, B., & Scholmerich, A. (1998). Culture and early infancy among Central African foragers and farmers *Developmental Psychology, 34,* 653–661.

Heywood, A., Oppenheimer, S., Heywood, P., & Jolley, D. (1989). Behavioral effects of iron supplementation in infants in Madang, Papua, New Guinea. *American Journal of Clinical Nutrition, 50,* 630–640.

Hinde, R. (1987). *Individuals, relationships and culture.* Cambridge, MA: Cambridge University Press.

Hinde, R. (1989). Ethological and relationship approaches. *Annals of Child Development, 6,* 251–285.

Hinde, R. (1990). The interdependence of the behavioral sciences. *Philosophical Transactions of the Royal Society of London: Series B—Biological Sciences, 329,* 217–227.

Hinde, R. (1991). When is an evolutionary approach useful? *Child Development, 62,* 671–675.

Hodges, J., & Tizard, B. (1989a). IQ and behavioral adjustment of ex-institutional adolescents. *Journal of Child Psychology and Psychiatry, 30,* 53–75.

Hodges, J., & Tizard, B. (1989b). Social and family relationships of ex-institutional adolescents. *Journal of Child Psychology and Psychiatry, 30,* 77–97.

Hofer, M. (1994). Hidden regulators in attachment, separation and loss. *Monographs of the Society for Research in Child Development, 59,* 192–207.

Hoffman, L. (1988). Cross-cultural differences in child rearing goals. In R. LeVine, P. Miller, & M. West (Eds.), *Parental behavior in diverse societies* (pp. 99–122). San Francisco: Jossey-Bass.

Hoffman, L. (1991). The influence of the family environment on personality. *Psychological Bulletin, 110,* 187–203.

Holaday, B., Swan, J., & Turner-Henson, A. (1997). Images of the neighborhood and activity patterns of chronically ill school age children. *Environment and Behavior, 29,* 348–373.

Holden, G., & West, M. (1990). Proximate regulation by mothers. *Child Development, 60,* 64–69.

Holloman, H., Dobbins, D., & Scott, K. (in press). The effect of biological and social risk factors in special education placement. *Research in Developmental Disabilities.*

Holloway, S. (1986). The relationship of mother's beliefs to children's mathematics achievement. *Merrill Palmer Quarterly, 32,* 231–250.

Holloway, S., & Gorman, K. (1988). Child rearing beliefs within diverse social structures. *International Journal of Psychology, 23,* 303–327.

Homel, R., Burns, A., & Goodnow, J. (1987). Parental social networks and child development. *Journal of Social and Personal Relationships, 4,* 159–177.

Hooker, K. (1991). Change and stability in self during the transition to retirement. *International Journal of Behavioral Development, 14,* 209–233.

Horowitz, F. (1987). *Exploring developmental theories.* Hillsdale, NJ: Erlbaum.

Horowitz, F. (1992). The concept of risk. In S. Friedman & M. Sigman (Eds.), *The psychological development of low-birthweight children* (pp. 61–90). Norwood, NJ: Ablex.

Howe, G., Feinstein, C., Reiss, D., Molock, S., & Berger, K. (1993). Adolescent adjustment to chronic physical disorders: I. Comparing neurological and non-neurological conditions. *Journal of Child Psychology and Psychiatry, 34,* 1153–1171.

Howrigan, G. (1988). Fertility, infant feeding and change in Yucatan. In R. LeVine, P. Miller, & M. Maxwell (Eds.), *Parental behavior in diverse societies* (pp. 37–50). San Francisco: Jossey-Bass.

Huber, A. (1991). Nutrition and mental retardation. In J. Matson & J. Mulick (Eds.), *Handbook of mental retardation* (2nd ed., pp. 308–326). Elmsford, NY: Pergamon Press.

Hunt, J., Tooley, W., & Cooper, B. (1992). Further investigations of intellectual status at age 8 years. In S. Friedman & M. Sigman (Eds.), *The psychological development of low-birthweight children* (pp. 315–337). Norwood, NJ: Ablex.

Hurtado, E., Claussen, A., & Scott, K. (1999). Early childhood anemia and mild or moderate mental retardation. *American Journal of Clinical Nutrition, 69,* 115–119.

Huttunen, M., & Niskanen, P. (1978). Prenatal loss of fathers and psychiatric disorders. *Archives of General Psychiatry, 35,* 429–431.

Immink, M. (1988). Methodology of field studies related to socioeconomic effects of chronic energy deficiency. In B. Schurch & N. Schrimshaw (Eds.), *Chronic energy deficiency* (pp. 153–174). Lausanne, Switzerland: International Dietary Energy Correlative Group.

Imperato-McGinley, J., Peterson, R., Gautier, T., & Sturla, E. (1979). Androgens and the evolution of male-gender identity among male pseudohermaphrodites with 5 alpha reductase deficiency. *New England Journal of Medicine, 300,* 1233–1237.

Infant Health and Development Program. (1990). Enhancing the outcomes of low birth weight premature infants. *Journal of the American Medical Association, 263,* 3035–3042.

Irons, W. (1980). Is Yomut social behavior adaptive? In G. Barlow & J. Silverberg (Eds.), *Sociobiology: Beyond nature/nurture* (pp. 417–463). Boulder, CO: Westview Press.

Isabella, R. (1993). Origins of attachment. *Child Development, 64*, 605–621.

Israel, M. (1987). Autosomal supressor gene for fragile X: An hypothesis. *American Journal of Medical Genetics, 26*, 19–31.

Jacklin, C. (1989). Female and male issues of gender. *American Psychologist, 44*, 127–133.

Jacklin, C., & Reynolds, C. (1993). Gender and childhood socialization. In A. Beall & R. Sternberg (Eds.), *The psychology of gender* (pp. 197–214). New York: Guilford Press.

Jacob, R. (1998). Individual variability in homocysteine response to folate depletion. *Nutrition Reviews, 56*, 212–217.

Jacobson, J., Boersma, D., Fields, R., & Olson, K. (1983). Paralinguistic features of adult speech to infants and small children. *Child Development, 54*, 436–442.

Jacobson, J., Jacobson, S., Fein, G., Schwartz, P., & Dowler, J. (1984). Prenatal exposure to an environmental toxin. *Developmental Psychology, 20*, 523–532.

Jacobson, J., Jacobson, S., Padgett, R., Brumitt, G., & Billings, R. (1992). Effects of prenatal PCB exposure on cognitive processing efficiency and sustained attention. *Developmental Psychology, 28*, 297–306.

Jacobvitz, D., & Bush, N. (1996). Reconstruction of family relationships. *Developmental Psychology, 32*, 732–743.

Jacoby, E., Cueto, S., & Pollitt, E. (1996). Benefits of a school breakfast program among Andean children in Huarez. *Food and Nutrition Bulletin, 17*, 54–64.

Joffe, J. (1982). Approaches to prevention of adverse developmental consequences of genetic and prenatal factors. In L. Bond & J. Joffe (Eds.), *Facilitating infant and early childhood development*. Hanover, NH: University Press of New England.

Johnson, S. (1988). Psychological aspects of childhood diabetes. *Journal of Child Psychology and Psychiatry, 29*, 729–738.

Jones, C., & Nesselroade, J., (1990). Multivariate replicated single subject repeated measures designs and *P* technique factor analysis. *Experimental Aging Research, 16*, 171–183.

Jones, C., Nesselroade, J., & Birkel, R. (1991). Examination of staffing level effects in the family household. *Journal of Environmental Psychology, 11*, 59–73.

Jose, P., Anna, C., Cafasso, L., Bryant, F., Chiker, V., Gein, N., & Zhezner, N. (1998). Stress and coping among urban Russian and American early adolescents. *Developmental Psychology, 34*, 757–769.

Juraska, J. (1990). The structure of the rat cerebral cortex: Effects of gender and the environment. In B. Kolb & R. Tees (Eds.), *The cerebral cortex of the rat* (pp. 483–505). Cambridge, MA: MIT Press.

Kagan, J. (1994). On the nature of emotion. *Monographs of the Society for Research in Child Development, 59*(2–3, Serial No. 240).

Kagan, J., Arcus, D., & Snidman, N. (1993). The idea of temperament: Where do we go from here? In R. Plomin & G. McClearn (Eds.), *Nature, nurture, and psychology* (pp. 197–212). Washington, DC: American Psychological Association.

Kagan, S., & Ender, P. (1975). Maternal response to success and failure of Anglo-American, Mexican-American and Mexican children. *Child Development, 46,* 452–458.

Kagitcibasi, C. (1989). Family and socialization in a cross-cultural perspective. *Nebraska Symposium on Motivation, 37,* 135–200.

Kagitcibasi, C. (1990). Family and home based intervention. In R. Brislin (Ed.), *Family and home based intervention* (pp. 121–141). Newbury Park, CA: Sage.

Kagitcibasi, C., & Berry, J. (1989). Cross-cultural psychology. *Annual Review of Psychology, 40,* 493–532.

Kandel, D. (1978). Homophily, selection and socialization in adolescent friendships. *American Journal of Sociology, 84,* 427–436.

Kandel, E., Brennan, P., Mednick, S., & Michelson, N. (1989). Minor physical anomalies and recidivistic adult violent criminal behavior. *Acta Psychiatrica Scandanavia, 79,* 103–107.

Kandel, E., & Mednick, S. (1991). Perinatal complications predict violent offending. *Criminology, 29,* 519–529.

Kandel, E., Mednick, S., Sorenson, L., Hutchings, B., Knop, J., Rosenberg, R., & Schulsinger, F. (1988). IQ as a protective factor for subjects at high risk for antisocial behavior. *Journal of Consulting and Clinical Psychology, 56,* 224–226.

Kaniel, S., & Fisherman, S. (1991). Level of performance and distribution of errors in the Progressive Matrices Test. *International Journal of Psychology, 26,* 25–33.

Kaplan, B. (1988). The relevance of food for children's cognitive and behavioral health. *Canadian Journal of Behavioral Sciences, 20,* 359–373.

Kaplan, H., & Dove, H. (1987). Infant development among the Ache of Eastern Paraguay. *Developmental Psychology, 23,* 190–198.

Kaplan-Sanoff, S., & Leib, A. (1995). Model intervention programs for mothers and children impacted by substance abuse. *School Psychology Review, 24,* 186–199.

Karlberg, J., Jalil, F., Lam., B., Low, L., & Yeung, C. (1994). Linear growth retardation in relation to three phases of growth. *European Journal of Clinical Nutrition-Supplement, 48,* S25–S34.

Karp, R. (1993). *Malnourished children in the United States.* New York: Springer.

Karp, R., Qazi, Q., Hittleman, J., & Chabrier, L. (1993). Fetal alcohol syndrome. In R. Karp (Ed.), *Malnourished children in the United States* (pp. 101–108). New York: Springer.

Keele, S., & Ivry, R. (1990). Does the cerebellum provide a common computation for diverse tasks? *Annals of the New York Academy of Sciences, 608,* 179–211.

Keller, E. (1987). Reproduction and the central project of evolutionary theory. *Biology and Philosophy, 2,* 383–396.

Kelly, G. (1955). *The psychology of personal constructs.* New York: Norton.

Kendler, K., & Eaves, J. (1986). Models for the joint effect of genotype and environment on liability to psychiatric illness. *American Journal of Psychiatry, 14,* 279–289.

Kendler, K., Kessler, R., Walters, E., MacLean, C., Neale, M., Heath, A., & Eaves, L. (1995). Stressful life events, genetic liability and onset of an episode of major depression in women. *American Journal of Psychiatry, 152,* 833–842.

Kendler, K., Neale, M., Kessler, R., Heath, A., & Eaves, L. (1992). Childhood parental loss and adult psychopathology in women. *Archives of General Psychiatry, 49,* 109–116.

Kermoian, R., & Campos, J. (1988). Locomotor experience: A facilitator of spatial–cognitive development. *Child Development, 59,* 908–917.

Kerr, M. (1996, June). *Temperament and culture.* Paper presented to the Netherlands Institute for Advanced Studies at the Conference on Temperament in Context, Wassenaer, The Netherlands.

Kerr, M., Lambert, W., & Bem, D. (1996). Life course sequelae of childhood shyness in Sweden. *Developmental Psychology, 32,* 1100–1105.

Keusch, G. (1977). Impact of infection on nutrition status. *American Journal of Clinical Nutrition, 30,* 1233–1235.

Keusch, G. (1990). Malnutrition, infection and immune function. In R. Suskind & L. Lewinter-Suskind (Eds.), *The malnourished child* (pp. 37–55). New York: Raven Press.

Killackey, H. (1990). Neocortical expansion. *Journal of Cognitive Neuroscience, 2,* 1–17.

Kim, U. (1990). Indigenous psychology. In R. Brislin (Ed.), *Applied cross-cultural psychology* (pp. 142–160). Newbury Park, CA: Sage.

Kim, U., & Chun, M. (1994). Educational "success" of Asian-Americans. *Journal of Applied Developmental Psychology, 15,* 329–343.

Kimura, D. (1987). Are men's and women's brains really different? *Canadian Psychology, 28,* 133–147.

Kindermann, T. (1993). Natural peer groups as contexts for individual development. *Developmental Psychology, 29,* 970–977.

Kinzie, J., Sack, W., Angell, R., & Rath, B. (1986). The psychiatric effects of massive trauma on Cambodian children. *Journal of the American Academy of Child Psychiatry, 25,* 377–383.

Kirksey, A., Rahmanifar, A., Wachs, T. D., McCabe, G., Bassily, N., Bishry, Z., Galal, O., Harrison, G., & Jerome, N. (1991). Determinants of pregnancy outcome and newborn behavior of a semirural Egyptian population. *American Journal of Clinical Nutrition, 49,* 657–667.

Kirksey, A., Wachs, T. D., Srinath, U., Rahmanifar, A., McCabe, G., Galal, O., Bassily, N., Bishry, Z., Yunis, F., Harrison, G., & Jerome, N. (1994). Relation of maternal zinc nutriture to pregnancy outcome and early infant development in an Egyptian village. *American Journal of Clinical Nutrition, 60,* 782-792.

Kitcher, P. (1985). *Vaulting ambition.* Cambridge, MA: MIT Press.

Klebanoff, M., Meirik, O., & Berendes, H. (1989). Second generation consequences of small for date births. *Pediatrics, 84,* 343–347.

Kleinman, J. (1992). The epidemiology of low birthweight. In S. Friedman & M. Sigman (Eds.), *The psychological development of low birthweight children* (pp. 21–36). Norwood, NJ: Ablex.

Kobayashi-Winata, H., & Power, T. (1989). Child rearing and compliance. *Journal of Cross-Cultural Psychology, 20,* 333–356.

Kochanska, G. (1990). Maternal beliefs as long-term predictors of mother–child interaction and report. *Child Development, 61,* 1934–1943.

Kochanska, G. (1993). Toward a synthesis of parental socialization and child temperament in early development of conscience. *Child Development, 64,* 325–347.

Kochanska, G. (1995). Children's temperament, mothers' discipline and security of attachment: Multiple pathways to emerging internalization. *Child Development, 66,* 597–615.

Kochanska, G., Murray, K., & Coy, K. (1997). Inhibitory control as a contributor to conscience in childhood. *Child Development, 68,* 263–277.

Kohn, M. (1983). Unresolved interpretative issues. In M. Kohn & C. Schooler (Eds.), *Work and personality* (pp. 296–314). Norwood, NJ: Ablex.

Kohn, M., & Schooler, C. (1983). *Work and personality.* Norwood, NJ: Ablex.

Kohnstamm, G., Halverson, C., Havill, V., & Mervielde, I. (1996). Parents free descriptions of child characteristics. In S. Harkness & C. Super (Eds.), *Parents' cultural belief systems* (pp. 27–55). New York: Guilford Press.

Kostelny, K., & Garbarino, J. (1994). Coping with the consequences of living in danger. *International Journal of Behavioral Development, 17,* 595–611.

Krassner, M. (1986). Diet and brain function. *Nutrition Reviews Supplement, 44,* 12–15.

Krebs, D. (1996). The value of evolutionary perspectives on social relations among children. *International Journal of Behavioral Development, 19,* 75–80.

Kuczynski, L., & Kochanska, G. (1995). Function and content of maternal demands. *Child Development, 66,* 616–628.

Kuhl, P., Andruski, J., Chistovich, I., Chistovich, L., Kozhevnikova, E., Ryskina, V., Stolyarova, E., Sundberg, U., & Lacerda, F. (1997). Cross-language analysis of phonetic units in language addressed to infants. *Science, 277,* 684–686.

Kuhn, T. (1970). *The structure of scientific revolutions* (2nd ed.). Chicago: University of Chicago Press.

Kupersmidt, J., Griesler, P., DeRosier, M., Patterson, C., & Davis, P. (1995). Childhood aggression and peer relations in the context of family and neighborhood factors. *Child Development, 66,* 360–375.

Kvalsvig, J., & Becker, P. (1988). Selective exposure of active and sociable children to schistosomiasis. *Annals of Tropical Medicine and Parasitology, 82,* 471–474.

Ladd, G., & Cairns, E. (1996). Children: Ethnic and political violence. *Child Development, 67,* 14–18.

LaFromboise, T., Coleman, H., & Gerton, J. (1993). Psychological impact of biculturalism. *Psychological Bulletin, 114,* 395–412.

Lahey, B., McBurnett, K., Loeber, R., & Hart, E. (1995). Psychobiology. In P. Sholevar (Ed.), *Conduct disorders in children and adolescents* (pp. 27–44). Washington, DC: American Psychiatric Press.

Landry, S., Smith, K., Miller-Loncar, C., & Swank, P. (1998). The relation of change in maternal interactive style to the developing social competence of full term and preterm children. *Child Development, 69*, 105–123.

Landsberg, C., & Young, J. (1983). The role of the sympathetic nervous system and catecholamines in the regulation of energy metabolism. *American Journal of Clinical Nutrition, 38*, 1018–1024.

Langlois, J., Ritter, J., Casey, R., & Sawin, D. (1995). Infant attractiveness predicts maternal behavior and attitudes. *Developmental Psychology, 31*, 464–472.

Langmeier, J., & Matejcek, Z. (1975). *Psychological deprivation in childhood.* New York: Wiley.

Largo, R., Pfister, D., Molinari, L., Knundu, S., Lipp, A., & Duc, G. (1989). Significance of prenatal, perinatal and postnatal factors in the development of AGA preterm infants at five to seven years. *Developmental Medicine and Child Neurology, 31*, 440–456.

Latham, M. (1998). Policy implications of the effects of health and nutrition on child development. In *Nutrition, health and child development* (Pan-American Health Organization Scientific Monograph, No. 566). Washington, DC: Pan-American Health Organization.

Lau, S., & Cheung, P. (1987). Relations between Chinese adolescents' perception of parental control and organization and their perception of parental warmth. *Developmental Psychology, 23*, 726–729.

Launer, L., & Habicht, J. (1989). Concepts about infant health, growth, and weaning: A comparison between nutritional scientists and Madurese mothers. *Social Science and Medicine, 29*, 13–22.

Lavigne, J., Faier, R., & Routman, J. (1992). Psychological adjustment to pediatric physical disorders. *Journal of Pediatric Psychology, 17*, 133–157.

Lawton, M. (1999). Environmental taxonomy: Generalizations from research with older adults. In S. Friedman & T. D. Wachs (Eds.), *Measuring environment across the life span* (pp. 91–126). Washington, DC: American Psychological Association.

Lee, L., & Zhan, Q. (1991). Political socialization and parental values in the Peoples Republic of China. *International Journal of Behavioral Development, 14*, 337–373.

Leftwich, M., & Collins, F. (1994). Parental smoking, depression and child development. *Journal of Pediatric Psychology, 19*, 557–569.

Leiderman, J. (1988). Misconceptions and new conceptions about early brain damage, functional asymmetry and behavioral outcome. In D. Molfese & S. Segalowitz (Eds.), *Brain lateralization in children* (pp. 375–399). New York: Guilford Press.

Lepore, S., Evans, G., & Schneider, M. (1991). Dynamic role of social support in the link between chronic stress and psychological distress. *Journal of Personality and Social Psychology, 61*, 899–909.

Lepowsky, M. (1987). Food taboos and child survival. In N. Scheper-Hughes (Ed.), *Child survival* (pp. 71–92). Dordrecht, The Netherlands: Reidel.

Lerner, R. (1984). *On the nature of human plasticity*. New York: Cambridge University Press.

Leslie, J. (1989). Women's work and child nutrition in the third world. In J. Leslie & M. Paolisso (Eds.), *Women, work and child welfare in the third world* (pp. 19–40). Boulder, CO: Westview.

Lester, B., & Brazelton, T. (1982). Cross-cultural assessment of neonatal behavior. In D. Wagner & H. Stevenson (Eds.), *Cultural perspectives on child development* (pp. 20–53). San Francisco: Freemont.

LeVine, R. (1988). Parental care. In R. LeVine, P. Miller, & M. West (Eds.), *Parental behavior in diverse societies* (pp. 3–10). San Francisco: Jossey-Bass.

LeVine, R. (1989). Cultural environments in child development. In W. Damon (Ed.), *Child development today and tomorrow* (pp. 52–68). San Francisco: Jossey-Bass.

LeVine, R., & LeVine, S. (1988). Parental strategies among the Gusii of Kenya. In R. LeVine, P. Miller, & M. West (Eds.), *Parental behavior in diverse societies* (pp. 27–36). San Francisco: Jossey-Bass.

LeVine, R., Miller, P., Richman, A., & LeVine, S. (1996). Education and mother–infant interaction. In S. Harkness & C. Super (Eds.), *Parents' cultural belief systems* (pp. 254–269). New York: Guilford Press.

Levins, R. (1973). The limits of complexity. In H. Pattee (Ed.), *Hierarchy theory: The challenge of complex systems* (pp. 111–127). New York: Braziller.

Levitsky, D., & Strupp, B. (1995). Malnutrition and the brain. *Journal of Nutrition, 125*(Suppl. 85), 2212S–2220S.

Levy, R. (1996). Essential contrasts: Differences in parental ideas about learning and teaching in Tahiti and Nepal. In S. Harkness & C. Super (Eds.), *Parents' cultural belief systems* (pp. 123–142). New York: Guilford Press.

Levy-Shiff, R. (1982). The effects of father absence on young children in mother headed families. *Child Development, 53*, 1400–1405.

Lewin, K. (1952). *Field theory in social science*. London: Social Science Paperbacks.

Lewis, M. (1995). Cognition–emotion feedback and the self-organization of developmental paths. *Human Development, 38*, 71–102.

Lewis, M., Ramsay, D., & Kawakami, K. (1993). Differences between Japanese infants and Caucasian American infants in the behavioral and cortisol response to inoculation. *Child Development, 64*, 1722–1731.

Lewis, M., Worobey, J., Ramsay, D., & McCormack, M. (1992). Prenatal exposure to heavy metals. *Pediatrics, 89*, 1010–1015.

Lickliter, R., & Berry, T. (1990). The phylogenic fallacy: Developmental psychology's misapplication of evolutionary theory. *Developmental Review, 10*, 348–364.

Liddell, C. (1988). The social interaction and activity patterns of children from two San groups living as refugees on a Namibian military base. *Journal of Cross-Cultural Psychology, 19*, 341–360.

Liddell, C. (1994). South African children in the year before school. *International Journal of Psychology, 29,* 409–430.

Liddell, C., Kemp, J., & Moema, M. (1993). The young lions: South African children and youth in political struggle. In L. Leavitt & M. Fox (Eds.), *The psychological effects of war and violence on children* (pp. 199–214). Hillsdale, NJ: Erlbaum.

Liddell, C., Kvalsvig, J., Qotyana, P., & Shabalala, A. (1994). Community violence and young South African children's involvement in aggression. *International Journal of Behavioral Development, 17,* 613–628.

Liddell, C., Kvalsvig, J., Shabalala, A., & Masilela, P. (1991). Historical perspectives on South African childhood. *International Journal of Behavioral Development, 14,* 1–19.

Liddell, C., & McConville, C. (1994). Starting at the bottom: Towards the development of an indigenous school-readiness program for South African children being reared at home. *Early Child Development and Care, 97,* 1–15.

Liddell, C., Rapodile, J., & Masilela, P. (1991). The design and evaluation of a preschool enrichment package for Black South African children in day care. *Early Child Development and Care, 66,* 1–13.

Liddell, C., Strydom, M., Qotyana, P., & Shabalala, A. (1993). An observational study of 5-year old South African children in the year before school. *International Journal of Behavioral Development, 16,* 537–561.

Lightfoot, C., & Valsiner, J. (1992). Parental belief systems under the influence. In I. Sigel, A. DeLisi, & J. Goodnow (Eds.), *Parental belief systems* (pp. 393–414). Hillsdale, NJ: Erlbaum.

Livingstone, F. (1980). Cultural causes of genetic change. In G. Barlow & J. Silverberg (Eds.), *Sociobiology: Beyond nature/nurture* (pp. 307–329). Boulder, CO: Westview Press.

Lloyd-Morgan, C. (1902). New statement. In J. Baldwin (Ed.), *Development and evolution* (pp. 347–348). New York: Macmillan.

Lockman, J., & Thelen, E. (1993). Developmental biodynamics. *Child Development, 64,* 953–959.

Loehlin, J. (1992). *Genes and environment in personality development.* Newbury Park, CA: Sage.

Long, J., & Vaillant, G. (1984). Natural history of male psychological health. *American Journal of Psychiatry, 141,* 341–346.

Lovaas, O. (1987). Behavioral treatment and normal educational and intellectual functioning in young autistic children. *Journal of Consulting and Clinical Psychology, 55,* 3–9.

Lozoff, B. (1998). Explanatory mechanisms for poorer development in iron deficient anemic infants. In *Nutrition, health and child development* (Pan-American Health Organization Scientific Monograph No. 566). Washington, DC: Pan-American Health Organization.

Lozoff, B., Felt, B., Nelson, E., Wolf, A., Meltzer, H., & Jimenez, E. (1995). Serum prolactin levels and behavior in infants. *Biological Psychiatry, 37,* 4–12.

Luborsky, L. (1995). The first trial of the P technique in psychotherapy research. *Journal of Consulting and Clinical Psychology, 63*, 6–14.

Lumsden, C. (1983). Gene–culture linkages and the developing mind. In C. Brainerd (Ed.), *Recent advances in cognitive developmental theory* (pp. 123–166). New York: Springer-Verlag.

Luster, T., & McAdoo, H. (1996). Family and child influences on educational attainment. *Developmental Psychology, 32*, 26–39.

Luster, T., Rhodes, K., & Haas, B. (1989). The relations between parenting values and parenting behavior. *Journal of Marriage and the Family, 51*, 139–147.

Luthar, S., Doernberger, C., & Zigler, E. (1993). Resilience is not a unidimensional construct. *Development and Psychopathology, 5*, 703–717.

Lyon, G., & Gadisseaux, J. (1991). Structural abnormalities of the brain in developmental disorders. In M. Rutter & P. Casaer (Eds.), *Biological risk factors for psychosocial disorders* (pp. 1–19). Cambridge, England: Cambridge University Press.

Lytton, H., & Romney, D. (1991). Parental differential socialization of boys and girls. *Psychological Bulletin, 109*, 267–296.

Ma, H. (1988). The Chinese perspective on moral judgment development. *International Journal of Psychology, 23*, 201–227.

Ma, H., & Leung, M. (1990). The adaptation of the Family Environment Scale to Chinese children and adolescents in Hong Kong. *International Journal of Psychology, 25*, 545–555.

Maccoby, E. (1988). Gender as a social category. *Developmental Psychology, 24*, 755–765.

Maccoby, E., Snow, M., & Jacklin, C. (1984). Children's disposition and mother–child interaction at 12 and 18 months. *Developmental Psychology, 20*, 459–472.

MacDonald, K. (1996). What do children want? A conceptualization of evolutionary influences on children's motivation in the peer group. *International Journal of Behavioral Development, 19*, 53–74.

MacDonald, K. (1987). Biological and psychological interactions in early adolescence: A sociobiological perspective. In R. Lerner & T. Foch (Eds.), *Biological–psychosocial interactions in early adolescence* (pp. 90–110). Hillsdale, NJ: Erlbaum.

Mack, K., & Mack, P. (1992). Induction of transcription factors in somatosensory cortext after tactile stimulation. *Molecular Brain Research, 12*, 141–147.

MacKinnon-Lewis, C., Starnes, R., Volling, B., & Johnson, S. (1997). Perceptions of parenting as predictors of boys' sibling and peer relations. *Developmental Psychology, 33*, 1024–1031.

Magnusson, D. (1988). *Individual differences from an interactional perspective*. Hillsdale, NJ: Erlbaum.

Magnusson, D. (1993). Human ontogeny: A longitudinal perspective. In D. Magnusson & P. Casaer (Eds.), *Longitudinal research on individual development* (pp. 1–25). Cambridge, England: Cambridge University Press.

Magnusson, D., & Bergman, L. (1990). A pattern approach to the study of pathways from childhood to adulthood. In L. Robbins & M. Rutter (Eds.), *Straight and devious pathways from childhood to adulthood* (pp. 101–115). Cambridge, England: Cambridge University Press.

Magyary, D., Brandt, P., Hammond, M., & Barnard, K. (1992). School age follow-up of the development of preterm infants. In S. Friedman & M. Sigman (Eds.), *The psychological development of low birthweight infants* (pp. 215–238). Norwood, NJ: Ablex.

Maier, S., Watkins, L., & Fleshner, M. (1994). Psychoneuroimmunology. *American Psychologist, 49,* 1004–1017.

Malhotra, S. (1989). Varying risk factors and outcomes: An Indian perspective. In W. Carey & S. McDevitt (Eds.), *Clinical and educational applications of temperament research* (pp. 91–96). Amsterdam: Swets & Zeitlinger.

Manetti, M., & Schneider, B. (1996). Stability and change in patterns of parental social support and their relation to children's school adjustment. *Journal of Applied Developmental Psychology, 17,* 101–116.

Mann, J. (1992). Nurturance of negligance: Maternal psychology and behavioral preference among preterm twins. In J. Barkow, L. Cosmides, & J. Tooby (Eds.), *The adapted mind* (pp. 367–390). New York: Oxford University Press.

Martin, J. (1992). The effect of maternal use of tobacco products or amphetamines on offspring. In T. Snoderegger (Ed.), *Perinatal substance abuse* (pp. 274–305). Baltimore: Johns Hopkins University Press.

Martorell, R. (1989). Body size, adaptation and function. *Human Organization, 48,* 15–20.

Martorell, R., Khan, L., & Schroeder, D. (1994). Reversibility of stunting: Epidemiological findings in children from developing countries. *European Journal of Clinical Nutrition, 48,* S45–S57.

Martorell, R., Ramakrishnana, U., Schroeder, D., Melgar, P., & Neufeld, L. (1998). Intrauterine growth retardation, body size, body composition and physical performance in adolescence. *European Journal of Clinical Nutrition, 52,* S43–S53.

Martorell, R., Yarbrough, S., & Klein, R. (1980). The impact of ordinary illnesses on the dietary intakes of malnourished children. *American Journal of Clinical Nutrition, 33,* 345–350.

Marvin, R., & Stewart, R. (1990). A family systems framework for the study of attachment. In M. Greenberg, D. Cichetti, & E. Cummings (Eds.), *Attachment in the preschool years* (pp. 51–86). Chicago: University of Chicago Press.

Masten, A., Best, K., & Garmezy, N. ()1990). Resilience and development. *Development and Psychopathology, 2,* 425–444.

Matheny, A. (1986). Injuries among toddlers. *Journal of Pediatric Psychology, 11,* 163–176.

Matheny, A., Wachs, T. D., Ludwig, J., & Phillips, K. (1995). Bringing order out of chaos: Psychometric characteristics of the Louisville Chaos Scale. *Journal of Applied Developmental Psychology, 16,* 429–444.

Matheny, A., Wilson, R., & Thoben, A. (1987). Home and mother: Relations with infant temperament. *Developmental Psychology, 23,* 323–331.

Matsueda, R., & Heimer, K. (1987). Race, family structure and delinquency. *American Sociological Review, 52,* 826–840.

Maughn, B. (1994). School influences. In M. Rutter & D. Hay (Eds.), *Development through life* (pp. 134–158). Oxford, England: Blackwell.

May, R. (1976). Simple mathematical models with very complicated dynamics. *Nature, 261,* 459–467.

May, R., & Oster, G. (1976). Bifurcations and dynamic complexity in simple ecological models. *The American Naturalist, 110,* 573–599.

Mayes, L., Granger, R., Frank, M., Schottenfeld, R., & Bornstein, M. (1993). Neurobehavioral profiles of neonates exposed to cocaine prenatally. *Pediatrics, 91,* 778–783.

Mayr, E. (1980). Epilogue: Some thoughts on the history of the evolutionary synthesis. In E. Mayr & W. Provine (Eds.), *The evolutionary synthesis* (pp. 1–50). Cambridge, MA: Harvard University Press.

McCall, R. (1981). Nature–nurture and the two realms of development. *Child Development, 52,* 1–12.

McCall, R. (1991). So many interactions, so little evidence. Why? In T. D. Wachs & R. Plomin, (Eds.), *Conceptualization and measurement of organism–environment interaction* (pp. 142–161). Washington, DC: American Psychological Association.

McCall, R., & Appelbaum, M. (1991). Some issues of conducting secondary analyses. *Developmental Psychology, 27,* 911–917.

McCartney, K., Harris, M., & Bernieri, F. (1990). Growing up and growing apart: A developmental meta-analysis of twin studies. *Psychological Bulletin, 107,* 226–237.

McClearn, G. (1993). Behavioral genetics. In R. Plomin & G. McClearn (Eds.), *Nature, nurture, and psychology* (pp. 27–54). Washington, DC: American Psychological Association.

McClearn, G., Plomin, R., Gora-Maslak, G., & Crabbe, J. (1991). The gene chase in behavioral science. *Psychological Sciences, 2,* 222–229.

McClelland, G., & Judd, C. (1993). Statistical difficulties of detecting interactions and moderator effects. *Psychological Bulletin, 114,* 376–390.

McCloskey, L., Figueredo, A., & Koss, M. (1995). The effects of systematic family violence on children's mental health. *Child Development, 66,* 1239–1261.

McConkie-Rosell, A., Lachiewicz, A., Spiridigliozzi, G., Tarleton, J., Schoenwald, S., Phelan, M., Goonewardena, P., Ding, X., & Brown, W. (1993). Evidence that methylation of the FMR-I locus is responsible for variable phenotypic expression of the fragile X syndrome. *American Journal of Human Genetics, 53,* 800–809.

McCormick, M. (1992). Advances in neonatal intensive care technology and their possible impact on the development of low birthweight infants. In S. Friedman & M. Sigman (Eds.), *The psychological development of low birthweight children* (pp. 37–60). Norwood, NJ: Ablex.

McCurry, C., Silverton, L., & Mednick, S. (1991). Psychiatric consequences of pregnancy and birth complications. In J. Gray & R. Dean (Eds.), *Neuropsychology of perinatal complications* (pp. 186–203). New York: Springer.

McDonald, M., Sigman, M., Espunosa, M., & Neumann, C. (1994). Effect of a temporary food shortage on children and their mothers. *Child Development, 65,* 404–415.

McEwen, B. (1989). The role hormones acting in the brain play in linking nature and nurture. In A. Galaburda (Ed.), *From reading to neurons* (pp. 463–472). Cambridge, MA: MIT Press.

McGarry-Roberts, P., Stelmack, R., & Campbell, K. (1992). Intelligence, reaction time and event related potentials. *Intelligence, 16,* 289–313.

McGillicuddy-DeLisi, A., & Subramanian, S. (1996). How do children develop knowledge? In S. Harkness & C. Super (Eds.), *Parents' cultural belief systems* (pp. 143–168). New York: Guilford Press.

McGue, M. (1993). From proteins to cognitions: The behavioral genetics of alchoholism. In R. Plomin & G. McClearn (Eds.), *Nature, nurture, and psychology* (pp. 245–268). Washington, DC: American Psychological Association.

McGue, M., Bouchard, T., Iacono, W., & Lykken, D. (1993). Behavioral genetics of cognitive ability. In R. Plomin & G. McClearn (Eds.), *Nature, nurture, and psychology* (pp. 59–76). Washington, DC: American Psychological Association.

McGuffin, P., & Huckle, P. (1990). Simulation of Mendelism revisited: The recessive gene for attending medical school. *American Journal of Human Genetics, 46,* 994–999.

McGuffin, P., & Katz, R. (1993). Genes, adversity, and depression. In R. Plomin & G. McClearn (Eds.), *Nature, nuture, and psychology* (pp. 217–230). Washington, DC: American Psychological Association.

McHale, S., Crouter, A., McGuire, S., & Updegraff, K. (1995). Congruence between mothers' and fathers' differential treatment of siblings. *Child Development, 66,* 116–128.

McLeod, J., & Shanahan, M. (1993). Poverty, parenting and children's mental health. *American Sociological Review, 58,* 351–366.

McMichael, A., Baghurst, P., Vimpani, G., Robertson, E., Wigg, N., & Tong, S. (1992). Sociodemographic factors modifying the effect of environmental lead on neuropsychological development in early childhood. *Neurology and Teratology, 14,* 321–327.

McNeil, T. (1987). Perinatal influences in the development of schizophrenia. In H. Helmchen & F. Henn (Eds.), *Biological perspectives on schizophrenia* (pp. 125–138). Chichester, England: Wiley.

McSwain, R. (1981). Care and conflict in infant development. *Infant Behavior and Development, 4,* 225–246.

McWhirter, L., & Trew, K. (1982). Children in Northern Ireland. In E. Anthony & C. Chiland (Eds.), *The child in his family* (Vol. 7, pp. 47–61). New York: Wiley.

Mednick, S., Brennan, P., & Kandel, E. (1988). Predisposition to violence. *Aggressive Behavior, 14*, 25–33.

Mednick, S., Gabrielli, W., & Hutchings, B. (1984). Genetic influences in criminal convictions. *Science, 224*, 891–893.

Mednick, S., Machon, R., Huttunen, M., & Bonett, D. (1988). Adult schizophrenia following prenatal exposure to an influenza epidemic. *Archives of General Psychiatry, 45*, 189–192.

Meeks-Gardner, J., Grantham-McGregor, S., Chang, S., Himes, J., & Powell, C. (1995). Activity and behavioral development in stunted and nonstunted children and response to nutritional supplementation. *Child Development, 66*, 1785–1797.

Mehler, J., Jusczyk, P., Lambertz, G., Halsted, N., Bertoncini, J., & Amiel-Tison, C. (1988). A precursor of language acquisition in young infants. *Cognition, 29*, 143–178.

Meisel, R., & Sachs, B. (1994). The physiology of male sexual behavior. In E. Knobil & J. Neill (Eds.), *The physiology of reproduction* (pp. 3–105). New York: Raven Press.

Menke, J., McClead, R., & Hansen, N. (1991). Perspectives on perinatal complications associated with mental retardation. In J. Matson & J. Mulick (Eds.), *Handbook of mental retardation* (2nd ed., pp. 139–150). Elmsford, NY: Pergamon Press.

Merialdi, M., Caulfield, L., Zavaleta, N., Figueroa, A., & DiPietro, J. (1998). Adding zinc to prenatal iron and folate tablets improves fetal neurobehavioral development. *Federation of American Societies for Experimental Biology Journal, 12*, A346.

Merzenich, M., Allard, T., & Jenkins, W. (1991). Neural ontogeny of higher brain functions. In O. Franzen & J. Westman (Eds.), *Information processing in the somatosensory system* (pp. 193–209). New York: Stockton Press.

Merzenich, M., Jenkins, W., Johnston, P., Schreiner, C., Miller, S., & Tallal, P. (1996). Temporal processing deficits of language-learning impaired children ameliorated by training. *Science, 271*, 77–81.

Meyer-Bahlberg, H., Ehrhardt, A., Rosen, L., Gruen, R., Veridiano, N., Vann, F., & Neuwalder, H. (1995). Prenatal estrogens and the development of homosexual orientation. *Developmental Psychology, 31*, 12–21.

Meyer-Bahlburg, H., Feldman, J., Cohen, P., & Ehrhardt, A. (1988). Perinatal factors in the development of gender related play behavior. *Psychiatry, 51*, 260–271.

Milar, C., Schroeder, S., Mushak, A., Dolcourt, J., & Grant, L. (1980). Contribution of the caregiving environment to increased lead levels of children. *American Journal of Mental Deficiency, 84*, 339–344.

Miller, B. (1987). Female infanticide and child neglect in rural North India. In N. Scheper-Hughes (Ed.), *Child survival* (pp. 95–112). Dordrecht, The Netherlands: Reidel.

Miller, C., & White, R. (1995, March). *Vulnerability and resilience in preterm infants*. Paper presented at the annual meeting of the Society for Research in Child Development, Indianapolis, IN.

Miller, D. (1997). The effects of nonobvious forms of experience on the development of instinctive behavior. In C. Dent-Read & P. Zukow-Goldring (Eds.), *Evolving explanations of development* (pp. 457–508). Washington DC: American Psychological Association.

Miller, G., Massaro, T., & Massaro, E. (1990). Interactions between lead and essential elements. *Neurotoxicology, 11*, 99–120.

Miller, J. (1978). *Living systems*. New York: McGraw Hill.

Miller, K. (1996). The effects of state terrorism and exile on indigenous Guatemalan refugee children. *Child Development, 67*, 89–106.

Miller, L., Kiernan, M., Mathers, M., & Klein-Gitelamn, M. (1995). Developmental and nutritional status of internationally adopted children. *Archives of Pediatric and Adolescent Medicine, 149*, 40–44.

Miller, S. (1988). Parents' beliefs about children's cognitive development. *Child Development, 59*, 259–285.

Miller, S. (1995). Parent's attributions for their children's behavior. *Child Development, 66*, 1557–1584.

Mills, R., & Rubin, K. (1993). Socialization factors in the development of social withdrawal. In K. Rubin & J. Asendorpf (Eds.), *Social withdrawal, inhibition and shyness in childhood* (pp. 117–148). Hillsdale, NJ: Erlbaum.

Minde, K. (1992). The social and emotional development of low birthweight infants and their families up to age 4. In S. Friedman & M. Sigman (Eds.), *The psychological development of low birthweight children* (pp. 157–187). Norwood, NJ: Ablex.

Minde, K., Shosenberg, N., Marton, P., Thompson, J., Ripley, J., & Burns, S. (1980). Self-help groups in a premature nursery—A controlled evaluation. *Journal of Pediatrics, 96*, 933–940.

Mink, I., & Nihara, K. (1986). Family lifestyles and child behaviors. *Developmental Psychology, 22*, 610–616.

Mize, J., Pettit, G., & Brown, E. (1995). Mothers' supervision of their children's peer play. *Developmental Psychology, 31*, 311–331.

Mizuta, I., Zahn-Waxler, C., Cole, P., & Hiruma, N. (1996). A cross-cultural study of preschoolers' attachment. *International Journal of Behavioral Development, 19*, 141–160.

Moen, P., Elder, G., & Luscher, K. (1995). *Examining lives in context*. Washington, DC: American Psychological Association.

Moffitt, T. (1990). The neuropsychology of juvenile delinquency. In M. Tonry & N. Morris (Eds.), *Crime and justice*. (Vol. 12, pp. 99–170). Chicago: University of Chicago Press.

Moffitt, T. (1993). Adolescence limited and life course persistent antisocial behavior. *Psychological Review, 100*, 674–701.

Moffitt, T., Caspi, A., Belsky, J., & Silva, P. (1992). Childhood experience and the onset of menarche. *Child Development, 63*, 47–58.

Moffitt, T., & Henry, B. (1989). Neuropsychological assessment of executive functions in self-reported delinquents. *Development and Psychopathology, 1*, 105–118.

Molfese, D., & Betz, J. (1988). Electrophysiological indices of the early development of language and cognition and their implications of predicting later development. In D. Molfese & S. Segalowitz (Eds.), *Brain lateralization in children* (pp. 171–190). New York: Guilford Press.

Molfese, V., DiLalla, L., & Lovelace, L. (1996). Perinatal, home environment and infant measures as successful predictors of preschool cognitive and verbal abilities. *International Journal of Behavioral Development, 19*, 101–120.

Molfese, V., Holcomb, L., & Helwig, S. (1994). Biomedical and social-environmental influences on cognitive and verbal abilities in children 1–3 years of age. *International Journal of Behavioral Development, 17*, 271–287.

Molina, B., & Chassin, L. (1996). The parent–adolescent relationship at puberty. *Developmental Psychology, 32*, 675–686.

Morelli, G., & Tronick, E. (1991). Parenting and child development in the Efe foragers and Lese farmers of Zaire. In M. Bornstein (Ed.), *Cultural approaches to parenting* (pp. 91–113). Hillsdale, NJ: Erlbaum.

Morisset, C., Barnard, K., & Booth, C. (1995). Toddler's language development: Sex differences within social risk. *Developmental Psychology, 31*, 851–865.

Morrison, F., Griffith, E., & Alberts, D. (1997). Nature–nurture in the classroom. *Developmental Psychology, 33*, 254–262.

Morrison, F., Smith, L., & Dow-Ehrensberger, M. (1995). Education and cognitive development. *Developmental Psychology, 31*, 789–799.

Moskovitz, S. (1985). Longitudinal follow-up of child survivors of the Holocaust. *Journal of the American Academy of Child Psychiatry, 24*, 401–407.

Mounts, N., & Steinberg, L. (1995). An ecological analysis of peer influence on adolescent grade point average and drug use. *Developmental Psychology, 31*, 915–922.

Mueller, W., & Malina, R. (1980). Genetic and environmental influences on growth of Philadelphia Black and White schoolchildren. *Annals of Human Biology, 7*, 441–448.

Mull, D. (1991). Traditional perceptions of Marasmus in Pakistan. *Social Science and Medicine, 32*, 175–191.

Munroe, R., Skimmer, H., & Pitzer, R. (1984). Gender understanding and sex role preference in four cultures. *Developmental Psychology, 20*, 673–682.

Muret-Wagstaff, S., & Moore, S. (1989). The Hmong in America: Infant behavior and rearing practices. In J. Nugent, B. Lester, & T. Brazelton (Eds.), *The cultural context of infancy* (Vol. 1, pp. 319–338). Norwood, NJ: Ablex.

Myers, R. (1992). *The twelve who survived*. London: Routledge.

My-Lien, N., Meyer, K., & Winick, N. (1997). Early malnutrition and later adoption. *American Journal of Clinical Nutrition, 30*, 1734–1735.

Nadel, L., Wilson, L., & Kurz, E. (1993). Effects of alterations in timing of development. In G. Turkewitz & D. Devenny (Eds.), *Developmental time and timing* (pp. 233–252). Hillsdale, NJ: Erlbaum.

Naipaul, V. (1997). After the revolution. *The New Yorker, 73*, 46–69.

Natori, Y., & Oka, T. (1997). Vitamin B$_6$ modulation of gene expression. *Nutrition Research, 7*, 1199–1207.

Needleman, H., & Gatsonis, C. (1990). Low-level lead exposure and the IQ of children. *Journal of the American Medical Association, 263*, 673–678.

Neisser, U., Boodoo, G., Bouchard, T., Boykin, A., Brody, N., Cesi, S., Halpern, D., Loehlin, J., Perloff, R., Sternberg, R., & Urbina, S. (1996). Intelligence: Knowns and unknowns. *American Psychologist, 51*, 77–101.

Nelson, C. (1994). Neural basis of infant temperament. In J. Bates & T. D. Wachs (Eds.), *Temperament: Individual differences at the interface of biology and behavior* (pp. 47–82). Washington, DC: American Psychological Association.

Nelson, C. (1995). The ontogeny of human memory. *Developmental Psychology, 31*, 723–738.

Nelson, C. (in press). The neurobiological bases of early intervention. In S. Meisels & J. Shonkoff (Eds.), *Handbook of early childhood intervention* (2nd ed.). Cambridge, England: Cambridge University Press.

Nelson, C., & Bloom, F. (1997). Child development and neuroscience. *Child Development, 68*, 970–987.

Nelson, K., & Ellenberg, J. (1986). Antecedents of cerebral palsy. *New England Journal of Medicine, 315*, 81–86.

Netley, C., & Rovet, J. (1988). The development of cognition and personality in X aneuploids and other subject groups. In D. Molfese & S. Segalowitz (Eds.), *Brain lateralization in children* (pp. 401–416). New York: Guilford Press.

Nettles, J., & Pleck, J. (1994). Risk, resilience and development. In R. Haggerty, L. Sherrod, N. Garmezy, & M. Rutter (Eds.), *Stress, risk and resilience in children and adolescents* (pp. 147–182). Cambridge, England: Cambridge University Press.

Neumann, C., & Harrison, G. (1994). Onset and evolution of stunting in infants and children. *European Journal of Clinical Nutrition , 48*(Suppl.), S90–S102.

New, R., & Richman, A. (1996). Maternal beliefs and infant care practices in Italy and the United States. In S. Harkness & C. Super (Eds.), *Parental cultural belief systems* (pp. 385–404). New York: Guilford Press.

Newcombe, N., & Dubos, J. (1987). Individual differences in cognitive abilities: Are they related to timing of puberty? In R. Lerner & T. Foch (Eds.), *Biological–psychosocial interactions in early adolescence* (pp. 249–302). Hillsdale, NJ: Erlbaum Press.

Newman, D., Caspi, A., Silva, P., & Moffitt, T. (1997). Antecedents of adult interpersonal functioning. *Developmental Psychology, 33*, 206–217.

Newport, E. (1990). Maturational constraints on language learning. *Cognitive Science, 14*, 11–28.

Nicassio, P. (1985). The psychosocial adjustment of the Southeast Asian refugee. *Journal of Cross-Cultural Psychology, 16,* 153–173.

Ninio, A. (1990). Early environmental experiences and school achievement in the second grade. *International Journal of Behavioral Development, 13,* 1–22.

Noonan, K. (1987). Evolution: A primer for psychologists. In C. Crawford, M. Smith, & D. Krebs (Eds.), *Sociobiology and psychology* (pp. 31–60). Hillsdale, NJ: Erlbaum Press.

Norgan, N. (1988). Chronic energy deficiency and the effect of energy supplementation. In B. Schurch & N. Schrimshaw (Eds.), *Chronic energy deficiency* (pp. 59–76). Lausanne, Switzerland: International Dietary Energy Consultive Group.

Nowak, A., & Lewenstein, M. (1994). Dynamical systems: A tool for social psychology. In R. Vallacher & A. Nowak (Eds.), *Dynamical systems in social psychology* (pp. 17–54). San Diego: Academic Press.

Nowak, A., Vallacher, R., & Lewenstein, M. (1994). Toward a dynamical social psychology. In R. Vallacher & A. Nowak (Eds.), *Dynamical systems in social psychology* (pp. 279–293). San Diego: Academic Press.

Nsamenang, A. (1992). *Human development in cultural context.* Newbury Park, CA: Sage.

Odum, H. (1983). *Systems ecology.* New York: Wiley.

Ogbu, J. (1983). Minority status and schooling in plural societies. *Comparative Education Review, 27,* 168–190.

Okagaki, L., & Sternberg, R. (1993). Parental beliefs and children's school performance. *Child Development, 64,* 36–56.

Olson, H., Streissguth, A., Bookstein, F., Barr, H., & Sampson, P. (1994). Developmental research in behavioral teratology. In S. Friedman & H. C. Haywood (Eds.), *Developmental follow-up* (pp. 67–112). San Diego: Academic Press.

Olweus, D. (1993). Victimization by peers. In K. Rubin & J. Asendorpf (Eds.), *Social withdrawal, inhibition and shyness in childhood* (pp. 315–342). Hillsdale, NJ: Erlbaum.

Osofsky, J., Culp, A., & Ware, L. (1988). Intervention challenges with adolescent mothers and their infants. *Psychiatry, 51,* 236–241.

Oster, G., & Alberch, P. (1982). Evolution and bifurcation of developmental programs. *Evolution, 36,* 444–459.

Oyama, S. (1989). Ontogeny and the central dogma. In M. Gunnar & E. Thelen (Eds.), *Systems and development: The Minnesota Symposium on Child Psychology: Vol. 22,* (pp. 1–34). Hillsdale, NJ: Erlbaum.

Paikoff, R., & Brooks-Gunn, J. (1991). Do parent–child relationships change during maturity? *Psychological Bulletin, 110,* 47–66.

Paikoff, R., Brooks-Gunn, J., & Warren, M. (1991). Effects of girls' hormonal status on depressive and aggressive symptoms over the course of one year. *Journal of Youth and Adolescence, 20,* 191–215.

Palacios, J., Gonzalez, M., & Moreno, M. (1992). Stimulating the child in the zone of proximal development. In I. Sigel, A. DeLisi, &. J. Goodnow (Eds.), *Parental belief systems* (pp. 71–94). Hillsdale, NJ: Erlbaum.

Palmer, H., & Paulson, K. (1997). Reactive oxygen species and antioxidants in signal transduction and gene expression. *Nutrition Reviews, 55*, 353–361.

Pandey, J. (1990). The environment, culture and behavior. In R. Brislin (Ed.), *Applied cross-cultural psychology* (pp. 254–277). Newbury Park, CA: Sage.

Papousek, H., & Papousek, M. (1991). Innate and cultural guidance of infants integrative competencies. In M. Bornstein (Ed.), *Cultural approaches to parenting* (pp. 23–44). Hillsdale, NJ: Erlbaum Press.

Park, S., Belsky, J., Putnam, S., & Crnic, K. (1997). Infant emotionality, parenting, and 3-year inhibition. *Developmental Psychology, 33*, 218–227.

Parke, R., & Bhavnagri, N. (1989). Parents as managers of children's peer relationships. In D. Belle (Ed.), *Children's social networks and social supports* (pp. 241–259). New York: Wiley.

Parker, J., & Asher, S. (1987). Peer relations and later personal adjustment. *Psychological Bulletin, 102*, 357–389.

Parmelee, A. (1986). Children's illness: Their beneficial effects on behavioral development. *Child Development, 57*, 1–10.

Partridge, L. (1983). Genetics and behavior. In T. Haliday & P. Slater (Eds.), *Genes, development and learning* (pp. 11–51). London: Blackwell.

Pattee, H. (1973a). The physical basis and origin of hierarchical control. In H. Pattee (Ed.), *Hierarchy theory: The challenge of complex systems* (pp. 73–108). New York: Braziller.

Pattee, H. (1973b). Unsolved problems and potential applications of hierarchy theory. In H. Pattee (Ed.), *Hierarchy theory: The challenge of complex systems* (pp. 131–156). New York: Braziller.

Patten, B. (1982). Environs: Relativistic elementary particles for ecology. *The American Naturalist, 119*, 172–219.

Patterson, C., Griesler, P., Vaden, N., & Kupersmidt, J. (1992). Family economic circumstances, life transitions and children's peer relations. In R. Parke & G. Ladd (Eds.), *Family–peer relations* (pp. 385–424). Hillsdale, NJ: Erlbaum.

Patterson, C., & Newman, J. (1993). Reflectivity and learning from aversive events. *Psychological Review, 100*, 716–736.

Patterson, G., & Bank, L. (1989). Some amplifying mechanisms for pathologic processes in families. In M. Gunnar & E. Thelen (Eds.), *The Minnesota Symposium on Child Psychology: Vol. 22. Systems and development* (pp. 167–209). Hillsdale, NJ: Erlbaum.

Patterson, J., & McCubbin, H. (1983). The impact of family life events and changes on the health of a chronically ill child. *Family Relations, 32*, 255–264.

Pavenstedt, E. (1967). *The drifters: Children of disorganized lower class families.* Boston: Little, Brown.

Pawson, I., & Jest, C. (1978). The high altitude areas of the world and their cultures. In P. Baker (Ed.), *The biology of high altitude people* (pp. 17–46). Cambridge, England: Cambridge University Press.

Pearson, D., & Dietrich, K. (1985). The behavioral toxicology and teratology of childhood. *Neurotoxicology, 6,* 165–182.

Pedersen, D., & Moran, G. (1995). A categorical description of infant–mother relationship in the home and its relation to Q-sort measures of mother–infant interaction. *Monographs of the Society for Research in Child Development, 60,* 111–132.

Pedersen, E., Faucher, T., & Eaton, W. (1978). A new perspective on the effects of first-grade teachers on children's subsequent adult status. *Harvard Educational Review, 48,* 1–31.

Pembrey, M. (1991). Chromosomal abnormalities. In M. Rutter & P. Casaer (Eds.), *Biological risk factors for psychosocial disorders* (pp. 67–100). Cambridge, England: Cambridge University Press.

Perez-Escamilla, R., Lutter, C., Segall, A., Rivera, A., Trevino-Siller, S., & Sanghvi, T. (1995). Exclusive breast-feeding duration is associated with attitudinal, socioeconomic and biocultural determinants in three Latin American countries. *Journal of Nutrition, 125,* 2972–2984.

Perrin, E., Ayoub, C., & Willett, J. (1993). In the eyes of the beholder: Family and maternal influences on perceptions of adjustment of children with a chronic illness. *Journal of Developmental and Behavioral Pediatrics, 14,* 94–105.

Petersen, A. (1988). Adolescent development. *Annual Review of Psychology, 39,* 583–607.

Petersen, A., Sariagiani, P., & Kennedy, R. (1991). Adolescent depression: Why more girls? *Journal of Youth and Adolescence, 20,* 247–271.

Petrill, S., Saudino, K., Cherny, S., Emde, R., Fulker, D., Hewitt, J., & Plomin, R. (1998). Exploring the genetic and environmental etiology of high general ability in fourteen to thirty-six month old twins. *Child Development, 69,* 68–74.

Petrill, S., Saudino, K., Cherny, S., Emde, R., Hewitt, J., Fulker, D., & Plomin, R. (1997). Exploring the genetic etiology of low cognitive ability from 14 to 36 months. *Developmental Psychology, 33,* 544–548.

Pianta, R., & O'Connor, T. (1996). Developmental systems challenges to the study of specific environment effects. In D. Detterman (Ed.), *Current topics in human intelligence: The environment* (Vol. 5, pp. 45–58). Norwood, NJ: Ablex.

Pianta, R., Sroufe, L., & Egeland, B. (1989). Continuity and discontinuity in maternal sensitivity at 6, 24 and 42 months in a high risk sample. *Child Development, 60,* 481–487.

Pickles, A. (1993). Stages, precursors and causes in development. In D. Hay & A. Angold (Eds.), *Precursors and causes in development and psychopathology* (pp. 23–49). New York: Wiley.

Pike, A., McGuire, S., Hetherington, E., Reiss, D., & Plomin, R. (1996). Family environment and adolescent depressive symptoms and antisocial behavior. *Developmental Psychology, 32,* 590–604.

Pine, J. (1995). Variation in vocabulary development as a function of birth order. *Child Development, 66*, 272–281.

Pless, I., Power, C., & Peckham, C. (1993). Long term psychosocial sequelae of chronic physical disorders in childhood. *Pediatrics, 91*, 1131–1136.

Plomin, R. (1990). *Nature and nurture: An introduction to human behavioral genetics*. Pacific Grove, CA: Brooks-Cole.

Plomin, R. (1991). Genetic risk and psychosocial disorder. In M. Rutter & P. Casaer (Eds.), *Biological risk factors for psychosocial disorders* (pp. 101–138). Cambridge, England: Cambridge University Press.

Plomin, R. (1994). *Genetics and experience*. Thousand Oaks, CA: Sage.

Plomin, R., & Daniels, D. (1987). Why are children in the same family so different from each other? *Behavioral and Brain Sciences, 10*, 1–16.

Plomin, R., DeFries, J., & Loehlin, J. (1977). Genotype environment interaction and correlation in the analysis of human development. *Psychological Bulletin, 84*, 309–322.

Plomin, R., DeFries, J., McClearn, G., & Rutter, M. (1997). *Behavioral genetics* (3rd ed.). New York: Freeman.

Plomin, R., Fulker, D., Corley, R., & DeFries, J. (1997). Nature, nurture and cognitive development from 1 to 16 years. *Psychological Science, 8*, 442–447.

Plomin, R., & McClearn, G. (1993). *Nature, nurture, and psychology*. Washington, DC: American Psychological Association.

Plomin, R., & Rende, R. (1991). Human behavioral genetics. *Annual Review of Psychology, 42*, 161–190.

Plomin, R., & Saudino, K. (1994). Quantitative genetics and molecular genetics. In J. Bates & T. D. Wachs (Eds.), *Temperament: Individual differences at the interface of biology and behavior* (pp. 143–174). Washington, DC: American Psychological Association.

Plomin, R., & Thompson, L. (1993). Genetics and high cognitive ability. In G. Brock & K. Ackrill (Eds.), *CIBA Foundation Symposium 718: The origins and development of high ability* (pp. 67–79). Chichester, UK: Wiley.

Pollitt, E. (1983). Morbidity and infant development. *International Journal of Behavioral Development, 6*, 461–475.

Pollitt, E. (1988). A critical view of three decades of research on the effects of chronic energy malnutrition on behavioral development. In B. Schurch & N. Scrimshaw (Eds.), *Chronic energy deficiency* (pp. 77–94). Lausanne, Switzerland: International Dietary Energy Consultive Group.

Pollitt, E. (1993). Iron deficiency and cognitive function. *Annual Review of Nutrition, 13*, 521–537.

Pollitt, E. (1995). Functional significance of the covariance between protein energy malnutrition and iron deficiency anemia. *Journal of Nutrition, 125*(Suppl.), 2272S–2277S.

Pollitt, E. (1996). Timing and vulnerability in research on malnutrition and cognition. *Nutrition Reviews, 54*, 549–555.

Pollitt, E., Cueto, S., & Jacoby, E. (1998). Fasting and cognition in well and under-nourished school children. *American Journal of Clinical Nutrition, 67*(Suppl.), 779S–784S.

Pollitt, E., & Gorman, K. (1994). Nutritional deficiencies as developmental risk factors. In C. Nelson (Ed.), *Threats to optimal development* (pp. 121–144). Hillsdale, NJ: Erlbaum.

Pollitt, E., Gorman, K., Engle, P., Martorell, R., & Rivera, J. (1993). Early supplementary feeding and cognition. *Monographs of the Society for Research in Child Development, 58*(7, Serial No. 235).

Pollitt, E., & Mathews, R. (1998). Breakfast and cognition: An integrative summary. *American Journal of Clinical Nutrition, 67*(Suppl.), 804S–813S.

Pollitt, E., & Saco-Pollitt, C. (1996). On the role of the physical environment in the development of intelligence. In D. Detterman (Ed.), *Current topics in human intelligence* (Vol. 5, pp. 163–172). Norwood, NJ: Ablex.

Pomerleau, A., Malcuit, G., & Sabatier, C. (1991). Child rearing practices and parental beliefs in three cultural groups of Montreal. In M. Bornstein (Ed.), *Cultural approaches to parenting* (pp. 45–68). Hillsdale, NJ: Erlbaum.

Potter, S. (1987). Birth planning in rural China. In N. Scheper-Hughes (Ed.), *Child survival* (pp. 33–58). Dordrecht, The Netherlands: Reidel.

Powell, C., & Grantham-McGregor, S. (1985). The ecology of nutritional status and development in young children in Kingston, Jamaica. *American Journal of Clinical Nutrition, 41*, 1322–1331.

Powell, C., & Grantham-McGregor, S. (1989). Home visiting of varying frequency and child development. *Pediatrics, 84*, 157–164.

Power, T., Kobayashi-Winata, H., & Kelley, M. (1992). Child rearing patterns in Japan and the United States. *International Journal of Behavioral Development, 15*, 185–205.

Prasad, A. (1996). Zinc deficiency in women, infants and children. *Journal of the American College of Nutrition, 15*, 113–120.

Prentice, A., & Bates, C. (1994). Adequacy of dietary mineral supply for human bone growth and mineralization. *European Journal of Clinical Nutrition, 48*, S161–S177.

Prentice, A., Cole, T., Foord, F., Lamb, W., & Whitehead, R. (1987). Increased birthweight after prenatal dietary supplementation of rural African women. *American Journal of Clinical Nutrition, 49*, 912–925.

Prigogine, I., & Stengers, I. (1984). *Order out of chaos*. Toronto, Ontario, Canada: Bantam.

Pueschel, S., & Goldstein, A. (1991). Genetic counseling. In J. Matson & J. Mulick (Eds.), *Handbook of mental retardation* (2nd ed., pp. 279–291). Elmsford, NY: Pergamon Press.

Pueschel, S., & Thuline, H. (1991). Chromosome disorders. In J. Matson & J. Mulick (Eds.), *Handbook of mental retardation* (2nd ed., pp. 115–138). New York: Pergamon Press.

Pulkkinen, L. (1982). Self-control and continuity from childhood to late adolescence. In P. Baltes & O. Brim (Eds.), *Life-span development and behavior* (Vol. 4, pp. 64–102). San Diego: Academic Press.

Punamaki, R. (1988). Historical, political and individualistic determinants of coping modes and fears among Palestinian children. *International Journal of Psychology, 23*, 721–739.

Punamaki, R., Qouta, S., & Sarraj, E. (1997). Models of traumatic experience and children's psychological adjustment. *Child Development, 64*, 718–728.

Pungello, E., Kupersmidt, J., Burchinal, M., & Patterson, C. (1996). Environmental risk factors and children's achievement from middle childhood to early adolescence. *Developmental Psychology, 32*, 755–767.

Putallaz, M., & Heflin, M. (1990). Parent–child interaction. In S. Asher & J. Coie (Eds.), *Peer rejection in childhood* (pp. 189–216). Cambridge, England: Cambridge University Press.

Quinton, D. (1994). Cultural and community influences. In M. Rutter & D. Hay (Eds.), *Development through life* (pp. 159–184). Oxford, England: Blackwell.

Quinton, D., & Rutter, M. (1976). Early hospital admissions and later disturbances of behavior. *Developmental Medicine and Child Neurology, 18*, 447–459.

Quinton, D., & Rutter, M. (1988). *Parenting breakdown.* Aldershot, England: Avebury.

Quinton, D., Rutter, M., & Gulliver, L. (1990). Continuities in psychiatric disorders from childhood to adulthood in the children of psychiatric patients. In L. Robins & M. Rutters (Eds.), *Straight and devious pathways from childhood to adulthood* (pp. 259–278). Cambridge, England: Cambridge University Press.

Radke-Yarrow, M., & Sherman, T. (1990). Hard growing: Children who survive. In J. Rolf & A. Masten (Eds.), *Risk and protective factors in the development of psychopathology* (pp. 97–119). New York: Cambridge University Press.

Radke-Yarrow, M., Zahn-Waxler, C., Richardson, D., Susman, A., & Martinez, P. (1994). Caring behaviors in children of clinically depressed and well mothers. *Child Development, 65*, 1405–1414.

Rahim, S., & Cederblad, M. (1984). Effects of rapid urbanization on child behavior and health in a part of Khartoum, Sudan. *Journal of Child Psychology and Psychiatry, 25*, 629–641.

Rahmanifar, A., Kirksey, A., Wachs, T. D., McCabe, G., Bishry, Z., Galal, O., Harrison, G., & Jerome, N. (1993). Diet during lactation associated with infant behavior and caregiver infant interaction in a semirural Egyptian village. *Journal of Nutrition, 123*, 164–175.

Raine, A., Venables, P., & Williams, M. (1996). Better autonomic conditioning and faster electrodermal half recovery time at age 15 years as possible protective factors against crime at age 29 years. *Developmental Psychology, 32*, 624–630.

Rakic, P. (1988). Specification of cerebral cortical areas. *Science, 241*, 170–176.

Rakic, P. (1989). Competitive interactions during neuronal and synaptic development. In A. Galaburda (Eds.), *From reading to neurons* (pp. 443–459). Cambridge, MA: MIT Press.

Ramey, C., & Ramey, S. (1998). Early intervention. *American Psychologist, 53,* 210–225.

Rao, P., & Inbaraj, S. (1977). Inbreeding effects on human reproduction in Tamil Nadu of South India. *Annals of Human Genetics, 41,* 87–98.

Rauh, V., & Brennan, J. (1992). An interactionist perspective on interventions with low birthweight infants. In S. Friedman & M. Sigman (Eds.), *The psychological development of low birthweight children* (pp. 435–470). Norwood, NJ: Ablex.

Raup, D. (1986). Biological extinction in earth history. *Science, 231,* 1528–1533.

Raz, S., Lauterbach, M., Hopkins, T., Glogowski, B., Porter, C., Riggs, W., & Sander, C. (1995). A female advantage in cognitive recovery from early cerebral insult. *Developmental Psychology, 31,* 958–967.

Reed, T., & Jensen, A. (1992). Conduction velocity in a brain measure pathway of normal adults correlates with intelligence level. *Intelligence, 16,* 259–272.

Reed, T., & Jensen, A. (1993). Choice reaction time and visual pathway nerve conduction velocity both correlate with intelligence but appear not to correlate with each other. *Intelligence, 17,* 191–203.

Reinisch, J., Ziemba-Davis, M., & Sanders, S. (1991). Hormonal contributions to sexually dimorphic behavioral development in humans. *Psychoneuroendocrinology, 16,* 213–278.

Reynolds, A. (1994). Effects of a preschool plus follow-on intervention for children at risk. *Developmental Psychology, 30,* 787–804.

Reynolds, A., Mavrogenes, N., Bezruczko, N., & Hagemann, M. (1996). Cognitive and family support mediators of preschool effectiveness. *Child Development, 67,* 1119–1140.

Reynolds, A., & Temple, J. (1998). Extended early childhood intervention and school achievement. *Child Development, 69,* 231–246.

Ricciuti, H. (1993). Nutrition and mental development. *Current Directions in Psychological Sciences, 2,* 43–46.

Richard, B., & Dodge, K. (1982). Social maladjustment and problem solving in school-age children. *Journal of Clinical and Consulting Psychology, 50,* 226–233.

Richards, M., Abell, S., & Petersen, A. (1993). Biological Development. In P. Tolan & B. Cohler (Eds.), *Handbook of clinical research and practice with adolescents* (pp. 21–44). New York: Wiley.

Richman, A., LeVine, R., New, R., Howrigan, G., Wells-Nystrom, B., & LeVine, S. (1988). Maternal behavior to infants in five cultures. In R. LeVine, P. Miller, & M. Maxwell (Eds.), *Parental behavior in diverse societies* (pp. 81–98). San Francisco: Jossey-Bass.

Richman, A., Miller, P., & LeVine, R. (1992). Cultural and educational variations in maternal responsiveness. *Developmental Psychology, 28,* 614–621.

Roberts, J., Burchinal, M., & Clarke-Klein, S. (1995). Otitis media in early childhood and cognitive, academic and behavior outcomes at 12 years of age. *Journal of Pediatric Psychology, 20,* 645–660.

Rodgers, B. (1990). Influences of early life and recent factors on affective disorders in women. In L. Robins & M. Rutter (Eds.), *Straight and devious pathways from childhood to adulthood* (pp. 314–327). Cambridge, England: Cambridge University Press.

Rogoff, B. (1980). Transitions in children's roles and capabilities. *International Journal of Psychology, 15,* 181–200.

Rogoff, B. (1990). *Apprenticeship in thinking.* New York: Oxford University Press.

Rogoff, B. (1991). The joint socialization of development by young children and adults. In M. Lewis & S. Feinman (Eds.), *Social influences and socialization in infancy* (pp. 253–280). New York: Plenum Press.

Rogoff, B., Mistry, J., Goncu, A., & Mosier, C. (1991). Cultural variation in the role relations of toddlers and their families. In M. Bornstein (Ed.), *Cultural approaches to parenting* (pp. 73–183). Hillsdale, NJ: Erlbaum.

Roopnarine, J., Talukder, E., Jain, D., Joshi, P., & Srivastav, P. (1992). Personal well being, kinship tie and mother-infant and father–infant interactions in single-wage and dual-wage families in New Delhi, India. *Journal of Marriage and the Family, 54,* 293–301.

Roper, T. (1983). Learning as a biological phenomena. In T. Halliday & P. Slater (Eds.), *Genes, development and learning* (pp. 178–212). London: Blackwell.

Rose, R. (1995). Genes and human behavior. *Annual Review of Psychology, 46,* 625–654.

Rose, S., & Feldman, J. (1996). Memory and processing speed in preterm children at eleven years. *Child Development, 67,* 2005–2021.

Rose-Krasnor, L., Rubin, K., Booth, C., & Caplan, R. (1996). The relation of maternal directiveness and child attachment security to social competence in preschoolers. *International Journal of Behavioral Development, 19,* 309–326.

Rosenberg, I., Solomons, N., & Schneider, R. (1977). Malabsorption associated with diarrhea and intestinal infections. *American Journal of Clinical Nutrition, 30,* 1248–1253.

Rosenblatt, D., & Whitehead, V. (1999). Cobalamin and folate deficiency: Acquired and hereditary disorders in children. *Seminars in Hematology, 36,* 19–34.

Rosenblum, L. (1998). Effective mothering in a familial context: A nonhuman primate perspective. In M. Lewis & C. Feiring (Eds.), *Families, risk and competence* (pp. 71–88). Mahwah, NJ: Erlbaum.

Rosenthal, D., Bell, R., Demetriou, A., & Efklides, A. (1989). From collectivism to individualism? *International Journal of Psychology, 24,* 57–71.

Rosnow, R., & Georgoudi, M. (1986). *Contextualism and understanding in behavioral science.* New York: Praeger.

Rossi, L., Candini, G., Scarlatti, G., Rossi, G., Prina, E., & Alberti, S. (1987). Autosomal dominant microcephaly without mental retardation. *American Journal of Diseases of Children, 141*, 655–659.

Roth, J. (1995, April). *Dropping out of high school among low-income adolescents*. Paper presented at a symposium of the Society of Research on Child Development, Indianapolis, IN.

Rothbart, M. (1989). Temperament in childhood: A framework. In G. Kohnstamm, J. Bates, & M. Rothbart (Eds.), *Temperament in childhood* (pp. 59–76). New York: Wiley.

Rothbart, M., & Bates, J. (1998). Temperament. In N. Eisenberg (Ed.), *Handbook of child psychology: Social, emotional and personality development* (Vol. 3, pp. 105–176). New York: Wiley.

Rothbart, M., Derryberry, D., & Posner, M. (1994). A psychobiological approach to the development of temperament. In J. Bates & T. D. Wachs (Eds.), *Temperament: Individual differences at the interface of biology and behavior* (pp. 82–116). Washington, DC: American Psychological Association.

Rowe, D. (1993). Genetic perspectives on personality. In R. Plomin & G. McClearn (Eds.), *Nature, nurture, and psychology* (pp. 179–195). Washington, DC: American Psychological Association.

Rowe, D. (1994). *The limits of family influence*. New York: Guilford Press.

Rubenstein, J., Lotspeich, L., & Ciaranello, R. (1990). The neurobiology of developmental disorders. In B. Lahey & A. Kazdin (Eds.), *Advances in clinical child psychology* (Vol. 13, pp. 1–52). New York: Plenum Press.

Rubin, K., LeMare, L., & Lollis, S. (1990). Social withdrawal in childhood. In S. Asher & J. Coie (Eds.), *Peer rejection in childhood* (pp. 217–249). Cambridge, England: Cambridge University Press.

Rush, D., & Callahan, K. (1989). Exposure to passive cigarette smoking and child development. *Annals of the New York Academy of Sciences, 562*, 74–100.

Rushton, J. (1984). Sociobiology: Toward a theory of individual and group differences in personality and behavior. In J. Royce & L. Mos (Eds.), *Annals of theoretical psychology* (Vol. 2, pp. 1–48). New York: Plenum Press.

Rushton, J., & Ankney, C. (1996). Brain size and cognitive ability. *Psychomomic Bulletin and Review, 3*, 21–36.

Rutter, M. (1983). Statistical and personal interactions. In D. Magnusson & V. Allen (Eds.), *Human development: An interactional perspective* (pp. 296–319). New York: Academic Press.

Rutter, M. (1988). Epidemiological approaches to developmental psychopathology. *Archives of General Psychiatry, 45*, 486–495.

Rutter, M. (1993). Developmental psychopathology as a research perspective. In D. Magnusson & P. Casaer (Eds.), *Longitudinal research on individual development* (pp. 127–152). Cambridge, England: Cambridge University Press.

Rutter, M. (1996). Transitions and turning points in developmental psychopathology. *International Journal of Behavioral Development, 19*, 603–626.

Rutter, M. (1997). Comorbidity: Concepts, claims and choices. *Criminal Behavior and Mental Health, 7*, 265–285.

Rutter, M., Bailey, A., Bolton, P., & LeCouteur, A. (1993). Autism. In R. Plomin & G. McClearn (Eds.), *Nature, nurture, and psychology* (pp. 285–306). Washington, DC: American Psychological Association.

Rutter, M., Chadwick, O., & Shaffer, D. (1984). Head injury. In M. Rutter (Ed.), *Developmental neuropsychiatry* (pp. 83–111). Edinburgh, Scotland: Churchill Livingstone.

Rutter, M., Dunn, J., Plomin, R., Simonoff, E., Pickles, A., Maughn, B., Ormel H., Meyer, J., & Eaves, L. (1997). Integrating nature and nurture. *Development and Psychopathology, 9*, 335–364.

Rutter, M., Macdonald, H., LeCouteur, A., Harrington, R., Bolton, P., & Bailey, A. (1990). Genetic factors in child psychiatric disorders II: Empirical findings. *Journal of Child Psychology and Psychiatry, 31*, 39–83.

Rutter, M., & Pickles, A. (1991). Person–environment interactions: Concepts, mechanisms and implications for data analysis. In T. D. Wachs & R. Plomin (Eds.), *Conceptualization and measurement of organism–environment interaction* (pp. 105–141). Washington, DC: American Psychological Association.

Rutter, M., Quinton, D., & Hill, J. (1990). Adult outcome of institution reared children: Males and females compared. In L. Robins & M. Rutter (Eds.), *Straight and devious pathways from childhood to adulthood* (pp. 135–167). Cambridge, England: Cambridge University Press.

Rutter, M., & Rutter, M. (1992). *Developing minds.* London: Penguin Press.

Sack, W., Clarke, G., & Seeley, J. (1996). Multiple forms of stress in Cambodian adolescent refugees. *Child Development, 67*, 107–116.

Sackett, G. (1991). Toward a more temporal view of organism–environment interaction. In T. D. Wachs & R. Plomin (Eds.), *Conceptualization and measurement of organism–environment interaction* (pp. 11–28). Washington, DC: American Psychological Association.

Saco-Pollitt, C. (1989). Ecocultural context and developmental risk. In J. Nugent, B. Lester, & T. Brazelton (Eds.), *The cultural context of infancy* (Vol. 1, pp. 3–25). Norwood, NJ: Ablex.

Salthe, S. (1985). *Evolving hierarchical systems.* New York: Columbia University Press.

Salzinger, S. (1990). Social networks in child rearing and child development. *Annals of the New York Academy of Science, 602*, 171–188.

Sameroff, A. (1989). General systems and the regulation of development. In M. Gunnar & E. Thelen (Eds.), *Minnesota Symposium on Child Psychology: Vol. 22. Systems and development* (pp. 219–235). Hillsdale, NJ: Erlbaum.

Sameroff, A. (1994). Ecological perspectives on longitudinal follow-up studies. In S. Friedman & H. C. Haywood (Eds.), *Developmental follow-up* (pp. 45–66). San Diego: Academic Press.

Sameroff, A. (1995). General systems theory and developmental psychopathology. In D. Cicchetti & D. Cohen (Eds.), *Developmental psychopathology: Vol 1. Theory and method* (pp. 659–695). New York: Wiley.

Sameroff, A., & Chandler, M. (1975). Reproductive risk and the continuum of caretaking causality. In F. Horowitz (Ed.), *Review of child development research* (Vol. 4, pp. 187–244). Chicago: University of Chicago Press.

Sameroff, A., & Fiese, B. (1990). Transactional regulation and early intervention. In S. Meisels & J. Shonkoff (Eds.), *Handbook of early childhood intervention* (pp. 119–149). Cambridge, England: Cambridge University Press.

Sameroff, A., Seifer, R., Baldwin, A., & Baldwin, C. (1993). Stability of intelligence from preschool to adolescence. *Child Development, 64*, 80–97.

Sameroff, A., Seifer, R., Barocas, R., Zax, M., & Greenspan, S. (1987). Intelligence quotient scores of 4 year old children: Social environmental risk factors. *Pediatrics, 79*, 343–350.

Sampson, R., & Groves, W. (1989). Community structure and crime. *American Journal of Sociology, 94*, 774–802.

Sampson, R., & Laub, J. (1994). Urban poverty and the family context of delinquency. *Child Development, 65*, 523–540.

Sandiford, P., Cassel, J., Sanchez, G., & Coldham, C. (1997). Does intelligence account for the link between maternal literacy and child survival. *Social Science and Medicine, 45*, 1231–1239.

Sandler, I., Miller, P., Short, J., & Wolchik, S. (1989). Social support as a protective factor for children in stress. In D. Belle (Ed.), *Children's social networks and social supports* (pp. 277–303). New York: Wiley.

Satz, P., Zaucha, K., McCleary, C., Light, R., Asarnow, R., & Becker, D. (1997). Mild head injury in children and adolescents. *Psychological Bulletin, 122*, 107–131.

Savin-Williams, R. (1995). An exploratory study of pubertal maturation timing and self-esteem among gay and bisexual male youths. *Developmental Psychology, 31*, 56–64.

Scarr, S. (1992). Developmental theories for the 1990's. *Child Development, 63*, 1–19.

Scarr, S., & McCartney, K. (1983). How people make their own environments. *Child Development, 54*, 424–435.

Schaefer, E., & Edgerton, M. (1985). Parent and child correlates of parental modernity. In I. Sigel (Ed.), *Parental belief systems* (pp. 287–318). Hillsdale, NJ: Erlbaum.

Scheper-Hughes, N. (1987a). A basic strangeness: Maternal estrangement and infant death. In C. Super (Ed.), *The role of culture in developmental disorder* (pp. 131–153). San Diego: Academic Press.

Scheper-Hughes, N. (1987b). Culture, scarcity and maternal thinking. In N. Scheper-Hughes (Ed.), *Child survival* (pp. 187–208). Dordrecht, The Netherlands: Reidel.

Scheper-Hughes, N. (1991). Social indifference to child death. *The Lancet, 337*, 1144–1147.

Schmitz, S. (1994). Personality and temperament. In J. DeFries, R. Plomin, & D. Fulker (Eds.), *Nature and nurture during middle childhood* (pp. 120–140). Oxford, England: Blackwell.

Schoggen, P. (1991). Ecological psychology. In R. Cohen & A. Siegel (Eds.), *Contexts in development* (pp. 281–301). Hillsdale, NJ: Erlbaum.

Schonfeld, I., Shaffer, D., & O'Connor, P. (1988). Conduct disorder and cognitive functioning. *Child Development, 59,* 993–1007.

Schooler, C. (1984). Psychological effects of complex environments. *Intelligence, 8,* 259–281.

Schooler, C. (1999). The workplace environment. In S. Friedman & T. D. Wachs (Eds.), *Measuring environment across the life span* (pp. 229–248). Washington, DC: American Psychological Association.

Schroeder, S., & Hawk, B. (1987). Psycho-social factors, lead exposure and IQ. In S. Schroeder (Ed.), *Toxic substances and mental retardation* (Monographs of the American Association on Mental Deficiency, Vol. 8, pp. 97–138). Washington, DC: American Association on Mental Deficiency.

Schulenberg, J., Wadsworth, K., O'Malley, P., Bachman, J., & Johnston, L. (1996). Adolescent risk factors for binge drinking during the transition to young adulthood. *Developmental Psychology, 32,* 659–674.

Schurch, B. (1995). Malnutrition and behavioral development: The nutrition variable. *Journal of Nutrition, 125*(Suppl.), 2255S–2262S.

Schwartz, D., Dodge, K., Pettit, G., & Bates, J. (1997). The early socialization of aggressive victims of bullying. *Child Development, 68,* 665–675.

Scola, P. (1991). Infections. In J. Matson & J. Mulick (Eds.), *Handbook of mental retardation* (2nd ed., pp. 151–157). Elmsford, NY: Pergamon Press.

Scott, K., Shaw, K., & Urbano, J. (1994). Developmental epidemiology. In S. Friedman & H. Haywood (Eds.), *Developmental follow-up: Concepts, domains and methods* (pp. 351–377). San Diego, CA: Academic Press.

Scrimshaw, N., & Young, V. (1989). Adaptation to low protein and energy intakes. *Human Organization, 48,* 20–30.

Seginer, R. (1983). Parents' educational expectations and children's academic achievement. *Merrill Palmer Quarterly, 29,* 1–23.

Sepulveda, J., Willett, N., & Munoz, A. (1988). Malnutrition and diarrhea. *American Journal of Epidemiology, 127,* 365–376.

Sewell, K., Adams-Webber, J., Mitterer, J., & Cromwell, R. (1992). Computerized repertory grids. *International Journal of Personal Construct Psychology, 5,* 1–23.

Shaheen, S. (1984). Neuromaturation and behavior development. *Developmental Psychology, 20,* 542–550.

Sham, P., O'Callaghan, E., Takei, N., Murray, G., Hare, E., & Murray, R. (1992). Schizophrenia following prenatal exposure to influenza epidemics between 1939–1960. *British Journal of Psychiatry, 160,* 461–466.

Sharma, A. (1996). Learning at school: The Indian scene. *Newsletter of the International Society for the Study of Behavioral Development, 29,* 4–5.

Sharp, D., Cole, M., & Lave, C. (1979). Education and cognitive development. *Monographs of the Society for Research in Child Development, 44*(1–2, Serial No. 178).

Shatz, M. (1985). An evolutionary perspective on plasticity in language development. *Merrill Palmer Quarterly, 31*, 211–222.

Sher, K., & Trull, T. (1996). Methodological issues in psychopathology research. *Annual Review of Psychology, 47*, 371–400.

Shonkoff, J. (1994). Health surveillance and the development of children. In S. Friedman & H. C. Haywood (Eds.), *Developmental follow-up* (pp. 113–128). San Diego: Academic Press.

Sigel, I. (1985). A conceptual analysis of beliefs. In I. Sigel (Ed.), *Parental belief systems* (pp. 345–371). Hillsdale, NJ: Erlbaum.

Sigel, I. (1992). The belief–behavior connection. In I. Sigel, A. DeLisi, & J. Goodnow (Eds.), *Parental belief systems* (2nd ed., pp. 433–456). Hillsdale, NJ: Erlbaum.

Sigman, M., Cohen, S., Beckwith, L., Asarnow, R., & Parmelee, A. (1992). The prediction of cognitive abilities at 8 and 12 years from neonatal assessments of preterm infants. In S. Friedman & M. Sigman (Eds.), *The psychological development of low birthweight children* (pp. 299–314). Norwood, NJ: Ablex.

Sigman, M., McDonald, M., Neumann, C., & Bwibo, N. (1991). Prediction of cognitive competence in Kenyan children from toddler nutrition, family characteristics and abilities. *Journal of Child Psychology and Psychiatry, 32*, 307–320.

Signorelli, N. (1990). Children, television and gender roles. *Journal of Adolescent Health Care, 11*, 50–58.

Silberg, J., Rutter, M., Meyer, J., Maes, H., Hewitt, J., Simonoff, E., Pickles, A., Loeber, R., & Eaves, L. (1996). Genetic and environmental influences on the covariation between hyperactivity and conduct disturbance in juvenile twins. *Journal of Child Psychology and Psychiatry, 37*, 803–816.

Simeon, D., & Grantham-McGregor, S. (1990). Nutritional deficiencies and children's behavior and mental development. *Nutritional Research Reviews, 3*, 1–24.

Simon, H. (1973). The organization of complex systems. In H. Pattee (Ed.), *Hierarchy theory: The challenge of complex systems* (pp. 3–27). New York: Braziller.

Simons, R., Lorenz, F., Wu, C., & Conger, R. (1993). Social network and marital support as mediators and moderators of the impact of stress and depression on parental behavior. *Developmental Psychology, 29*, 368–381.

Singer, L., Arendt, R., Farkas, K., Minnes, S., Huang, J., & Yamashita, T. (1997). Relationship of prenatal cocaine exposure and maternal postpartum psychological distress to child developmental outcome. *Development and Psychopathology, 9*, 473–489.

Singer, L., Yamashita, T., Hawkins, S., Cairns, D., Baley, J., & Kliegman, R. (1994). Increased incidence of intraventricular hemorrhage and developmental delay in cocaine-exposed very low birth weight infants. *Journal of Pediatrics, 124*, 765–771.

Singer, L., Yamashita, T., Lilien, L., Collin, M., & Baley, J. (1997). A longitudinal study of developmental outcome of infants with bronchopulmonary dysplasia and very low birth weight. *Pediatrics, 100,* 987–993.

Sinha, D. (1990). Intervention for development out of poverty. In R. Brislin (Ed.), *Applied cross-cultural psychology* (pp. 77–97). Newbury Park, CA: Sage.

Sinha, G. (1988). Exposure to industrial and urban environments and formal schooling as factors in psychological differentiation. *International Journal of Psychology, 23,* 707–719.

Skarda, C., & Freeman, W. (1987). How brains make chaos in order to make sense of the world. *Behavioral and Brain Sciences, 10,* 161–195.

Skuse, D. (1984). Extreme deprivation in early childhood. *Journal of Child Psychology and Psychiatry, 25,* 543–572.

Skuse, D. (1987). The psychological consequences of being small. *Journal of Child Psychology and Psychiatry, 28,* 641–650.

Skuse, D., Reilly, S., & Wolke, D. (1994). Psychosocial adversity and growth during infancy. *European Journal of Clinical Nutrition, 48,* S113–S130.

Slabach, E., Morrow, J., & Wachs, T. D. (1991). Questionnaire measurement of infant and child temperament. In J. Strelau & A. Angleitner (Eds.), *Explorations in temperament* (pp. 205–234). New York: Plenum Press.

Slater, P. (1983). The development of individual behavior. In T. Halliday & P. Slater (Eds.), *Genes, development and learning* (pp. 82–113). Oxford, England: Blackwell.

Slaughter-DeFoe, D., Nakagawa, K., Takanishi, R., & Johnson, D. (1990). Toward cultural/ecological perspectives on schooling and achievement in African and Asian-American children. *Child Development, 61,* 363–383.

Smith, J., Burian, R., Kauffman, S., Alberch, P., Campbell, J., Goodwin, B., Lande, R., Raup, D., & Wolpert, L. (1985). Developmental constraints and evolution. *Quarterly Review of Biology, 60,* 265–287.

Smith, M. (1987). Evolution and developmental psychology. In C. Crawford, M. Smith, & D. Krebs (Eds.), *Sociobiology and psychology* (pp. 225–252). Hillsdale, NJ: Erlbaum.

Smith, P. (1996). Strategies of cooperation. *International Journal of Behavioral Development, 19,* 81–88.

Sober, E., & Lewontin, R. (1982). Artifact, cause and genetic selection. *Philosophy of Science, 47,* 157–180.

Solan, H. (1991). Metabolic screening programs. In J. Matson & J. Mulick (Eds.), *Handbook of mental retardation* (2nd ed., pp. 292–307). New York: Pergamon.

Soliman, A., Hassan, A., Aref, M., Hintz, R., Rosenfeld, R., & Rogol, A. (1986). Serum insulin-like growth factors I and II concentrations and growth hormone and insulin responses to arginine infusion in children with protein-energy malnutrition before and after nutritional rehabilitation. *Pediatrics Research, 20,* 1122–1130.

Solter, D. (1988). Differential imprinting and expression of maternal and paternal genes. *Annual Review of Genetics, 22,* 127–146.

Somogyi, A., & Beck, H. (1993). Nutrition and breast feeding: Exposure to chemicals in breast milk. *Supplement to Environmental Health Perspectives, 101*, 45–52.

Soorani-Lunsing, R., Hadders-Algra, M., Olinga, A., Huisjes, H., & Touwen, B. (1993). Is minor neurological dysfunction at 12 years related to behavior and cognition? *Developmental Medicine and Child Neurology, 35*, 321–330.

Sorensen, H., Sabroe, S., Olsen, J., Rothman, K., Gillman, M., & Fischer, P. (1997). Birth weight and cognitive function in young adult life. *British Medical Journal, 315*, 401–403.

Sostek, A., (1992). Prematurity as well as intraventricular hemorrhage influence developmental outcome at 5 years. In S. Friedman & M. Sigman (Eds.), *The psychological development of low birthweight children* (pp. 259–274). Norwood, NJ: Ablex.

Spear, N., & Hyatt, L. (1993). How the timing of experience can affect the ontogeny of learning. In G. Turkewitz & D. Devenny (Eds.), *Developmental time and timing* (pp. 167–208). Hillsdale, NJ: Erlbuam.

Spitz, H. (1996). Commentary on the contributions of this volume. In D. Detterman (Ed.), *Current topics in human intelligence: The environment* (Vol. 5, pp. 173–178). Norwood, NJ: Ablex.

Squire, L., & Zola-Morgan, S. (1991). The medial temporal lobe memory system. *Science, 253*, 1380–1386.

Sroufe, A. (1983). Infant caregiving attachment and patterns of adaptation and competence. In M. Perlmutter (Ed.), *Minnesota Symposium on Child Psychology* (Vol. 16, pp. 41–84). Hillsdale, NJ: Erlbaum.

Sroufe, A., & Egeland, B. (1991). Person and environment. In T. D. Wachs & R. Plomin (Eds.), *Conceptualization and measurement of organism–environment interaction* (pp. 68–86). Washington, DC: American Psychological Association.

Sroufe, A., Egeland, B., & Kreutzer, T. (1990). The fate of early experience following developmental change. *Child Development, 61*, 1363–1373.

Sroufe, A., & Jacobvitz, D. (1989). Diverging pathways, developmental transformations, multiple etiologies and the problem of continuity in development. *Human Development, 32*, 196–203.

Sroufe, A., Jacobvitz, D., Mangelsdorf, S., De Angelo, E., & Ward, M. (1985). Generational bonding dissolution between mothers and their preschool children. *Child Development, 56*, 317–325.

Stansbury, K., & Gunnar, M. (1994). Adrenocortical activity and emotion regulation. *Monographs of the Society for Research in Child Development, 59*, 108–134.

Steinberg, G., Dornbusch, S., & Brown, B. (1992). Ethnic differences in adolescent achievement. *American Psychologist, 47*, 723–729.

Steinberg, L., Lamborn, S., Darling, N., & Dornbusch, S. (1994). Over-time changes in adjustment and competence among adolescents from authoritative, authoritarian, indulgent and neglected families. *Child Development, 65*, 754–770.

Steinberg, L., Mounts, N., Lamborn, S., & Dornbusch, S. (1991). Authoritative parenting and adolescent adjustment across varied ecological niches. *Journal of Research on Adolescence, 1,* 19–36.

Steinberg, L., & Silverberg, S. (1986). The vicissitudes of autonomy in early adolescence. *Child Development, 57,* 841–851.

Steinhausen, H., Edinsel, E., Fegert, J., Gobel, D., Reister, E., & Rentz, A. (1990). Child psychiatric disorders and family dysfunction in migrant workers and military families. *European Archives of Psychiatry and Neurological Sciences, 239,* 257–262.

Steinhausen, H., & Rauss-Mason, C. (1991). Epilepsy and anticonvulsive drugs. In M. Rutter & P. Casaer (Eds.), *Biological risk factors for psychosocial disorders* (pp. 311–339). Cambridge, England: Cambridge University Press.

Steinmetz, J. (1994). Brain substrates of emotion and temperament. In J. Bates & T. D. Wachs (Eds.), *Temperament: Individual differences at the interface of biology and behavior* (pp. 17–46). Washington, DC: American Psychological Association.

Stevenson, H., Parker, T., Wilkinson, A., Bonnevaux, B., & Gonzalez, M. (1978). Schooling, environment and cognitive development. *Monographs of the Society for Research in Child Development, 43*(1–2, Serial No. 175).

Stice, E., & Barrera, M. (1995). A longitudinal examination of the reciprocal relations between perceived parenting and adolescent substance use and externalizing behaviors. *Developmental Psychology, 31,* 332–334.

Stoolmiller, M. (1999). Implications of the restricted range of family environments for estimates of heritability and nonshared environment in behavior–genetic adoption studies. *Psychological Bulletin, 125,* 1–17.

Stouthamer-Loeber, M., Loeber, R., Farrington, D., Zhang, Q., Van Kammen, W., & Maguin, A. (1993). The double edge of protective and risk factors for delinquency. *Developmental and Psychopathology, 5,* 683–701.

Streissguth, A., Sampson, P., & Barr, H. (1989). Dose-response effects of prenatal alcohol exposure in humans from infancy to adulthood. *Annals of the New York Academy of Sciences, 562,* 123–132.

Strelau, J. (1994). The concepts of arousal and arousability as used in temperament studies. In J. Bates & T. D. Wachs (Eds.), *Temperament: Individual differences at the interface of biology and behavior* (pp. 117–142). Washington, DC: American Psychological Association.

Stromquist, N. (1989). Determinants of educational participation and achievement of women in the third world. *Review of Educational Research, 59,* 143–183.

Strupp, B., & Levitsky, D. (1995). Enduring cognitive effects of early malnutrition. *Journal of Nutrition, 125*(Suppl.), 2221S–2232S.

Super, C. (1976). Environmental effects on motor development. *Developmental Medicine and Child Neurology, 18,* 561–567.

Super, C. (1980). Behavioral development in infancy. In R. Munroe, R. Munroe, & B. Whiting (Eds.), *Handbook of cross-cultural human development* (pp. 181–270). New York: Garland.

Super, C., & Harkness, S. (1986). The developmental niche. *International Journal of Behavioral Development, 9,* 545–569.

Super, C., & Harkness, S. (1999). The environment in cultural and developmental research. In S. Friedman & T. D. Wachs (Eds.), *Measuring environment across the life span* (pp. 279–336). Washington, DC: American Psychological Association.

Super, C., Harkness, S., van Tijen, N., van der Vlugut, Dykstra, J., & Fintelman, M. (1996). The three r's of Dutch child rearing and the socialization of infant arousal. In S. Harkness & C. Super (Eds.), *Parents' cultural belief systems:* Their origins, expressions, and consequences (pp. 447–466). New York: Guilford Press.

Super, C., Herrera, M., & Mora, J. (1990). Long term effects of food supplementation and psychosocial intervention on the physical growth of Colombian infants at risk for malnutrition. *Child Development, 61,* 29–49.

Sur, M., Pallas, S., & Roe, A. (1990). Cross-modal plasticity in cortical development. *Trends in Neurosciences, 13,* 227–233.

Susser, E., Neugebauer, R., Hoek, H., Brown, A., Lin, S., Labovitz, D., & Gorman, J. (1996). Schizophrenia after prenatal famine. *Archives of General Psychiatry, 53,* 25–31.

Susser, M., & Stein, Z. (1994). Timing in prenatal nutrition: A reprise of the Dutch Famine Study. *Nutritional Reviews, 52,* 84–94.

Sutton-Smith, B. (1986). Play interactions and developmental processes. In A. Gottfried & C. Brown (Eds.), *Play interactions* (pp. 313–322). Washington, DC: Heath.

Sutton-Smith, B., & Roberts, J. (1980). Play, toys, games and sports. In H. Triandis & A. Heron (Eds.), *Handbook of cross-cultural psychology* (Vol. 4, pp. 425–471). Boston: Allyn & Bacon.

Symons, D. (1992). On the use and misuse of Darwinism in the study of human behavior. In J. Barkow, L. Cosmides, & J. Tooby (Eds.), *The adapted mind* (pp. 137–162). New York: Oxford Press.

Talbert, J., & McLaughlin, M. (1999). Assessing the school environment. In S. Friedman & T. D. Wachs (Eds.), *Measuring environment across the life span* (pp. 197–228). Washington, DC: American Psychological Association.

Tamis-LeMonda, C., & Bornstein, M. (1994). Specificity in mother–toddler play reactions across the second year. *Developmental Psychology, 30,* 283–292.

Tarullo, L., DeMulder, E., Ronsaville, D., Brown, E., & Radke-Yarrow, M. (1995). Maternal depression and maternal treatment of siblings as predictors of child psychopathology. *Developmental Psychology, 31,* 395–405.

Task Force on Joint Assessment of Prenatal and Perinatal Factors Associated With Brain Disorders. (1985). National Institutes of Health report on causes of mental retardation and cerebral palsy. *Pediatrics, 76,* 457–458.

Taylor, E. (1991). Toxins and allergens. In M. Rutter & P. Casaer (Eds.), *Biological risk factors for psychosocial disorders* (pp. 199–232). Cambridge, England: Cambridge University Press.

Taylor, H., Hack, M., Klein, N., & Schatschneider, C. (1995). Achievement in children with birth weights less than 750 grams with normal cognitive abilities. *Journal of Pediatric Psychology, 20,* 703–719.

Taylor, R., & Roberts, D. (1995). Kinship support and maternal and adolescent well-being in economically disadvantaged African American families. *Child Development, 66,* 1585–1597.

Telzrow, C. (1991). Impact of perinatal complications on education. In J. Gray & R. Dean (Eds.), *Neuropsychology of perinatal complications* (pp. 161–185). New York: Springer.

Temple, C. (1997). Cognitive neuropsychology and its application to children. *Journal of Child Psychology and Psychiatry, 38,* 27–52.

Teti, D., Gelfand, D., Messinger, D., & Isabella, R. (1995). Depression and the quality of early attachment. *Developmental Psychology, 31,* 364–376.

Thatcher, R., Walker, R., & Guidice, S. (1987). Human cerebral hemispheres develop at different rates and ages. *Science, 236,* 1110–1113.

Thelen, E. (1989). Self-organization in developmental processes. In M. Gunnar & E. Thelen (Eds.), *Minnesota Symposium on Child Psychology* (Vol. 22, pp. 77–177). Hillsdale, NJ: Erlbaum.

Thelen, E., & Smith, L. (1994). *A dynamic systems approach to the development of cognition and action.* Cambridge, MA: MIT Press.

Thelen, E., & Ulrich, B. (1991). Hidden skills. *Monographs of the Society for Research in Child Development, 56*(1, Serial No. 223).

Thoman, E. (1990). Sleeping and waking states of infants. *Neuroscience and Biobehavioral Reviews, 14,* 93–107.

Thoman, E., Acebo, C., & Becker, P. (1983). Infant crying and stability in the mother–infant relationship. *Child Development, 54,* 653–659.

Thompson, L. (1996). Where are the environmental influences on IQ? In D. Detterman (Ed.), *Current topics in human intelligence: The environment* (Vol. 5, pp. 179–184). Norwood, NJ: Ablex.

Thompson, L., Detterman, D., & Plomin, R. (1993). Differences in heritability across groups differing in ability, revisited. *Behavior Genetics, 23,* 331–336.

Thompson, W., & Grusec, J. (1970). Studies of early experience. In P. Mussen (Ed.), *Carmichael's manual of child psychology* (Vol. 1, pp. 565–566). New York: Plenum Press.

Tienari, P., Sorri, A., Lahti, I., & Naarala, M. (1987). Genetic and psychosocial factors in schizophrenia. *Schizophrenia Bulletin, 13,* 477–484.

Tietjen, A. (1989). The ecology of children's social support networks. In D. Belle (Ed.), *Children's social networks and social supports* (pp. 37–69). New York: Wiley.

Toller, S. (1992). Biochemistry, individual differences and psychonutrition. In A. Gale & M. Eysenck (Eds.), *Handbook of individual differences* (pp. 19–44). New York: Wiley.

Tomasello, M., Savage-Rumbaugh, S., & Kruger, A. (1993). Imitative learning of actions on objects by children, chimpanzees and encultured chimpanzees. *Child Development, 64,* 1688–1705.

Tooby, J., & Cosmides, L. (1992). The psychological foundations of culture. In J. Barkow, L. Cosmides, & J. Tooby (Eds.), *The adapted mind* (pp. 19–136). New York: Oxford University Press.

Triandis, H. (1989). Cross-cultural studies of individualism and collectivism. *Nebraska Symposium on Motivation, 37*, 41–135.

Triandis, H. (1990). Theoretical concepts that are applicable to the analysis of ethnocentrism. In R. Brislin (Ed.), *Applied cross-cultural psychology* (pp. 35–55). Newbury Park, CA: Sage.

Tronick, E., Morelli, G., & Winn, S. (1987). Multiple caretaking of Efe (pygmy) infants. *American Anthropologist, 89*, 96–106.

Tronick, E., Thomas, R., & Daltabuit, M. (1994). The Quechua Manta pouch: A caregiving practice for buffering the Peruvian infant against the multiple stressors of high altitude. *Child Development, 5*, 1005–1013.

Turkewitz, G., & Kenny, P. (1985). The role of developmental limitations of sensory input on sensory/perceptual organization. *Journal of Developmental and Behavioral Pediatrics, 6*, 302–306.

Uauy, R., & deAndraca, I. (1995). Human milk and breast feeding for optimal development. *Journal of Nutrition, 125*(Suppl. 85), 2278S–2280S.

Uauy, R., Peirano, P., Hoffman, D., Mena, P., Birch, D., & Birch, E. (1996). Role of essential fatty acids in the function of the developing nervous system. *Lipids, 31*(Suppl.), S167–S176.

Uchino, B., Cacioppo, J., & Kiecolt-Glaser, J. (1996). The relationship between social support and physiological processes. *Psychological Bulletin, 119*, 488–531.

Ulijaszek, S. (1994). Between population variation in pre-adolescent growth. *European Journal of Clinical Nutrition, 48*(Suppl.), S5–S14.

Ungerleider, L. (1995). Functional brain imaging mechanisms of cortical mechanisms for memory. *Science, 270*, 769–775.

Unvas-Moberg, K. (1989). The gastrointestinal tract in growth and reproduction. *Scientific American, 261*, 60–65.

Valsiner, J., & Litvinovic, G. (1996). Processes of generalization in parental reasoning. In S. Harkness & C. Super (Eds.), *Parents' Cultural belief systems* (pp. 56–82). New York: Guilford Press.

van Aken, M. (1995, March). *Personality characteristics, psychological adjustment and perceived social support in 12 year olds.* Paper presented at the annual meeting of the Society for Research in Child Development, Indianapolis, IN.

van Geert, P. (1991). A dynamic systems model of cognitive and language growth. *Psychological Review, 98*, 3–53.

van Ijzendoorn, M., & Kroonenberg, P. (1988). Cross-cultural patterns of attachment. *Child Development, 59*, 147–156.

Vernon-Feagans, L., Emmanuel, D., & Blood, I. (1997). The effect of otitis media and quality of daycare on children's language development. *Journal of Applied Developmental Psychology, 18*, 395–409.

Viken, R., Rose, R., Kaprio, J., & Koshenvino, M. (1994). A developmental genetic analysis of adult personality. *Journal of Personality and Social Psychology, 66,* 722–730.

Vogt, L., Jordan, C., & Tharp, R. (1987). Explaining school failure, producing school success. *Anthropology and Education Quarterly, 18,* 276–286.

von Bertalanffy, I. (1968). *General systems theory.* New York: Braziller.

Vorhees, C., & Mollnow, E. (1987). Behavioral teratogenesis: Long term influences on behavior from early exposure to environmental agents. In J. Osofsky (Ed.), *Handbook of infant development* (2nd ed., pp. 913–971). New York: Wiley.

Vuchinich, S., Bank, L., & Patterson, G. (1992). Parenting, peers, and the stability of antisocial behavior in preadolescent boys. *Developmental Psychology, 28,* 510–521.

Wachs, T. D. (1979). Proximal experience and early cognitive–intellectual development: The physical environment. *Merrill Palmer Quarterly, 25,* 3–41.

Wachs, T. D. (1987). Specificity of environmental action as manifest in environmental correlates of infants mastery motivation. *Developmental Psychology, 23,* 782–790.

Wachs, T. D. (1989). Temperament, activity and behavioral development of infants and children. In B. Schurch & N. Scrimshaw (Eds.), *Activity, energy expenditure and energy requirements of infants and children* (pp. 297–320). Lausanne, Switzerland: International Dietary Energy Consultive Group.

Wachs, T. D. (1991). Synthesis: Promising research designs, measures, and strategies. In T. D. Wachs & R. Plomin (Eds.), *Conceptualization and measurement of the organism–environment interaction* (pp. 162–182). Washington, DC: American Psychological Association.

Wachs, T. D. (1992). *The nature of nurture.* Newbury Park, CA: Sage.

Wachs, T. D. (1993a). Determinants of intellectual development: Single determinant research in a multidetermined universe. *Intelligence, 17,* 1–10.

Wachs, T. D. (1993b). Nature of relations between the physical and social microenvironment of the two year old child. *Early Development and Parenting, 2,* 81–87.

Wachs, T. D. (1994). Fit, context and the transition between temperament and personality. In C. Halverson, G. Kohnstamm, & R. Martin (Eds.), *The developing structure of personality from infancy to adulthood* (pp. 209–222). Hillsdale, NJ: Erlbaum.

Wachs, T. D. (1995a). Genetic and family influences on individual development: Both necessary, neither sufficient. *Psychological Inquiry, 6,* 161–173.

Wachs, T. D. (1995b). Relation of mild-to-moderate malnutrition to human development: Correlational studies. *Journal of Nutrition, 125*(Suppl. 8S), 2245S–2254S.

Wachs, T. D. (1996a). Environment and intelligence. In D. Detterman (Ed.), *Current topics in human intelligence* (Vol. 5, pp. 68–86). Norwood, NJ: Ablex.

Wachs, T. D. (1996b). Known and potential processes underlying developmental trajectories in childhood and adolescence. *Developmental Psychology, 32,* 796–801.

Wachs, T. D. (1996c). Environmental influences on intelligence: Would that it were that simple. In D. Detterman (Ed.), *Current topics in human intelligence: The environment* (Vol.5, pp. 235–246). Norwood, NJ: Ablex.

Wachs, T. D. (1998). Family environmental influences and the development of undernourished children. In M. Lewis & C. Feiring (Eds.), *Families, risk and competence* (pp. 245–268). Hillsdale, NJ: Erlbaum.

Wachs, T. D. (1999). Celebrating complexity: Conceptualization and assessment of the environment. In S. Friedman & T. D. Wachs (Eds.), *Measuring environment across the life span* (pp. 357–392). Washington DC: Amercan Psychological Association.

Wachs, T. D. (in press). Linking nutrition and temperament. In D. Molfese & V. Molfese (Eds.), *Temperament and personality development across the life span.* Hillsdale, NJ: Erlbaum.

Wachs, T. D., Bishry, Z., Moussa, W., Yunis, F., McCabe, G., Harrison, G., Swefi, I., Kirksey, A., Galal, O., Jerome, N., & Shaneen, F. (1995). Nutritional intake and context as predictors of cognition and adaptive behavior of Egyptian school age children. *International Journal of Behavioral Development, 18,* 425–450.

Wachs, T. D., Bishry, Z., Sobhy, A., McCabe, G., Galal, O., & Shaheen, F. (1993). Relation of rearing environment to adaptive behavior of Egyptian toddlers. *Child Development, 64,* 586–604.

Wachs, T. D., & Gruen, G. (1982). *Early experience and human development.* New York: Plenum Press.

Wachs, T. D., & King, B. (1994). Behavioral research in the brave new world of neuroscience and temperament. In J. Bates & T. D. Wachs (Eds.), *Temperament: Individual differences at the interface of biology and behavior* (pp. 307–336). Washington, DC: American Psychological Association.

Wachs, T. D., & McCabe, G. (1998). The role of the environment in human nutritional research and intervention. In *Nutrition, health and child development* (Pan-American Health Organization Scientific Monograph No. 566). Washington, DC: Pan-American Health Organization.

Wachs, T. D., McCabe, G., Moussa, W., & Yunis, F. (1999, April). *Maternal intelligence and education level as infuences on the nutritional intake of Egyptian toddlers.* Paper presented at the annual meeting of the Society for Research in Child Development, Albuquerque, NM.

Wachs, T. D., McCabe, G., Yunis, F., Kirksey, A., Harrison, G., Galal, O., & Jerome, N. (1996). Relation of nutritional intake and context to cognitive performance of Egyptian adults. *International Journal of Behavioral Development, 22,* 129–154.

Wachs, T. D., & Plomin, R. (1991). *Conceptualization and measurement of organism environment interaction.* Washington, DC: American Psychological Association.

Wachs, T. D., Sigman, M., Bishry, Z., Moussa, W., Jerome, N., Neumann, C., Bwibo, N., & McDonald, M. (1992). Caregiver child interaction patterns in two cultures in relation to nutrition. *International Journal of Behavioral Development, 15*, 1–18.

Wachs, T. D., & Weizmann, F. (1992). Prenatal and genetic influences upon behavior and development. In C. Walker & M. Roberts (Eds.), *Handbook of clinical child psychology* (2nd ed., pp. 183–198). New York: Wiley.

Waddington, C. (1966). *Principles of development and differentiation.* New York: Macmillan.

Waddington, C. (1972). Form and information. In C. Waddington (Ed.), *Toward a theoretical biology* (Vol. 4, pp. 109–141). Chicago: Aldine.

Wadsworth, S. (1994). School achievement. In J. DeFries, R. Plomin, & D. Fulker (Eds.), *Nature and nurture during middle childhood* (pp. 86–101). London: Blackwell.

Wagner, D. (1978). Memories of Morocco. *Cognitive Psychology, 10*, 1–28.

Wahlsten, D. (1990). Insensitivity of the analysis of variance to heredity–environment interaction. *Behavioral and Brain Sciences, 13*, 109–161.

Wainryb, C. (1995). Reasoning about social conflicts in different cultures. *Child Development, 66*, 390–401.

Walker, E., Downey, G., & Bergman, A. (1989). The effects of parental psychopathology and maltreatment on child behavior. *Child Development, 60*, 15–24.

Warner, R. (1980). The coevolution of behavioral and life history characteristics. In G. Barlow & J. Silverberg (Eds.), *Sociobiology: Beyond nature/nurture* (pp. 151–180). Boulder, CO: Westview.

Wasserman, G., Graziano, J., Factor-Litvak, P., Popovac, D., Morina, N., Musabegovic, A., Vrenezi, N., Capuni-Paracka, S., Lekic, V., & Preteni-Redjepi, E. (1994). Consequences of lead exposure and iron supplementation on childhood development at age 4 years. *Neurotoxicology and Teratology, 16*, 233–240.

Wasserman, T. (1984). The effect of cognitive development on the use of cognitive behavioral techniques with children. *Child and Family Behavior Therapy, 5*, 37–50.

Waterlow, J. (1994a). Causes and mechanisms of linear growth retardation (stunting). *European Journal of Clinical Nutrition-Supplement, 48*, S1–S4.

Waterlow, J. (1994b). Summary of causes and mechanisms of linear growth retardation. *European Journal of Clinical Nutrition-Supplement, 48*, S210.

Watkins, W., & Pollitt, E. (1996). Effect of removing ascaris on the growth of Guatemalan school children. *Pediatrics, 97*, 871–876.

Watkins, W., & Pollitt, E. (1997). Stupidity or worms: Do intestinal worms impair mental performance? *Psychological Bulletin, 121*, 171–191.

Watkins, W., & Pollitt, E .(1998). Iron deficiency and cognition among school age children. In *Nutrition, health and child development* (Pan-American Health Organization Scientific Monograph No. 566). Washington, DC: Pan-American Health Organization.

Watson-Gegeo, K., & Gegeo, D. (1989). The role of sibling interaction in child socialization. In P. Zukow (Ed.), *Sibling interaction across cultures* (pp. 54–76). New York: Springer-Verlag.

Webster, A., Bamford, J., Thyer, N., & Ayles, R. (1989). The psychological, educational and auditory sequelae of early persistent secretory otitis media. *Journal of Child Psychology and Psychiatry, 30,* 529–546.

Weinberg, J., Zimmerberg, J., & Sonderegger, T. (1992). Gender specific effects of perinatal exposure to alcohol and drugs. In T. Sonderegger (Ed.), *Perinatal substance abuse* (pp. 51–89). Baltimore: Johns Hopkins University Press.

Weinstein, C. (1991). The classroom as a social context for learning. *Annual Review of Psychology, 42,* 493–525.

Weisner, T. (1989a). Comparing sibling relationships across cultures. In P. Zurkow (Ed.), *Sibling interaction across cultures* (pp. 11–25). New York: Springer-Verlag.

Weisner, T. (1989b). Cultural and universal aspects of social support for children. In D. Belle (Ed.), *Children's social networks and social supports* (pp. 70–90). New York: Wiley.

Weisner, T., Matheson, C., & Bernheimer, L. (1996). American cultural models of early influence and parent recognition of developmental delay. In S. Harkness & C. Super (Eds.), *Parents' cultural belief systems* (pp. 496–531). New York: Guilford Press.

Weisner, T., & Wilson-Mitchel, J. (1990). Non-conventional family life styles and sex typing in six-year-old girls. *Child Development, 61,* 1915–1933.

Weiss, P. (1971). The basic concept of hierarchic systems. In P. Weiss (Ed.), *Hierarchically organized systems in theory and practice* (pp. 1–44). New York: Hafner.

Welles-Nystrom, B. (1996). Scenes from a marriage. Equality ideology in Swedish family policy, maternal ethotheories and practices. In S. Harkness & C. Super (Eds.), *Parents' cultural belief systems* (pp. 192–214). New York: Guilford Press.

Welsh, M., Pennington, B., Ozanoff, S., Rouse, B., & McCabe, E. (1990). Neuropsychology of early treated phenylketonuria. *Child Development, 61,* 1697–1713.

Werner, E. (1979). *Cross-cultural child development.* Monterey, CA: Brooks-Cole.

Werner, E. (1988). A cross-cultural perspective on infancy. *Journal of Cross-Cultural Psychology, 19,* 96–113.

Werner, E. (1990). Protective factors and individual resilience. In S. Meisels & J. Shonkoff (Eds.), *Handbook of early childhood intervention* (pp. 97–116). Cambridge, England: Cambridge University Press.

Werner, E. (1994). Overcoming the odds. *Developmental and Behavioral Pediatrics, 15,* 131–136.

Werner, E., & Smith, R. (1982). *Vulnerable but invincible.* New York: McGraw-Hill.

Werner, E., & Smith, R. (1992). *Overcoming the odds.* Ithaca, NY: Cornell University Press.

White, K. (1982). The relation between socioeconomic status and academic achievement. *Psychological Bulletin, 20,* 76–99.

Whitehead, A. (1925). *Science and the modern world.* New York: Macmillan.

Whitefield, G., Hsieh, J., Jurutka, P., Selznick, S., Haussler, C., MacDonald, P., & Haussler, M. (1995). Genomic actions of 1,25-dihydroxyvitain D3. *Journal of Nutrition-Supplement, 125*, 1690S–1694S.

Whiting, B. (1980). Culture and social behavior. *Ethos, 8*, 95–116.

Whiting, B., & Edwards, C. (1988). *Children of different worlds.* Cambridge, MA: Harvard University Press.

Whiting, B., & Whiting, J. (1975). *Children of six cultures.* Cambridge, MA: Harvard University Press.

Whiting, J. (1981). Environmental constraints on infant care practices. In R. Munroe, R. Munroe, & B. Whiting (Eds.), *Handbook of cross-cultural human development* (pp. 155–179). New York: Garland.

Willerman, T., Schultz, R., Rutledge, J., & Bigler, E. (1992). Hemisphere size asymmetry predicts relative verbal and non-verbal intelligence differentially in the sexes. *Intelligence, 16*, 315–328.

Williams, B. (1980). Kin selection, fitness and cultural evolution. In G. Barlow & J. Silverberg (Eds.), *Sociobiology: Beyond nature/nurture* (pp. 573–587). Boulder, CO: Westview Press.

Williams, C., & Berry, J. (1991). Primary prevention of acculturative stress among refugees. *American Psychologist, 46*, 632–641.

Williams, T. (1977). Infant development and supplemental care. *Human Development, 20*, 1–30.

Wilson, D. (1994). Adaptive genetic variation and human evolutionary plasticity. *Ethology and Sociobiology, 15*, 219–235.

Wilson, D., Near, D., & Miller, R. (1996). Machiavellianism: A synthesis of the evolutionary and psychological literature. *Psychological Bulletin, 119*, 285–299.

Wilson, E. (1980). A consideration of the genetic foundation of human social behavior. In G. Barlow & J. Silverberg (Eds.), *Sociobiology: Beyond nature/nurture* (pp. 295–306). Boulder, CO: Westview Press.

Wilson, E. (1998). Back from chaos. *Atlantic Monthly, 281*, 41–62.

Wilson, G. (1989). Clinical studies of infants and children exposed prenatally to heroin. *Annals of the New York Academy of Sciences, 562*, 123–132.

Wilson, G. (1992). Heroin use during pregnancy. In T. Sonderegger (Ed.), *Perinatal substance abuse* (pp. 224–238). Baltimore: Johns Hopkins University Press.

Wilson, J. (1977). Embryotoxicity of drugs in man. In J. Wilson & F. Fraser (Eds.), *Handbook of teratology* (Vol. 1, pp. 104–136). New York: Plenum Press.

Winick, M., Meyer, K., & Harris, R. (1975). Malnutrition and environmental enrichment by early adoption. *Science, 190*, 1173–1175.

Winter, D. (1993). Slot rattling: From law enforcement to lawbreaking. *International Journal of Personal Construct Psychology, 6*, 253–267.

Witelson, S. (1991). Neural sexual mosaicism: Sexual differentiation of the human temporo-parietal region for functional asymmetry. *Psychoneuro-Endrocinology*, *16*, 131–153.

Witelson, S., Glezer, I., & Kigar, D. (1995). Women have greater density of neurons in posterior temporal cortex. *Journal of Neuroscience, 15*, 3418–3428.

Witkin, H., & Berry, J. (1975). Psychological differentiation in cross-cultural perspectives. *Journal of Cross-Cultural Psychology, 6*, 4–87.

Wohlwill, J. (1973). The concept of experience: S or R. *Human Development, 16*, 90–107.

Wohlwill, J., & Heft, H. (1987). The physical environment and the development of the child. In I. Altman & D. Stokols (Eds.), *Handbook of environmental psychology* (pp. 281–328). New York: Wiley.

Wolff, P. (1977) Biological variations and cultural diversity. In R. Leiderman, S. Tulkin, & A. Rosenfeld (Eds.), *Culture and infancy* (pp. 357–381)

Wright, J., & Mischel, W. (1987). A conditional approach to dispositional constructs. *Journal of Personality and Social Psychology, 53*, 1159–1177.

Yamazaki, K., Inomata, J., & MacKenzie, J. (1987). Self-expression, interpersonal relations and juvenile delinquency in Japan. In C. Super (Ed.), *The role of culture in developmental disorder* (pp. 180–206). San Diego: Academic Press.

Yip, R., & Dallman, P. (1996). Iron. In E. Ziegler & L. Filer (Eds.), *Present knowledge in nutrition* (7th ed., pp. 277–292). Washington, DC: International Life Sciences Institute Press.

Youdim, M., Ben-Shachar, D., & Yehuda, S. (1989). Putative biological mechanisms of the effect of iron deficiency on brain biochemistry and behavior. *American Journal of Clinical Nutrition, 50*, 607–617.

Young, M. (1998). Policy implications of early childhood development programs. In *Nutrition, health and child development* (Pan-American Health Organization Scientific Monograph No. 566). Washington, DC: Pan-American Health Organization.

Zajonc, R., & Mullally, P. (1997). Birth order: Reconciling conflicting results. *American Psychologist, 52*, 685–699.

Zeitlin, M. (1991). Nutritional resilience in a hostile environment. *Nutrition Reviews, 49*, 259–268.

Zeitlin, M. (1996). My child is my crown: Yoruba parental theories and practices in early childhood. In S. Harkness & C. Super (Eds.), *Parents' cultural belief systems* (pp. 407–427). New York: Guilford Press.

Zeskind, P., & Iacino, R. (1987). The relation between length of hospitalization and the mental and physical development of preterm infants. *Infant Behavior and Development, 10*, 217–221.

Zigler, E. (1967). Familial mental retardation: A continuing dilemma. *Science, 155*, 292–298.

Zuckerman, M. (1994). Impulsive unsocialized sensation seeking. In J. Bates & T. D. Wachs (Eds.), *Temperament: Individual differences at the interface of biology and behavior* (pp. 219–258). Washington, DC: American Psychological Association.

Zukow, P. (1989). Siblings as effective socializing agents. In P. Zukow (Ed.), *Sibling interaction across cultures* (pp. 79–105). New York: Springer-Verlag.

AUTHOR INDEX

A

Abel, E., 189
Abell, S., 63, 64, 65
Aber, L., 159, 180
Aboud, F., 161
Abuelo, D., 6, 7, 37, 38, 185
Acebo, C., 269
Ackerman, L., 162
Adair, L., 28, 189
Adamson, L., 149
Adams-Webber, J., 290
Adan, A., 179
Affleck, G., 102
Aguayo, V., 27
Ahadi, S., 297
Albalak, R., 28
Alberch, P., 2, 3, 15, 199, 277, 278
Alberti, S., 57
Alberts, D., 101, 118
Aldwin, C., 152, 226
Alemu, T., 161
Alexander, K., 171, 300
Allard, T., 48, 203
Allen, L., 74, 86, 88, 90, 94
Als, H., 25, 72, 80, 82, 137, 264, 288, 298, 319, 329
Altman, I., 167
Alva, S., 177
Amiel-Tison, C., 137
Anderson, J., 15, 19, 22, 26
Anderson, P., 2, 213, 276, 307, 318
Anderson, V., 73
Andrew, J., 231, 234
Andruski, J., 26
Angell, R., 147, 177, 180
Ankney, C., 54, 105
Anna, C., 179
Aotaki-Phenice, L., 158, 162, 163
Appelbaum, M., 98, 101, 208, 255
Archer, J., 15, 26
Arcus, D., 66, 107, 120
Aref, M., 200
Aronowitz, M., 178, 179
Asarnow, R., 55, 60
Asendorpf, J., 103, 105, 106, 109, 167, 218, 300, 306
Asher, S., 111
Ashworth, A., 70

Assuncao, A., 70
Ayles, R., 74
Aylward, G., 71
Ayoub, C., 74, 83
Azuma, H., 130, 179

B

Bachevalier, J., 46, 62, 64
Bachman, J., 113
Baghurst, P., 83, 189
Bailey, A., 6–7, 39, 40, 43, 71, 116, 123, 145, 184, 189, 238, 254
Bakeman, R., 149
Baldwin, A., 145, 186
Baldwin, C., 145, 186
Ballabriga, A., 50, 85
Bamford, J., 74
Bancroft, J., 60, 61, 63, 64, 65, 66, 189
Bandura, A., 102, 110, 113, 122
Bank, L., 103, 133, 146, 197, 231, 234, 252, 310, 331
Barbaranelli, C., 110, 122
Bargh, J., 288
Barker, D., 234, 243
Barker, R., 280, 301, 302
Barlow, G., 14
Barnard, K., 104, 145, 186
Barocas, R., 145
Bar-On, D., 6
Baron, R., 208
Barr, H., 5, 77, 79, 80, 82
Barr, R., 49, 81, 149
Barrera, M., 150, 151
Barrett, D., 163
Barrett, M., 75
Barsky, V., 57
Barton, S., 265, 269, 273, 274, 277, 288
Bassily, N., 90
Bates, C., 74
Bates, J., 4, 107, 109, 118, 120, 149, 186, 188, 255, 298, 312, 324, 329
Bateson, P., 9, 10, 18, 19, 22, 133, 186, 188, 202, 245, 298
Baumgardner, T., 39
Baxter, A., 80
Beagle, J., 291
Beaton, G., 162, 163
Beautrais, A., 82

Beck, H., 76
Becker, D., 271
Becker, J., 60, 64, 65, 66, 101, 102
Becker, P., 81, 197, 269
Beckwith, L., 55, 60, 233, 234, 319
Bell, J., 85
Bell, M., 55, 56, 58
Bell, R., 150, 158, 179
Bellinger, D., 78, 320
Belmont, J., 37, 75
Belsky, J., 20, 21, 116, 121, 128, 162, 242, 296
Bem, D., 103, 117, 118, 121, 167, 218, 296, 308
Benasich, A., 131
Benbow, C., 54, 55
Bender, B., 44
Ben-Shachar, D., 85
Berenbaum, S., 62, 63
Berendes, H., 233
Berger, J., 27
Berger, K., 74
Bergman, A., 150
Bergman, L., 210, 234, 291
Bernhardt, P., 65
Bernheimer, L., 153, 163
Bernieri, F., 36, 41
Berry, J., 29, 127, 155, 160, 174, 177, 179, 186
Berry, T., 15, 17, 23
Bertoncini, J., 137
Best, D., 178, 180
Best, K., 4, 46, 104, 106, 110, 119, 133, 142, 179, 186, 239, 255
Betz, J., 55
Beydouin, S., 70
Bezruczko, N., 236
Bhavnagri, N., 170
Bicego, G., 161
Bigler, E., 54
Birch, D., 85
Birch, E., 85
Bird, Y., 9
Biringen, Z., 98, 101
Birkel, R., 291
Bisanz, J., 179
Bishry, Z., 74, 90, 94, 163, 179, 189, 197, 198, 257
Bjorklund, D., 98
Black, J., 7, 49, 52
Black, K., 25, 224, 256
Black, M., 89

Blatt, S., 24
Bleichrodt, N., 121
Bleske, A., 26
Block, J., 109, 299, 306
Bloom, F., 48, 49, 50
Blue, J., 128
Boerma, J., 161
Boersma, D., 25
Bohman, M., 41
Bolger, K., 145
Bolton, P., 39, 40, 43, 71, 116, 123, 145, 184, 189, 238, 254
Bond, L., 73
Bonett, D., 28
Bonnevaux, B., 177
Bonta, B., 167
Boodoo, G., 105
Bookstein, F., 77, 80, 82
Booth, C., 104
Borawski-Clark, E., 70
Born, M., 121
Bornschein, R., 77, 80, 98, 224
Bornstein, M., 163, 178, 218, 221, 257
Bouchard, T., 38, 105
Bourgeois, J., 49
Bower, P., 291
Boyce, J., 178
Boyce, M., 5, 74, 83, 104
Boyce, W., 4, 49, 81, 178, 239, 320, 328
Boykin, A., 105
Bradley, R., 133, 142, 186, 211, 225, 241
Brand, S., 179
Brandt, P., 145, 186
Braungart, J., 150
Brazelton, T., 180
Breedlove, M., 54, 55, 61, 61n, 64
Brennan, J., 70, 102, 133
Brennan, P., 58, 83
Breslau, N., 70
Brinker, R., 80
Brody, G., 104, 122, 129, 141, 160, 177, 180, 306
Brody, N., 41, 105
Bronfenbrenner, U., 8, 36, 125, 139, 142, 154, 178, 201, 236, 280, 299, 301, 322
Brook, J., 71, 82, 105, 255
Brooks-Gunn, J., 20, 65, 66, 71, 99, 101, 131, 133, 218
Brophy, J., 129

Brown, B., 133, 145, 149
Brown, E., 126, 128, 255
Brown, J., 317, 318
Brown, K., 81
Brown, W., 9
Brutsaert, T., 28
Bryant, B., 160, 180
Bryant, F., 179
Buchanan, C., 60, 64, 65, 66, 100, 101,
    102
Bugental, D., 128
Buka, S., 11, 70, 71
Bulux, J., 79
Bulux, J., 79
Burchinal, M., 8, 75, 186
Burian, R., 15
Buriel, R., 158, 171
Burn, J., 9
Burns, A., 102, 170
Burns, S., 324
Buss, D., 15, 16, 17, 19, 22, 23, 26, 197,
    241, 255, 256
Butler, L., 80
Bwibo, N., 90, 94, 197
Byne, W., 54, 61n

C
Cadman, D., 5, 74, 83, 104
Cadoret, R., 151, 255
Cafasso, L., 179
Cain, K., 110
Cairns, B., 111, 301
Cairns, E., 159, 160, 177
Cairns, R., 16, 36, 42, 111, 200, 212, 218,
    229, 231, 302
Caldwell, B., 144, 225, 241
Calkins, S., 56, 57, 58, 106, 116, 187, 280
Callahan, K., 79
Callender, G., 38, 47, 75, 258
Campbell, J., 15
Campbell, K., 55
Campos, J., 98, 101
Candini, G., 57
Cannon, T., 255
Capara, G., 110, 122
Caplan, A., 14, 185
Capron, C., 43, 255
Capuni-Paracka, S., 77
Cardon, L., 34, 38, 41
Carlin, M., 202
Carmichael-Olson, H., 70, 188

Caro, T., 9, 19, 188
Carran, D., 70
Casaer, P., 43, 50, 69–70, 72, 82
Case, R., 294
Casey, P., 133, 142, 186, 211
Cashdan, E., 30
Caspi, A., 20, 21, 102, 103, 107, 111, 116,
    117, 118, 121, 122, 141, 150, 160,
    167, 174, 177, 188, 218, 220, 225,
    229, 233, 236, 255, 273, 296, 305,
    306, 308, 312
Cassel, J., 161
Cassidy, J., 116, 121, 296
Cather, A., 29
Catroppa, C., 73
Cauffman, E., 141
Caughy, M., 72, 83, 133, 149
Caulfield, L., 90
Cavalli-Sforza, L., 36, 154
Caviness, V., 49, 50
Ceci, S., 36, 105, 125, 133, 142, 163, 218,
    236, 280
Cederblad, M., 167
Cen, G., 163, 166
Chabrier, L., 77
Chadwick, O., 241
Chagnon, N., 17
Chambon, P., 185
Chan, S., 158, 171
Chandler, M., 4, 82, 116
Chang, F., 25, 224
Chang, S., 85, 311, 319, 322, 331
Chao, R., 170
Chapais, B., 14
Chapman, M., 150
Charlesworth, W., 15, 24
Chase-Lansdale, P., 231, 234
Chassin, L., 101, 158, 163
Chen, C., 132, 163, 177, 180, 308
Chen, H., 163, 166
Chen, X., 163, 166, 178
Cherny, S., 34, 41, 42
Chess, S., 311
Chesterman, E., 4
Cheung, P., 141
Chiker, V., 179
Childs, C., 29, 166, 181
Chinese Cultural Connection, 168
Chipperfield, J., 126
Chisholm, J., 14, 19, 27, 30, 173, 180
Chistovich, I., 26
Chistovich, L., 26

Chiu, M., 165, 178
Chow, J., 159, 184, 186
Ciaramitaro, V., 37
Ciaranello, R., 5, 37, 48, 80, 133
Cillessen, A., 111
Clarke, A., 6, 184, 225, 254, 303, 307
Clarke, G., 234, 241, 303, 307
Clarke, J., 75
Clarke-Klein, S., 75
Clarke-Stewart, K., 45, 133
Clausen, J., 102, 111, 117, 118, 120, 225, 309
Claussen, A., 88
Cloniger, R., 41
Cochran, M., 170
Cohen, F., 4
Cohen, H., 52, 64
Cohen, J., 255
Cohen, P., 61, 61n, 62, 63n, 71, 82, 105, 255
Cohen, S., 55, 60
Coie, J., 116, 136
Coldham, C., 161
Cole, M., 24, 92, 153, 154, 161, 167, 170, 179, 231
Cole, P., 121
Cole, T., 28
Coleman, H., 110, 166, 177, 178, 179, 326
Coleman, J., 287, 293
Collaer, M., 60, 62, 63, 66, 67, 103, 256
Colombo, M., 225
Compas, B., 110, 111
Conger, K., 160, 180, 211
Conger, R., 46, 102, 104, 118, 141, 151, 160, 180, 211, 255
Connolly, K., 75, 76, 80, 88
Contreras, J., 162
Conyers, O., 104, 160, 180
Cook, J., 84
Cooper, B., 80
Cooper, C., 145, 201
Cooper, R., 145, 201
Coplan, R., 56
Corley, R., 41
Cornblatt, B., 43
Cornelius, M., 82
Corsaro, W., 146
Cosmides, L., 15, 16, 17, 22, 23–24
Costa, P., 282
Coulton, C., 159, 184, 186
Cousins, R., 280

Crabbe, J., 31, 33, 34
Crane, J., 173, 179
Crawford, C., 15, 19, 22, 26
Criqui, M., 133
Crnic, K., 70, 105, 128, 158, 168, 188, 269
Crockenberg, S., 193
Cromwell, R., 290
Cronbach, L., 187, 188, 207, 209
Cronk, L., 119
Cropper, S., 199
Crouter, A., 8, 126, 177
Crow, T., 28
Crutchfield, J., 9, 264, 265, 273, 274
Cruz-Sosa, M., 128
Cueto, S., 311
Culp, A., 102
Cupples, L., 29

D
Dallman, P., 271, 322
Daltabuit, M., 29
Dalterio, S., 79
Daly, M., 21
Dance, K., 6, 252
D'Andrade, R., 128, 166
Daniels, D., 138
Daniels, M., 36, 41, 42
Darby, B., 79
Darling, N., 125, 128, 132, 141, 145
Davidson, J., 66, 197
Davidson, R., 56
Davies, P., 188
DaVila, V., 170
Davis, P., 179
Dawes, A., 142, 160, 177, 188
Dawes, R., 11, 122
Dawkins, R., 14, 15, 18, 19, 20, 211n, 288
Dawson, G., 46, 57
Day, N., 82
Day, R., 121, 163
deAndraca, I., 89, 199
De Angelo, E., 139
Deater-Deckerd, K., 149
DeCasper, A., 137
DeFries, J., 32, 34, 37, 38, 40, 41, 42, 196, 201
DeKay, W., 16, 17, 22
DeKlyen, M., 112
de la Parra, A., 225
Dell, P., 233

DeLong, G., 84, 88, 199
Demetriou, A., 158, 179
DeMorris, K., 160, 180
DeMulder, E., 126, 255
Dennenberg, V., 233
DeRosier, M., 179
Derryberry, D., 56, 109, 198, 203, 298
Detterman, D., 38, 41, 126, 138
Devlin, B., 36, 41, 42
DeVries, L., 43, 69–70, 72, 82
DeVries, M., 93, 107, 121, 163
Dewey, K., 79
Diamond, A., 37, 38, 46, 47, 49, 50, 75,
    258
Diaz-Guerrero, R., 110
Dickson, W., 130, 179
Diener, M., 162
Dietrich, K., 77, 79, 80, 98, 224, 320
DiLalla, L., 255
Ding, X., 9
DiPietro, J., 90, 133, 149
Dishion, T., 145, 231, 302
Disney, E., 79
Djali, S., 37
Dodge, K., 112, 116, 149, 163, 179, 180,
    186, 198, 255
Doernberger, C., 118
Doherty, W., 188
Dong, Q., 178
Donner, E., 37
Dornbusch, S., 141, 145, 149, 188, 302
Douglas, J., 81
Dove, H., 30
Downey, G., 5, 150, 288, 294
Draper, P., 20, 30
Druin, D., 38, 47, 75, 258
DuBois, D., 179, 280
Dubos, J., 37, 101
Duc, G., 70, 188
Dunn, J., 139, 205
Dunn, M., 179
Duyme, M., 43, 255
Dykstra, J., 167

E
Earls, F., 257
Easter, S., 52n
Eaton, W., 102, 126, 146, 238
Eaves, J., 198, 280, 298, 299
Eaves, L., 40, 133, 205
Eccles, J., 60, 64, 65, 66, 100, 101, 102

Eckenrode, J., 146, 186, 209, 211, 218,
    219, 256
Eckerman, C., 70, 236
Edelman, G., 10, 15, 24, 49, 52n, 185,
    186, 201, 218, 241, 252, 294
Edgerton, M., 127
Edwards, C., 25, 30, 99, 119, 154, 167,
    168, 172, 173, 174, 293
Efklides, A., 158, 179
Egeland, B., 112, 133, 145, 148, 151, 180,
    197, 226
Ehrhardt, A., 61, 61n, 62, 63, 63n
Eisenberg, N., 109, 113, 299
Ekblad, S., 16
Eland, J., 6
Elder, G., 102, 103, 104, 118, 141, 150,
    159, 160, 174, 177, 180, 188, 218,
    225, 229, 233, 276, 305, 306
Eldridge, N., 276
Elicker, J., 3, 5, 151, 219, 239
Ellenberg, J., 6, 186, 319
Elman, J., 98, 289
Ember, S., 14, 18
Emde, R., 42, 98, 101, 107
Ender, P., 172
Engfer, A., 120, 147
Engle, P., 74, 79, 84, 85, 86, 89, 92, 94,
    95, 119, 128, 129, 161, 178, 322
Englund, M., 3, 5, 151, 219, 239
Ensminger, M., 177
Entwisle, D., 171, 300
Epting, F., 291
Erhardt, A., 61n, 62, 63, 65, 66
Erickson, M., 113
Erikson, E., 218
Erlenmeyer-Kimling, L., 43
Espunosa, M., 89, 92
Esrachi, A., 43
Evans, E., 179
Evans, G., 104, 137–138, 142, 212, 212n

F
Fabes, R., 109, 113, 299
Factor-Litvak, P., 77
Faier, R., 74
Falbo, T., 162
Falkner, F., 4, 86, 181
Fanaroff, A., 70, 71
Farber, E., 133
Farmer, J., 9, 264, 265, 273, 274
Farrington, D., 138

Farver, F., 121, 163, 189
Faucher, T., 146, 238
Feingold, A., 121
Feinstein, A., 188
Feinstein, C., 74
Feldman, E., 112, 116, 186, 198
Feldman, J., 61, 61n, 62, 63n
Feldman, M., 36, 154
Feldman, S., 163, 165, 166, 172, 178, 179, 180
Felner, R., 179, 280
Fergusson, D., 82
Fergusson, F., 77
Fergusson, P., 77
Fernald, A., 167
Fernald, L., 88
Ferro-Luzzi, A., 28
Field, T., 109, 329
Fields, R., 25
Fiese, B., 150, 185, 234
Figueredo, A., 4, 21, 180, 197
Figueroa, A., 90
Finchim, F., 110
Finn, J., 105
Fintelman, M., 167
Fischbein, S., 43
Fischer, P., 70
Flanagan, C., 100
Fleshner, M., 81
Fletcher, A., 141, 145
Fletcher, P., 319, 331
Flor, D., 104, 122, 129, 141, 160, 177, 180, 305, 306
Fogel, A., 153, 173, 201, 261, 262, 264, 265, 272, 273, 277
Folkman, S., 4
Fonagy, T., 233
Foord, F., 28
Forget, H., 52, 64
Fox, N., 55, 56, 57, 58, 120, 187, 280
Frank, D., 29
Frankel, D., 164, 165, 322
Freeman, W., 265
Freitas, A., 5, 288, 294
Freund, L., 39
Fried, P., 79
Friedman, H., 71, 133
Friedman, J., 81
Frisancho, A., 27, 28
Frisancho, H., 28
Frosch, D., 121, 163, 189
Fry, D., 158, 174

Fuchs, G., 95
Fuggle, P., 37, 62
Fulker, D., 38, 41, 42, 150

G
Gable, S., 128
Gabrielli, W., 40, 44
Gadisseaux, J., 49, 50, 57, 229
Gadisseux, J., 49, 50
Galal, O., 74, 90, 161, 163, 179, 189, 198, 257
Galler, J., 233
Gandini, L., 173
Garbarino, J., 159, 160, 170, 171, 177, 186, 280
Garcia, H., 105, 158, 168
Garcia, L., 84, 92, 94, 119, 128, 129, 161, 178, 322
Garcia, M., 255
Garcia-Coll, C., 105, 158, 168
Gardner, S., 66
Gariepy, J., 16, 111, 301
Garmezy, N., 4, 104, 106, 110, 119, 133, 142, 179, 186, 239, 282
Gates, R., 75
Gatz, M., 138
Gautier, T., 62, 67
Gavida-Payne, S., 322
Ge, X., 102, 104, 118, 141, 151, 160, 255
Gegeo, D., 24
Gein, N., 179
Gelfand, D., 120
Georgieff, M., 199, 221
Georgoudi, M., 178
Gershwin, M., 89
Gersten. M., 4, 107, 150–151
Gerton, J., 110, 166, 177, 178, 179, 326
Gest, S., 111, 301
Geva, D., 82
Ghandour, M., 163
Gillis, J., 38, 42
Gillman, M., 70
Giovaninni, D., 173
Gleick, J., 10, 264, 265, 270, 273, 274, 276, 296
Glezer, I., 54
Goduka, I., 158, 162, 163
Goldberg, G., 70
Goldberg, S., 38
Golden, M., 74, 86, 224, 233, 331
Goldschmidt, L., 82
Goldsmith, H., 4, 7, 32, 39, 40, 43

Goldstein, A., 188
Goldstein, M., 43, 252, 310, 319
Golub, M., 89
Goncu, A., 168
Gonzalez, M., 127, 177
Goodman, R., 9, 10, 48, 49, 50, 51, 52,
    73, 138, 186, 188, 229, 256
Goodnow, J., 29, 30, 102, 127, 128, 129,
    130, 167, 170, 171, 201, 231
Goodwin, B., 15, 185, 242, 288,
    289
Goonewardena, P., 9
Gora-Maslak, G., 31, 33, 34
Gore, S., 146, 186, 209, 211, 218, 219,
    256
Gorman, K., 74, 84, 85, 88, 89, 94, 95,
    136, 161, 173, 322
Gottesman, I., 4, 7, 8, 32, 36, 39, 40, 43
Gottfried, A., 81
Gottlieb, G., 26, 233
Gottman, J., 216, 298, 299, 325, 326
Gould, S., 3, 16, 17, 20n, 23, 53, 154,
    252, 274, 276
Graber, J., 20, 101
Graham, P., 37, 62, 73
Grantham-McGregor, S., 70, 85, 86, 87,
    88, 89, 93, 94, 95, 133, 136, 150,
    311, 319, 322, 331
Gray, J., 46
Graziano, J., 77
Greenberg, M., 70, 112, 120, 188, 269
Greenberger, E., 308
Greenfield, P., 29, 166, 181
Greenough, W., 7, 25, 49, 52, 224, 256,
    299
Greenspan, S., 145
Griesler, P., 141, 145, 179, 180, 186
Griffith, E., 101, 118
Grimwood, K., 73
Groff, J., 199, 212
Gropper, S., 199, 212
Gross, R., 71, 133
Groves, W., 170, 171, 179
Gruber, H., 186, 252, 307
Gruen, G., 142, 221, 225
Gruen, R., 61n, 63
Grundman, M., 141, 218
Gualtieri, T., 105
Guidice, S., 49
Guilarte, T., 199
Guisinger, S., 24
Gulliver, L., 103, 111

Gunnar, M., 45, 60, 64, 65–66, 110, 113,
    120, 306
Gutierrez, J., 174
Guttman, R., 43

H
Haas, B., 126, 128, 129
Habicht, J., 181, 322
Hack, M., 70, 71, 86
Hagemann, M., 236
Hagerman, R., 34, 37
Hagger, C., 62, 64
Hallberg, L., 90
Halpern, D., 23, 54, 105, 282, 312
Halsted, N., 137
Halverson, C., 178
Hambidge, K., 327
Hammond, M., 145, 186
Hammond, P., 98, 224
Hampson, E., 64
Hans, S., 83
Hansen, N., 71, 72, 224
Harding, R., 180
Hardy-Brown, K., 8
Hare, E., 28
Harkness, S., 128, 145, 153, 155, 163,
    167, 168, 172, 174, 204, 304
Harnish, J., 149, 163, 179, 180
Harper, K., 9
Harrington, R., 39, 40, 43, 116, 123, 145,
    184, 189, 238, 254
Harris, J., 132, 133, 139
Harris, L., 98, 224
Harris, M., 36, 41
Harris, R., 225
Harrison, A., 158, 171
Harrison, G., 42, 74, 88, 90, 161, 163,
    181, 189, 198
Hart, C., 179
Hart, E., 56, 57
Hartup, W., 4, 111, 145, 152, 172, 312
Hasan, K., 167
Haselton, M., 26
Hassan, A., 200
Hastings, L., 104, 160, 180
Hastings, P., 163, 166
Hauser-Cram, P., 331
Haussler, C., 199
Haussler, M., 199
Havill, V., 178
Hawk, B., 77, 150

Hawley, T., 79
Hazelwood, L., 162
Heath, A., 133
Heft, H., 137
Helwig, S., 241
Hendricks, A., 89
Henry, B., 106, 116, 255, 257
Herbener, E., 116, 117, 122
Herdt, G., 66, 197
Herrera, M., 331
Hertgaard, L., 113
Hess, R., 179
Hetherington, E., 45, 104, 132, 138, 151,
    162, 189
Hewitt, J., 40, 42
Heywood, A., 95
Heywood, P., 95
Hill, J., 5, 119
Himes, J., 85
Hinde, R., 1, 14n, 15, 16, 18, 22, 23, 24,
    118, 125, 148, 178, 201, 261,
    307
Hines, M., 60, 62, 63, 66, 67, 103,
    256
Hintz, R., 200
Hiruma, N., 121
Hittleman, J., 77
Hodges, J., 226, 234
Hodgman, J., 81
Hofer, M., 116, 212, 228, 236
Hoffman, D., 85
Hoffman, L., 119, 132, 138, 139, 150
Hogan, S., 75
Holcomb, L., 241
Holloway, S., 173
Holzgreve, W., 4, 86
Homel, R., 102, 170
Hood, K., 16
Hooker, K., 291
Horowitz, F., 7, 120, 139, 184, 185, 221,
    257
Horwood, L., 77
Howe, G., 74
Howrigan, G., 154, 162, 195
Hsieh, J., 199
Huckle, P., 33
Hunt, J., 80
Hunt, S., 199, 212
Hurtado, E., 88
Hutchings, B., 4, 40, 44, 106
Huttunen, M., 28, 66, 137
Hyatt, L., 52, 218, 219, 245

I
Iacino, R., 81
Iacono, W., 38
Immink, M., 91, 333
Imperato-McGinley, J., 62, 67
Inbaraj, S., 24
Irons, W., 23
Isabella, R., 120
Israel, M., 6, 9

J
Jacklin, C., 39, 104, 119, 150
Jacob, R., 6
Jacobson, J., 25
Jacobson, N., 177
Jacobvitz, D., 5, 10, 139, 312
Jacoby, E., 311
Jain, D., 154, 160, 166
Jastreboff, P., 49
Jemerin, J., 4, 81, 239, 320, 328
Jenkins, R., 105, 158, 168
Jenkins, W., 48, 59, 203
Jensen, A., 55
Jerome, N., 90, 94, 161, 163, 189, 197,
    198
Jest, C., 27
Joffe, J., 150
Johnson, D., 105, 154
Johnson, S., 75, 132, 133
Johnston, L., 113
Johnston, P., 59
Jolley, D., 95
Jones, C., 291
Jordan, C., 322
Jose, P., 179
Joshi, P., 154, 160, 166
Judd, C., 188, 209
Juraska, J., 52, 226
Jurutka, P., 199
Jusczyk, P., 137

K
Kagan, J., 3, 56, 107, 120
Kagan, S., 172
Kagitcibasi, C., 127, 154, 166, 179, 322
Kandel, E., 4, 58, 71, 83, 106
Kaplan, B., 83
Kaplan, H., 30
Kaplan-Sanoff, S., 79
Kaprio, J., 39, 41
Karbon, M., 109
Karp, R., 76, 77, 159

Kashiwagi, K., 130, 179
Katz, R., 40
Kauffman, S., 15, 277
Kawakami, K., 24, 109
Keen, C., 89
Keir, E., 73
KeKlyen, M., 120
Kelleher, K., 133, 142, 186, 211, 280
Keller, E., 14
Kelley, M., 173
Kelly, G., 291
Kemp, J., 160, 162, 177
Kendler, K., 133, 198, 280, 298, 299
Kennedy, R., 99, 101, 189, 211
Kenny, D., 208
Kenny, P., 98, 219
Kermoian, R., 98
Kerr, M., 121, 122, 167
Kessler, R., 133
Keusch, G., 74, 94, 199–200, 200, 212
Keyes, S., 299, 306
Khan, L., 86
Kiernan, K., 231, 234
Kiernan, M., 74
Kigar, D., 54
Killackey, H., 48, 49
Kim, U., 168
Kimura, D., 53, 54, 64
Kindermann, T., 99
King, B., 120, 225
Kinzett, N., 77
Kinzie, J., 147, 177, 180
Kirksey, A., 90, 161, 163, 189, 198
Kitcher, P., 17
Klebanoff, M., 233
Kleber, R., 6
Klein, N., 70, 71
Klein, R., 163, 200
Klein-Gitelamn, M., 74
Kleinman, J., 70, 158, 233
Kliewer, W., 137–138
Knop, J., 4, 106
Knundu, S., 70, 188
Kobayashi-Winata, H., 164, 173, 179
Kochanska, G., 99, 108, 128, 131, 151, 198, 329
Kohn, M., 128, 197
Kohnstamm, G., 178
Konner, M., 149
Korbin, J., 159, 184, 186
Koshenvino, M., 39, 41
Koss, M., 4, 21, 180, 197

Kostelny, K., 160, 186
Kozhevnikova, E., 26
Kraft, K., 77, 80, 98, 224
Krassner, M., 47, 84
Krebs, D., 18, 20
Krell, R., 6
Kreutzer, T., 148
Krier, M., 280
Kroonenberg, P., 154
Kruger, A., 164
Kuczynski, L., 99, 151
Kuhl, P., 26
Kuhn, T., 1
Kupersmidt, J., 8, 141, 145, 179, 180, 186
Kurz, E., 245, 255, 258
Kvalsvig, J., 76, 80, 81, 154, 158, 160, 161, 163, 171, 172, 180, 19

L
Lacerda, F., 26
Lachiewicz, A., 9
Ladd, G., 159
LaFromboise, T., 110, 166, 177, 178, 179, 326
Lahey, B., 56, 57
Lahti, I., 43
Lamb, W., 28
Lambert, W., 167
Lamberty, G., 105, 158, 168
Lambertz, G., 137
Lamborn, S., 188
Lamkin, R., 177
Lanborn, S., 133, 145
Lande, R., 15, 277
Landry, S., 82
Landsberg, C., 84, 199
Langmeier, J., 8
Largo, R., 70, 188
Latham, M., 82, 333
Lau, S., 141, 163, 179, 180
Laub, J., 159
Launer, L., 181, 322
Lave, C., 161, 179
Lavigne, J., 74
Law, C., 243
Lawton, M., 226
LeCouteur, A., 39, 40, 43, 71, 116, 123, 145, 184, 189, 238, 254, 311
Lee, L., 154, 172, 173
Leib, A., 79
Leiderman, J., 51

Lekic, V., 77
LeMare, L., 136, 146
Leonard, J., 291
Lepore, S., 104, 142, 212, 212n
Lepowsky, M., 91, 92
Lerner, R., 226
Leslie, J., 92
Lester, B., 180
Leung, K., 163, 179, 180
LeVine, R., 29, 128, 154, 161, 162, 166,
    167, 168, 169, 180
LeVine, S., 29, 128, 154, 161, 166
Levins, R., 256
Levitsky, D., 53, 85, 199, 228
Levy, R., 166
Lewenstein, M., 9, 274, 279, 301,
    307
Lewin, K., 204, 208, 282, 287
Lewis, M., 24, 109, 265, 275, 277, 278,
    282, 295, 297
Lewontin, R., 14
Lickliter, R., 15, 17, 23
Lickliter & Gottlieb 1985, 25
Liddell, C., 154, 158, 160, 161, 162, 163,
    171, 172, 174, 77, 180, 322, 325
Light, R., 271
Lightfoot, C., 130
Linden, M., 44
Lindsay, C., 231, 234
Lipp, A., 70, 188
Lipsitt, L., 11, 71
Lira, P., 70
Litvinovic, G., 177
Livingstone, F., 24, 231, 302
Lloyd-Morgan, C., 212
Lockman, J., 98
Loeber, R., 40, 56, 57, 138
Loehlin, J., 39, 105, 196, 282, 312
Lollis, S., 136, 146
Long, J., 4, 56, 106
Looney, J., 180
Lopez, I., 225
Lorenz, F., 104, 160, 180, 211
Lotspeich, L., 5, 37, 48, 80, 133
Lovaas, O., 7
Lovelace, L., 255
Lozoff, B., 85, 88, 89, 199
Lubinski, D., 54, 55
Luborsky, L., 291
Ludwig, J., 137
Lujan, C., 27
Lumsden, C., 15, 19, 24

Luscher, K., 276
Luster, T., 6, 126, 128, 129
Luthar, S., 118
Lutter, C., 91
Lykken, D., 38
Lyman, D., 102, 150
Lyon, G., 49, 50, 57, 229
Lytton, H., 132

M
Ma, H., 168
Maarten, S., 81
Maccoby, E., 119, 150, 173, 178
MacDonald, G., 75
Macdonald, H., 39, 40, 43, 116, 123, 145,
    184, 189, 238, 254
MacDonald, K., 14, 16, 17, 19
MacDonald, P., 199
Machon, R., 28
MacIver, D., 100
Mack, K., 42
Mack, P., 42
MacKinnon-Lewis, C., 132, 133
Maes, H., 40
Magnusson, D., 2, 4, 102, 111, 113, 118,
    210, 233, 234, 262, 273, 291, 307
Maguin, A., 138
Magyary, d., 145, 186
Maier, S., 81
Malcuit, G., 163, 179
Malhotra, S., 167
Malina, R., 42
Manetti, M., 162
Mangelsdorf, S., 139, 162
Mann, J., 21
Manson, S., 147, 177, 180
Marcovitch, S., 38
Marlow, N., 43, 69–70, 72, 82
Marshall, T., 56
Martin, J., 79, 80, 137–138, 142
Martin, K., 84
Martin, L., 133
Martin, N., 4
Martinez, P., 146
Marton, P., 324
Martorell, R., 74, 85, 86, 89, 93, 94, 95,
    200
Marvin, R., 264, 269, 308
Masilela, P., 154, 160, 161, 171, 325
Massaro, E., 77
Massaro, T., 77

Masten, A., 4, 104, 106, 110, 119, 133, 142, 179, 186, 239, 282
Maszk, P., 109
Matejcek, Z., 8
Matheny, A., 57, 137
Mathers, M., 74
Matheson, C., 153, 163
Mathews, R., 89
Maughn, B., 136, 146, 151, 174, 205, 218, 323
Mavrogenes, N., 236
May, R., 265
Mayr, E., 1
Mazzocco, M., 39
McAdoo, H., 6, 105, 158, 168
McBurnett, K., 56, 57
McCabe, E., 75
McCabe, G., 74, 90, 161, 163, 179, 189, 198, 257, 319, 332
McCall, R., 8, 188, 197, 208, 255
McCartney, K., 36, 41, 117, 302
McClead, R., 71, 72, 224
McClearn, G., 3, 31, 32, 33, 34, 37, 38, 40, 138, 201
McCleary, C., 271
McClelland, G., 188, 209
McCloskey, L., 4, 21, 180, 197
McConkie-Rosell, A., 9
McConville, C., 322
McCormick, M., 70
McCrae, R., 282
McCrary, C., 104, 160, 180
McCurry, C., 71, 83
McDonald, M., 89, 90, 92, 94, 197
McEwen, B., 60, 65
McGarry-Roberts, P., 55
McGillicuddy-DeLisi, A., 127, 166, 177
McGue, M., 38, 41, 111
McGuffin, P., 33, 40
McGuire, S., 45, 126, 138
McHale, S., 126, 177
McLaughlin, M., 174, 201, 215
McLeod, J., 159, 160, 163, 179, 241
McMichael, A., 83, 189
McNeil, T., 71, 83
McNeilly-Chogue, M., 179
McSwain, R., 30
McWhirter, L., 160
Meares, H., 280
Mednick, S., 4, 28, 40, 44, 58, 71, 83, 106, 255

Medrano, Y., 84, 92, 94, 119, 128, 129, 161, 178, 322
Meeks-Gardner, J., 85
Mehle, J., 137
Meirik, O., 233
Meisel, R., 65, 66
Melgar, P., 86
Mena, P., 85
Menke, J., 71, 72, 224
Merialdi, M., 90
Mervielde, I., 178
Merzenich, M., 48, 59, 203
Messinger, D., 120
Meyer, J., 40, 205
Meyer, K., 225
Meyer-Bahlberg, H., 61, 61n, 62, 63, 63n
Meyers, A., 29
Michelson, N., 58
Midgley, C., 100
Miguel, J., 27
Miller, B., 21, 119
Miller, C., 82
Miller, D., 7, 25, 136
Miller, G., 77
Miller, J., 265, 268, 271, 272, 274, 275, 282, 288, 295, 297, 301
Miller, K., 234
Miller, L., 74
Miller, P., 128, 161
Miller, R., 14, 19
Miller, S., 59, 126, 127, 128, 129, 131
Miller-Loncar, C., 82
Milotick, M., 28
Minde, K., 82, 197, 198, 233, 324
Mink, I., 151, 258
Mischel, W., 103, 273
Misson, J., 49, 50
Mistry, J., 168
Mitterer, J., 290
Mize, J., 128
Mizuta, I., 121
Moema, M., 160, 162, 177
Moen, P., 276
Moffitt, T., 3, 20, 21, 100, 102, 103, 105, 106, 107, 108, 111, 116, 118, 136, 150, 200, 212, 217, 255, 257, 258, 273, 306, 319, 325, 331
Molfese, D., 55
Molfese, V., 241, 255
Molina, B., 101, 158, 163
Molinari, L., 70, 188

Mollnow, E., 76, 79, 234
Molock, S., 74
Mont-Reynaud, R., 163, 179, 180
Moore, A., 6
Moore, S., 168
Mora, J., 331
Morelli, G., 121, 173, 174
Moreno, M., 127
Morikawa, H., 167
Morina, N., 77
Morisset, C., 104
Morris, S., 70
Morrison, F., 101, 118, 179
Morrow, J., 123, 151, 193
Mosier, C., 168
Moskovitz, S., 6, 177
Mounts, N., 133, 145, 188
Moussa, W., 90, 94, 163, 189, 197
Mueller, W., 42
Mulhall, P., 179
Mull, D., 92, 107, 322
Mullally, P., 126
Mundfrom, D., 133, 142, 186, 211, 280
Munoz, A., 28
Munro, E., 9
Munroe, R., 178
Muret-Wagstaff, S., 168
Murphy, B., 109
Murray, G., 28
Murray, R., 28
Musabegovic, A., 77
Myers, R., 319, 323

N
Naarala, M., 43
Nachmias, M., 113
Nadel, L., 245, 255, 258
Naipaul, V. S., 233
Nakagawa, K., 105, 154
Napoleone, M., 29
Nathan, M., 43
Natori, Y., 42
Neale, M., 133
Near, D., 14, 19
Neckerman, H., 111, 301
Needle, R., 188
Neiderhiser, J., 151, 255
Neisser, U., 105, 282, 312
Nelson, C., 46, 47, 48, 49, 50, 52, 57,
        201, 280
Nelson, D., 179
Nelson, K., 6, 186, 319

Nesselroade, J., 138, 291
Netley, C., 37, 38
Neufeld, L., 86
Neufeld, R., 6
Neumann, C., 74, 88, 89, 90, 92, 94, 181,
        197
Neuwalder, H., 61n, 63
New, R., 128
Newcombe, N., 37, 101
Newman, D., 107, 111
Newman, J., 106
Newport, E., 218
Nguyen, T., 160, 177
Nihara, K., 151, 258
Ninio, A., 179
Niskanen, P., 66, 137
Nolan, T., 73
Noonan, K., 15, 17, 18, 19, 20, 21, 24
Norgan, N., 94, 95
Nowak, A., 9, 274, 276, 279, 301,
        307
Nsamenang, A., 308

O
O'Callaghan, E., 28
O'Connor, P., 105, 106
O'Connor, T., 301
Odum, H., 153, 261, 301, 302
Oehler, J., 70, 236
Offord, D., 5, 74, 83, 104
Ogbu, J., 158, 171
Oka, T., 42
Okamoto, Y., 294
Olsen, J., 70
Olsen, S., 179
Olson, H., 77, 80, 82
Olson, K., 25
Olweus, D., 107, 111, 148, 229
O'Malley, P., 113
Oppenheimer, S., 95
Orband-Miller, L., 85
Ormel, H., 205
Osmond, C., 243
Osofsky, J., 102
Oster, G., 2, 3, 199, 265, 277, 278
Oyama, S., 36, 287
Ozanoff, S., 75

P
Packard, N., 9, 264, 265, 273, 274
Paikoff, R., 66, 99, 101, 218
Palacios, J., 127

Pallas, S., 241, 255
Palmer, H., 199, 255
Palsane, M., 104, 142
Pandey, J., 29, 30
Papousek, H., 23, 25
Papousek, M., 23, 25
Parke, R., 170
Parker, J., 111
Parker, T., 177
Parmelee, A., 55, 60, 73
Parnas, J., 255
Parsons, B., 54, 61n
Partridge, L., 18, 19, 42
Pastore, G., 28
Pastorelli, C., 110, 122
Pattee, H., 265, 270, 276
Patten, B., 201
Patterson, C., 8, 106, 141, 145, 179, 180, 186
Patterson, G., 103, 133, 141, 145, 146, 197, 231, 234, 252, 310, 331
Paulson, K., 199
Pavenstedt, E., 110, 228
Pawson, I., 27
Pearson, D., 79, 98, 224, 320
Peckham, C., 74, 83
Pedersen, E., 146, 238
Pedersen, N., 138
Peerson, J., 79
Peirano, P., 85
Pembrey, M., 32, 34, 36
Pennington, B., 75
Perez-Escamilla, R., 91
Perloff, R., 105, 282, 312
Perrin, E., 74, 83
Petersen, A., 63, 64, 65, 99, 100, 101, 189, 211, 217
Peterson, K., 29
Peterson, R., 62, 67
Petrill, S., 42
Pettit, G., 128, 149, 255
Pfeiffer, S., 71
Pfister, D., 70, 188
Pharoah, P., 88
Phelan, M., 9
Phillips, K., 137
Phillips, W., 6–7, 40
Pianta, R., 151, 180, 301
Pickles, A., 40, 148, 188, 198, 202, 205, 207, 238, 310
Pierson, D., 331

Pike, A., 45, 138
Pine, C., 158, 171
Pine, J., 126
Pitzer, R., 178
Pless, I., 74, 83
Plomin, R., 3, 31, 32, 33, 34, 36, 37, 38, 39, 40, 41, 42, 43, 44, 45, 52n, 138, 150, 151, 185, 188, 189, 193, 196, 201, 205, 209, 242, 254
Pollitt, E., 27–28, 28, 74, 75, 76, 84, 85, 88, 89, 90, 93, 94, 95, 136, 150, 161, 163, 189, 199, 311, 319, 322
Pomerleau, A., 163, 179
Poole, D., 158, 162, 163
Pope, S., 133, 142, 186, 211, 280
Popovac, D., 77
Porges, S., 56
Posner, M., 56, 109, 198, 203, 298
Poston, D., 162
Potter, S., 21
Povey, S., 9
Powell, C., 85, 150, 319, 331
Power, C., 74, 83
Power, T., 164, 173, 179
Prasad, A., 327
Preece, M., 104
Prentice, A., 28, 70, 74
Preteni-Redjepi, E., 77
Prevor, M., 38, 47, 75, 258
Price, G., 130, 179
Prichard, S., 291
Prigogine, I., 270, 273, 276, 277, 278
Prina, E., 57
Propert, K., 233
Pueschel, S., 6, 36, 188
Punamaki, R., 160, 177, 180, 189, 198, 218
Pungello, E., 8, 186, 241
Purves, D., 52n

Q
Qazi, Q., 77
Qotyana, P., 158, 174, 180
Qouta, S., 160, 180, 189, 198
Queen, K., 85
Quinton, D., 5, 81, 103, 111, 119, 136, 154, 155, 158, 173, 174, 180

R
Radke-Yarrow, M., 111, 113, 126, 146, 151, 163, 255
Rahim, S., 167

Rahmanifar, A., 90, 198
Raine, A., 106, 310
Rakic, P., 48, 49, 52, 52n, 241, 256
Ramakrishnana, U., 86
Ramey, C., 133, 330
Ramey, S., 133, 330
Ramsay, D., 24, 109
Rao, P., 24
Rapodile, J., 325
Rath, B., 147, 177, 180
Rauh, V., 70, 102, 133
Raup, D., 15, 277
Rauss-Mason, C., 225
Reed, T., 55
Reilly, S., 87
Reinisch, J., 54, 61, 63n, 198, 212
Reiss, A., 39
Reiss, D., 45, 74, 138
Rende, R., 34, 38, 39, 41, 42
Reyman, D., 100
Reynolds, A., 236, 331, 332
Reynolds, C., 39, 119
Rhodes, J., 162
Rhodes, K., 126, 128, 129
Ricciuti, H., 83, 85, 94
Richards, B., 112
Richards, M., 63, 64, 65
Richardson, D., 146
Richardson, G., 82
Richman, A., 128, 161
Ripley, J., 324
Ritchot, K., 102
Rivera, A., 91
Rivera, J., 74, 85, 89, 94, 95
Rizzo, T., 146
Robels, N., 82
Roberts, D., 180
Roberts, J., 75
Robertson, E., 83, 189
Robins, L., 257
Robinson, A., 44
Robinson, C., 179
Robinson, M., 37
Rock, S., 144, 225, 241
Rodgers, B., 207
Rodning, C., 233, 234, 319
Roe, A., 241, 255
Roeder, K., 36, 41, 42
Roer-Bronstein, D., 164, 165, 322
Rogoff, B., 99, 167, 168, 210
Rogol, A., 200
Romero-Abal, M., 79

Romney, D., 132
Ronsaville, D., 126, 255
Roopnarine, J., 154, 160, 166
Roos, N., 29
Roscher, B., 102
Rose, F., 233
Rose, R., 36, 38, 39, 41, 46, 52, 139
Rosen, L., 61n, 63
Rosenberg, I., 75, 83, 93, 200
Rosenberg, K., 233
Rosenberg, R., 4, 106
Rosenblatt, D., 199
Rosenblum, L., 10
Rosenfeld, R., 200
Rosenthal, D., 158, 163, 165, 166, 172,
    178, 179, 180
Rosnow, R., 178
Rossi, G., 57
Rossi, L., 57
Roth, J., 163
Rothbart, M., 56, 109, 120, 186, 188, 198,
    203, 297, 298, 312, 329
Rothman, K., 70
Rouse, B., 75
Routman, J., 74
Rovet, J., 37, 38
Rowe, D., 39, 45, 132, 133, 138,
    139
Rowe, J., 102
Rubenstein, J., 5, 37, 48, 80, 133
Rubin, K., 56, 136, 146, 163, 166
Rush, D., 79
Rushton, J., 14, 15, 17, 54, 105, 288
Rutledge, J., 54
Rutter, M., 5, 6–7, 32, 39, 40, 43, 45, 71,
    81, 101, 103, 111, 116, 119, 120,
    123, 133, 145, 146, 147, 148, 184,
    186, 188, 189, 190, 196, 198, 202,
    205, 207, 216, 218, 220, 224, 225,
    226, 228, 234, 238, 239, 241, 251,
    254, 257, 280, 307, 311, 312
Ryskina, V., 26

S
Sabatier, C., 163, 179
Sabroe, S., 70
Sachs, B., 65, 66
Sack, W., 147, 177, 180, 234, 241
Sackett, G., 188, 233, 234, 252
Saco-Pollitt, C., 27–28, 75, 88
Sagi, A., 6
Salthe, S., 192, 213, 265, 270, 274, 275, 309

Salzinger, S., 141, 301
Sameroff, A., 4, 82, 116, 145, 150, 174,
    185, 186, 234, 264, 265, 268, 269,
    275, 280, 288, 290, 297, 301, 323,
    324, 331
Sampson, P., 5, 77, 79, 80, 82
Sampson, R., 159, 170, 171, 179
Sanchez, G., 161
Sanders, S., 54, 61, 63n, 198, 212
Sandiford, P., 161
Sanghvi, T., 91
Sariagiani, P., 99, 101, 189, 211
Sarraj, E., 160, 180, 189, 198
Satz, P., 271
Saudino, K., 31, 41, 42
Savage-Rumbaugh, S., 164
Savin-Williams, R., 100
Scarlatti, G., 57
Scarr, S., 45, 117, 122, 132, 151, 211n,
    302
Schaefer, E., 127
Schatschneider, C., 71
Scheper-Hughes, N., 93, 121, 322
Schloo, R., 4, 86
Schmidt, L., 42
Schmitz, A., 39
Schneider, B., 162
Schneider, M., 142
Schneider, R., 75, 83, 93, 200
Schoenwald, S., 9
Schonfeld, I., 105, 106
Schooler, C., 127, 197
Schreiner, C., 59
Schroeder, D., 86
Schroeder, S., 77, 150
Schulenberg, J., 113
Schulsinger, F., 4, 106
Schultz, R., 54
Schurch, B., 62, 85, 88, 89, 90
Schwartz, D., 255
Schwartz, J., 133
Scola, P., 5, 72, 80
Scott, K., 11, 70, 72, 88
Scrimshaw, N., 85, 93, 94, 163, 272,
    280
Seeley, J., 234, 241
Segall, A., 91
Seginer, R., 129
Seifer, R., 145, 186
Selznick, S., 199
Sepulveda, J., 28
Serrano, J., 79

Sethuraman, K., 88
Sette, S., 28
Sewell, K., 291
Shabalala, A., 154, 158, 160, 161, 163,
    171, 172, 174, 180
Shackelford, T., 26
Shaffer, D., 105, 106, 241
Shaheen, A., 77, 225
Shaheen, F., 74, 90, 163, 179, 189, 257
Sham, P., 28
Shanahan, M., 159, 160, 163, 179, 241
Shannon, F., 82
Sharma, A., 161
Sharp, D., 161, 179
Shatz, M., 3, 25
Shaw, K., 11, 70, 72
Shaw, R., 9, 264, 265, 273, 274
Shejwal, B., 104
Sher, K., 241, 255
Sherman, D., 159, 170, 171
Sherman, L., 29, 319, 320
Sherman, T., 111, 113, 151
Shonkoff, J., 74, 75, 82, 327
Shosenberg, N., 324
Shukla, R., 77, 80
Siegel, L., 57
Sigel, I., 126, 127, 128
Sigman, M., 55, 60, 89, 90, 92, 94, 197
Signorelli, N., 133
Sigvardsson, S., 41
Silberg, J., 40
Silva, P., 20, 21, 102, 107, 111, 116, 150,
    255, 257
Silverberg, S., 8
Silverton, L., 71, 83
Simeon, D., 85, 87, 88, 89, 94, 95
Simon, H., 262, 270
Simonoff, E., 40, 205
Simons, R., 46, 104, 160, 180, 211, 255
Singbeil, C., 126
Sinha, D., 171
Sinnamon, H., 81
Sirevang, A., 25, 224, 298
Skarda, C., 265
Skimmer, H., 178
Skinner, M., 145, 231, 301
Skuse, D., 5, 87, 102
Slabach, E., 123, 151, 193
Slater, P., 16, 154
Slaughter-DeFoe, D., 105, 154
Slotkin, T., 85
Smith, J., 15, 71, 82, 105, 277

Smith, K., 82
Smith, L., 10, 242, 265, 269, 273, 279, 282
Smith, M., 17, 20, 21, 22, 23, 27, 109
Smith, P., 24
Smith, R., 106, 161, 328
Snidman, N., 107, 120
Snow, M., 150
Snow, R., 188
Snyder, E., 62, 63
Sober, E., 14
Sobhy, A., 74, 179, 257
Solan, H., 322
Soliman, A., 200
Solomons, N., 75, 79, 83, 93, 200
Solter, D., 34
Somogyi, A., 76
Sonderegger, T., 189
Sorenson, H., 70
Sorenson, L., 4, 106
Soria, R., 28
Soriano, E., 6
Sorri, A., 43
Sostek, A., 311
Spear, N., 52, 218, 219, 245
Spelz, M., 112, 120
Spence, M., 137
Spielvogel, H., 28
Spiker, D., 71, 133
Spiridigliozzi, G., 9
Spitz, H., 2
Spitzer, N., 52n
Srivastav, P., 154, 160, 166
Sroufe, A., 3, 5, 10, 112, 139, 145, 148, 151, 180, 197, 219, 226, 228, 239, 312
Stansbury, K., 60, 64, 65–66, 110
Starnes, R., 132, 133
Steele, H., 233
Steele, N., 233
Stein, Z., 233
Steinberg, G., 149, 302
Steinberg, L., 8, 125, 128, 132, 133, 141, 145, 188
Steinhausen, H., 225
Steinmetz, J., 46
Stelmack, R., 55
Stengers, I., 270, 273, 276, 277, 278
Sternberg, R., 105, 282, 312
Stevenson, H., 132, 163, 177, 180
Stewart, M., 151, 255

Stewart, R., 264, 269, 308
Stewart, S., 56, 163, 166
Stice, E., 150, 151
Stoffer, D., 82
Stokols, D., 152, 226
Stolyarova, E., 26
Stoneman, Z., 104, 129, 141, 160, 180, 305, 306, 322
Stoolmiller, M., 36, 145, 231, 301
Stouthamer-Loeber, M., 138
Streisel, I., 81
Streissguth, A., 5, 77, 79, 80, 82
Strelau, J., 108, 304
Strobino, D., 133, 149
Stromquist, N., 119, 120, 154, 159, 171, 174
Strupp, B., 53, 85, 199, 228
Strydom, M., 174
Sturla, E., 62, 67
Su, M., 159, 184, 186
Subramanian, S., 127, 166, 177
Succop, P., 77, 80, 98, 224
Suedfeld, P., 6
Sundbert, U., 26
Super, C., 7, 24, 128, 145, 153, 155, 163, 167, 168, 172, 174, 204, 304, 331
Sur, M., 241, 255
Susman, A., 104, 146
Susser, M., 233
Swank, P., 82
Swefi, L., 90, 163, 189
Symons, D., 13, 23, 26
Symons 1987, 17
Szatmari, P., 5, 74, 83, 104

T
Takanishi, R., 105, 154
Takei, N., 28
Tal, J., 163, 178
Talbert, J., 174, 201, 215
Tallal, P., 59
Talukder, E., 154, 160, 166
Tamis-LeMonda, C., 163, 178
Tarleton, J., 9
Tarullo, L., 126, 255
Task Force on Joint Assessment of Prenatal and Perinatal Factors Associated with Brain Disorders, 5
Taylor, E., 83
Taylor, H., 71

Taylor, P., 82
Taylor, R., 180
Tellegen, A., 106, 282
Tellez, W., 27
Telzrow, C., 71, 82
Temple, J., 332
Tennen, H., 102
Teti, D., 120
Tharp, R., 322
Thatcher, R., 49
Thelen, E., 10, 10n, 98, 242, 264, 265,
    269, 270, 273, 277, 279, 282
Thoman, E., 5, 262, 269, 298
Thomas, A., 311
Thomas, D., 9
Thomas, R., 29
Thompson, J., 324
Thompson, L., 2, 38, 41, 42, 138, 202
Thompson, W., 145
Thuline, H., 6, 36
Thyer, N., 74
Tienari, P., 43
Tietjen, A., 155, 159, 168, 170, 174, 301
Tivan, T., 331
Tizard, B., 226, 234
Toller, S., 83
Tomasello, M., 164
Tomlinson-Keasey, C., 133
Tong, S., 83, 189
Tooby, J., 15, 16, 17, 22, 23–24
Tooley, W., 80
Traissac, P., 27
Tredoux, C., 188
Trevino-Siller, S., 91
Trew, K., 160
Triandis, H., 155, 293
Tronick, E., 29, 121, 173, 174
Troughton, E., 151, 255
Trull, T., 241, 255
Tsuang, M., 71
Tucker, J., 133
Turkewitz, G., 98, 219
Tylee, A., 291

U
Uauy, R., 85, 89, 199
Ulijaszek, S., 17
Ulrich, B., 270
Ungerleider, L., 58, 241
Unvas-Moberg, K., 64
Updegraff, K., 126

Urbano, J., 11, 72
Urbina, S., 105, 282, 312

V
Vaden, N., 141, 145, 180, 186
Vaillant, G., 4, 106
Valente, E., 149, 163, 179, 180
Valez, N., 255
Vallacher, R., 274, 276
Valsiner, J., 130, 177
Van Aken, M., 103, 167, 300, 306
Van den Bos, G., 324
Van der Flier, H., 121
Van der Velden, P., 6
van der Vlugut, 167
van Geert, P., 264, 265, 270, 301
Van Ijzendoorn, M., 6, 111, 154
Van Kammen, W., 138
van Lieshout, C., 4, 111, 145, 152, 172, 312
Vann, F., 61n, 63
Van Tijen, N., 167
Vargas, E., 28
Vele, C., 71, 82, 105
Venables, P., 106, 310
Veridiano, N., 61n, 63
Viken, R., 39, 41
Villena, M., 28
Vimpani, G., 83, 189
Vogt, L., 322
Volling, B., 132, 133
von Bertalanffy, I., 202, 261, 262, 265, 271,
    275, 276, 282, 288, 293, 295
Von Eye, A. 104
Von-Knorring, A., 41
Vorhees, C., 76, 79, 234
Vrenezi, N., 77
Vuchinich, S., 103, 231, 234

W
Wachs, T. D., 2, 43, 44, 45, 74, 85, 88, 89,
    90, 93, 94, 95, 104, 107, 117, 120,
    122, 123, 125, 126, 132, 137, 138,
    139, 141, 142, 145, 149, 150, 151,
    152, 161, 163, 178, 179, 186, 188,
    189, 193, 197, 198, 203, 209, 210
    215, 216, 221, 225, 228, 231, 236,
    240, 242, 255, 256, 257, 302, 304,
    319, 324, 332
Waddington, C., 186, 199, 212, 241–242,
    272, 298

Wadsworth, K., 113
Wadsworth, S., 38
Wagner, D., 161
Wahlsten, D., 188
Wainryb, C., 173, 179
Wakefield, J., 26
Walker, D., 331
Walker, E., 150
Walker, L., 102
Walker, R., 49
Walker, S., 136, 311, 319, 322, 331
Wallace, C., 256
Walper, S., 120, 147
Wara, D., 4
Ward, M., 139
Ware, L., 102
Warner, R., 9, 23
Warren, M., 20, 65, 66, 101
Wasik, B., 105, 158, 168
Wasserman, G., 77
Wasserman, T., 225
Waterlow, J., 84, 86
Watkins, L., 81
Watkins, W., 75, 76, 90
Watson-Gegeo, K., 24
Webster, A., 74
Weinberg, J., 189
Weinstein, C., 106, 142
Weisner, T., 153, 163, 173
Weiss, P., 261, 262, 276
Weissman, B., 70
Welles-Nystrom, B., 233
Welsh, M., 75
Werner, E., 6, 45, 82, 106, 110, 113, 133,
        161, 164, 186, 188, 240, 269, 282,
        319, 320, 328
West, L., 9
Whitbeck, L., 160, 180, 211
White, K., 156
White, R., 82
Whitehead, A., 261, 288
Whitehead, R., 28
Whitehead, V., 199
Whiteside, L., 133, 142, 186, 211, 280
Whitfield, G., 199
Whiting, B., 30, 99, 119, 153, 164, 166,
        167, 168, 170, 172, 173, 174,
        177
Whiting, J., 29, 173
Whitmore, W., 85
Wigfield, A., 100

Wigg, N., 83, 189
Wiggins, S., 291
Wilkinson, A., 177
Willerman, T., 54
Willett, J., 74, 83
Willett, N., 28
Williams, B., 162
Williams, C., 174, 177
Williams, J., 178, 180
Williams, M., 106, 310
Williams, T., 330
Williams, W., 163
Wilson, D., 14, 18, 19, 23
Wilson, E., 20, 183
Wilson, G., 5, 79, 80
Wilson, J., 79
Wilson, L., 245, 255, 258
Wilson, M., 21, 158, 171
Wilson, R., 160, 177
Wilson-Mitchel, J., 173
Windle, M., 188
Wingard, D., 133
Winick, M., 225
Winn, S., 121, 173, 174
Winter, D., 291
Witelson, S., 52, 54, 61, 104
Witkin, H., 29, 160, 179
Wohlwill, J., 137, 139, 218, 221
Wolff, P., 162
Wolke, D., 87
Wolpert, L., 15, 277
Wright, J., 103, 273
Wu, C., 160

Y
Yarbrough, S., 200
Yates, W., 151, 255
Yehuda, S., 85
Yip, R., 271, 322
Youdim, M., 85
Young, J., 84, 199
Young, M., 280, 333
Young, V., 85, 93, 94, 163, 272, 280
Yunis, F., 90, 161, 163, 189

Z
Zahn-Waxler, C., 104, 121, 146
Zajonc, R., 126
Zaucha, K., 271
Zavaleta, N., 90
Zax, M., 145

Zeitlin, M., 5, 84, 92, 94, 95, 119, 128,
129, 161, 168, 171, 178, 195, 322
Zeltzer, L., 49, 81
Zeskind, P., 81
Zhan, Q., 154, 172, 173
Zhang, Q., 138
Zhezner, N., 179

Zhou, H., 178
Ziemba-Davis, M., 54, 61, 63n, 198,
212
Zigler, E., 118, 242
Zimmerberg, J., 189
Zuckerman, M., 56
Zukow, P., 201

SUBJECT INDEX

A

academic achievement. *See* school achievement
acculturation, 155, 164, 171–172, 177–178
adaptiveness, problem of, 22–23
adaptive strategies
  hunter-gatherer, 22–23
  of minority children, 158
additive coaction, 186–187, 207
additive genetic contributions, 26–27
adolescence, 63–67, 111. *See also* puberty
age, genetic influences and, 41
age-related processes. *See* temporal processes
age specificity, 221–225
aggressive behavior, and adult criminality, 111
alcoholism, genetic contribution to, 40–41. *See also* fetal alcohol syndrome
androgen, 61–64
Angelman syndrome, 34
anorexia, 89
anticipatory socialization, and proximal environmental influences, 146
antisocial behavior, 40, 55–56, 105–106, 136, 150
arguments from design, 16–17
assessment strategies, 333–334
  principles for, 319–332
asymmetrical relations, in general system, 274–275
attachment, 3, 112–113, 121, 148
attractors, in DST, 269, 272, 282, 289. *See also* strong deep attractors
autism, 40, 71
autocorrelation, and individual characteristics, 103

B

balance, as metaphor, 280–282
behavior
  consequences of malnutrition, 86–87
  genetic pathway to, 32–33, 42
  parental, 99, 122–123, 127–128, 131, 137–138, 170
behavioral range, 312

behavioral variability, interrelation with CNS variability, 53–56
behavior patterns, evolutionary significance of, 17
behaviors, universal, 7–8, 167, 265
  and experience-expectant development, 25–26
  problem of, in evolutionary approaches, 23–24
belief systems, parental, 126–132
  and individual variability, 128–129
  nature of, 130
  necessary but not sufficient, 129–132
  and parental behaviors, 127–128, 131
  and work characteristics, 160
bidirectionality
  and causal linkages, 199–200, 212–213
  and general system, 274
  of individuals and niches, 301–304
  in moderation of proximal environmental influences, 142
  of relation of parental beliefs to individual behavioral development, 129
  of SCA and self–stabilization, 300
  of temporal moderation, 226
  of transactional processes, 150–151
bifurcation point, 277–280
  conditions leading to, 278–279
  identifying, 279
  and multiple influences, 311–312
  response to, 279–281
biological influences
  and causal chains, 239
  as predictors, 5
biomedical influences, 69–83
  disease, 72–76
  necessary but not sufficient, 79–83
  pre- and perinatal complications, 69–72
  toxic conditions, 76–79
birth order, as social address, 125–126
birth weight, 69–71, 93. *See also* growth retardation
blunting, 226–229

bronchopulmonary dysplasia (BPD), 71–72
buffering, 226–229

C
catastrophe theory. *See* dynamic systems theory (DST)
categorization, and development of stable central attractors (SCA), 293
causal-chain processes, and intervention strategies, 330–332
causal chains, 236–240
    of CNS influences, 58–60
    and covarying multiple influences, 195
    of gene-environment interaction, 45–46
    hypotheses for, 238–240
    and individual characteristics, 122–123
    mediated, 211–213
    negative, 240, 330–331
    positive, 240
    probabilistic nature of, 237–238
    and proximal environmental influences, 147–148
    of undernutrition, 91–93
causal linkages, 191–192, 198–200
    and covariance linkages, 200, 210
    and research design, 211–213
central conceptual structures, and stable central attractors (SCA), 294
centralization, 295
    and behavioral range, 312
    and developmental trajectory, 282–283
    in GST, 268, 272, 275, 277, 289
    and individual as system, 287
    and potential for change, 307
    and reaction to perturbation, 308–309
    and SCA, 296
central nervous system, human (CNS)
    and age specificity, 221, 225
    amygdala, 46, 49
    and balance, 280
    biochemical links to temperament, 47
    corpus callosum, 54
    cortex, 46, 48–49
    damage caused by oxygen deprivation, 71
    degenerate neuronal groupings, 185
    development, 48–50

evolutionary influences on, 24–25
fetal, 72–73, 88
as final common pathway for individual behavioral–developmental variability, 58
frontal lobe, 56
function, 51–52n, 60–63
as general system, 272
hippocampus, 46, 49
and hormonal influences, 60–63, 61n, 199
and individual differences, 46–60
and infection, 73
links between structures, 46–47
massa intermedia, 54
neurons, 48–49
and nutritional influences, 84–85
organization, 60–63, 61n
processing, 55–57
and specificity, 241, 256
structure, 57, 60–63
and temporal deviations, 219
and temporal persistence, 229
central nervous system (CNS) influences, necessary but not sufficient, 56–60
central nervous system (CNS) variability
    etiology of, 50
    and gender differences, 53–55
    interrelation with behavioral variability, 53–56
    nature of, 48–50
chance events, and individual characteristics, 102
change, sudden, in dynamic system, 269, 274, 276
change potential, as function of self–stabilization, centralization, and niche potential, 306–308
chaos theory. *See* dynamic systems theory (DST)
child conduct disorder, and perinatal complications, 71
child coping strategies, 228
child rearing, 132, 167–169
child–rearing patterns, influence of physical ecology on, 29–30
children
    actual *vs.* potential risk, 321
    adjustment to environmental chaos, 137

and cognitive maturation, 98–99
and early physical maturation, 98
extremely low birth weight (ELBW),
71
as force in their own development,
326
iron-deficiency anemia (IDA), 88–89
and internal working models,
114–116
low birth weight (LBW), 69–70
malnutrition in, 86–89
very low birth weight (VLBW),
70–71
zinc deficiency in, 89
children, at-risk, and proximal
environmental influences, 133
chromosomal deviations, and mental
retardation, 36–37
chromosomal transmission processes,
disruptions in, 32
chromosomes, 32
cluster analysis, 210, 290–291
CNS. *See* central nervous system, human
(CNS)
coevolution, 180–181, 231
coexistence, of generalizable and specific
processes, 255–256
cognitive capacity, 105–106
cognitive performance, 62, 64, 76, 88,
129–130, 161. *See also* maturation,
cognitive
competition, in general systems theory
(GST), 268. *See* general systems
theory
complexity, 202–206, 214, 259, 332–334
growth of, in systems, 294–295
and specificity, 257
conduct disorders, and cognitive deficits,
105–106
congenital adrenal hyperplasia, 61, 63
consilience, 183
context, and assessment/intervention
strategies, 321–324
contextual reactivation, 231–233
contextual theory, 178
contiguity, criterion of, 192
control
ego, 109–110
parental, 170
covariance
active, 196–197, 231
and biomedical influences, 80–82

and causal chains, 239–240
of distal and nondistal influences,
162–163, 180–181
higher order, 193–195
of individual characteristics and other
influences, 118–120
and interaction processes, 197–198
and intervention strategies, 327–328
of maturational and other influences,
101–102
and multiple influences, 192–198,
238–240
and nutritional influences, 88, 93–95
organism–environment, 229–231
passive, 195–197
and perinatal complications, 72
and proximal environmental
influences, 142–145, 149–150
reactive, 196–198, 231
across time, 197
covariance linkages, 192–198
and causal linkages, 200, 210
and research design, 210–211
covariance processes, probabilistic nature
of, 192–193
Cri du Chat syndrome, 202
criminal behavior, 40, 58, 71
critical (sensitive) periods, 218
cross-generational influences, 233–234
culture, 155. *See also* distal environmental
influences
and attachment characteristics, 121
coevolution with CNS, 24–25
and difficult temperament, 107
as distal environmental influence,
155, 167–173
and family structure, 168–169
and gender, 121
and individual characteristics,
121–122
individual fit with, 166–167
and inhibition, 121–122
and nutritional influences, 91–93, 181
and parental values, 126–127
and proximal environmental
influences, 141–142, 149
and school characteristics, 136
stability of, 165–166
cultures, collectivist *vs.* individualistic,
155, 166, 168, 293
cumulative influences, 234–236
and bifurcation points, 278–279

and intervention strategies,
330–332
and temporal persistence, 234
cumulative spirals, 236

D
depression, adult, genetic influence on,
40
developmental niche theory, 172–173,
204. *See also* niche
developmental psychopathology theory,
204–205
developmental specialists, and
developmental generalists, 19
dietary quality, 90–91
discontinuity, in dynamic system, 273
distal environmental influences, 126,
153–155
heterogeneous nature of, 173–174
individual reactivity to, 176–178
and individual variability, 173–176
linkages among, 174–176
moderation of, 176–178
as moderators, 163
necessary but not sufficient, 162–167,
176–181
not always there, 178–180
parallels with individual change,
164–166
processes for, 167–176
and proximal environmental
influences, 178–180
types of, 155–162
unique variance associated with,
162–163
distal environmental processes
at individual level, 173–176
at population level, 167–173
drug use, maternal, 77–80, 82
dynamic systems theory (DST), 9–10, 10n,
229, 231–233, 242, 264–270. *See
also* general systems theory (GST);
system
applied to developmental variability,
272–274, 276–277
and concept of bifurcation, 277–280
key concepts in, 274–276

E
ecology, 14. *See also* physical ecology
economic conditions, as distal
environmental influence, 160

education, 119–120, 161. *See also*
cognitive performance; school
achievement
effect size
and biomedical influences, 80
for individual characteristics, 118
ego resilience model, 299. *See also*
resilience
environment, proximal, as moderating
factor for individual
characteristics, 120. *See also*
proximal environmental
influences
environment, psychosocial, and
nutritional influences, 95
environment, reactivity to, and CNS
variability, 56
environmental chaos, 137–138
environmental influences. *See also*
biomedical influences; distal
environmental influences;
gene–environment interaction;
proximal environmental
influences
and CNS influences, 58–60
environmental chaos, 137–138
as predictors, 5
environmental specificity, 142–144
environmental stress, and immune system
functioning, 81–82
environmental toxins, exposure to, 77
equifinality, in GST, 268, 277
estrogen, 64–65
ethnicity, 105, 131–132. *See also* minority
status
ethology, and evolutionary approaches,
14
event chains
and individual characteristics,
122–123
as mechanism, 116–117
in proximal environmental
influences, 136
evolution
cultural, 154
and specificity, 221, 241, 256
evolutionary approaches, 13–27
experimental studies on infrahuman
populations, 15–16
necessary but not sufficient, 22–27
testing of, 20–21
evolutionary genetics, 14

evolutionary model, for stable central attractors (SCA), 294
evolutionary theory, 13–17
  contribution to individual behavioral development, 17–21
  proper unit of analysis in, 14, 20n
experience, early *vs.* late, 225–234
experience-expectant development, and evolutionary approaches, 25–26
experiences, universal, 7–8
extreme groups, study of, and outcome variability, 4–5

F
family structure, undernutrition and, 92
father absence, as test of evolutionary approaches, 20–21
fetal alcohol syndrome, 76–77
five-alpha-reductase syndrome, 61–62
fragile X syndrome, 34, 37
fragmentation, in human developmental sciences, 1–2
functional capacities, levels of, and age specificity, 224–225
functional linkages, 184. *See also* linkages; structural linkages
  and development of stable central attractors (SCA), 294
  among multiple influences, 185–190
  strategies for, 207–209
  and structural linkages, 200–213

G
gastrointestinal illness
  and delayed growth, 74
  and malnutrition, 93–94
gender
  and CNS structure and function, 60–63
  and CNS variability, 53–55
  and culture, 121
  and detection of interaction processes, 188–189
  and educational opportunities, 119–120
  and effects of social disruption, 160
  and hormonal influences, 66–67
  and individual characteristics, 118–119
  and undernutrition, 92
gender differences, 103–105
gene-environment interaction, 43–46

generalizability, and specificity, 255–256
general systems theory (GST), 264–270. *See also* dynamic systems theory (DST); system
  applied to developmental variability, 275–277
  key concepts, 275–276
generational shifts, and distal environmental influences, 154. *See also* cross–generational influences
genes, 32
genetic change, and evolutionary changes, 26–27
genetic disorders, and outcome variability, 6–9
genetic influences, 3, 31–46, 184–185
  chromosomal and single–gene processes, 33–34
  and CNS development, 48
  covariance with proximal environmental influences, 149–150
  on intelligence, 36–38
  moderated by non–genetic factors, 43–44
  multiple gene processes, 34–36
  and nutritional influences, 199
  on personality, 38–39
  on psychopathology, 39–41
  unanswered questions, 41–42
genetic predisposition, 42–43
genomic imprinting, 34
growth patterns, and parental beliefs, 129
growth recovery, 86
growth retardation, 74, 86

H
heterogeneity. *See also* individual variability
  individual, 118
  population, 19
  of predictors, 8–9
hierarchy
  of explanatory principles, 2
  in GST, 268, 270, 274, 296–297
  of proximal environment, 139–142, 149
high-altitude living, as potential biological stressor, 27–28
hormonal exposure, prenatal
  prenatal, 60–63

and cognitive performance, 62
social and behavioral consequences,
62–63
hormonal influences, 60–67
bidirectionality of, 65–66
and CNS, 199
nature of, 65
postnatal, 63–65
puberty, 99–101
hormone production, regulation of, 60
human capital, 333
human developmental sciences, use of
term, 2
human ecological theory, 178
hunter–gatherer solutions, persistence
of, as explanatory framework,
22–23
hypothalamic–pituitary–adrenal (HPA)
axis, 63
hypothalamic–pituitary–adrenocortical
(HPA) system, 65

I
illness, chronic postnatal, 73–75
immune processes, and CNS function, 52n
immune system, and environmental stress,
81–82
individual, and culture, 166–167
individual as system, 284–289
and contextual niches, 300–309
criteria for, 288
and ongoing role of multiple
influences, 309–312
reaction to perturbation, 308–309
and SCA, 289–297
self-stabilization processes, 297–300
individual behavioral development,
evolutionary contributions to,
17–21
individual change, and distal
environmental influences,
164–166
individual characteristics, 3, 102–124
and causal chains, 240
and centralization, 283
and distal environmental influences,
163
mechanisms for, 114–117
as moderator of biomedical
influences, 83
as moderator of distal environmental
influences, 176–178

as moderator of temporal deviation
impact, 219
necessary but not sufficient, 117–124
and niche selection, 304–305
and proximal environmental
influences, 151–152
and range specificity, 254
and response to bifurcation point, 280
and stable central attractors (SCA),
291–293
types of, 103–114
and undernutrition, 92–93
individual differences
and stable central attractors (SCA),
295–297
and self-stabilization, 298–300
individual variability. *See also* outcome
variability; variability
in CNS, 48–50
and group-level explanations, 17–18
and parental beliefs, 128–129
infection, 72–73, 75–76
influence, isolated single, 184–185, 203,
207, 210–211, 213–214. *See also*
multiple influences
information processing, CNS variability
and, 55
infrahuman acculturation, 164
infrahuman studies
and CNS, 49, 52–52n, 54
and cross–generational influence,
233
and cultural evolution, 154
and developmental specificity,
244–245
and early physical maturation, 98
and effects of malnutrition, 84–85
and evolutionary influences, 16, 25
and hormonal influences, 61–61n, 62,
64
and interaction processes, 188
and proximal environmental
influences, 133, 136
and sensitization, 228
inheritance, in evolutionary approaches,
14–15
inhibition, 107–109
culture and, 121–122
initial conditions
and dynamic system, 270, 274, 278
and individual as system, 287
instability, as risk factor, 236

intelligence, 36–38, 41–42, 54, 105–106, 312. *See also* cognitive performance

interaction
and covariance, 197–198
detecting, 188–189, 209
as functional linkage, 187–190
and strategies for functional linkages, 207–209
types of, 190–191

interconnection density, 203

internal working model, 114–116, 148, 228, 296

interpersonal relations, and behavioral range, 312

interpersonal style, 111–113

intervention
controlled, and outcome variability, 6
cumulative, 330–332
evaluating outcome, 324, 330
goal of, 324
multidimensional, 319

intervention strategies, 333–334
principles for, 319–332

intrinsic *vs.* extrinsic factors, 31
in undernutrition, 91

iron-deficiency anemia (IDA), 87–89

IT–AT, 332

K

kin selection, 24

L

lead exposure, 77, 98

legitimate reductionism, 318

lifestyle changes, and multiple traits, 113

life themes, 277

linkage patterns, 202–205, 214–215

linkages. *See also* functional linkages; structural linkages
and development of stable central attractors (SCA), 293
in general system, 272
and SCA, 291–292
among strong attractors, 269
in systems, 261, 275

linked multiple-influence structure
conceptual implications, 201–203
implications for research design, 203–213
as research framework, 213–216

long–term effects, of proximal environmental influences, 145–148

M

macrosystem specificity, 179

male aggression, evolutionary processes and, 22

malnutrition, 84–89. *See also* micronutrient deficits; undernutrition
and behavioral consequences, 94–95
and culture, 91–93
and other risk factors, 93–94

maturation, 98. *See also* temporal processes
cognitive, 98–99
differential, in CNS, 49–50

maturational influences, 98–102
necessary but not sufficient, 101–102

measurement
direct, of proximal environmental influences, 133
imprecise, 8–9
precision of, and CNS influences, 57–58

mediational analysis, 211–213

menstruation, 64, 100

mental retardation, 36–38, 62, 69, 72–73, 88

micronutrient deficits, 87–91

midlevel processes, 11, 183. *See also* linked multiple–influence structure; specificity processes; system–level processes; temporal processes
and development of stable central attractors (SCA), 293–295
and development of self–stabilization, 297
necessary but not sufficient, 313–315

migration
and distal environmental influences, 164
involuntary, 159–160, 171

minority status, 171
as distal environmental influence, 158
and family structure, 168–169

moderation
of biomedical influences, 82–83
of distal environmental influences, 180
of genetic influences, 43–44

of hormonal influences, 66
of maturational influences, 101–102
of parental belief systems, 131–132
of proximal environmental
   influences, 141–142, 149
temporal, 225–229
moderators
   distal environmental influences as,
      163
   proximal cultural, and individual
      characteristics, 120
   temporal and cultural, and individual
      characteristics, 120–122
molecular genetics, 31–32
multidimensional approach, for assessment
      and intervention, 319
multiple-influence models, 3
multiple influences, 213–216. *See also*
      influence, isolated single; linked
      multiple-influence structure
   covariance among, 192–198
   and development of stable central
      attractors (SCA), 293–295
   and development of self–stabilization,
      297
   functional linkages among, 185–190
   and functional *vs.* structural linkages,
      200–213
   and midlevel and system-level
      processes, 284–312
   necessary but not sufficient, 313–315
   and niche position, 302
   ongoing role of, 309–312
   probabilistic nature of, 318
   as system, 262–264
   and temporal moderation, 228
multiple states, in systems, 276
multiple trait characteristics, 113–114
mutual influences model, for proximal
      environmental influences and
      individual characteristics, 151

N
neighborhood, as distal environmental
      influence, 159
nesting, of belief systems, 129
neurochemical processes, in CNS, 47
niche, 117, 300–305
   cultural, 174
   and individual as system, 305–309
   and individual development, 301–304
   necessary but not sufficient, 313–315

operation of, 304–305
positive *vs.* negative valence,
   301–302, 305
niche availability, and behavioral range,
   312
niche characteristics, and stable central
   attractors (SCA), 306
niche potential, 284–286
   and assessment, 322
   and intervention strategies, 325–326
   and potential for change, 307
   and reaction to perturbation,
      308–309
niche restriction, 117, 302, 304–306,
   311–312
niche selection, 231, 240, 302, 304–305
nutritional influences, 83–95
   and balance, 280
   and culture, 91–93, 163
   and genetic influences, 199
   malnutrition, 86–89
   mild nutrient deficits, 89–91
   necessary but not sufficient, 91–96
   scope of problem, 84–85
nutritional rehabilitation, 85, 87
nutritional risk, culture and, 181
nutritional status, and gastrointestinal
      illness, 199–200
nutritional supplementation, 89, 94–95

O
organism-environment interaction,
      151–152, 189, 229–231
   and assessment/intervention
      strategies, 328–330
otitus media, chronic, 74–75
outcome variability, 3, 6–11. *See also*
      variability; individual variability
   and CNS influences, 57–58
   as "fact of nature," 9–10
   group, 13
   and postnatal hormonal influences,
      64–65
   among siblings, 138–139
   and variability in individual
      characteristics, 97

P
paradigms, scientific, 1–2
parental-resource allocation, as test of
      evolutionary approaches, 21
parsimony, 2–3, 334

partitioning, of variance, 36
pattern analysis, 210–211
peer-group influences, 133
peer rejection, 111–112
peer relations, 170
    and parent–child relations, 145
perinatal complications, 71–72
Personal Construct Theory, 290–291
personality
    and behavioral range, 312
    genetic influences on, 38–39
personality characteristics, 107–110
perturbations
    in general system, 271
    individual reaction to, 308–309
    multiple influences as, 310–311
phenocopies, 185
phenylketonuria (PKU), 37–38, 75
physical characteristics, 103–105
    as mechanism, 114
physical ecology
    direct consequences of, 27–29
    indirect influence of, 29–30
    necessary but not sufficient, 30
physical sciences, example of, 2–3
planfullness, 111
pleiotropy, 184–185
postnatal risk factors, as predictors, 5–6
poverty, as distal environmental influence, 159
predictability
    of change potential, 306–308
    in dynamic system, 273
    in systems, 276
prediction, proper use of, 10–11
predictors, individual, and outcome variability, 4–6
predispositions, and development of stable central attractors (SCA), 293–294
pregnancy, and hormonal treatments, 61
prematurity, and perinatal complications, 71–72
prenatal stimulation, 136–137
principles
    for assessment and intervention, 319–332
    systems, 264–269
probability
    and causal chains, 237–238
    and covariance processes, 192–193
    and multiple influences, 318

and proximal environmental influences, 147–148
process specificity, 142–144, 242, 252–254
progesterone, 64–65
progressive mechanization, in GST, 268
proximal environment
    structure of, 139–142
proximal environmental influences, 125–126, 132–152
    and cross–generational influences, 233
    and distal environmental influences, 170, 178–180
    emerging domains, 136–139
    necessary but not sufficient, 132–134, 148–152
    nonextreme, 132–134
    probabilistic nature of, 147–148
    processes of, 139–148
    shared vs. nonshared, 138–139
    specific, 134–136
psychopathology, genetic influences on, 39–41
psychosocial conditions, and hormonal influences, 66
psychosocial influences, and causal chains, 239
psychosocial interventions, and proximal environmental influences, 133
P-technique factor analysis, for stable central attractors (SCA) patterns, 290
puberty, 99–101

R

race. See minority status
rational choice theory, 168–169
reactivity, 108–109
    as mechanism, 114
reactivity, differential, 187–188
    and causal chains, 239–240
reactivity, individual
    and assessment/intervention strategies, 328–330
    to distal environmental influences, 176–178
redefinition, as goal of intervention, 324
reeducation, as goal of intervention, 324
remediation, as goal of intervention, 324
repertory grid technique, for SCA patterns, 290–291

reproductive strategies, as test of
    evolutionary approaches, 20–21
research cost, 214–215
research design, and linked
    multiple–influence structure,
    203–213
residence, as distal environmental
    influence, 158–159
resilience, 109–110, 151, 185
    in general system, 271–272, 275
    and multiple traits, 113–114
    and self–stabilization, 299
resources, differential access to,
    170–171
response patterns, universal, 15
risk, identifying, 319–321

S
SCA, salience, and linkage patterns,
    214–215
schizophrenia, 39, 43, 71, 73
school achievement, 38, 106, 129–130,
    146–147, 236
school attendance, and cognitive
    performance, 161
school characteristics, culture and, 136
schooling, as distal environmental
    influence, 161
schools, as moderating factor, 132
seasonal influences, 28–29
segregation, in systems, 272, 275, 295
selection
    in evolutionary approaches, 14–15
    frequency-dependent, 18–19
    at group level, 15
selectionist models, 52n
self-concept, 111, 155
self-efficacy, 110
self-organization, in dynamic system, 273
self-perceptions, 110–111
self-regulation, 109, 287
self-reorganization, and bifurcation points,
    278
self-stabilization
    and behavioral range, 312
    and bifurcation points, 278
    in GST, 271, 277
    and intervention strategies, 325–326
    and niches, 303–304, 306
    and potential for change, 307
    and reaction to perturbation,
    308–309

and stable central attractors (SCA),
    300
self-stabilization processes, 297–300
self-stabilizing mechanisms, 148
sensitization, 226–229
setting, 170. See also niche
sibling relationship patterns, as moderating
    factor, 132
siblings, and shared vs. nonshared
    environmental influences,
    138–139
side information, collecting, 209
single-gene disorders, and mental
    retardation, 37–38
single-influence models, limitations of,
    3
single-process models, limitations of, 3
sleeper effects, 229
social address, 125–126
    age as, 221
social-address predictors, and outcome
    variability, 8
social class, as moderator for proximal
    environmental influences, 149
social disruption, as distal environmental
    influence, 159–160
social support networks
    as distal environmental influence,
    161–162
    as proximal environmental influence,
    161
sociocultural groups, variability in,
    153–154
socioeconomic status (SES), as distal
    environmental influence, 159
specificity, 241. See also age specificity;
    environmental specificity; process
    specificity
    as artifact, 242
    developmental, 242–251
    environmental, 241
    etiology of, 256
    and generalizability, 255–256
    and individual differences in SCA,
    295
    interdoman, 252
    and intervention strategies, 322–325
    range, 252–254
    and systems processes, 277
    specificity principle, 205
specificity processes, 240–258
    implications of, 257–258

and other midlevel processes, 257–258
spiraling processes, and proximal environmental influences, 146–147
stability
cultural, 165–166
of influences over time, 234–236
in systems, 269–270, 275–276
stabilized central attractors (SCA), 289–297
development of, 293–295
and individual differences, 295–297
and intervention strategies, 325–326
nature of, 291–293
and niches, 306
and self-stabilization, 300
statistical modeling procedures, pitfalls of, 33
steeling, 226–229
strategies, shifting, evolutionary processes and, 19–20
stress
environmental, and immune system functioning, 81–82
gender and, 104–105
maternal, during pregnancy, 137
stress reactivity, and hormonal influences, 65–66
stress vulnerability, and multiple traits, 113
strong deep attractors, in DST, 269, 282, 289
structural linkages, 184, 191–200. *See also* functional linkages; linkages
and assessment process, 319–321
and functional linkages, 200–213
and intervention strategies, 327–328
and multiple influences, 202–205
strategies for, 209–213
structural model, 139–142, 153, 160, 201
structure, of proximal environment, 139–142, 149
stunting, cross-generational, 86
substance abuse. *See* drug use, maternal
subtractive coaction, 186
support, multiple influences as, 310–311
system, 262
dynamic, 266–269
environmental processes as, 141
three–level framework, 263–264, 284–286, 314
as unit of analysis, 261–262

system-level processes, 262–264. *See also* midlevel processes
and midlevel process specificity, 277
necessary but not sufficient, 284, 313–315
systems principles, 264–269
application of, 201–202
systems theories, and developmental variability, 272–276

T
temperament, 107–110
and behavioral range, 312
and CNS, 47
difficult, 107
genetic contribution to, 43–44
individual variability in, 56
infant, 163
and parental behavior, 122–123
temporal deviations, impact of, 218–221
hypotheses for, 220–221
temporal discontinuity, 192
temporal factor, in covariance, 197
temporal moderation, 146, 225–229
temporal persistence, 229–234
temporal processes, 217–240
testosterone, 64–65
time-locked developmental sequences, deviations from, 218–221
TORCH disorders, 72–73
trait distribution, and genetic influences, 41–42
transactional processes, and proximal environmental influences, 150–151
transition point
in dynamic system, 270, 274
and individual characteristics, 103
and individual differences in self–stabilization, 298
multiple influences and, 311–312
translation process, from CNS activity to individual behavioral variability, 58–60
turning point, 225, 277, 307
twin studies, 8–9, 34–36, 40

U
undernutrition, causes of, 91–93
unemployment, parental, as distal environmental influence, 160

urbanization, as distal environmental
   influence, 158–159

V
values
   culture and, 155
parental, 126–132
   variability. *See also* outcome
      variability; individual variability
   intracultural, 172–173

and system, 261–262
   within variability, 6–7
violence. *See* social disruption

W
warfare, as distal environmental influence,
   159–160
wholeness, in GST, 268
work characteristics, parental, as distal
   environmental influence, 160

ABOUT THE AUTHOR

Theodore D. Wachs, PhD, is a professor of psychological sciences at Purdue University. He received his PhD in child clinical psychology in 1968 from George Peabody College. Dr. Wachs is a Fellow of the American Psychological Association and was the 1995–1996 Golestan Fellow at the Netherlands Institute for Advanced Studies in the Humanities and Social Sciences. His current research concerns the relation between early development, environmental characteristics, and nutritional status in young children. He has authored or edited six books and has written numerous articles on developmental psychology.